I0819693

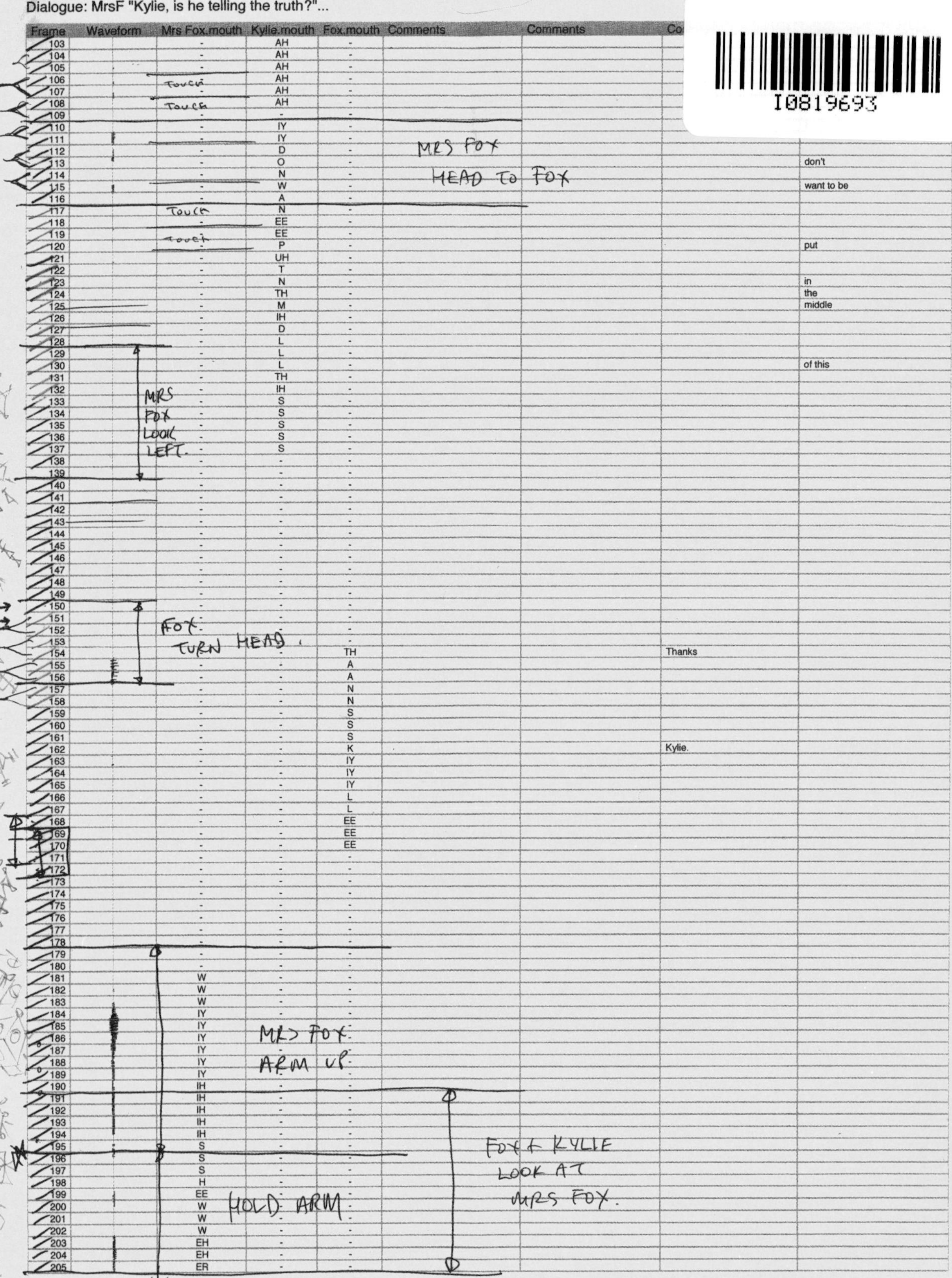

Frame	Waveform	Mrs Fox.mouth	Kylie.mouth	Fox.mouth	Comments	Comments	Co…	
103		-	AH	-				
104		-	AH	-				
105		-	AH	-				
106		-	AH	-				
107		-	AH	-				
108		-	AH	-				
109		-	-	-				
110		-	IY	-				
111		-	IY	-				
112		-	D	-				
113		-	O	-				don't
114		-	N	-				
115		-	W	-				want to be
116		-	A	-				
117		-	N	-				
118		-	EE	-				
119		-	EE	-				
120		-	P	-				put
121		-	UH	-				
122		-	T	-				
123		-	N	-				in
124		-	TH	-				the
125		-	M	-				middle
126		-	IH	-				
127		-	D	-				
128		-	L	-				
129		-	L	-				
130		-	L	-				of this
131		-	TH	-				
132		-	IH	-				
133		-	S	-				
134		-	S	-				
135		-	S	-				
136		-	S	-				
137		-	S	-				
138		-	-	-				
139		-	-	-				
140		-	-	-				
141		-	-	-				
142		-	-	-				
143		-	-	-				
144		-	-	-				
145		-	-	-				
146		-	-	-				
147		-	-	-				
148		-	-	-				
149		-	-	-				
150		-	-	-				
151		-	-	-				
152		-	-	-				
153		-	-	-				
154		-	-	TH			Thanks	
155		-	-	A				
156		-	-	A				
157		-	-	N				
158		-	-	N				
159		-	-	S				
160		-	-	S				
161		-	-	S				
162		-	-	K			Kylie.	
163		-	-	IY				
164		-	-	IY				
165		-	-	IY				
166		-	-	L				
167		-	-	L				
168		-	-	EE				
169		-	-	EE				
170		-	-	EE				
171		-	-	-				
172		-	-	-				
173		-	-	-				
174		-	-	-				
175		-	-	-				
176		-	-	-				
177		-	-	-				
178		-	-	-				
179		-	-	-				
180		-	-	-				
181		W	-	-				
182		W	-	-				
183		W	-	-				
184		IY	-	-				
185		IY	-	-				
186		IY	-	-				
187		IY	-	-				
188		IY	-	-				
189		IY	-	-				
190		IH	-	-				
191		IH	-	-				
192		IH	-	-				
193		IH	-	-				
194		IH	-	-				
195		S	-	-				
196		S	-	-				
197		S	-	-				
198		H	-	-				
199		EE	-	-				
200		W	-	-				
201		W	-	-				
202		W	-	-				
203		EH	-	-				
204		EH	-	-				
205		ER	-	-				

Handwritten annotations:
TOUCH (106, 108, 117, 119)
MRS FOX HEAD TO FOX (110–116)
MRS FOX LOOK LEFT. (128–139)
FOX TURN HEAD. (150–156)
MRS FOX ARM UP (179–195)
FOX + KYLIE LOOK AT MRS FOX. (190–205)
HOLD ARM (195–205)

THE MAKING OF

FANTASTIC MR. FOX

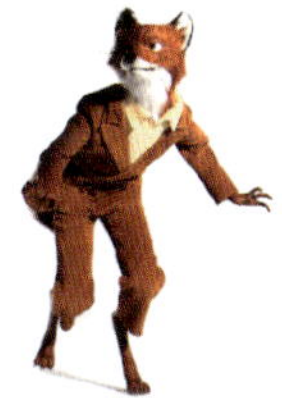

AN AMERICAN EMPIRICAL PICTURE BY

WES ANDERSON

INTRODUCTION AND INTERVIEWS BY
MICHAEL SPECTER

SET PHOTOGRAPHY BY
RAY LEWIS

Including drawings, designs, and photographs by Wes Anderson, Chris Appelhans, Christian De Vita, Turlo Griffin, Félicie Haymoz, Huy Vu, and Greg Williams

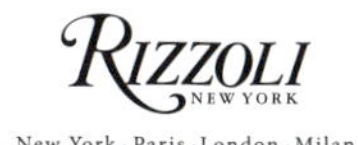

New York · Paris · London · Milan

First published in the United States of America
in 2009 by Rizzoli International Publications, Inc.
49 West 27th Street, New York, NY 10001
www.rizzoliusa.com

2026 2027 2028 / 20 19 18
Printed in Hong Kong
Design by Pentagram
ISBN-13: 978-0-8478-3354-2
Library of Congress Control Number: 2009934109

The authorized representative in the EU for product safety and compliance is Mondadori Libri S.p.A.via Gian Battista Vico 42, Milan, Italy, 20123
www.mondadori.it

Special thanks go to: Molly Cooper, Tina Chai, Jeremy Dawson, and Beni Hardiman at American Empirical Pictures; Masumi Briozzo, Angus Hyland, and Zara Moore at Pentagram; Jacob Lehman, Robb Pearlman, Rachel Selekman, and Chris McDonnell at Rizzoli; and especially special thanks to Liccy Dahl.

Front endpapers: A dope sheet used by animators to mark out the timing of puppet movements, as well as camera and lighting changes

Back endpapers: Pages of score composed by Alexandre Desplat and used at the music recording sessions at Abbey Road

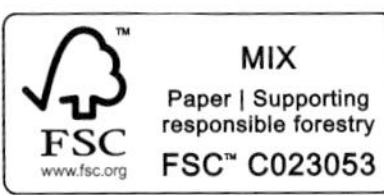

INTRODUCTION

BY MICHAEL SPECTER

The first time I met Wes Anderson, some years ago, I asked how he arrived at his particular approach to making movies. "I guess I try to think up a story," he said, "that I can sort of tell in a way that nobody else would tell it." He had just completed *The Life Aquatic with Steve Zissou*, which managed to be an adventure film about marriage, loss, and family life all at once—often carried out many leagues under the sea, and in a world populated by phosphorescent creatures, a single-minded but murderous shark, and, naturally enough, pirates.

We were eating dinner in the garden of a restaurant in Manhattan. "Now, I want to make a movie in India," he said. "On a train." I think he also mentioned his devotion to the great Indian filmmaker, Satyajit Ray. That was all he said, but it was enough to propel him toward *The Darjeeling Limited*, which revisited, in the most poignant way, Wes's blended themes of family anguish, yearning, and joy.

So when he told me that he had acquired the rights to one of the modern touchstones of children's literature, Roald Dahl's *Fantastic Mr. Fox*, I was a bit taken aback. After all, somebody had already told that story. Or so I thought. But Wes decided to make it his own—with the energetic approval of Liccy Dahl, Roald's intellectually adventurous widow. She was curious—perhaps even anxious—about how he might turn a book with a few characters and little dialogue into a full-length, stop-motion picture with a complicated family of foxes and friends. But she was eager to see him try. "I was so in love with his work," she told me, after having seen his first two films, *Bottle Rocket* and *Rushmore*, "I was dying for him to do *Fantastic Mr. Fox*, but I needed to know what his thoughts and his conceptual ideas were for the film."

Making the movie in stop-motion meant creating tens of thousands of individual photographs and running them together, each one an expression of Wes's highly specific vision. It didn't take Liccy Dahl long to realize that these two singular artists—a modernist from Texas and a Welsh fighter pilot born nearly a century go—would perform what amounts to a cinematic and artistic duet. "Wes has expanded it in the true spirit of the book, and of Roald particularly," she said.

Wes has often been called "quirky"—a term I loathe; it simply means he has a vision and that he is tenacious in his pursuit of bringing it to life. The same has to be said of Dahl, whose work always defied convention (ultimately, of course, creating a standard all its own). Wes's films don't pander; he doesn't create market-tested characters or see a reason to airbrush reality. Enhancing reality perhaps, even warping it: but there are no anodyne solutions or simplistic answers in Wes Anderson's toolbox. Or in Roald Dahl's.

Mr. Fox, for example, is a vain and slightly puffed-up character. A bit silly, which makes him—I have to say it—all the more human. The evil farmers—fat Boggis, squat Bunce, and skinny Bean—may be hated by readers (and viewers), but somehow they also manage to resonate with nearly every seven-year-old who has picked up the book, and with their parents as well. That's because Dahl's characters, and Wes's too, are imbued with a rare mix of fantasy and humanism.

Dahl began writing *Mr. Fox* in 1969, the year Wes was born, and completed it the following year. In one of those happy accidents that great art often demands, *Fantastic Mr. Fox* was the first book that Wes remembers having read. "It was not only the first Roald Dahl book I read," he recalls, "I think it was the first book I ever possessed." Wes loved the character of Mr. Fox for his foibles as much as for anything else. But he also loved digging. "My brothers and I were obsessed with being underground."

People might wonder how the work of two such distinctive artists can possibly be fused together. They can't be. But there are two types of interpreters: literalists who cleave to the text, and poets who make it their own. Boris Pasternak, who brought Shakespeare to the modern Russian reader with a particular intensity, was the latter. Taking nothing away from the Bard, he simply added a new layer of genius. In Wes Anderson's version of *Fantastic Mr. Fox*, loyal readers will have no trouble finding their cherished text. But they will also find more: a Roald Dahl story for modern times.

Style

8.18.02

Welcome To the Dahl House

It is not just kids who yearn to go to Gipsy House, where Roald Dahl wrote 'James and the Giant Peach,' among other classics. Grown-up children do, too. People like the director Wes Anderson.

Photographs by Tim Walker
Text by Wes Anderson

My brothers and I grew up reading Roald Dahl's stories. Our mother had gotten us nameplates to put in our books, and we used to steal one another's copies of "Charlie and the Chocolate Factory" and "The Wonderful Story of Henry Sugar," tear out the other's nameplates and replace them with our own. Dahl was our favorite.

For me the best were "Danny the Champion of the World" and "Fantastic Mr. Fox."

Last year I decided to find out what it would take to make a movie from "Mr. Fox." I arranged

Far right: The 19th-century English farmhouse in Great Missenden that Dahl named Gipsy House. His widow, Felicity, still lives there. Right: An avenue of pleached lime leading up to Dahl's writing hut.

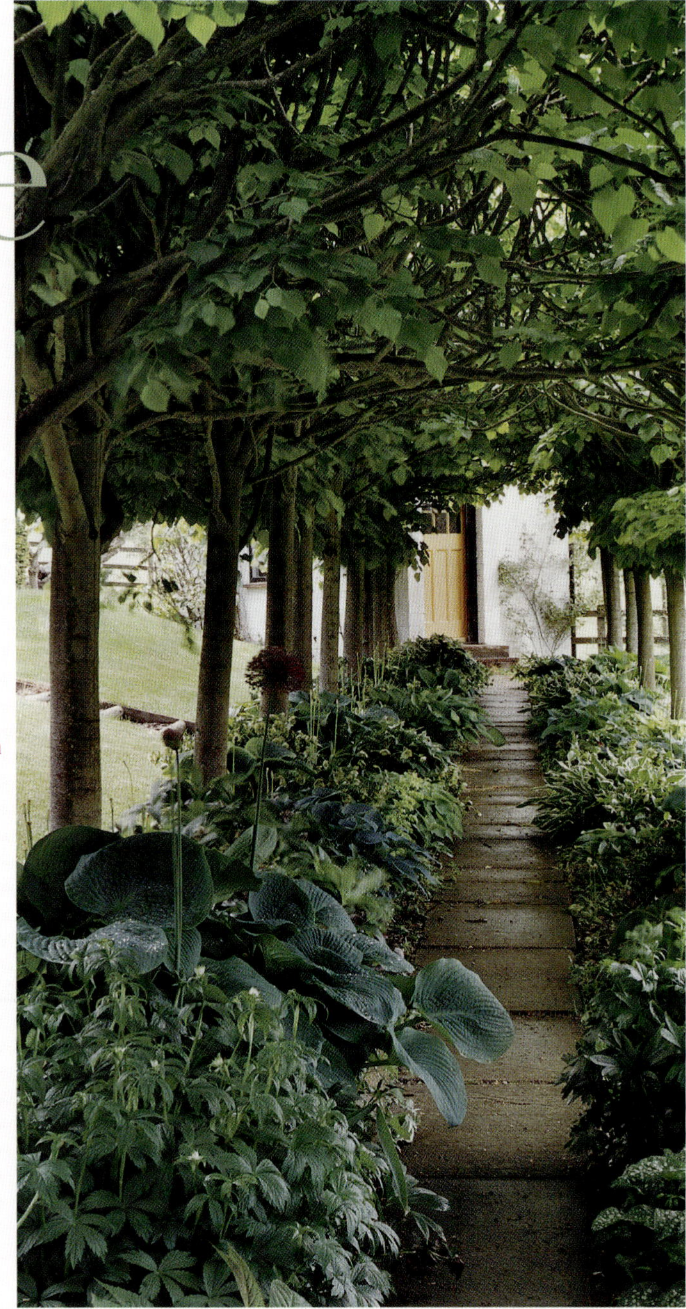

42

This article first appeared in the *Sunday Magazine* section of *The New York Times* on August 18, 2002

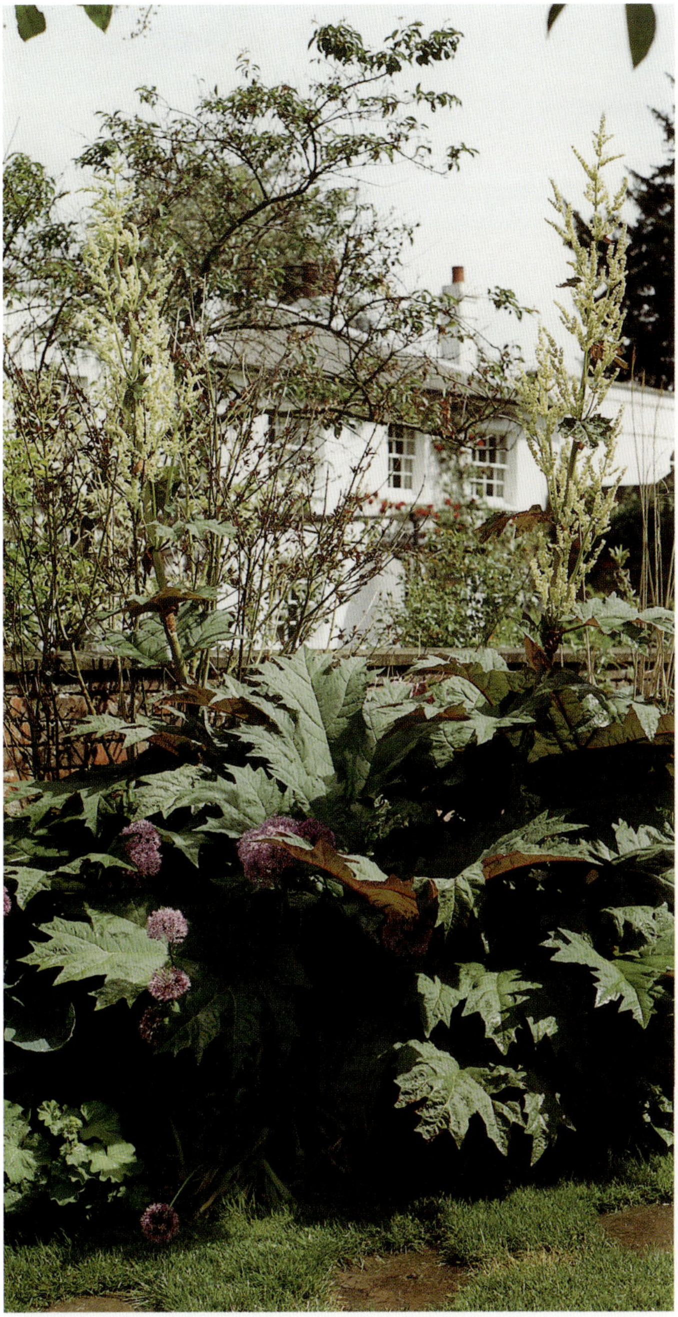

Far left: A poster advertising the opening of the garden for charity; it is open to the public about four times a year. Left: A part of the walled garden. There is also a kitchen garden, a formal garden and an orchard. Below: Roald Dahl, left, with a schoolmate at Repton, about 1933.

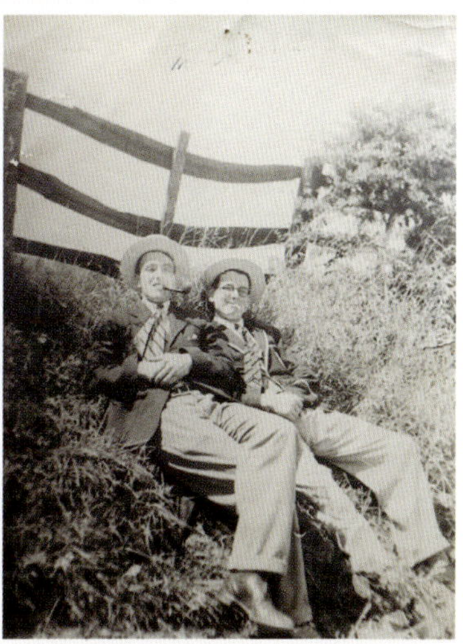

to meet with Dahl's wife, Felicity, or Liccy, who runs the Dahl estate and helps to produce the films, operas, etc., that have come from his books.

She is a very charming and energetic woman, with an infectious enthusiasm for her husband's work. She invited me to Gipsy House. I knew about Dahl's residence in Great Missenden near Oxford, and I was especially eager to see the tiny hut where he wrote for four hours each day in an armchair with a green-felt-upholstered board across his lap for a desk.

I went to Gipsy House in March, and it was drenched in mud. Liccy gave me a pair of rubber boots and one of Dahl's old fishing hats and took me around the property. There is a gigantic beech tree at the end of a fox run, which I immediately recognized from "Fantastic Mr. Fox." There is a

Right: A view of the potager, *with a topiary in the center and several ilex trees. Far right and below: The chair in the writing hut where Dahl composed his stories, in longhand, on yellow legal pads in pencil. The painting is by Penny Graham.*

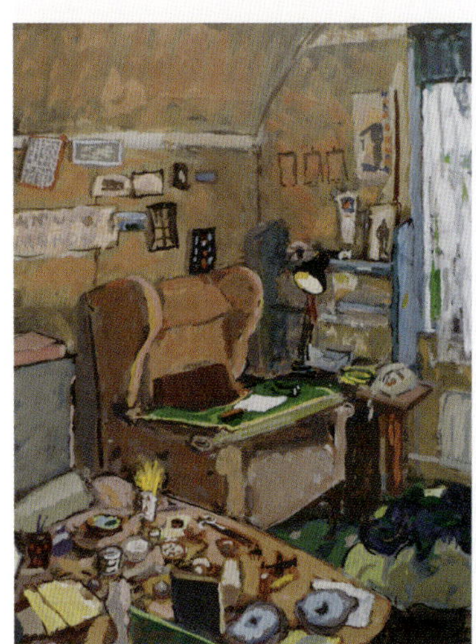

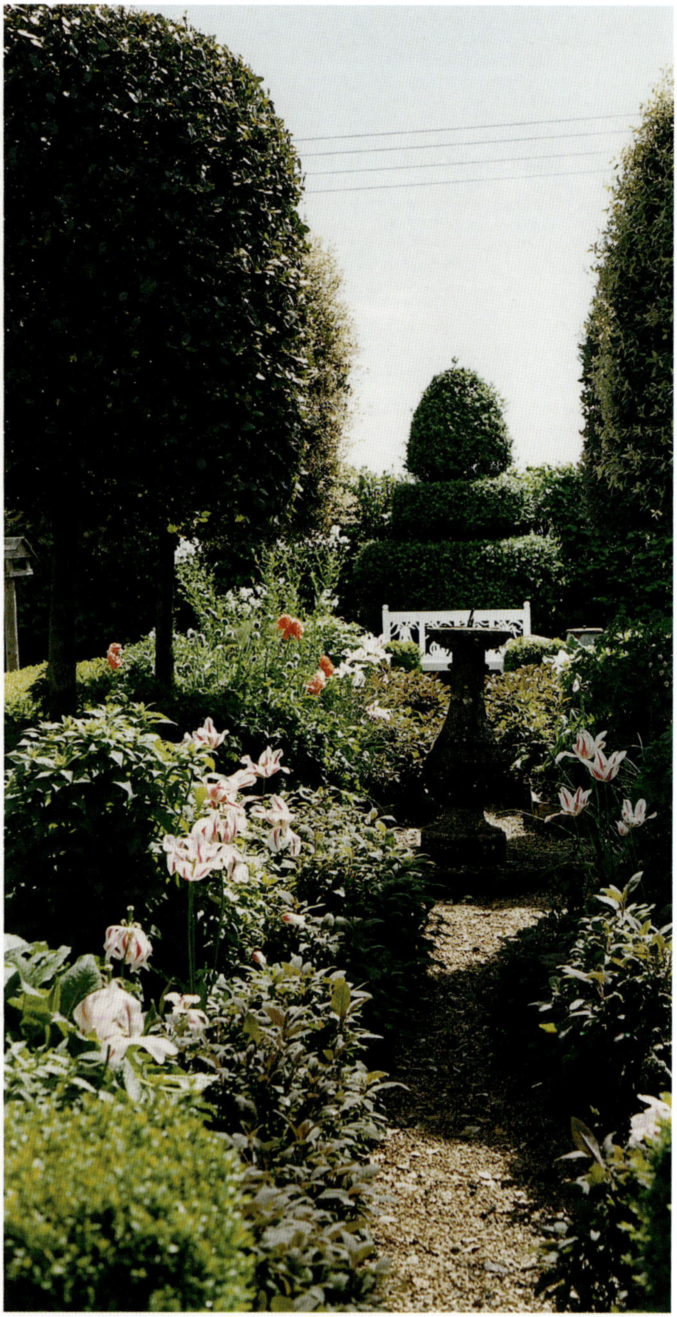

painted gypsy caravan under a tree, which I had seen in dust-jacket photographs. There is a stone half buried on the edge of the drive with the word "gipsy" carved into it.

Liccy showed me into Dahl's famous writing hut. There is part of a bone from his hip on the table next to his first metal hip replacement, which didn't take. There is a 10-pound ball of aluminum foil made from several years of Cadbury chocolate wrappers. There is a little surgical valve he invented that saved his son from hydrocephalus.

That night Liccy left me to examine Dahl's manuscripts in an office next to the guest house. An archivist made me wash my hands twice with special soap and told me to close all the curtains and lock the door when I was finished. I was

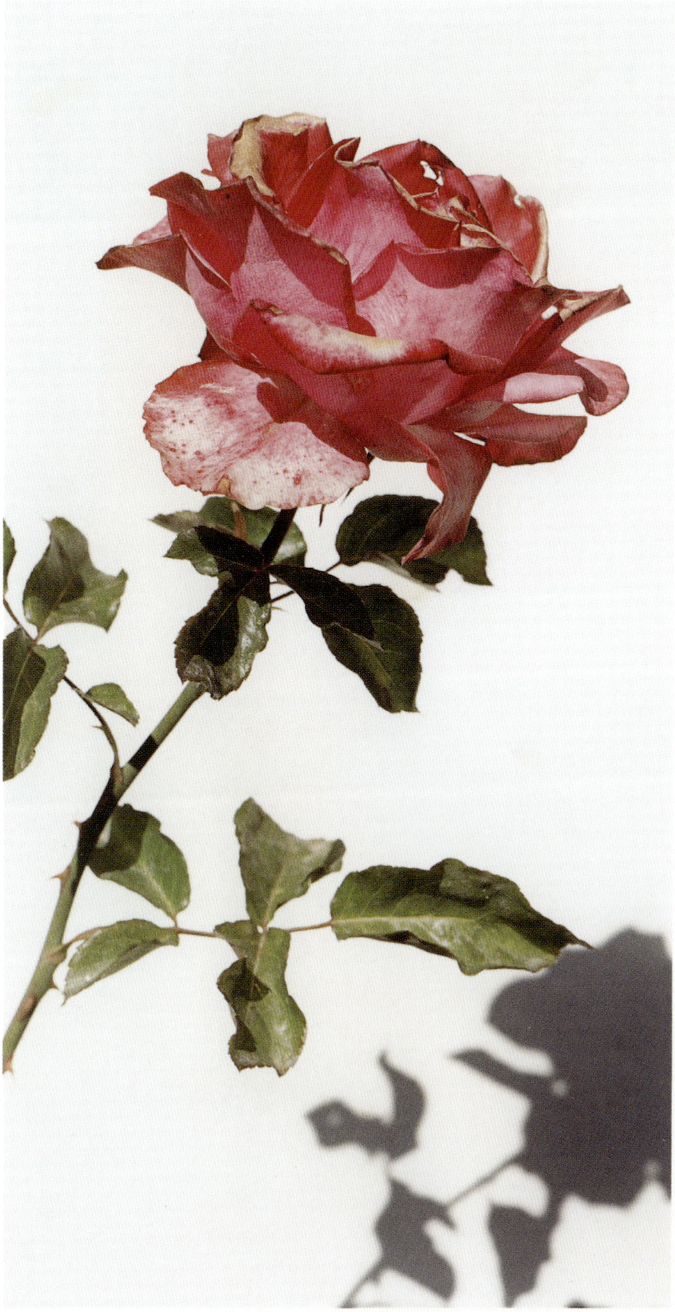

Far left: A wall of memorabilia in Dahl's writing hut. Left: The rose is one of the hundreds of antique varieties that populate the grounds. Old roses were one of Dahl's passions along with collecting 18th-century furniture and betting on the horses. Below: The door to Gipsy House. The sign is a family joke.

For more pilgrimages, see this week's Fashions of the Times.

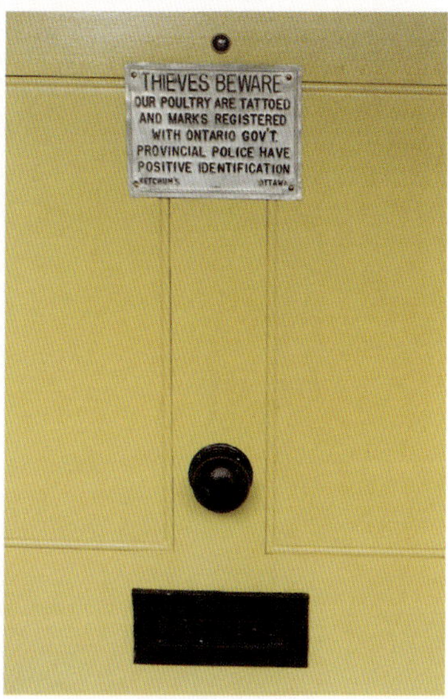

alone with dozens of handwritten drafts with Dahl's sketches in the margins, and I could see his whole process laid out in front of me. More than ever, I felt as if I were in his presence.

The next morning I walked with Liccy across a bridge over the highway to a church and the cemetery where Dahl is buried. The sky was dark, and it started to rain as we went to his grave. We shared an umbrella.

There is a monument made of a round wooden bench on a stone platform. Each of Dahl's eight children has a seat on the bench with his or her name carved into the back: Olivia, Tessa, Theo, Ophelia, Neisha, Charlotte, Lucy and Lorina. I wanted to sit for a while, but the bench was wet. Liccy and I walked back to the house in the rain. We had tea. ■

1. FANTASTIC MR FOX
AN AMERICAN ETC

TITLE SHOT IS LIKE THE COVER OF A BOOK. BIRDS, WIND BLOWING, CLOUDS MOVING, SUN GLIMMERS.

cut back to this after 3. then he says line & waits to meet her in 4.

EXT. WOODS. DAY

2. TIGHTER OF FOX. "WHAT'D THE ETC." BEFORE WE SEE:

An apple tree stands alone at the top of a hill. A handsome fox dressed in an Edwardian-style navy velvet suit leans against it with his arms folded and his legs crossed, chewing on a reed of wild grass. He holds an apple core in his paw. He spits out a seed. He looks off across a meadow that descends into the valley below.

A female fox strides briskly up the hill. Her coat is a paler, especially beautiful shade of fox-red, and she wears men's trousers and a dark tunic. Fox says as she approaches:

3. OVER TREE/ APPLE IN FOX'S HAND LOOKING DOWN HILL AT MRS. FOX

FOX
What'd the doctor say?

MRS. FOX
Nothing. Supposedly, it's just a twenty-four hour bug. He gave me some pills.

FOX
(reassuringly)
I told you. You probably just ate some bad gristle.

~~SHE JOINS HIM IN THIS~~

Fox brushes the fur on Mrs. Fox's ears with his paws. They walk together along the crest of the hill to a fork in the path.

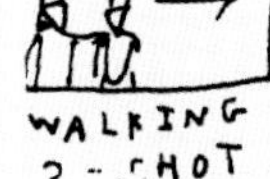

4. WALKING 2-SHOT

FOX (POINTING)
Should we take the short cut or the scenic route?

MRS. FOX
Let's take the short cut.

FOX
But the other way is so much more beautiful.

MRS. FOX
(shrugs)
OK, let's take the scenic route.

FOX
Great. It's actually slightly quicker, anyway.

Fox throws his apple core away over his shoulder and dances a quick circle around Mrs. Fox, wrapping his arm around her waist extravagantly and making her laugh as they start off down the scenic route.

AT END OF 4 CAMERA STOPS AS THEY PEEL AWAY FROM CAMERA & DOWN HILL:

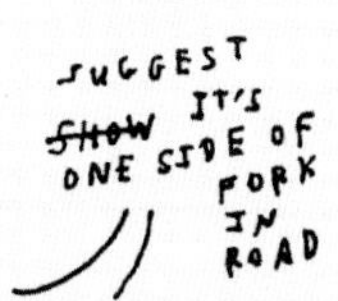

SUGGEST ~~SHOW~~ IT'S ONE SIDE OF FORK IN ROAD

I

A PINK SKY

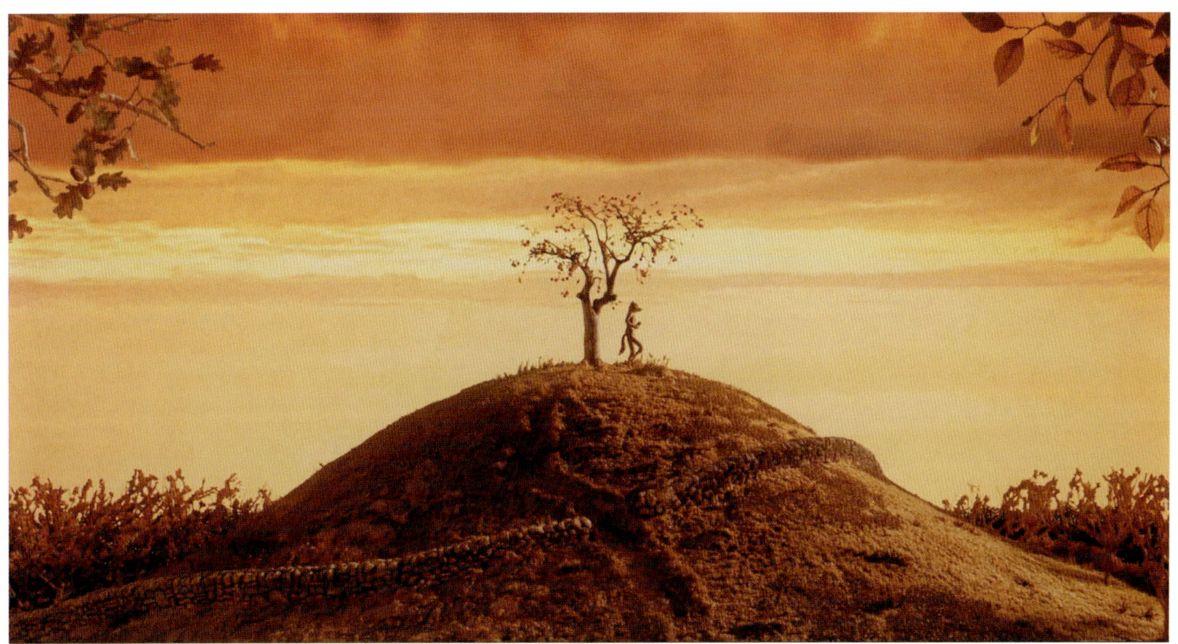

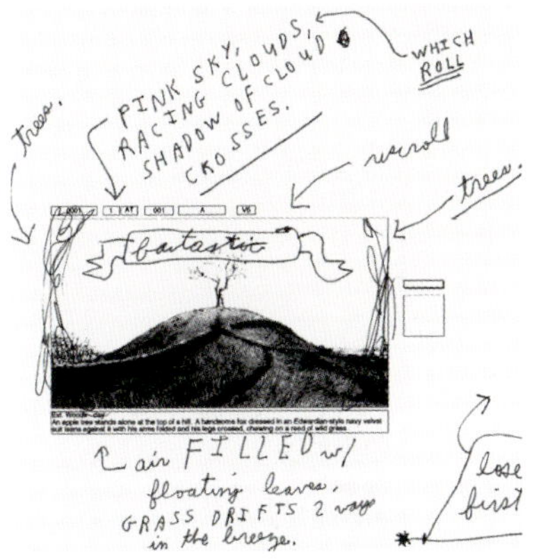

Opposite page: The first page of an early version of the screenplay annotated by Wes

Above: A shot from the opening of the movie

Left: Notes on the opening by Wes

Right: A book prop made for the film alongside an original edition of the book with artwork by Donald Chaffin

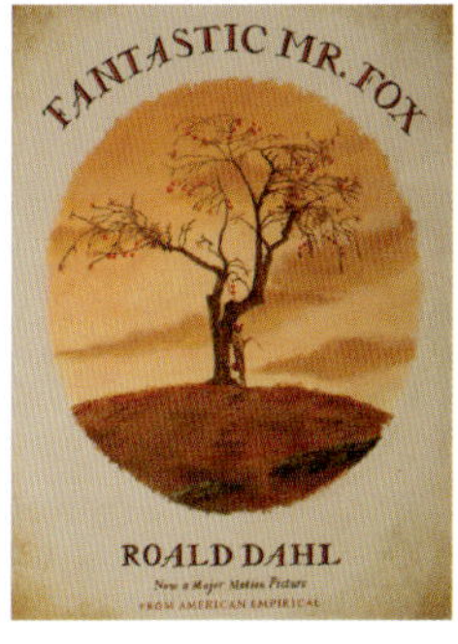

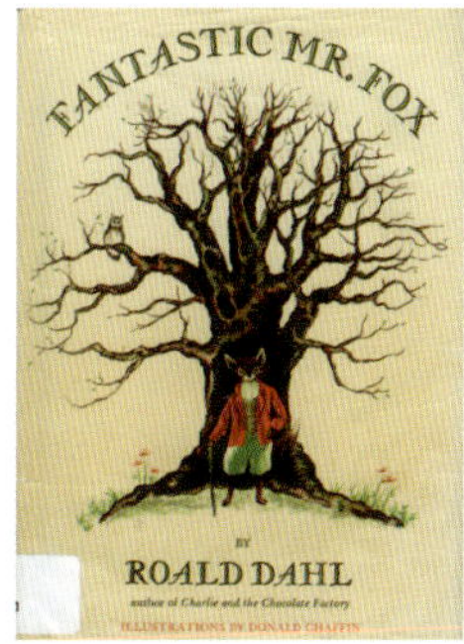

Right: Sketches and early artwork for the opening scene by Chris

Following pages: A photo by Greg of Wes with a Mr. Fox puppet in the puppet hospital at 3 Mills Studios in London

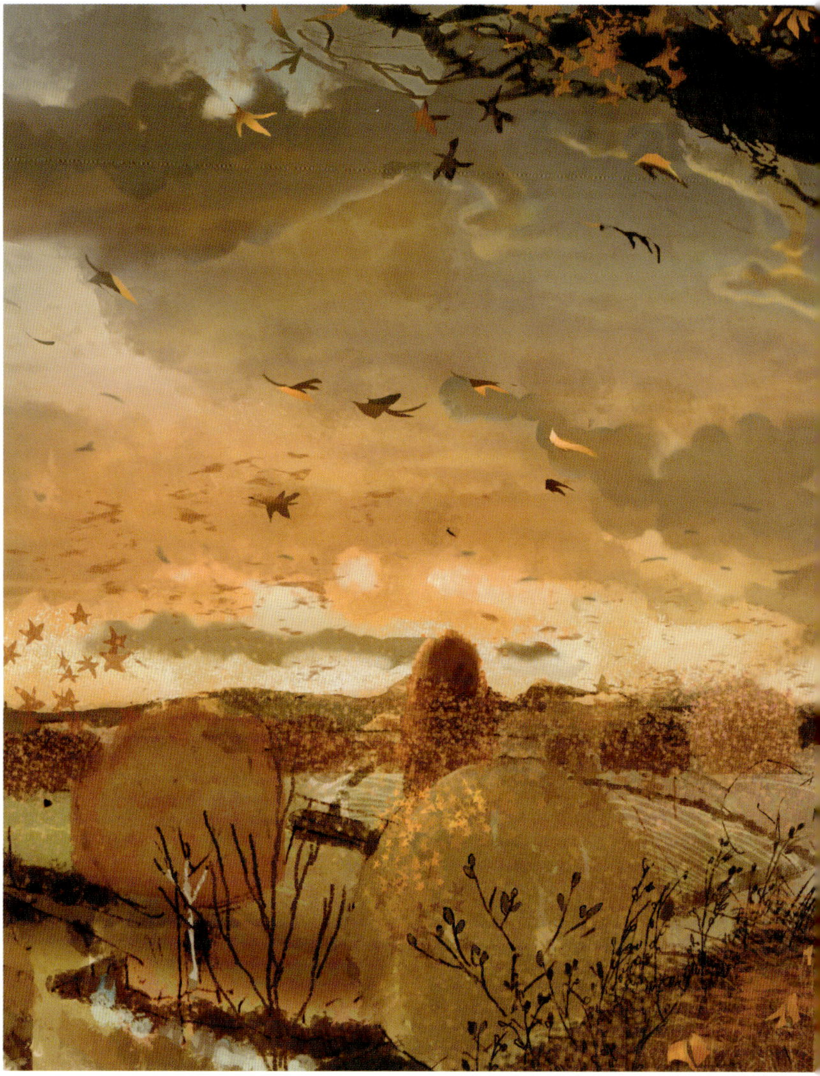

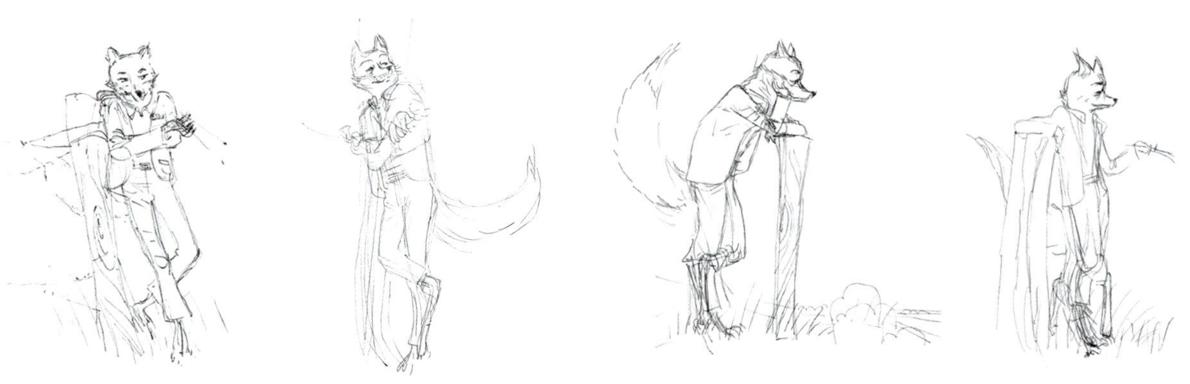

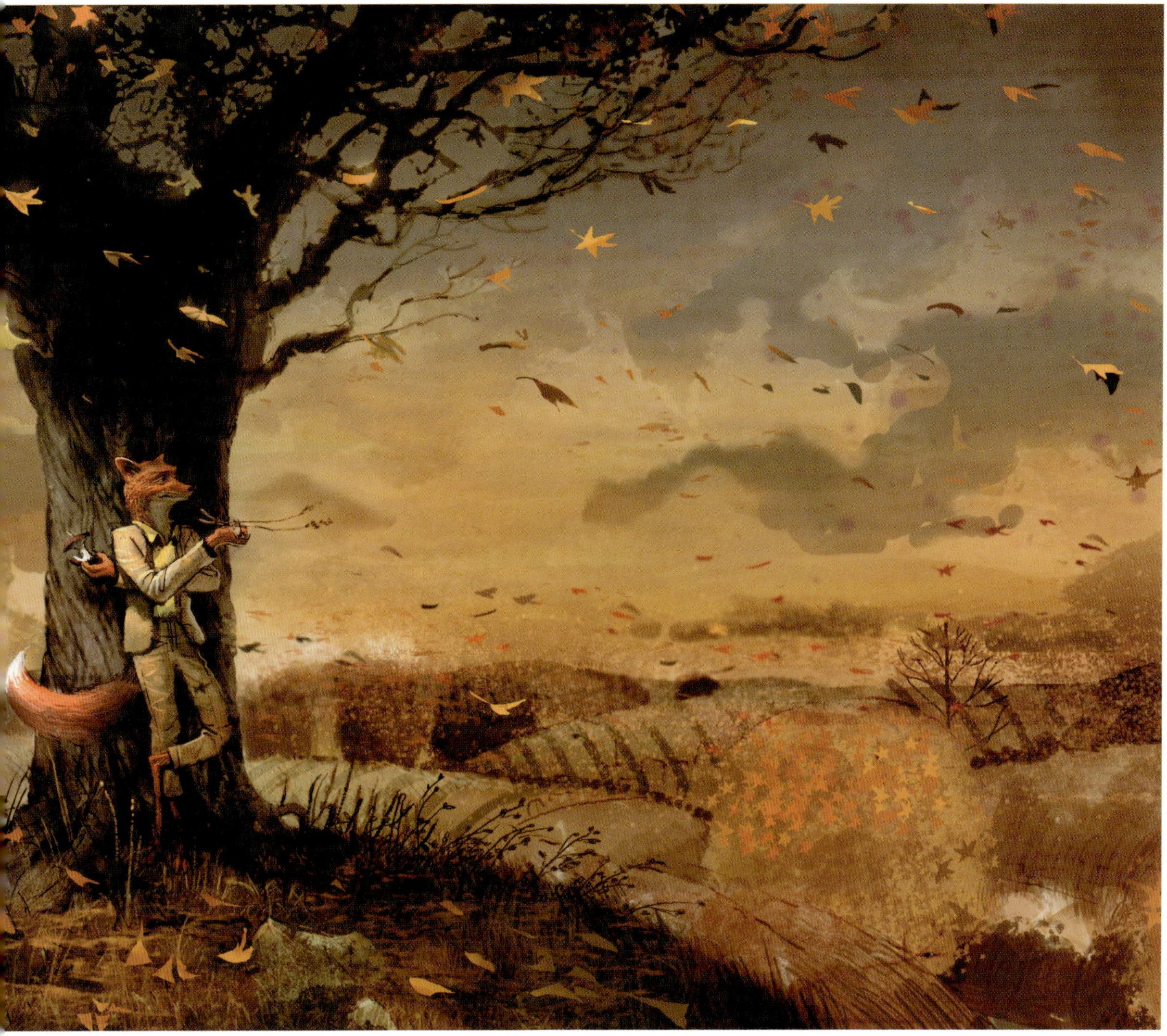

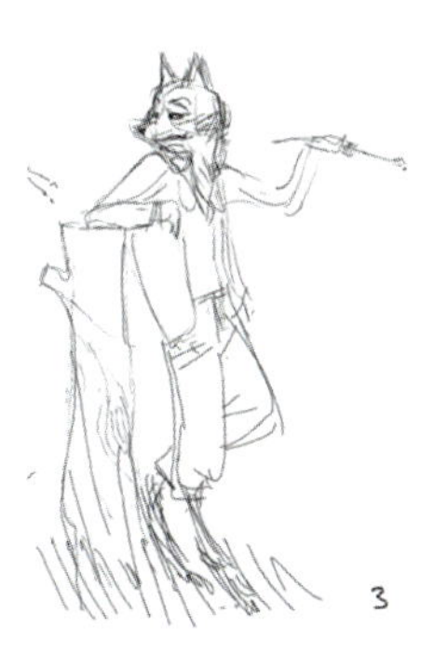
3

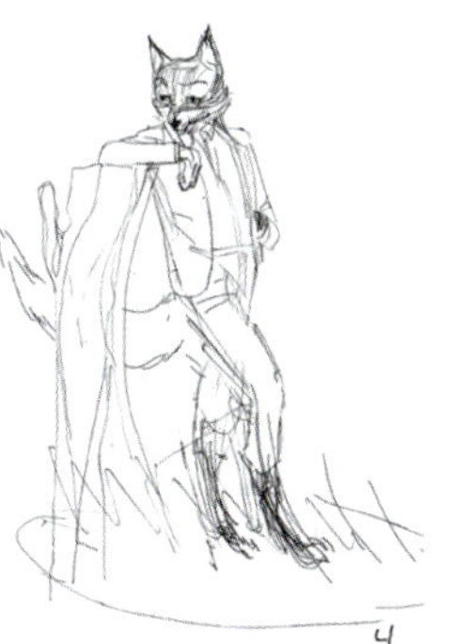
4

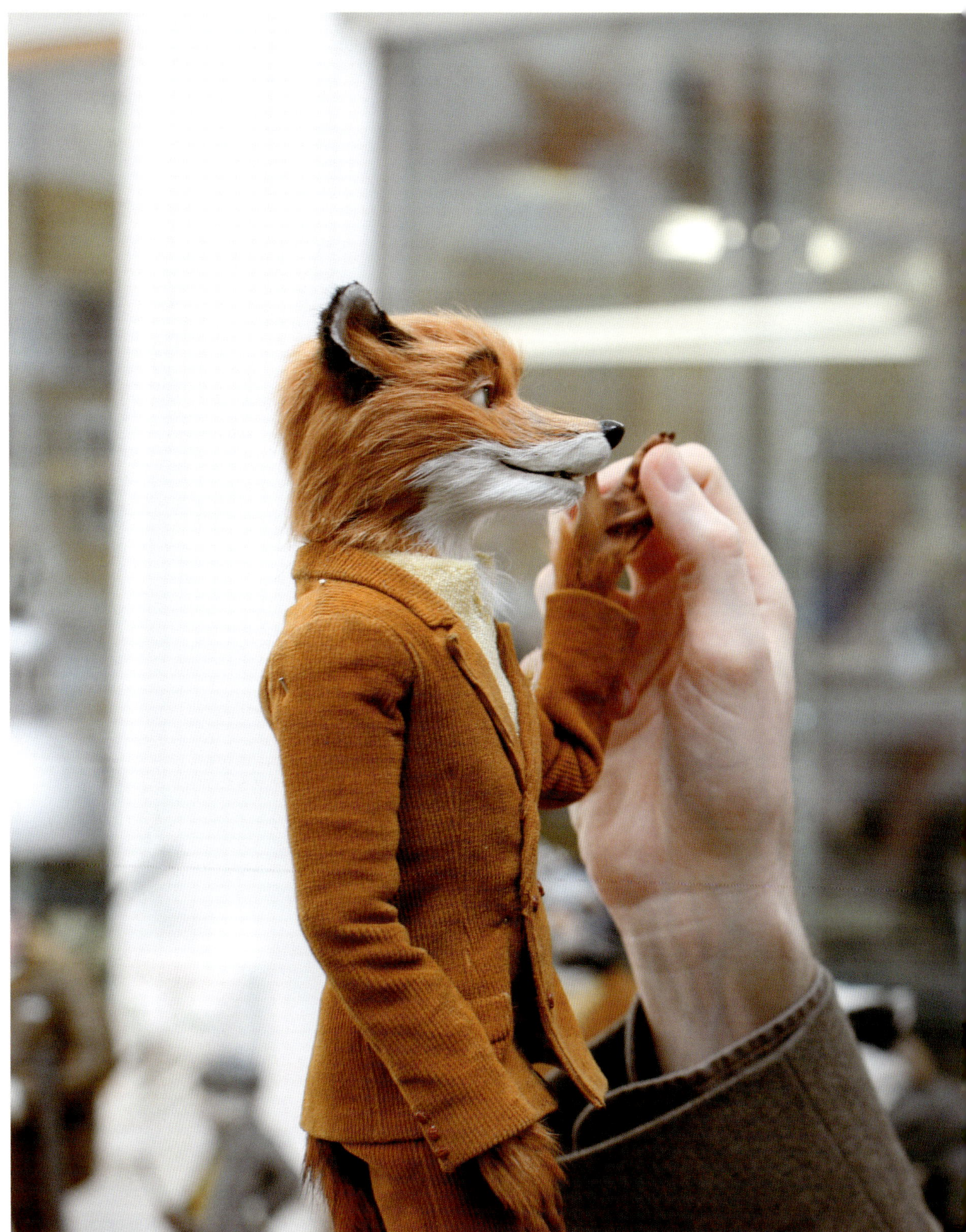

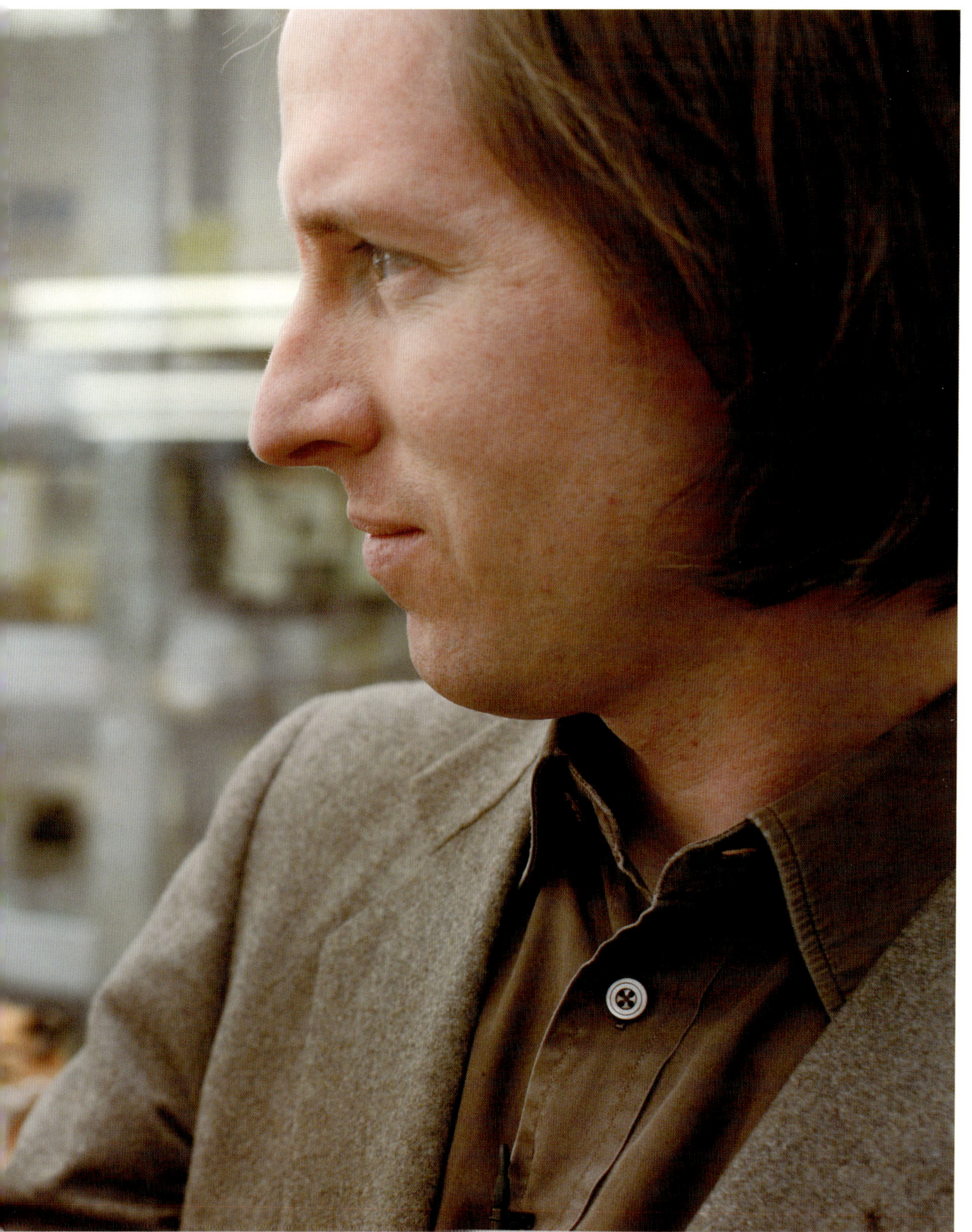

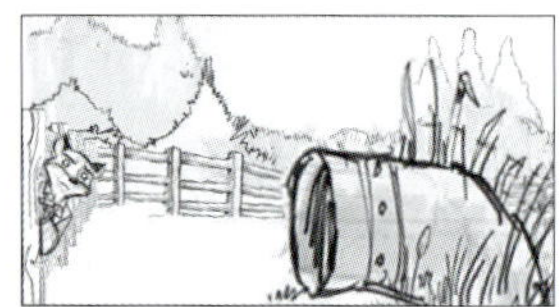

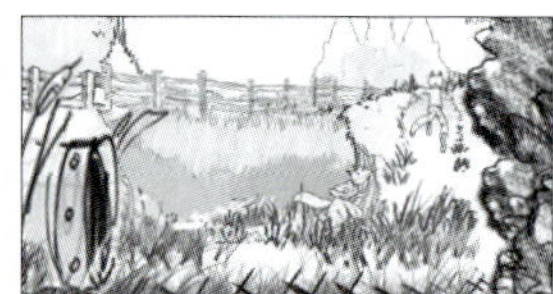

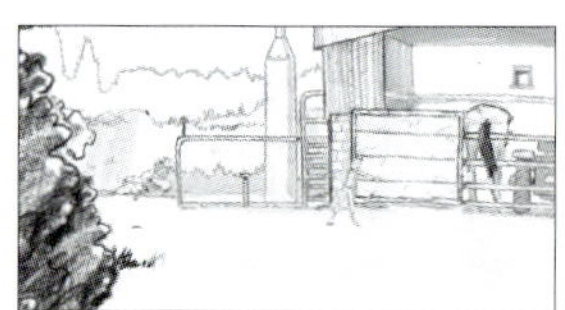

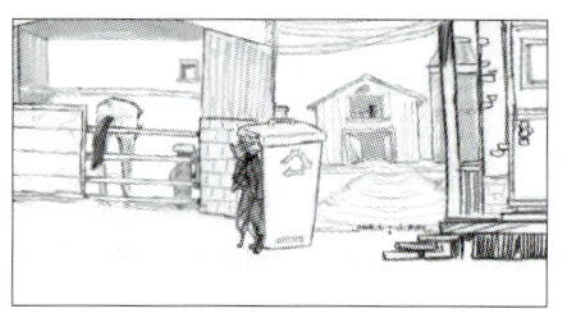

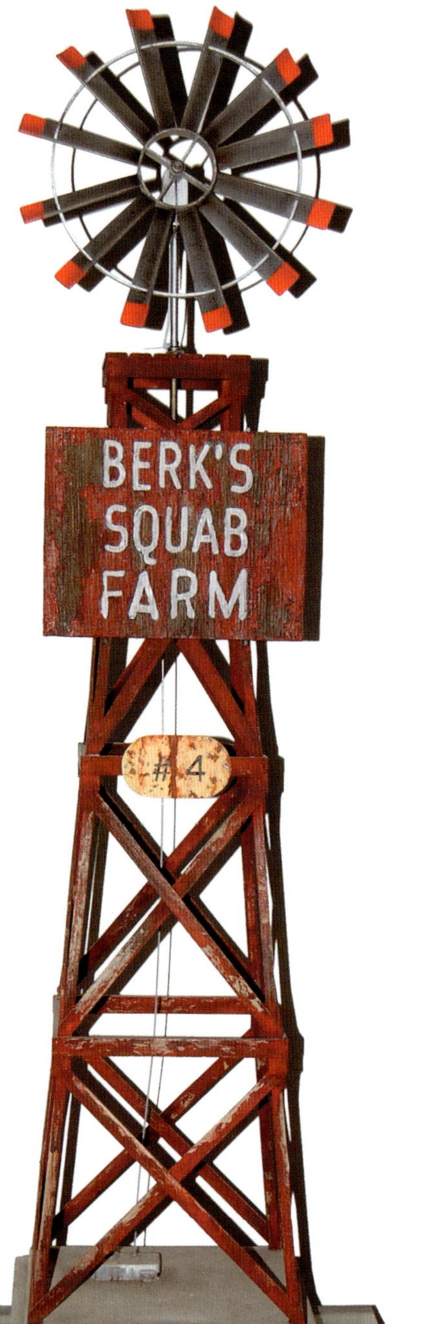

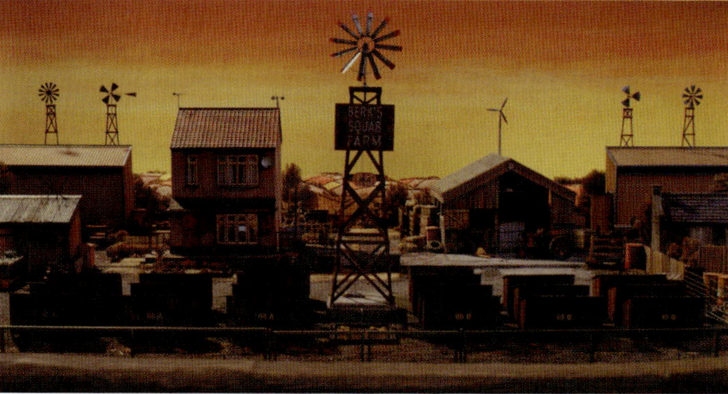

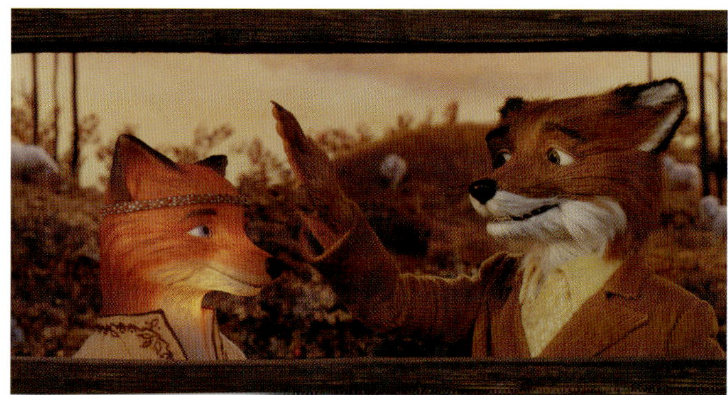

From: Wes Anderson
Subject: **Re: Tobias' Shot - Glowing Mrs Fox "Maybe it's the lighting"**
Date: 25 September 2008 13:15:40 BST
To: Tobias Fouracre

[Animator:] There is a specific line between the sun, his hand and her face that Fox is experimenting with.

[Wes] THIS SENTENCE COULD BE THE FIRST LINE OF A VERY SOPHISTICATED POEM AND ALSO VERY ACCURATELY DESCRIBES WHAT WE WANT HERE.

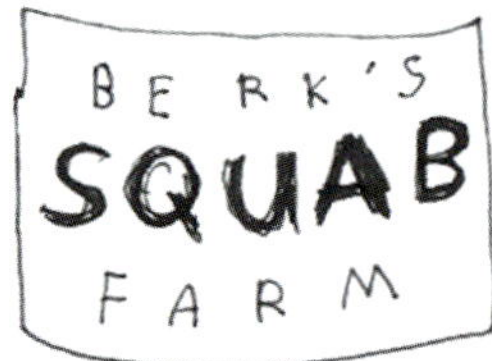

Above: Storyboards by Christian and stills from the squab farm raid scene

Far left: The windmill prop from the squab farm

Near left: A sketch by Wes of the farm sign

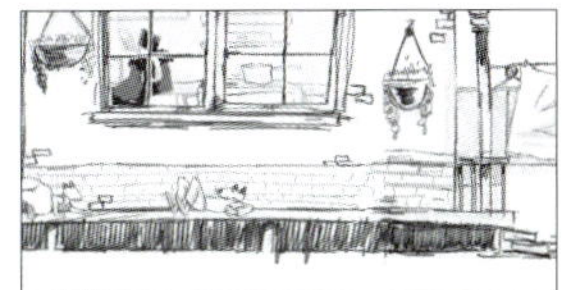

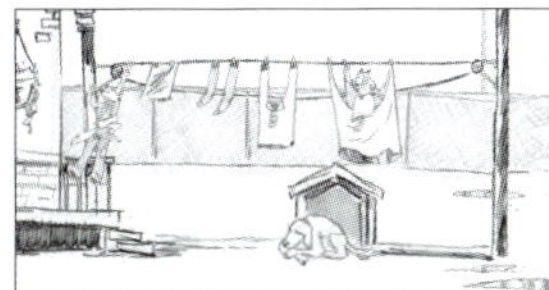

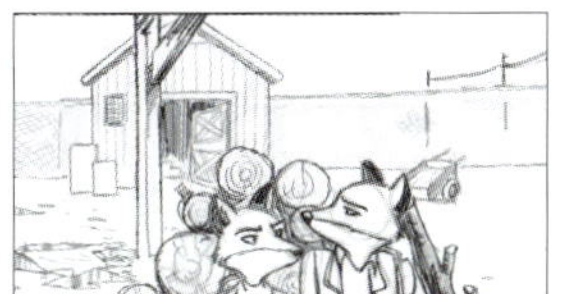

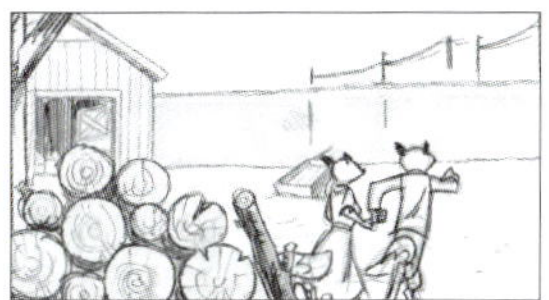

From: Wes Anderson
Subject:
Date: 15 November 2008 20:20:17 GMT
To: Nelson Lowry

Nelson and Mark, I had an idea for the shot of the Squab Farm—the thing we could do that would provide us more animation in the establishing shot is to add 6 more smaller windmills—each different and meant to be at different distances—some tin ones on little towers, one or 2 attached to rooftops, a more modern one somewhere—and then when we boom down we see one little one in the foreground that is maybe more like a pinwheel you know—so part of the idea for the shot is windmills everywhere.

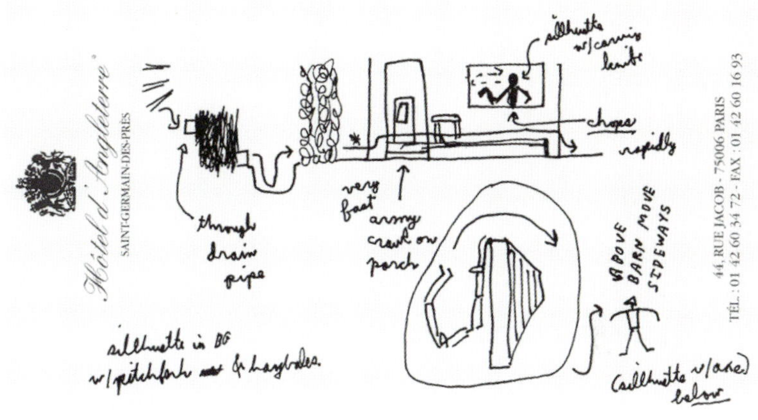

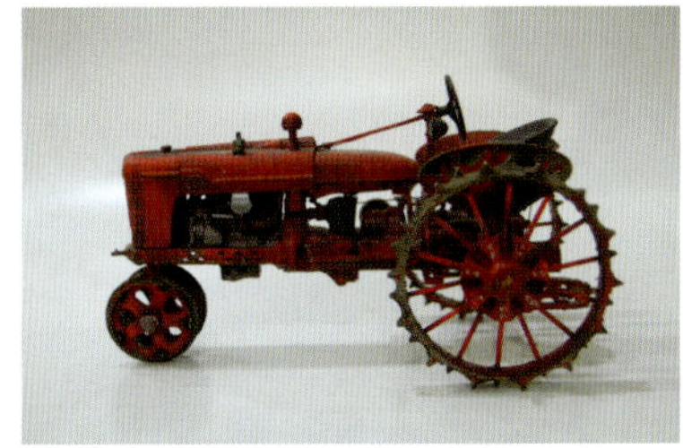

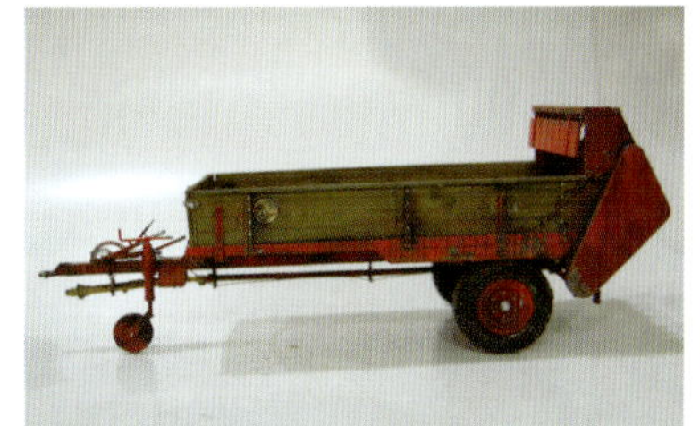

Above right: A sketch for the long dolly shot by Wes

Right: The "hairy hut" in the gardens of Roald Dahl's house, photographed by Wes, and a hut made for the film

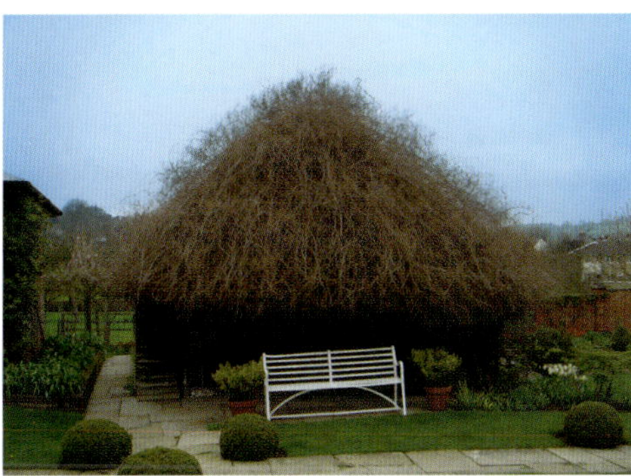

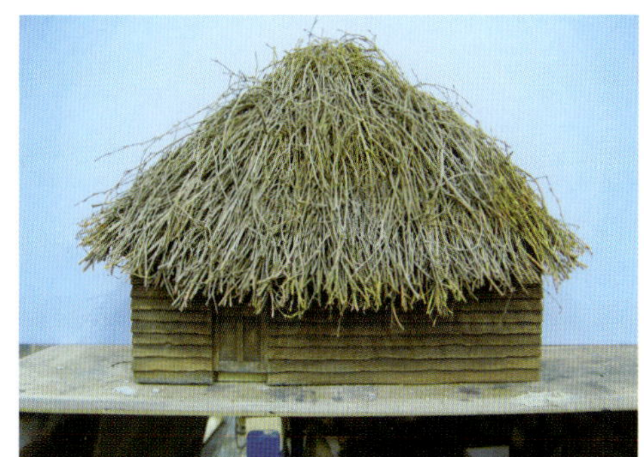

AN INTERVIEW WITH

WES ANDERSON

6/29/09

MS: *Now that I get to interview you after all the years we've known each other, I have all sorts of amazingly mean questions I can ask.*
WA: Oh, yes. Oh, good.

What I wanted to ask you first is if you could very briefly kind of describe your working day on this set, and I mean when you're wherever you are, and they're shooting in London.
Yes, yes, okay. Wherever I am. Yes, well during the shooting each day begins with all of us reviewing the previous day's work. For me, that happens the previous night. I get the dailies usually sometime between eleven and midnight or, depending on where I am, sometimes I've been operating on a completely different time zone from everyone else. But usually I watch the dailies at night, and then I send my notes by e-mail to the crew in London about the various shots, which have progressed a few seconds each. Then they watch the dailies in the next morning, and they review my notes, and then they write me back or call me, and we figure out what the game plan is. Then people go out on their sets and get to work, and when there's a new shot being organized I get e-mails with the images of the shots, so I can respond. I work with Jeremy, one of our producers, and Tristan, or whichever director of photography is on that particular shot, and I work with Mark, the director of our animation, and all the animators, and we figure out the blocking, and we get the lenses right and the shots right. We get it all set up and refine it and go back and forth a bit. We also have this software where I can look through any of the cameras on any of the units. At the most we had twenty-nine units, I think, and I can see what the camera's seeing on each unit, and I can also have a live image from those units. Then, at the same time, I work with Nelson, the production designer, on the upcoming sets, and Andy, who is in charge of the puppets department, sorting out whatever's left to sort out with the design and details of the puppets, and Alice in the art department on the costumes, and Andy Weisblum, our editor, plus Steve and Ralph and the rest of the editing gang, on the cut of the movie, and we have Christian, our storyboard artist, who's drawing the shots. The day just sort of makes its way along, interacting with all these different departments, and I just sit at my computer all day and am on the phone or looking at all these e-mails. But it's just a continuous thing throughout the day, and we've got all these systems worked out so it's very efficient. That was a long answer, but…

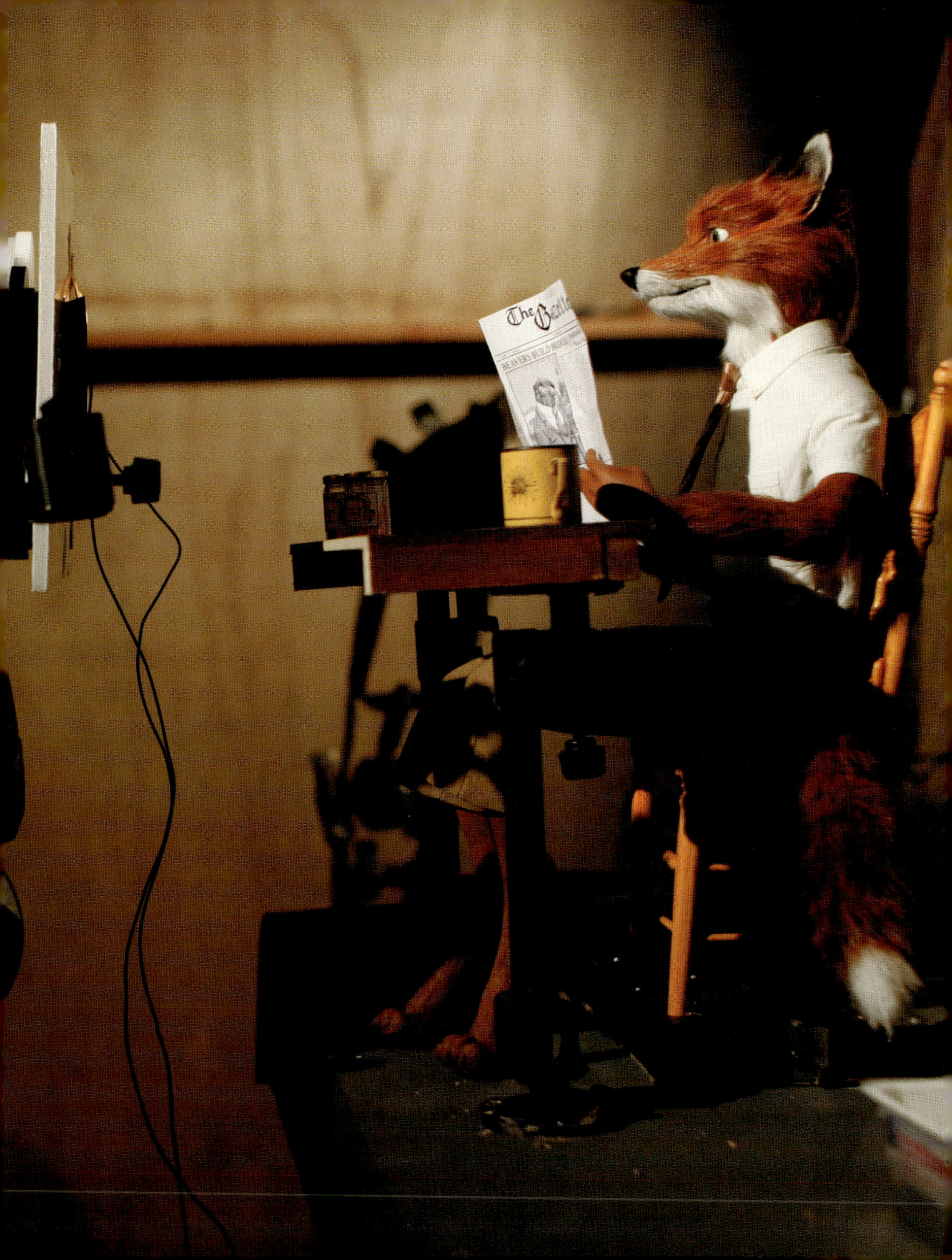
BEAVERS BUILD BRIDGES

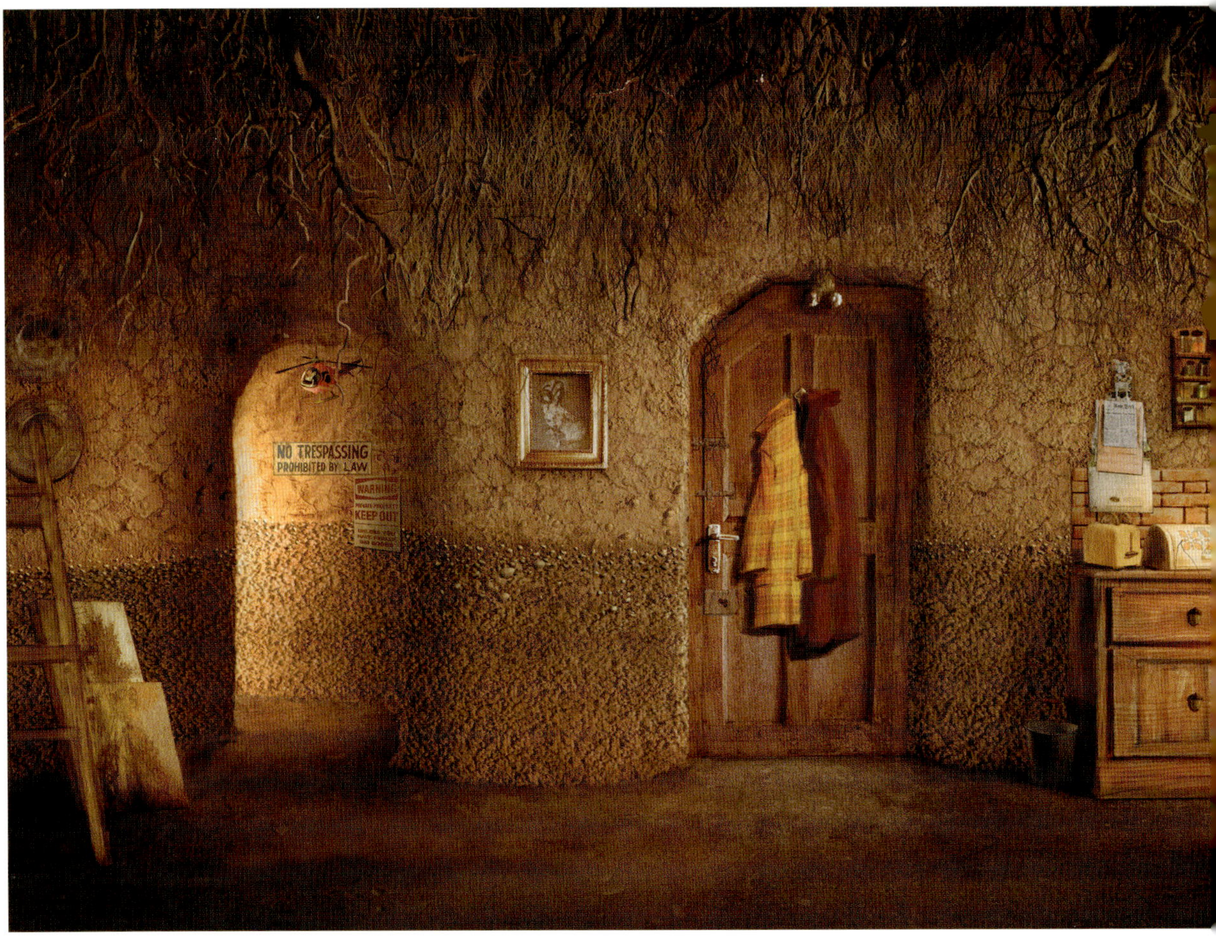

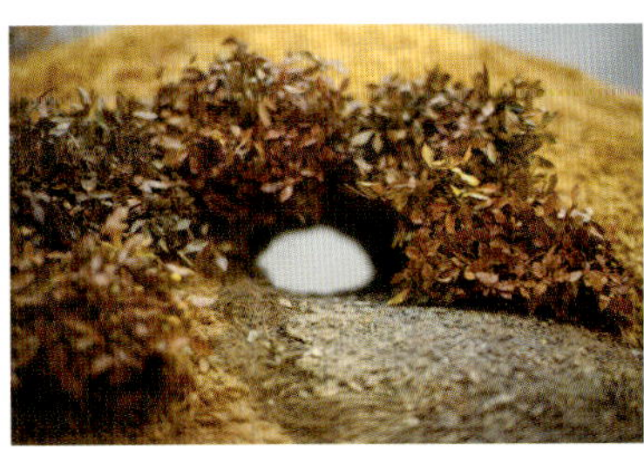

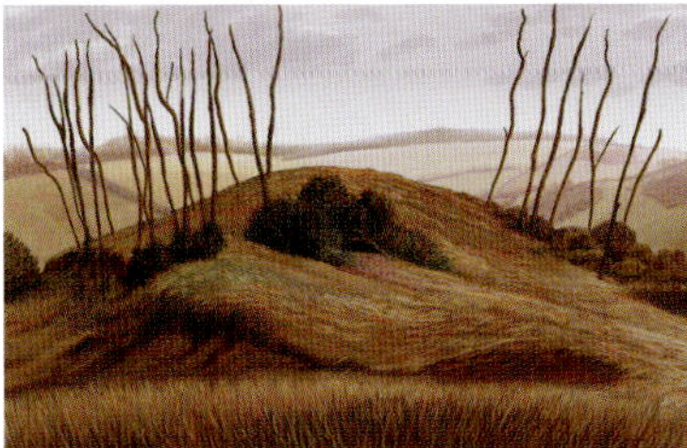

Above: The final concept artwork for the foxhole kitchen by Turlo

Left: A photograph of the foxhole exterior, alongside concept artwork by Turlo

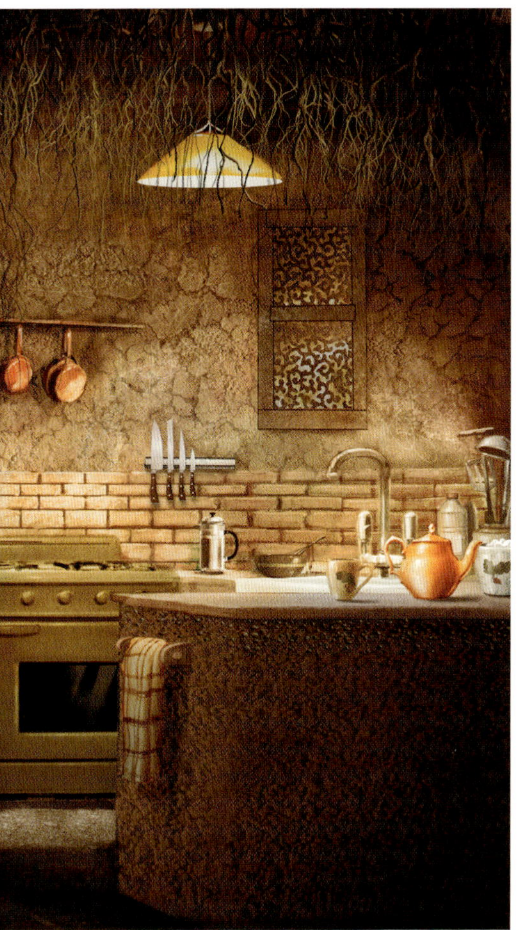

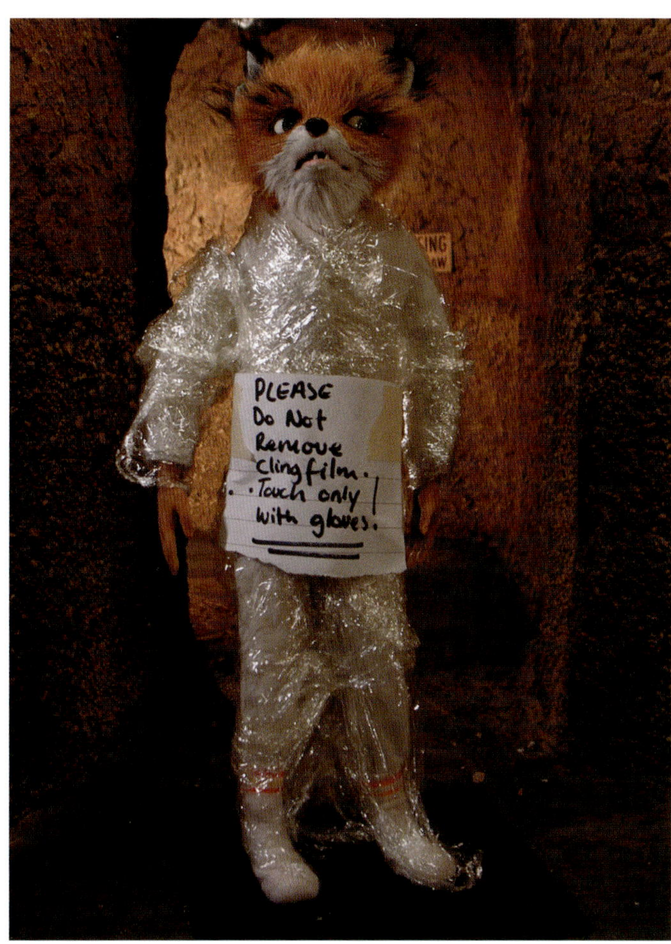

32 * The Gazette Wednesda

FOX About Town with Mr. Fox

It is the twig-runner's dilemma and always has been. When you face a burning pinecone

The breeze picks up and a change of season comes upon us. Once again, we find ourselves savouring the dusky, smoke filled air, the sweetest of the year, and scampering about, even as hibernation awaits just ahead, tapping its impatient hind paws-- and so we return to the whack-bat pitch.

Whack-bat metaphors never sound convincing, do they? Nevertheless, permit me to attempt one, or another, as my few regular readers may interject. I once knew a stoat who wore three undershirts in the summer. I used to call him Toasty, in fun, but he never failed to take offence. Can a fox on a hill smell fear in the

I have never crossed paths with an English Wolf, but pardon my French they scare the cuss out of me. What sort of creature sleeps with the windows open? Answer: one with long claws and about ten stone on yours truly. So we named our cheery little team the Wild English Wolves and had eleven T shirts made up. No elected body has ever actually "represented" its people in any sense other than the symbolic.

The batter never swings lest the pine cone is lit. A truism, yes -- but a potent one. When you face a burning pine cone do the hairs on your coat bristle? My drink is 85 proof rye, cool, in a nutshell, but you can never get it dry enough for me. So let it be with whack-bat, hops, reeds, thunderstorms and other matters of the vale.

Tomorrow I shall continue with these musings and if anyone out there is listening please chirp! I will hear you.

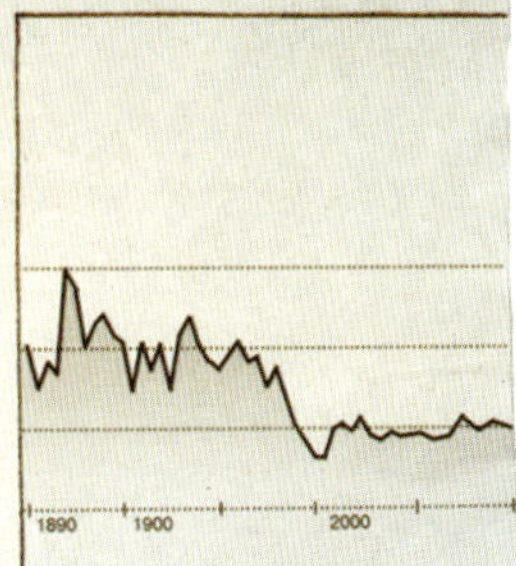

No tree virus yet discovered replicates during the monsoon.

Science

The noted molecular biologist Melvin L.T. Skunk-Ferret has published the fourth in his series of analytical reports

Above right: An Ash puppet awaiting a shot

Right: Mr. Fox's column in *The Gazette*, the newspaper prop made for the movie

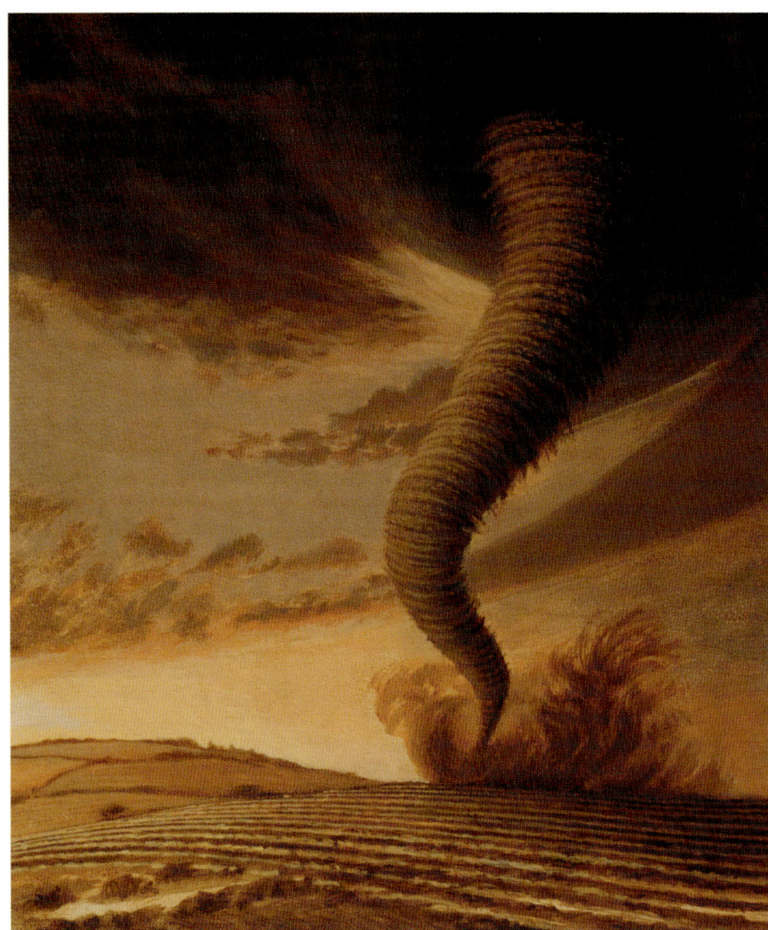

Artists Turlo Griffin and Roy Bell at work on Mrs. Fox's mural

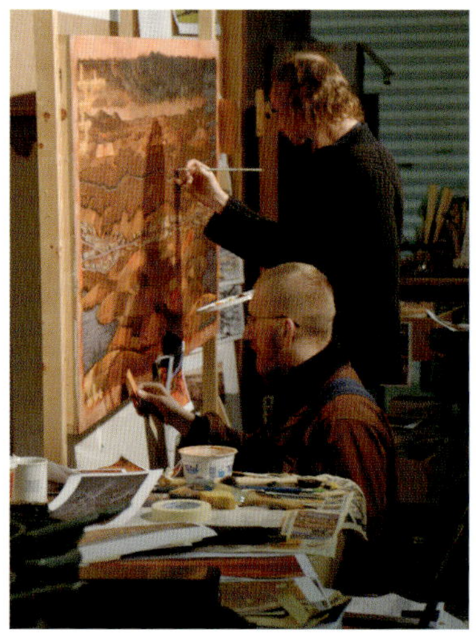

Felicity Fox

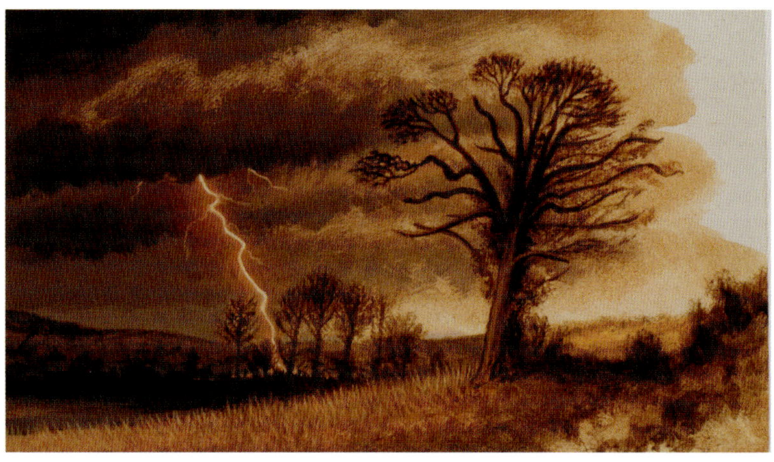

Mrs. Fox's miniature paintings. The paintings were made by Turlo Griffin, an environment designer on the movie; Mrs. Fox's signature was based on that of Albrecht Dürer.

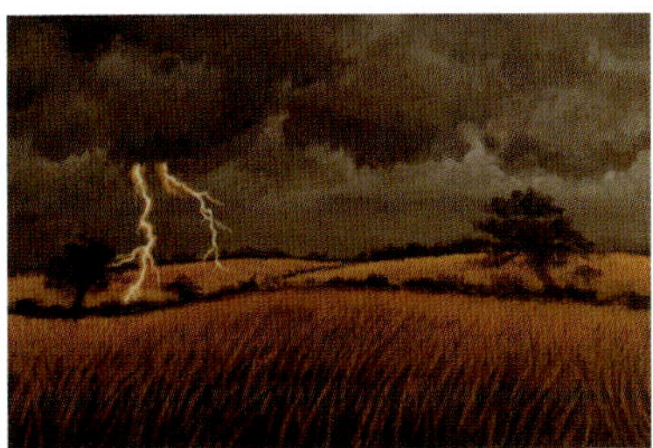
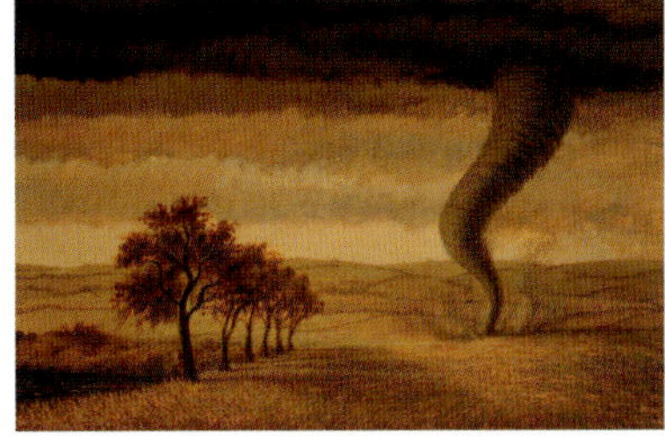
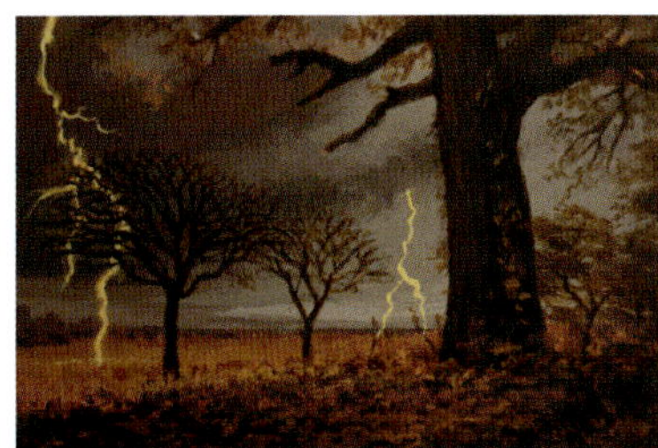
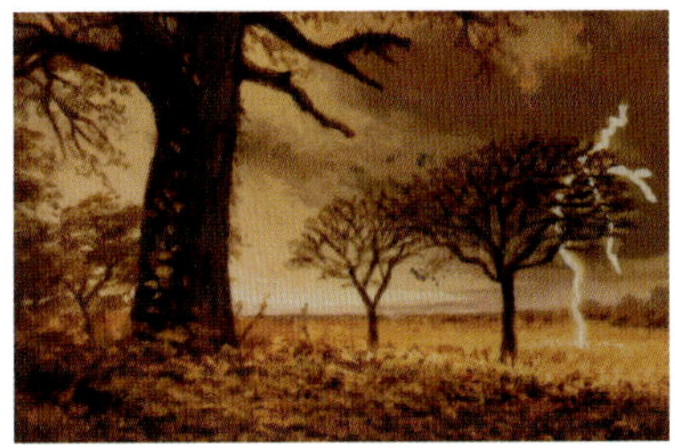
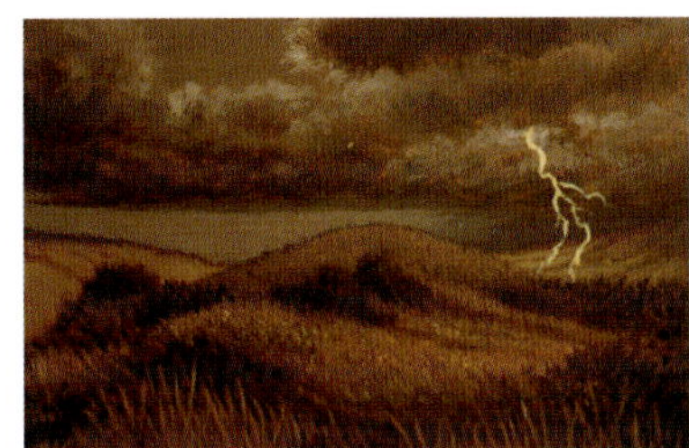
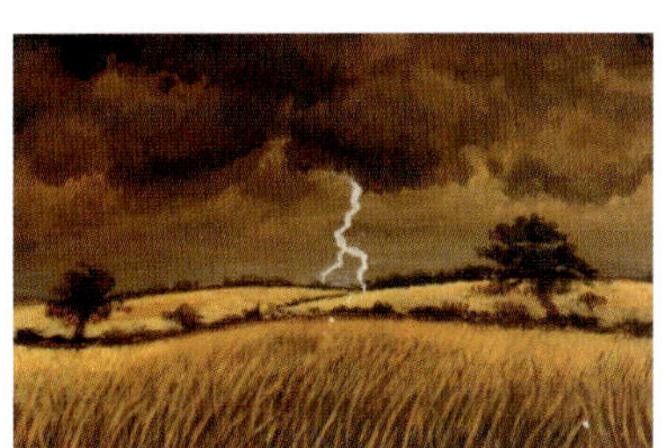

MS: *No, it's amazingly complex. I mean, it's simple, but in the most complex possible way, if you get that. But let's go back to the question of what drew you to this particular book of all the Dahls—I know that you've read others of his and that you care about him.*

WA: Yes. I love Dahl, and this was not only the first Roald Dahl book I ever read—I think it was the first book I ever possessed. It was published just after I was born. I think he was probably in the process of finishing writing it during the minute that I was born, and it was published shortly thereafter, although I don't suppose this registered with him, at the time. I loved this book as a child. I loved the character of Mr. Fox, this sort of heroic and slightly full of himself animal, and I also loved the digging. My brothers and I were obsessed with being underground.

And did you ever try personally in your life to dig that way?

Yes, we did. You know, at one point we got involved with an underground fort that we did not initiate, but that some friends of the family's sons, who were older and who had dirt bikes, like motorcycles and, you know, they hunted and had surfboards and they did more dangerous sports than we seemed to ever be involved in. They had built an underground fort that we sort of participated in that had tunnels, and it was in a large mound in a forest. It really was like a complex, it was like an anthill. We did some digging at our house, but we ran into some electrical pipes and things and did some damage and it didn't really work out that well. We also dug a hole through the roof of the house, which wasn't very popular, to try to make sort of a secret access to the attic.

Oh, parents really love that.

Yes, yes, they love that, when you open up the roof of the house.

Yeah. So do you see this movie as a movie for kids, for adults, for smart kids?

I've been thinking about this lately. Who is it for? I prefer not to ask that question, but, in fact, I didn't. There are lots of movies for kids that I like and have always liked. *The Bad News Bears* is one that I've always loved. I've always talked to people about how much I like that movie. That's a movie for kids, but it doesn't make any compromises based on the fact that it's for children. The movie ends with the Bears losing the game, drinking beers with the coach, and there's quite a lot of profanity, and one of the kids smokes cigarettes. And, you know, I don't really like the movement in children's movies toward—I'm not fond of this thing where it gets so clean and safe. It's just very unpleasant to me. And so I wanted to make a movie for kids, but I wanted to do one that—certainly our movie is not really violent, and instead of swearing they say the word "cuss." But it's not been made deliberately safe, and instead we tried to keep it free and a bit wilder like Dahl—and I would like to think it stands for something even though I couldn't tell you precisely what.

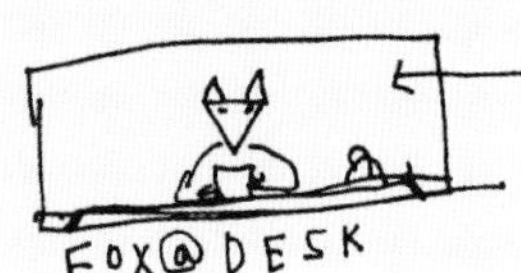

FOX@DESK

SOMETHING IN B.G. (OTHER OFFICES? water cooler. clock. file cabinet.)

FOX

I want to say I hate this job, but that would make it seem more important to me than I want people to think it is.

Fox starts typing again monotonously. The raccoon comes back and hands Fox a little torn slip of newspaper.

RACCOON

I almost forgot. I know you're looking.

INSERT:

A clipping from the real estate section. There is a photograph of a wide, sprawling beech tree at the top of a hill. A caption below it reads:

Tree Living, Great Views, Classic Beech

TIGHTER VERSION OF ABOVE

Fox stares at the advertisement.

CUT TO:

The wide, sprawling beech tree at the top of the hill. Fox stands next to it with a skinny weasel in a khaki outfit beside him. Weasel checks his watch and mutters to himself:

SHOT OF TREE (same as newspaper picture)

WEASEL

Kylie, where are you?

FOX

(vaguely)

Who's Kylie?

WEASEL & FOX (maybe tighter)

WEASEL

Kylie's the super. He's supposed to meet us with the key. He's a little --

Weasel makes a fluttering gesture with his paw. Fox nods. A twig snaps behind them, and Fox looks back, past Weasel. He says gently:

FOX

Catching anything, Mr. Kylie?

PAN ~~AFTER~~ ~~FOX~~ AFTER

Weasel turns and sees a heavy-set opossum with a cowlick approaching through the bushes with a fishing rod over his shoulder. He carries a bucket. He is Kylie.

KYLIE

Just minnows. You want one?

TO KYLIE COMING UP THE HILL.

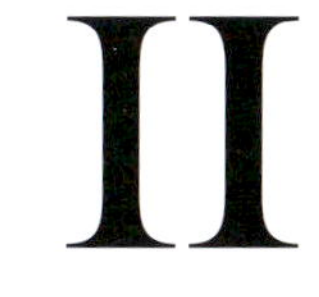

A TREE ON A HILL

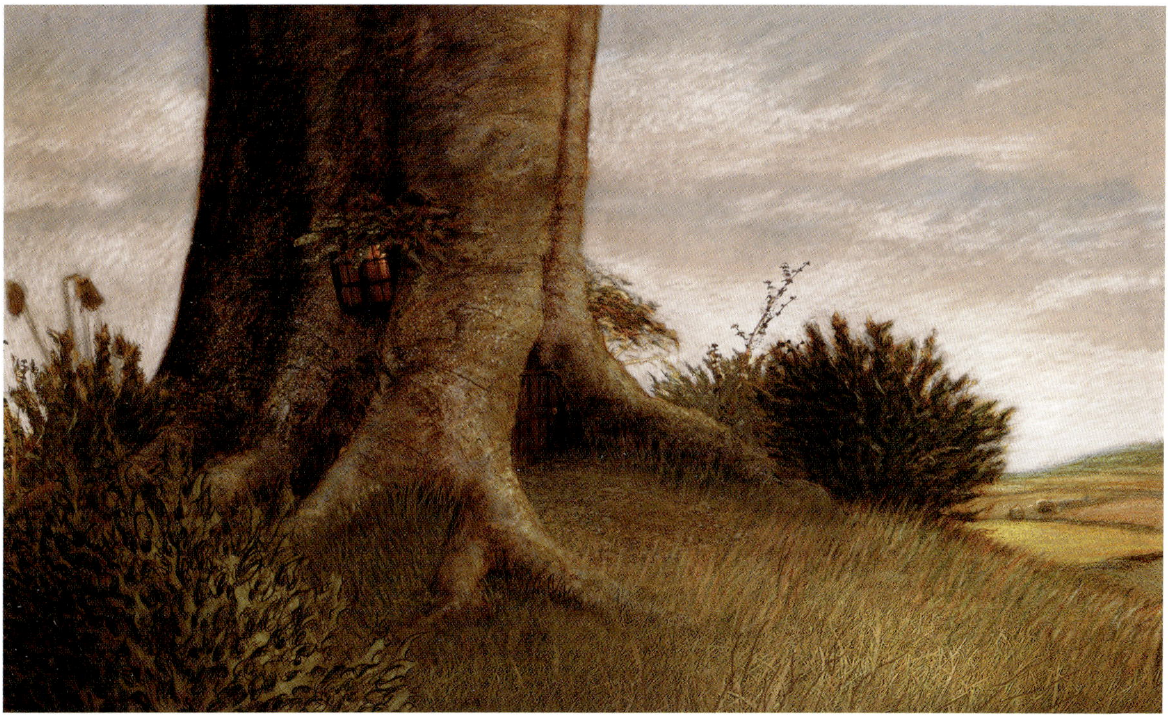

Sketches and early artwork for the tree base by Turlo

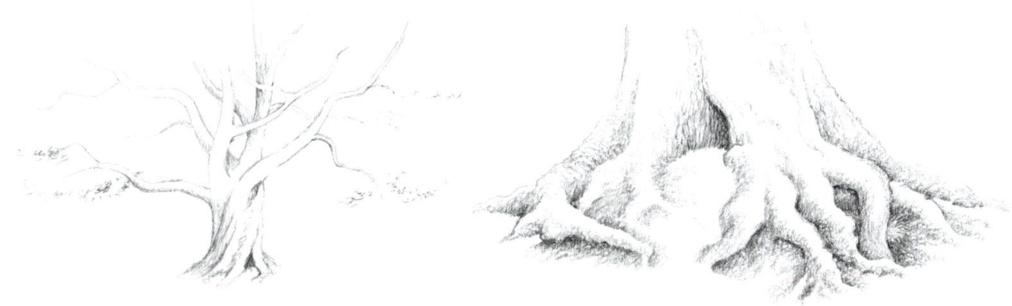

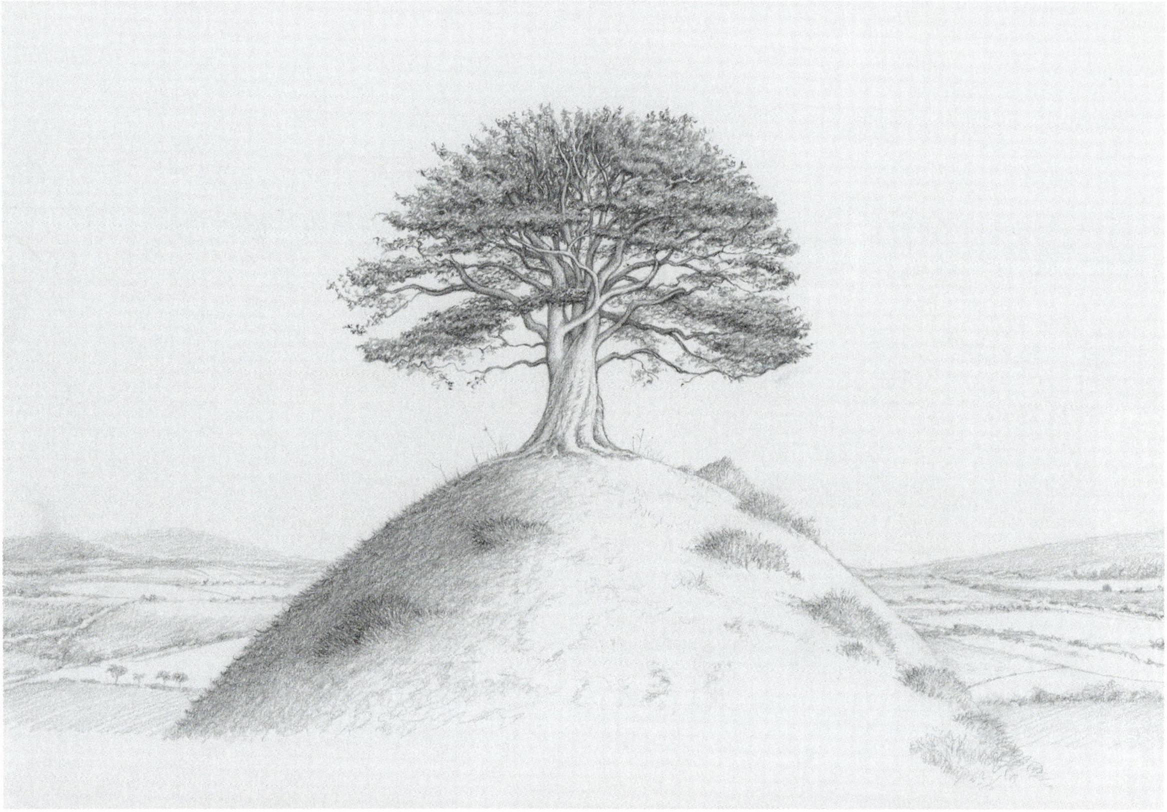

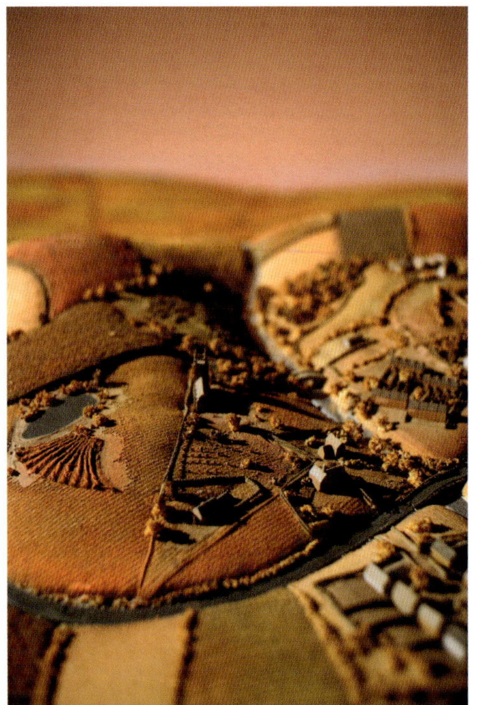

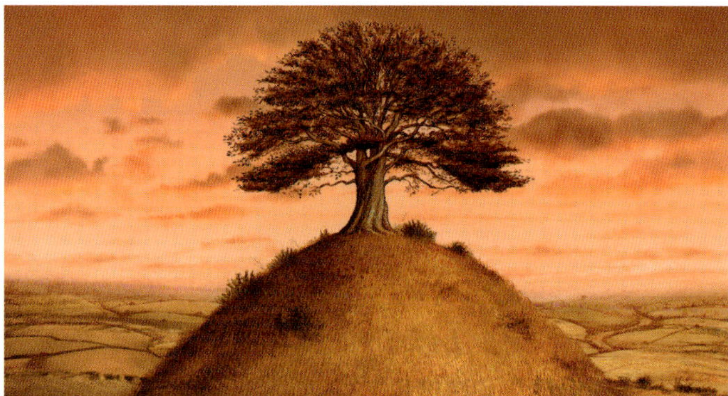

Artwork by Turlo for the tree and the hill

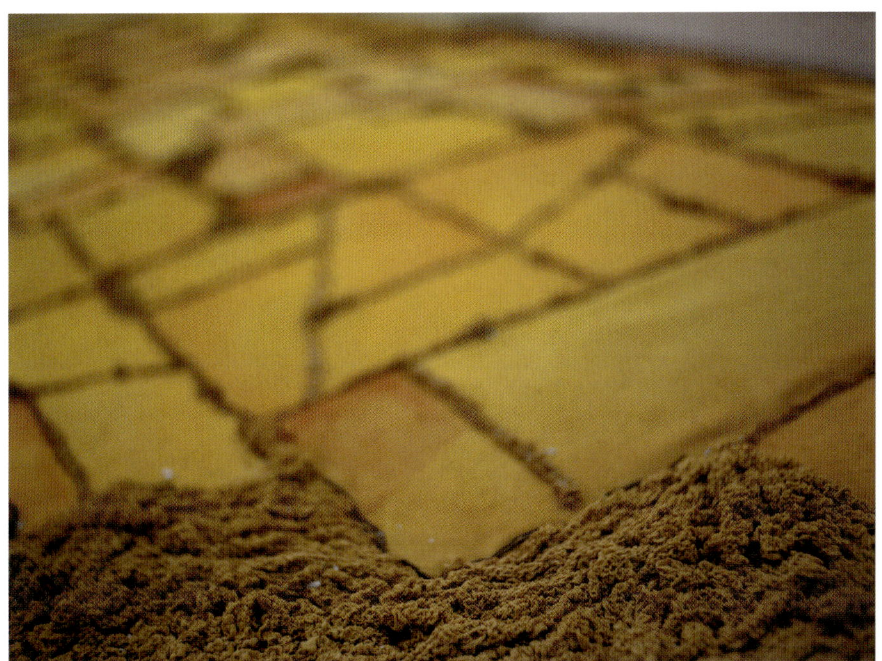

Photographs of the landscape and the tree being assembled in the workshop. The landscape was sculpted by hand and then covered with dyed towels, tea leaves, and cut-up air conditioner filters to create the texture of leaves and grass.

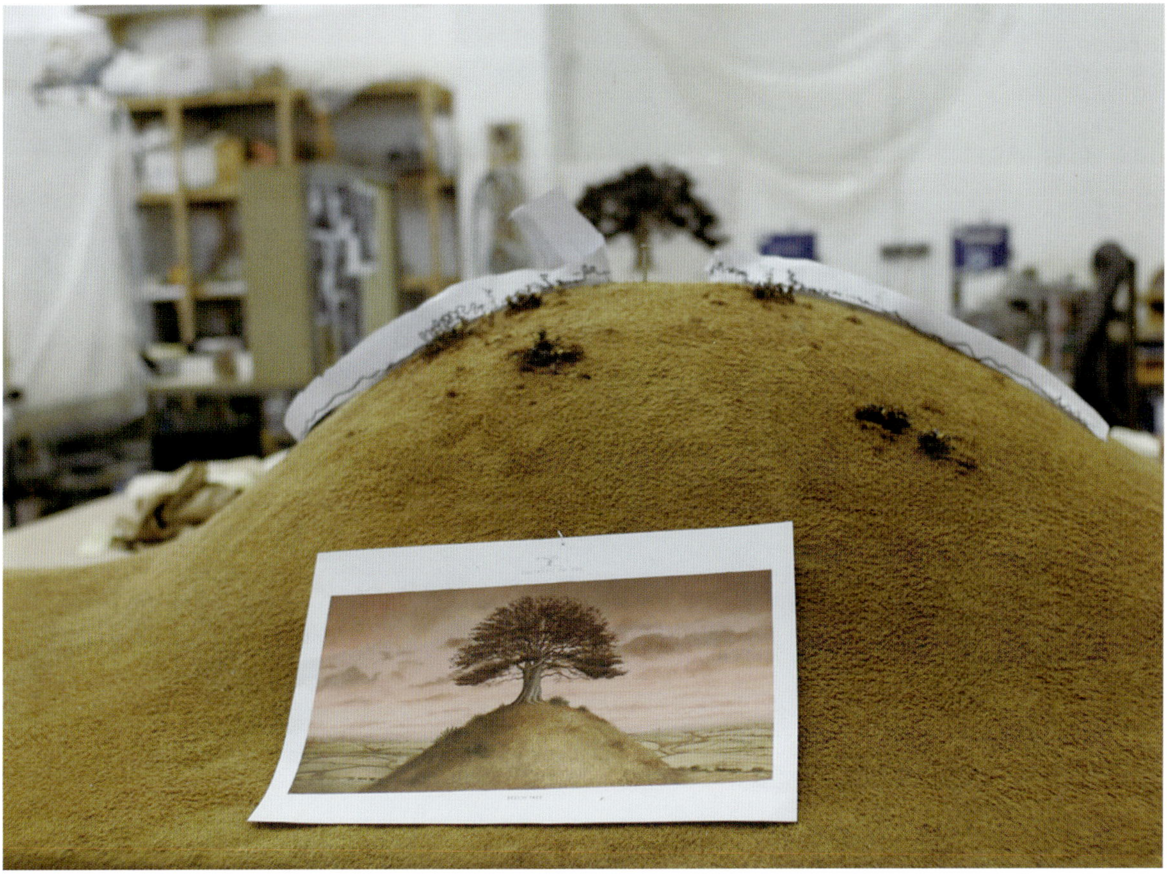

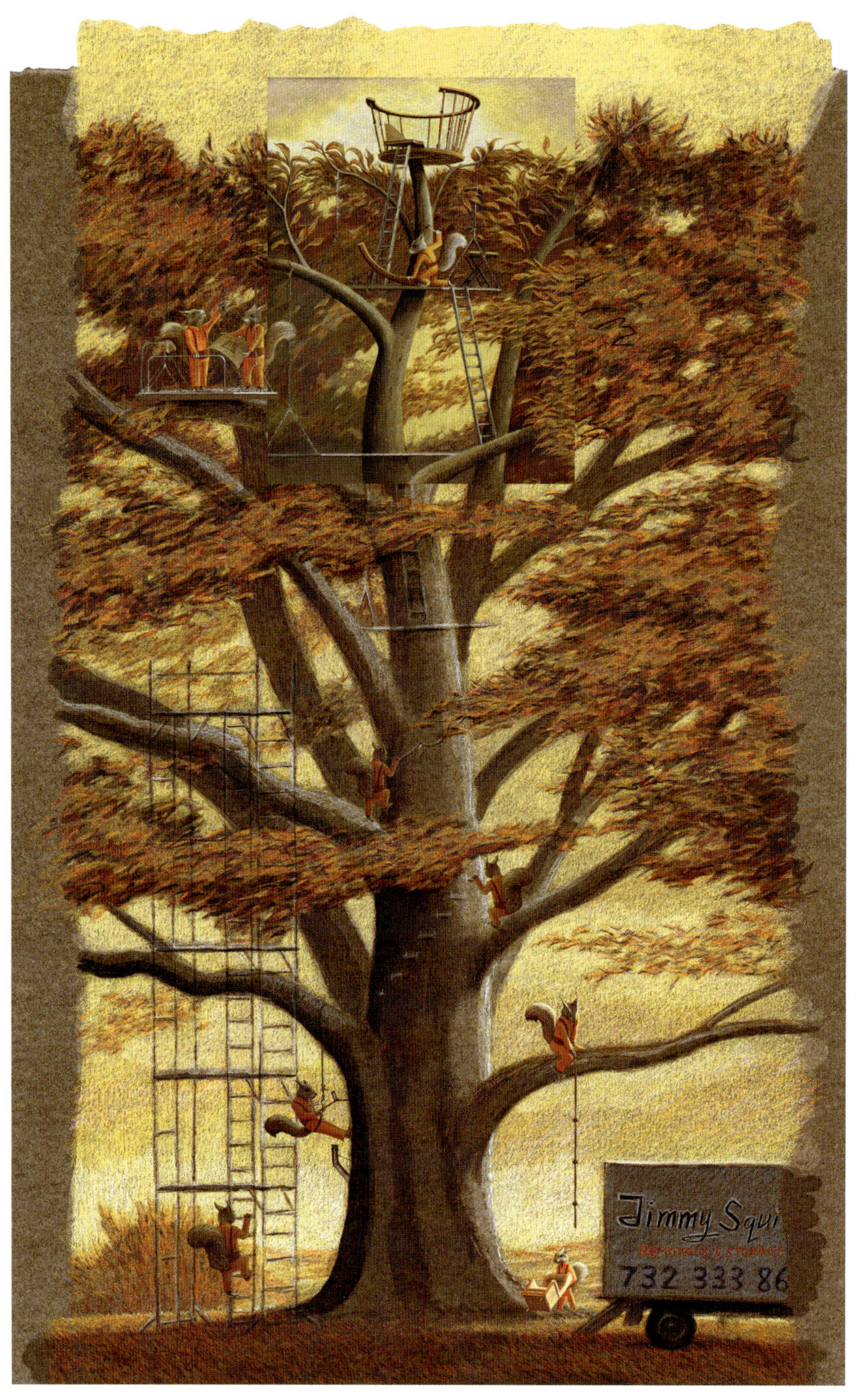

Left: Artwork by Turlo for a shot of squirrel workmen at work on the exterior of the tree

Right: The squirrel workmen puppets waiting off-set

Below: Notes and sketches for the squirrel shots by Wes

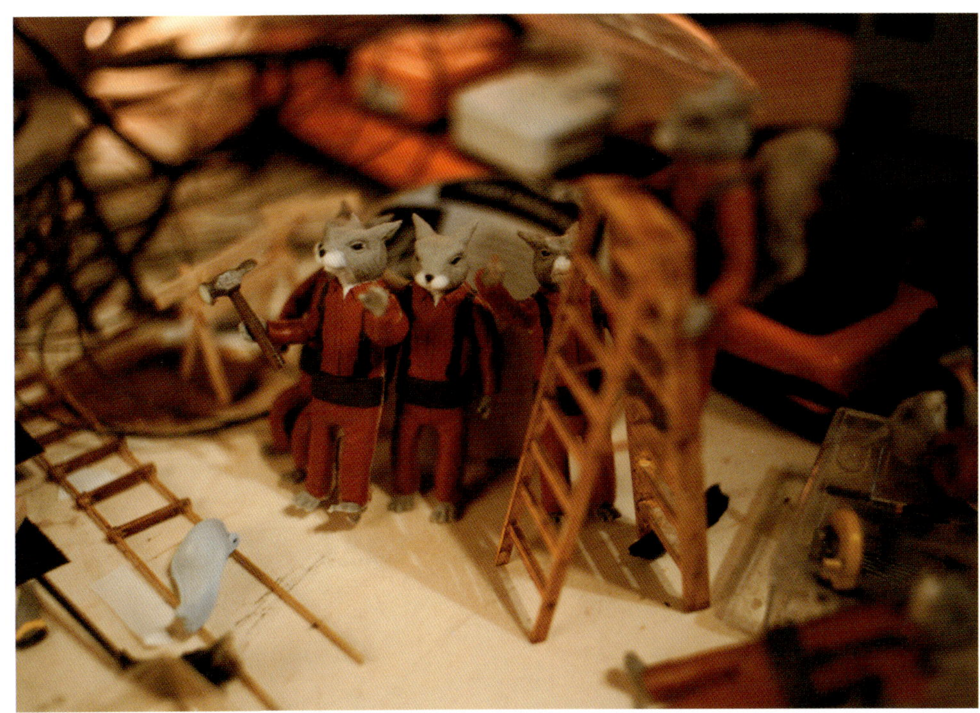

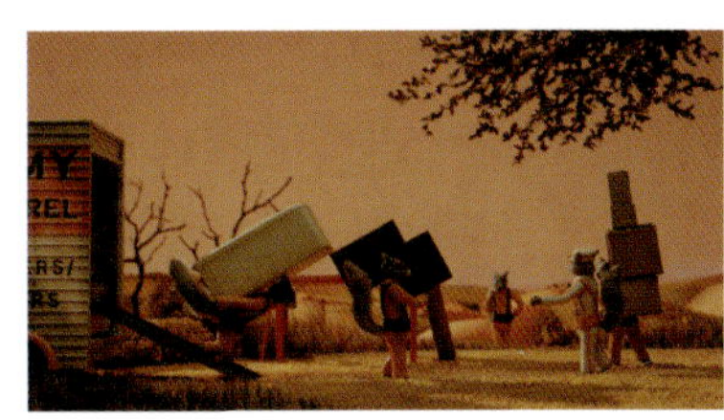

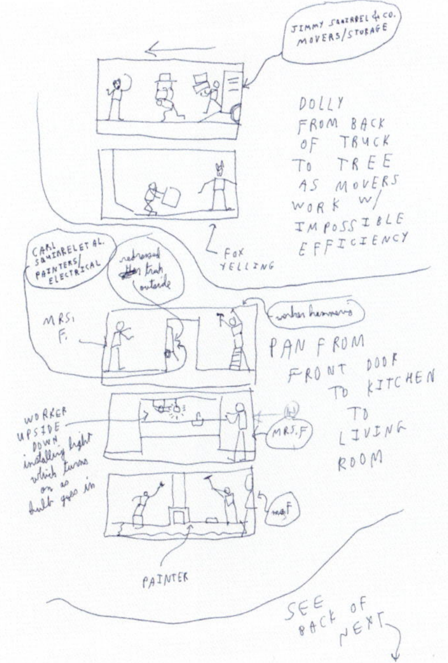

Above: A still from the movie of the squirrel workmen unloading the van

Left: Two squirrel vans made for the film

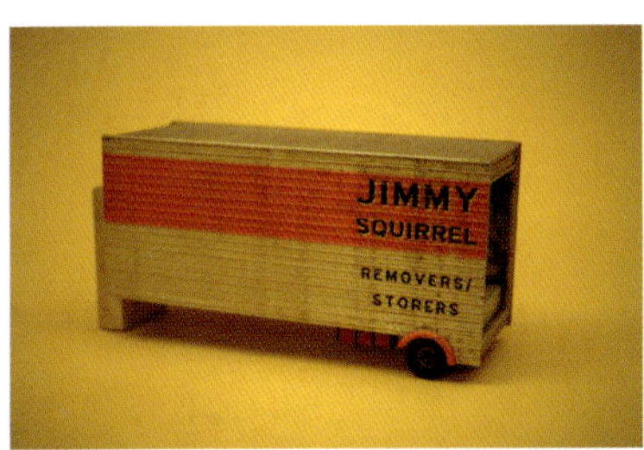

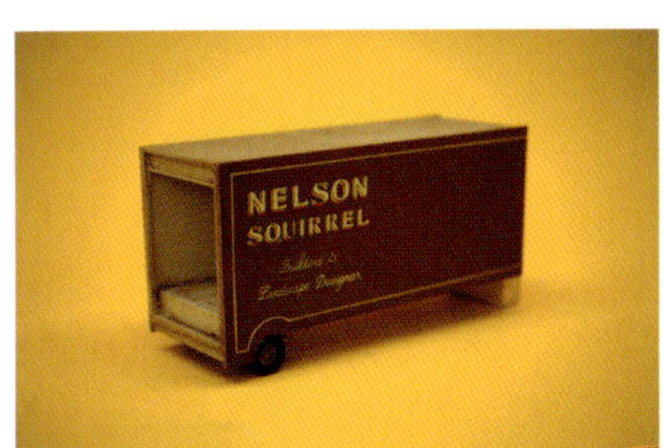

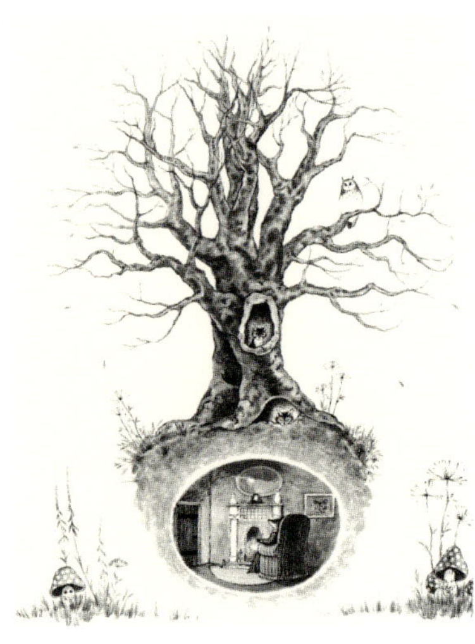

Left: Donald Chaffin's drawing of the tree

Right: Designs for the tree interior and exterior made for the film

Below: The final concept design for the tree interior

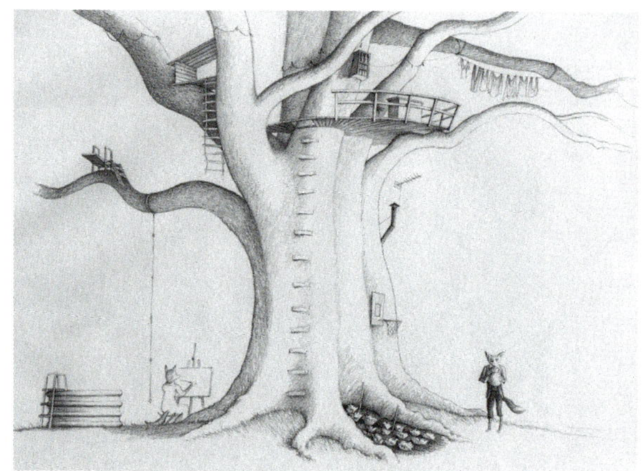

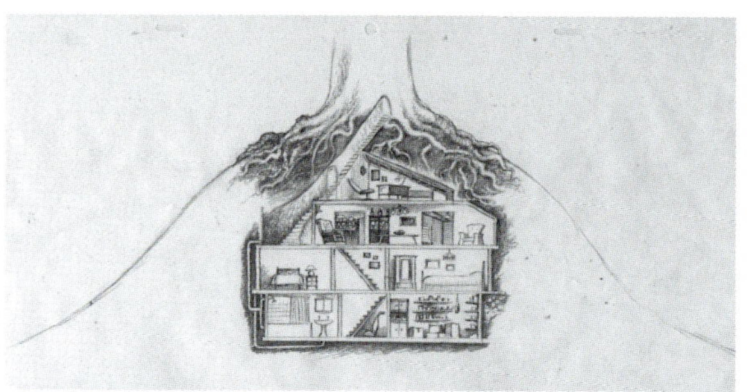

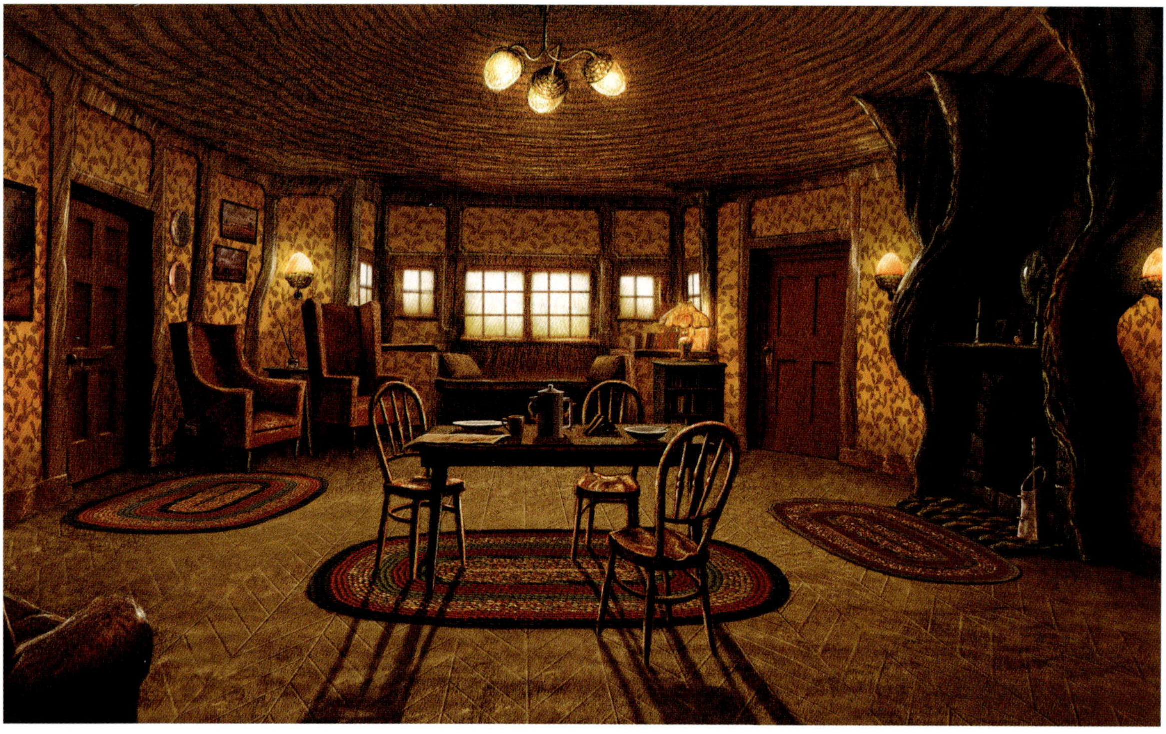

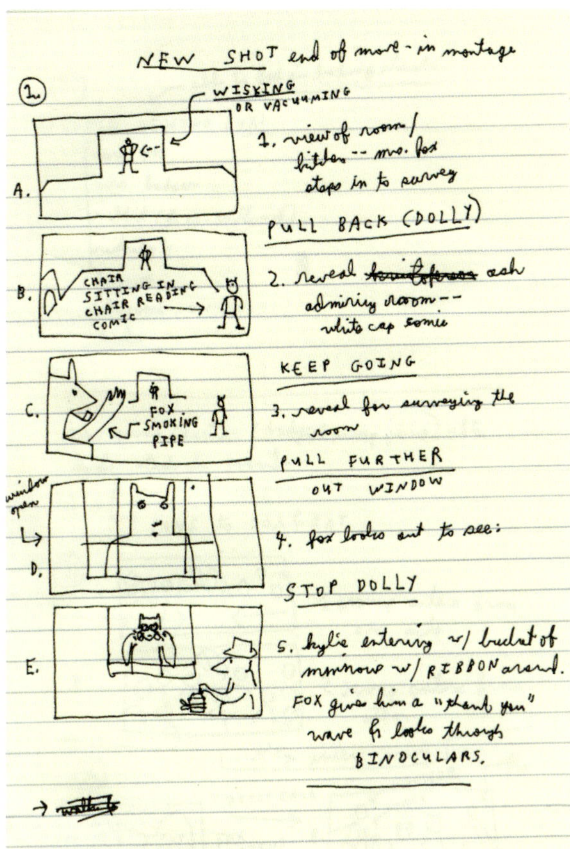

Above: Notes and sketches by Wes for the final shot of the moving-in sequence

Right: Kylie in the tree kitchen

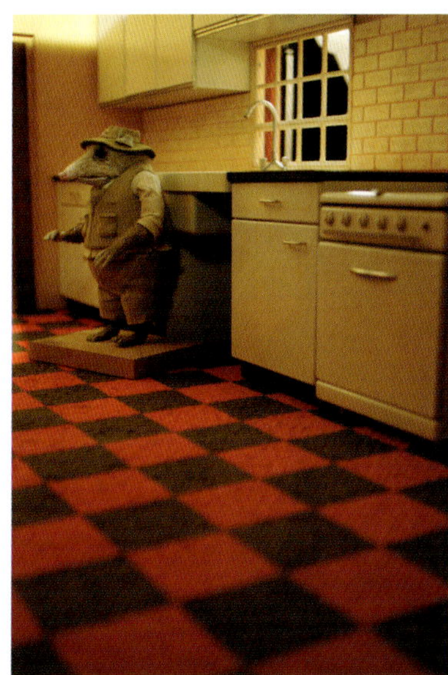

MS: *One of the things that I know you did is take people out to Connecticut to record the dialogue. I assume the attempt was to have natural conversation rather than a studio conversation. Is that true?*

WA: First, I thought it would be nice if we could have our cast together and try to make it a fun experience recording the voices, and that it might be nice if it sounded like when you were outside, that you were really outside—I mean, if we just did it for real, if for a scene in the forest we recorded the scene in the forest, and if we're going to set a scene by a river, we'll go over by a river, and if we're meant to be in an underground tunnel, we'll do it in somebody's basement. And that was sort of the way we recorded it.

Let me ask you about the animation, because there are lots of ways to animate a movie. What drew you to stop-motion particularly?

The thing I've always loved with stop-motion, more than anything else, is puppets that have fur, and actually not only that. I also like the fighting skeletons in, maybe it's Jason and the Argonauts, or maybe it's one of the Sinbad movies where they have the fighting skeletons. But I have always liked—I love the way King Kong, the old King Kong, looked, with his fur—the animators call it "boiling." And for some reason, the whole magical aspect of stop-motion was one of those things where you can see the trick—I mean, you know the Cocteau movies? The visual effects in *Beauty and the Beast*, for instance, are things where you can really see that a person is behind this wall sticking their arm through it, holding a torch, and the film is running backwards, and so that is how this light is coming on, or the mirror is actually water. You know, those kinds of effects, where you can see what it is, have always been the most fascinating and mesmerizing and moving to me. And with stop-motion, the whole film is that sort of thing in a way, to my mind. So I guess, to the degree that that makes any sense, that's more or less where it comes from for me. That magical effect where you can see how it is accomplished—where at one and the same time you are enchanted by the trick to the effect and by the story itself. I have no idea why this concept means so much to me.

MS: *Roald Dahl is a special kind of writer, and you are a special kind of director, and there's such a thing as a Wes Anderson movie. Is this a Wes Anderson movie or is it a Wes Anderson version of a Roald Dahl book?*
WA: Well, you know, the book is not very long so we had to invent a lot. And the book doesn't have very many characters who get enough story to actually have names, for instance. Like the children, Mr. Fox's children in the book, they don't have real characters. They're just sort of referred to, essentially. It's just much shorter. So we had to expand it, we had to expand it to have a whole cast and we had to expand it to make the story last the length of a feature film. But as we did it, all we wanted to do was to try to write something that we hoped Roald Dahl would think was suitable and fit with what he had invented in the first place. And, you know, we were trying to write a Roald Dahl movie. I think in the end—I was writing with Noah Baumbach and we have our own point of view, or whatever you want to call it. I mean, we're not going to think up the same jokes that Roald Dahl would, and we bring our own personalities to it. But our goal was to try to do a Roald Dahl story.

A table in Roald Dahl's writing shed, photographed by Wes, and props made for the film

1. Pencil case with pencils
2. Brush
3. Pencil sharpener
4. Balls of aluminum foil made by Roald Dahl from chocolate wrappers
5. Geodes
6. Roald Dahl's mug

Following pages: A still from the movie showing Mr. and Mrs. Fox at home in the tree, with Ash reading *White Cape*

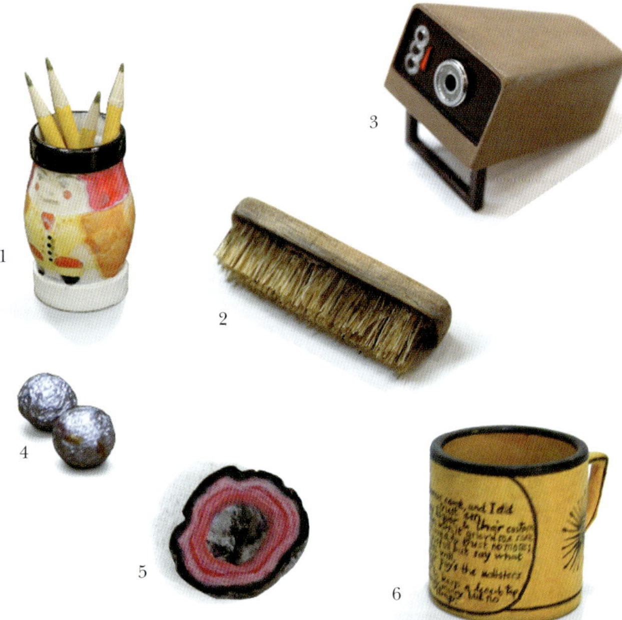

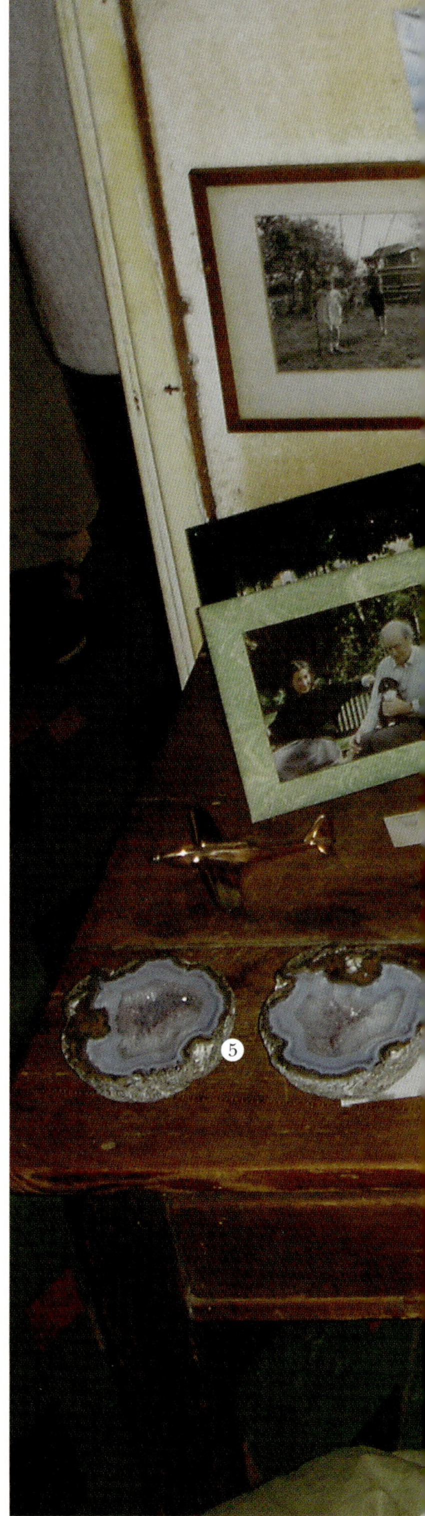

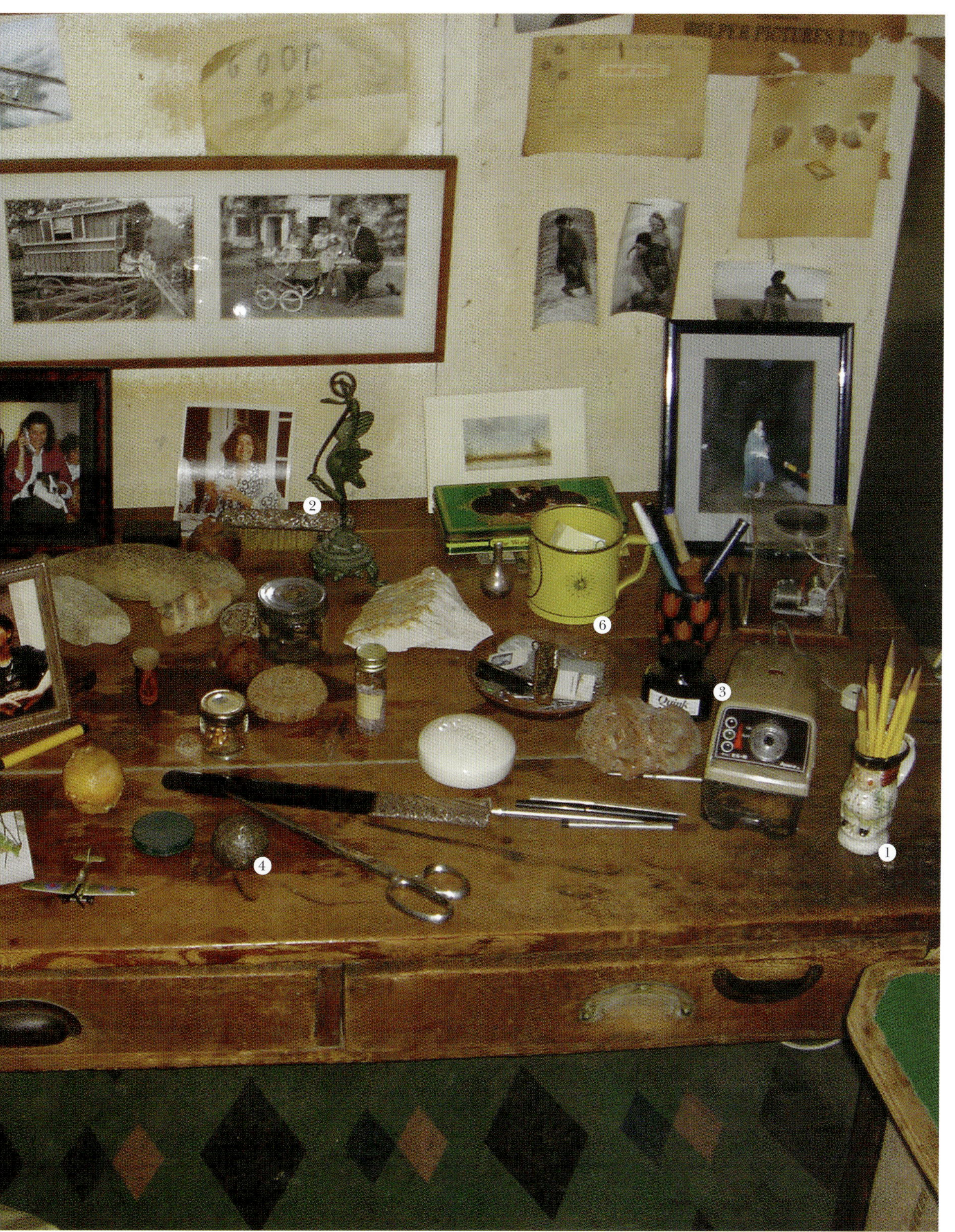
2
6
3
Quink
1
4

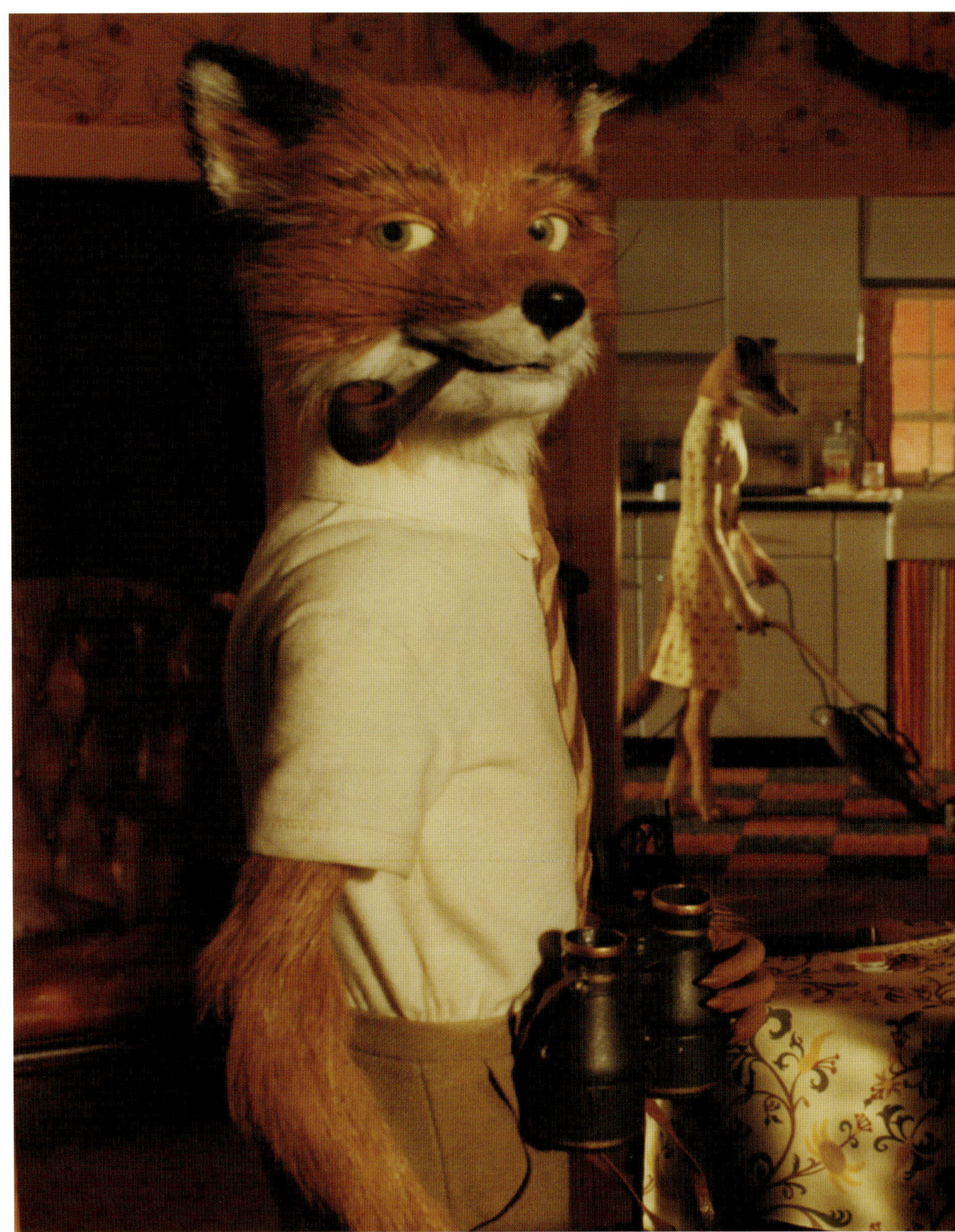

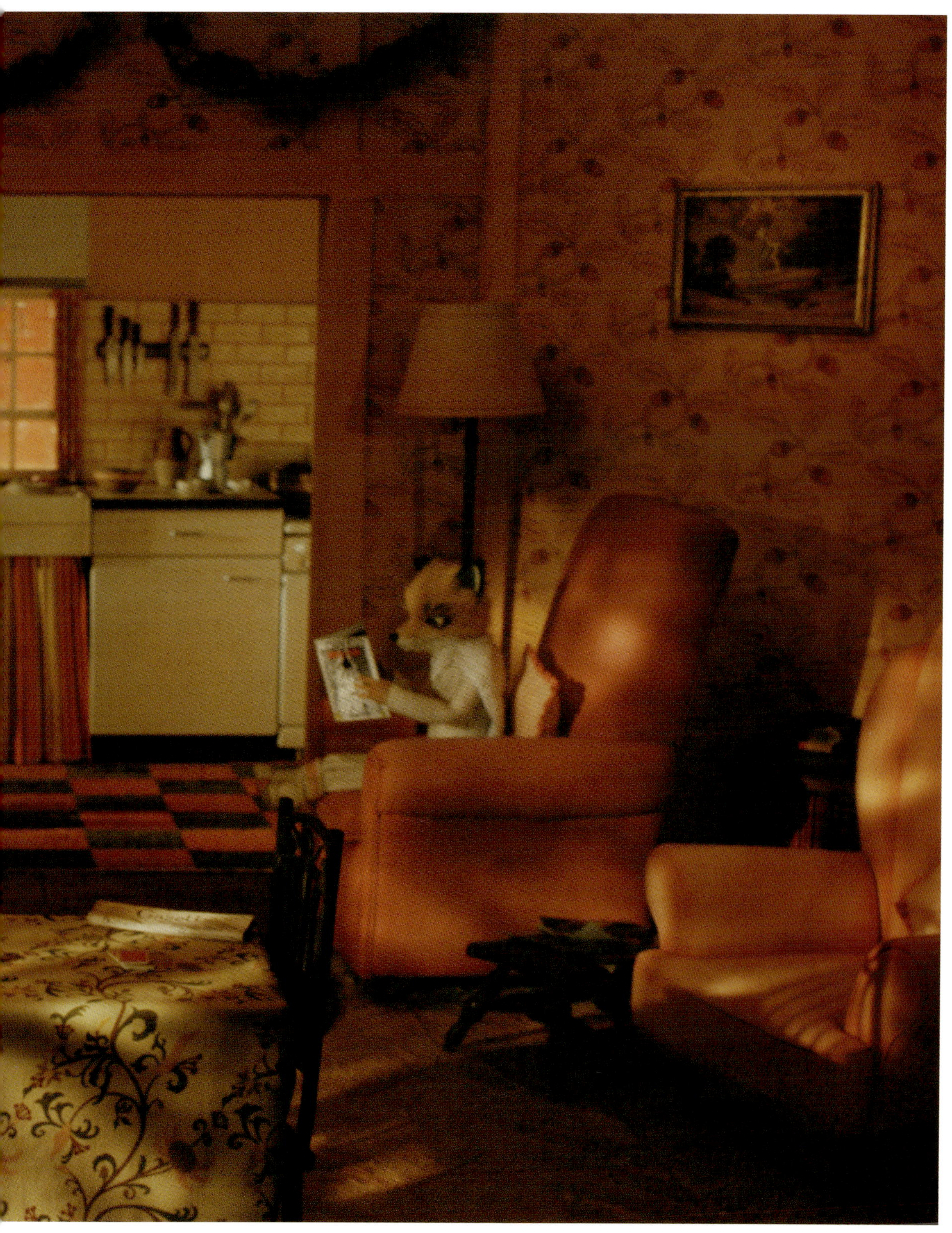

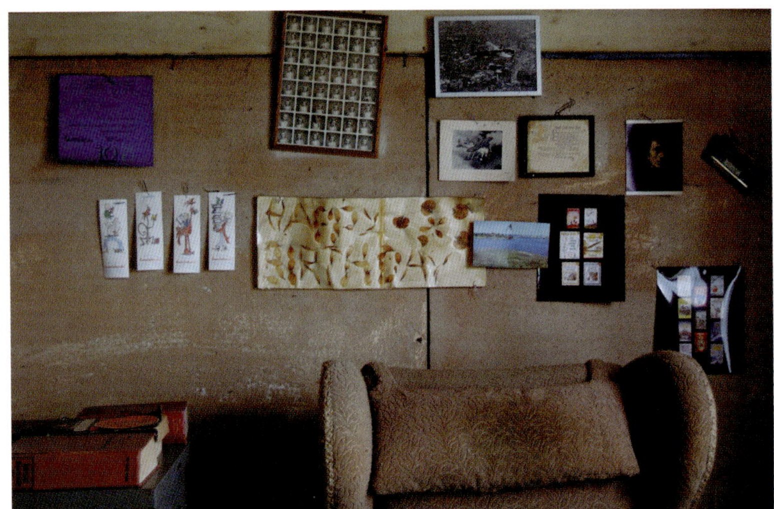

Left: A wall in Roald Dahl's writing shed, photographed by Wes

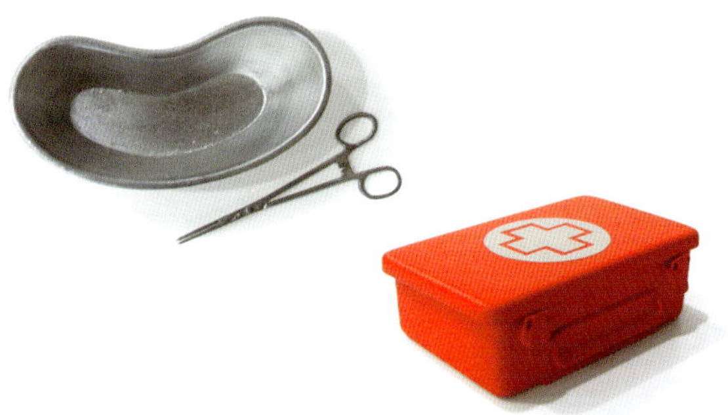

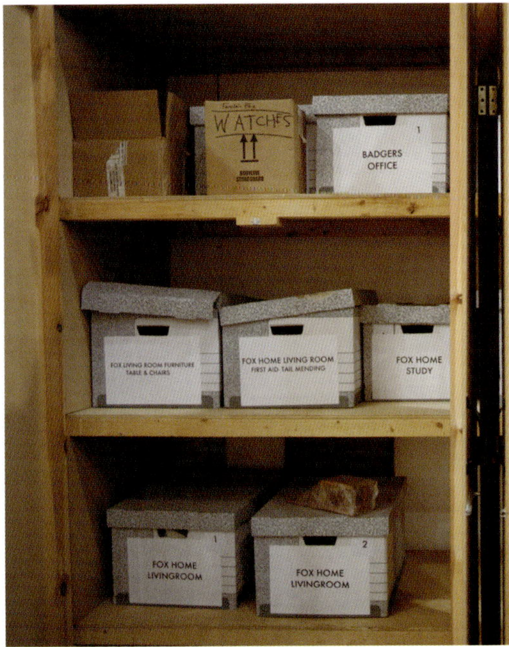

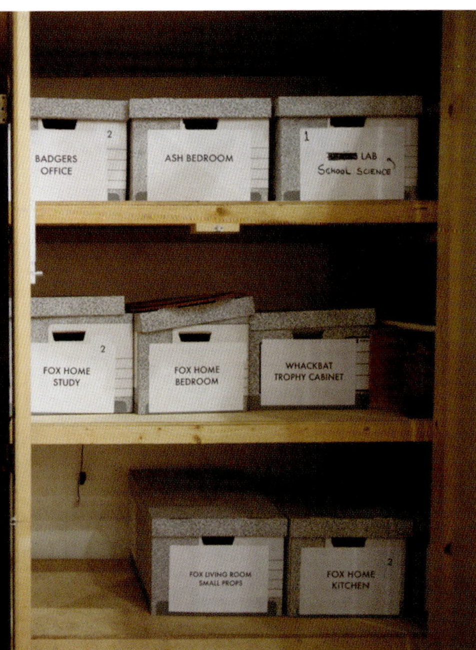

Clockwise from above left: Mrs. Fox's medical kit; Mr. Fox's chair; prop storage at the studio in London

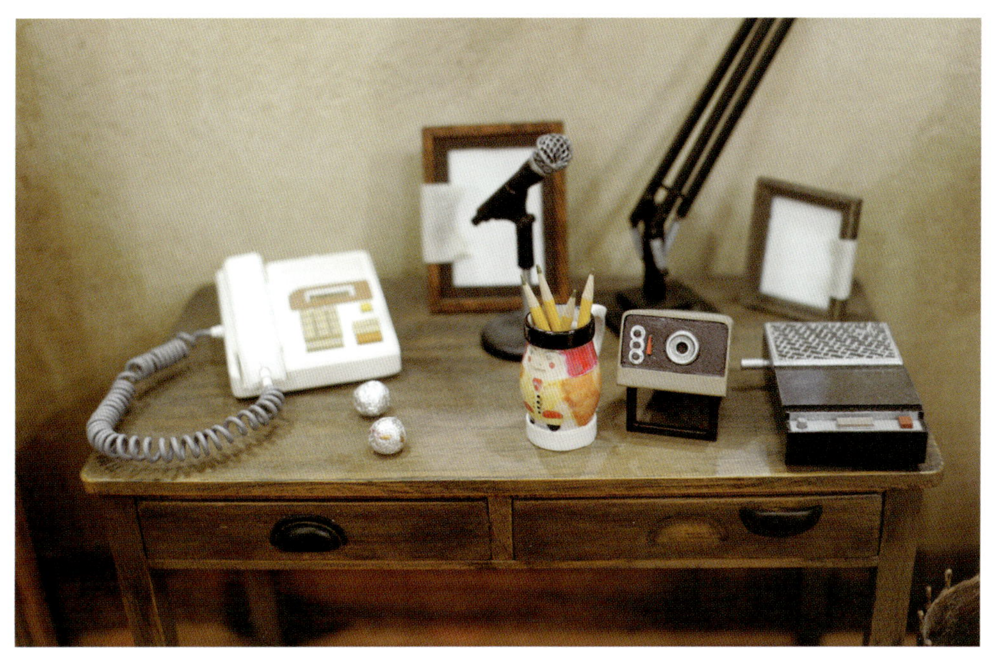

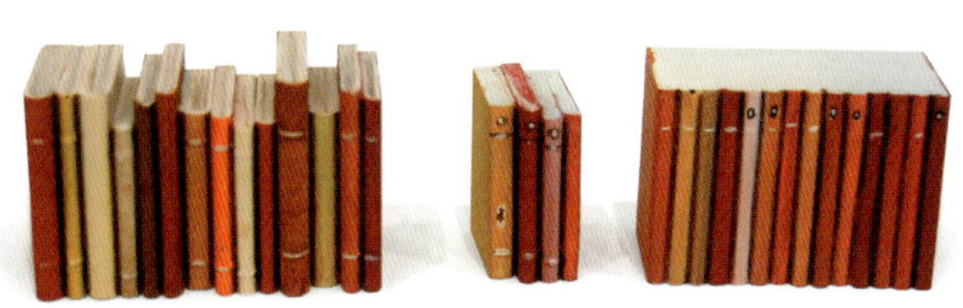

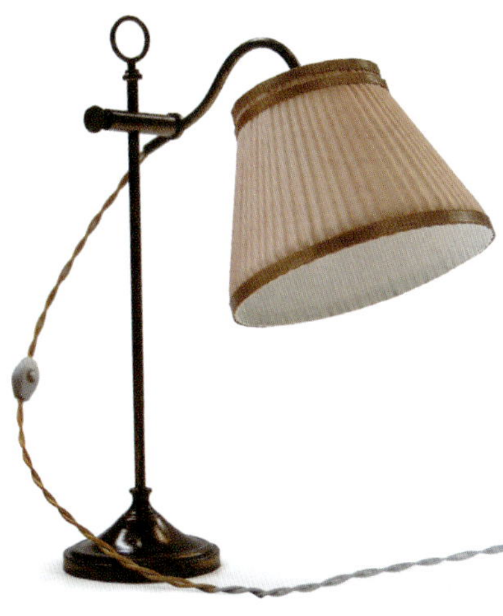

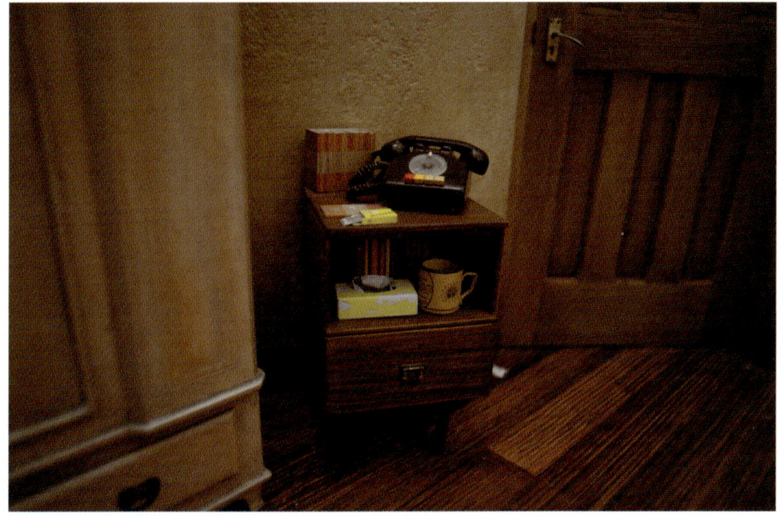

Clockwise from top left: The table in Mr. Fox's study; a lamp and a side-table in Mr. and Mrs. Fox's bedroom; books in Ash's bedroom based on a set of Roald Dahl books

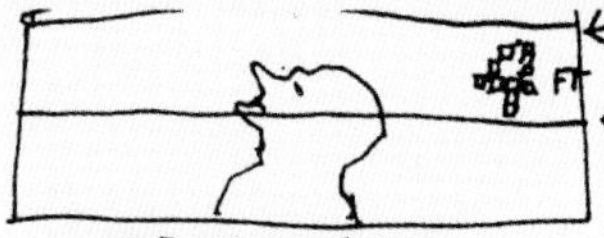

camera at water level, 1/2 & 1/2

EXT. SWIMMING POOL. DAY ~~[crossed out]~~ WIDER? waist-up

Bunce stands up to his nose in water. The depth reads 4FT.

BADGER (V.O.)
He's so short his chin would probably be under water in the shallow end of any swimming pool on the planet.

INT. BUNCE'S KITCHEN. DAY

Bunce sits on two stacked telephone books on a chair. He guts a dead goose, cutting out its liver and mashing it with a fork. A plate of doughnuts cools on the table.

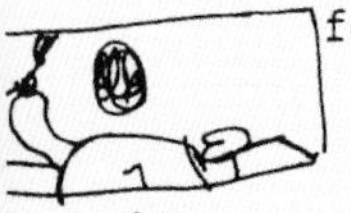

BADGER (V.O.)
He eats only doughnuts with smashed-up goose livers injected into them.

ACK OF UNCE, OOM UP FROM H. BOOKS TO THE ABOVE.

CUT TO:

A tall, skinny man in a long trench-coat. He holds a Luger pistol. He stands in front of his farm, which is an apple orchard that stretches over thousands of acres. He has a mean face. He is Bean.

title: franklin bean

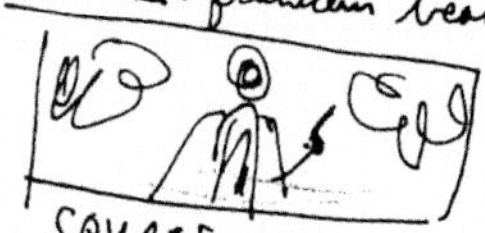

BADGER (V.O.)
Franklin Bean is a turkey and apple farmer. He keeps his birds in an orchard where they run around squawking and gobbling, surrounded by apples.

SQUARE ON

H. BOOKS SAY: IRECTORY ASSISTANCE GREAT AF SFORD, mother's RECTORY SSISTANCE INDERMERE & SSER ON VALLEY

Bean aims his Luger and shoots a humming bird. Crazy turkeys run about among the trees.

INT. BEAN'S SHED. DAY

Bean works at a moonshine-type cider still, boiling chemicals and sipping from a bottle.

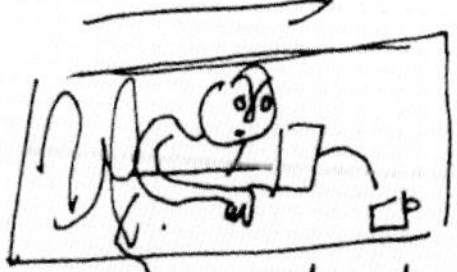

BADGER (V.O.)
He's probably anorexic, because he never eats anything. He's on a liquid diet of strong, alcoholic cider, which he makes from his apples. He's as skinny as a pencil, as smart as a whip -- and easily the biggest cusshole I've ever met in my life.

bean works at still -- track w/ him as he adds ingredients & liquid flows through glass tubes RUBE GOLDBERG style. AT end it goes into his MUG.

he drinks w/ A SICK SMILE.

CUT TO:

Fox and Badger in Badger's office.

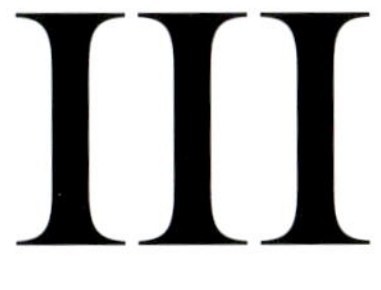

III

THREE FARMERS

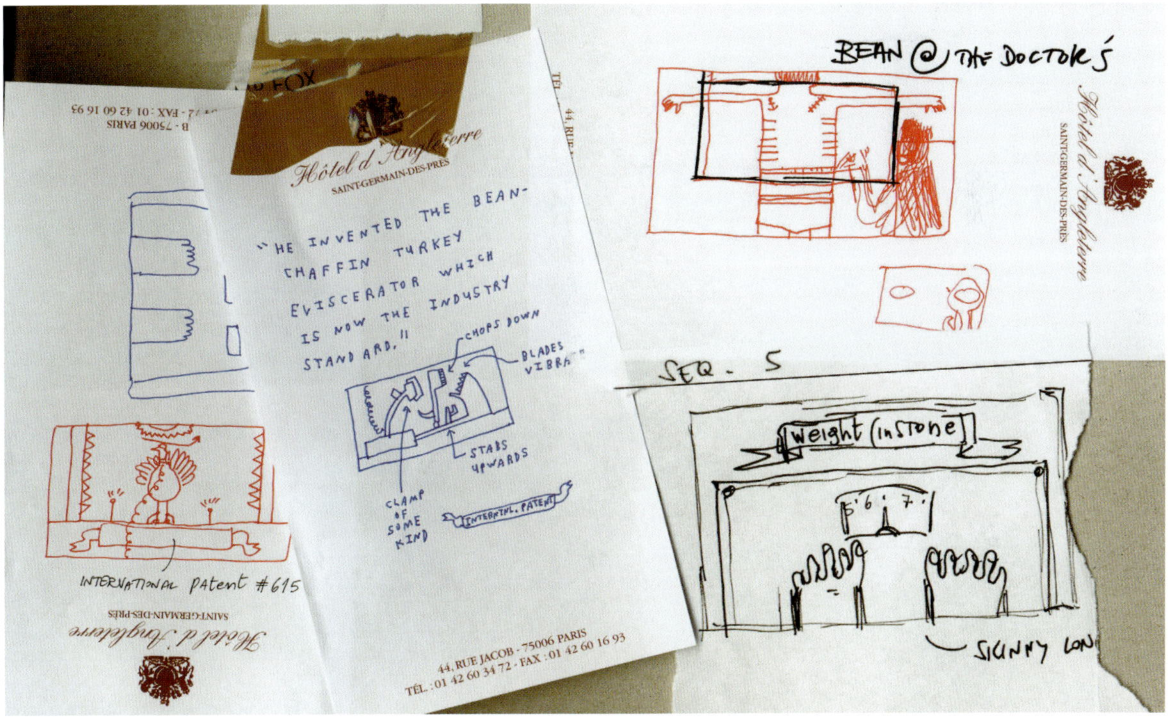

Above: A page from Christian's notebook, with notes and sketches by himself and Wes

Right: Donald Chaffin's drawings of the farmers and their favorite foods

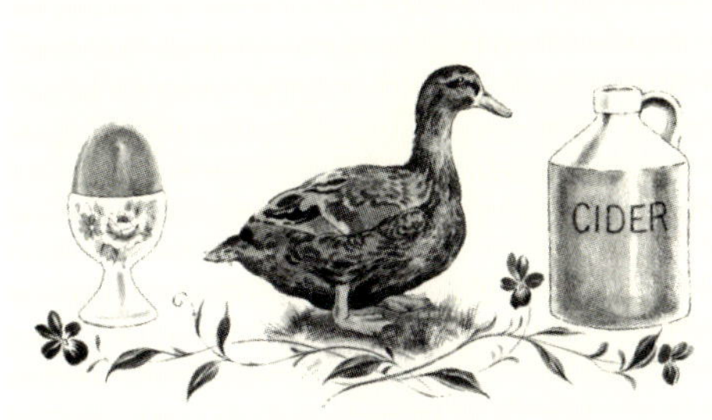

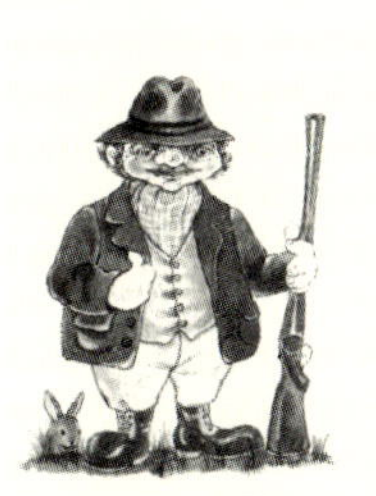

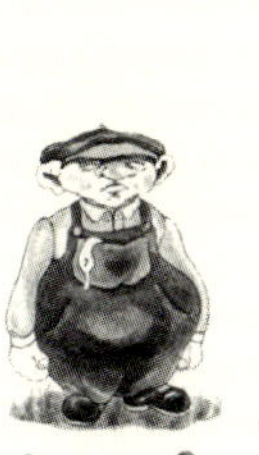

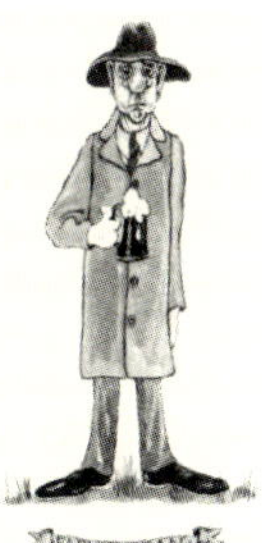

MS: *You know, creating new characters and situations in an intensely loved book is a little risky. Are you worried that people will see this movie and no matter what else they say they'll say, "But it isn't the same"?*
WA: Well, I feel like there's so many bad things that people could say about you, so why focus on one in particular? Who knows what people are going to think, and it's fine. I mean, if we didn't set them up with one thing, we would have to set them up with something else.

Jason Schwartzman described the way you directed him, and I presume others, and he said it must have been like a silent movie director because you would do the role, and you'd be throwing the script around, saying, "Now you do this and now you do that and now..." That's a different kind of directing than anyone really gets to do, isn't it?
Well, in the case of this film, all you need is the voice, so we're kind of doing whatever we need to do to make just the voices work. And part of that is trying to make it go someplace where it's a bit of an adventure to record it, or trying to create some situation where it's inspiring to the actors. In general, it's really just sort of pretending, and—I don't know. It's almost like you can just record, you can just rehearse together and try anything and do anything, and we record the rehearsal and we're done.

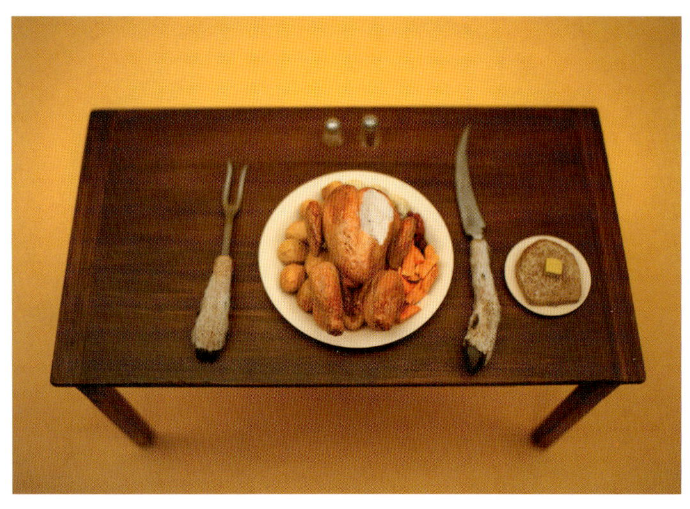

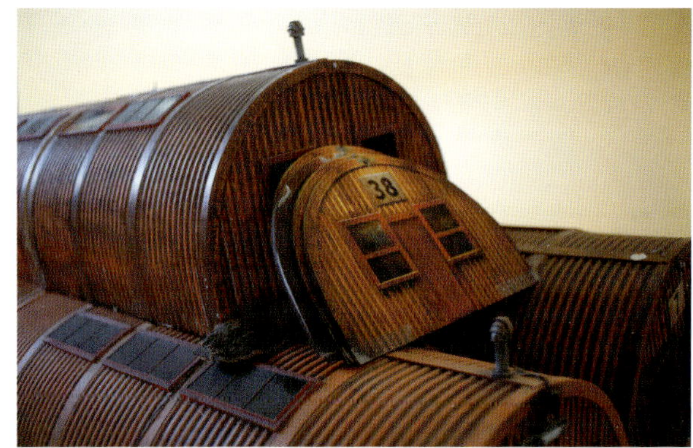

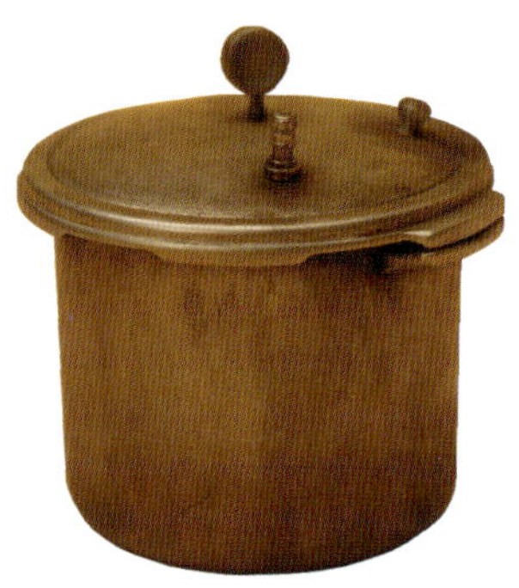

Left: The pressure cooker from the set of Boggis's kitchen

Above: Boggis's meal of baked chicken, with animal-hoof cutlery

Right: Boggis's chicken huts stacked in the workshop and a photograph of Boggis in front of his farm

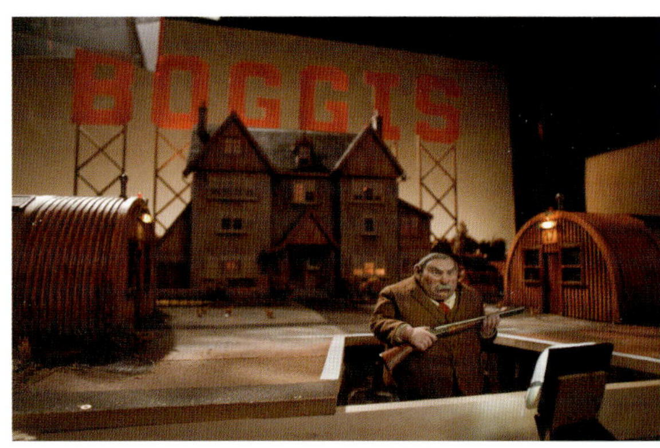

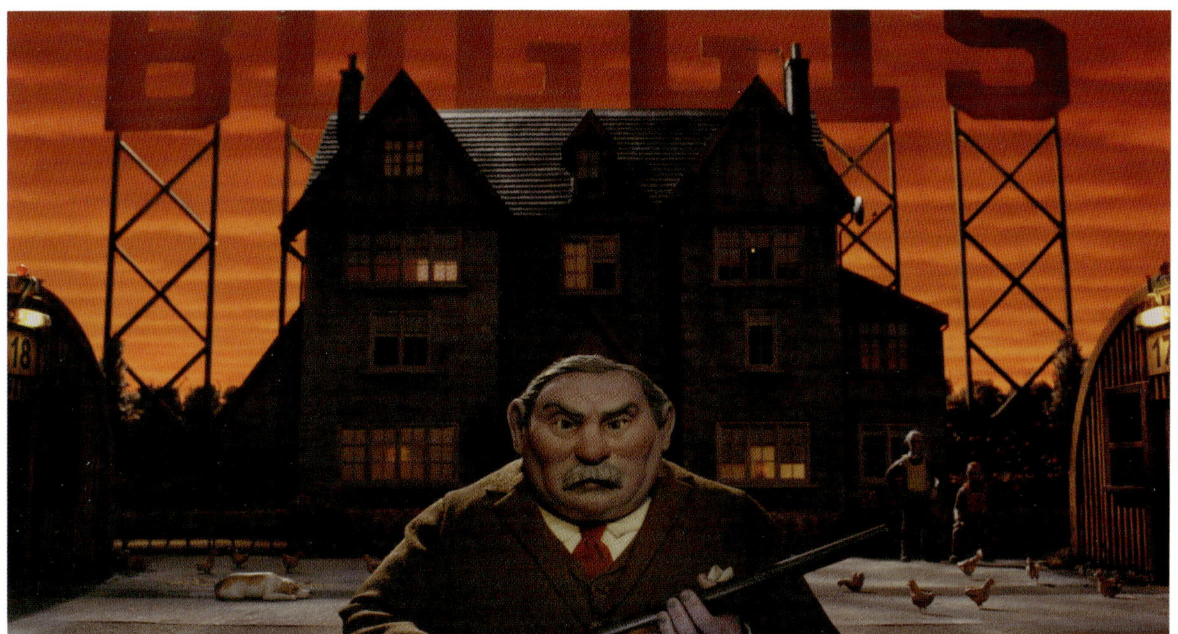

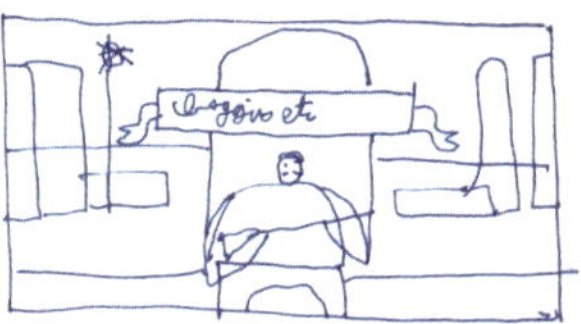

Above and right: A still from the movie and an early sketch for the shot by Wes

Below: Mr. Fox's beagle dossier

Following pages: The set for Bunce's farm in progress

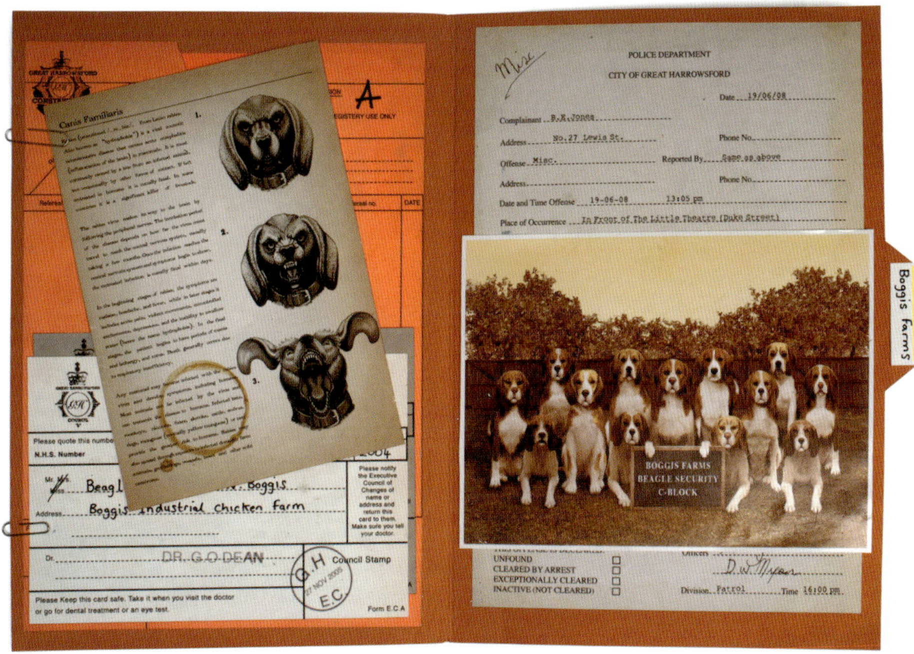

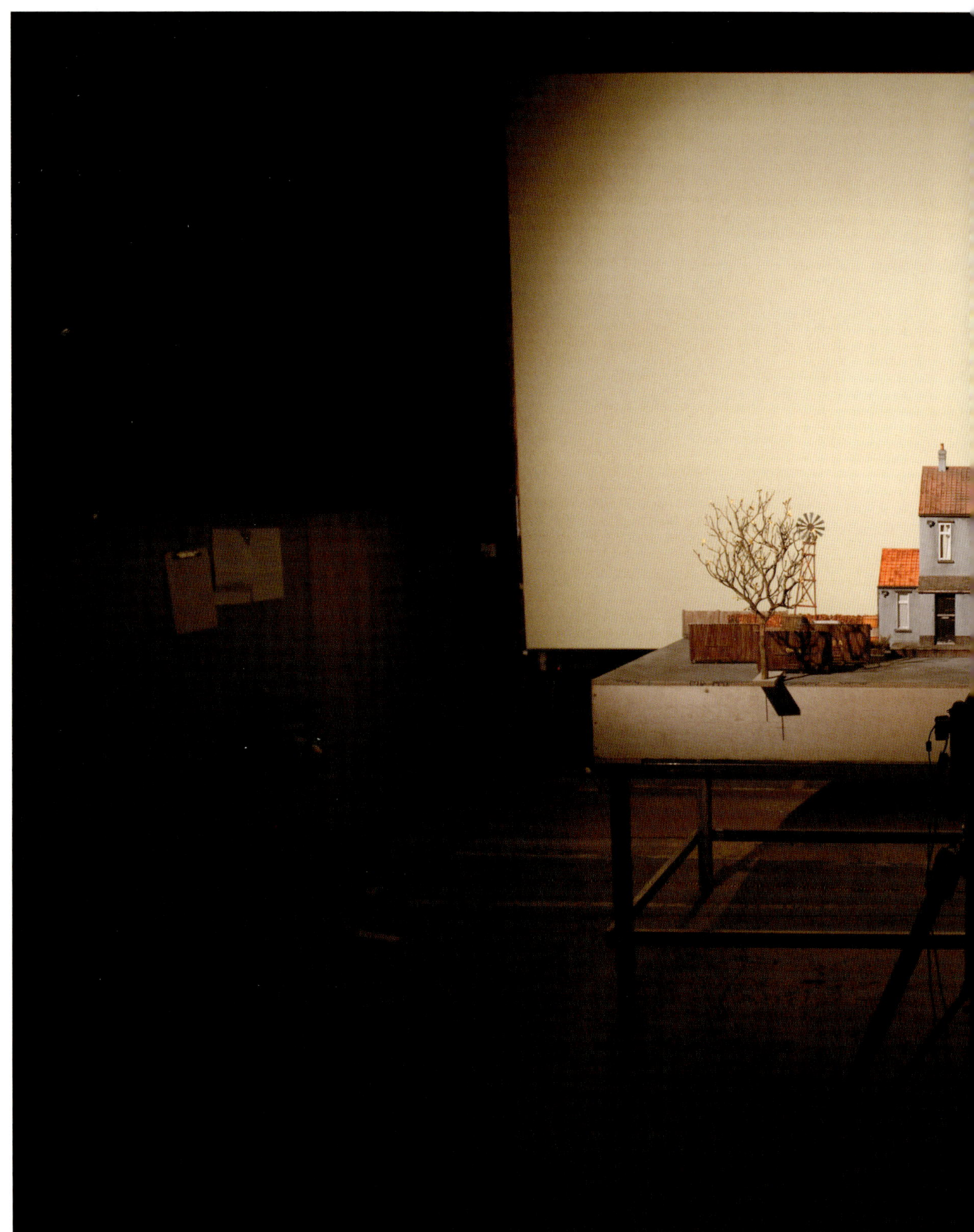

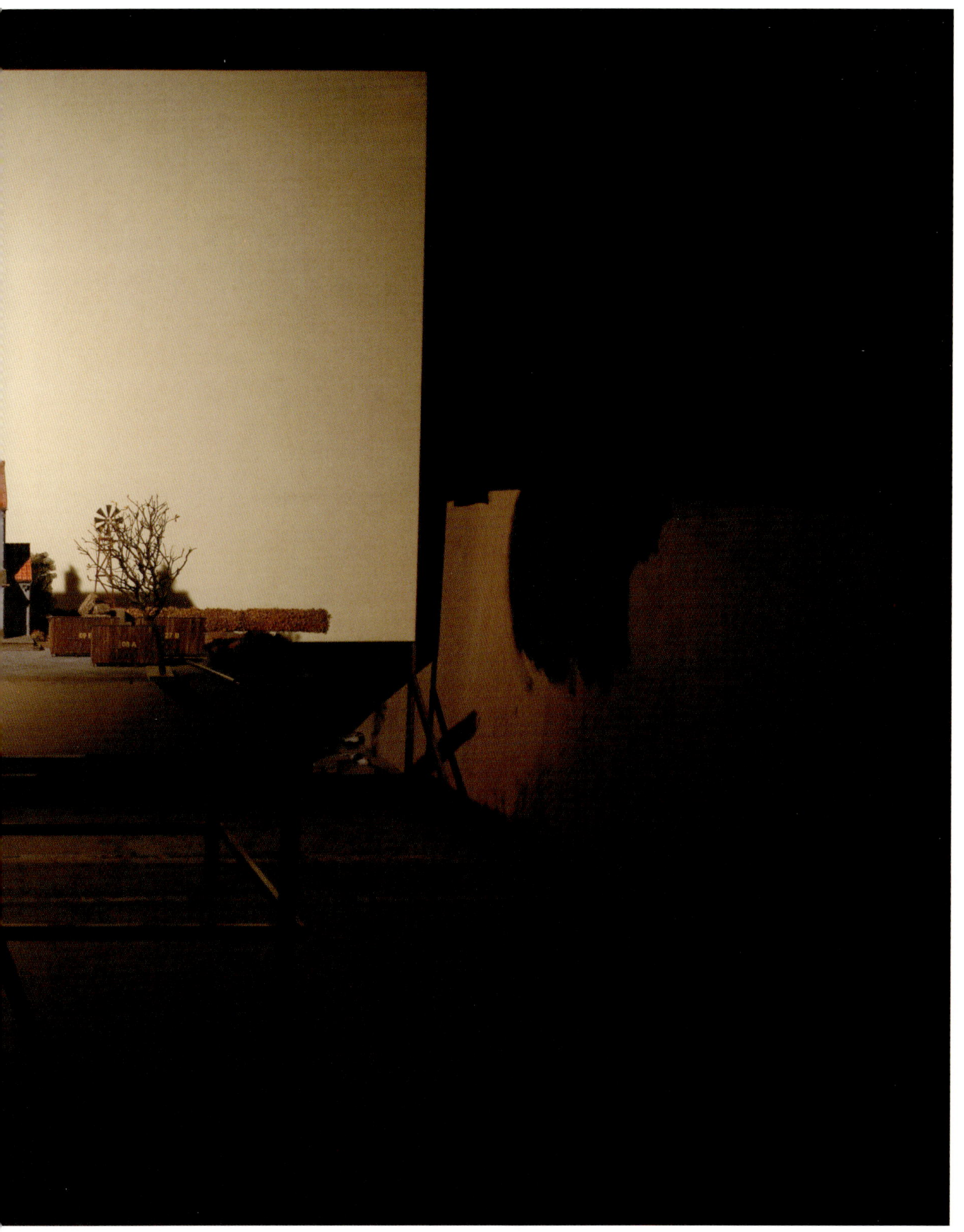

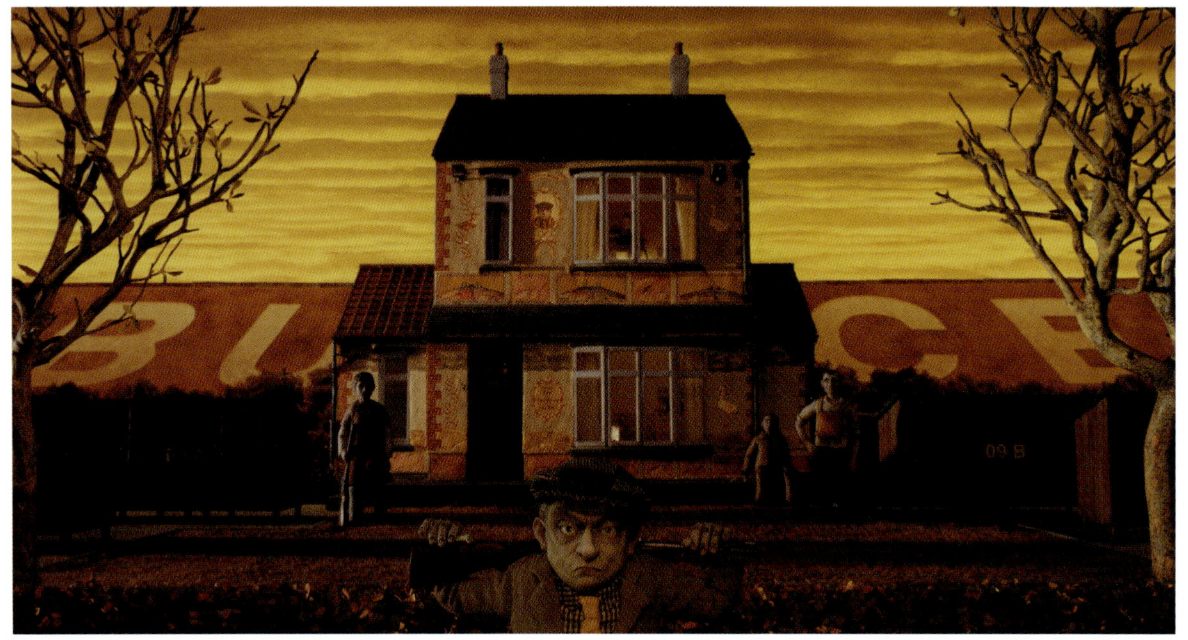

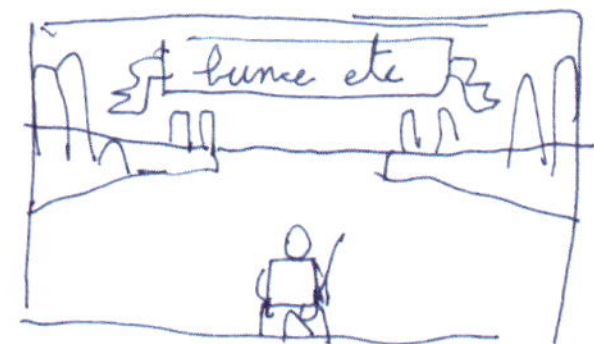

Above and right:
A still from the movie and an early sketch for the shot by Wes

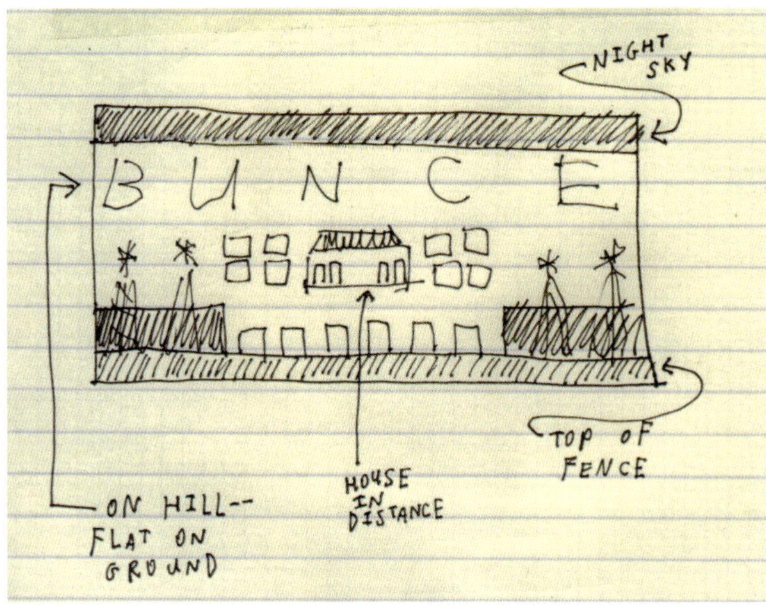

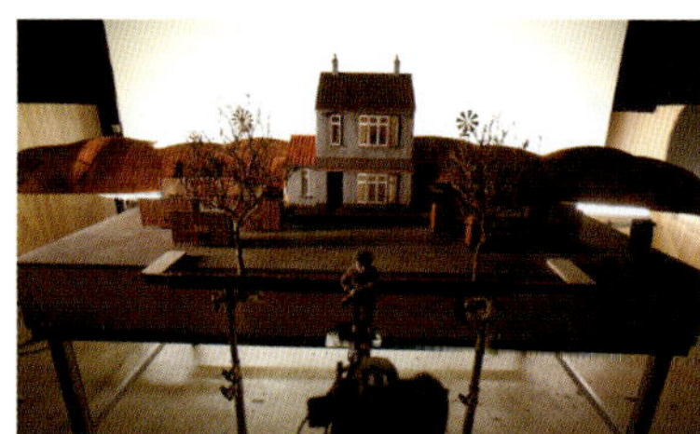

Above and left:
A photograph and a sketch by Wes of the set for Bunce's house

MS: *Jason said that sometimes he'd have like twelve words written down on a script and somehow you would make an entire conversation out of that. Was that done with other characters? You don't strike me as all that improvisational in general, but it seems as if that is what happened here.*
WA: I think some scenes want to be done very simply and, from my experience, the prepared version of the scene is what you want to get just right. And then other scenes want to be allowed to expand or go in circles and come back to something, or whatever that is. And sometimes, if you feel like the scene is not quite working, then you're sort of open to wherever it happens to go. So yeah, with this one we definitely had some things that went their own way.

Do you feel you have more control over a film like this, where you can kind of totally mold the characters—I mean, quite literally mold the characters in all the shots—whereas with humans, they'll do as much as you can get them to do, but they're still humans?
Isn't Jim Jarmusch's new movie called *The Limits of Control*? There are limits of control to any method, I would think, and that's something that you have to hope for. You have to have room for the accidents, and with this I was kind of wondering where's the room for the accidents going to come in? And part of recording the voices outside of a controlled environment was just so we'd have the opportunity for some things to go wrong, or some things to surprise us. And also, every animator brings their own perspective, and the same accidents happen on a stop-motion set. They just happen very slowly. [laughs] ♣

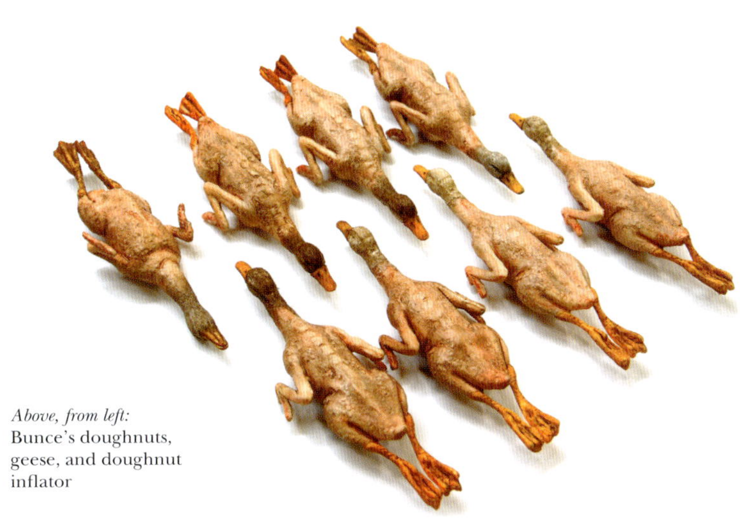

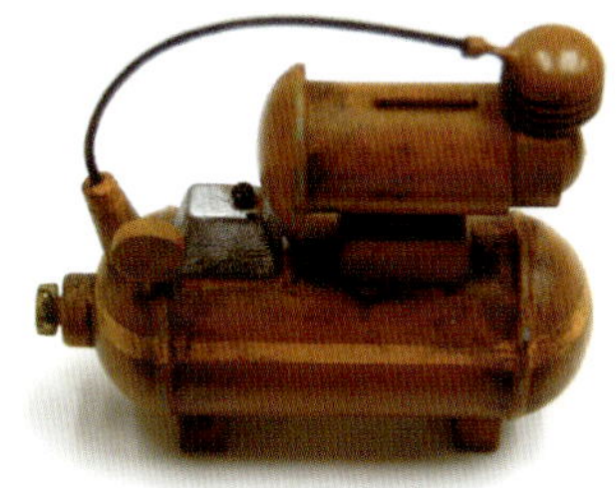

Above, from left:
Bunce's doughnuts, geese, and doughnut inflator

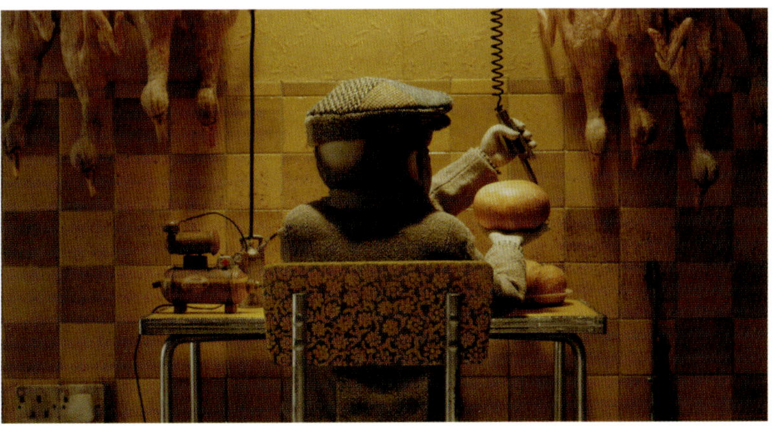

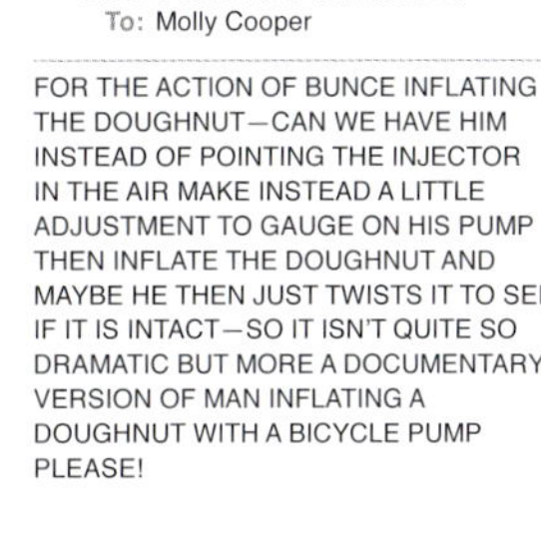

From: Wes Anderson
Subject: **Re: dailies send June 2**
Date: 3 June 2008 11:03:36 BST
To: Molly Cooper

FOR THE ACTION OF BUNCE INFLATING THE DOUGHNUT—CAN WE HAVE HIM INSTEAD OF POINTING THE INJECTOR IN THE AIR MAKE INSTEAD A LITTLE ADJUSTMENT TO GAUGE ON HIS PUMP THEN INFLATE THE DOUGHNUT AND MAYBE HE THEN JUST TWISTS IT TO SEE IF IT IS INTACT—SO IT ISN'T QUITE SO DRAMATIC BUT MORE A DOCUMENTARY VERSION OF MAN INFLATING A DOUGHNUT WITH A BICYCLE PUMP PLEASE!

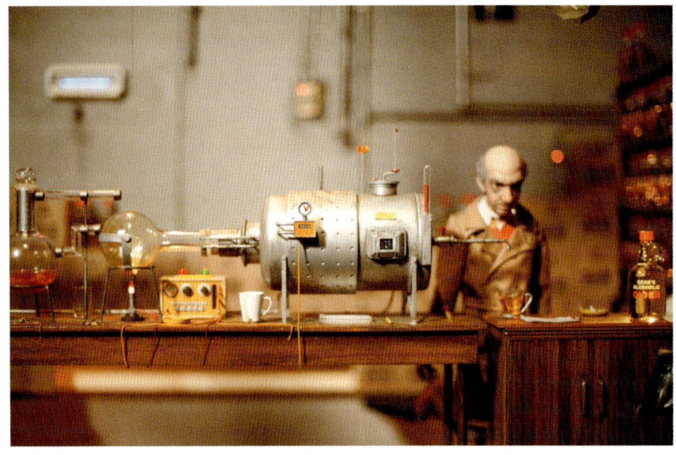

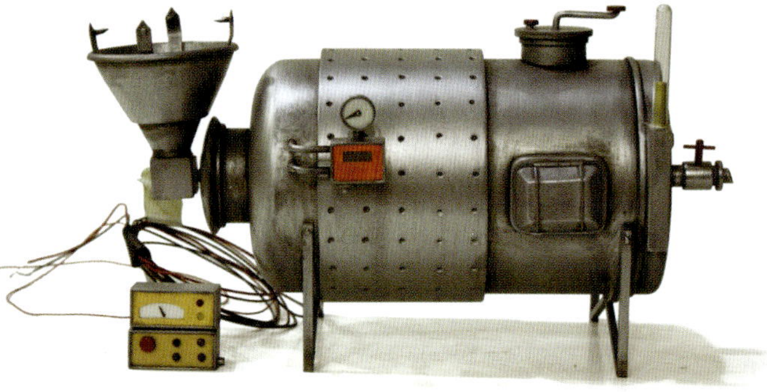

Above: Bean and his cider still

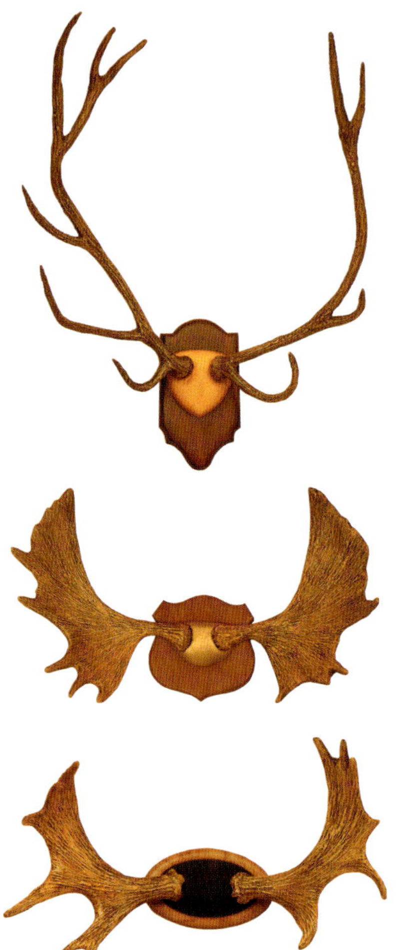

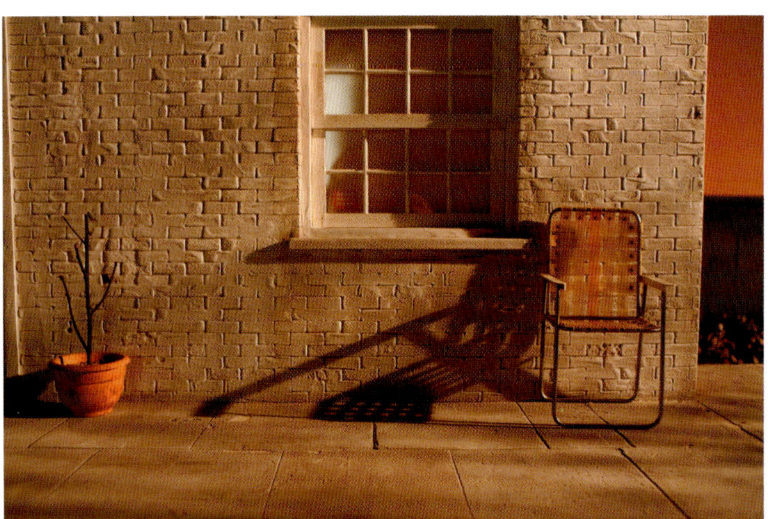

Above: Three sets of antlers from Bean's trophy wall

Left: Bean's porch

Opposite top: A still from the movie and an early sketch for the shot by Wes

Opposite right: A sketch and notes by Wes for the shot of Bean's invented species of turkey and the final turkey puppet

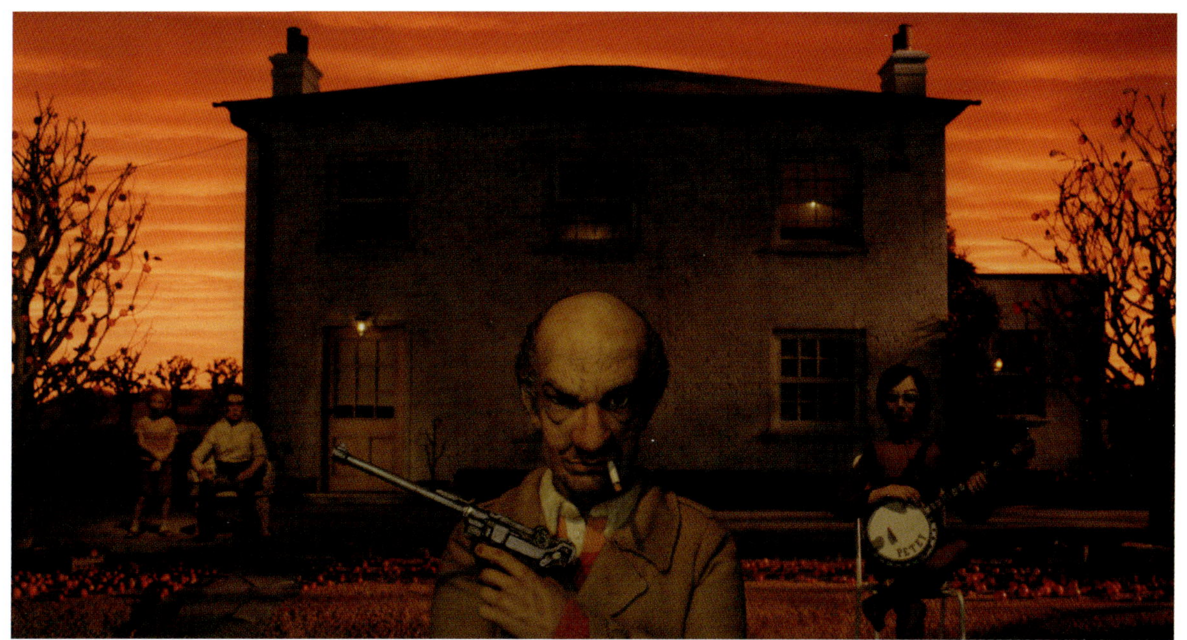

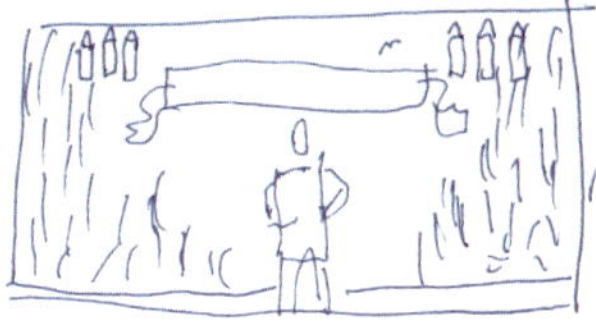

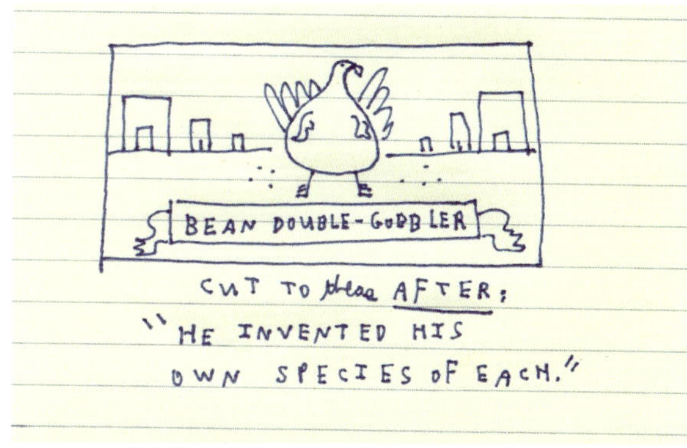

From: Wes Anderson
Subject:
Date: 28 January 2009 12:51:32 GMT
To: Nelson Lowry, Alice Bird, Mark Gustafson

For all the scenes with Boggis, Bunce, and Bean, more or less all anyway, I want to give Bunce a goose-liver doughnut and Boggis some portable version of one of his chicken dishes—so he can in one scene have a yakitori skewer, in another a fried chicken wing, in another a small baked leg with barbecue sauce on it, and in another maybe he has some version of the boiled, maybe chopped in a little bowl or something? And Bean always has a cigarette and as often as possible cider.

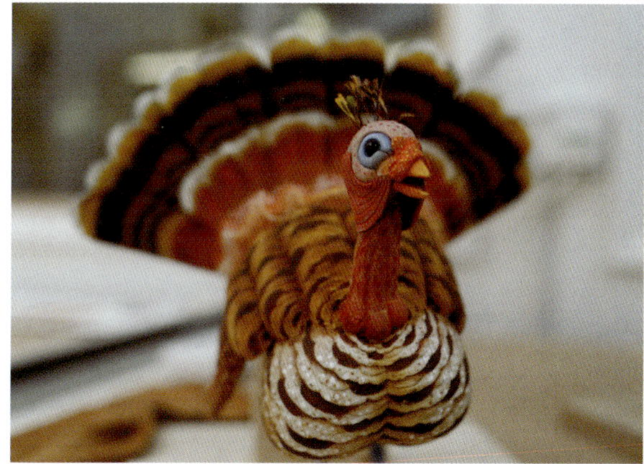

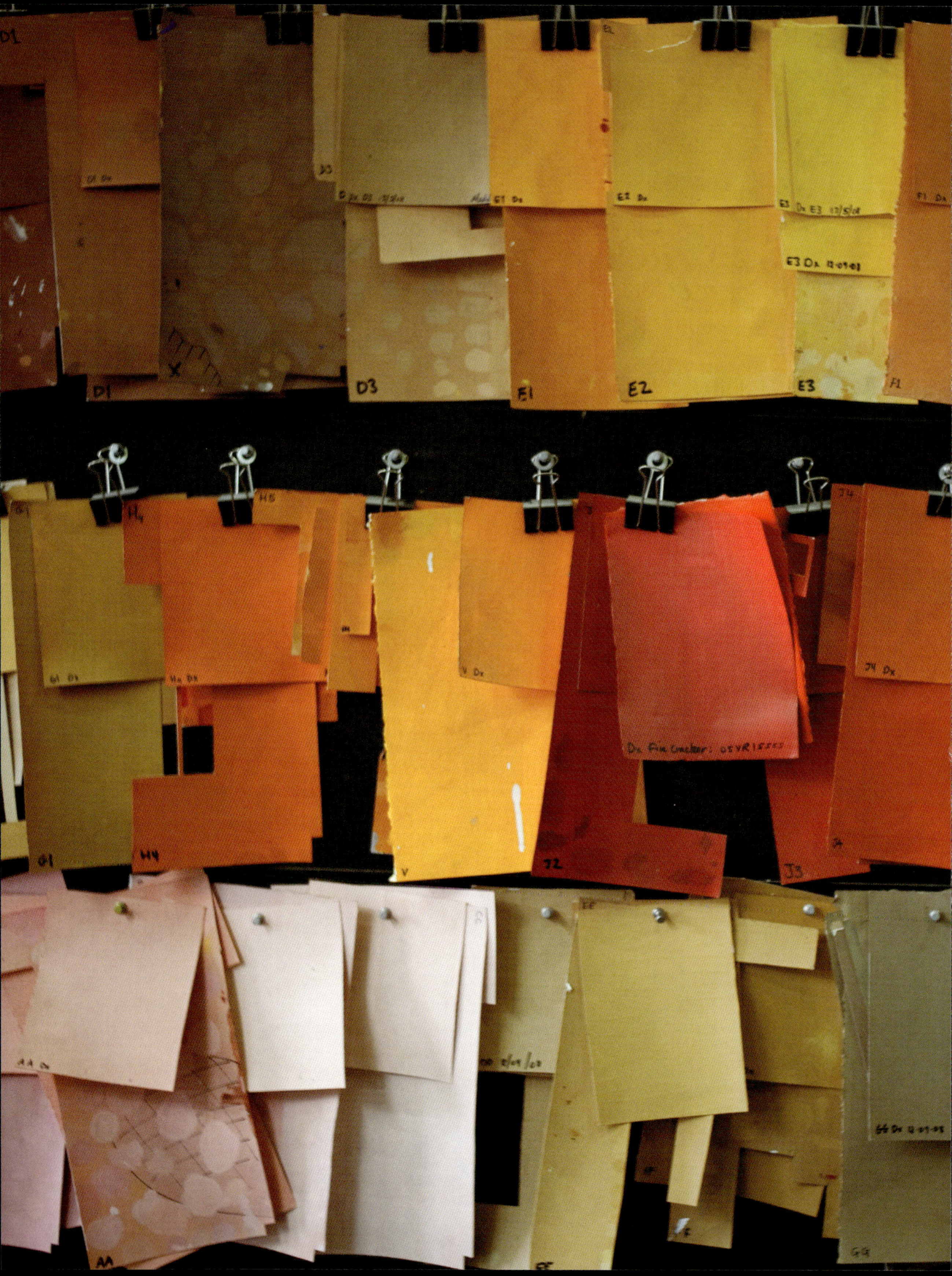
D1
D3
E1
E2
E3
F1
G1
H4
V
J2
J3
J4
AA
EE
GG

THE FOX FAMILY

MR. FOX

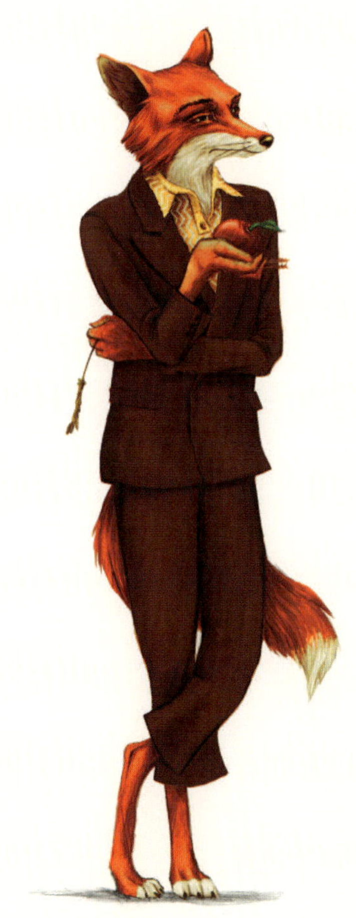

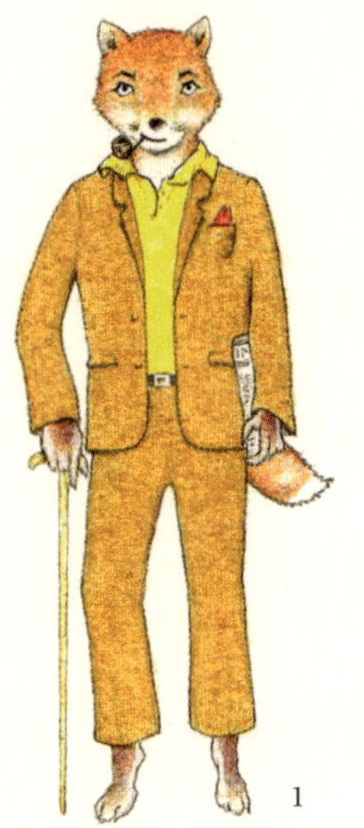

1

FOX
JULY 26 '06

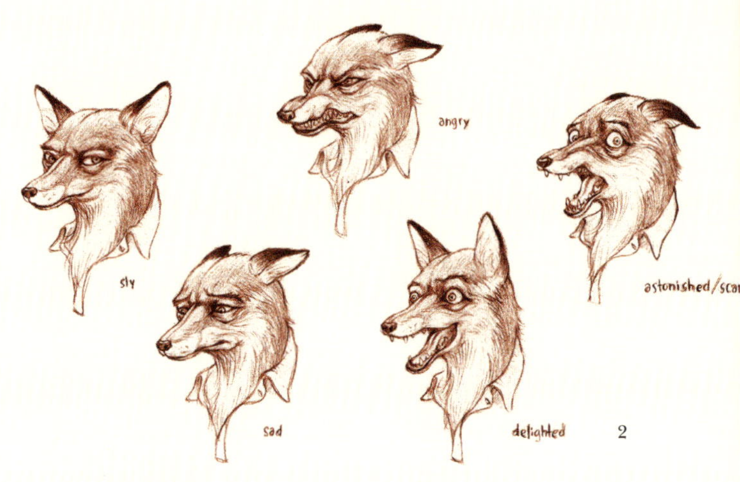

2

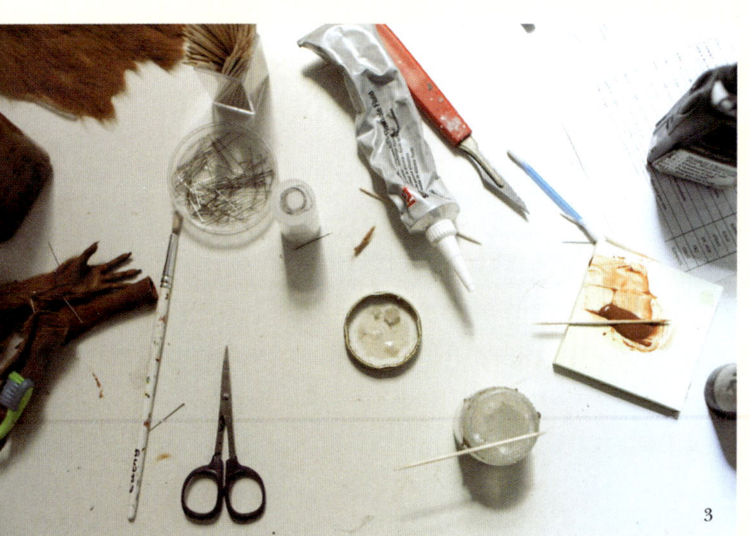

3

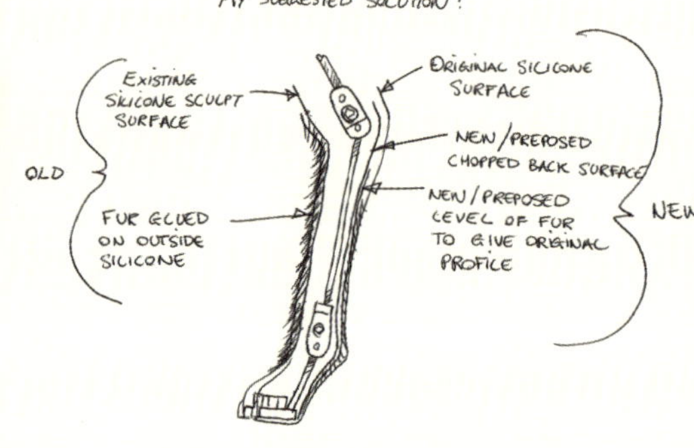

DEAR ALICE
MY SUGGESTED SOLUTION!

EXISTING SILICONE SCULPT SURFACE
ORIGINAL SILICONE SURFACE
NEW/PREPOSED CHOPPED BACK SURFACE
OLD
FUR GLUED ON OUTSIDE SILICONE
NEW/PREPOSED LEVEL OF FUR TO GIVE ORIGINAL PROFILE
NEW

BY SIMPLY CHOPPING BACK INTO THE SCULPTED FUR SILICONE LEG MORE WE WILL ACHIEVE THE LOOK OF THE CORRECT SIZE FOOT.

ANDY

4

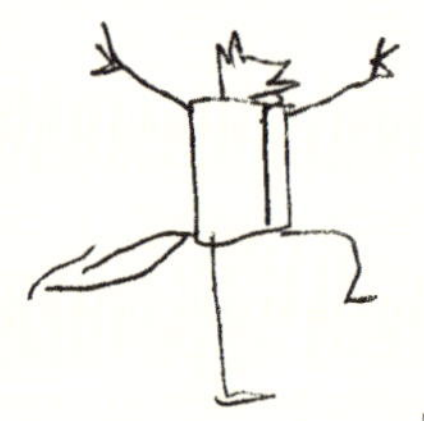

5

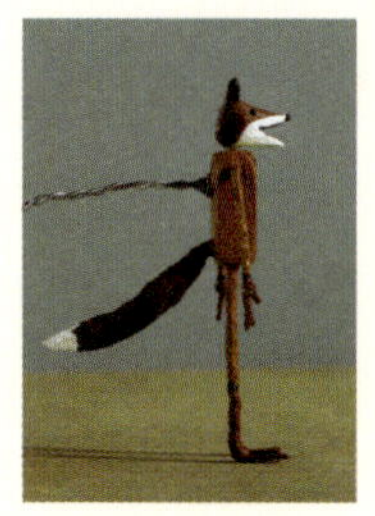

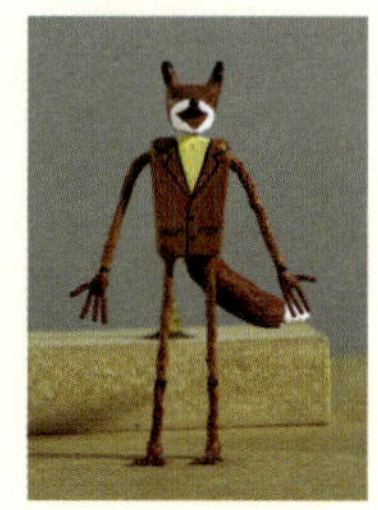

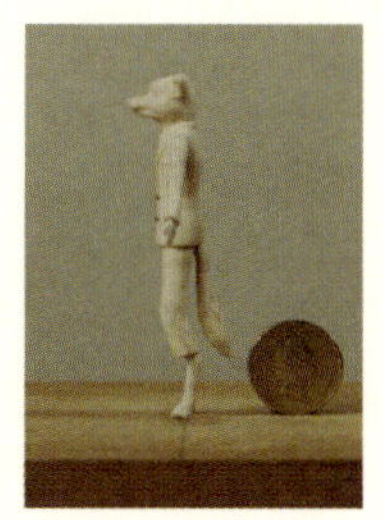

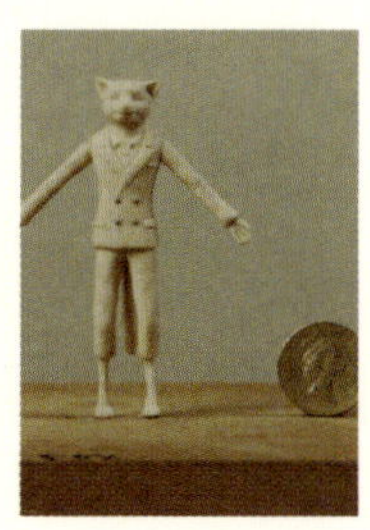

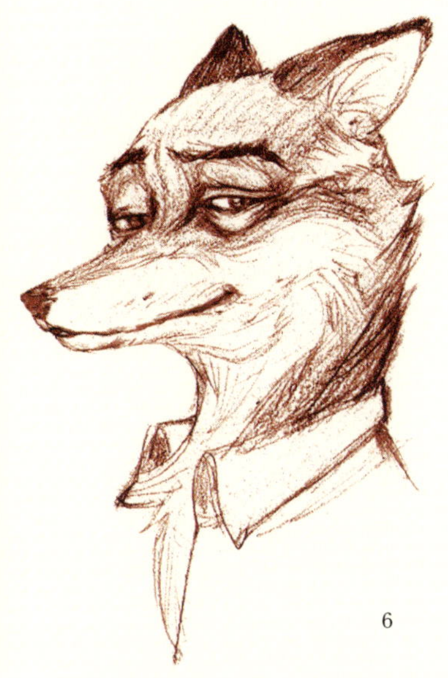

6

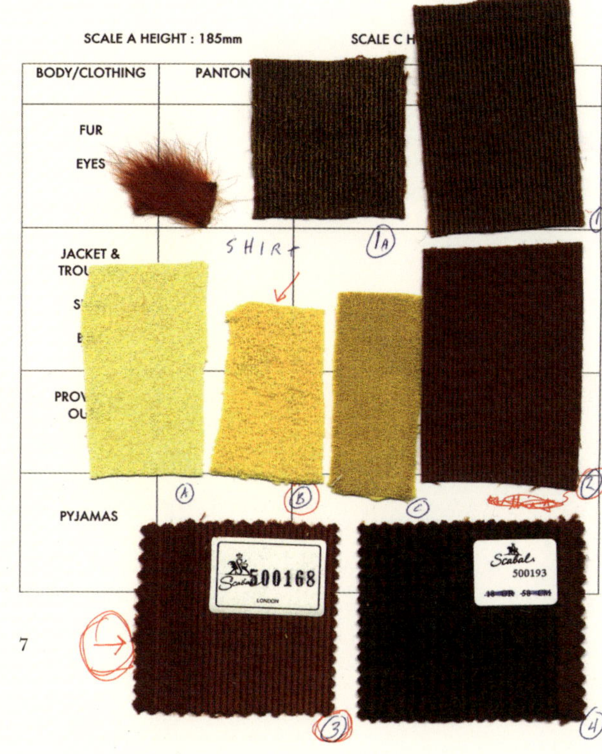

7

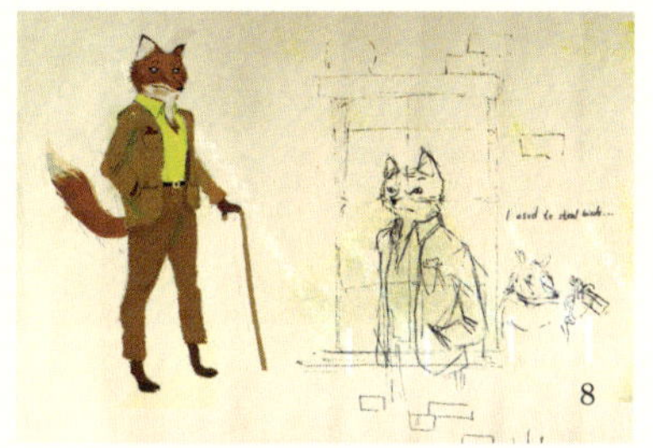

8

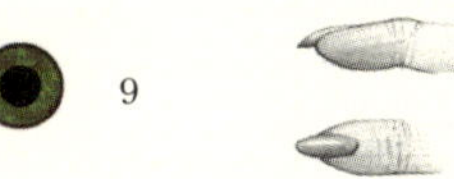

9

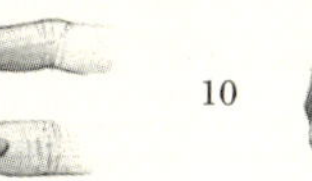

10

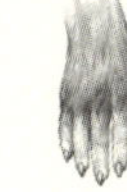

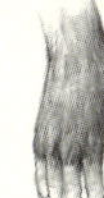

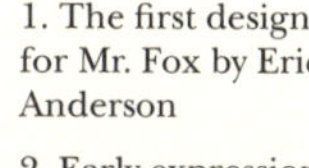

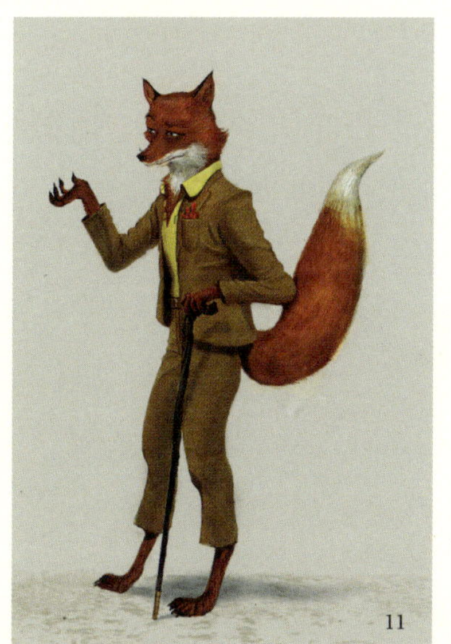

11

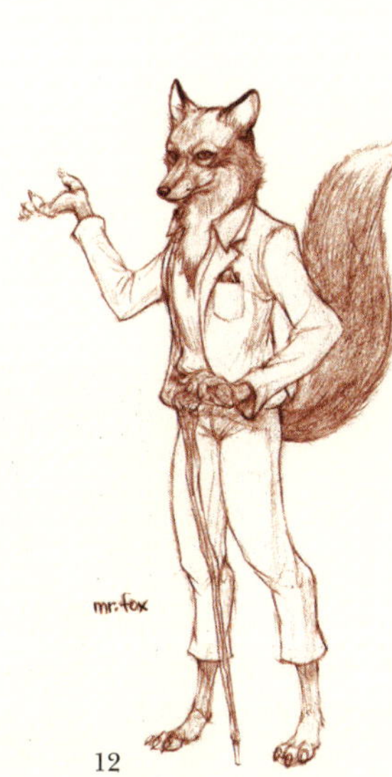

12

1. The first design for Mr. Fox by Eric Anderson

2. Early expression development for Mr. Fox by Huy

3. A worktable in the puppet hospital at the studio

4. Notes by puppet department head Andy Gent on a modification to Mr. Fox's leg

5. A sketch by Wes for a micro-scale puppet of Mr. Fox alongside early versions of the puppet

6. An early portrait of Mr. Fox by Huy

7. Fabric samples for Mr. Fox's costume, with selections annotated by Wes

8. Early concept art for Mr. Fox by Chris

9. The final eyeball design for Mr. Fox

10. Early ideas for Mr. Fox's fingers and paws

11. Early color concept for Mr. Fox by Chris

12. Early sketch of Mr. Fox

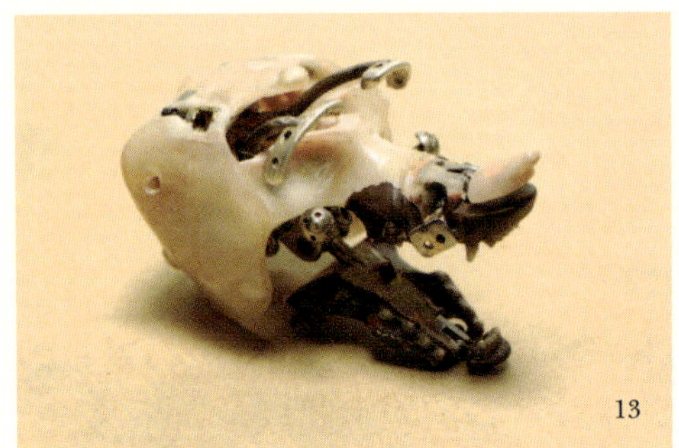

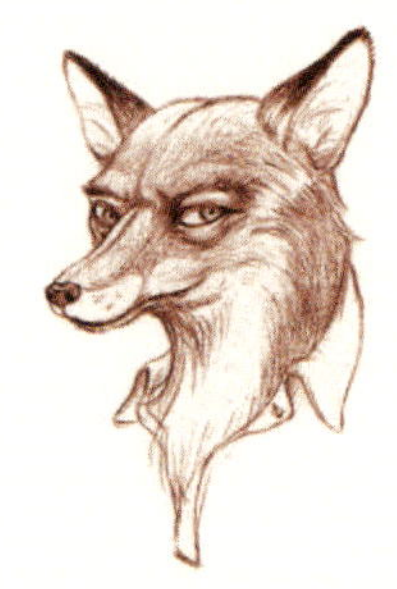

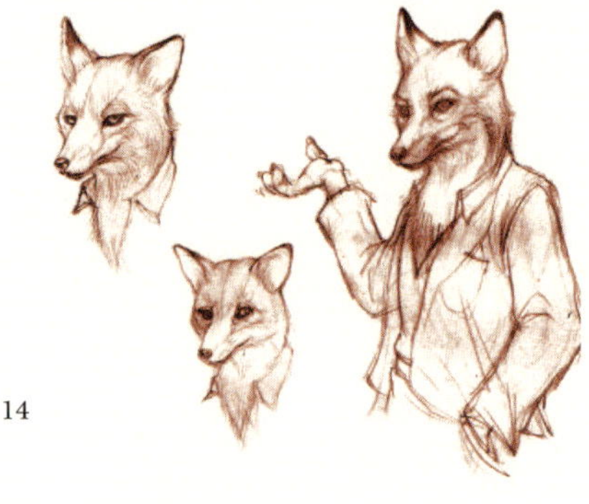

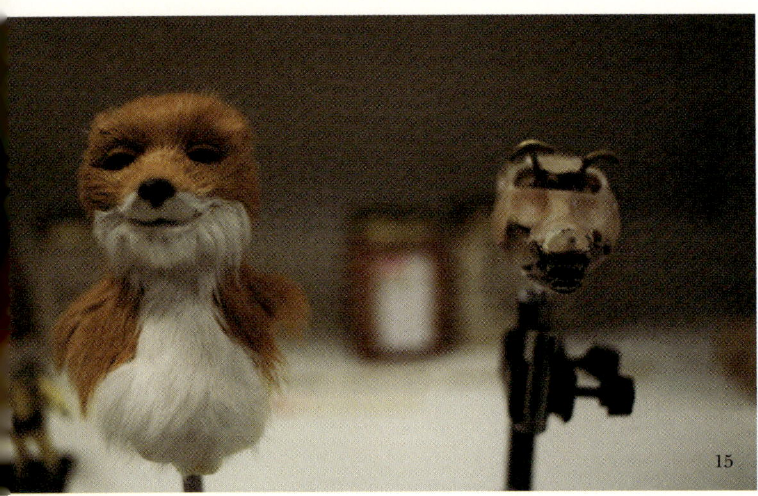

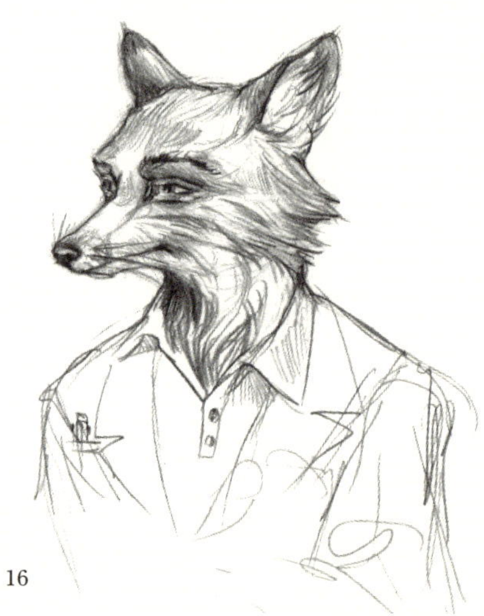

13. The head mechanism for a Mr. Fox puppet

14. Early concept sketches for Mr. Fox by Huy

15. One of the heads of Mr. Fox in progress alongside its mechanism

16 and 17. Concept art for Mr. Fox by Félicie

18. The approved turnaround for the Mr. Fox puppet construction

19. An animator working on movement development for Mr. Fox

20. Mr. Fox's internal armature

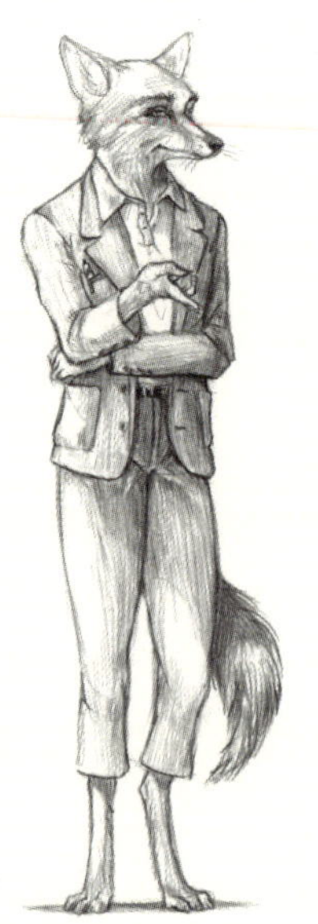

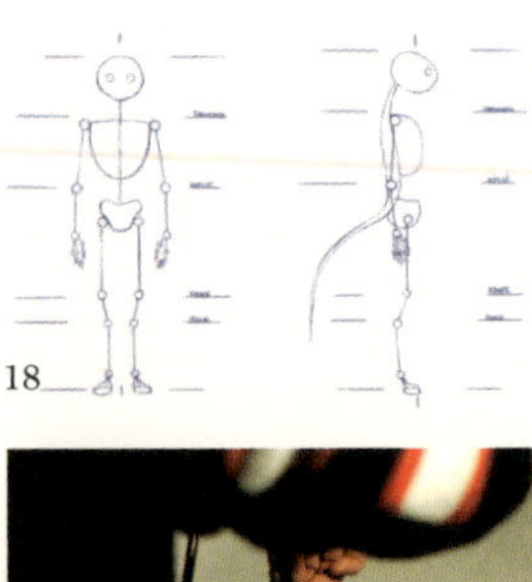

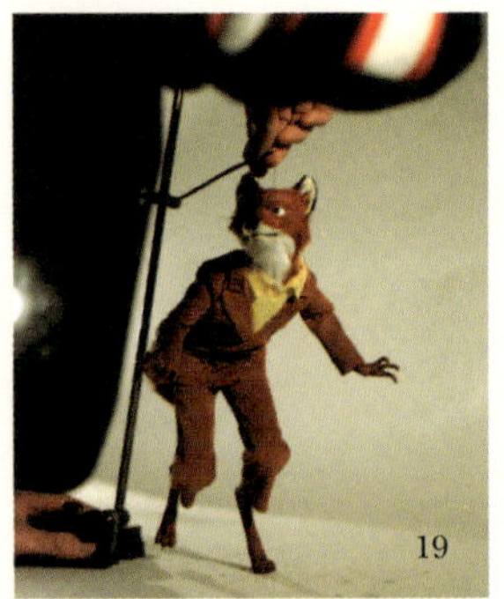

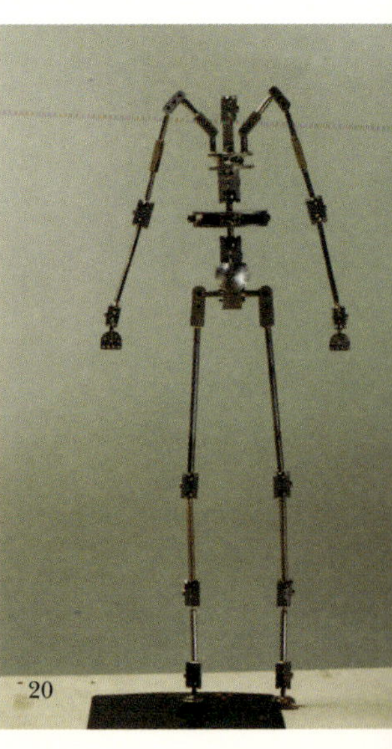

THE FOX FAMILY

MRS. FOX

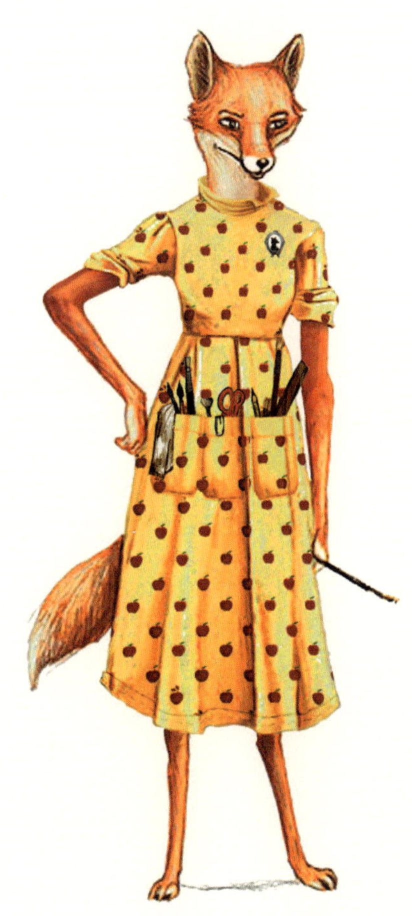

1. A design for Mrs. Fox's cameo brooch by Turlo

2. Early expression development for Mrs. Fox by Félicie

3. An early turnaround for Mrs. Fox

4. The first design for Mrs. Fox by Eric Anderson

5. A Mrs. Fox puppet on a table in the puppet hospital

6. Early pattern options for Mrs. Fox's apple-print dress

7. Working on the Mrs. Fox puppet in the puppet hospital

8. Modifications to Mrs. Fox's costume by Félicie

9. Fabric and color options for Mrs. Fox's costume

10. Early designs for Mrs. Fox's dress pattern

11. The final design for Mrs. Fox's pajamas

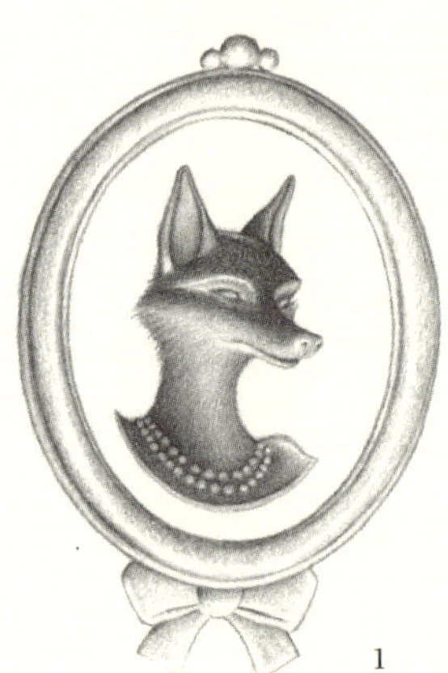

1

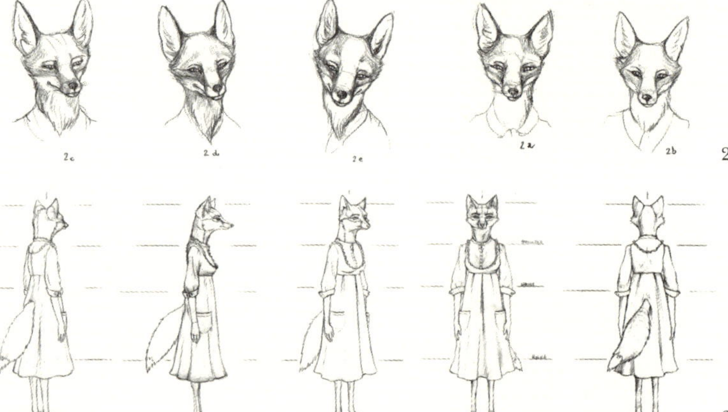

2

3

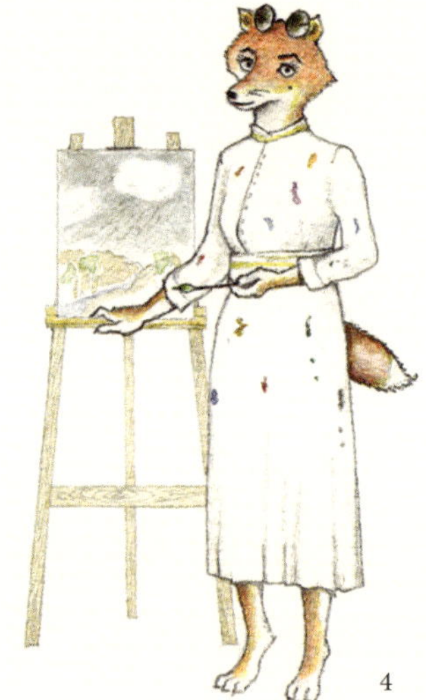

4

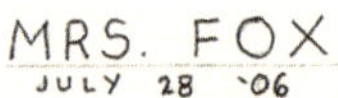

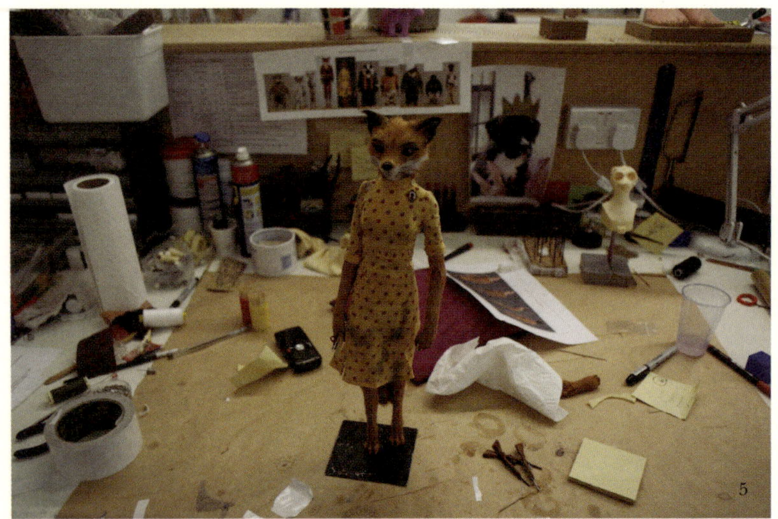

5

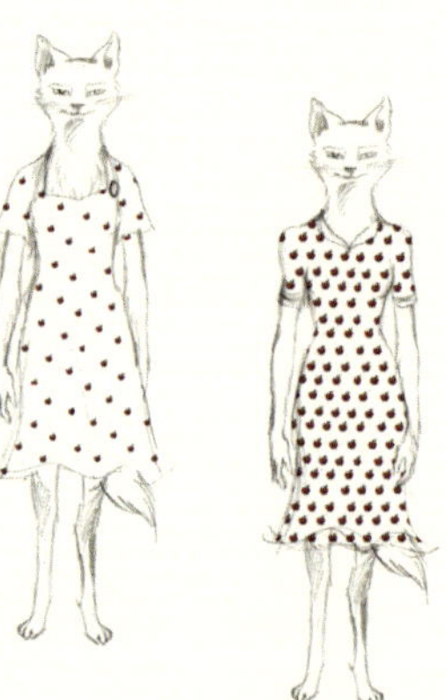

6

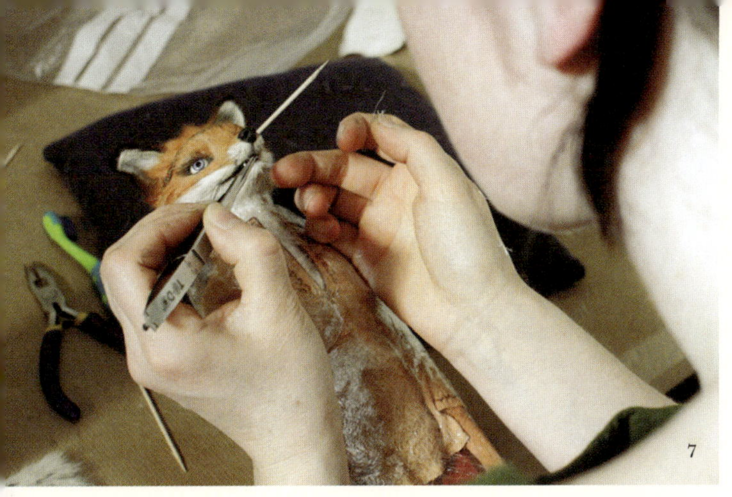

7

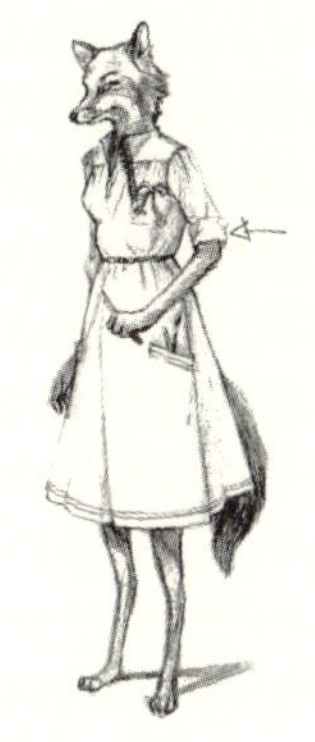

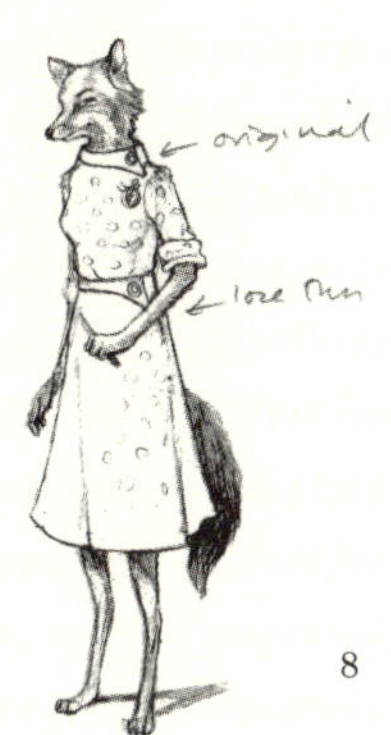

8

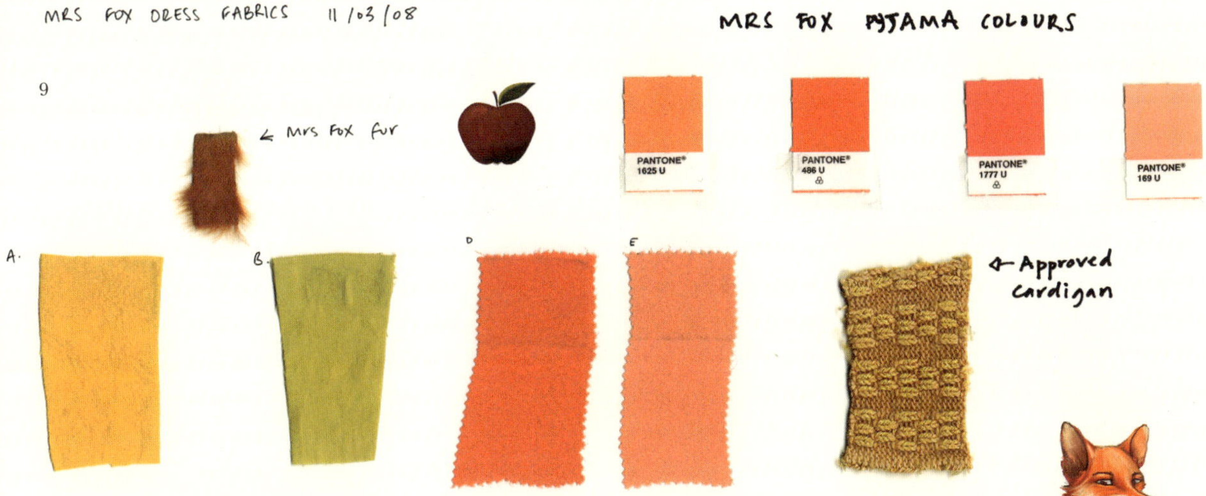

MRS FOX DRESS FABRICS 11/03/08

MRS FOX PYJAMA COLOURS

9

← Mrs Fox fur

PANTONE® 1625 U

PANTONE® 486 U

PANTONE® 1777 U

PANTONE® 169 U

A.

B.

D

E

← Approved cardigan

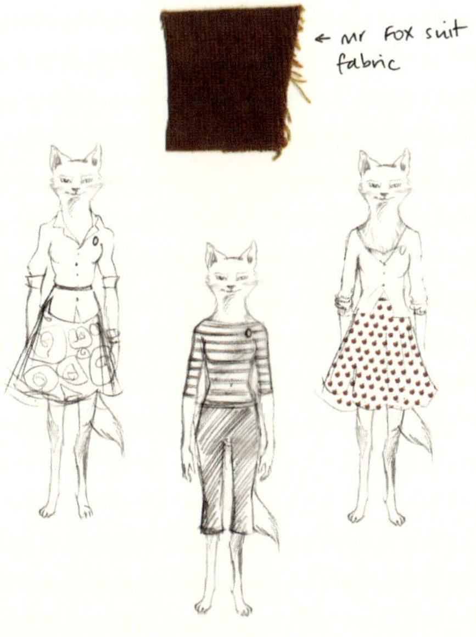

← Mr Fox suit fabric

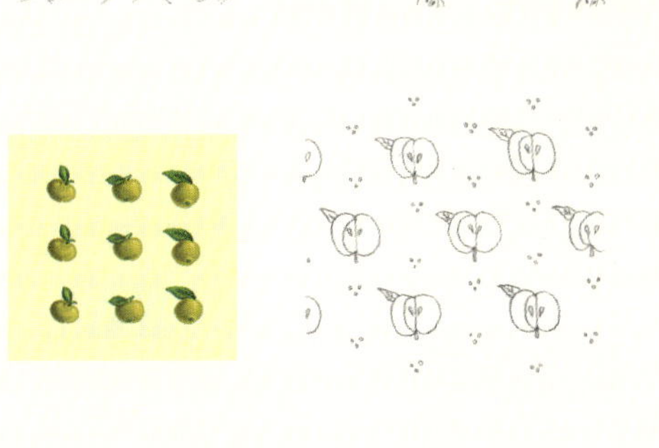

10

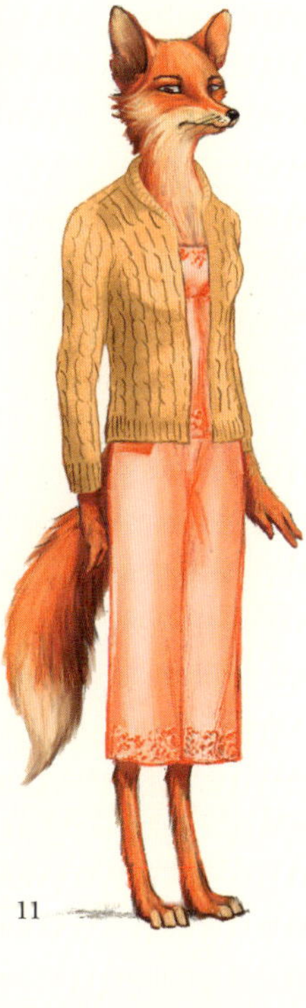

11

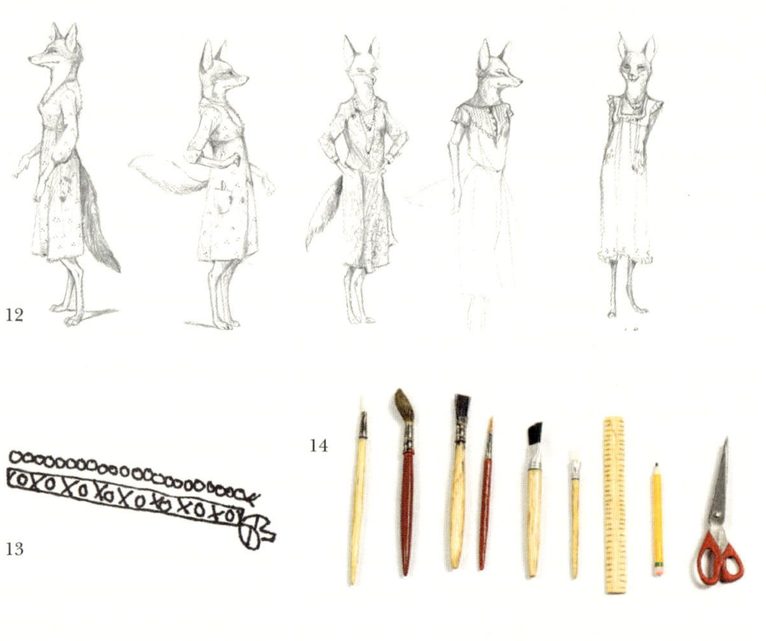

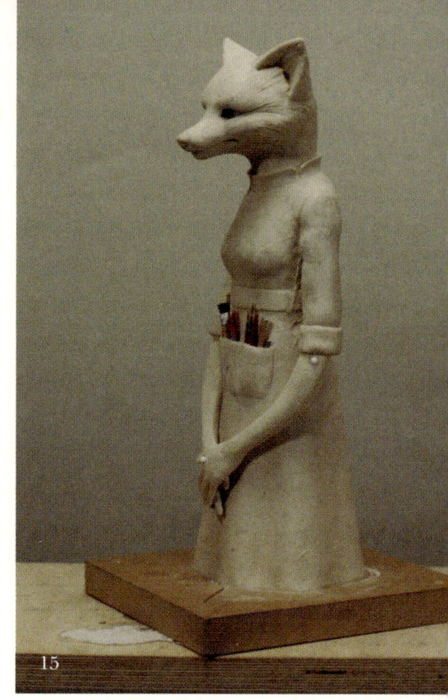

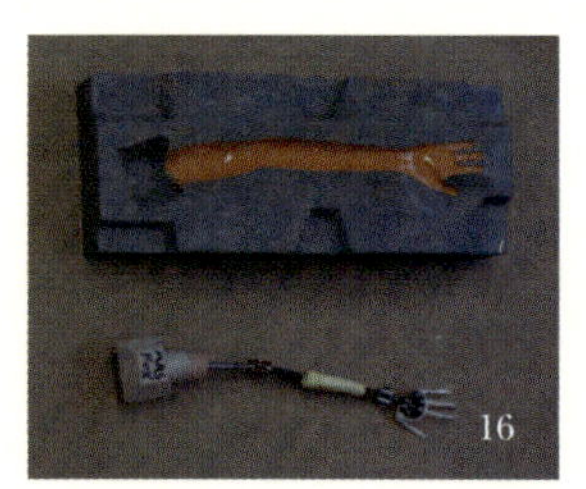

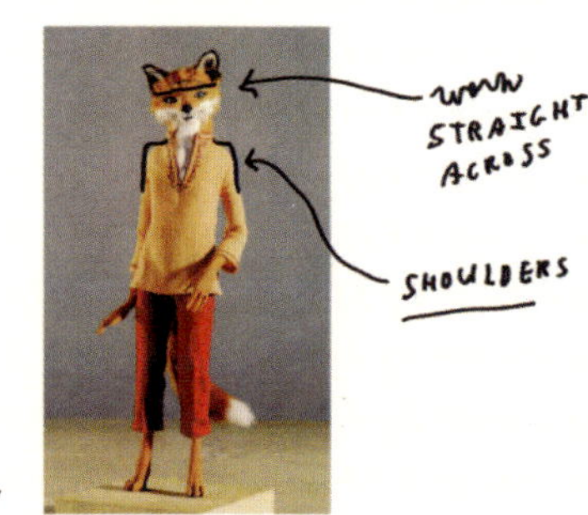

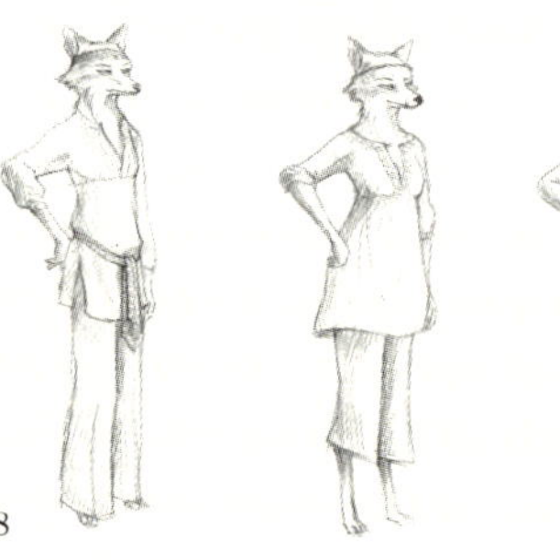

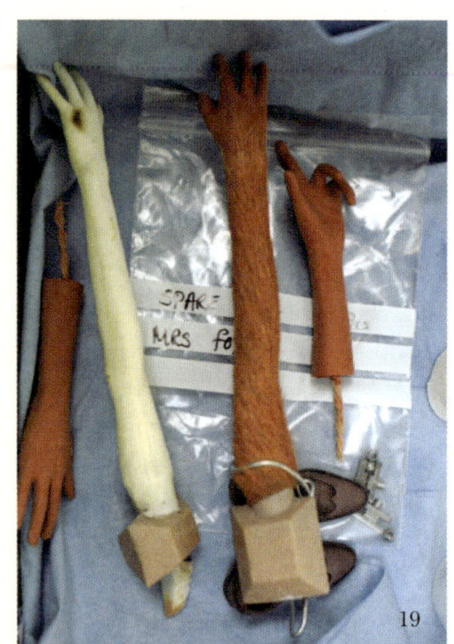

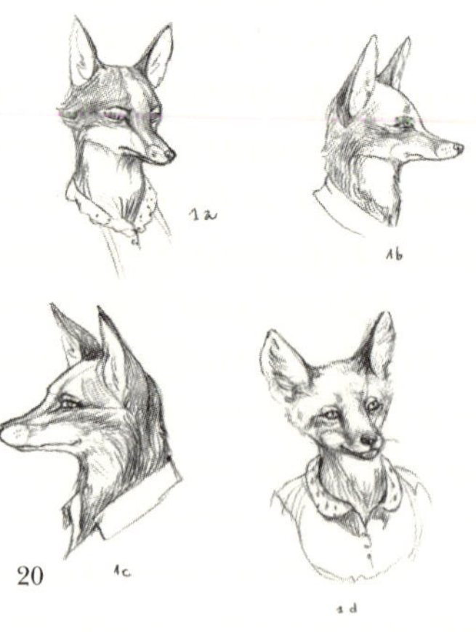

12. Designs for Mrs. Fox's dress by Félicie

13. A sketch for Mrs. Fox's headband by Wes

14. The props from Mrs. Fox's dress pocket

15. The sculpture for the glowing Mrs. Fox puppet used in the supermarket scene

16. The mold for Mrs. Fox's arm alongside its armature

17. Notes by Wes on the costume design for the young Mrs. Fox

18. Early artwork by Félicie for the costume for the young Mrs. Fox

19. Miscellaneous parts for the Mrs. Fox puppet

20. Early concept artwork for Mrs. Fox by Félicie

THE FOX FAMILY

ASH

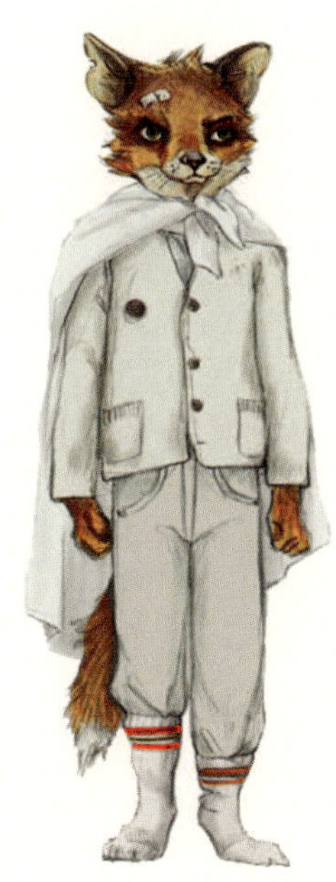

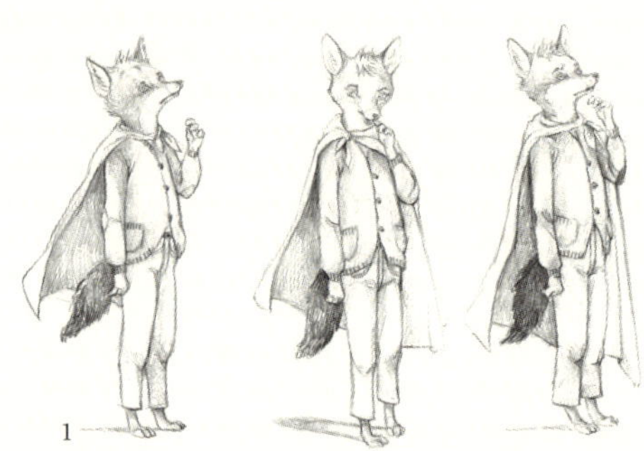
1

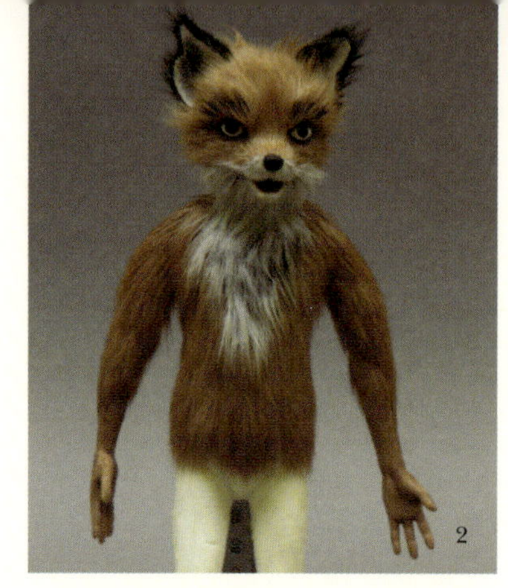
2

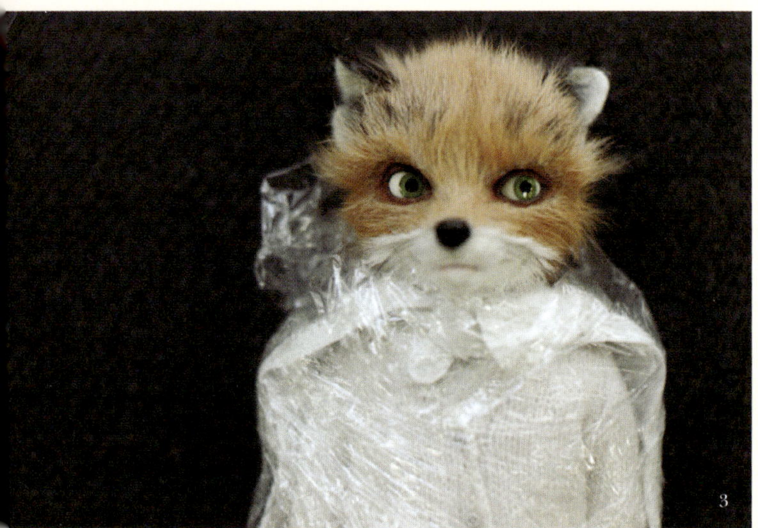
3

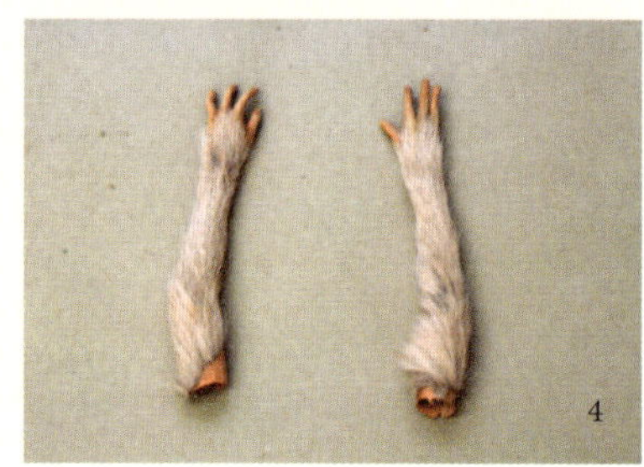
4

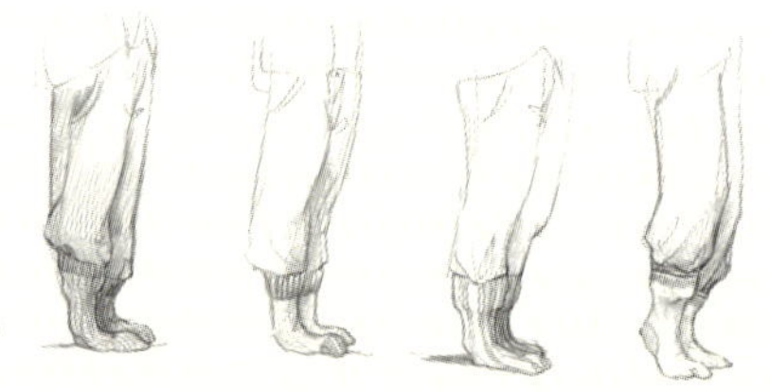
5

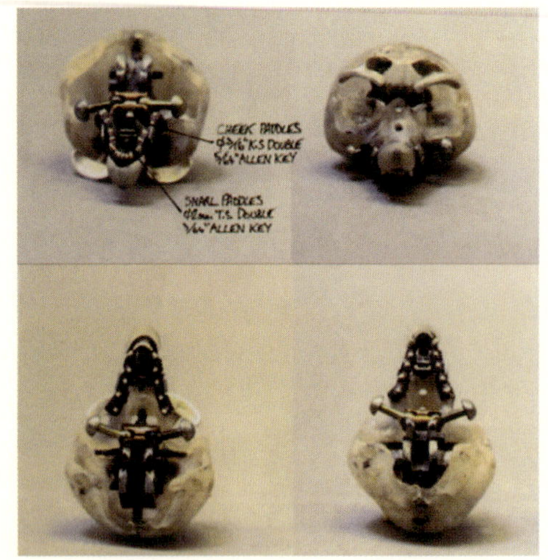

6

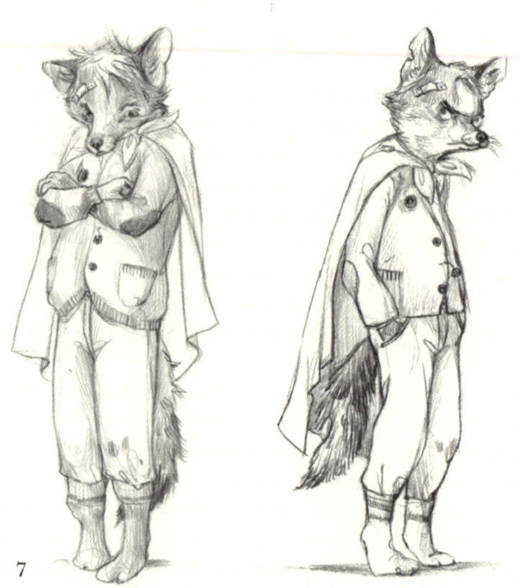
7

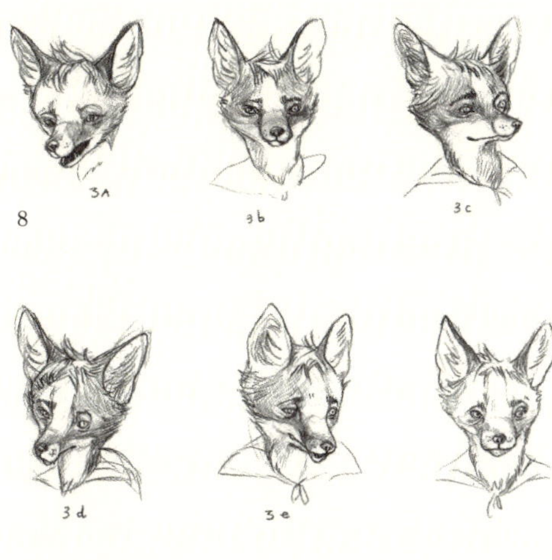

8

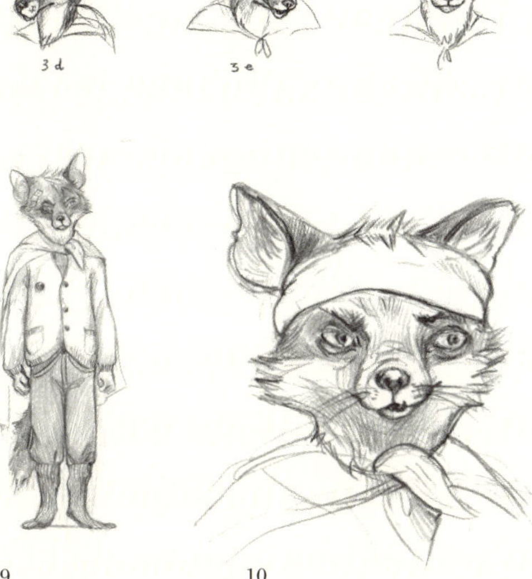

9

10

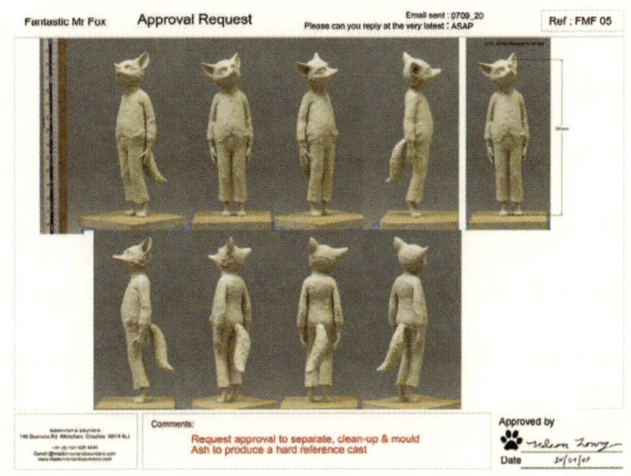

11

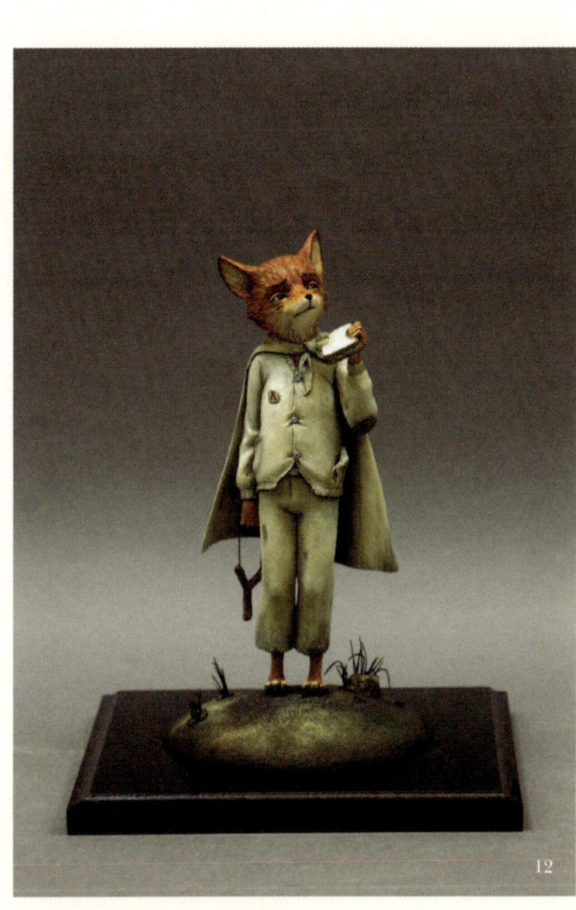

12

All concept art for Ash on these pages by Félicie

1. Early concept designs for Ash

2. Fur tests for Ash

3. Ash's costume protected between shots

4. A spare pair of arms for Ash

5. Early artwork for Ash's feet and paws

6. Instructions for Ash's head mechanism from the puppet bible

7. Early pose and expression development for Ash

8. Early head designs for Ash

9. and 10. Early concept art for Ash

11. Approved mold for the Ash puppet

12. The original painted sculpture of the Ash puppet

All concept art for Ash on these pages by Félicie

13. Early concept designs for Ash doing karate

14. Instructions for assembling Ash's armature from the puppet bible

15. Patterns and instructions for making Ash's swimsuit

16. Early designs for Ash's swimsuit

17. Instructions for assembling Ash's armature from the puppet bible

18. Designs for the sidecars on Ash's underpants

19. A digital mock-up of Ash's underpants

20. An early design for Ash's swimsuit

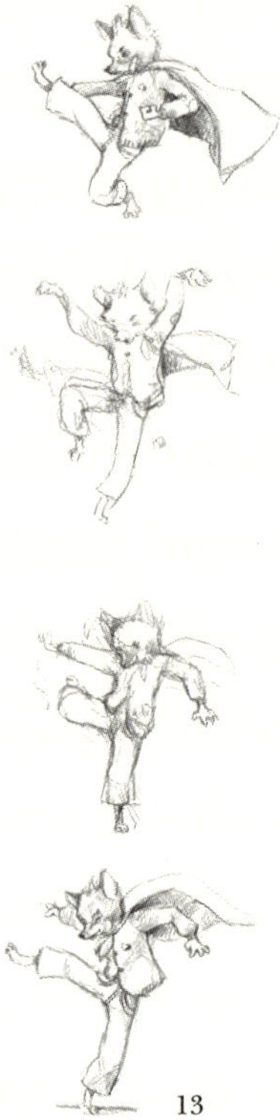

13

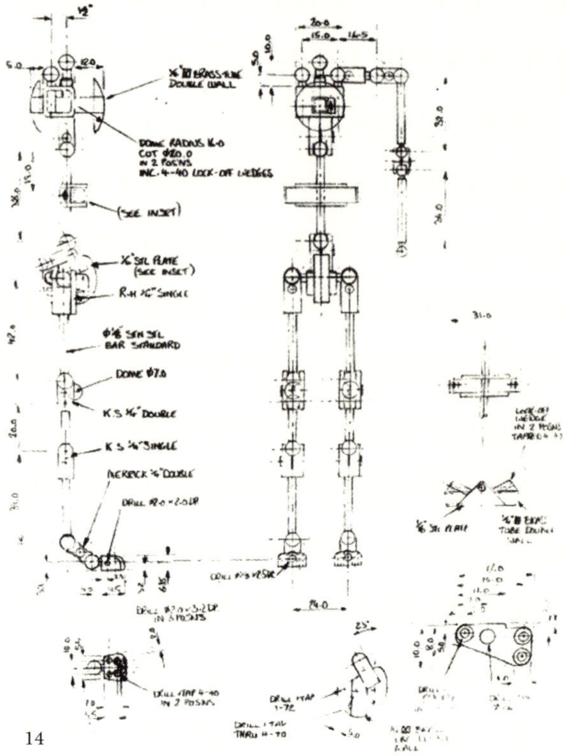

14

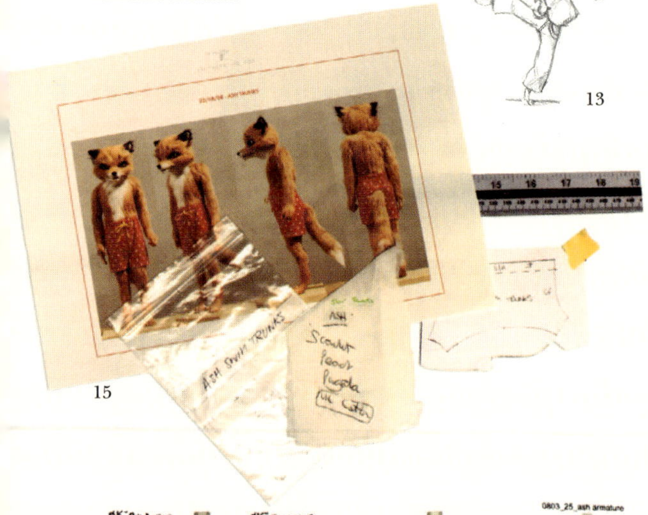

15

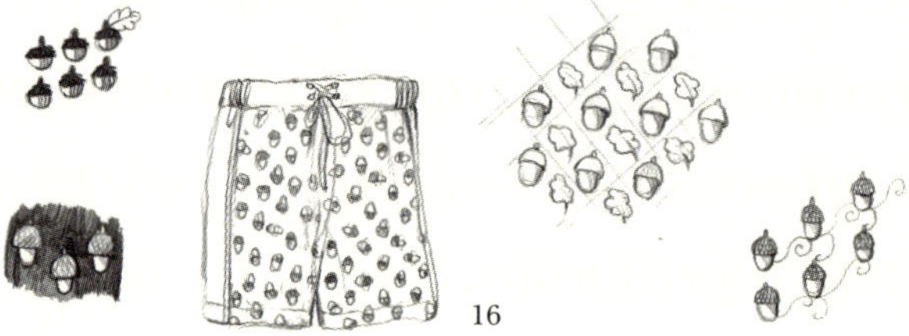

16

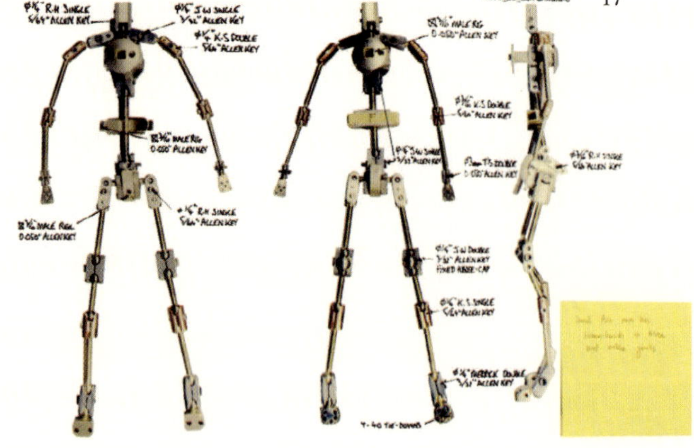

17

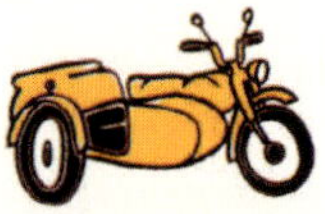

18

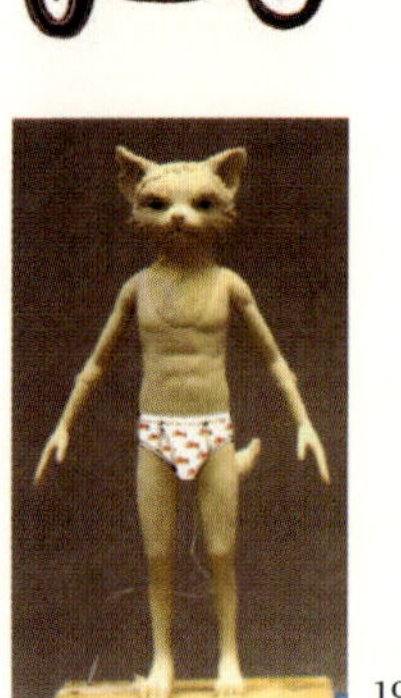

19

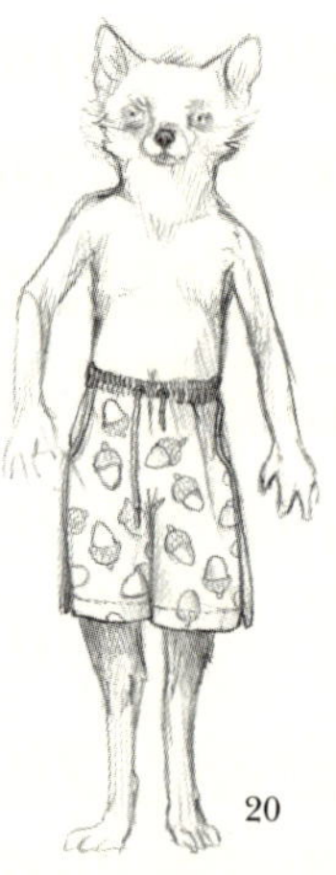

20

THE FOX FAMILY

KRISTOFFERSON

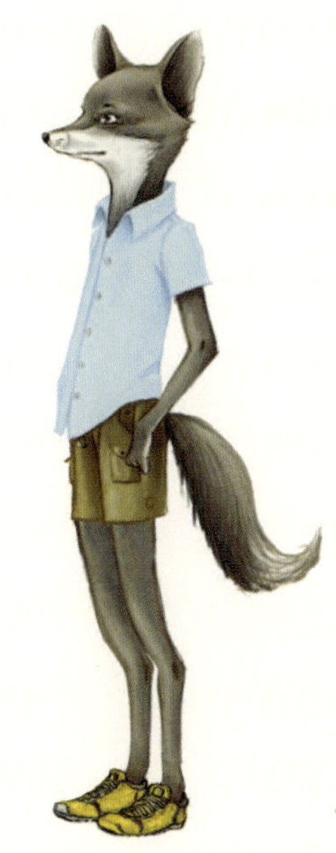

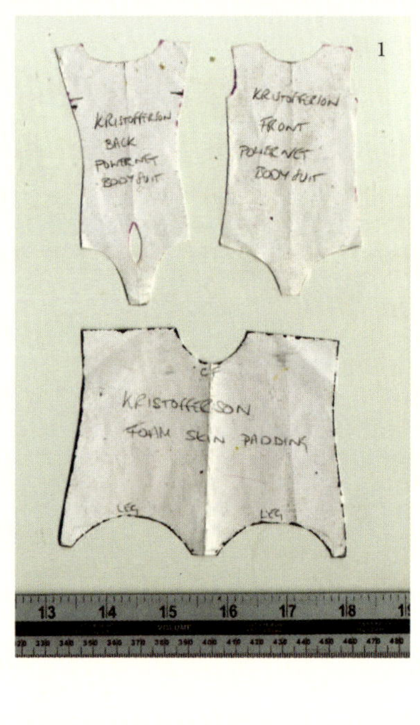

KRISTOFFERSON
BACK
POWERNET
BODYSUIT
KRISTOFFERSON
FRONT
POWERNET
BODYSUIT
KRISTOFFERSON
FOAM SKIN PADDING
LEG
LEG

1

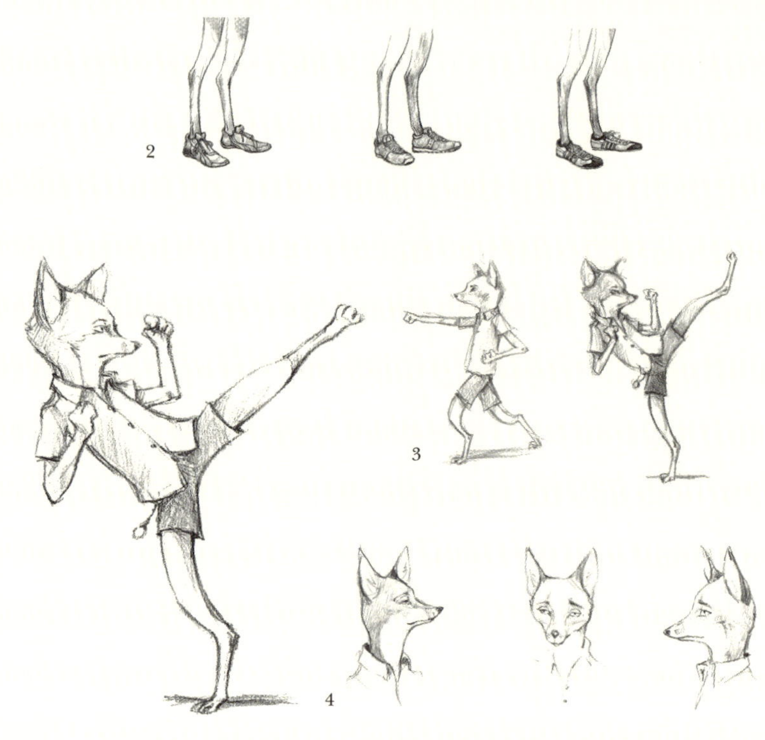

2

3

4

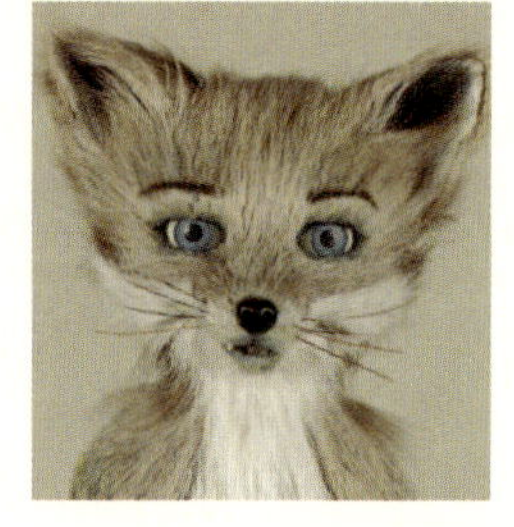

5

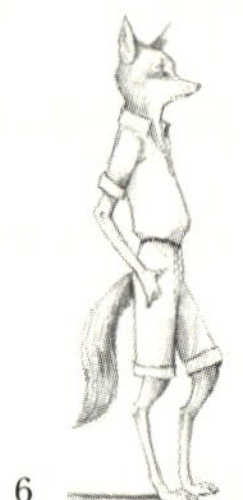

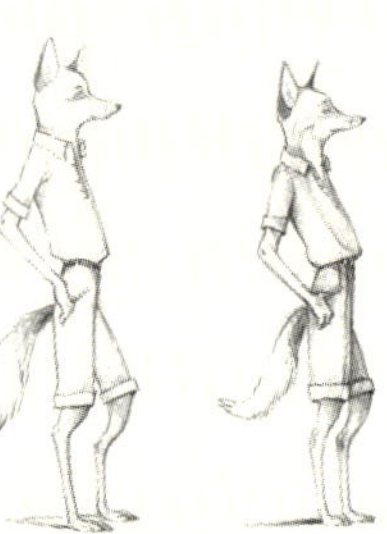

6

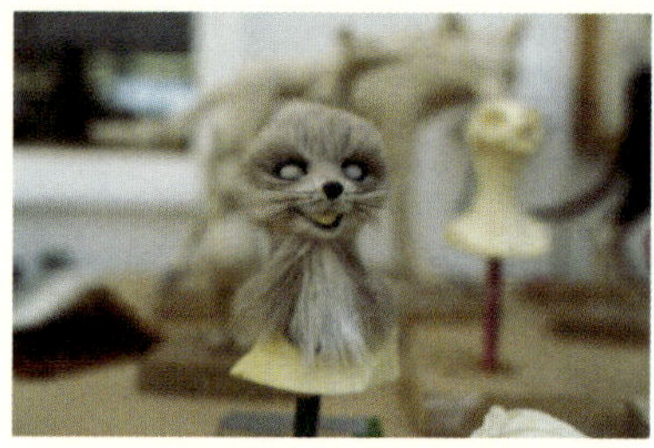

7

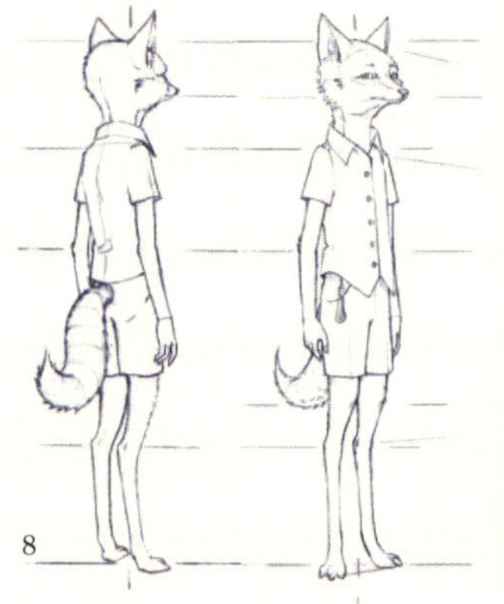

8

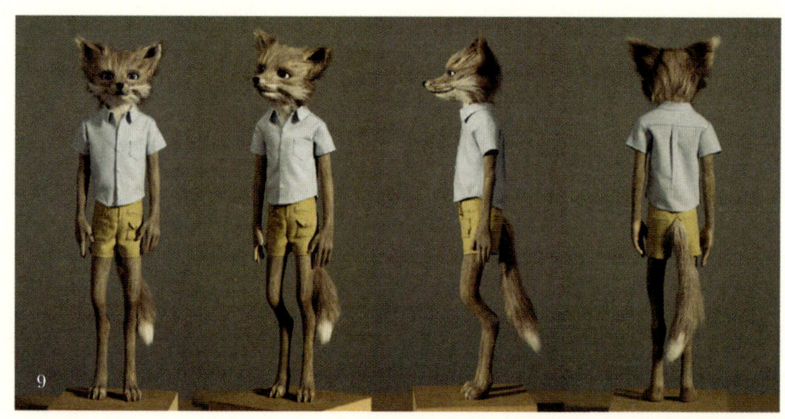

9

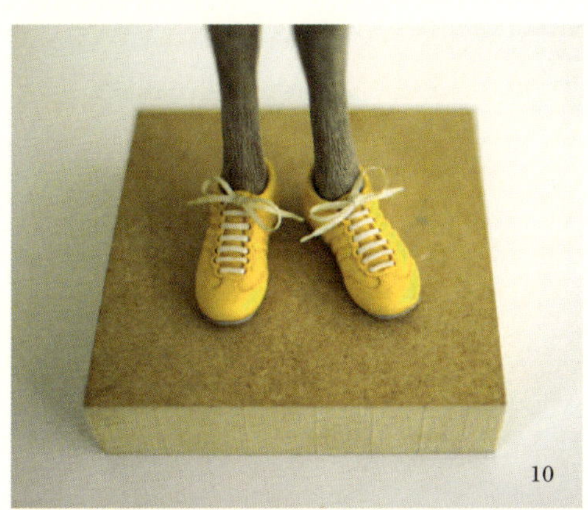

10

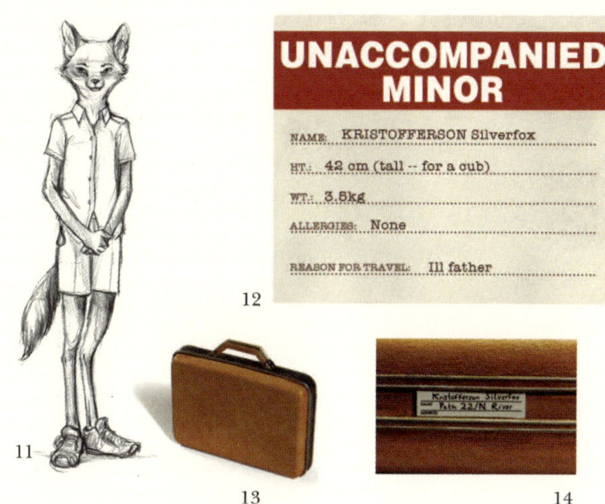

11

12

13

14

All concept art for Kristofferson on these pages by Félicie

1. The pattern for Kristofferson's torso fur

2. Designs for Kristofferson's sneakers

3. Early concept designs for Kristofferson doing karate

4. Early designs for Kristofferson's head

5. Approved eyes and eyebrows for Kristofferson

6. Early pose and expression development for Kristofferson

7. Kristofferson's furring in progress in the puppet hospital

8. A turnaround for the Kristofferson sculpture

9. The Kristofferson puppet prior to furring the arms and legs

10. Kristofferson's approved sneakers

11. Pose and expression development for Kristofferson

12. Kristofferson's travel tag

13. Kristofferson's suitcase

14. Kristofferson's luggage tag

15. Samples of Kristofferson's costume with notes from Wes

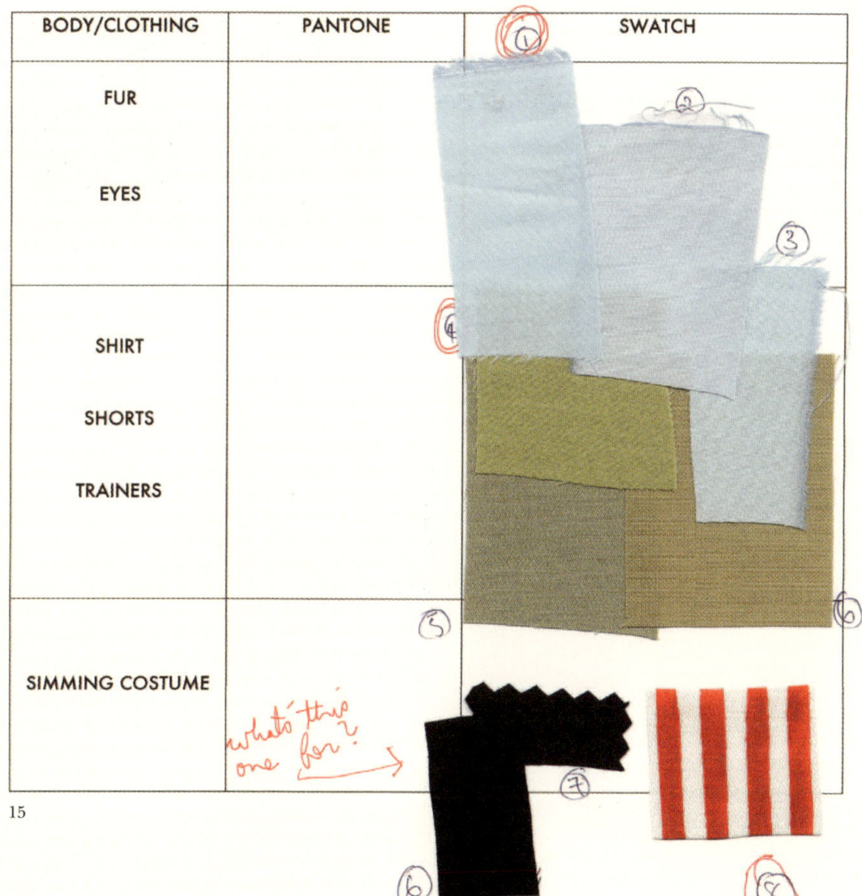

15

16. Lineup of four approved Kristofferson puppets, from full-scale to mini-micro

17. A sculpture of Kristofferson for eye detail reference

18. The mold for the miniature Kristofferson puppet

19. An early concept design for Kristofferson's swimsuit and dive pose

20. The pattern for Kristofferson's shorts

21. Early concept art for Kristofferson's swimsuit

22. Selections for Kristofferson's key ring and pocket-knife

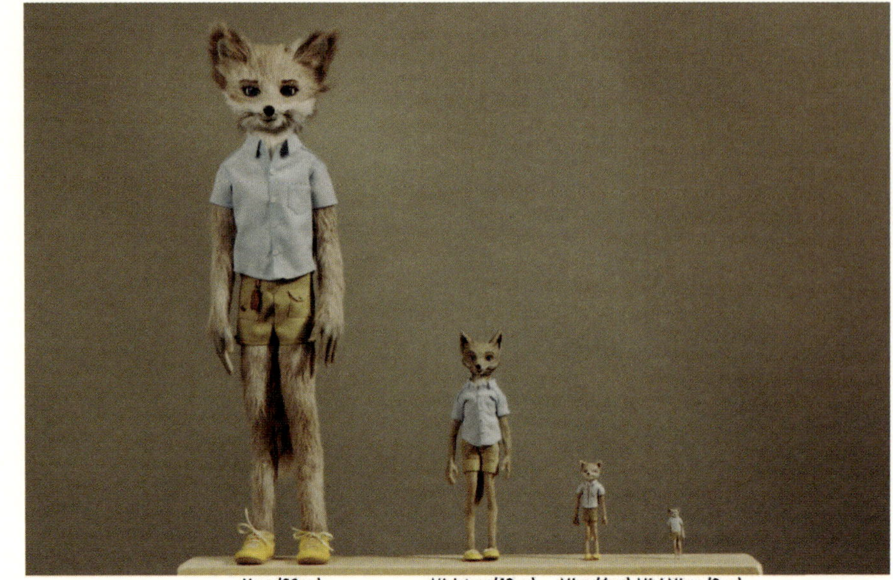

16

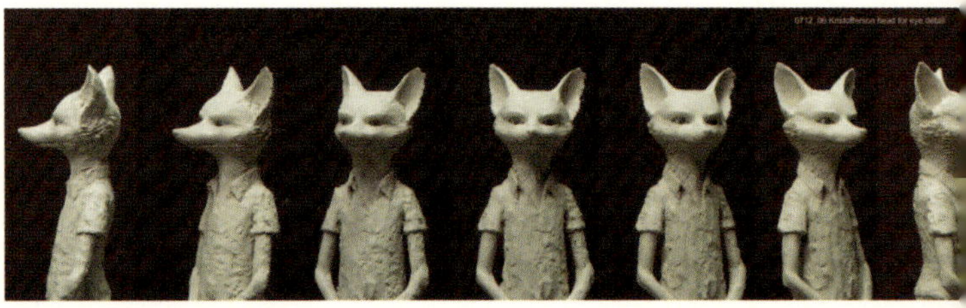

17

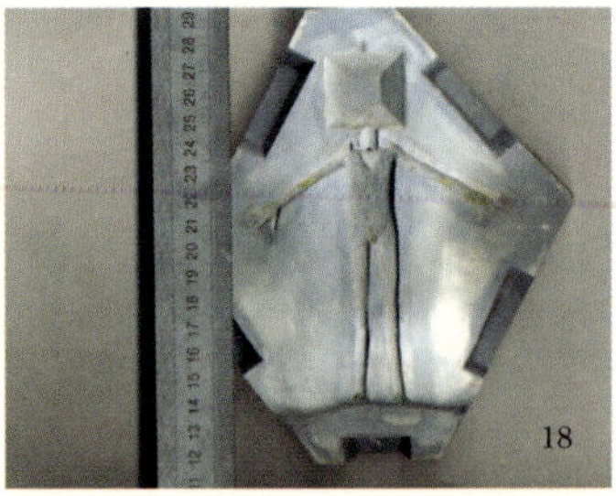

18

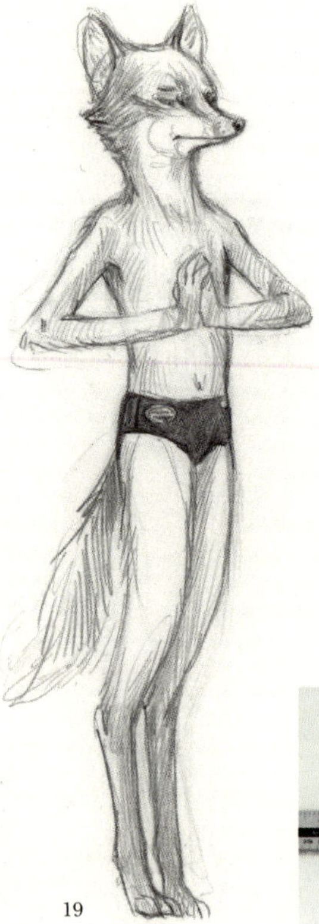

KEYRING

POCKET KNIFE

19

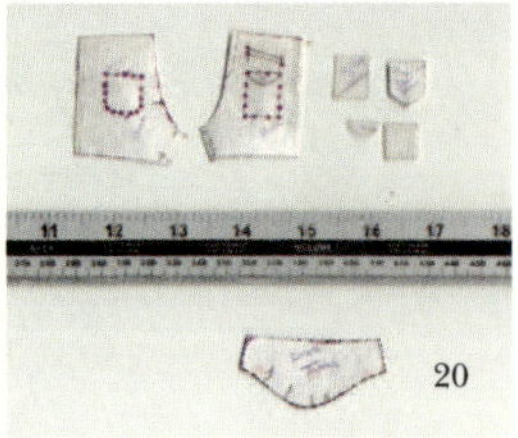

20

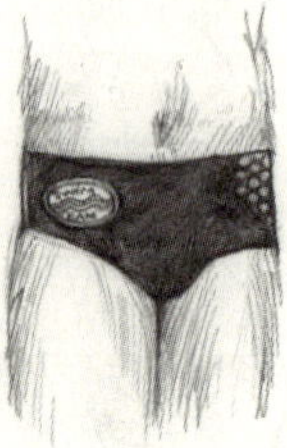

21

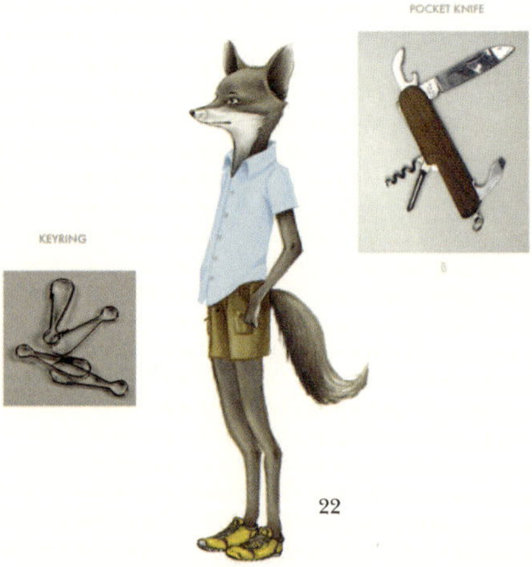

22

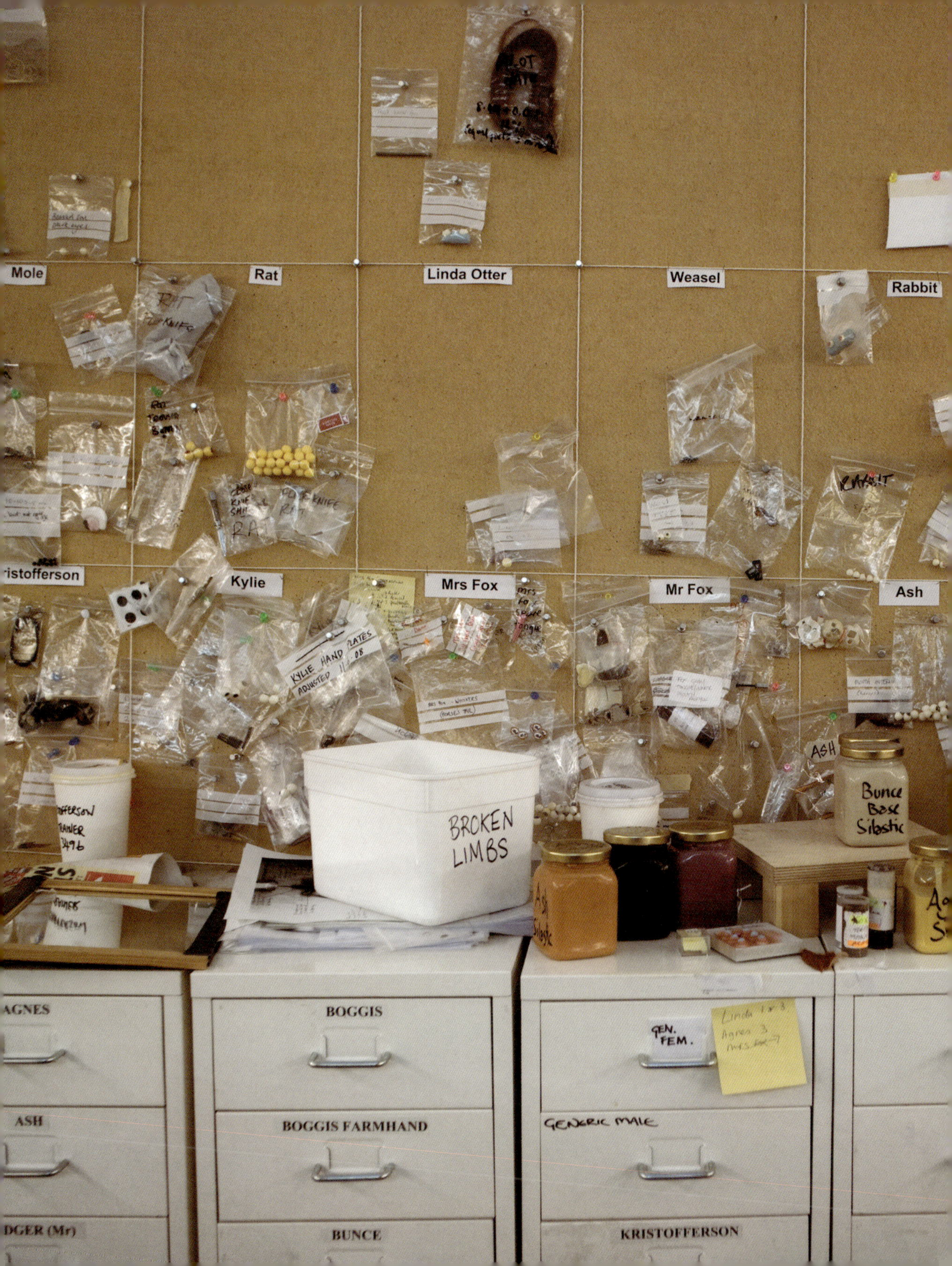

Mole
Rat
Linda Otter
Weasel
Rabbit
ristofferson
Kylie
Mrs Fox
Mr Fox
Ash
BROKEN
LIMBS
Bunce
Base
Silastic
AGNES
BOGGIS
GEN.
FEM.
ASH
BOGGIS FARMHAND
GENERIC MALE
DGER (Mr)
BUNCE
KRISTOFFERSON

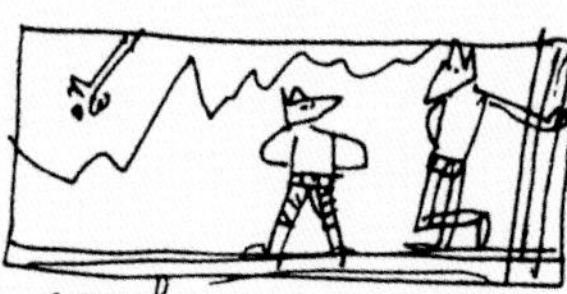

ASH & K. ON BRANCH

FOX

Kristofferson! Welcome to our little tree! I hope you brought your swimming trunks.

EXT. TREE. DAY

Ash and another fox cub stand together poised on a high branch over a pond behind Fox's tree. The second cub is taller, leaner, sleeker, and it is immediately apparent even by his posture that he is infinitely more graceful than Ash. He is Kristofferson.

Ash wears over-sized swim trunks with a pattern of acorns printed on them. Kristofferson wears a professional Speedo with a patch on it that says Swim Team.

Fox sits in the grass eating an apple on a quiet bank below with Mrs. Fox. She is painting at an easel. Fox's tree is just across the meadow behind them. Ash yells:

BOOM DOWN TO FOX & MRS. FOX.

ASH

Watch this, Dad!

WIDE AS ASH JUMPS BUT NOT TOO WIDE.

Fox looks up into the tree. Ash leaps into the air and does a spectacularly awkward back-flip during which he appears to have four arms and three legs randomly attached to his body, flailing wildly. He hits the water by the side of his head and smacks into the surface back-first with a pained yelp. Fox grimaces. He claps mildly.

SEE POND

(NOTE: an alternate version of Ash with four arms and three legs randomly attached to his body will be used for this stunt.)

SOME

FOX

Good jump, Ash! Remember to keep your tail tucked!

FOX CLAPPING

Fox looks at Mrs. Fox's canvas. It is a picture of the pond and landscape in severe weather with black clouds and lightning bolts. It is signed Felicity Fox. Fox raises an eyebrow.

FOX

Still painting thunderstorms, I see.

DOLLY TO MRS. F & HER CANVAS. FOX LEANS IN TO FRAME TO LOOK

Fox looks up into the tree again. Kristofferson steps off the branch and performs a reserved but perfect jack-knife. He enters the water splashlessly. Fox leaps to his feet, applauding with his paws above his head, whistling and hollering:

BACK TO CLAPPING SHOT.

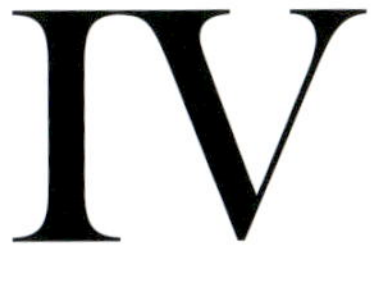

IV

THE VIEWS ABOVE GROUND

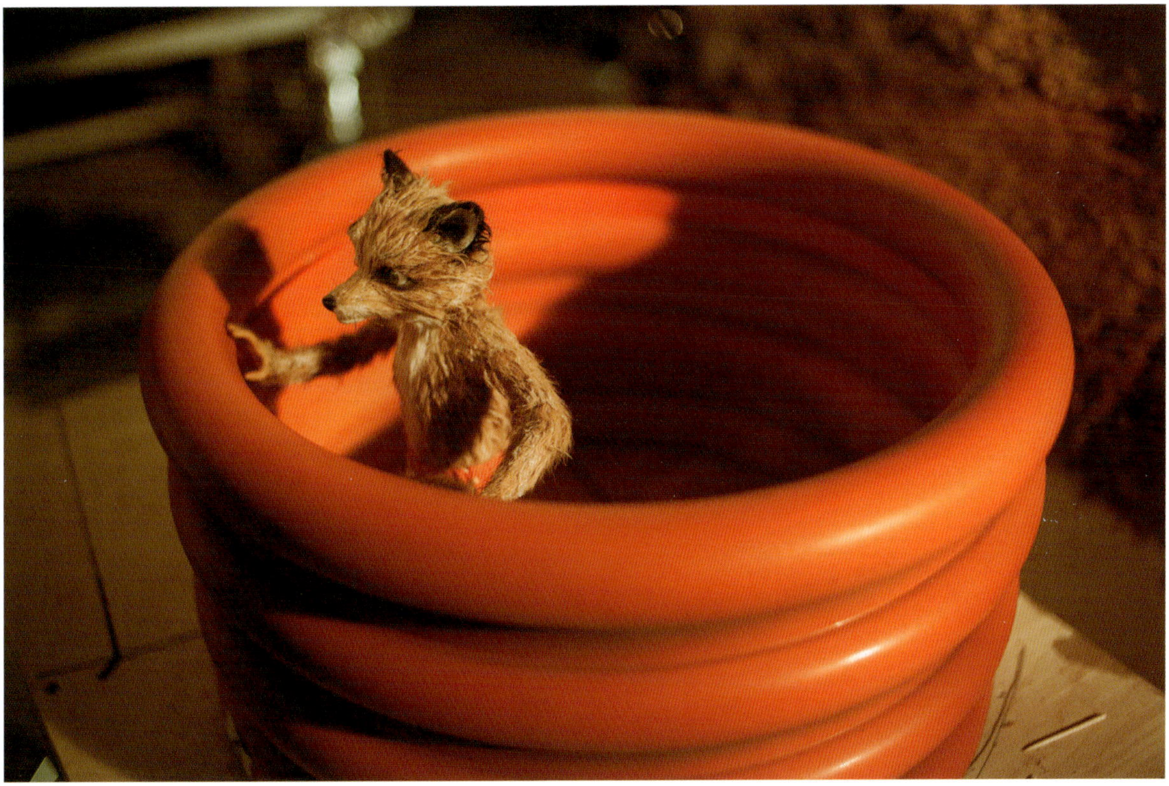

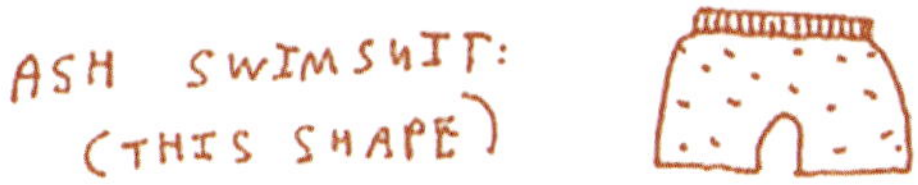

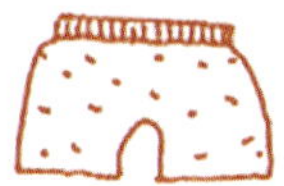

Above: Ash in the pool

Left: Sketch by Wes of Ash's swimsuit

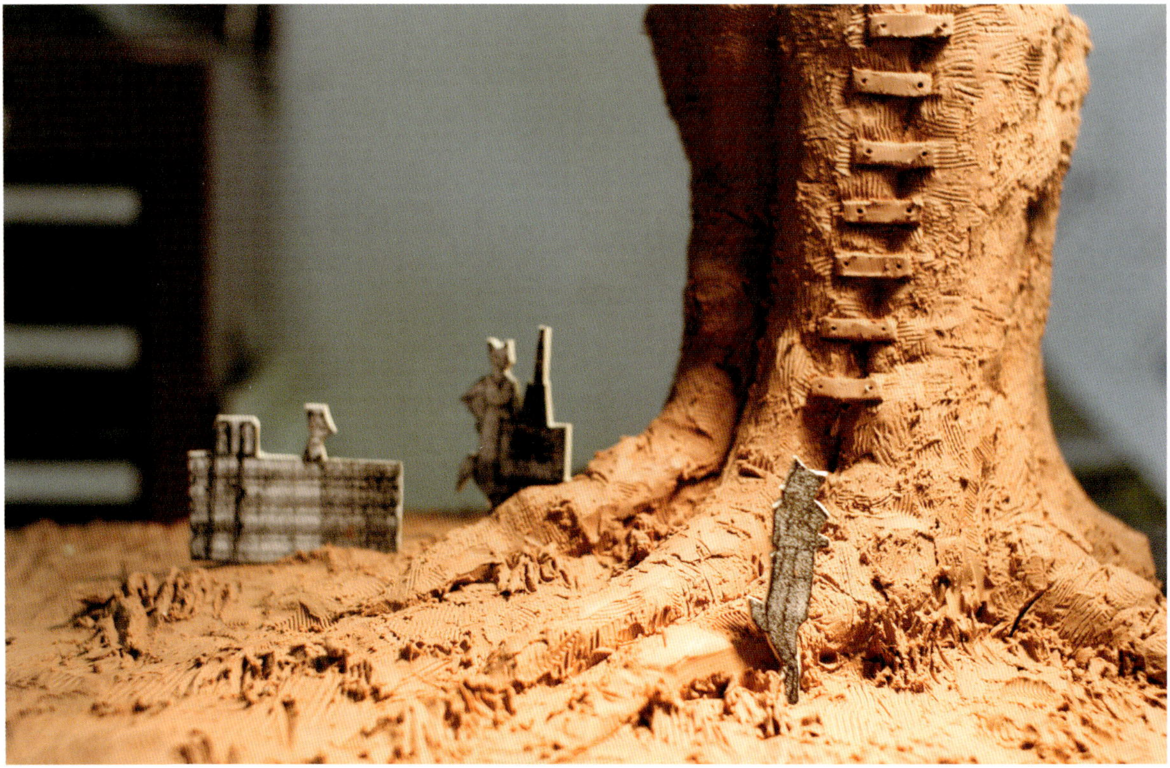

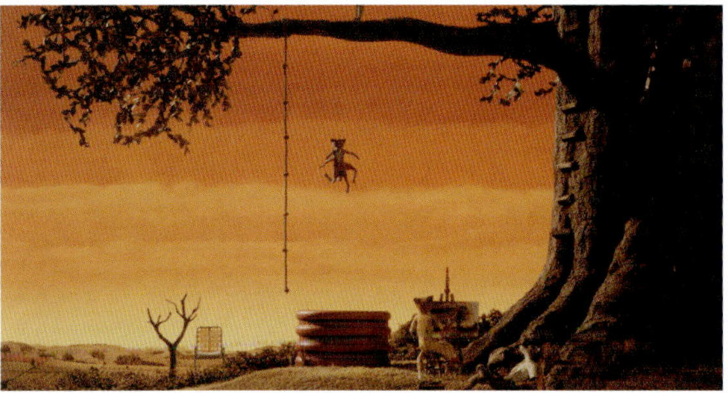

Above: Beech tree maquette with Fox family cutouts for scale reference in the workshop

Left: A still from the movie of Ash's dive

Below: Fleur-de-lis designs for Kristofferson's splash, and a note from Wes on the style of Ash's swimsuit.

Opposite page: Storyboard sketches for Ash's dive by Christian

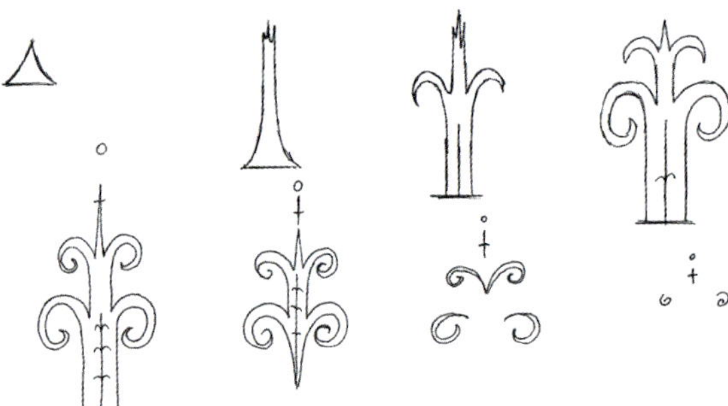

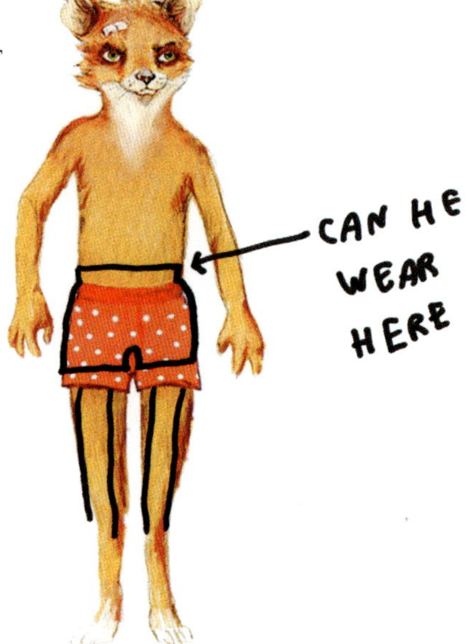

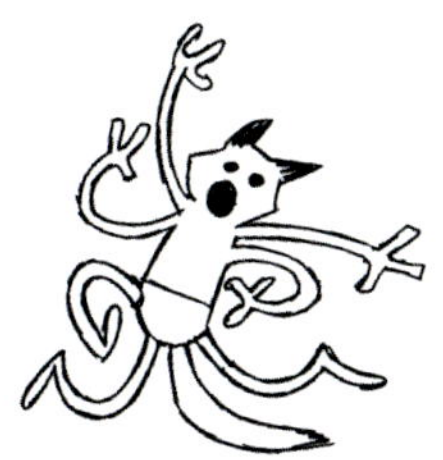

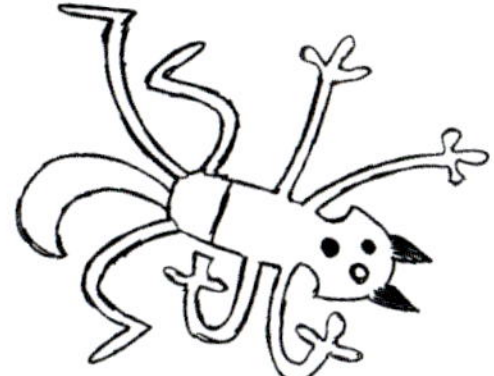

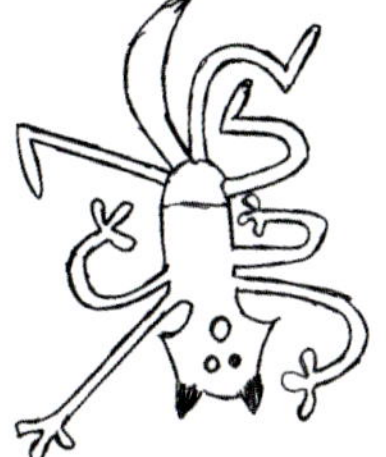

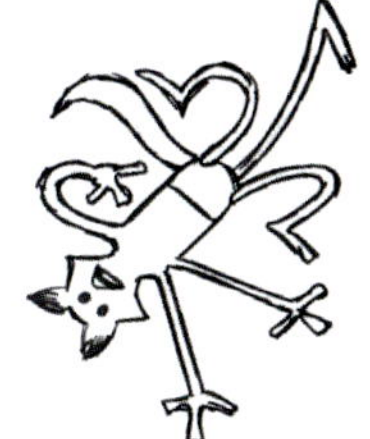

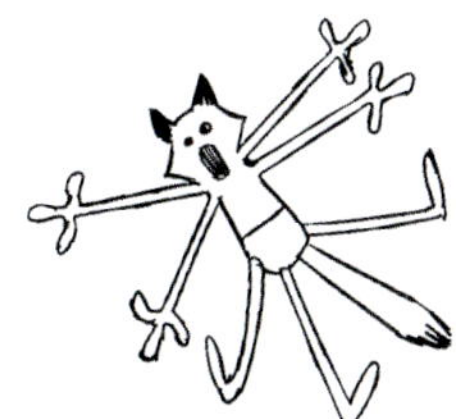

AN INTERVIEW WITH

ERIC ANDERSON

6/24/09

EA: You want me to try and sound natural and alive?

MS: *You can sound fake and dead, if that makes you more comfortable. What's the deal with that book for you guys? I mean, it's a great book, but there's a lot of great kids' books.*
There was a very nice edition one of my brother's had, and sometimes I think you sort of latch on to particular copies in certain situations, and I think that the illustrations—I think I have the name right, Donald Chaffin? I think the first edition was the one that came out like in the mid-sixties or around then, and that one was with magical drawings for a kid. So I think that stuck in the imagination. I can't say what Wes's relationship is with that book.

And was there any particular reason that you played Kristofferson? And with such conviction.
Probably—probably haphazardly, but maybe there was something going on deeper than I realize.

Brother situation?
Wes had me come up, and I was going to be, like, an additional dialogue foley artist – like the guy who makes sound effects – when we recorded at this farm in Connecticut. And there weren't enough people, maybe, or maybe there were, and there were just some new things that came up. I was on sound effects duty, and then I filled in for the as-yet-unhired cast actor for Kristofferson, and possibly through entropy there were enough screenings where I was playing the part where it was like, well, just get Eric to fill that in. I'd like to think it was more than that, but—

You were good.
—that's possibly what it was. I enjoyed it. Once I got into the process of it—which would be I would go to one of two sound recording studios in New York and put on headphones and speak into a microphone—Wes would be on these headphones from Europe and I would speak and it was like a telephone call in which I would just start doing dialogue. There was a test to see which Eric voice might sound like a thirteen-year-old or whatever he is. And so I tried higher voices and we got steadily, steadily back down to my regular one, and once I reached my voice he said just do that one.

And while you were talking was Wes giving directions?
He wasn't supposed to because it might have been picked up by the microphone. But sometimes he was on speakerphone, which actually took time—like, okay, we'd have to wait, be quiet, and then it cuts out and then I can do my lines. So sometimes it was a bit low-tech, but he was giving lots of directions. Sometimes we would interrupt each other, and it was fun. You know, I've been working with him for most of my life, of course, but it's fun working with him because everything else goes away, all the abstractions, and it gets done with very specific pieces of direction, which you're eager to accomplish. It's a very fun mini dynamic of carrot and stick.

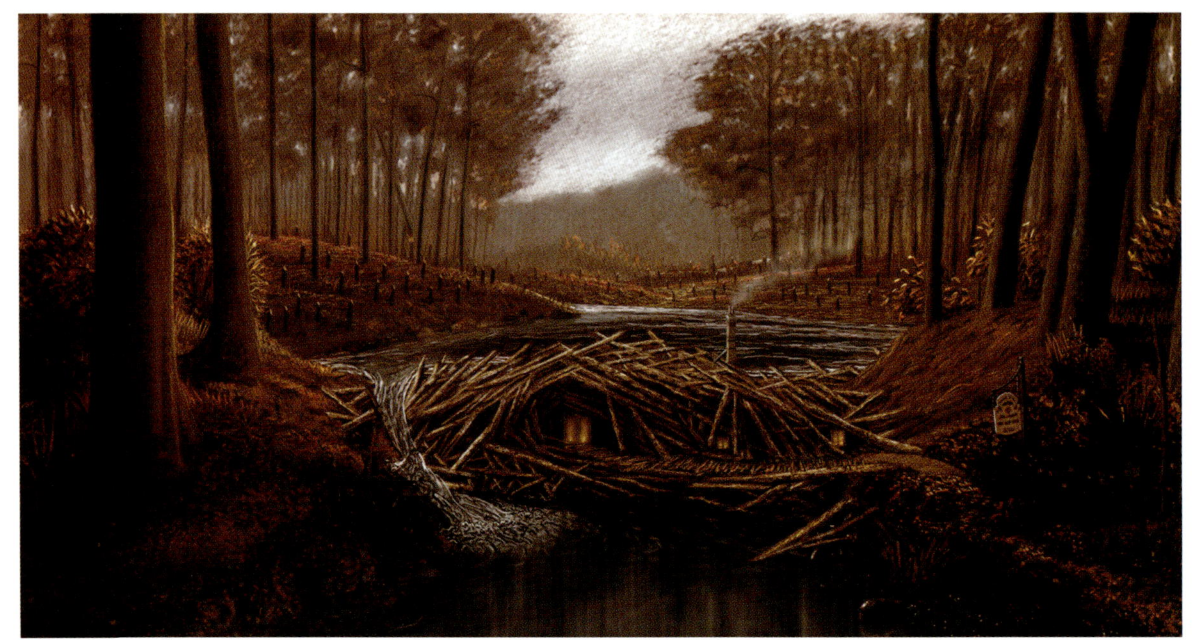

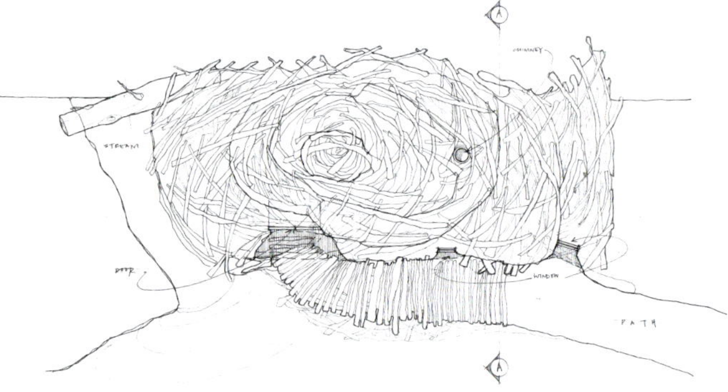

Top: Final concept design for the beaver dam by Turlo

Above: A draft for the beaver dam by Hannah Moseley

Right: The set for the beaver dam in progress in the workshop

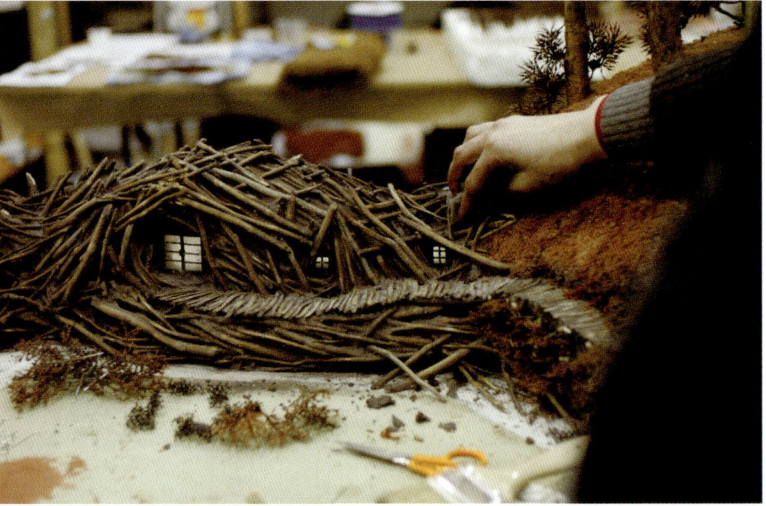

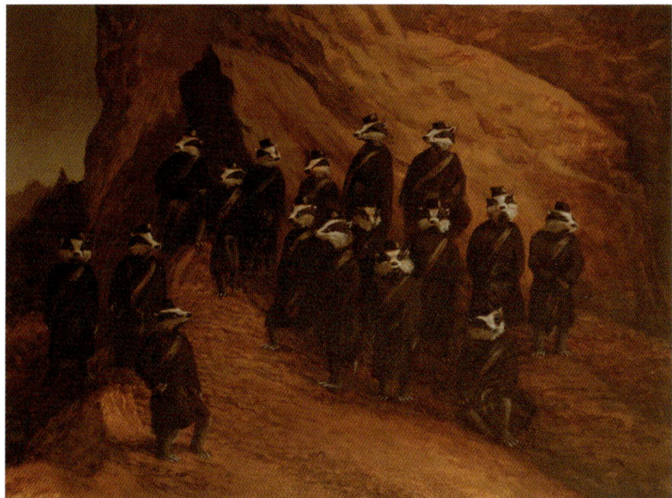

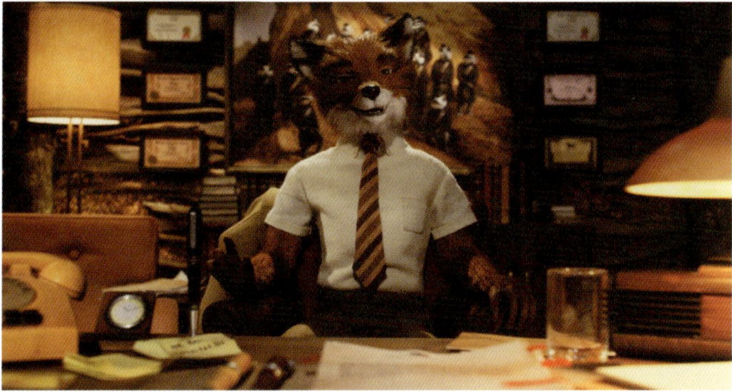

Top: A painting prop from Badger's office by Turlo

Above: A still from the movie of Mr. Fox at Badger's desk

Right: Sketches by Wes of the fight between Mr. Fox and Badger

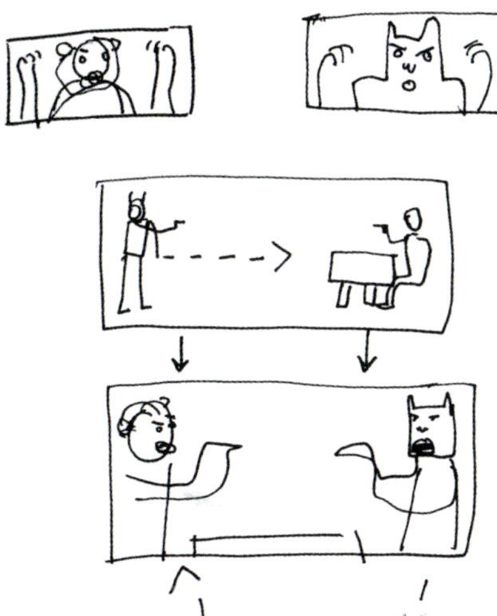

MS: *He told me you did the sort of original Mr. Fox character sketch.*
EA: I didn't manage to do too many because I'm extremely slow as an illustrator, but I did Fox, I think I did two views of him, and then I did his wife, which I don't think was used. But yeah, I did the early ones. I think he wanted me to do more, but I had a book to do.

Both of you are very visual artists, even for a film director he's a visual artist. And this movie is like a hundred trillion beautiful still paintings. What in your background got you guys so visual? Is it because your mom was in art?
Mom was never, I don't think she was a professional artist. She was a painter in addition to getting a degree in anthropology. But I'm not really sure. That's the clearest thing I have that I can point to, but I feel like Wes was—is—an extremely natural visual artist, who I had the opportunity to be around a lot. That's how I see it.

But you're an illustrator. That's like the most visual of artists.
He was one of those first. I feel like I'm trying to accomplish his thirteen-year-old artwork. He was very good at thirteen.

I think you've accomplished it. I think you're at least up to eighteen.
Well that's just it from my perspective, but no, it's—you know, it's also sometimes like the stories that you are exposed to, and that mean something to you, are kind of like shared experiences anyway. Life experience can lead you to these stories that you read, and it's possible that we had a shared taste in illustrated books, this being one of them.

1. Early concept art for Badger by Félicie

2. The final approved Badger color design

3. Early pose and expression development for Badger by Félicie

4. A badger costume turnaround

Opposite page: Bill Murray looks on to the set of Badger's office at the studio, photographed by Greg

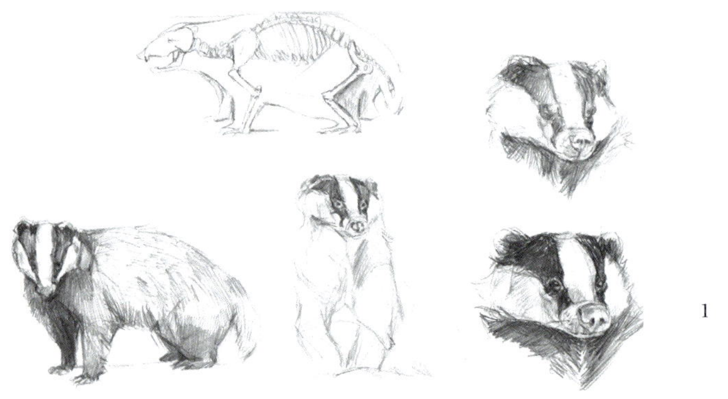

1

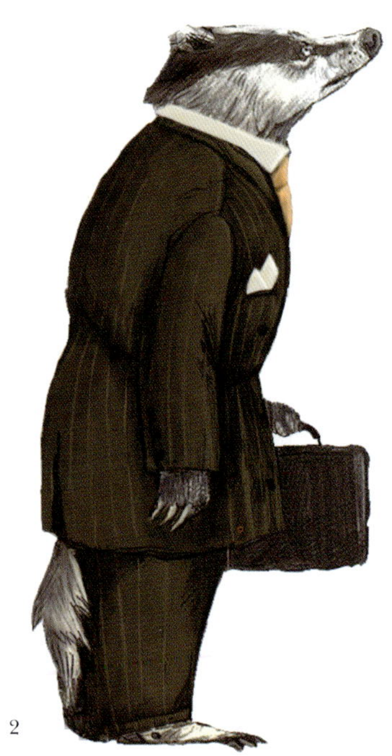

2

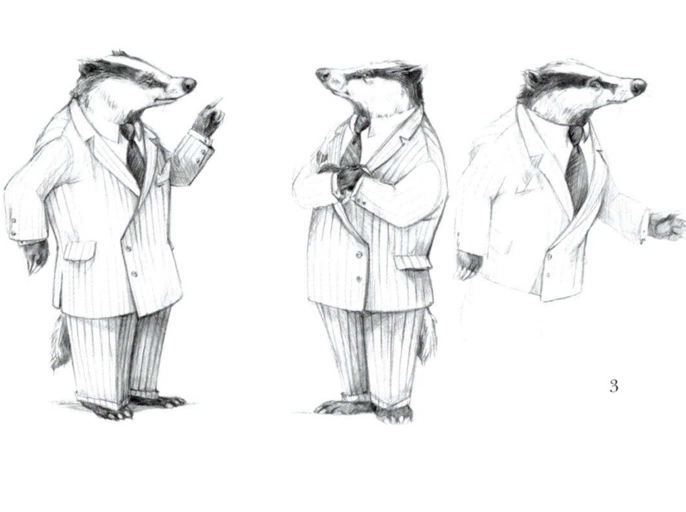

3

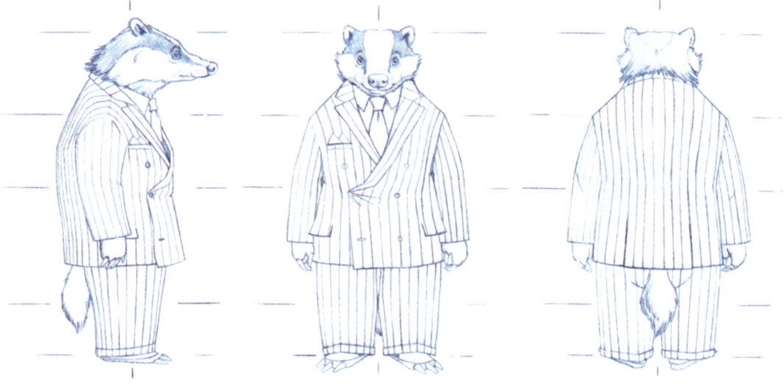

4

BADGER

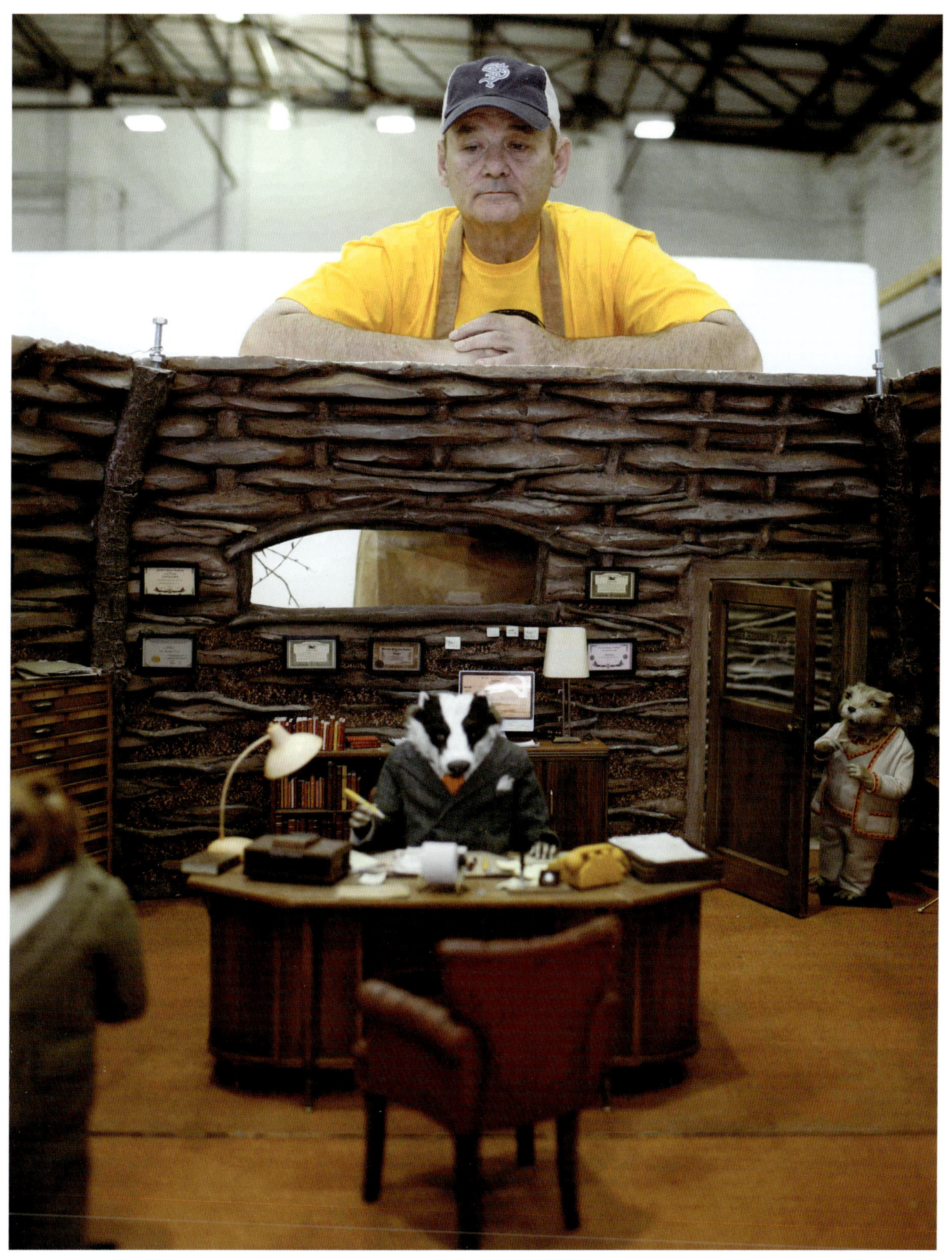

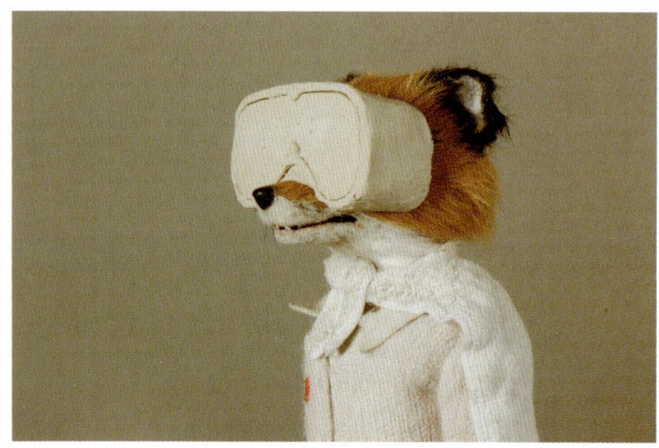

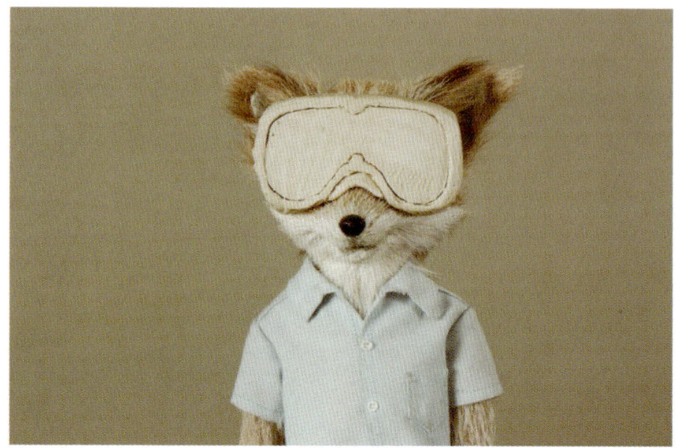

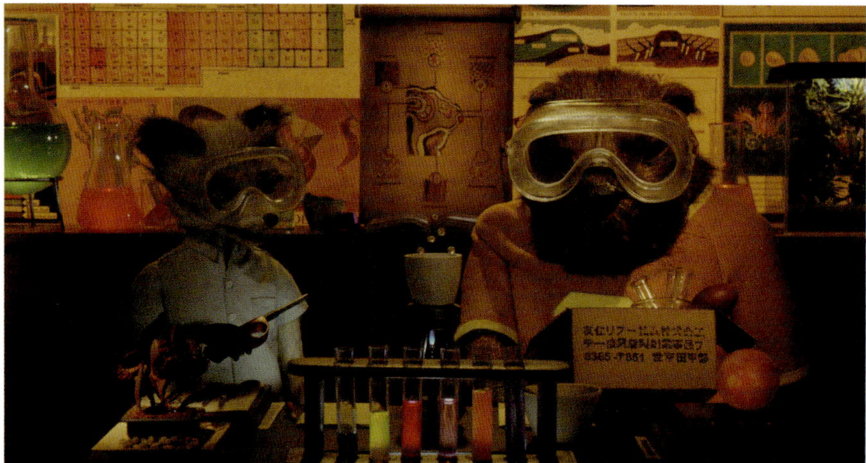

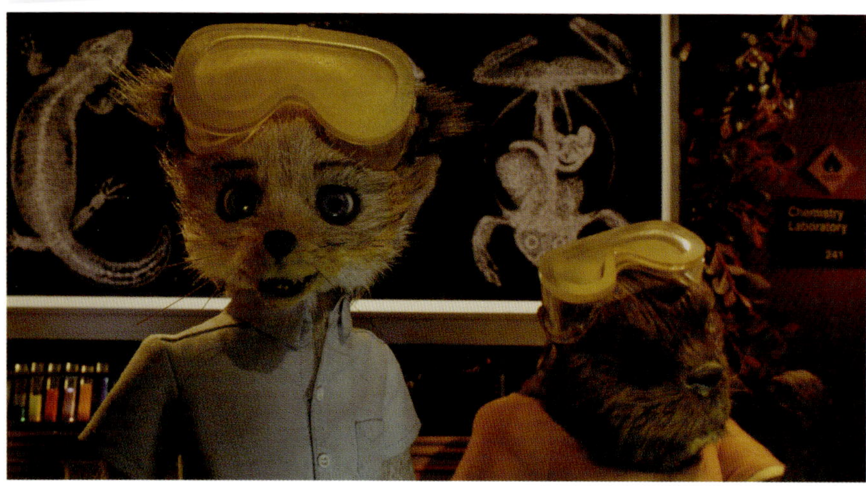

Above: Molds for Ash's and Kristofferson's chemistry lab goggles

Left: Stills from the movie of Kristofferson and Beaver's son in the lab

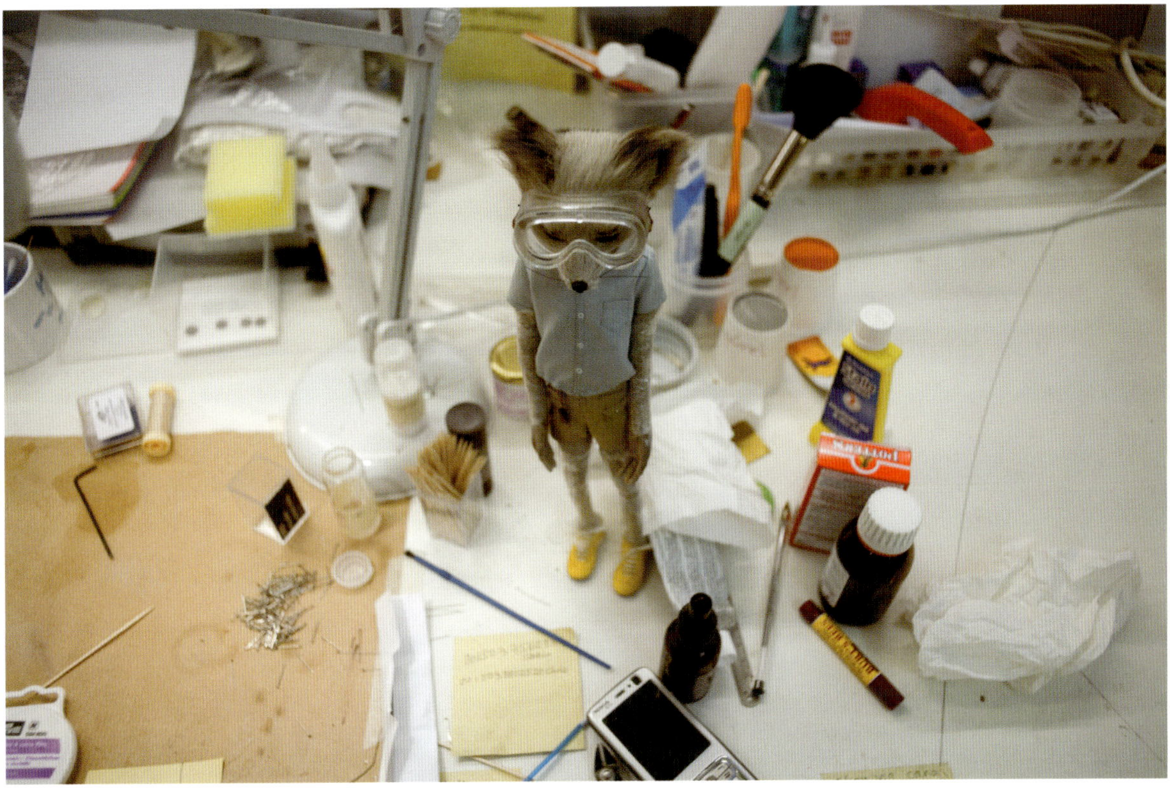

From: Wes Anderson
Subject: **Re: NELSON ON ALICE'S COMPUTER (just for this e-mail, please respond to my account)**
Date: 16 January 2009 11:07:33 GMT
To: Alice Bird

Ok—the more dynamic the better for this set—and we want lots and lots of props and science materials—we want to go overboard with this—also I think we want to darken the room and then light the different aspects—experiment light, aquarium light, light for poster, bunsen burner—so they are working in a darkened room with special lighting.

Let's in fact more or less entirely fill the back wall of the lab with these images—as down screens hung from ceiling, as posters taped on wall, as images tacked to bulletin board, so the entire space is completely filled with these things but we still have a sense of the architecture behind it, which is kind of 60s classroom style please.

Above: The Kristofferson puppet being worked on in the puppet hospital

Below: Posters from the set of the chemistry lab

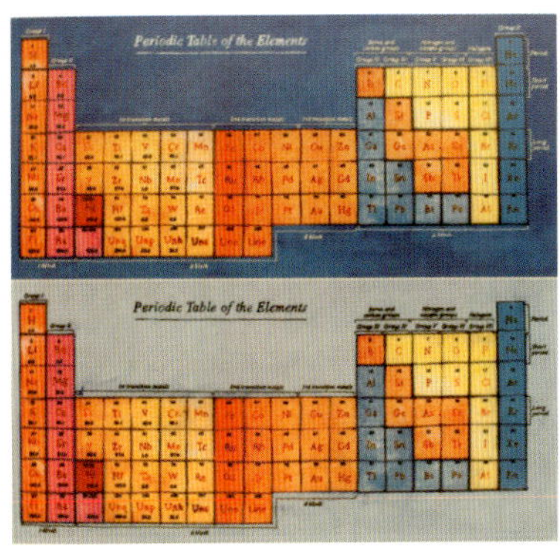

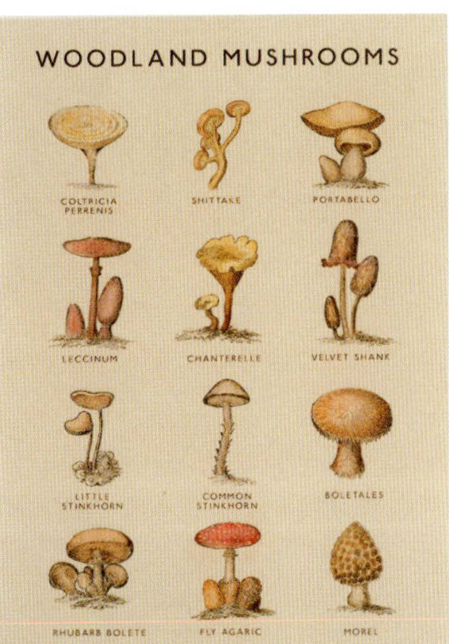

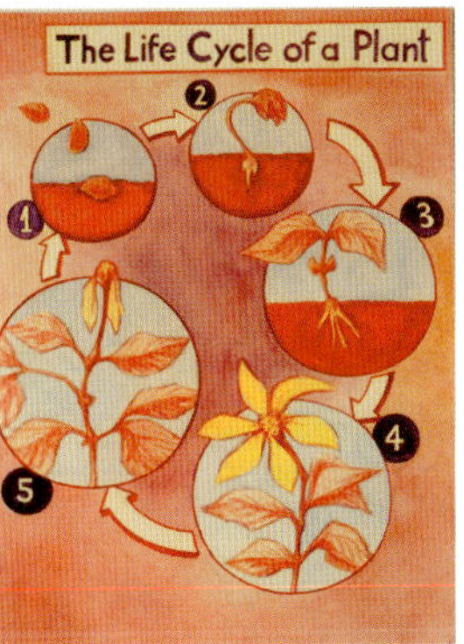

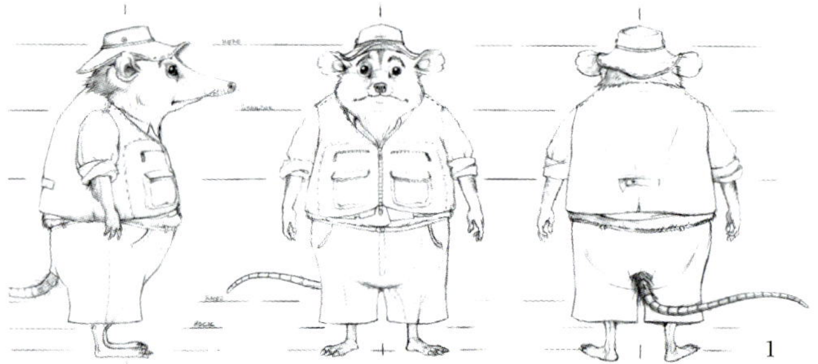

1

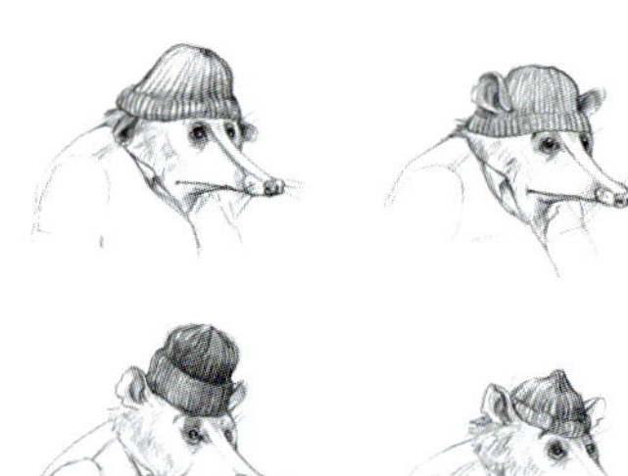

2

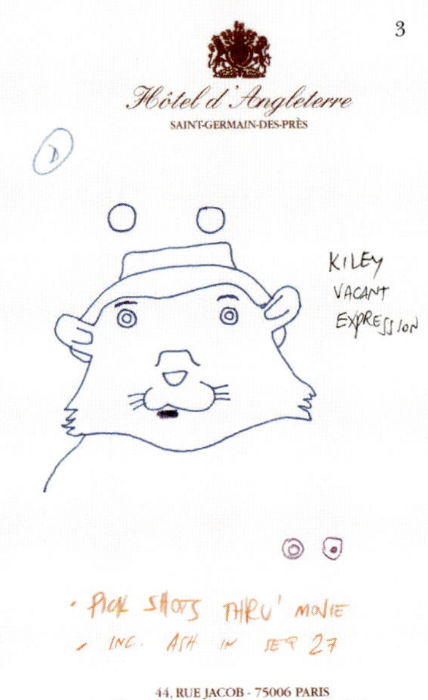

3

1. A Kylie costume turnaround

2. Early hat designs for Kylie by Félicie

3. A sketch by Wes for Kylie's vacant eyes

4. An unfinished mini-micro-scale Kylie puppet

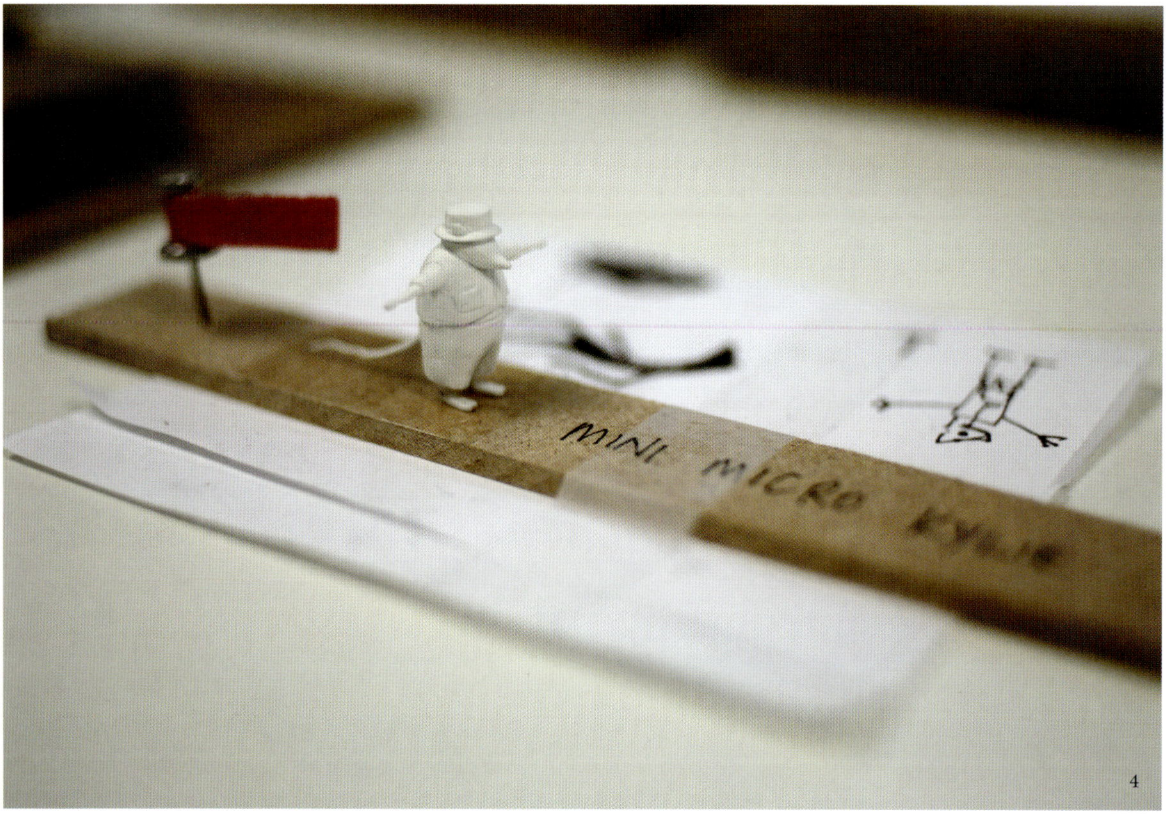

4

5. A full-scale Kylie puppet being worked on in the puppet hospital

6. An early version of the mini-micro-scale Kylie puppet

7. A full-scale costume reference for Kylie

8. The final approved color design for Kylie

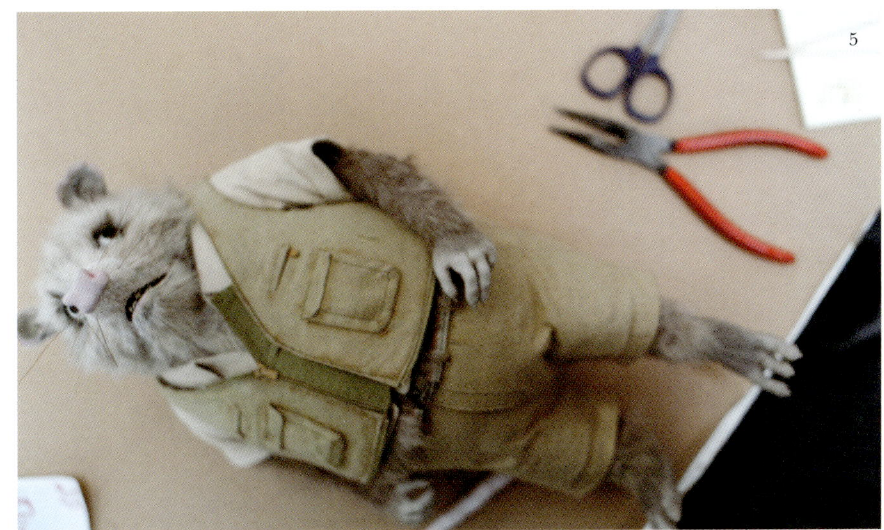

5

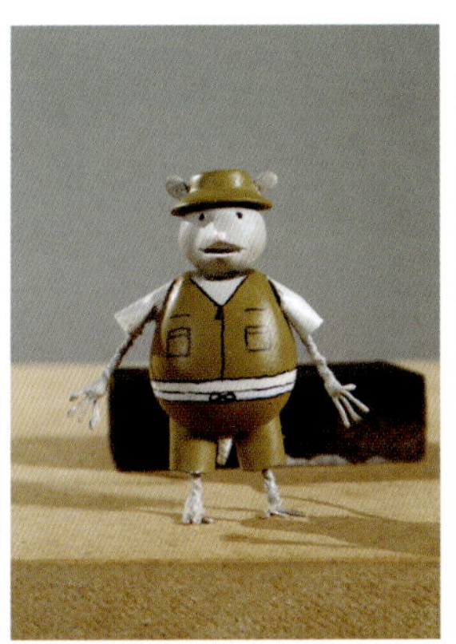

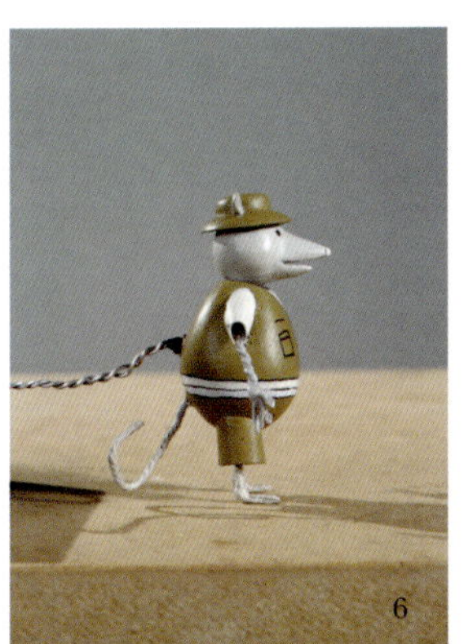

6

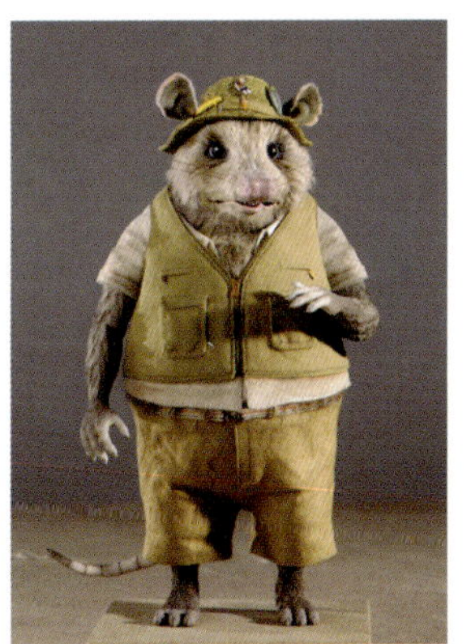

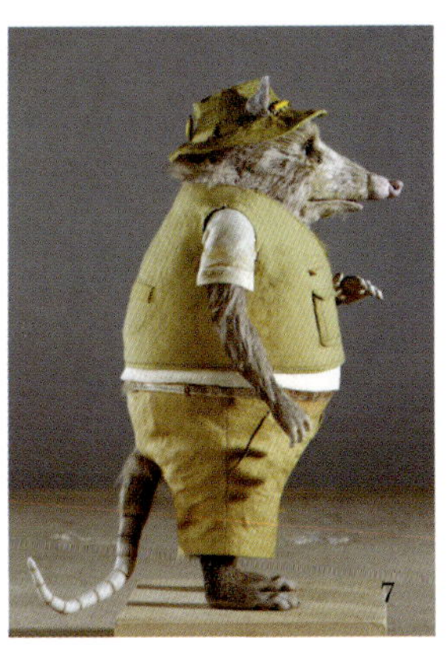

7

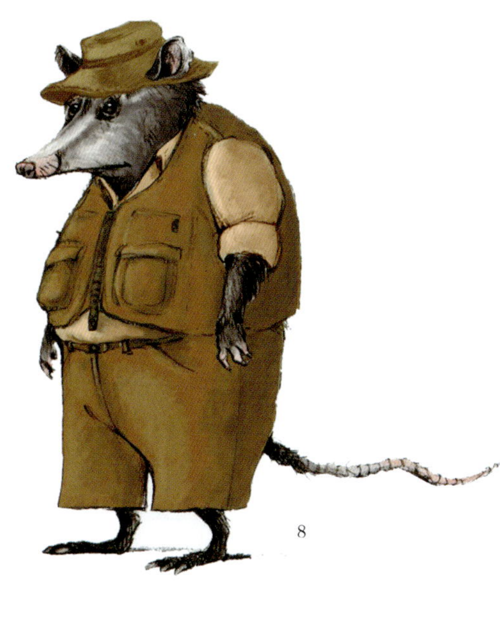

8

KYLIE

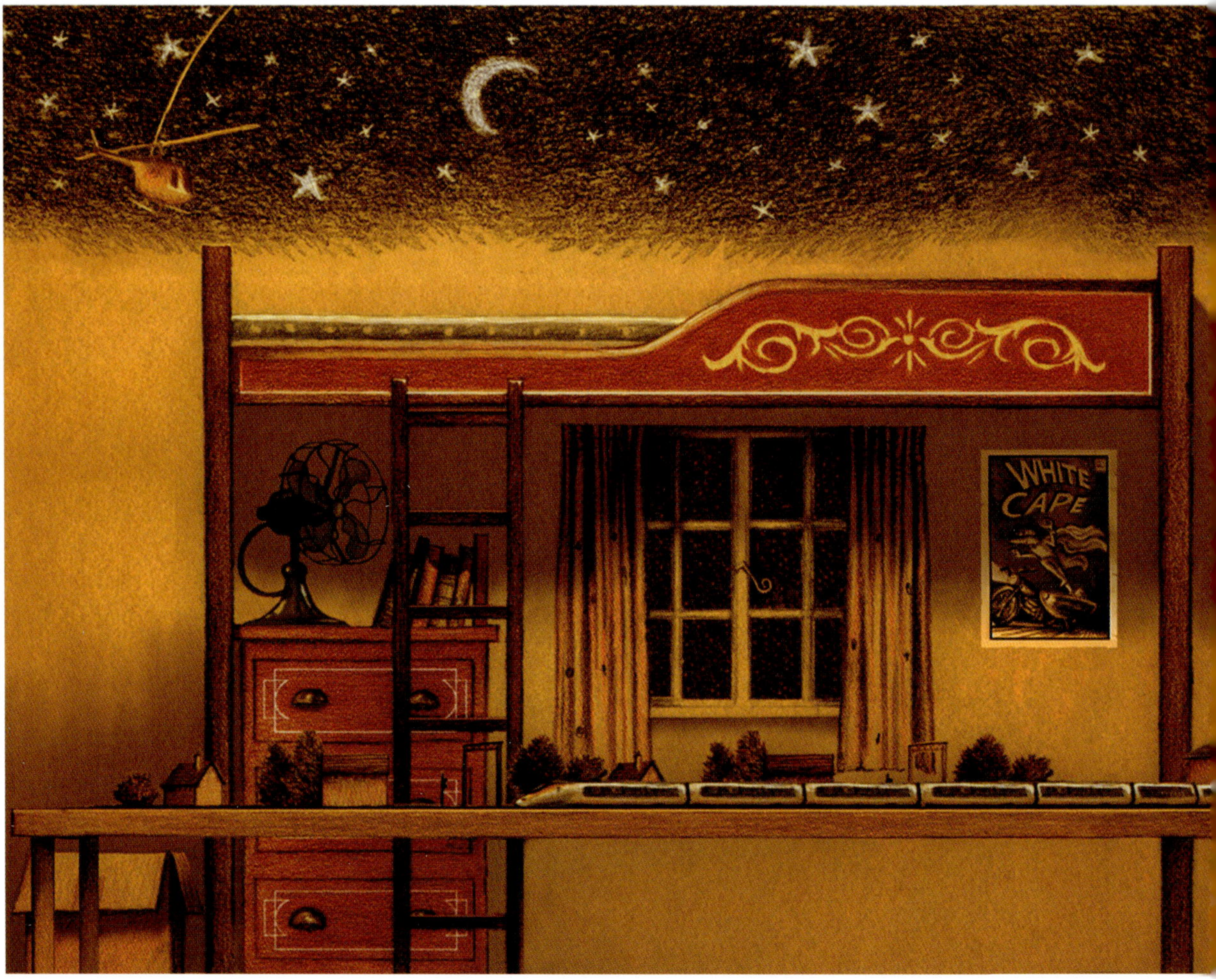

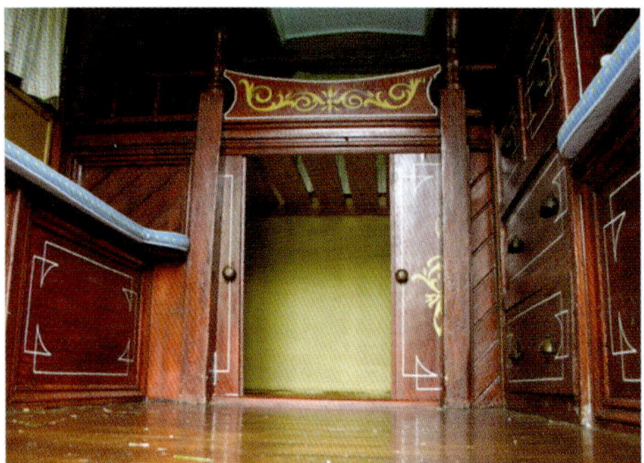

Above: Final concept art for Ash's bedroom by Turlo

Left: A caravan at Roald Dahl's house used as a reference for the design of Ash's bunk bed

Right: A sketch and notes by Wes for the scene in Ash's bedroom

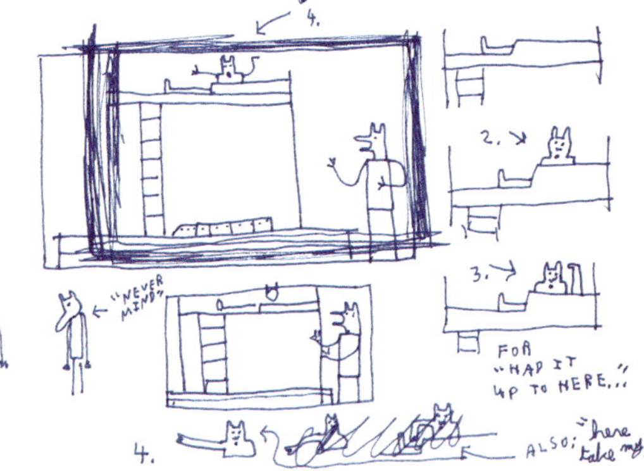

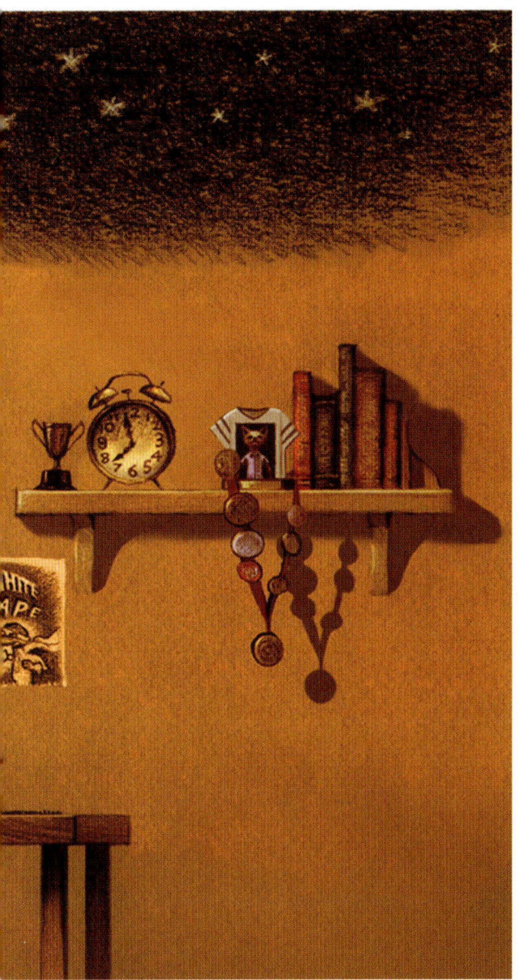

Right: Furniture and props from Ash's bedroom

Below right: A draft for the set of Ash's bedroom by Hannah Moseley

Below left: A still from the movie

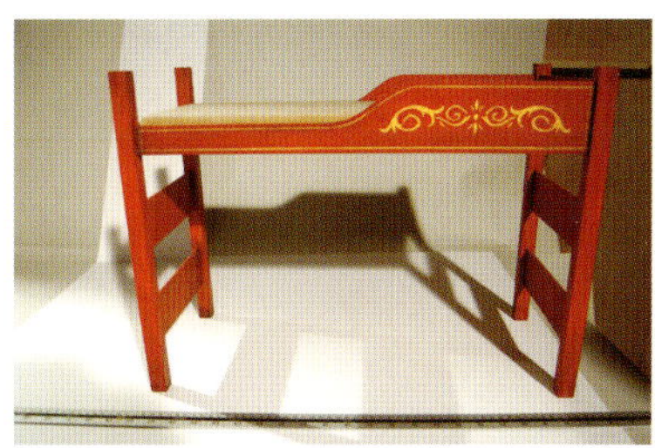

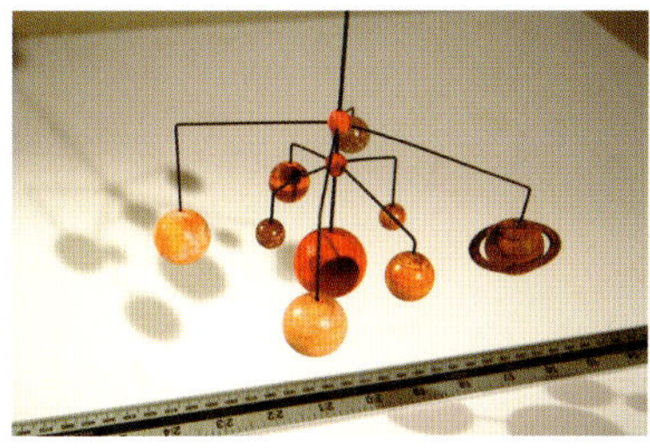

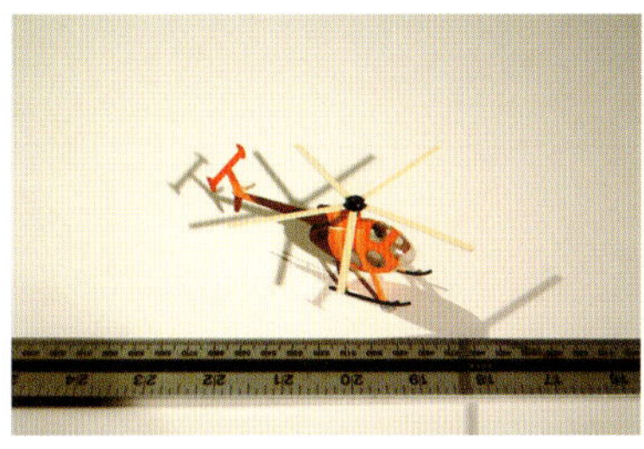

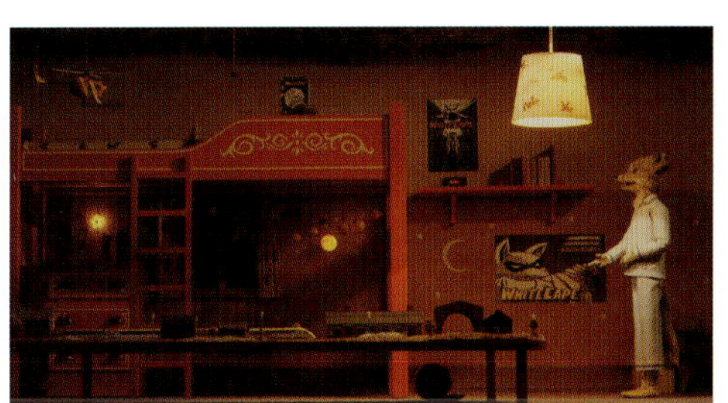

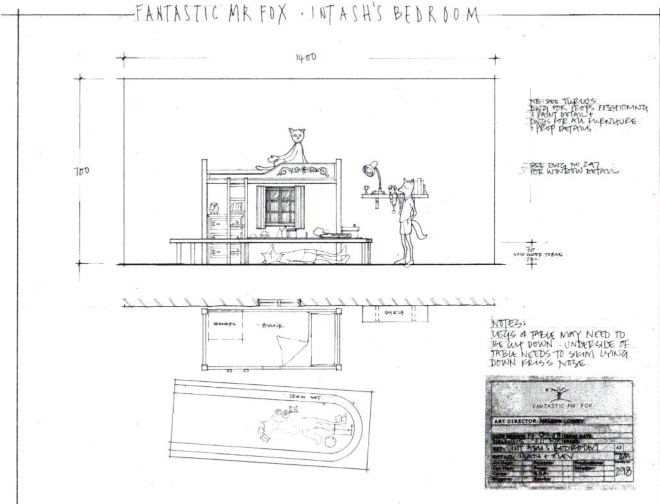

MS: *And what about kids' stuff? Do you see this as a kids' book?*
EA: I can't say that I'm an expert in what appeals to kids anymore. Kids probably say, "what appeals to us is good stuff," so they keep it open themselves. But I think if I was a kid I would be very excited about this. It's got some of the things that I think kids' movies tend to overlook these days, which are quiet bits. I can remember very clearly that when I first saw *Star Wars,* and I was very young, that what was enchanting—or I'll use a better example, *Mary Poppins.* The enchanting bits for me were the silent bits, and some books and some stories seem to have their own silent bits. Like *The Little Prince* seems to have bits where you're kind of aware of a sense of expansiveness and smallness in a large landscape. I don't want to get too abstract, but that's something about *Mr. Fox* that would have been appealing to me as a kid. And I think also I would've been aware that it's got a kind of urbanity, which would have made me feel very grown up, like it would've made me feel cool. Don't use that. [laughs]

Tell the tape recorder, not me.
Don't use that word. That's a smart bomb. That's a booby trap, that word. You know, it would've made me feel like I was being treated as a grown-up.

Better. Strike "cool."
Strike "cool." I'll disavow it.

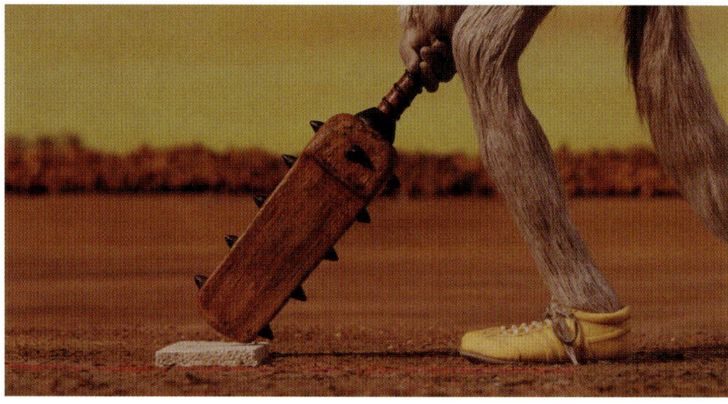

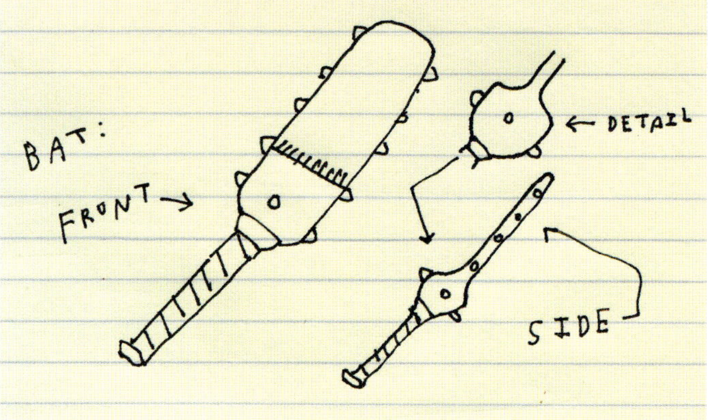

Top: A still from the whackbat scene

Above: A sketch by Wes of the whackbat

Below: The final whackbat prop

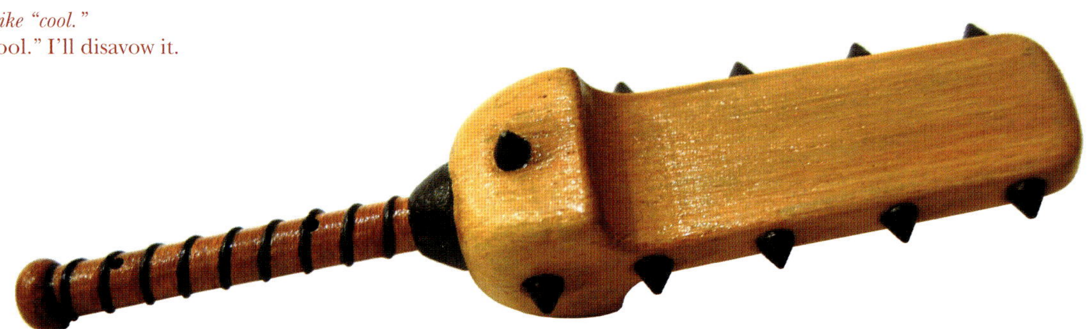

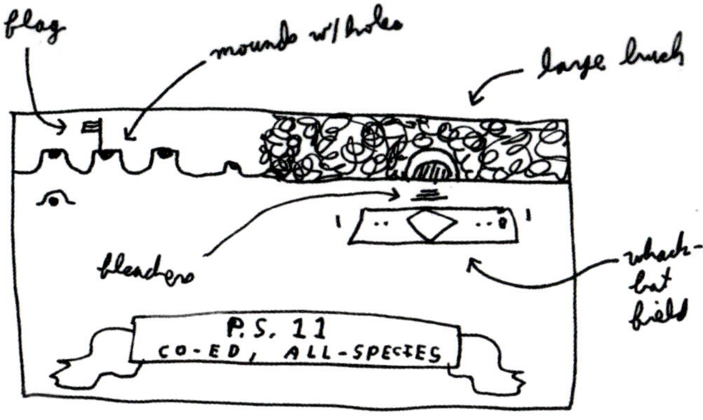

From: Wes Anderson
Subject: **Re: Whack Bat Trophy Cabinet**
Date: 9 December 2008 16:49:51 GMT
To: Molly Cooper

I THINK THE PLAQUE CAN SAY:

P.S. whatever it is
WHACK-BAT
Most Valuable Player
of the fox-year

'68 F.F. FOX
'68 1/2 F.F. FOX
'69 F.F. FOX
'69 1/2 F.F. FOX
'70 F.F. FOX
'70 1/2 F.F. FOX
'71 F.F. FOX
'71 1/2 J.T. RACOON
'72 H.K. SILVERY-MARMOSET

AND THEN CAN CONTINUE BELOW BUT WE DON'T SEE THAT PART IN CLOSEUP

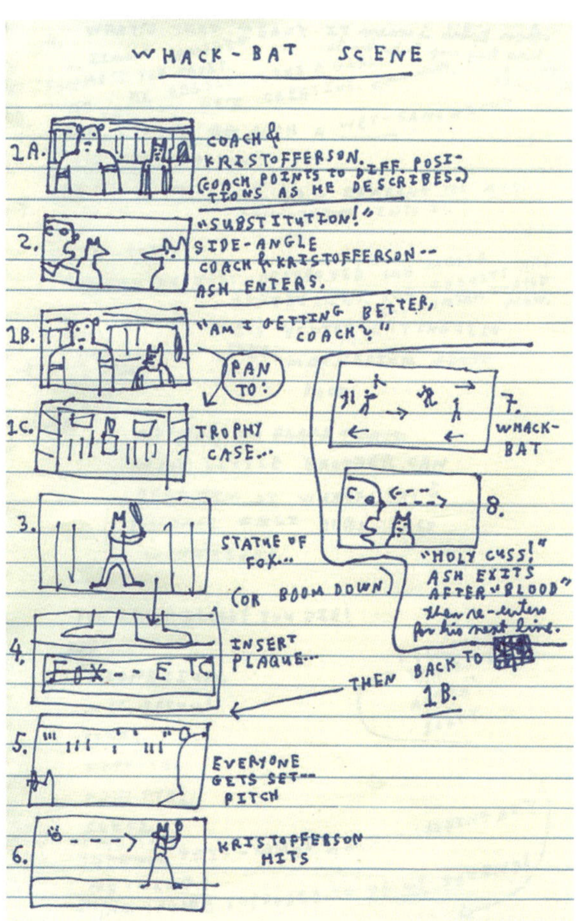

Above: A sketch by Wes of the whackbat field

Left: Notes and sketches by Wes for the whackbat scene

Right: Mr. Fox's whackbat trophy

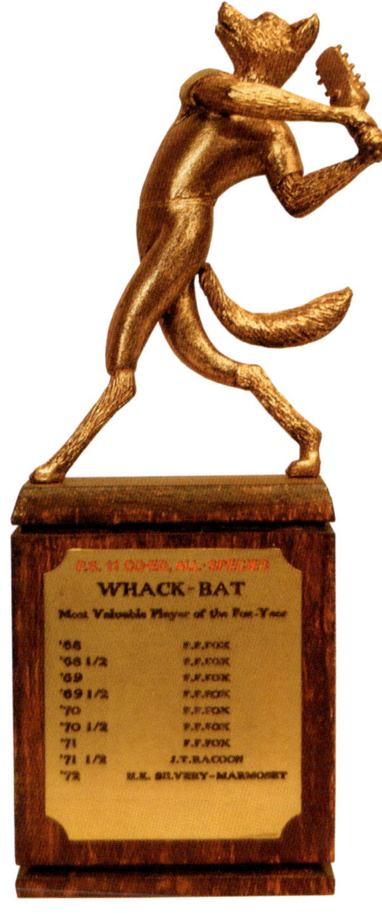

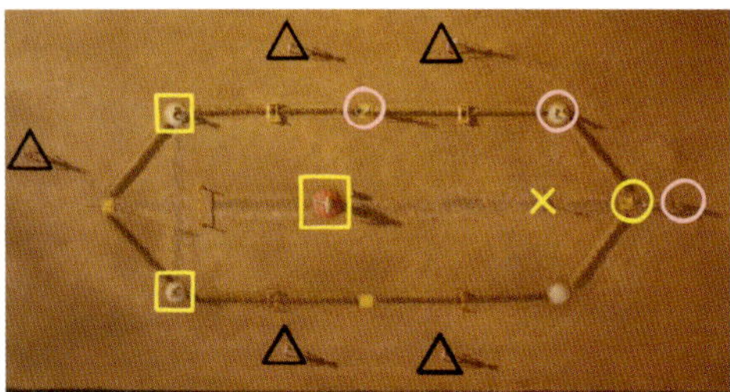

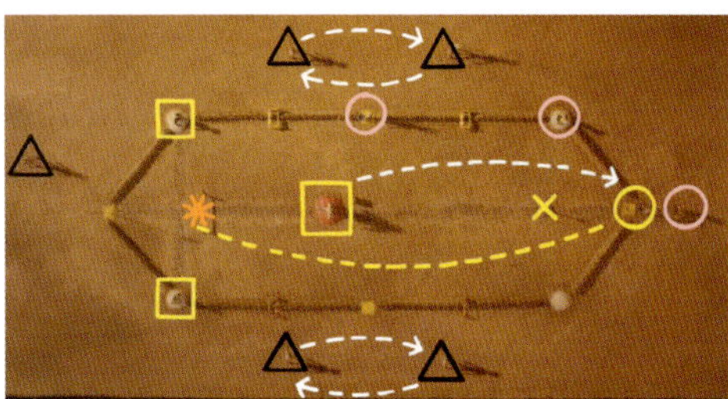

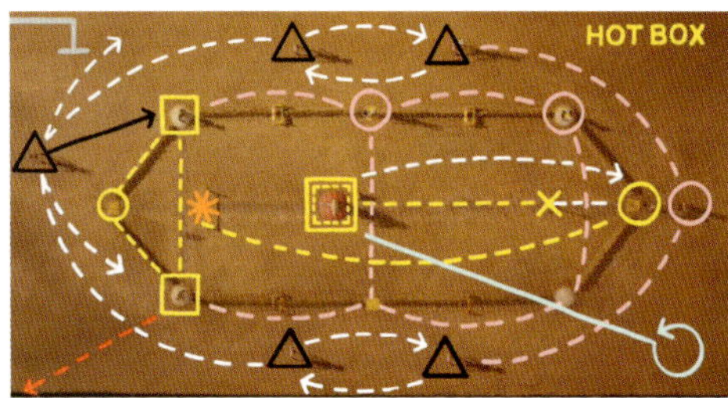

Above: Stills from the movie of the whackbat game

From: Wes Anderson
Subject: **Re: Whack bat rules**
Date: 24 March 2009 11:24:27 GMT
To: Brad Schiff

| KRISTOFFERSON, as discussed should and will be the focus of this entire thing. one way i will differentiate him from the others is by animating him on one's while everyone else is animated on two's. he will move much smoother and quicker that way automatically drawing the eye to him.

PERFECT

| as he runs back and forth touching his whack-bat to the base on each end (like they do in cricket) and knocking the cedar stick off the cross rock he will do some incredibly athletic moves in order to avoid the taggers. some thought i had, he could...

| -do a flips over the hurdle and the taggers?

YES! OVER HURDLE MAYBE NOT THE TAGGERS

| -some jukes and spins like great football running backs do in order to avoid the taggers?

YES LIKE WALTER PAYTON

| -he could jump clear over beaver maybe on his third trip down? that would be really humiliating to beaver and show how incredible kristofferson is?

YES MAYBE DOES ONE OF THOSE JUMPS WHERE YOU PUT YOUR HANDS ON TOP OF THEIR HEAD AND LEGS GO ON SIDES—LIKE JUMPING A POST

| -he could twist as he jumps over taggers like gymnast do when they jump over the pommel horse or when they do floor exercises?

MAYBE WE SAVE THE JUMPING OVER ANIMALS FOR ONLY BEAVERS SON AT THE END SO IT HAS MORE IMPACT—MAYBE HE IS THE ONLY ACTUAL LIVING CREATURE HE JUMPS OVER

| all of these things provide many options and would bring focus to kristofferson all the while showing his superior athleticism in the game.

| at the end, when "hotbox" is called, maybe he stops where ever he is, raises his arm with the bat in it and yells "divide that by nine please"?

PERFECT

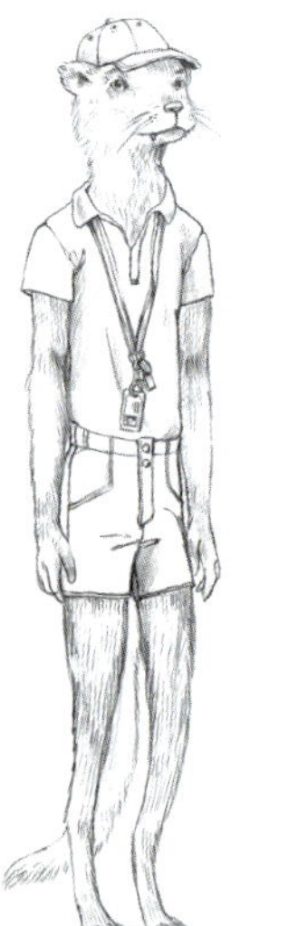

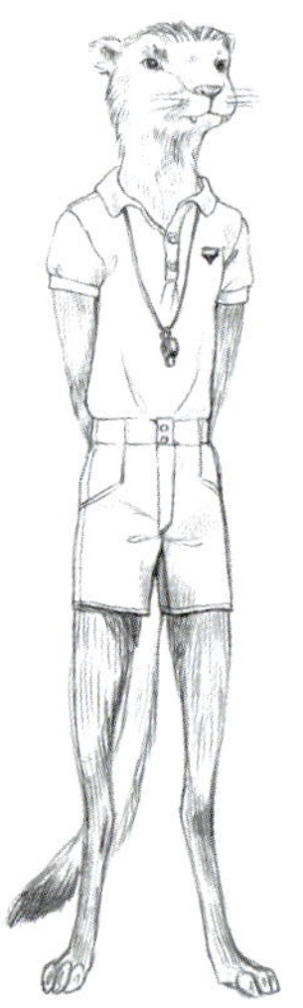

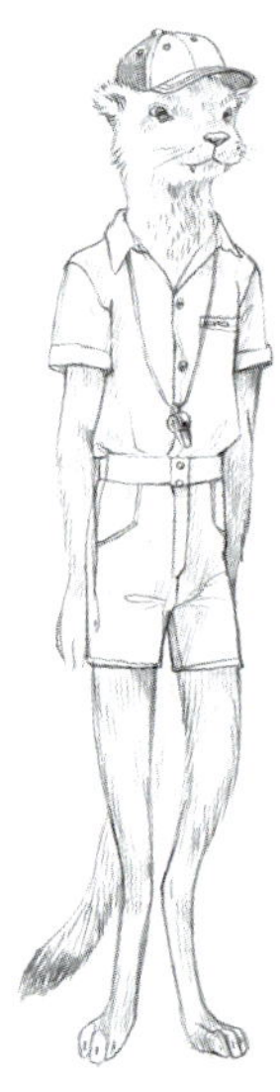

Right: The final color design for Coach Skip

Left: Early concept designs for Coach Skip by Félicie

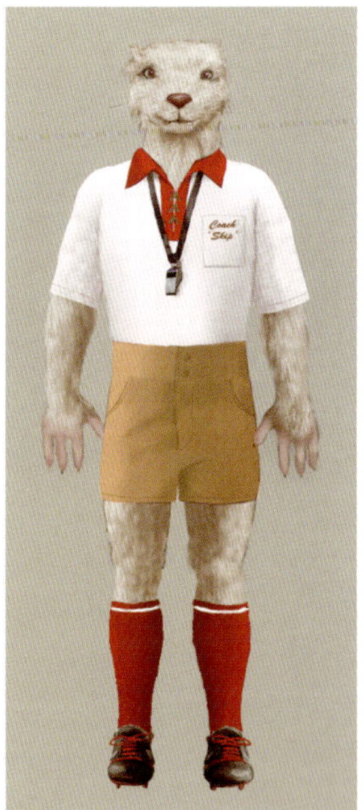

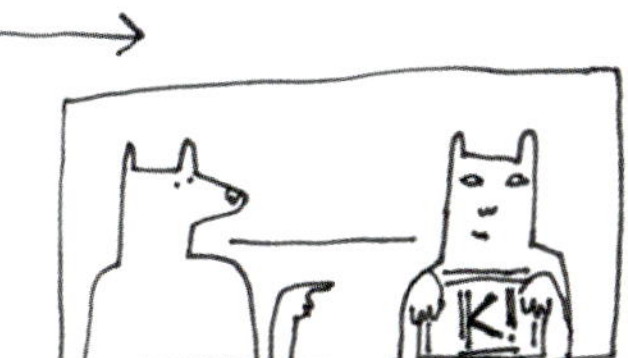

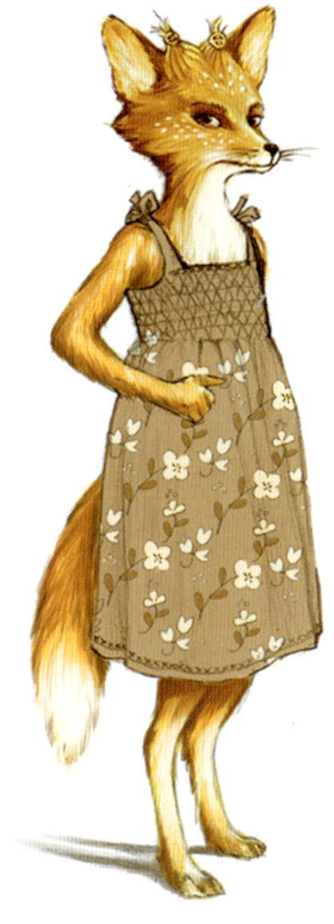

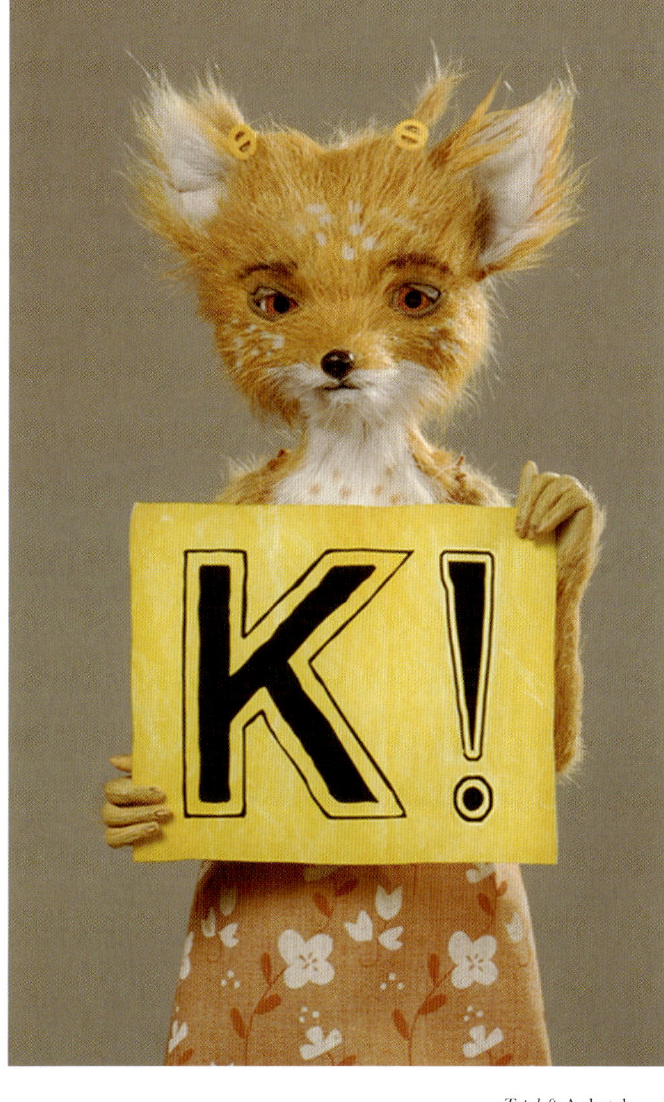

AGNES

Top left: A sketch by Wes for an exchange between Ash and Agnes on the sidelines of the whackbat field

Above left: The final approved color design for Agnes

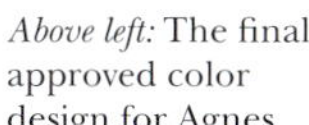

Above right: The approved design for Agnes's 'K' sign

Left: Early costume designs for Agnes by Félicie

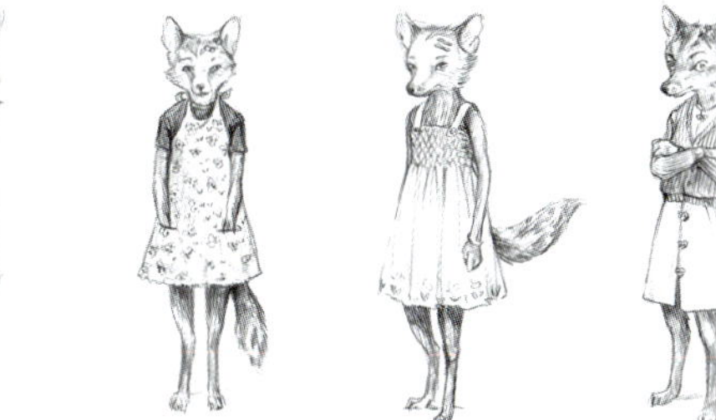

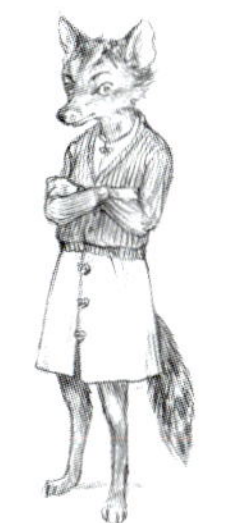

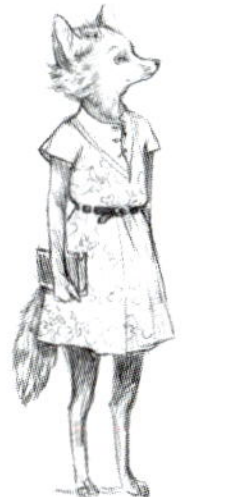

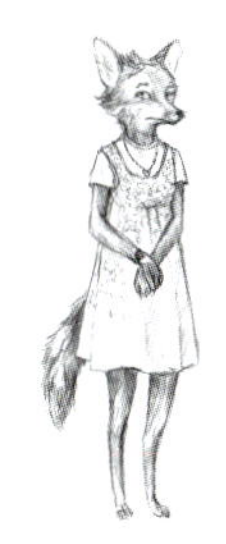

moment and listens. He steps out of the hole and says stonily:

FOX
Nice job covering for me. Next time try --

IT'S A HOLE, BUT W/A DOOR INSIDE?

A twig snaps. Fox freezes.

FRONT &

CUT TO:

Boggis, Bunce, and Bean frozen in the bushes.

~~THEY LOOK~~ LOOK, also alert

CUT TO:

The branches of the trees as the wind suddenly changes its direction.

TREETOPS

CUT TO:

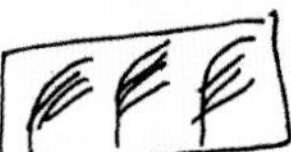

Fox on high alert. He rapidly sniffs the air three times in a row. He turns to a confused Kylie and says, panicking:

FOX
All three!

Fox and Kylie spin around and dart back into the hole as Boggis, Bunce, and Bean open fire wildly from the bushes. A barrage of bullets and buckshot rips into the tree-bark. Silence.

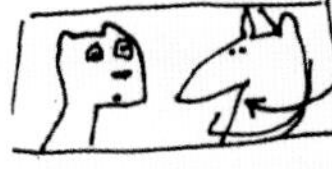

Smoke from the three guns floats upward in the night air. Boggis, Bunce, and Bean approach the tree. Bean shines his flashlight on Fox's hole. DOLLY FROM BUSHES TO TREE.

In the circle of light on the ground lies the tattered, blood-stained remains of Fox's tail. Bean picks it up and holds it in the air in front of Boggis and Bunce.

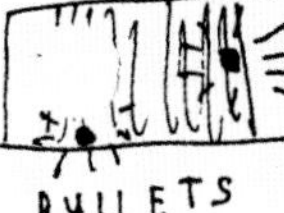

BULLETS

BEAN
We got the tail, but we missed the fox.

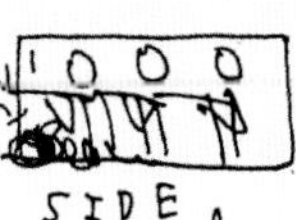

SIDE angle of guns blazing

Pause. Bean takes out his walkie-talkie.

BEAN
Petey? You and the boys sober up and get out here on the A.S.A.P. Bring eleven shovels, three pick-axes, 500 rounds of ammunition, and a bottle of apple cider.

OVER FARMERS OF FOX, KYLIE, TREE

1 - SHOT.

END ON TAIL ON GROUND. FLASH-LIGHT SEES IT. HAND PICKS IT UP. BOOM UP TO 3 FARMER.

V

STEALING BIRDS

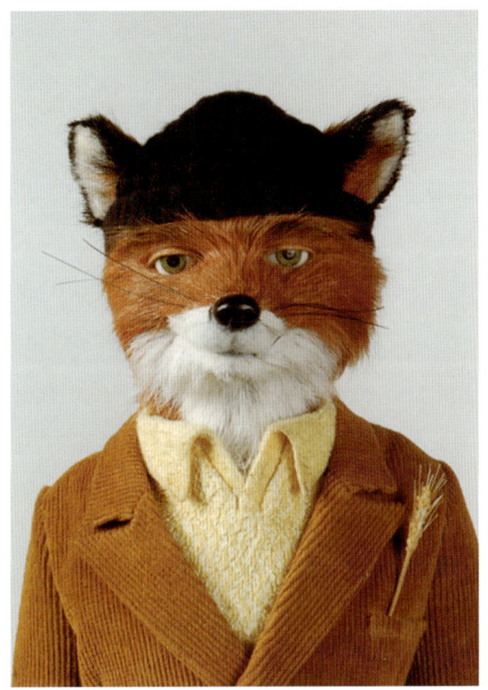

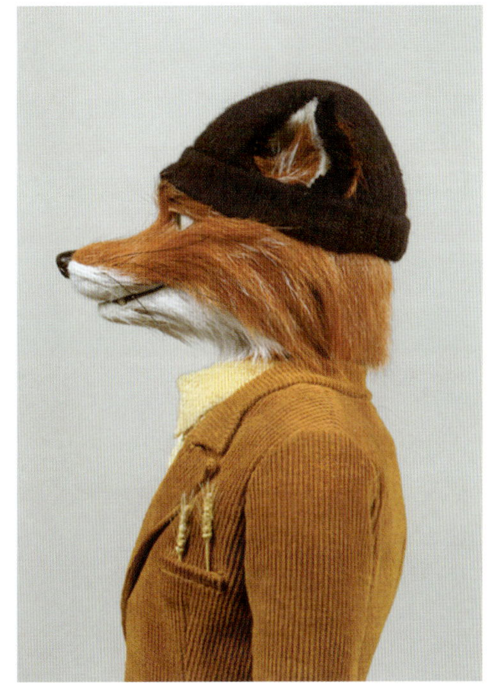

Above: A turn-around for Mr. Fox's raiding hat

Right: A sketch and notes by Wes for the scene where Mr. Fox briefs Kylie on the Bunce raid

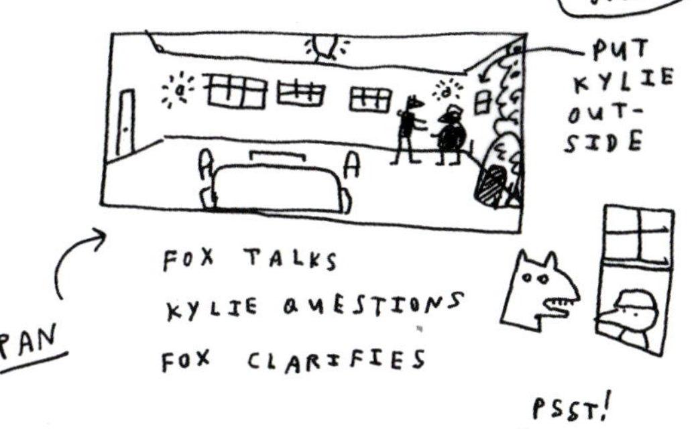

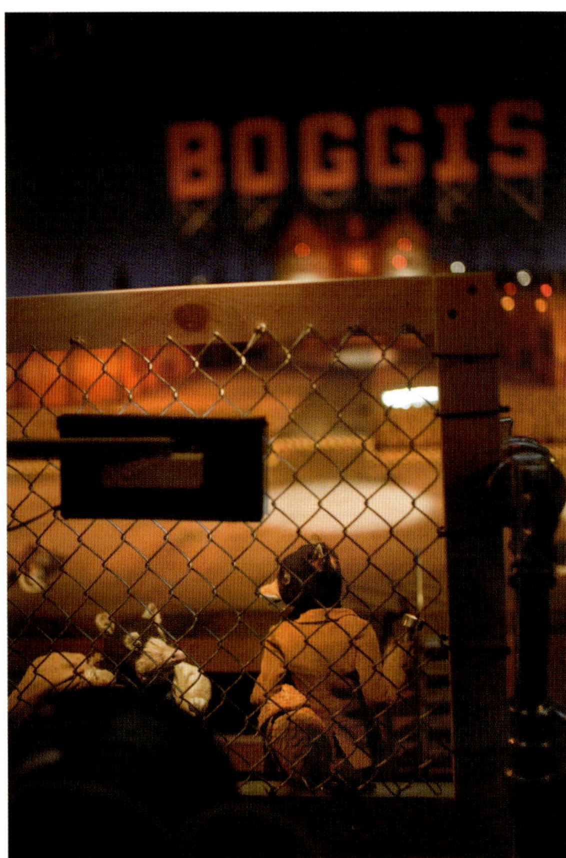

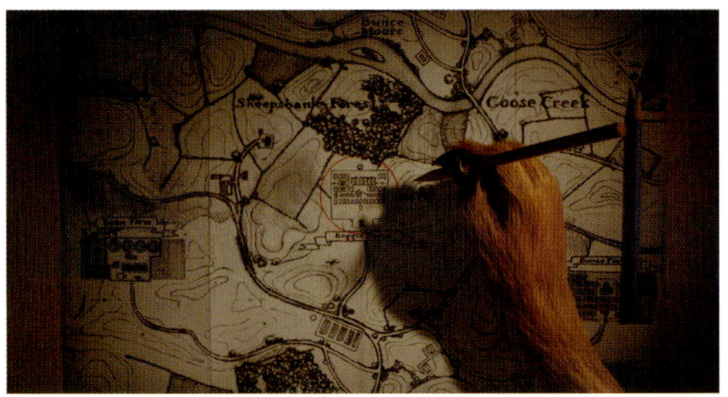

Above: A still from the movie showing a map of Boggis's farm

Left: A set still of Mr. Fox and Kylie at Boggis's farm

Right: The tranquilizing dust and glue props

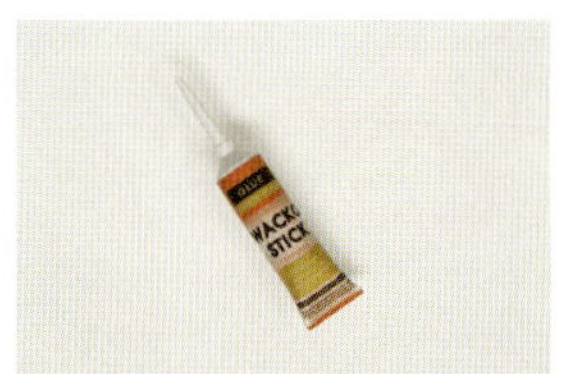

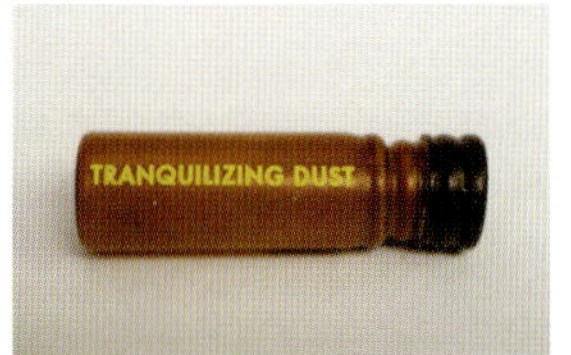

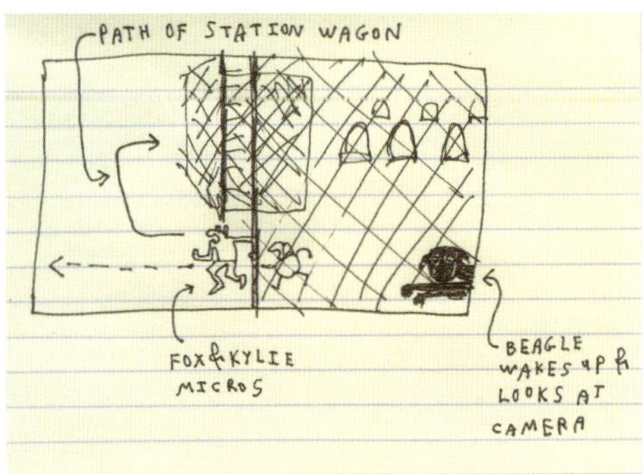

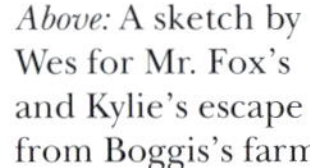

Above: A sketch by Wes for Mr. Fox's and Kylie's escape from Boggis's farm

Right: A set still of a tranquilized beagle

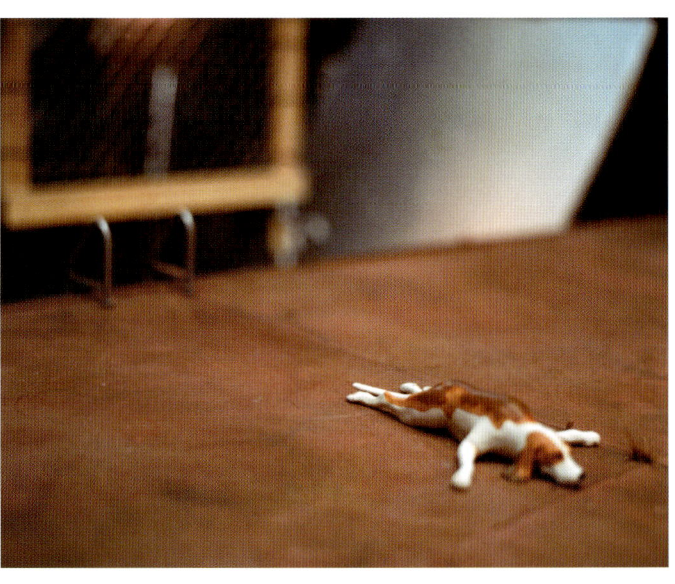

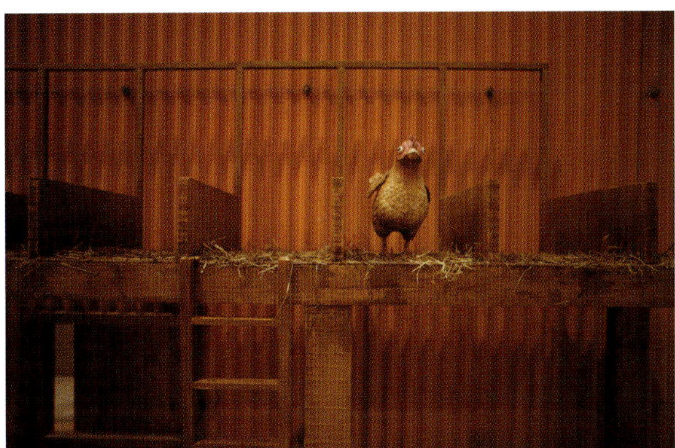

Left: A still of the set of Boggis's chicken hut

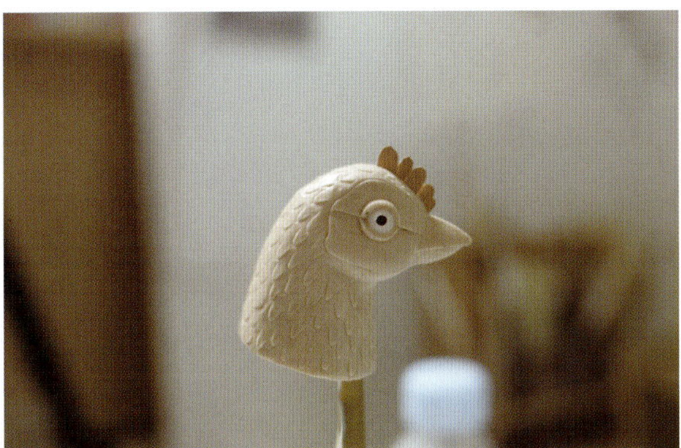

Below: A chicken puppet in progress in the puppet hospital

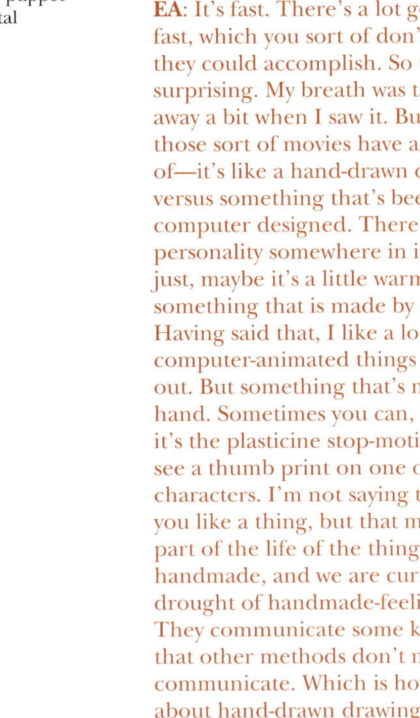

MS: *I don't know about you, but I've just never seen a movie that looks like this before. This is as close to—this is some combination of real movie and stop-motion. I was taken aback by that.*

EA: It's fast. There's a lot going on fast, which you sort of don't think they could accomplish. So that is surprising. My breath was taken away a bit when I saw it. But don't those sort of movies have a kind of—it's like a hand-drawn drawing versus something that's been computer designed. There's a little personality somewhere in it that's just, maybe it's a little warmer than something that is made by computer. Having said that, I like a lot of the computer-animated things that come out. But something that's made by hand. Sometimes you can, like, if it's the plasticine stop-motion, you'll see a thumb print on one of the characters. I'm not saying that's why you like a thing, but that might be part of the life of the thing that's so handmade, and we are currently in a drought of handmade-feeling things. They communicate some kind of life that other methods don't necessarily communicate. Which is how I feel about hand-drawn drawings.

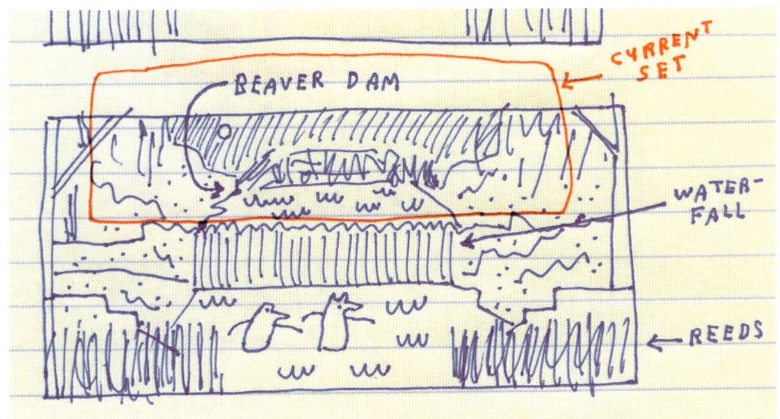

Above: Wes's notes for modifying the Beaver dam set for use in a shot of Fox and Kylie on their way to the Boggis raid

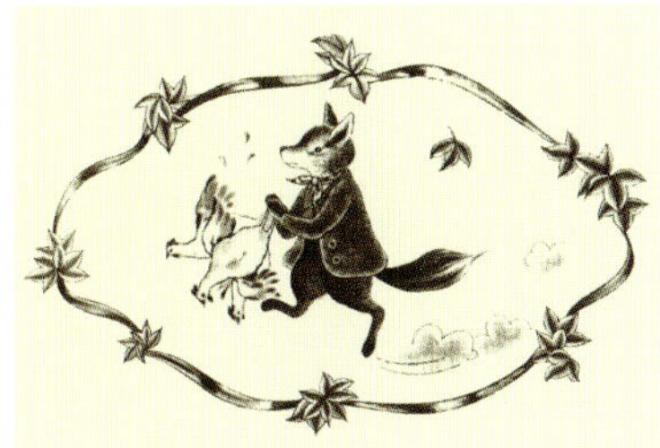

Above: Donald Chaffin's illustration of Mr. Fox stealing chickens

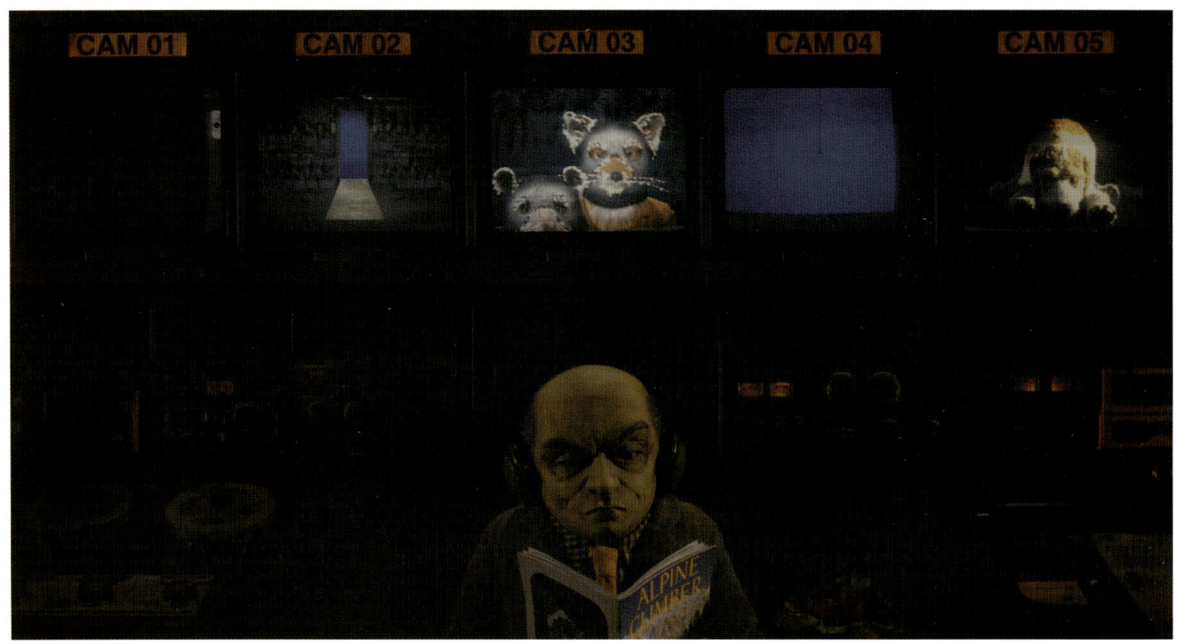

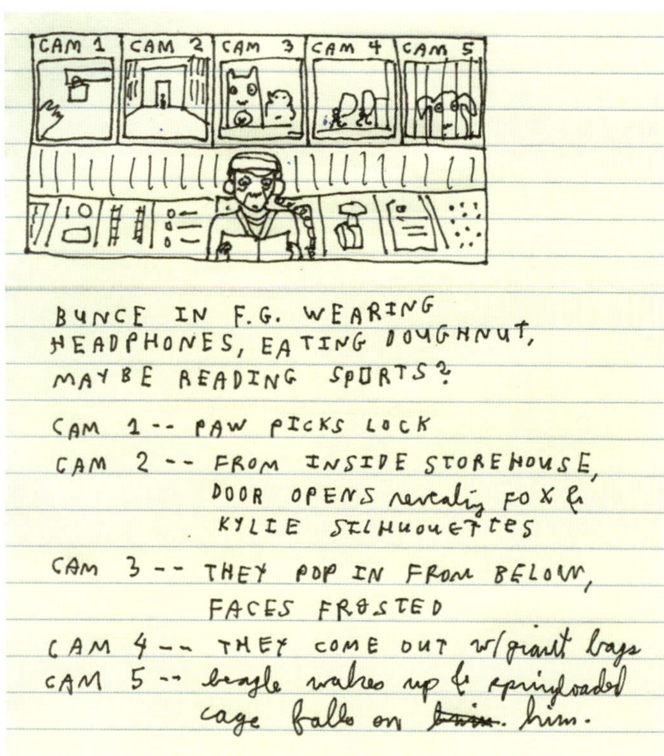

Above: Still from the movie of the Bunce raid

Left: A sketch by Wes for the Bunce raid

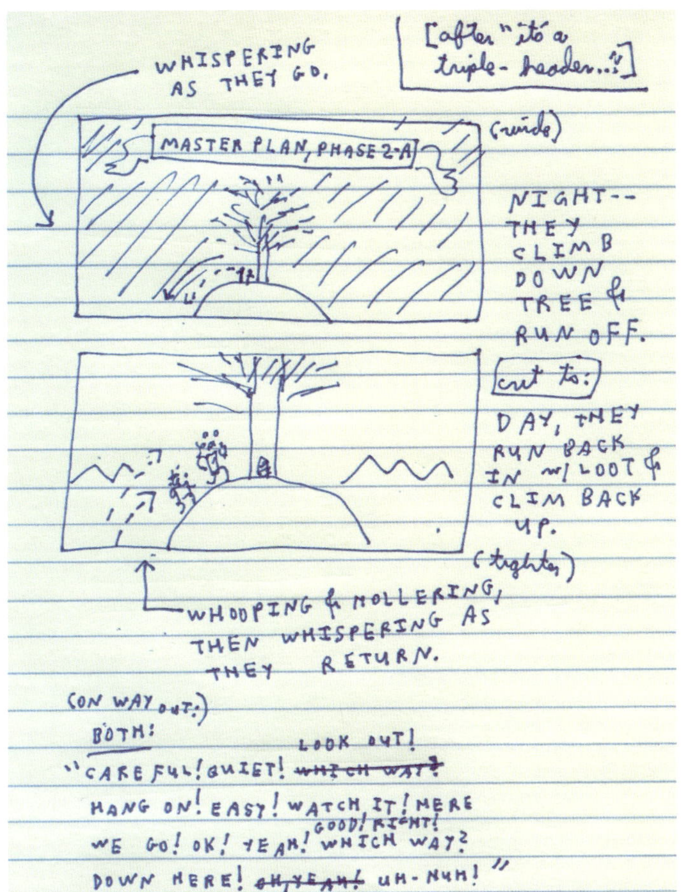

MS: *Yeah, you're right. We are definitely in a drought there. One of the things I think about Wes's movies is that he has this repertory relationship with the people who work with him, both actors and people like you. What you think that does for his work?*

EA: My guess would be that you develop creative relationships with people, and after a certain point you can sort of resort to a shorthand, which is incredibly liberating and brings a kind of confidence. It can be very awkward and exposing when you're trying to make something, which is a strange thing to do, necessarily, particularly with strangers. I've had the experience of being in that kind of moment with relative strangers and feeling incredibly homesick. And I know that if you can develop that with people, then you've got the kind of home feeling. That's my guess. And then also it's just, they're awesome, and you want to use those people because you've seen them be awesome and you want to have an awesome thing, so you get these people and off you go.

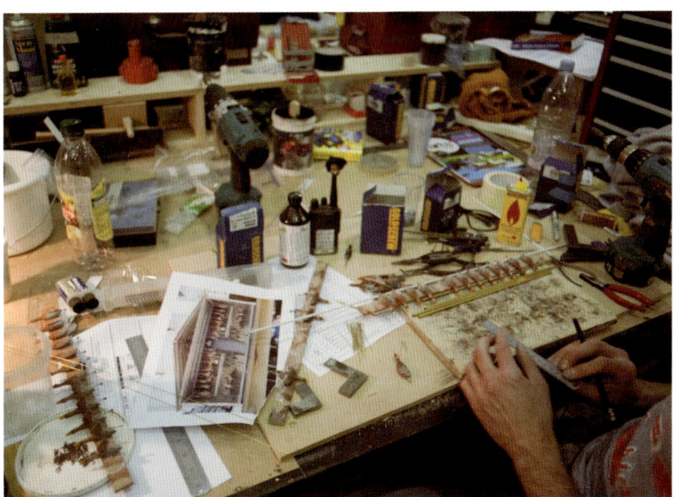

Above: A sketch and notes by Wes for Fox and Kylie on their way to and from the Bunce raid

Left: Making the geese for Bunce's storeroom in the workshop

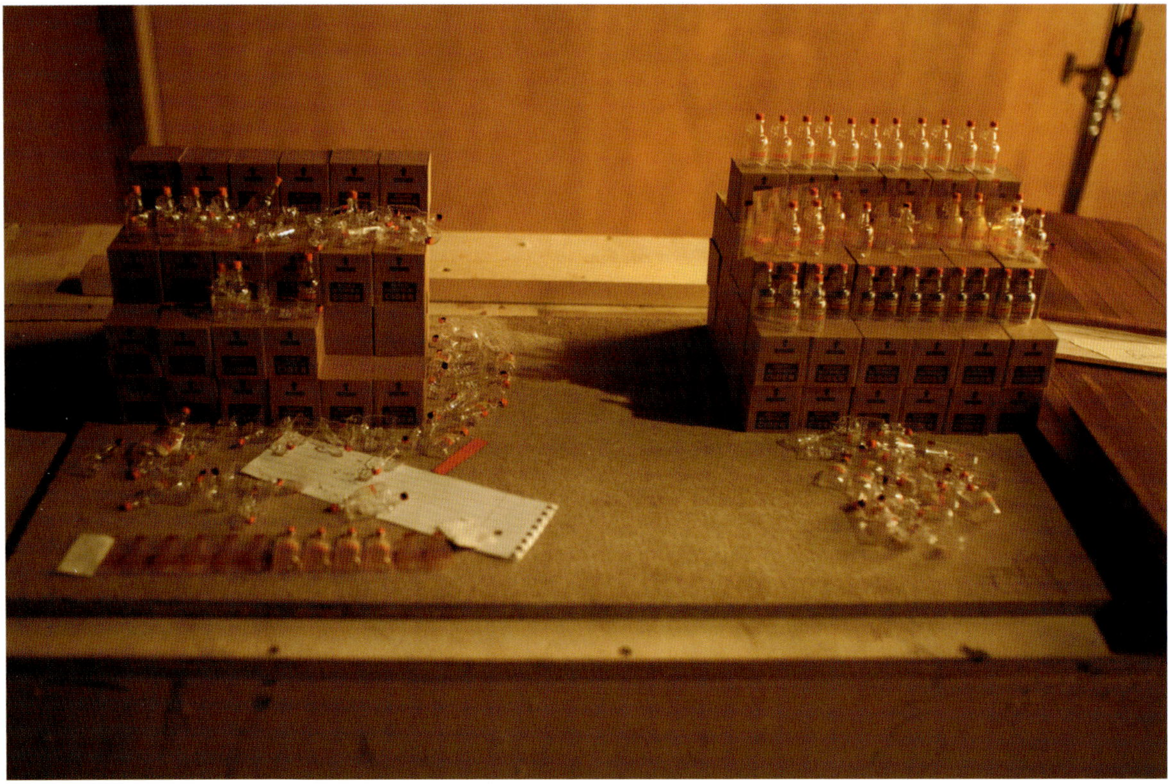

Above: The micro-scale set of Bean's cider cellar in progress

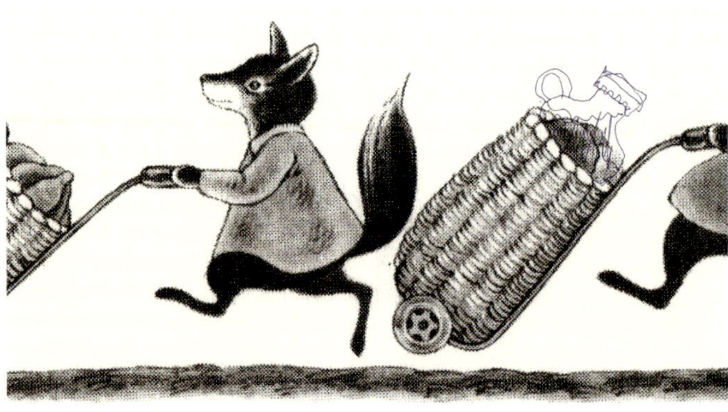

Above and right: Donald Chaffin's illustration of the foxes stealing cider, decorated with a sketch by Wes of a cider bottle

Far right: A cider cart prop from the movie

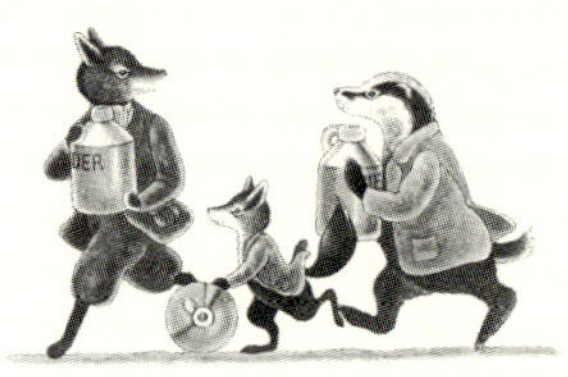

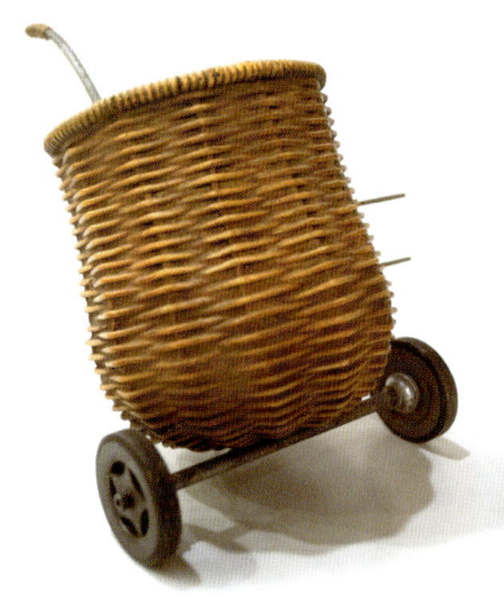

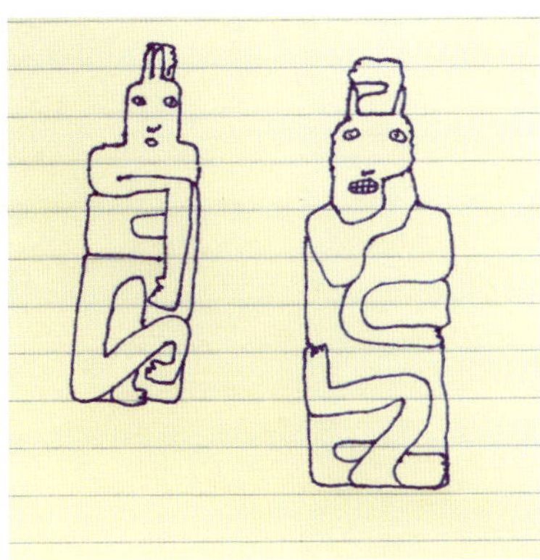

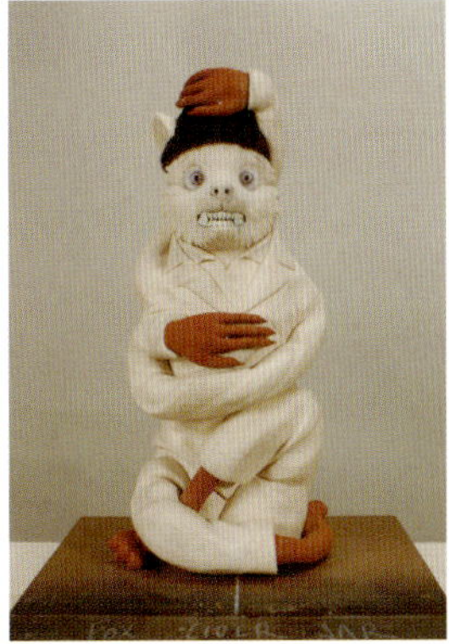

From: Wes Anderson
Subject: **Re: Cider bottle fox design**
Date: 5 August 2008 13:37:16 BST
To: Alice Bird

I would start with clay in the shape of the actual Mr. Fox, then contort it into the cider bottle shape so it is not made from one solid shape but instead has the gaps etc that come from arms and legs etc being pressed together.

Above left: A sketch by Wes for the bottle-shaped Mr. Fox

Above right: The bottle-shaped Mr. Fox model in progress

Right: The final approved bottle-shaped Mr. Fox

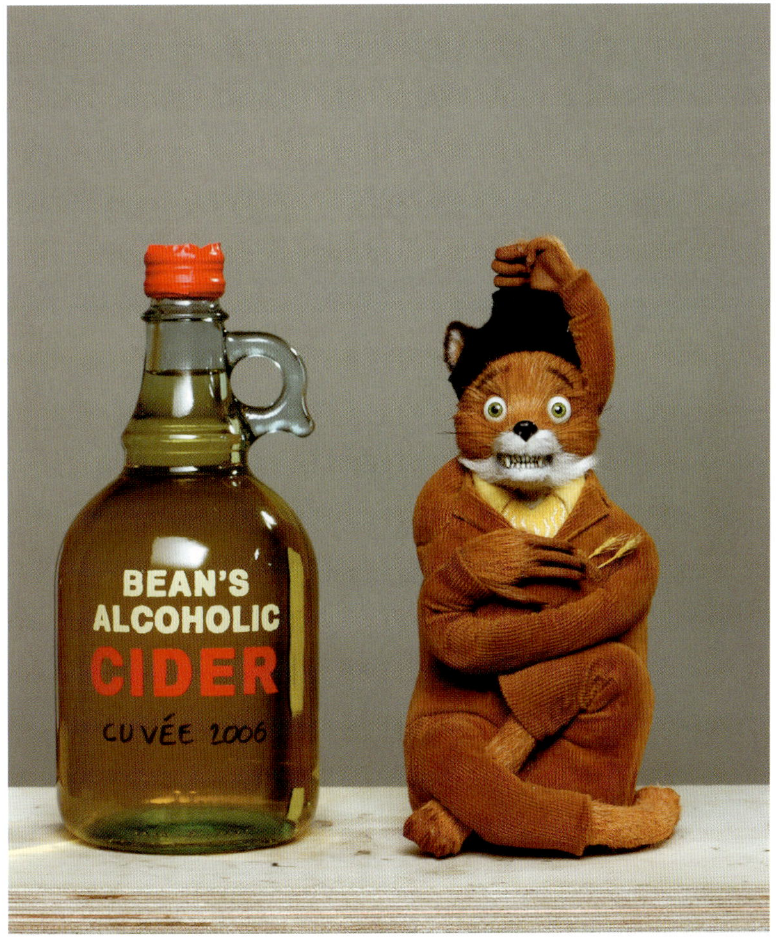

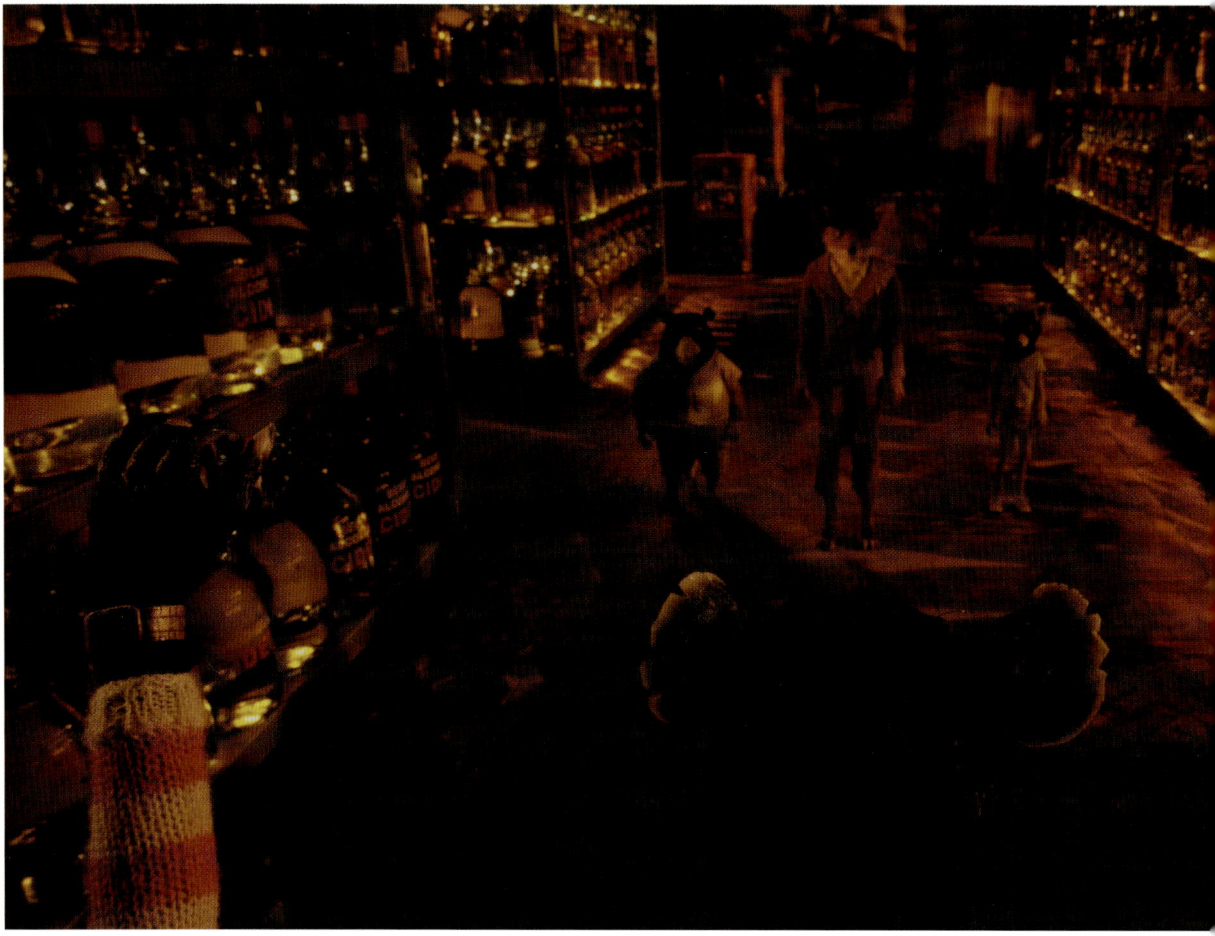

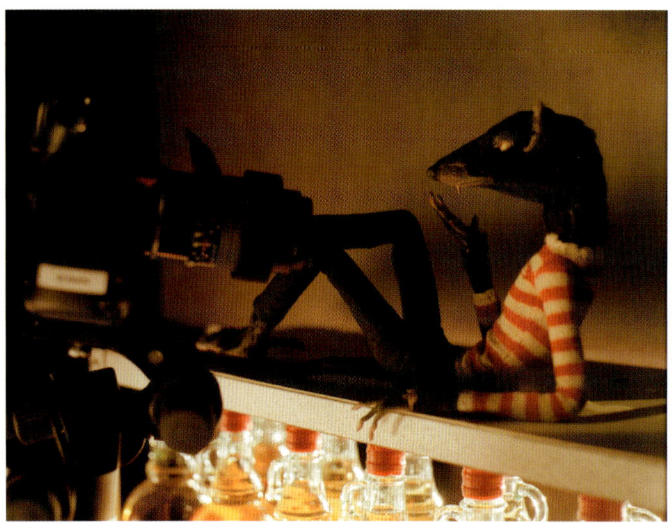

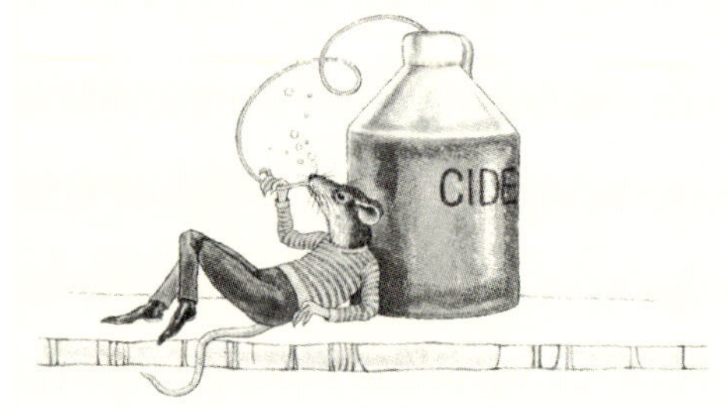

Left: A set still of Rat in Bean's cider cellar

Above: Donald Chaffin's illustration of Rat

Opposite page: A sketch by Wes of the fight between Rat and Mr. Fox

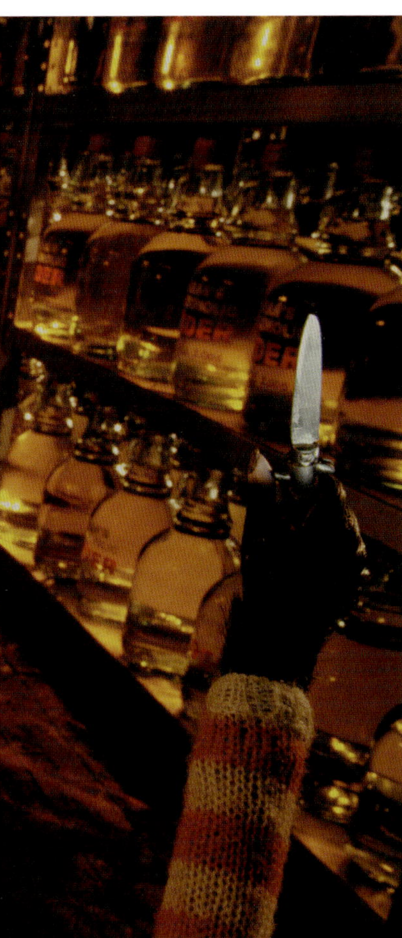

From: Wes Anderson
Subject: **Re: Art Department**
Date: 14 February 2008 12:38:03 GMT
To: Nelson Lowry

IMPORTANT NOTE: I think the cider cellar needs to be AT LEAST 2 levels of cider jar shelves higher plus still more space above the top shelf so the ceiling is more vaulted—it needs to be kind of a cathedral of cider—and I think we need to make these cider jars clear glass maybe? so we can get light bouncing behind them so the cider can glow in the jars OK?

Who animated bean at top of stairs by the way? That was done by somebody who has a wonderful way with smoke.

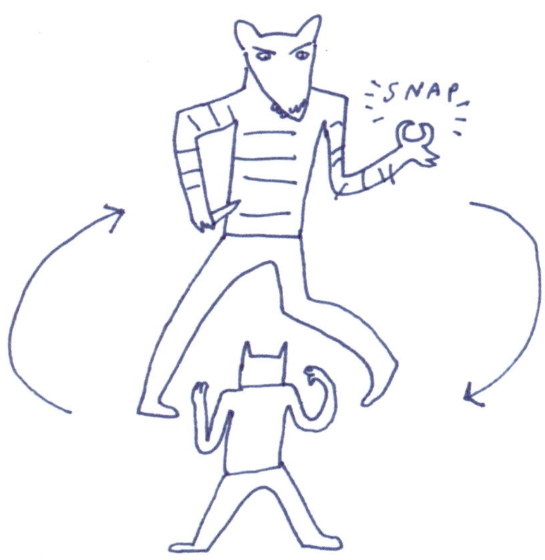

MS: *Kids sometimes figure they're going to be "X" when they grow up. Did Wes ever suggest, "I'm going to be a director"? Was there any of that between you guys?*
EA: I can remember a point where I was certainly going to be a fighter pilot for the U.S. Navy, and then I was going to be a submariner, and then I was going to be a classic surface warfare officer.

Of course.
There was always a tinge of unreality about those, which I think everybody who met me at the time saw and smiled about but didn't feel it was right to tell me about. They knew I needed to experience it on my own. But I think that there were enough artistic projects underway at the time that there wasn't a great feeling of mystery about where Wes was going, although maybe there was a period where he was going to be a tennis player… or maybe he would just play tennis.

Is he any good at tennis?
Well I think the last time I watched him play tennis I was probably thirteen myself, and my impression was that he was great. But he might not agree. It's easy for me to be glib about it, but I think there was a feeling of being writers and directors probably, even for me when I was like sort of in denial about it. I went to college and studied English. He was making movies when we were eleven years old.

Oh, he was? Where did that come from?
I don't know. Our father gave him a Yashica Super 8mm movie camera, and suddenly we were making movies.

Is that true? Yashica Super 8. That's the key to becoming a great director, huh?
Well, that's the key to making movies. I don't know. Next question. Lay it on me. ♣

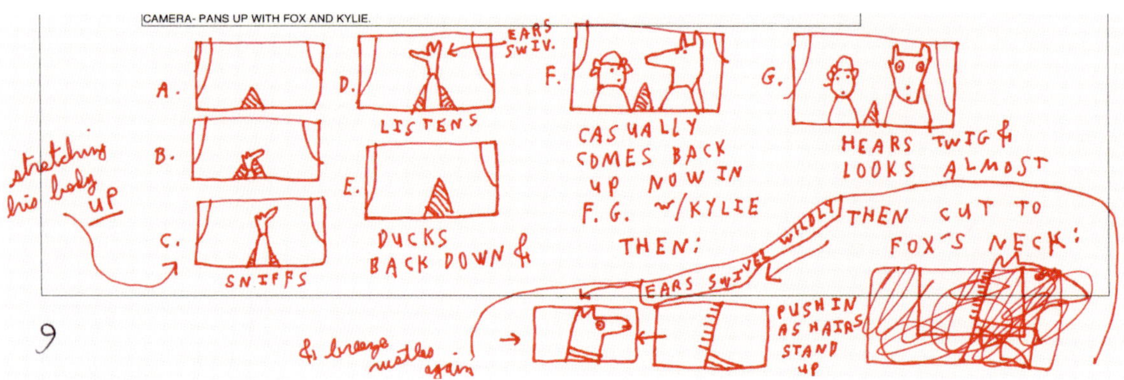

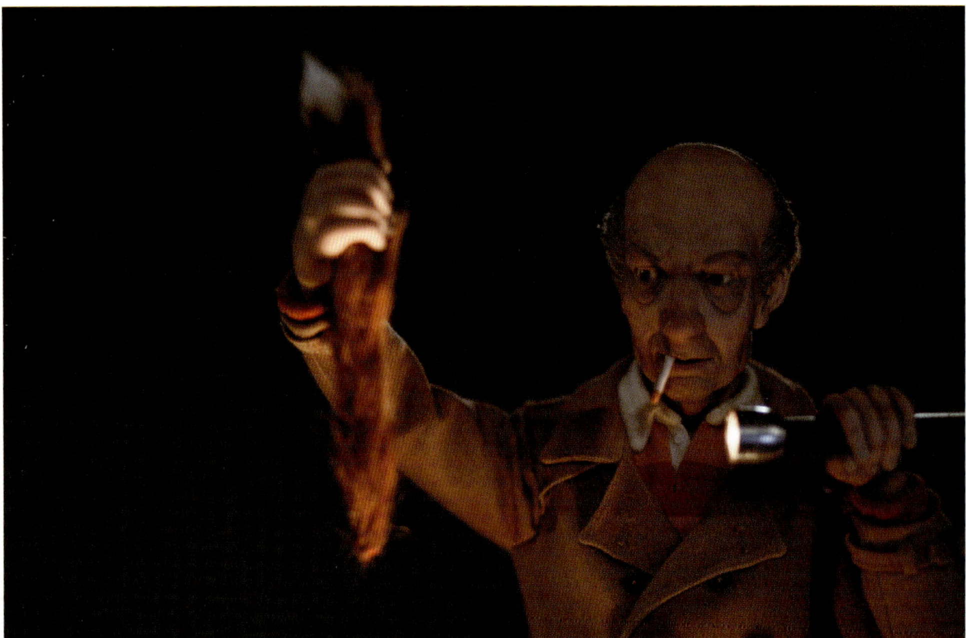

Above: Rough storyboards by Wes for Mr. Fox and Kylie coming out of the tree

Left: A still from the movie of Bean with Mr. Fox's tail

Below left: Donald Chaffin's illustration of the shooting

Below right: A sketch by Wes of Bean picking up Mr. Fox's tail

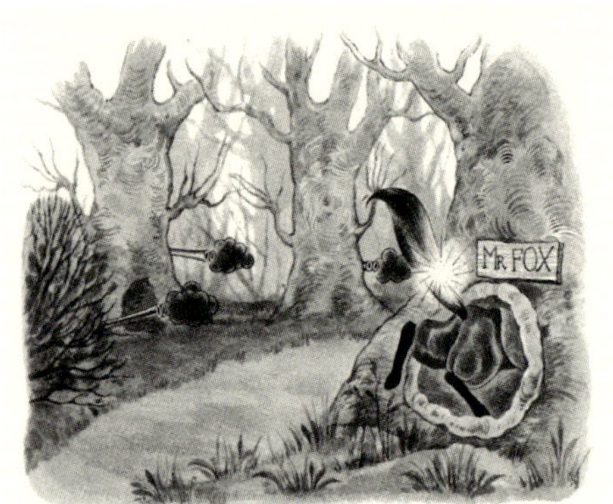

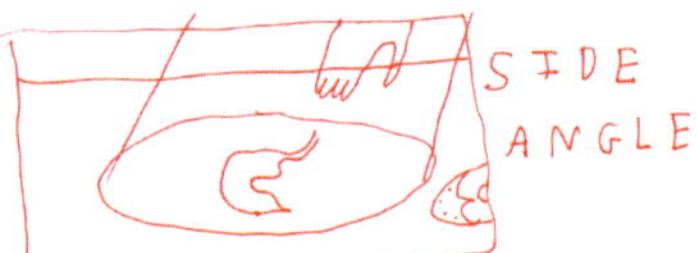

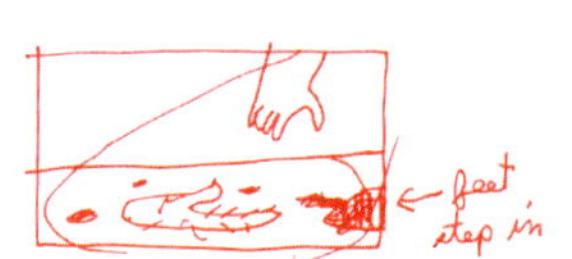

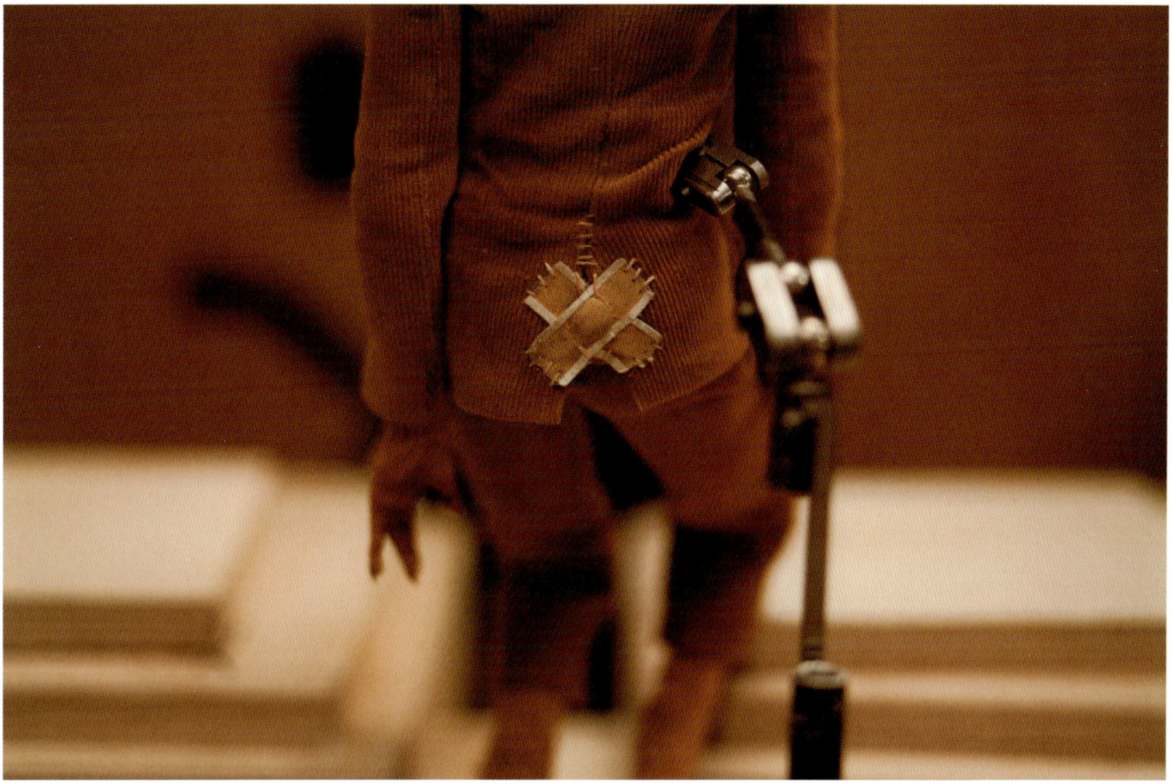

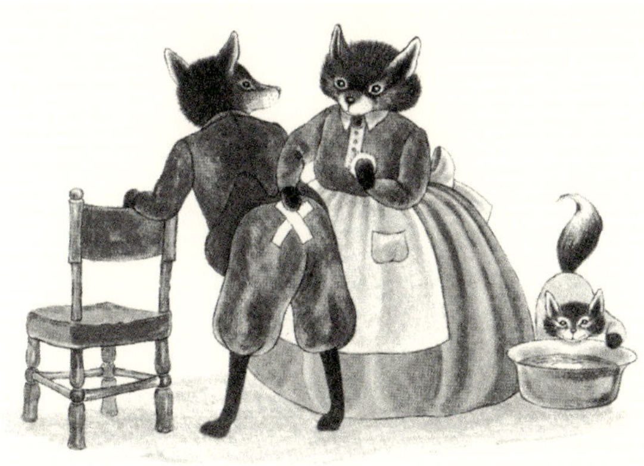

Above: The Mr. Fox puppet with tail bandage

Left: Donald Chaffin's illustration of Mrs. Fox bandaging Mr. Fox's tail

Below: A still from the movie of Mrs. Fox bandaging Mr. Fox's tail

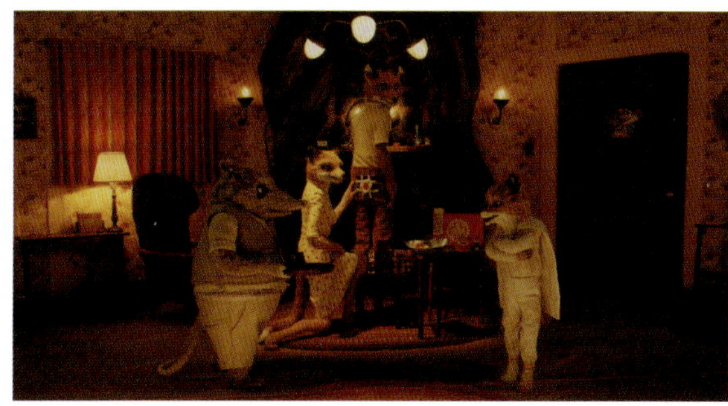

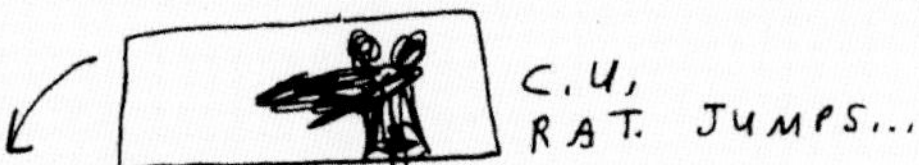

RAT
You're a little torn and tattered, but still a fine-lookin' woman, Mrs. Foxy.

Rat leaps across the hollow and lands poised on all four claws at Mrs. Fox's feet. She recoils against the wall and says with sudden venom:

MRS. FOX
You filthy beast!

RAT LEAPS INTO SHOT. DOLLY FAST IN TOWARD THEM TO:

RAT
(enthusiastically)
You're filthy, yourself! Covered in dirt and grime! Smothered in grease and spit -- all on account of your husband's doin's.

Rat circles around Mrs. Fox menacingly.

2-SHOT.
(they exit)

RAT
'Course, I can hardly blame the poor boy. He's got to be what he is.

Mrs. Fox considers this. She frowns.

MRS. FOX
And what is he?

RAT
(ominously)
A wild animal -- like you once were.

Mrs. Fox stares at Rat. Rat lunges at her, and she darts away.

CUT TO:

The diggers one hundred yards later. Fox suddenly whistles and raises his fist.

The diggers stop digging. Fox feels the ceiling with his paws. He knocks something hard. It sounds hollow. He looks at the others with a funny expression and raises an eyebrow.

FRONT ANGLE 2.

Fox carefully pushes up a floorboard. It creaks loudly. They all duck down and wait. Nothing happens. Fox pushes up a second floorboard. He cautiously pokes his head up through the gap. He lets out a shriek of excitement and whispers excitedly down to the others:

REVERSE OVER THEM. 3.

1A.

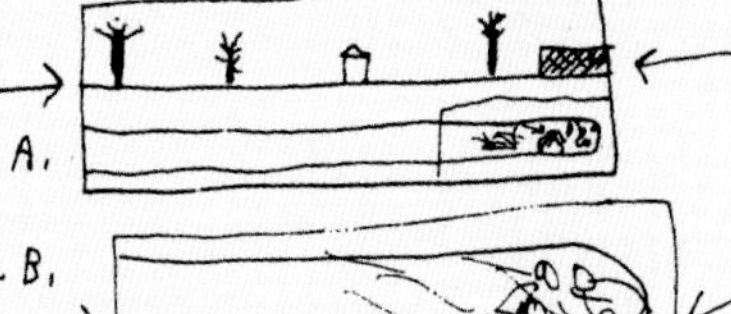

WIDE ABOVE & BELOW GROUND DOLLIES ~~BOOMS~~ IN FAST ON DIGGERS DIGGING & FINALLY TO:

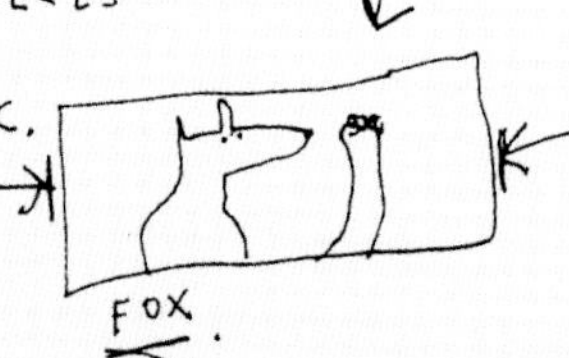

VI

DIGGING TUNNELS

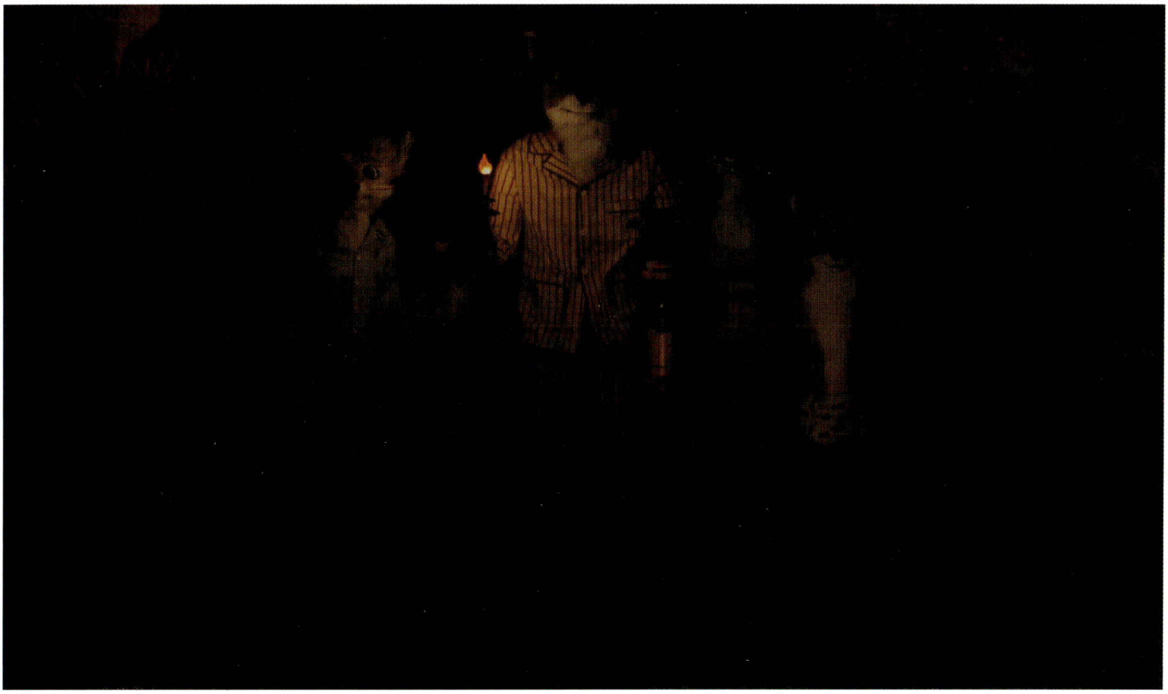

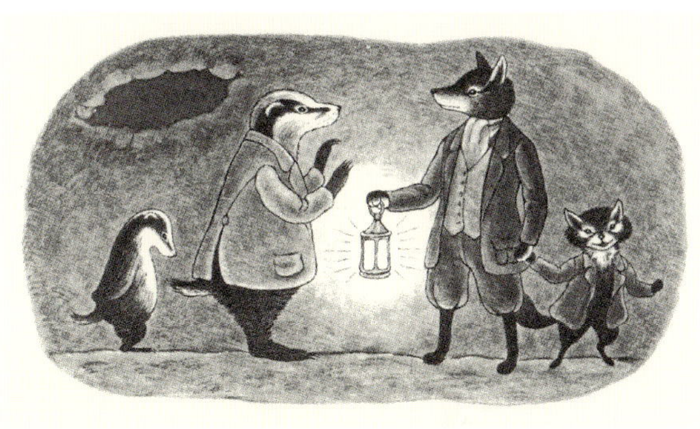

Above: A still from the movie of the Fox family meeting Badger

Left: Donald Chaffin's illustration of Mr. Fox meeting Badger underground

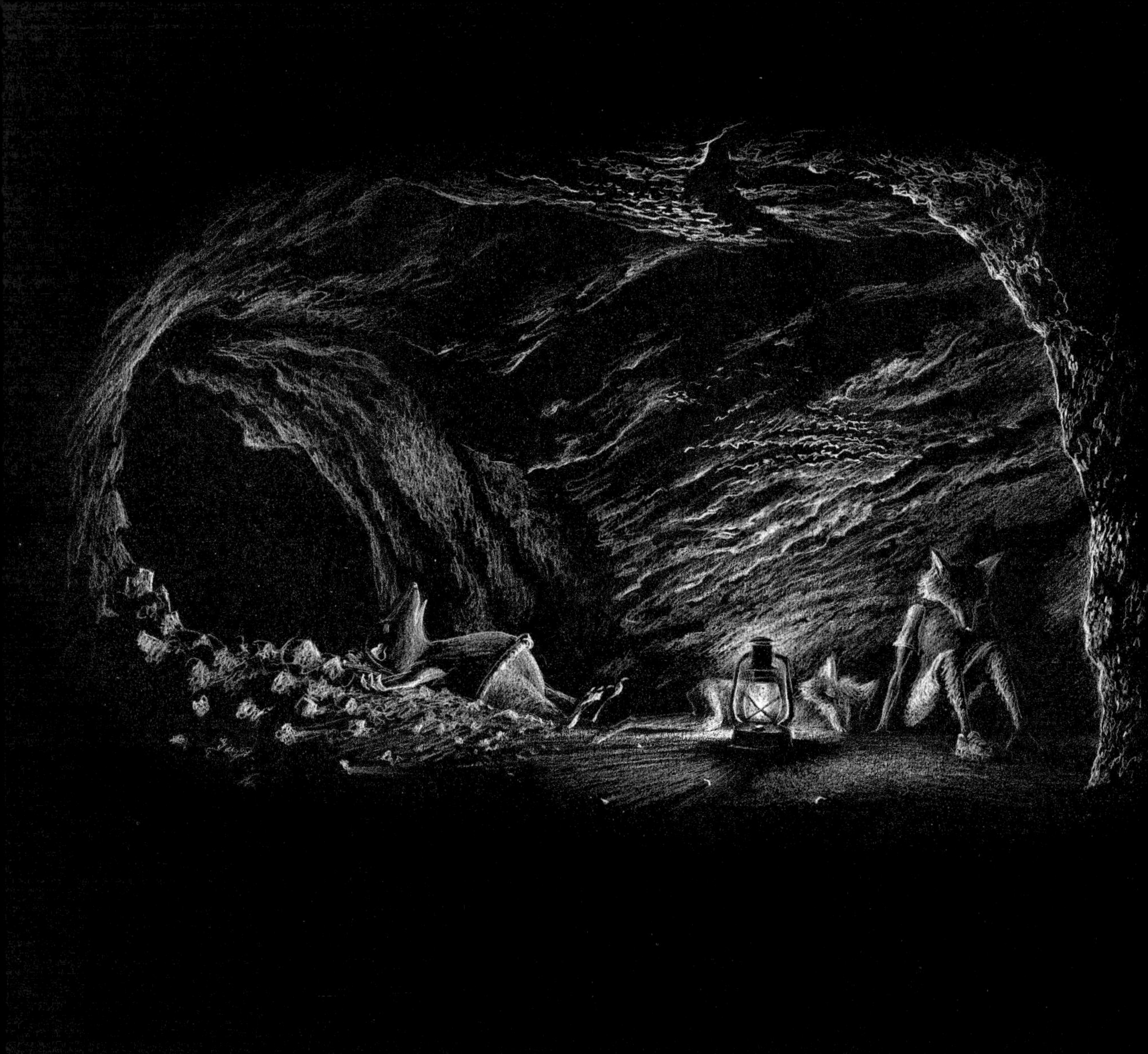

From: Wes Anderson
Subject: **Re: Stalagmite cave - wide and tighter**
Date: 16 October 2008 19:44:36 BST
To: Molly Cooper

how will the cave drawings be done? all as just outlines? need creams and yellows to read well—the outlines—lots of them would be great—add more i think

let's put 2 practicals up with fox and kylie—as flashlight and a lantern?

the backlight look is very nice but let's please make it quite a bit less bright

looks very good so far

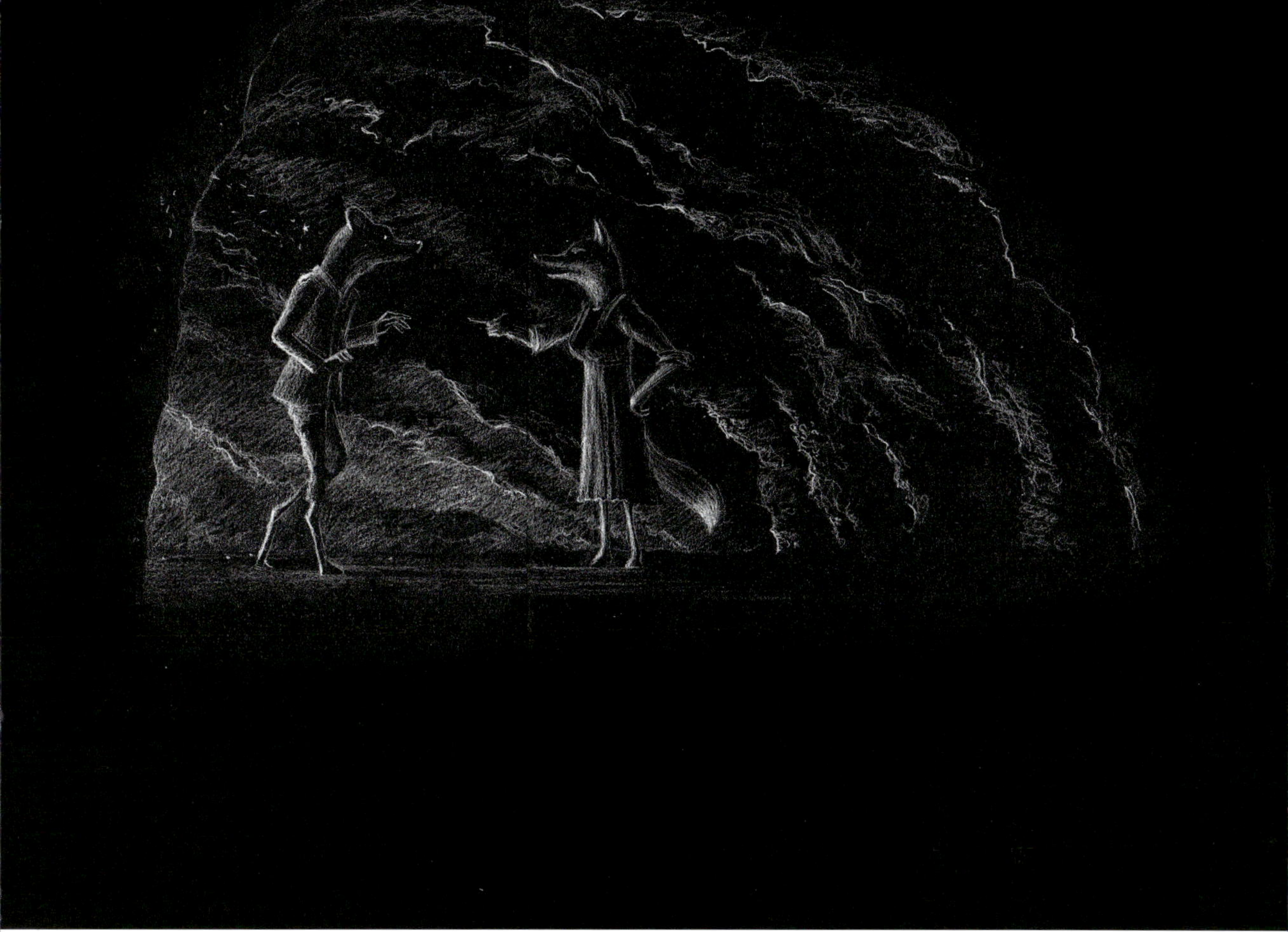

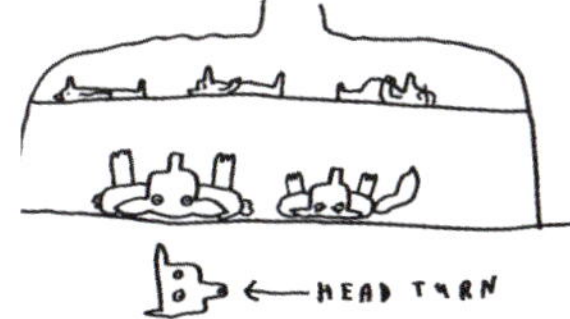

Above: A sketch by Wes for the Fox family and Kylie in an underground pocket

Above: Concept art by Turlo of the foxes underground

Right: Notes and sketches by Wes for the scene in the underground cave

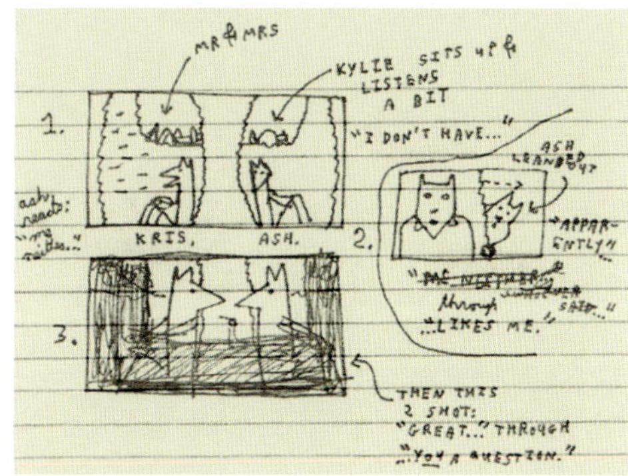

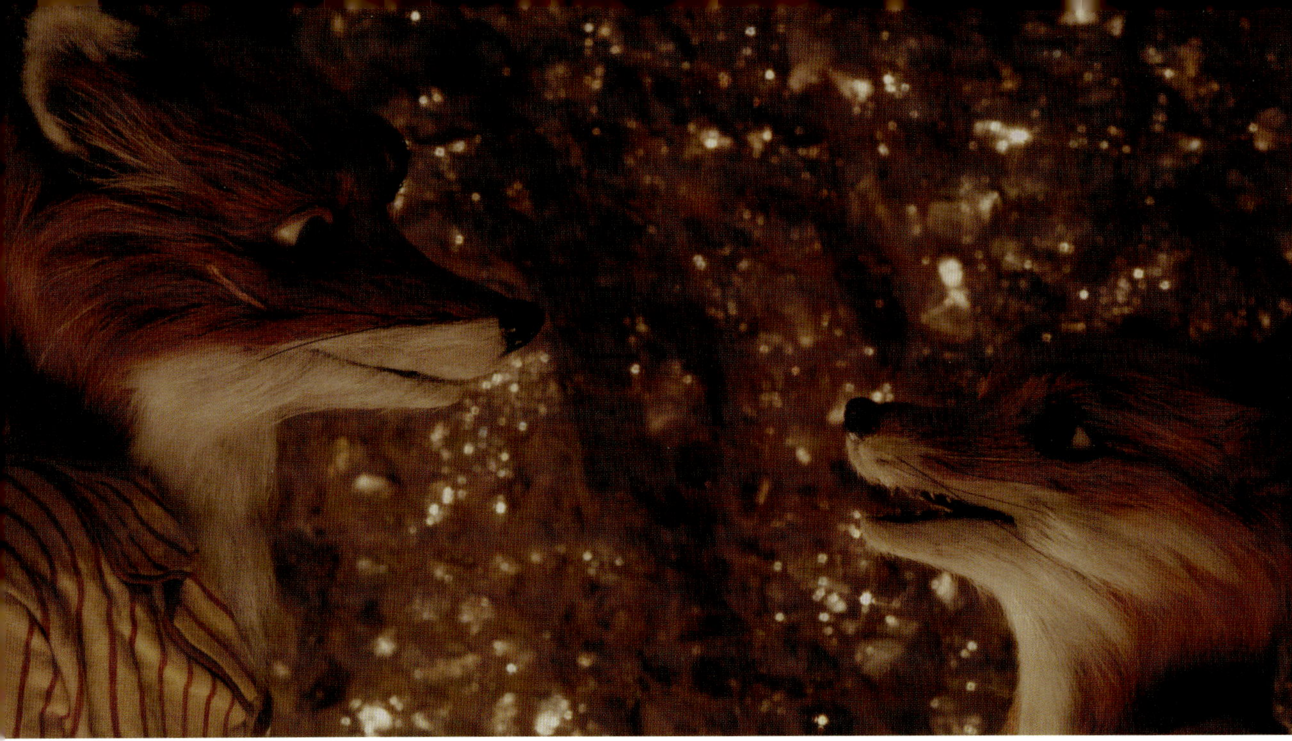

AN INTERVIEW WITH

LICCY DAHL

6/26/09

MS: *Had you ever thought about* Fantastic Mr. Fox *being made into a movie before Wes approached you?*
LD: Not really, no. I mean, this was a long time ago when Wes approached Michael Siegel, my film agent in L.A., and I think Wes had only just made *Bottle Rocket* and *Rushmore*. So I was slightly surprised that he was asking for *Fox*.

Why were you surprised?
Well, you look at those two films and then you think of *Fantastic Mr. Fox*. It couldn't be more distant. [laughs] I was very taken aback, you know, because I love those two films and I thought golly, how on earth would he make *Fantastic Mr. Fox*? It wasn't until much later that we met. He was just starting *The Royal Tenenbaums*, in fact. The production was just being put together. We met and I mean, I was so in love with his work, I was dying for him to do *Fantastic Mr. Fox*, but I needed to know what his thoughts and his conceptual ideas were for the film.

What did he tell you? I mean, how did he approach this when you talked? What was his conception?
Well at that point he wasn't at all sure, you know, whether it was going to be live or stop-motion or anything. And it wasn't until much later—because I have an absolute standard rule with all the films that are made of Roald's books that the first thing is the screenplay. I said to Wes, "Until we have a screenplay I can't begin to go down this path." And we gave him the options on the book for some time, and then he came to Gipsy House and we spent quite a long time walking around the countryside in the pouring rain. [laughs] Then I could see, and I showed him the original manuscript and indeed an original book, a notebook, in which Roald had done the drawings of the foxes and Boggis, Bunce, and Bean. And I think that inspired him enormously. And then he actually came to Gipsy House to write the screenplay. He stayed here for I think about two or three weeks.

Oh, I didn't even know that.
With Noah. They worked sort of all day and we had a wonderful time. He walked around the countryside with Noah, because obviously it was Buckinghamshire that inspired Roald for the book, and I think it certainly inspired Wes. Scott Rudin came over and I think he was here for about two days, or a day, I can't remember now exactly. And finally the screenplay, the first draft was done, and we went from there.

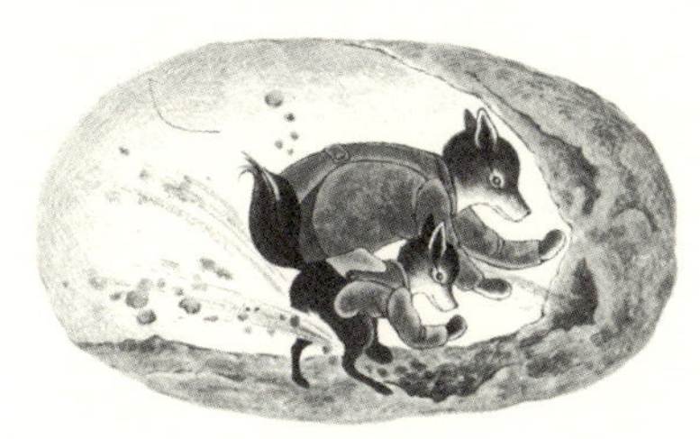

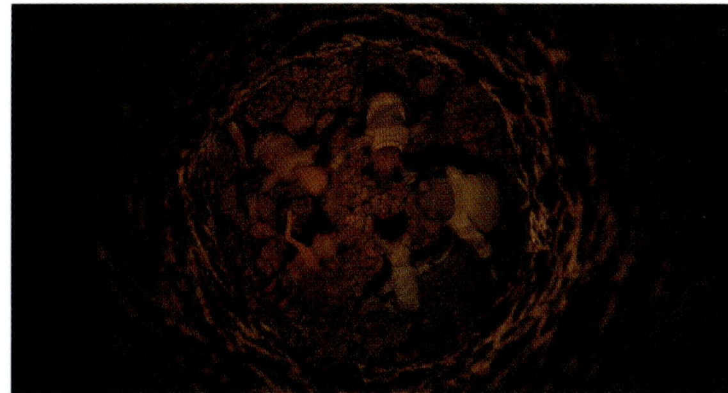

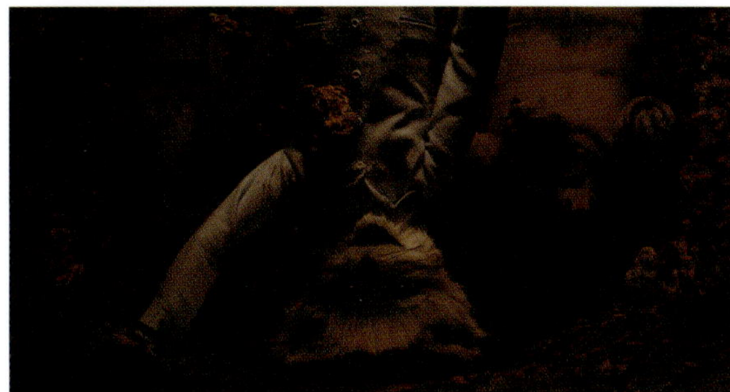

Opposite page: A still from the movie of Mr. and Mrs. Fox

Above: Donald Chaffin's illustration of the foxes digging

Right: Stills from the film of the foxes digging

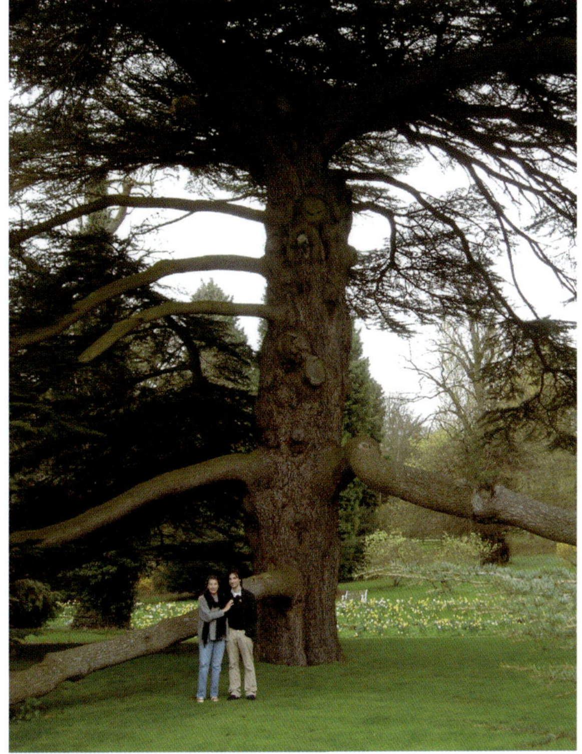

Right: Sketches by Wes of the foxes and Kylie looking up as the ceiling caves in

Left: A photograph taken by Wes of Liccy Dahl and Noah Baumbach, during one of Wes and Noah's visits to Gipsy House

Below: A sketch by Wes of Ash with mud on his face

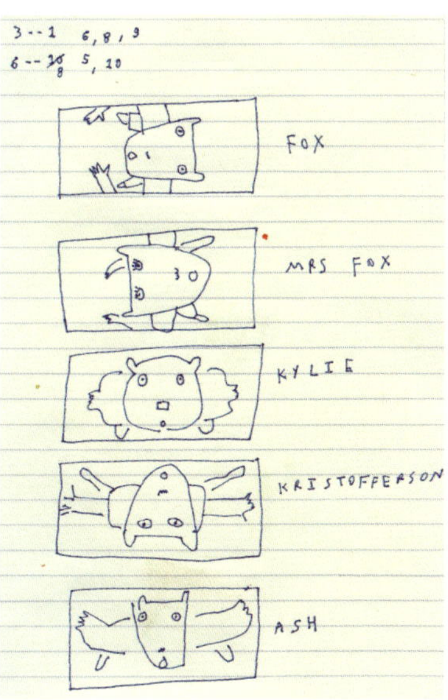

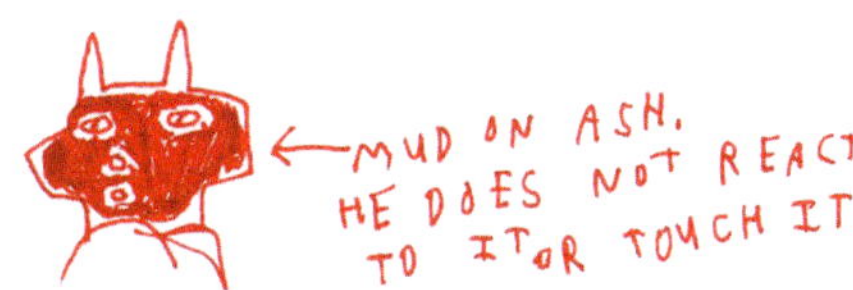

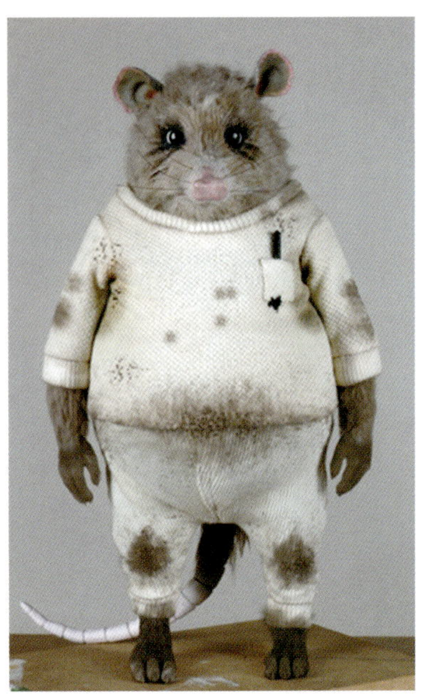

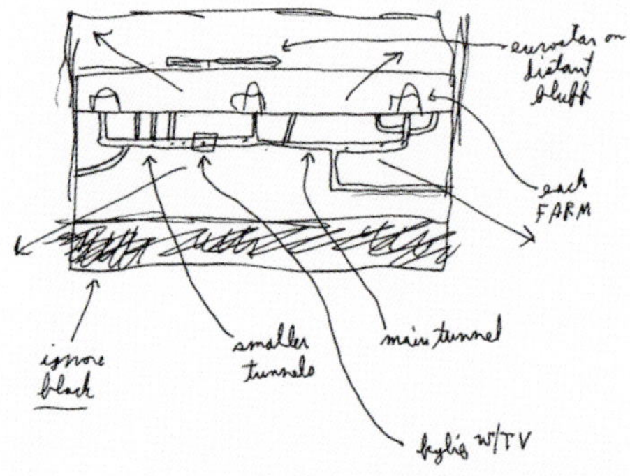

Left: Digital image showing dirt patches and ink stains on Kylie

Right: A sketch by Wes for a wide shot of the underground digging tunnels

Below: A still of the set built for digging under the farms

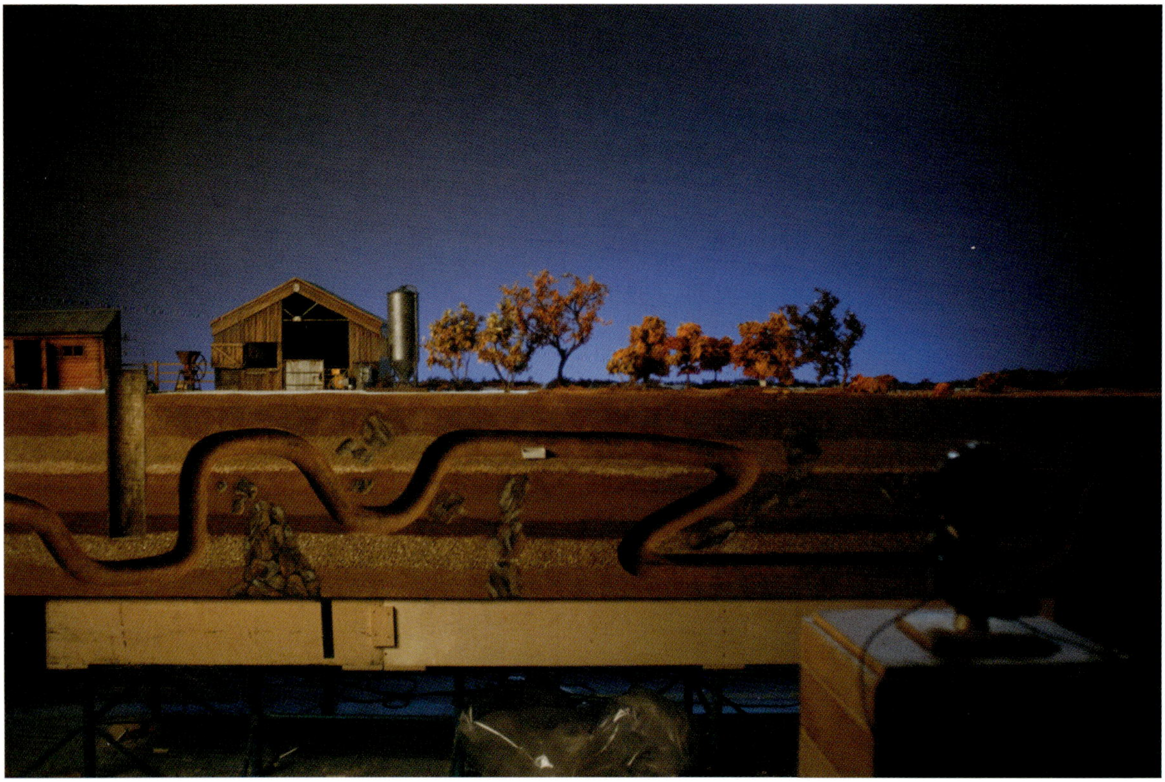

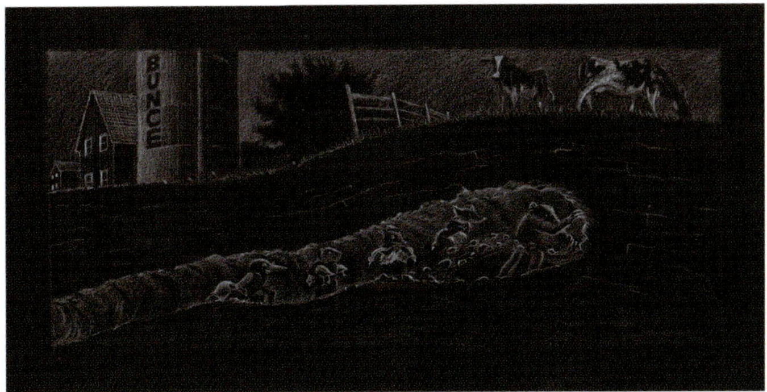

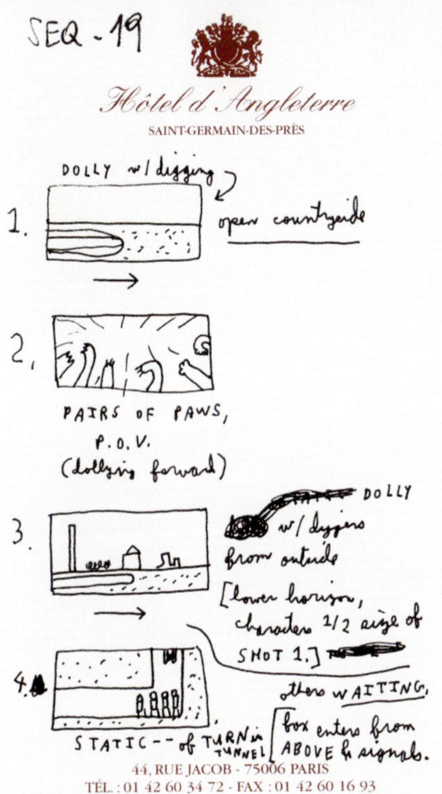

Above: Early concept art by Turlo for digging under the farms

Left: Rough storyboards by Wes for the digging shots

Below: Notes by Wes for digging under the farms

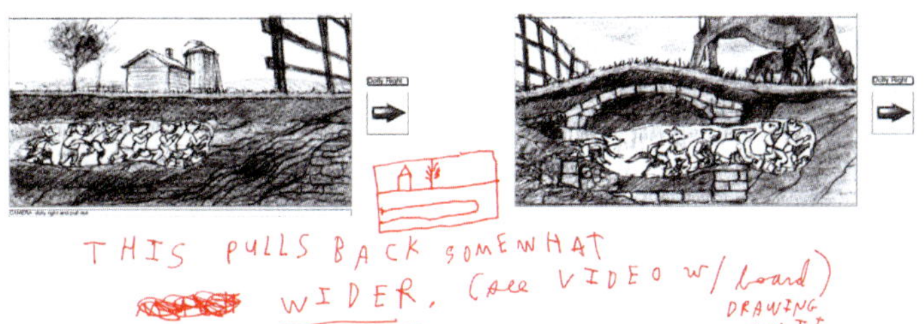

MS: *It's pretty remarkable, I think.*
LD: It's very difficult when you are the keeper of Roald's children's books. We have to be so careful whose hands they go into, because obviously it can have a good or a bad effect on those books. So it was quite a gamble for us because needless to say, the book had to be expanded, and Wes and Noah certainly took it into other realms. You get nervous because you think, will the readers, the young readers and the old readers of the book, be shocked, or excited? You never know.

Well that's what I was going to ask you. The thing with a book like this is that it means so much to so many readers that they kind of have their own conceptions of it. And sometimes that's hard—and this movie is so special and so different that it can't possibly match up with preconceptions because it's just its own thing. Now that can be very exciting, but there is a risk there.
I think Wes has expanded it in the true spirit of the book and of Roald, particularly.

You think Roald would be happy if he could see it?
Well until I see the final cut I can't say, but certainly the work that has been done in the studio was just fantastic. I mean, I was so staggered by the sets and the designers and the whole animation team down there, teams of many, many extremely talented people. And I mean, I'm just praying. You know, I can't say anything until the film's finished.

It is actually staggering how much work went into it and how beautiful the movie is. And it's humorous, it's smart. I think it's going to bring a major new generation of readers to your husband's work.
But also I think it's fantastic for Wes to have gone from live-action to stop-motion, which is a totally different, extremely difficult form of filmmaking. And what a leap for him to make.

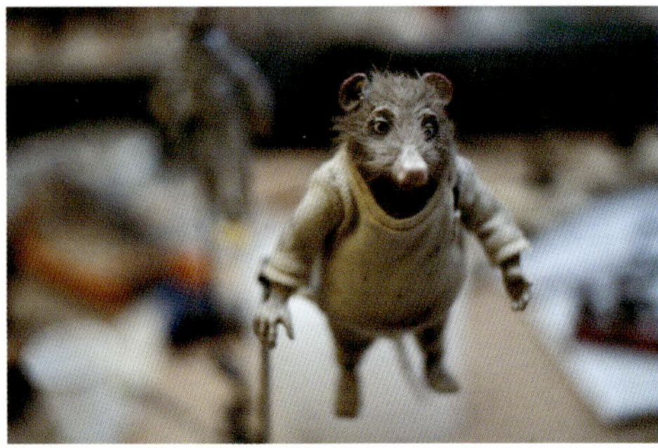

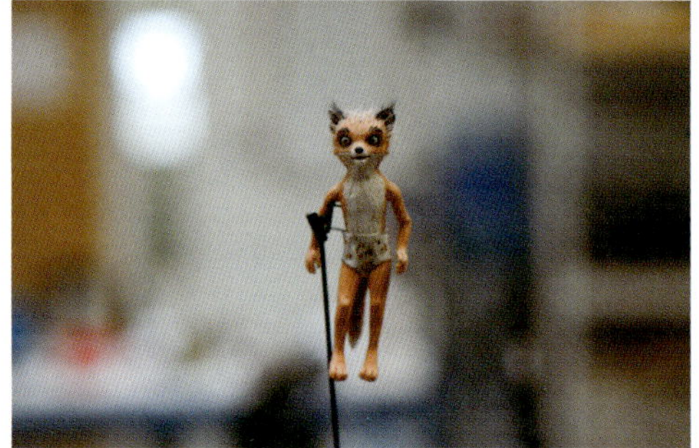

MS: *In the course of making this film, Wes exchanged 65,000 emails with the production.*
LD: [laughs] That does not surprise me. I think it's incredible. I really think the teams Wes has around him making this film are exceptional.

I agree. Would you think that any of Roald's other work is amenable to stop-motion?
Well I think the only way *James and the Giant Peach* could have been done was with stop-motion—I mean, we have live-action in it as well. When Wes mentioned to me, "Look, I think this is going to be stop-motion," I was somewhat taken aback, not because I didn't think *Fox* is ideal for stop-motion, but to get a live-action director to properly make his first—I mean, I know he'd worked with Henry Selick on *Life Aquatic* so he did have some experience. But for us I thought, oh, my God, a whole stop-motion film? And then I thought no, he's so clever and he wouldn't go into that field unless he was pretty certain he could do it, and I knew where he would win was getting a team of animation people that would have to work with him and who would be of the greatest talent in that world that existed. So I thought, no, he's right. This is ideal, this is an ideal book for stop-motion. But the rest of Roald's books—nothing comes to my mind. Of course *Charlie and the Chocolate Factory* was live. No, I can't think of anything, to be honest, but who knows? I might be wrong.

Are you concerned that loyal readers won't see the movie in the same way, or are you hoping it will bring people to the book who wouldn't have read it before? Is this going to be for kids or for adults?
Luckily I've got an incredible number of grandchildren, ranging from eight-year-olds up to thirty-year-olds. I've taken them all down to the studio and they've seen various sections of the film, and from the youngest to the oldest they just loved it. So on that ground I was happy. But of course I think there will be criticism from a lot of the parents who know the book very well and are now reading it to their children. We're bound to get that because they'll say, you know, "It's gone into other areas that are not in the book at all." But on the other hand, I think it will draw people into buying and reading the book. And I just hope Wes is not going to get criticized at all because that book, I think, it is one of the most loved Dahl books internationally. It has an enormous public, which is already in love with that book. But you never know. Until the film comes out, I don't know. When we were making *James and the Giant Peach*, Henry left out the cloud men in that book. I went to a screening in Los Angeles and at the end the audience's main criticism was, "You've left the cloud men out." Well, then Henry had to put them in, found some extra money and put them in. But it will be very interesting to see with *Fox*, there's not much that Wes has left out, but he has added an enormous amount. We'll just have to wait and see. ✤

Opposite page: Half-scale puppets of Kylie and Ash rigged for the digging scenes

Right: Donald Chaffin's illustration of the animals dancing in the chicken hut

Below: A still of Mr. Fox and other animals dancing in Bunce's storeroom

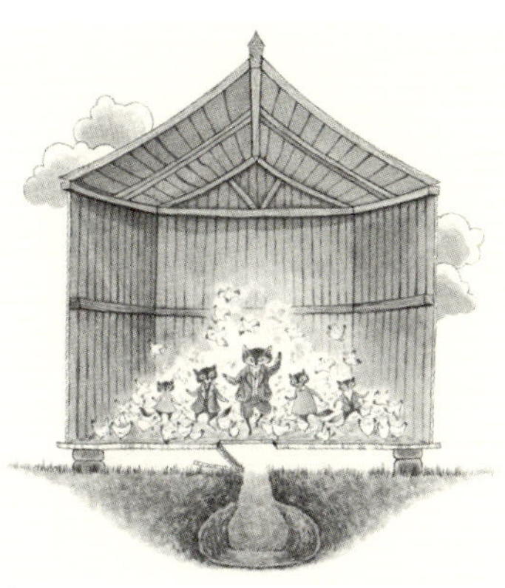

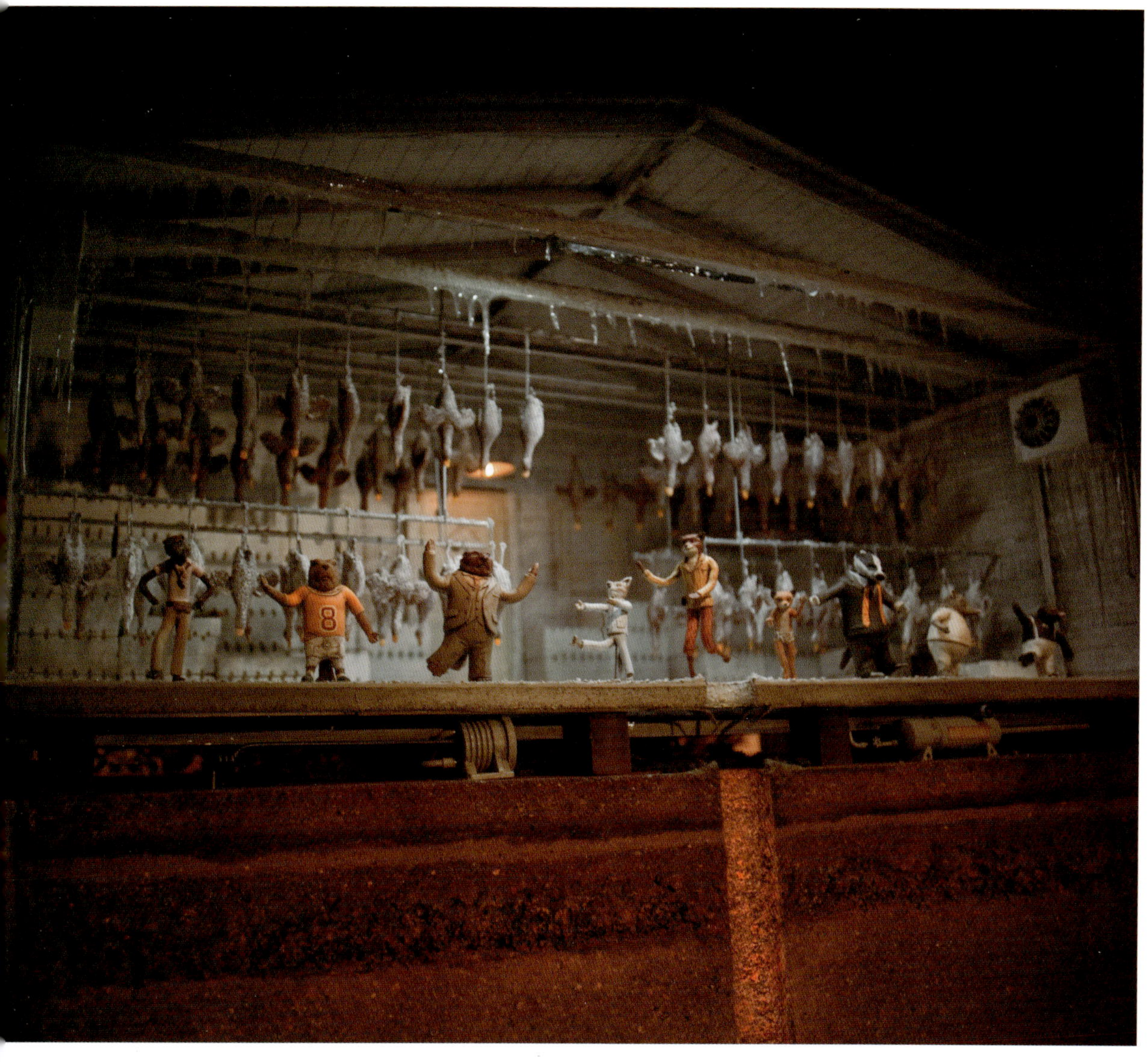

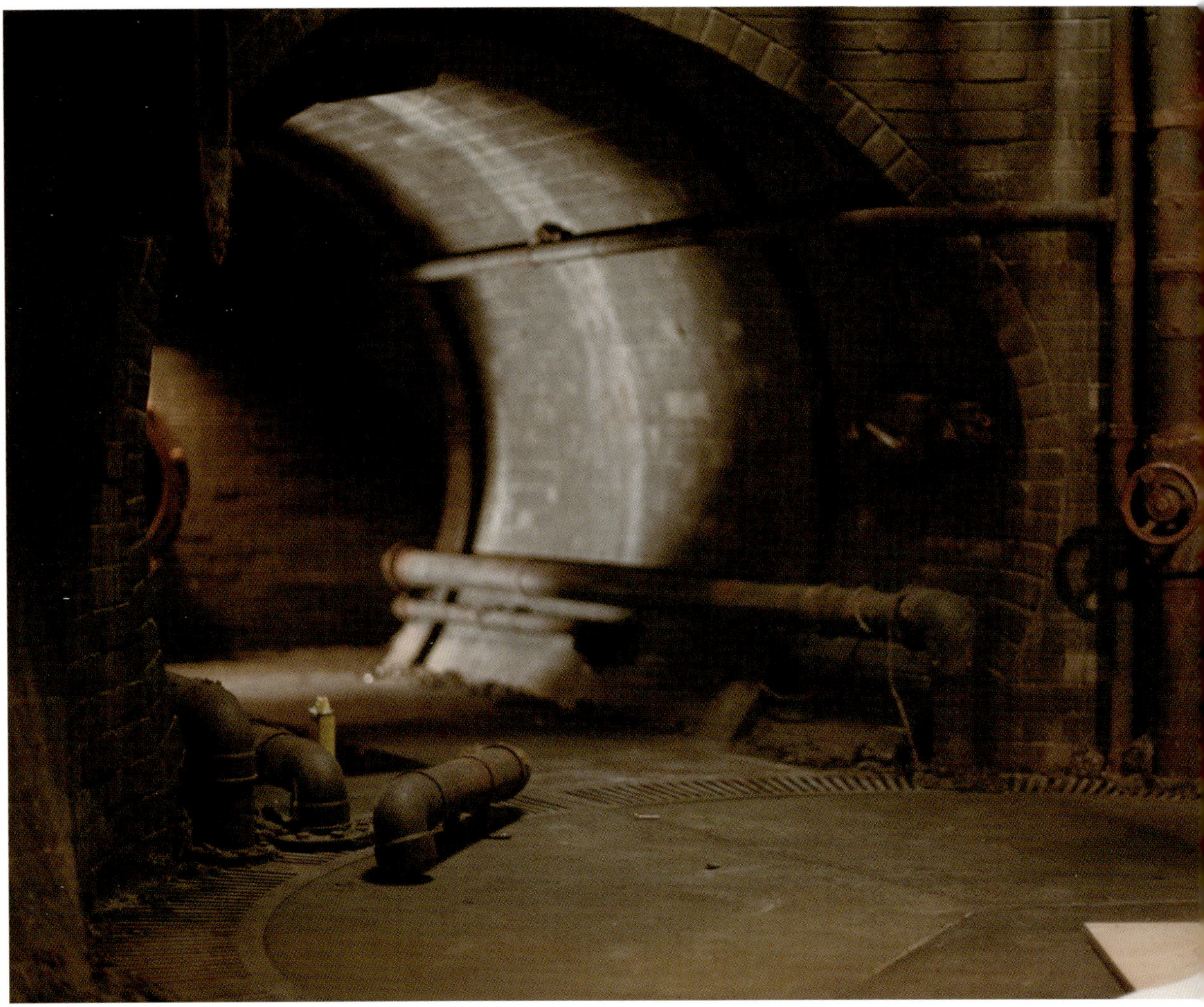

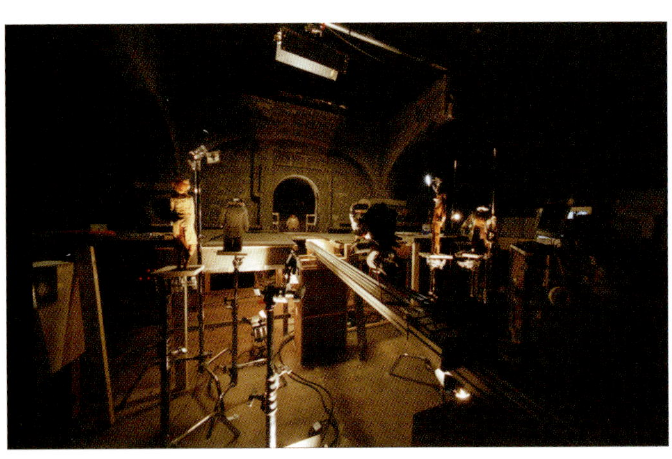

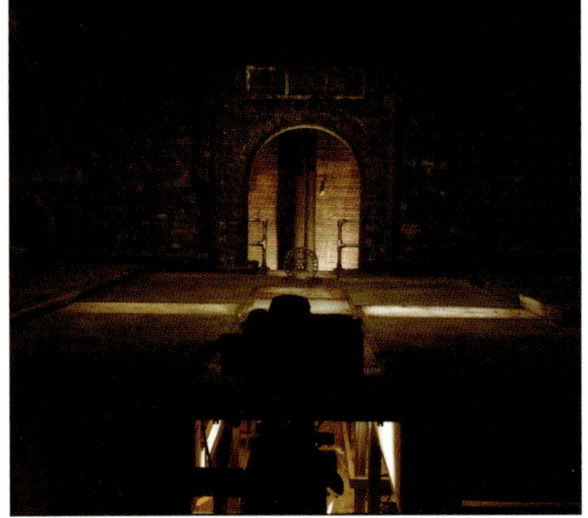

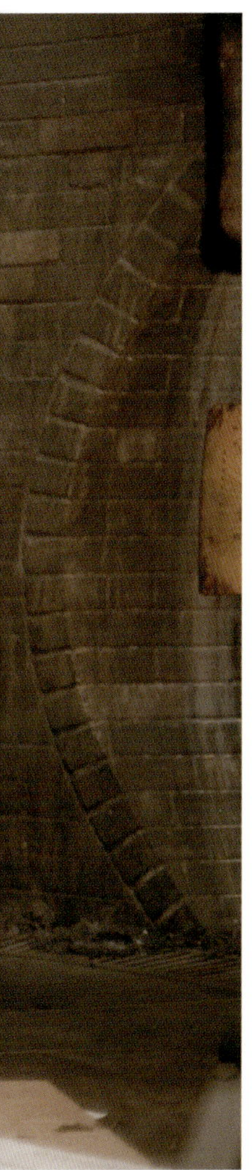

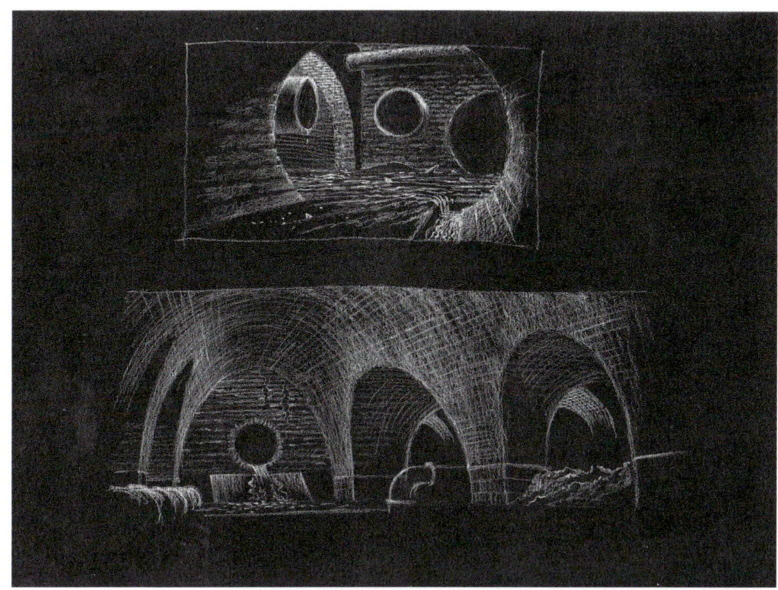

Opposite page: Photographs of the sewer sets

Above: Early concept art by Turlo for the sewer areas

Right: A Mrs. Fox puppet on the sewer set

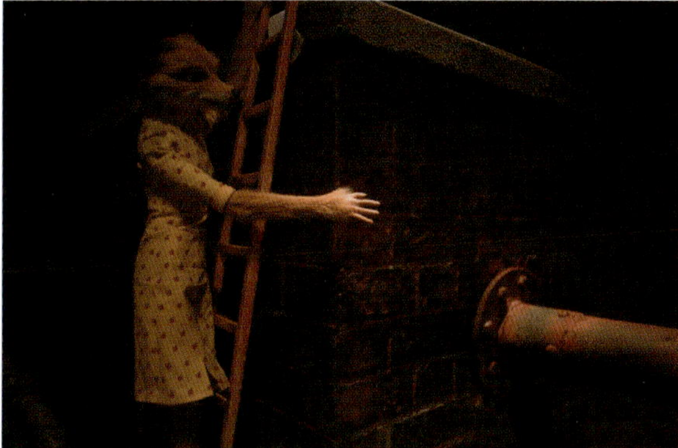

From: Wes Anderson
Subject: **Re: Art Department**
Date: 16 November 2008 21:28:22 GMT
To: Nelson Lowry

Nelson a couple of things for the sewer:

i think for the parts of the town square sequence that occur in the sewer we should have as a new visual element for that section underground street signs painted on the the tunnel walls—these to correspond with the streets above—and also there can be light that comes through gratings for this part—natural light—so in fact it is not as dark a section of the sewer? except for the mole/mural parts of that

also i think we should pick a section that can have steam coming from various pipes which we can do with our cotton technique—one chamber/one scene of the underground sequence

also maybe in the large chamber where fox gies the latin names speech we can include materials the city has stored there—traffic cones, dismantled roadblocks, a stack of doors of some kind, etc—stuff the city uses

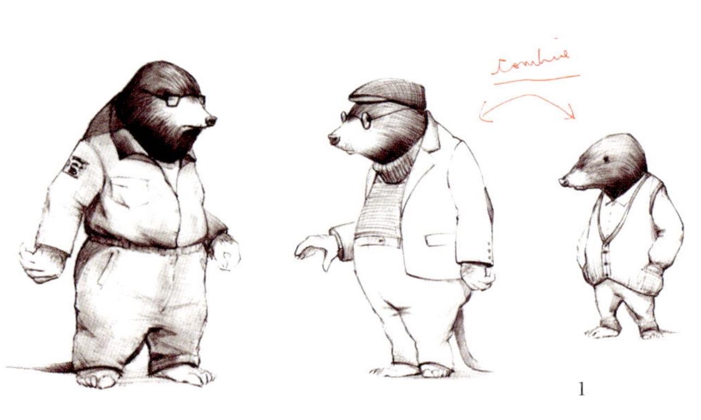

1. Early concept art for Mole by Victor Georgiev with a note from Wes

2. A sculpture for the Mole puppet

3. Notes by Wes on Mole's tie and suspenders

4. A turnaround for Mole's costume

5. Early designs for Mole's head by Félicie

6. The final approved color design for Mole

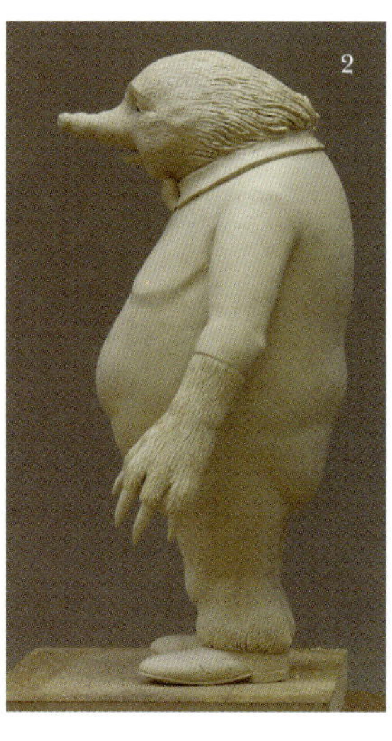

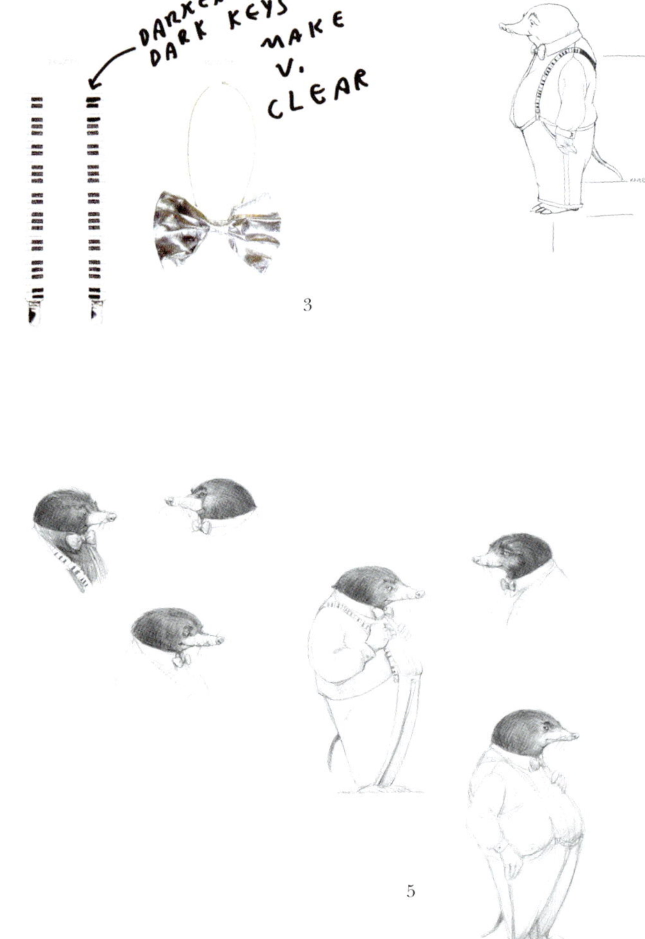

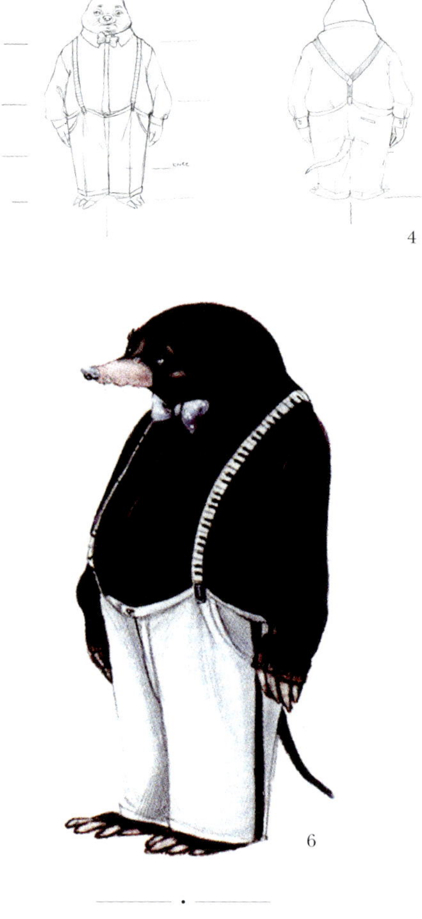

MOLE

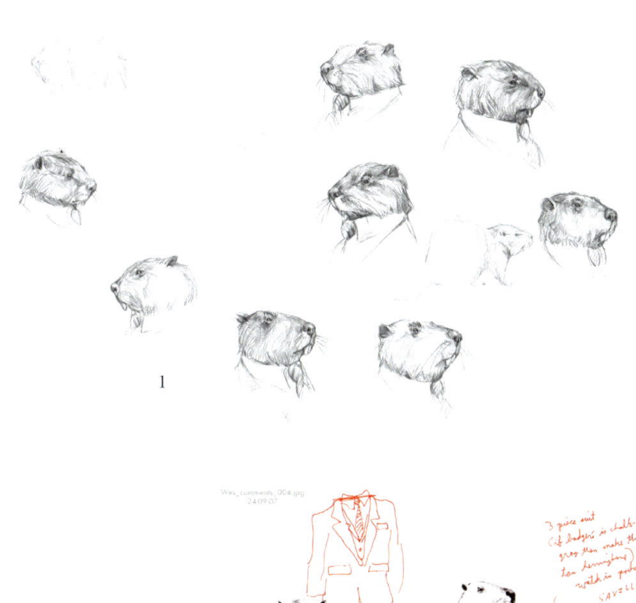

1

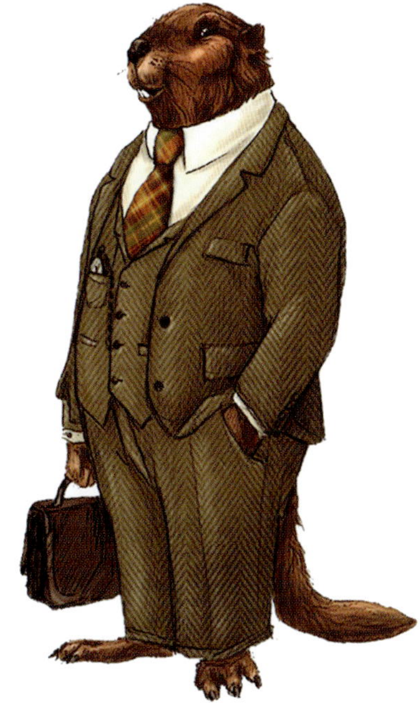

BEAVER

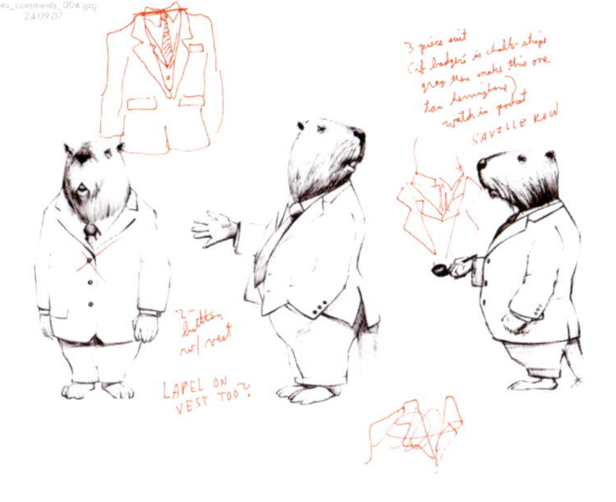

2

1. Early designs for Beaver's head by Félicie

2. Notes by Wes on Beaver's costume

3. The final approved color design for Beaver

4. Notes on Beaver's belly shape

5. An extra tail part for Beaver

6. The Beaver puppet in the puppet hospital

7. Early concept designs for Beaver by Félicie

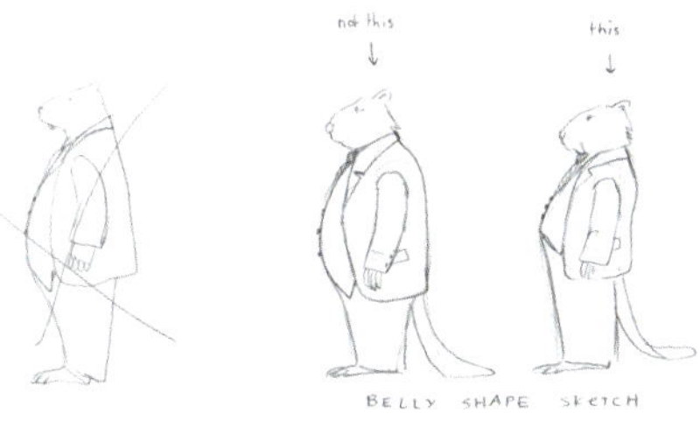

4

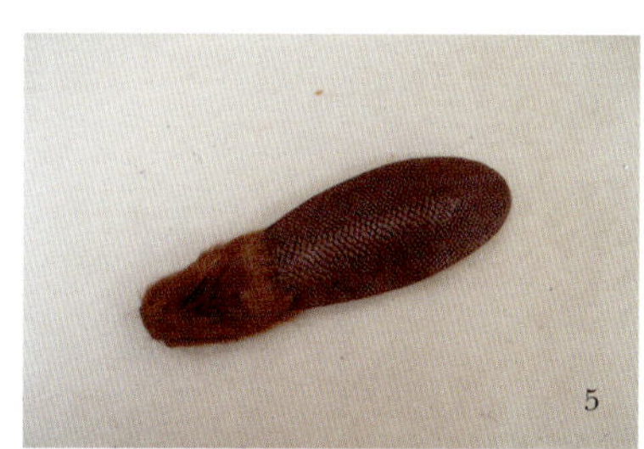

5

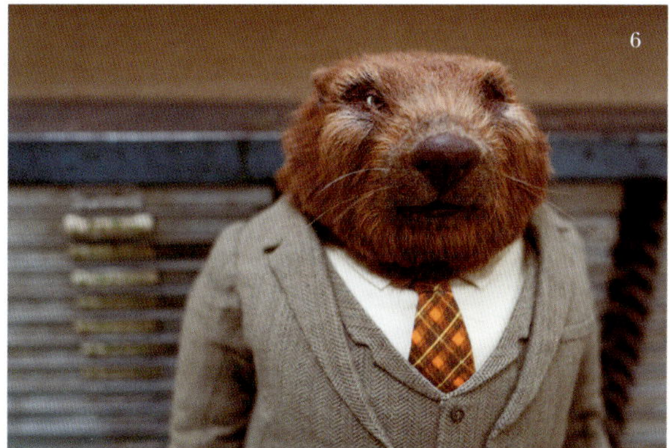

6

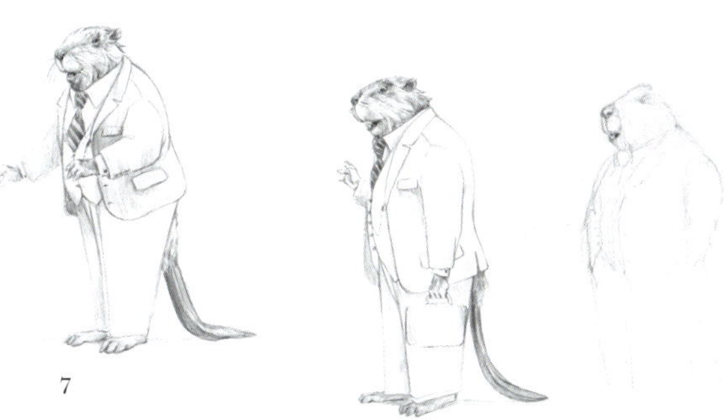

7

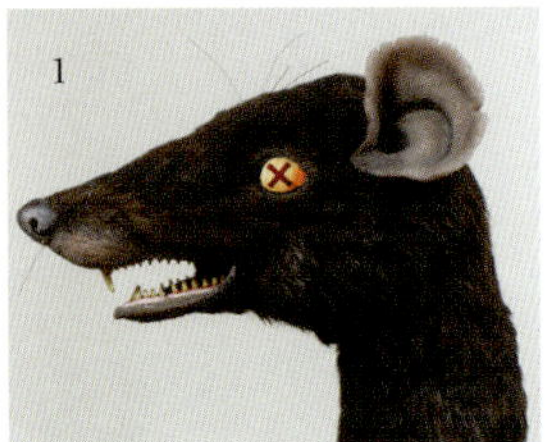

1

1. The final approved design for Rat's dead-eye look

2. The final approved design for Rat's sweater badge

3. Notes by Wes on Rat's costume

4. The final approved color design for Rat

5. A turnaround for Rat's costume

6. Notes by Wes on Rat's posture

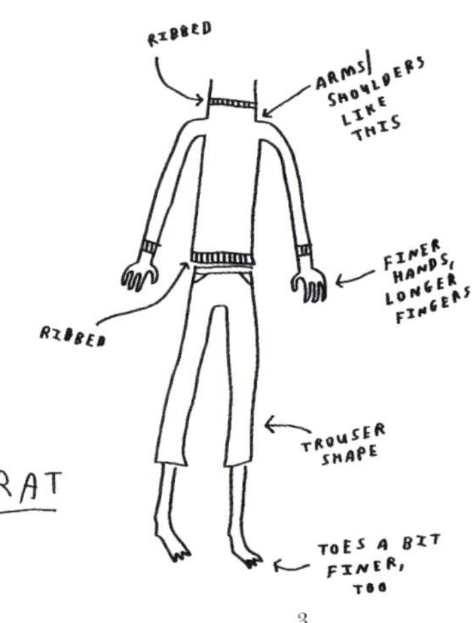

3

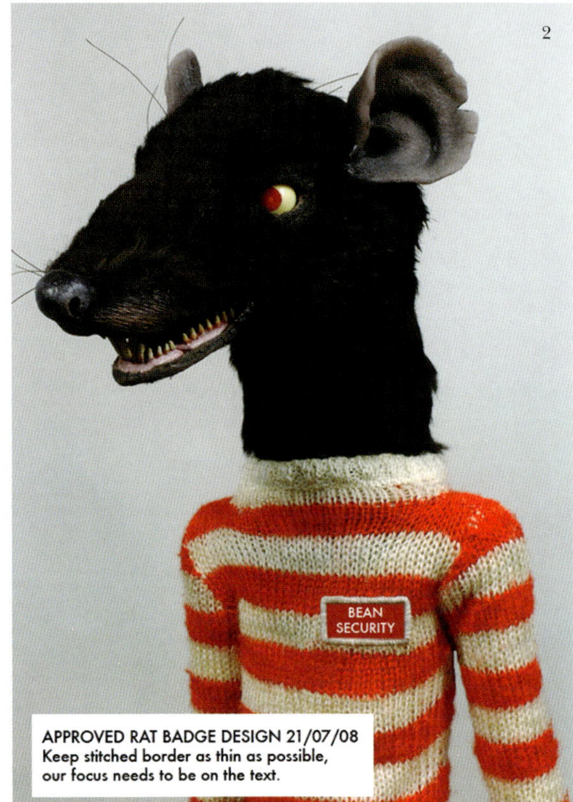

2

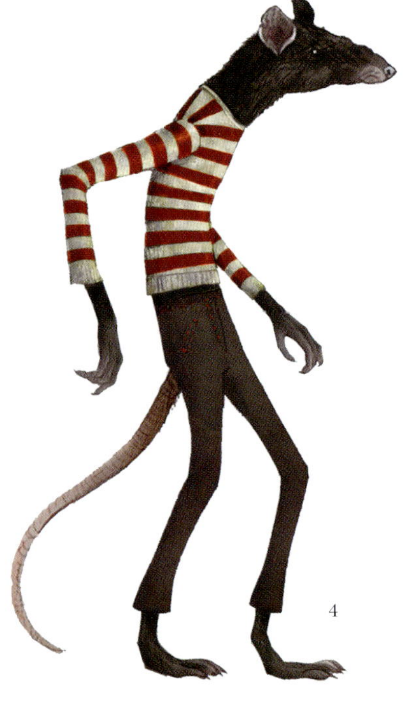

4

RAT

5

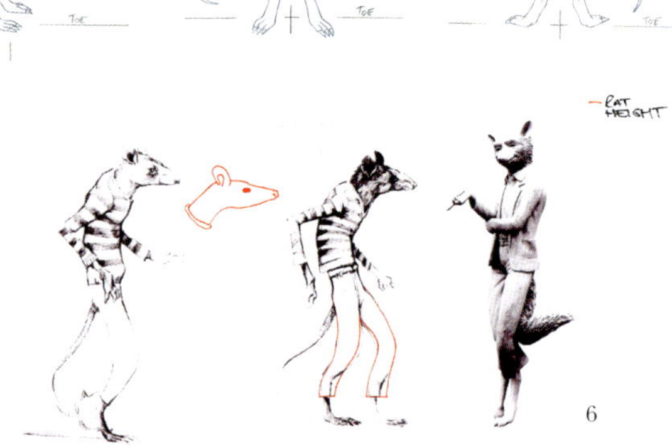

6

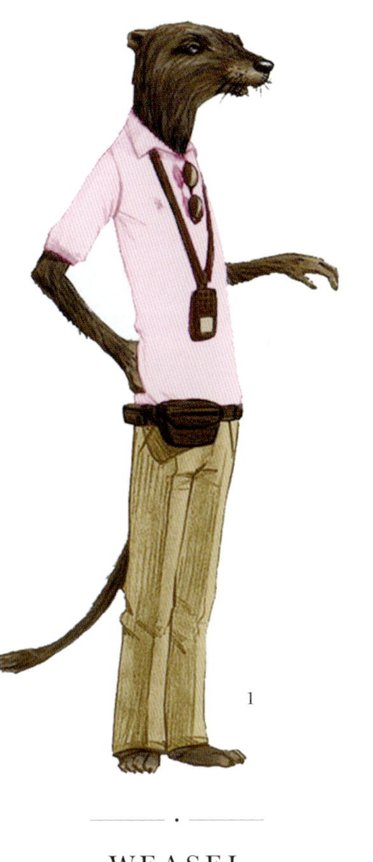

1

WEASEL

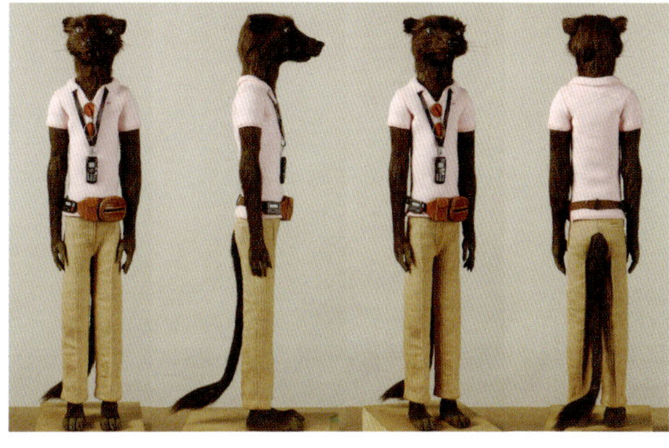

2

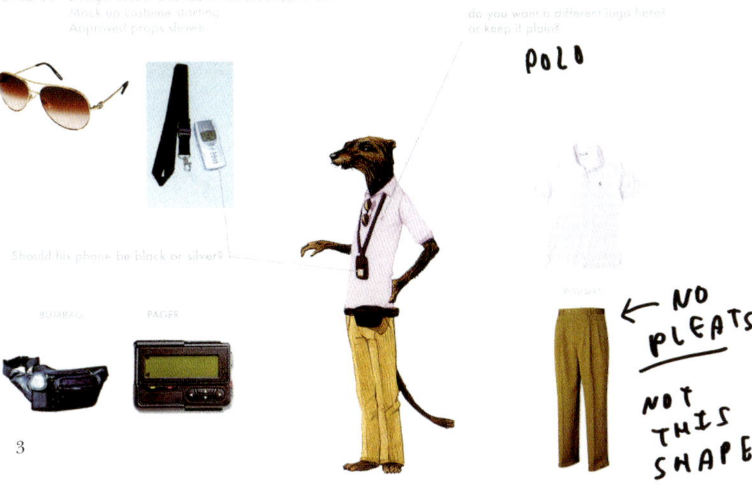

3

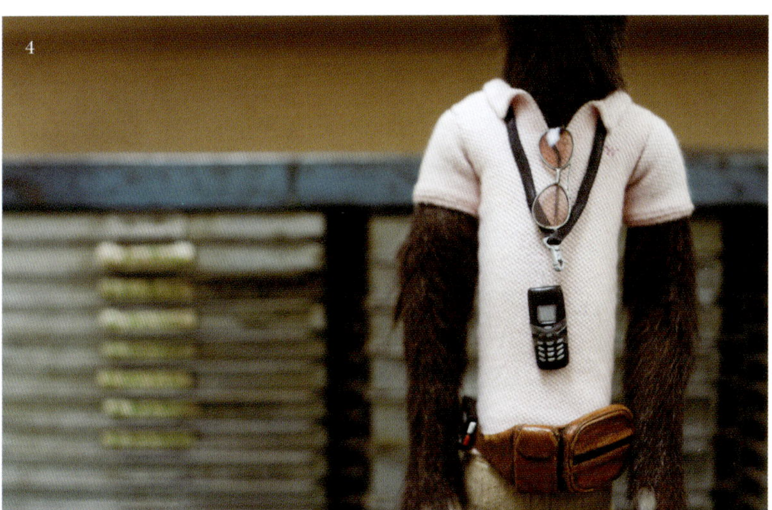

4

1. The final approved color design for Weasel

2. A full-scale Weasel puppet turnaround

3. The reference for Weasel's personal props and notes from Wes on Weasel's pants

4. The Weasel puppet in the puppet hospital

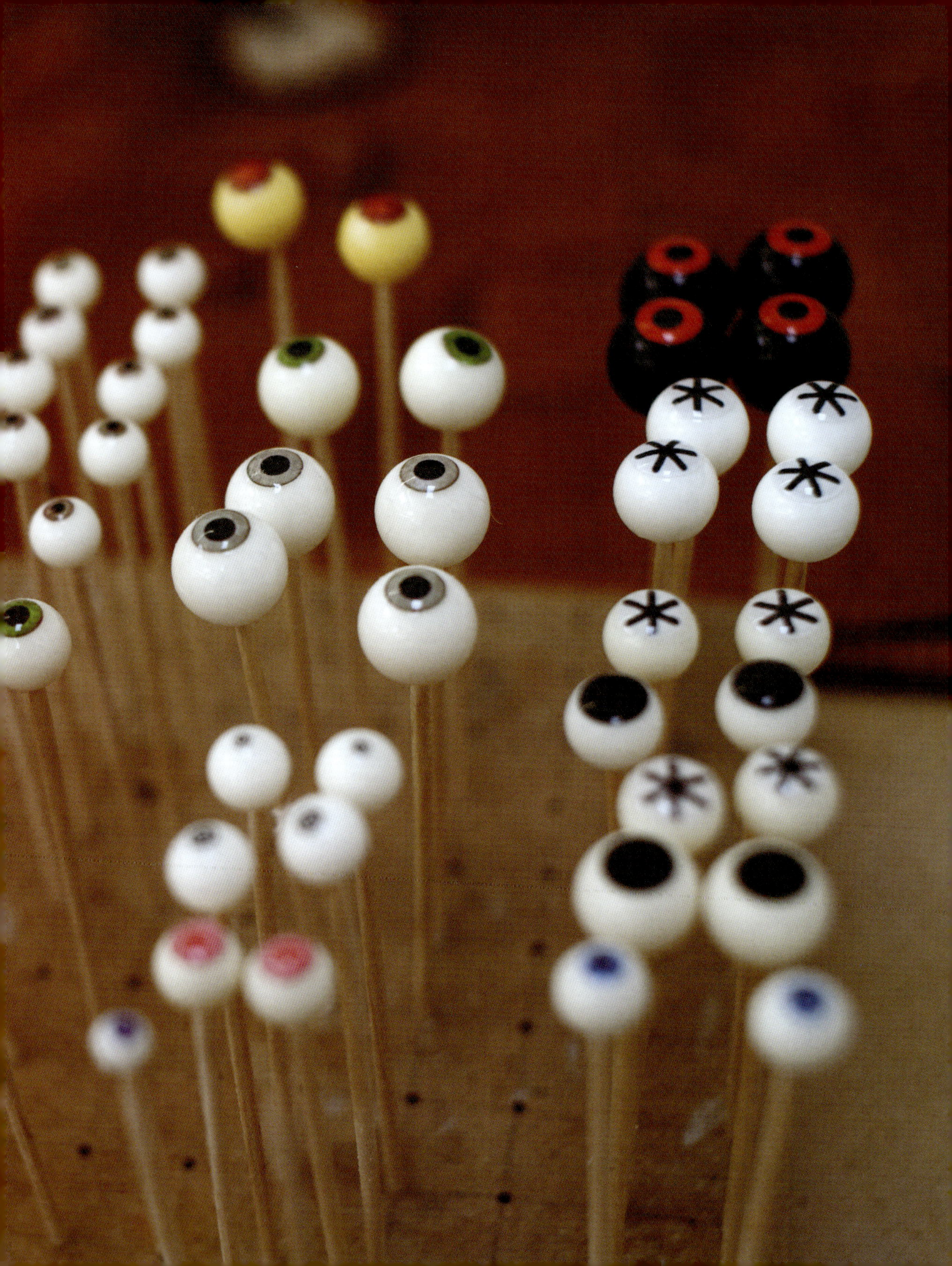

THE FARMERS

BOGGIS, BUNCE & BEAN

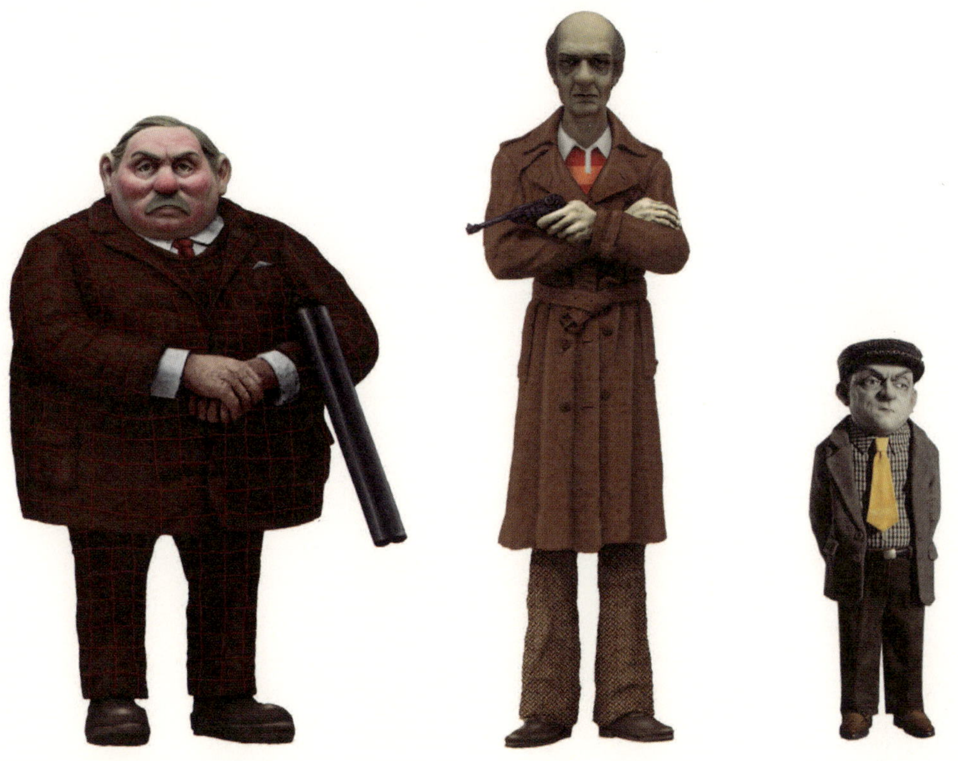

1. Boggis's head being painted in the puppet hospital

2. Boggis's hair being punched-in in the puppet hospital

3. A large-scale model made for a cut shot of an insect flying into Boggis's ear

4. Large-scale models of Boggis's feet made for a shot of his feet on scales

5. Art department notes on Boggis's costume

6. Boggis and Bunce in the puppet hospital

7. Boggis's shoes in progress

8. and 9. Fabric samples for Boggis's costume, with notes by Wes

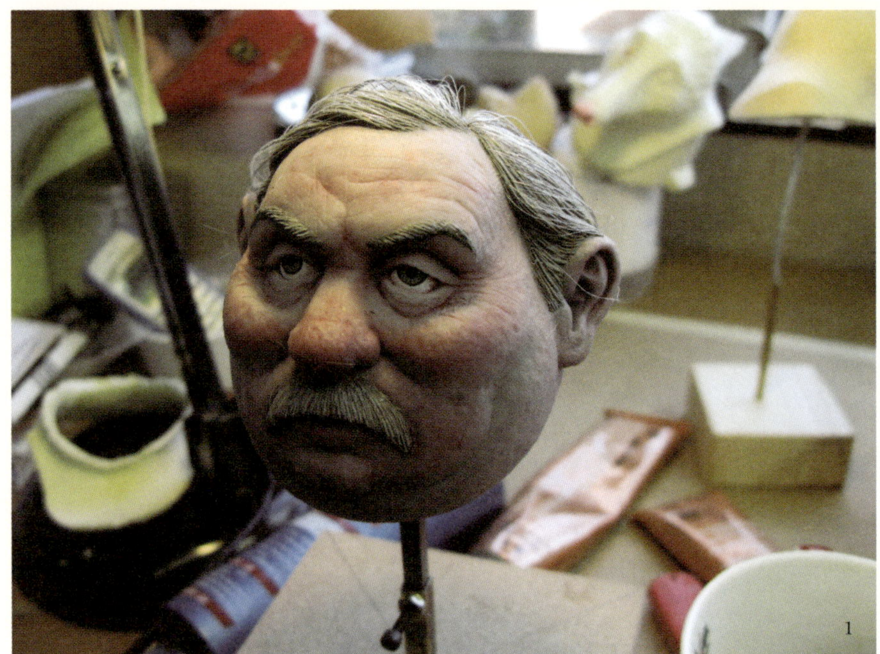

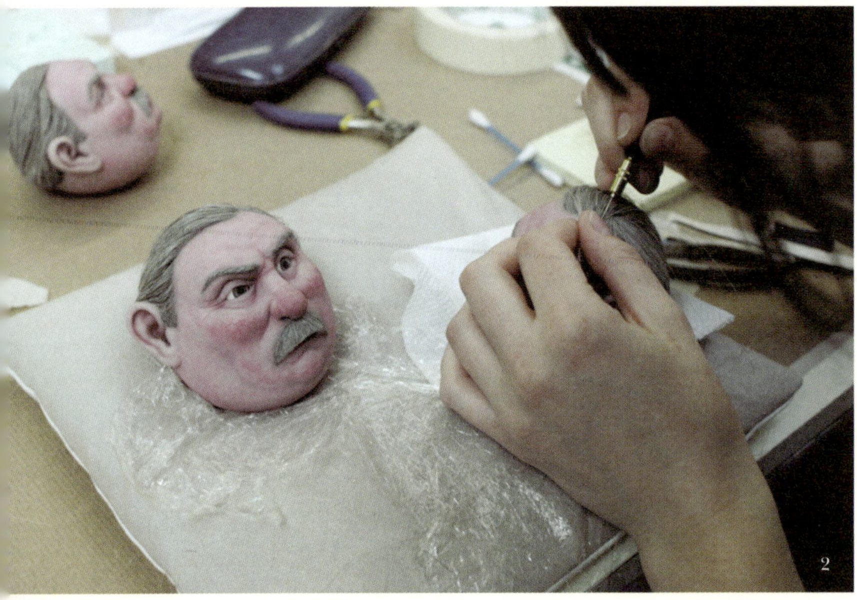

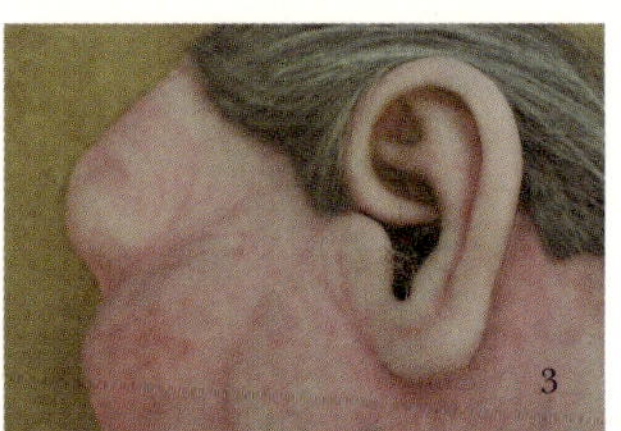

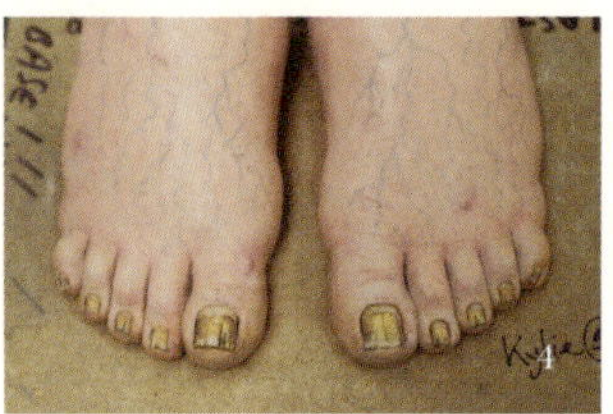

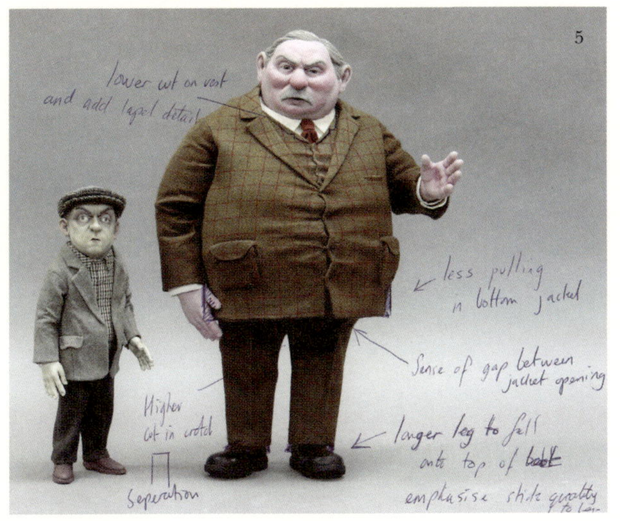

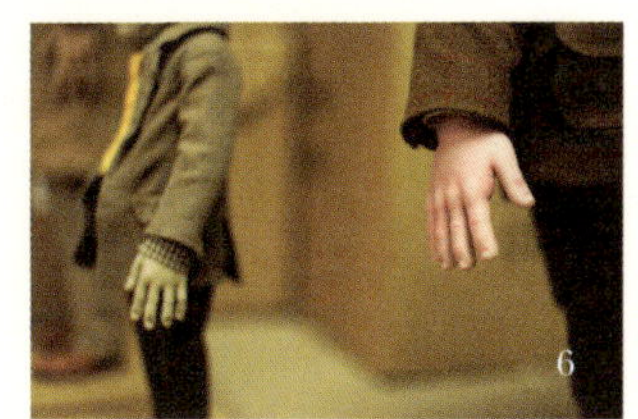

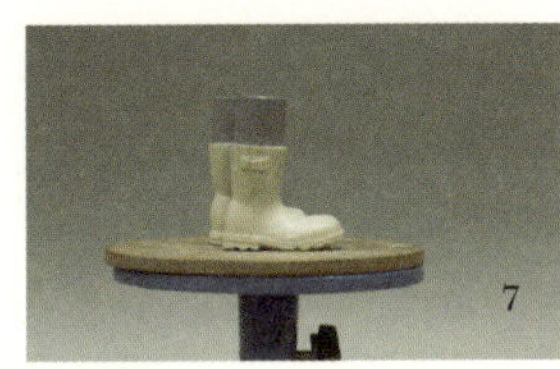

8 BOGGIS FABRIC SAMPLES

TIE Approved tie colour

Approved tie fabric

A B C D

JACKET A B C

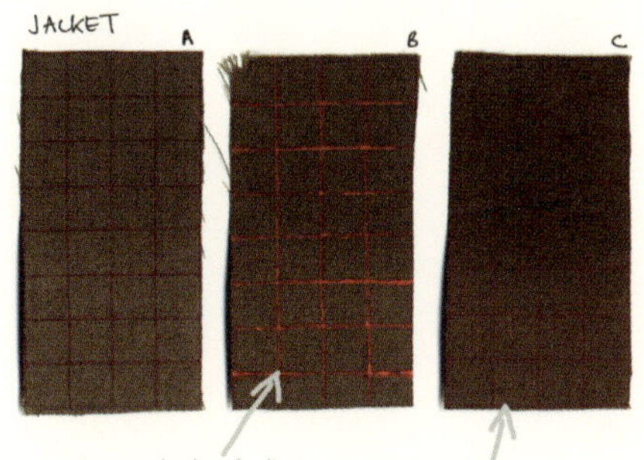

Approved colour for lines on suit

Approved suit fabric, but with finer lines on pattern

9 SCALE A HEIGHT : 384mm SCALE

NOT THESE

BODY/CLOTHING	PANTONE	
SKIN	691 U	
EYES		
VEINS	500 U	①
HAIR	10 U	
TROUSERS (BASE) PATTERN	464 U 174 U	②
JACKET (BASE) PATTERN	464 U 174 U	
SHIRT	7541 U	
TIE	200 U	
BOOTS	BLACK 6 U	

TIE

SHIRT

maybe knitted → let's see alt ties please

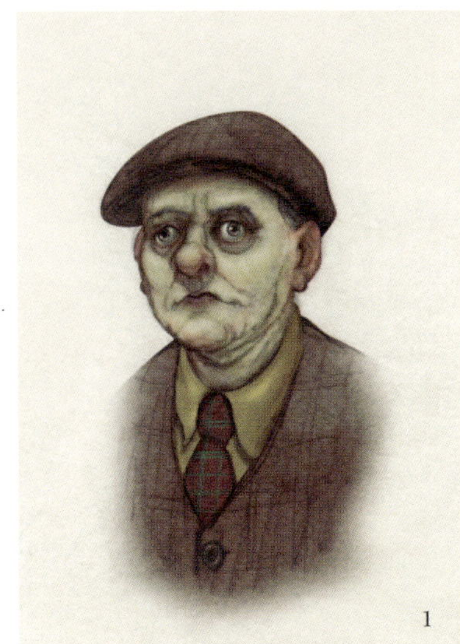

1

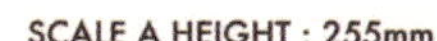

SCALE A HEIGHT : 255mm SCALE B HEIGHT : 106mm

BODY/CLOTHING	PANTONE	SWATCH
SKIN EYES HAIR	7500 U 462 U	① SLACKS
TROUSERS SHIRT JACKET TIE SHOES CAP GUN	431 U 1 U 7531 U 127 U 1817 U SHIRT → JACKET →	②
BU	← ①	② ?

SWIM SUIT ↑

4

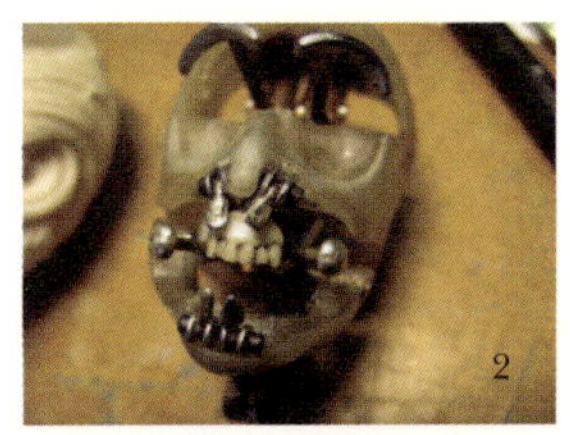

2

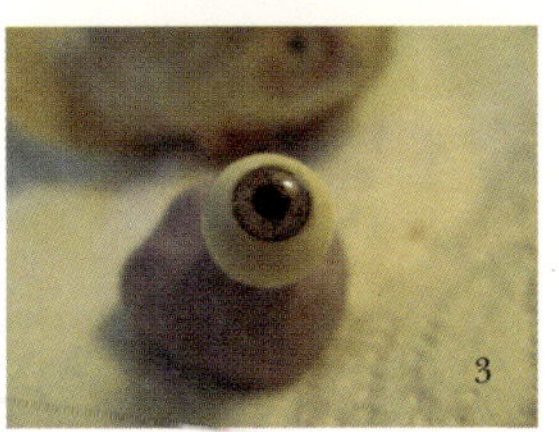

3

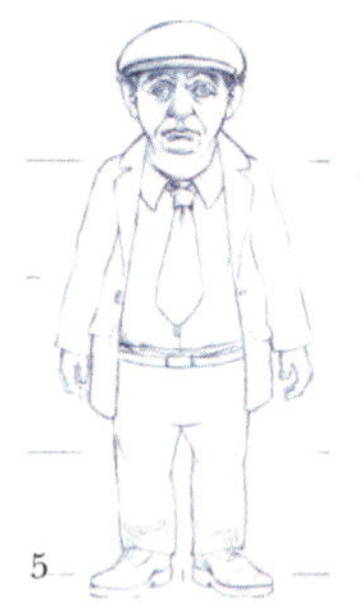

5

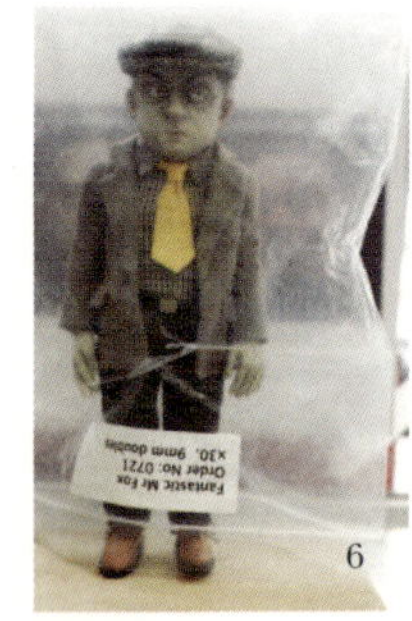

6

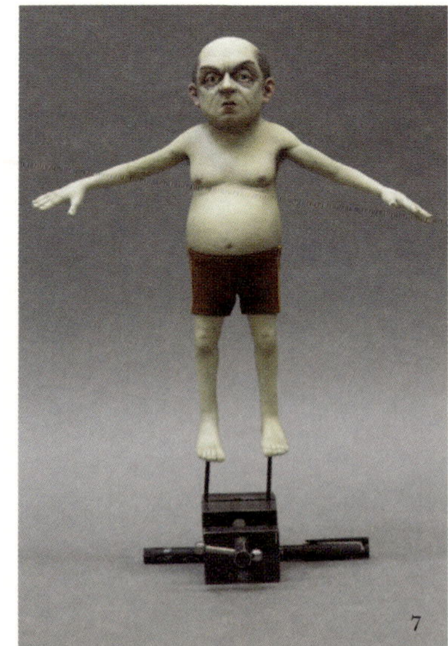

7

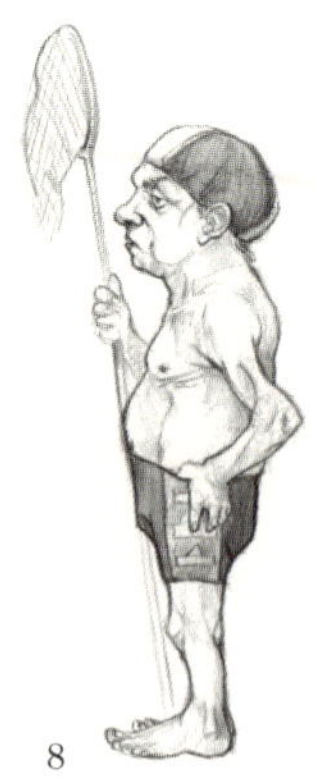

8

1. Early concept artwork for Bunce by Huy

2. Bunce's head mechanism

3. Bunce's eyeball

4. Selections by Wes for material for Bunce's costume

5. An early sketch of Bunce's costume

6. The Bunce puppet in its delivery case from Mackinnon & Saunders of Bristol

7. Bunce rigged for his swimming pool shot

8. Designs for Bunce's swimsuit by Félicie

9. An extra pair of Bunce's hands

10. The finished Bunce puppet in the puppet hospital

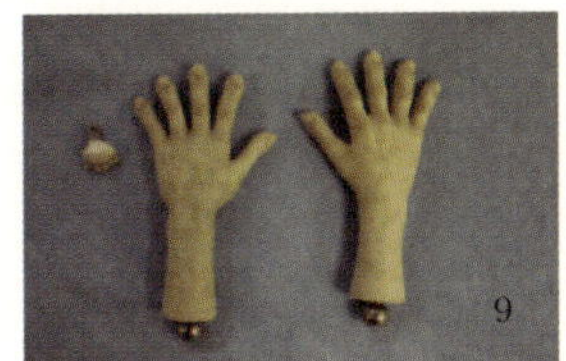

9

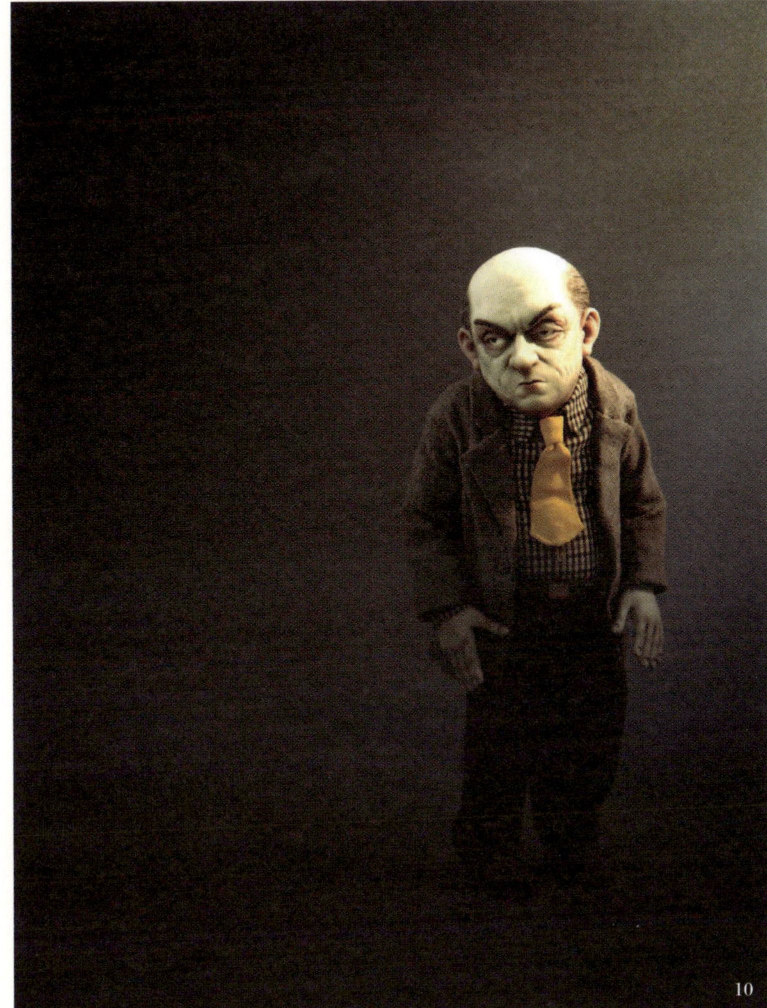

10

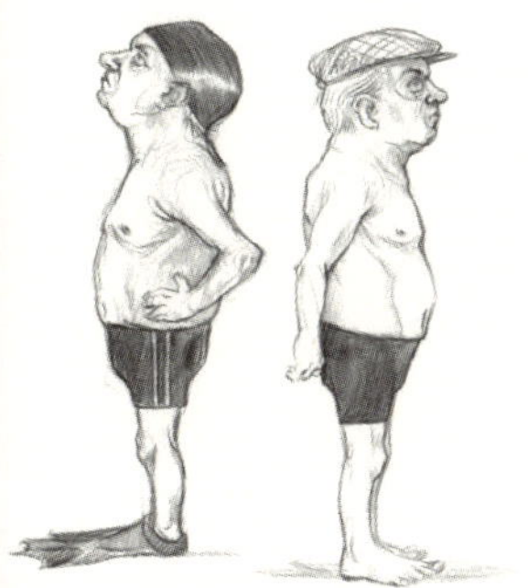

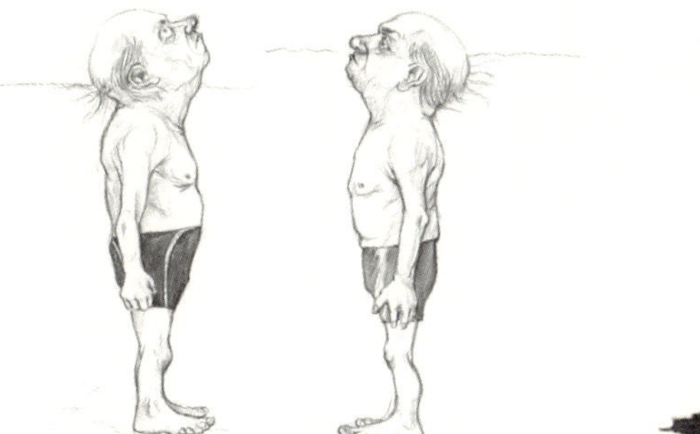

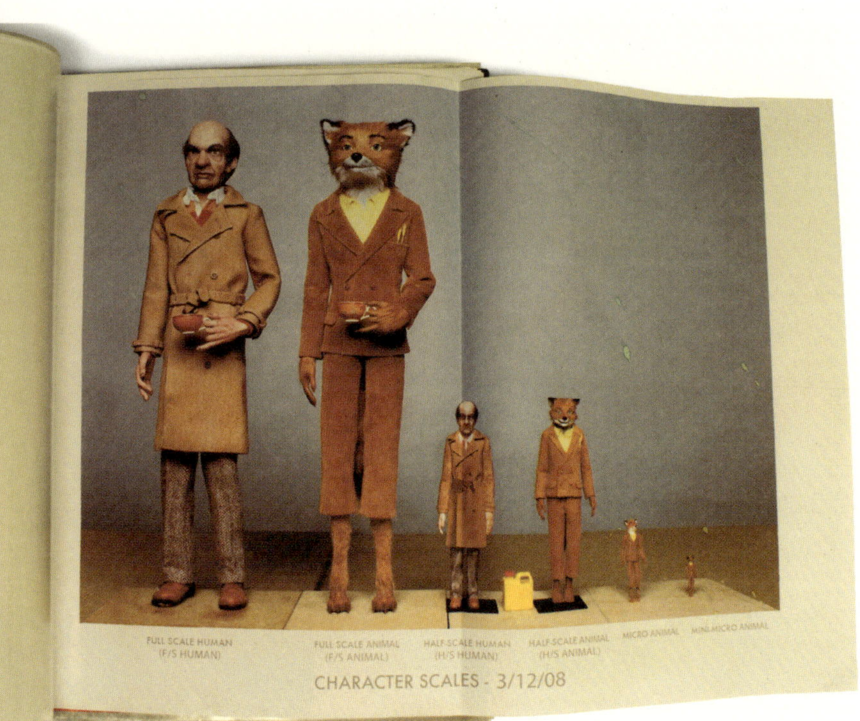

1

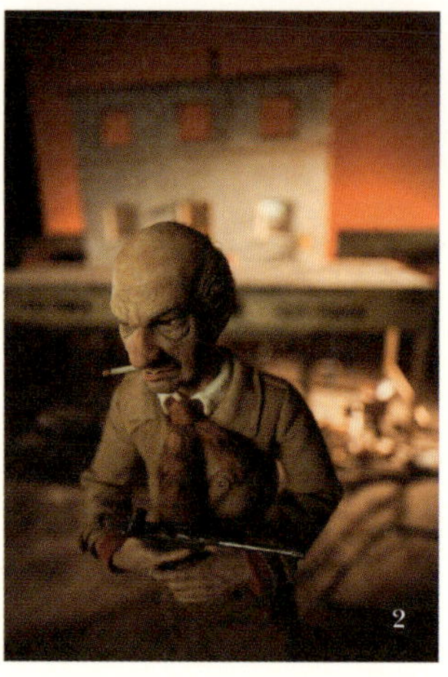

2

I LIKED THE FABRIC ON THE maquette coat— what was that one?

BALSA WOOD CORE
5mm HOLE IN CORE
12x5 WASHER
TS 3mm .050 ALLEN BOLT
TS 4mm 1/16 ALLEN BOLT
TS 3mm .050 ALLEN BOLT
TS 2mm SLOTTED SCREW
1/8+3/32 K&S
Ø 3/32
Ø 1/16
Ø 1/16
Ø 3/64
0.80 NUT
6.75x3.15 WASHER
19.5
6
24.5
21.5
3.5
JW 5mm DOUBLE 5/64 ALLEN BOLT
Note washer and rod set half way
7/32+3/16 K&S
KEEP NUT LONG FOR EASE OF ACCESS
2.56 NUT 5/64 ALLEN BOLT
JW 8mm DOUBLE 3/32 ALLEN BOLT
18
JW 6mm SINGLE 3/32 ALLEN BOLT
15
5
4.40 RIGGING POINT
45.5
Ø1/8
JW 5mm DOUBLE (FIXED) 5/64 ALLEN BOLT
Ø 3/32
5/32+1/8 K&S
46.5
JW 5mm DOUBLE (FIXED) 5/64 ALLEN BOLT
3/16 KEYSTEEL SHAPED TO FIT
0.80 0.80 RIGGING POINTS
TS 3mm .050 ALLEN BOLT
1.12mm PLATE
FOOT PLATE TEMPLATES

3

4

SCALE A HEIGHT : 468mm

SCALE B HEIGHT : 195mm

BODY/CLOTHING	PANTONE	SWATCH
SKIN	4685 U	
EYES		
HAIR	8 U	
TROUSERS	4685 U	
RUGBY SHIRT (COLLAR)	1 U 715 U 485 U	
TRENCHCOAT	7517 U	
	469 U	

maybe these are his trousers & maquette coat goes w/ the below?

JACKET

1

2

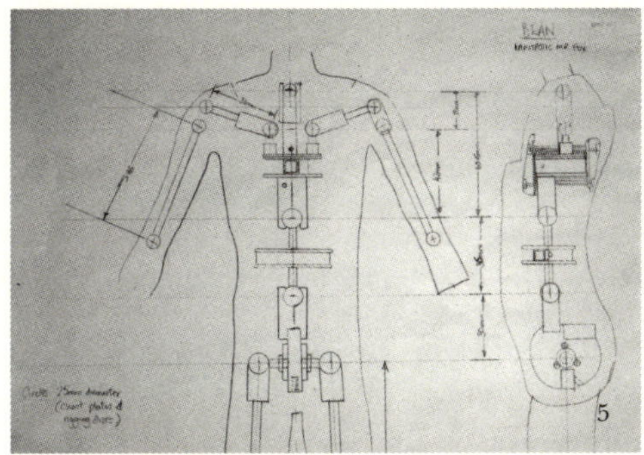
5

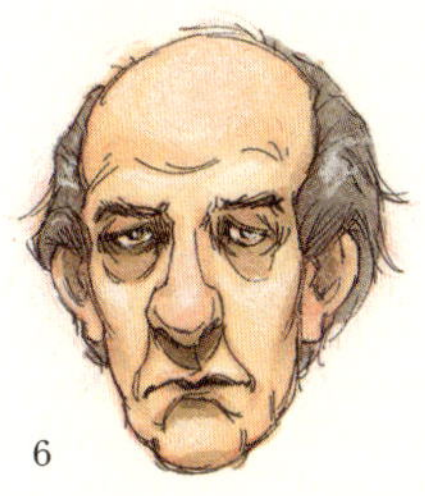
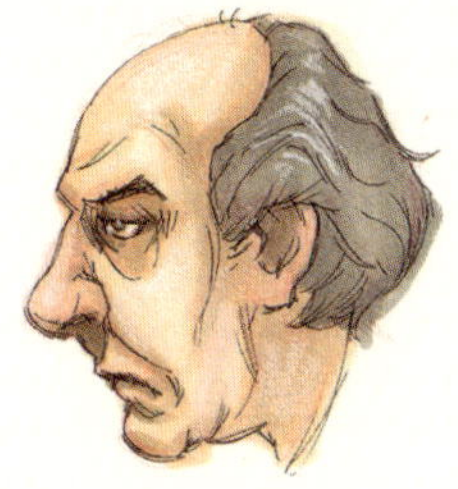
6

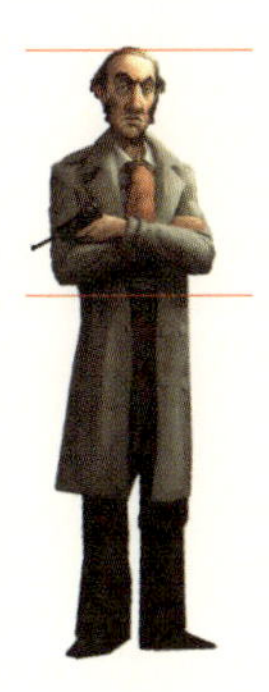
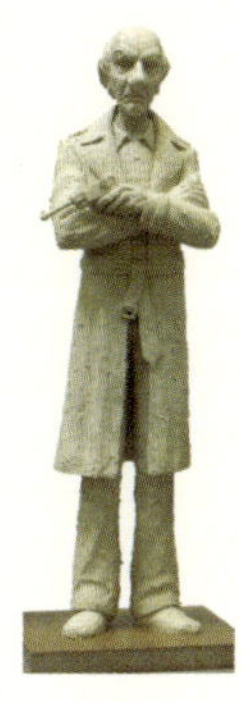
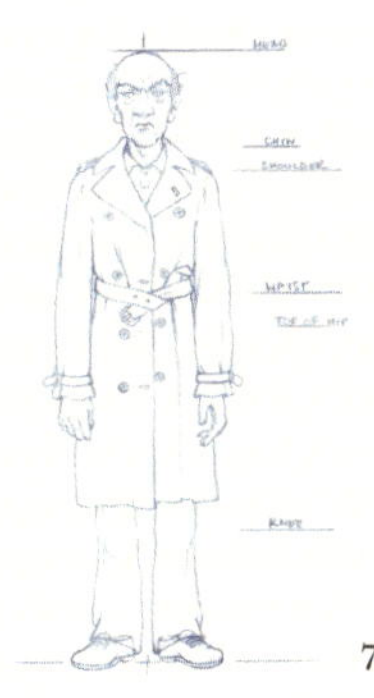
7

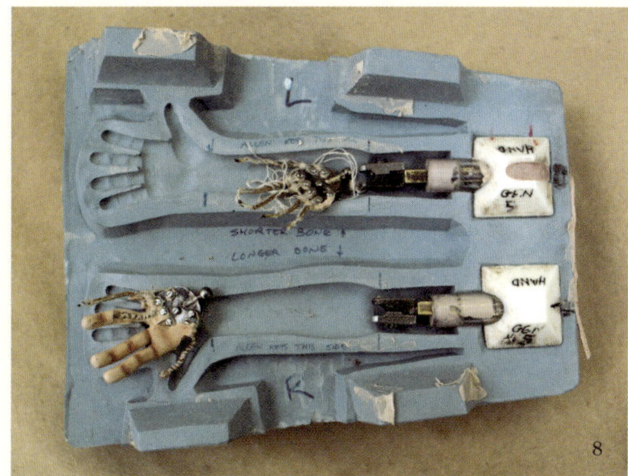

8

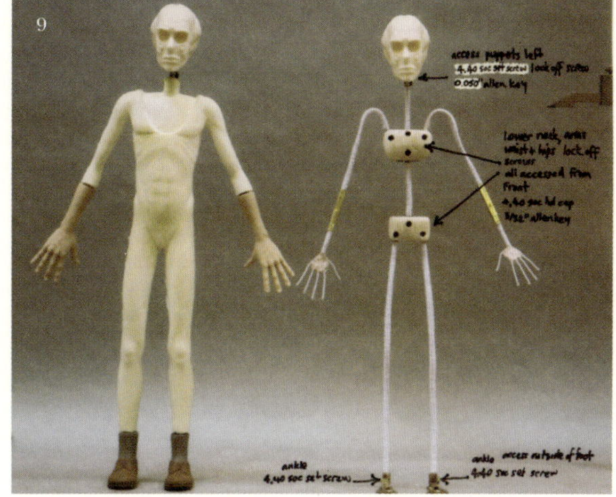

9

10
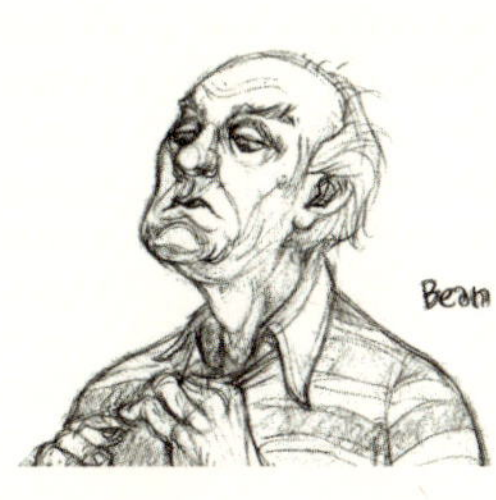

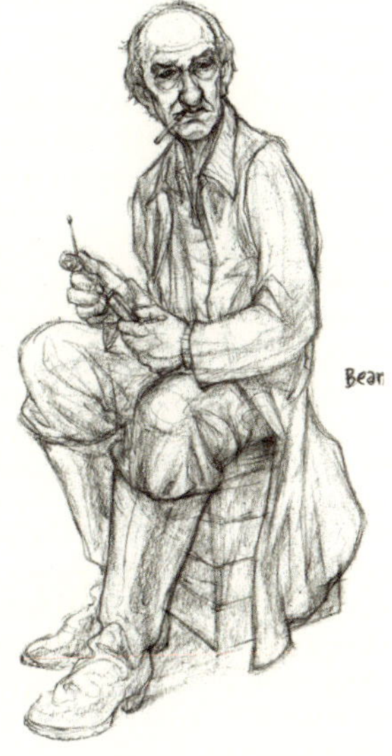

1. Scale comparisons between the Mr. Fox and Bean puppets

2. Bean on set in front of his house

3. Instructions for assembling the Bean armature from the puppet bible

4. Notes by Wes on fabric samples for Bean's costume

5. Instructions for fitting the Bean armature from the puppet bible

6. An early concept design for Bean by Huy

7. Concept designs and notes for Bean's costume

8. Molds for Bean's arm and hand

9. Instructions for assembling the Bean armature from the puppet bible

10. Early concept designs for Bean by Huy

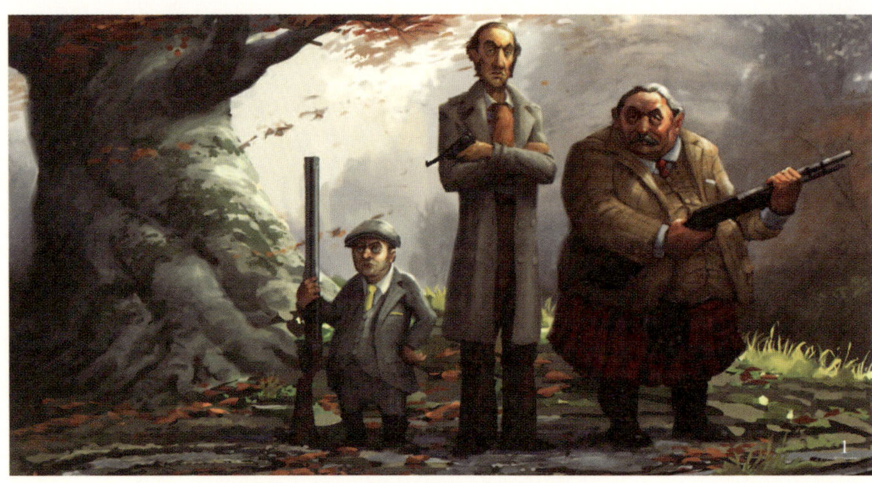

1. Early artwork for the three farmers by Ruben Hickman

2. The approved farmer sculptures

3. A comparison chart for the farmers' hands

4. The three farmers waiting outside the manhole in an unused shot from the movie

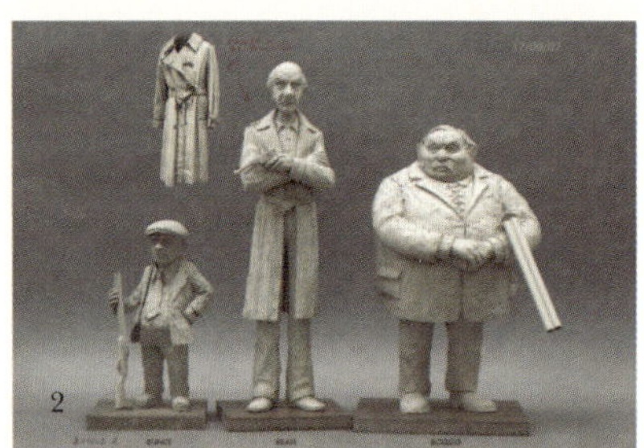

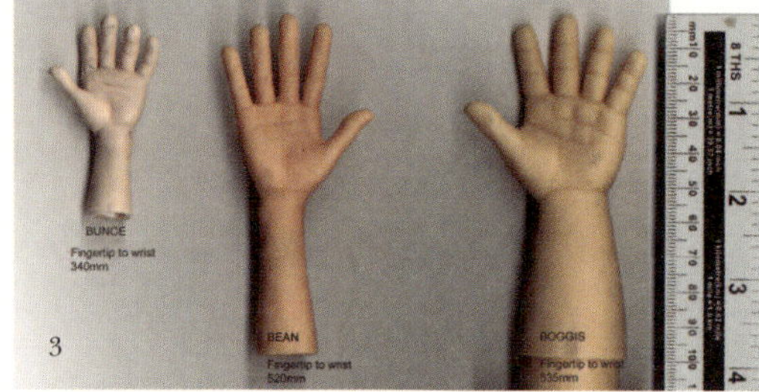

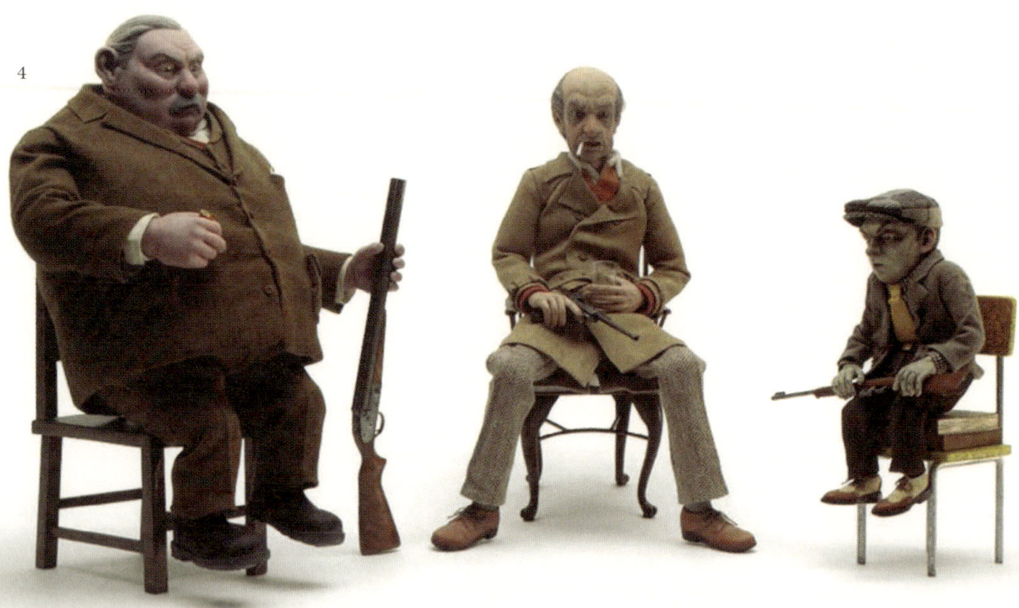

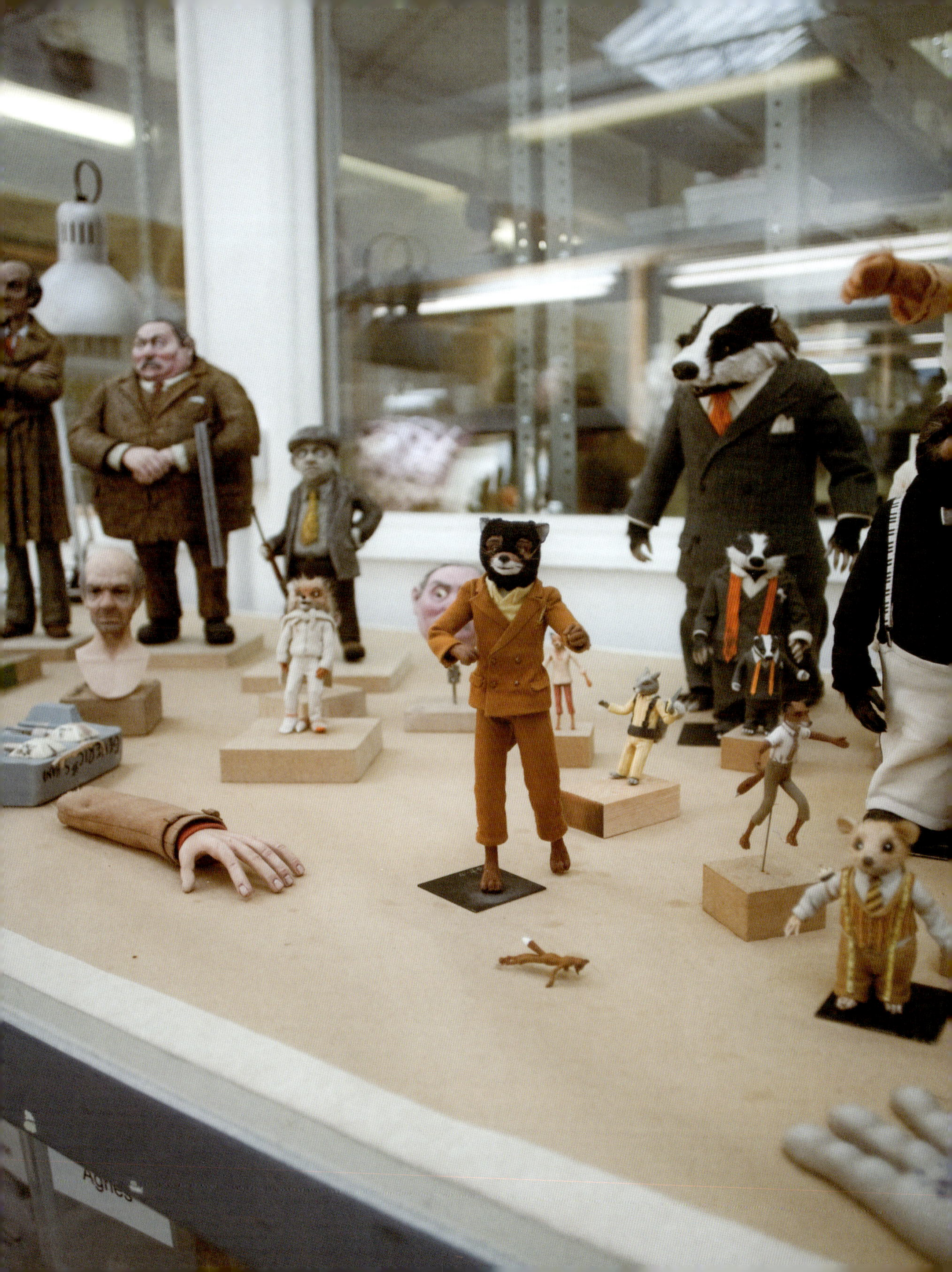
Agnes

of Mrs. Fox's paintings of landscapes in rainstorms. He says thoughtfully:

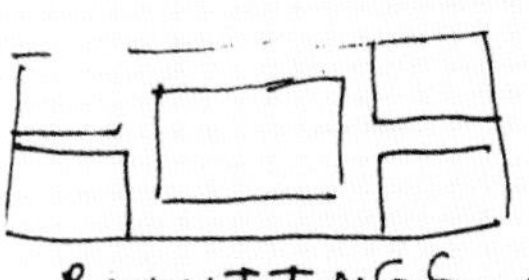

BEAN
She's got a good eye, but she's obviously very depressed.

BUNCE
These foxes dig like a bunch of hyperactive gophers.

BOGGIS
Franklin? You got another twist for this plot?

BEAN
(still staring at the paintings)
Say that again?

BOGGIS
I say you got another --

Bean whips out his walkie-talkie and twirls it like a six-shooter. He presses a button on it and says:

BEAN
Petey? Get me the current contact info for Earl Malloy on the A.S.A.P.

BUNCE
(intrigued)
Who's Earl Malloy?

CUT TO:

Three yellow and black, murderous, brutal bulldozer digging-tractors with Malloy Consolidated painted on the sides of them. They make a terrible, high-pitched growling noise and spit black grease and smoke.

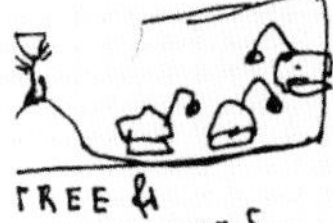

Boggis, Bunce, and Bean stand among the tractors nodding giddily to each other. They scramble into the drivers' seats and begin ripping into the hillside. Bunce sits on a dictionary to see over the dashboard.

INT. HOLE. DAY

Fox, Kylie, and Mrs. Fox sleep in the darkness. Kristofferson practices his tae-kwon-do in the air pocket behind the mineral deposit. Ash watches him through the crack in the bedrock. He says ominously:

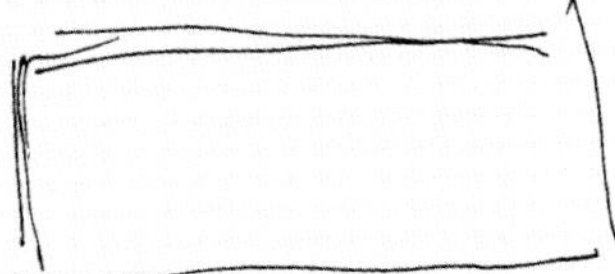

VII

THE TERRIBLE TRACTORS

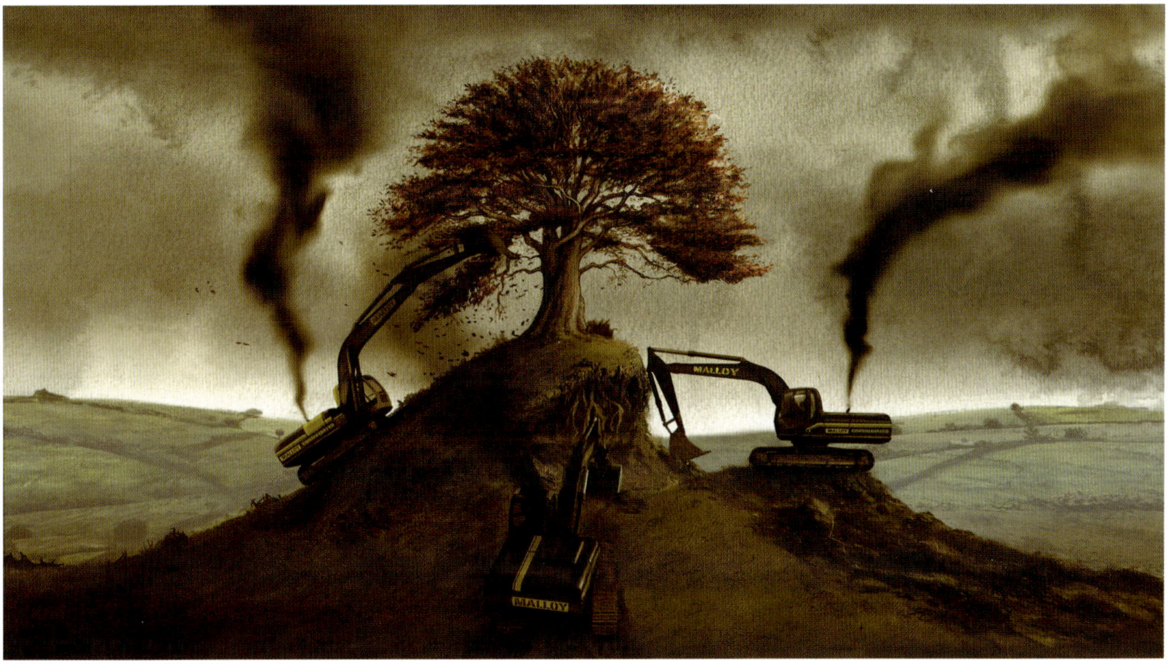

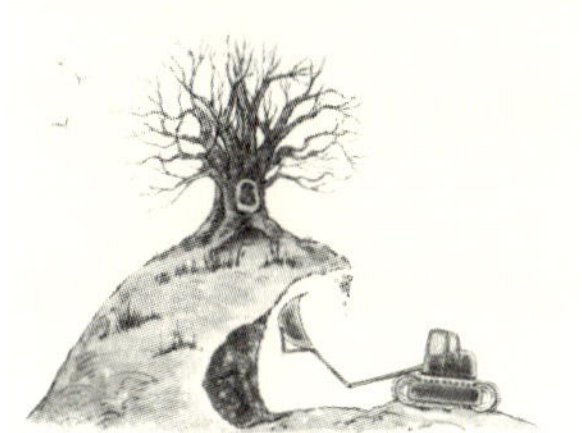

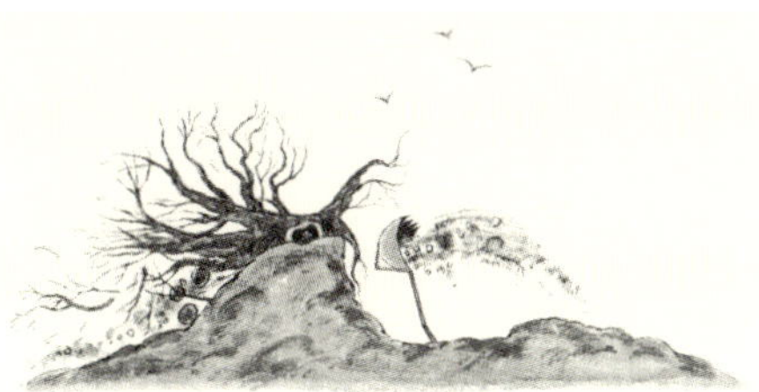

Above: Concept artwork for the farmers digging out the hill by Nelson Lowry

Left: Donald Chaffin's illustrations for the hill digging

Right: Thumbnail sketches by Wes of the hill digging

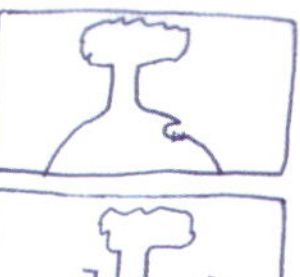

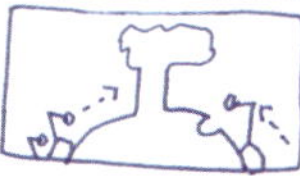

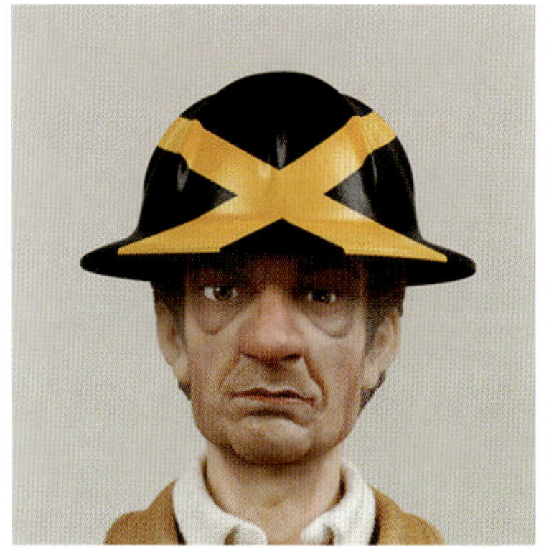

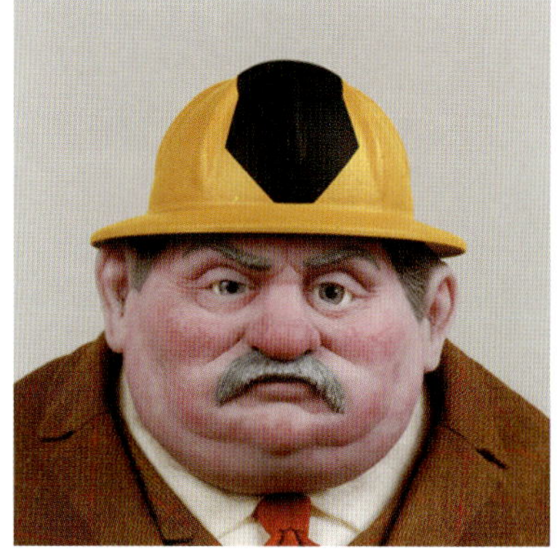

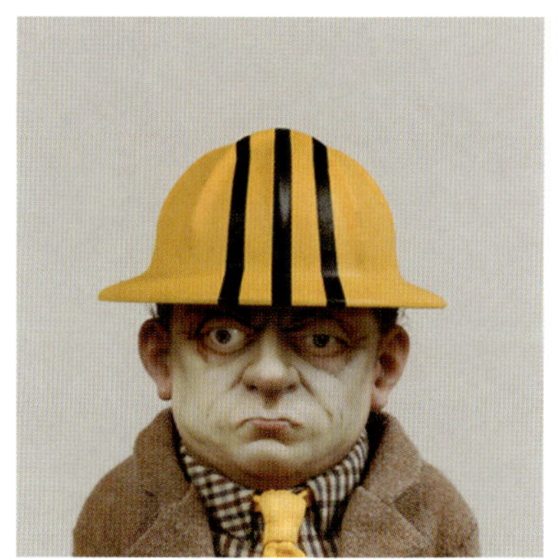

Above: The approved farmer helmets

Right: A sketch by Wes for the shot of diggers approaching the hill, and the actual still from the film

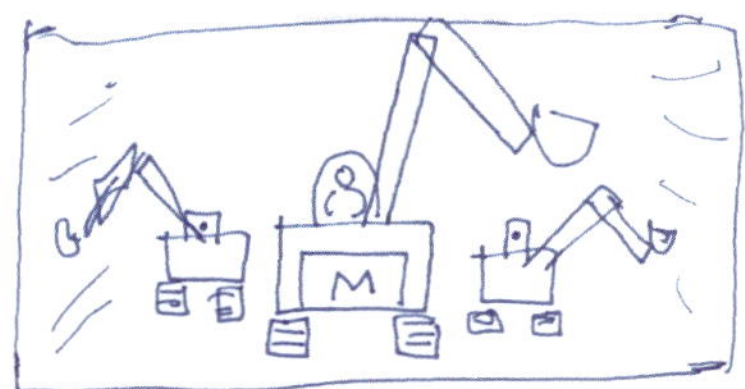

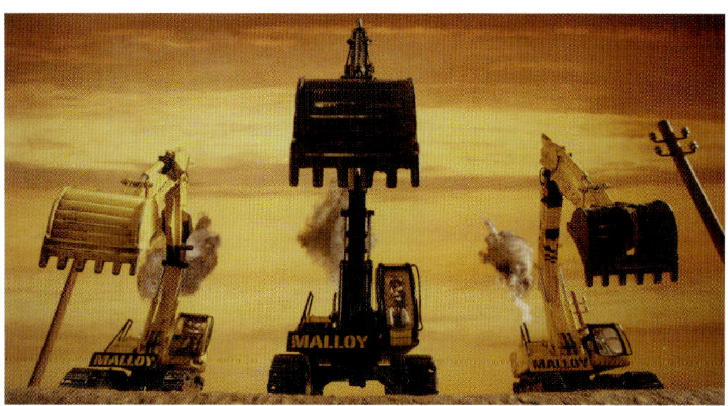

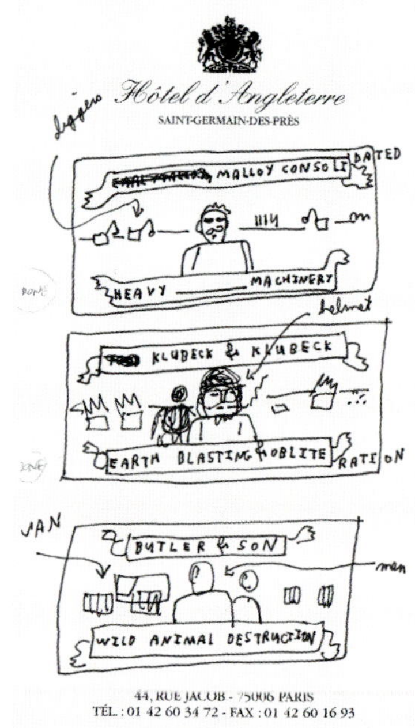

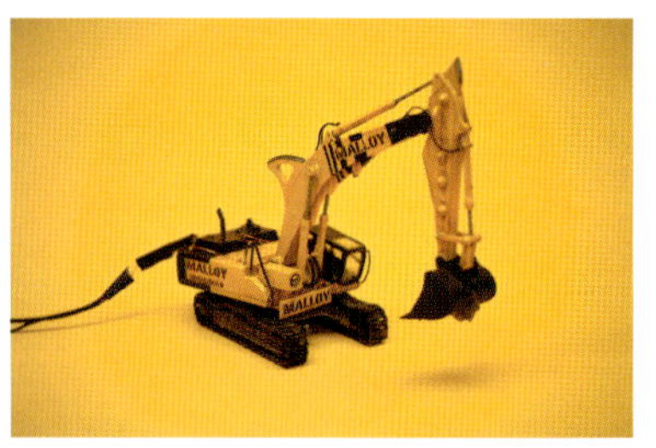

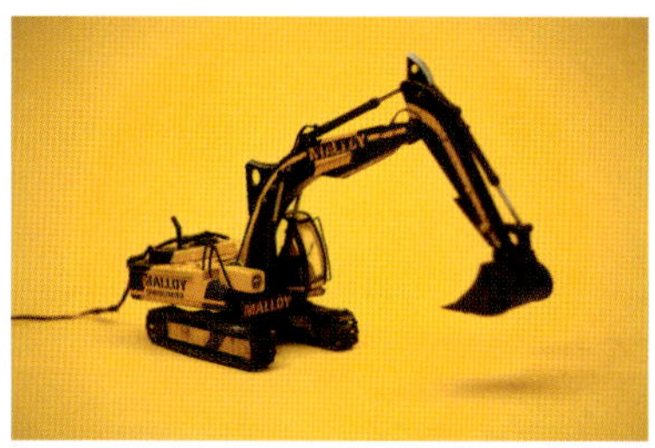

Above: Sketches by Wes for the introductory shots of Malloy, Klubeck, and Butler (a character that was cut from the movie)

Left: The diggers used in the movie, made from a set of toys made by JCB

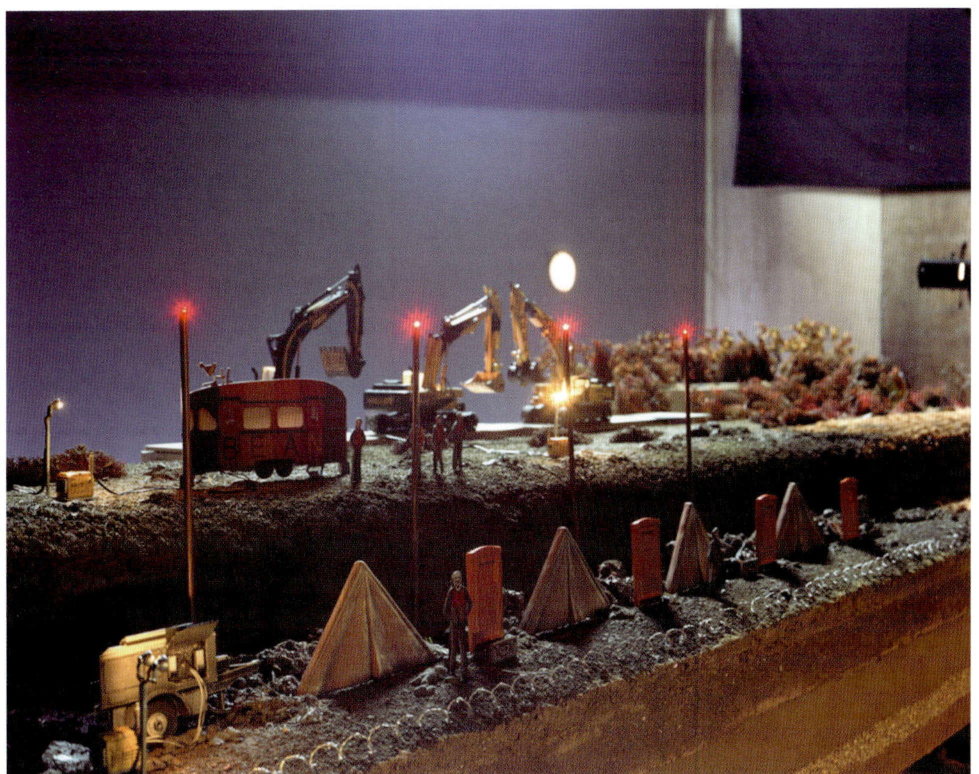

Left: A photograph of the miniature-scale set of the farmers' camp

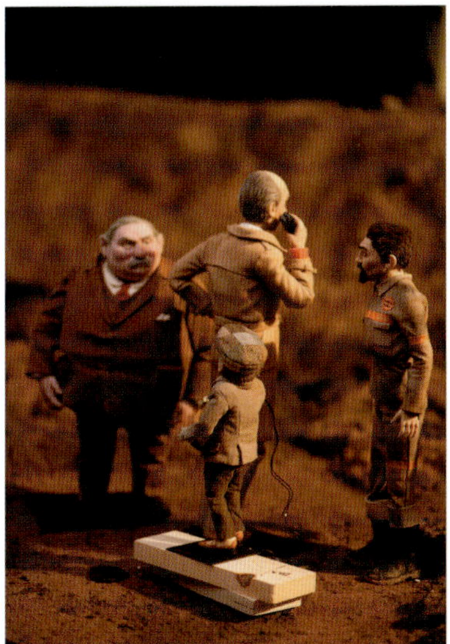

Above: A still of the farmers and Klubeck in the demolished hill

From: Wes Anderson
Subject: **Re: Digger hill - Klubeck runs over**
Date: 18 December 2008 19:01:43 GMT
To: Molly Cooper

How big does Klubeck get as he runs toward us before he disappears and re-appears? I wonder if this needs a double-stage approach for forced perspective—he could disappear and reappear twice and we use 3 scales?

I would make the text bigger on the dynamite KLUBECK NITRO-PLUS no.2

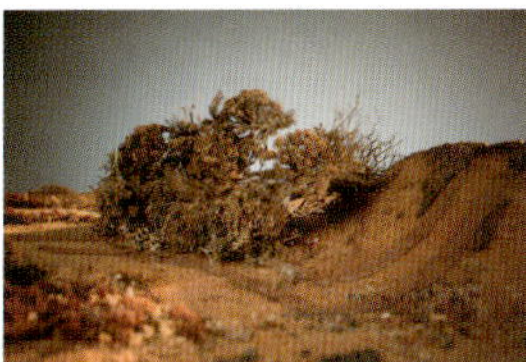

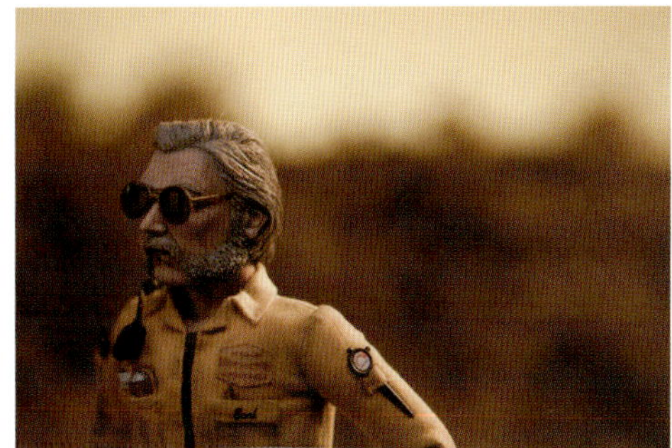

Right: The demolished hill set and Malloy in the demolished hill

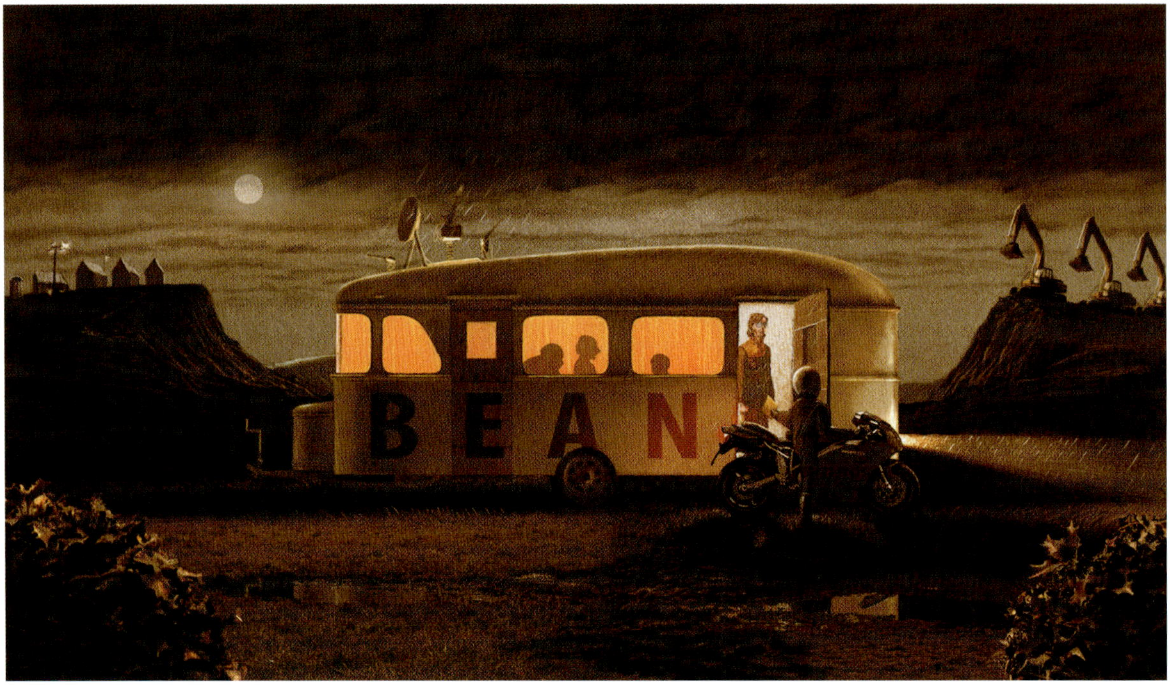

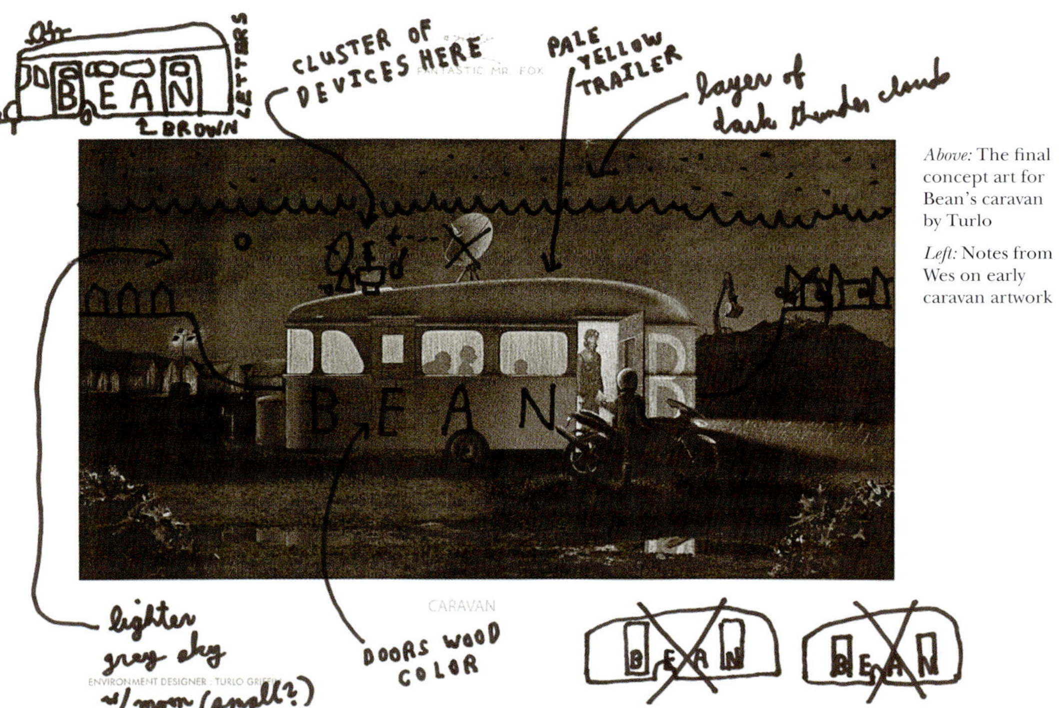

Above: The final concept art for Bean's caravan by Turlo

Left: Notes from Wes on early caravan artwork

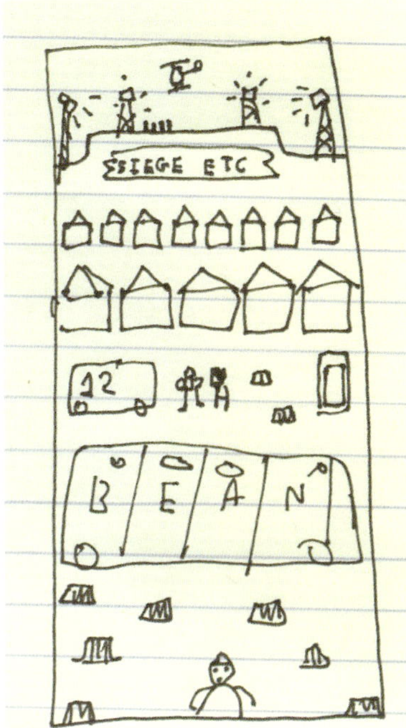

Above: A sketch by Wes for the long vertical shot of the farmers' camp

Right: The final shot from the movie

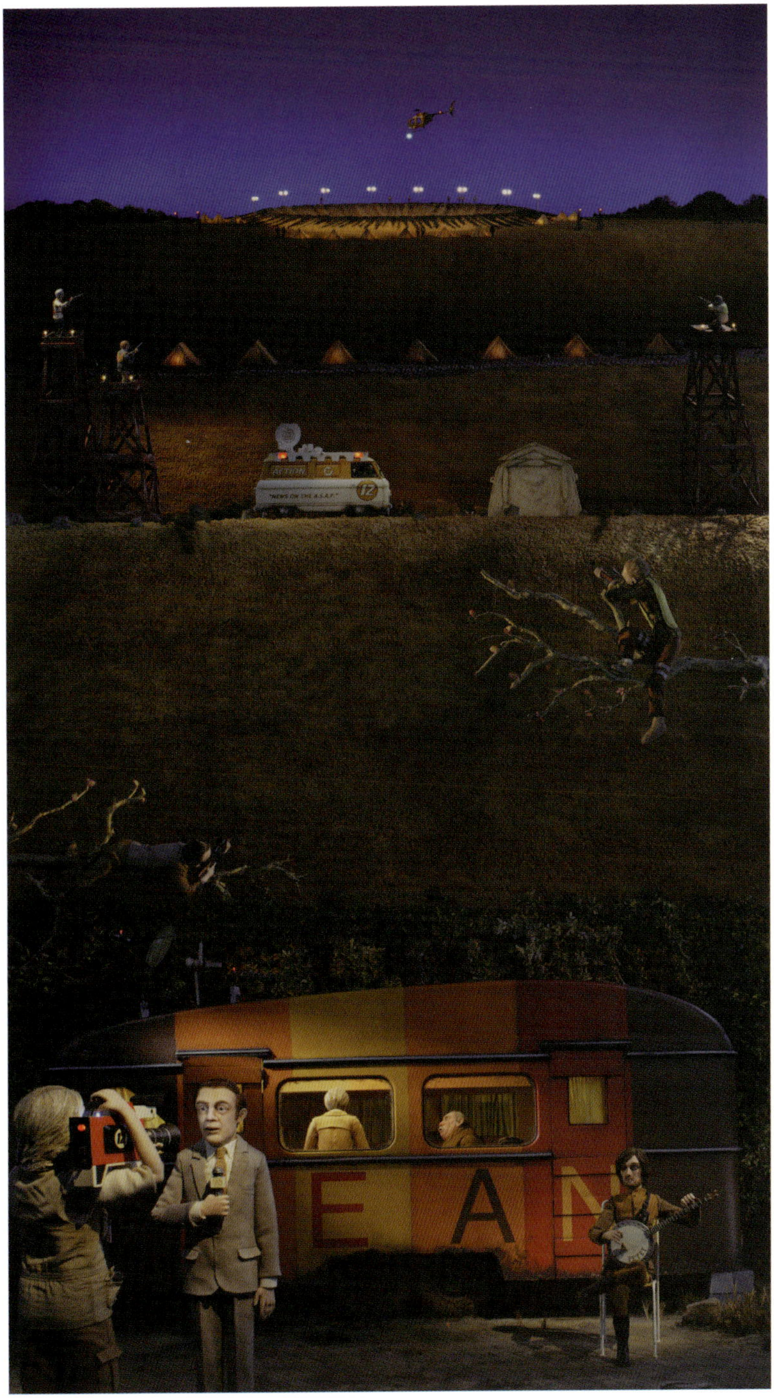

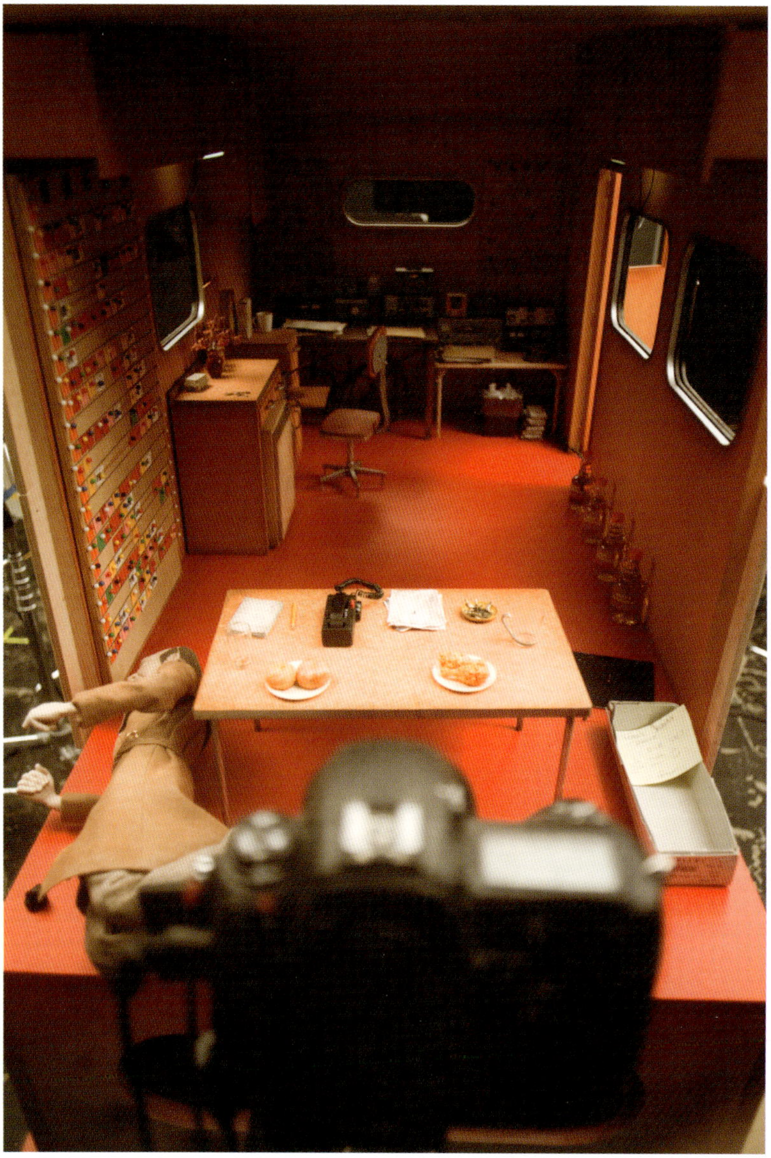

From: Wes Anderson
Subject: **Re: Caravan boards for new shot**
Date: 28 January 2009 11:34:47 GMT
To: Chris DeVita

Actually for the end of Bean's flip out one adjustment: rather than the moment I described with the cup etc instead—

Bean can smash all the books etc off the shelves and then lunges across the room toward the door (let's say side of frame)

Then we cut to exterior of caravan. Let's say the caravan is filling 3/4 of the left part of the frame
On far right of frame is just that little part of the cider still
On closer right part in front of caravan is Petey repairing an upside down bicycle using a wrench. He has other tools on ground
On left of frame is a large trashcan next to the door and 2 farmhands with sandwiches watching nervously

Bean bursts open the door turns and kicks the trashcan out of the frame as the farmhands duck out of the way and quickly exit left
Then bean grabs the bicycle and throws it towards the camera—it goes out top of frame and smashes back down through frame and out in FG then he grabs Petey's wrench out of his hand and darts past Petey toward the cider still
He raises the wrench up into the air to smash it
Boggis and Bunce appear in the doorway

We cut to close-up of Bean on LEFT side of camera—Boggis and Bunce and Petey enter in BG smaller on right.
Bean says "I've got an idea."

Above: A photograph of the interior of Bean's caravan in its original form

Right: Photographs of the caravan interior while Bean pulls it apart

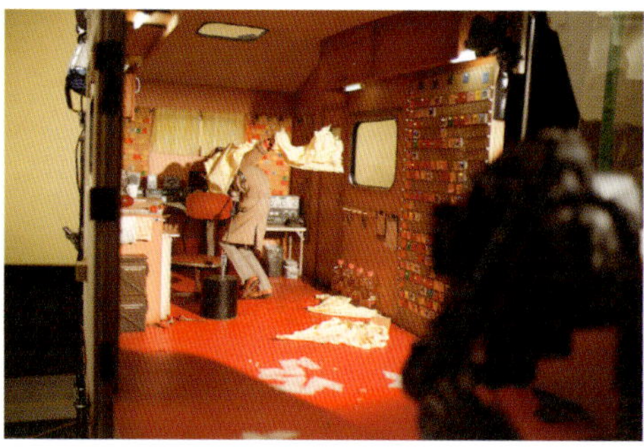

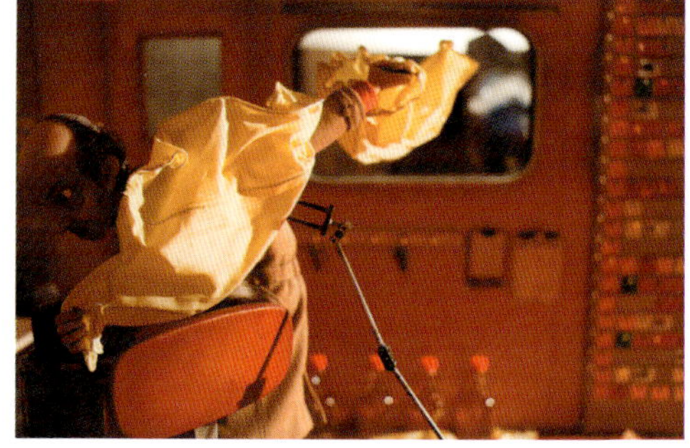

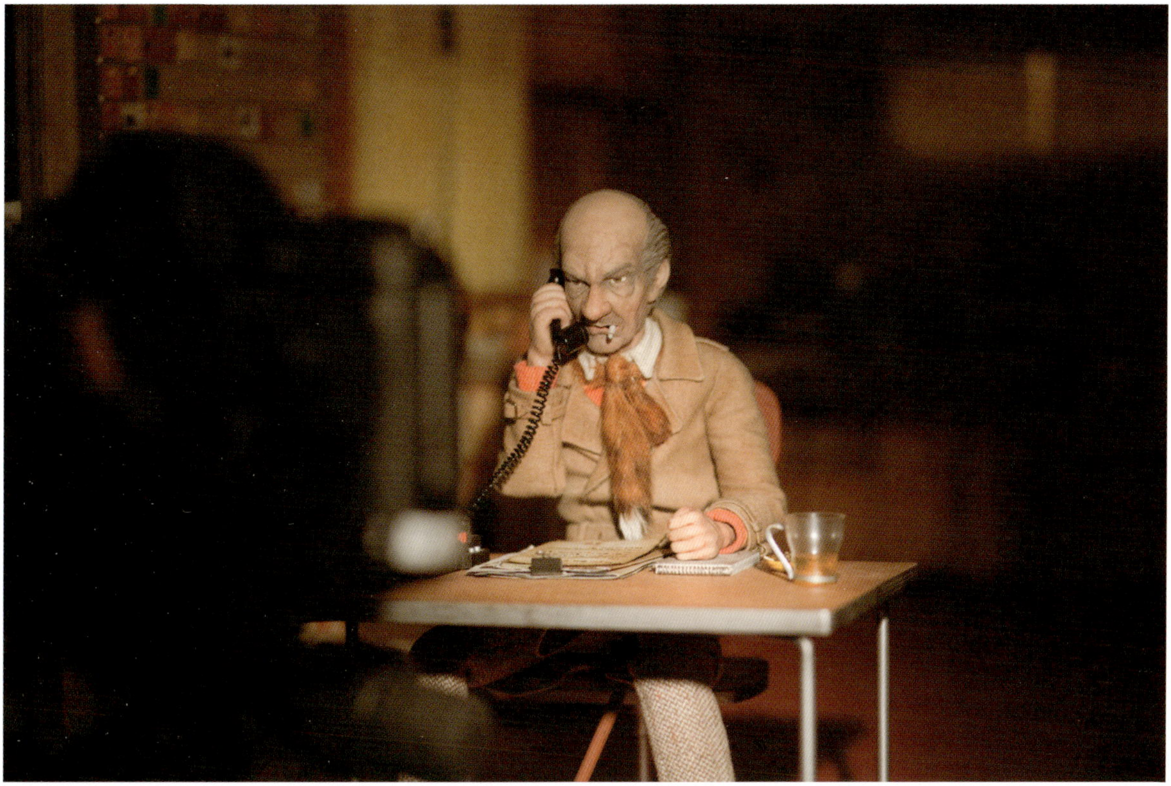

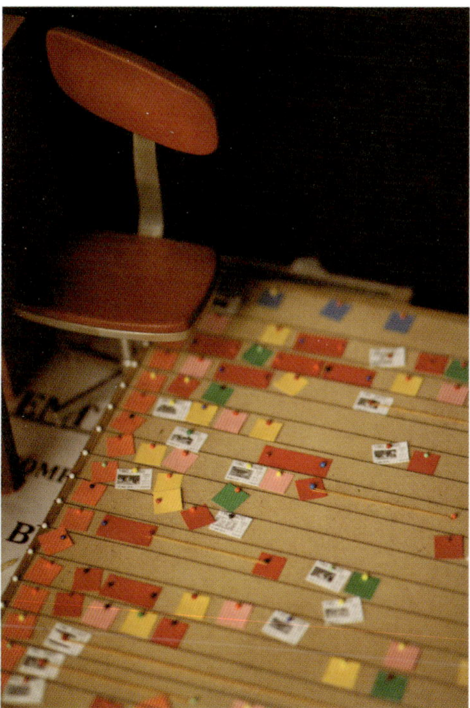

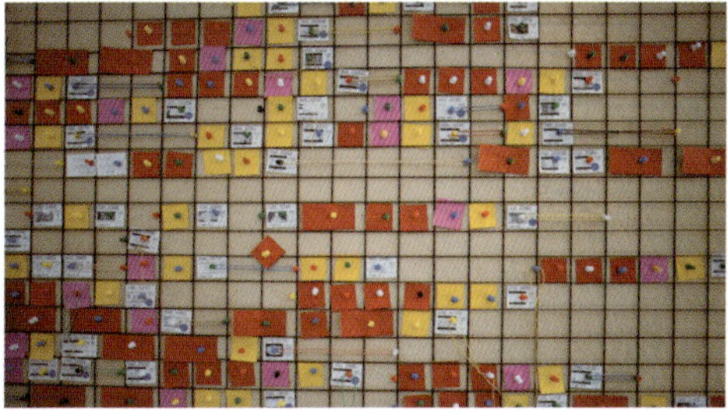

Top: A photograph of Bean at his desk in the caravan

Above: Scheduling boards for the film, used as a reference for the boards in Bean's caravan

Left: Set dressing from the interior of Bean's caravan

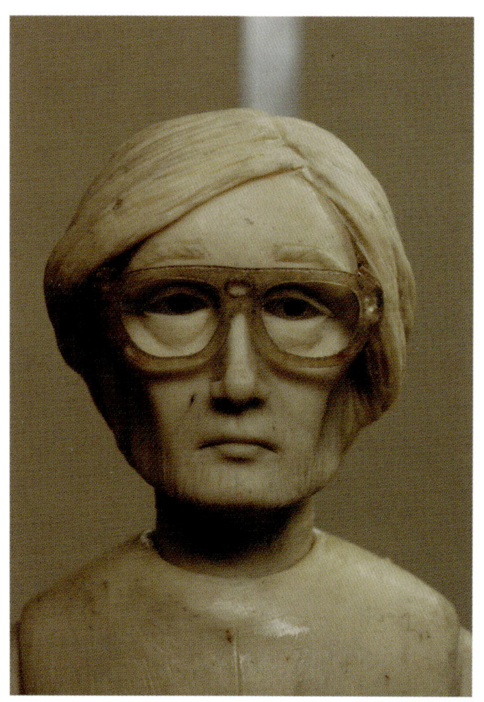

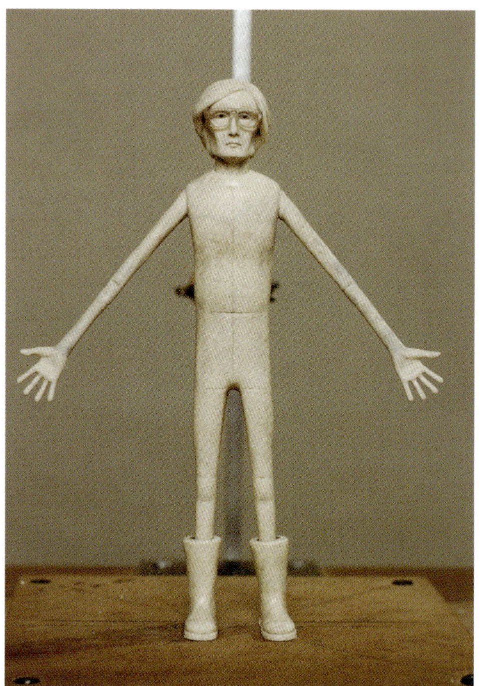

Above: An early sculpture of Petey

Right: Early concept art for Petey by Félicie

Below: The final color design and head sculpture for Petey

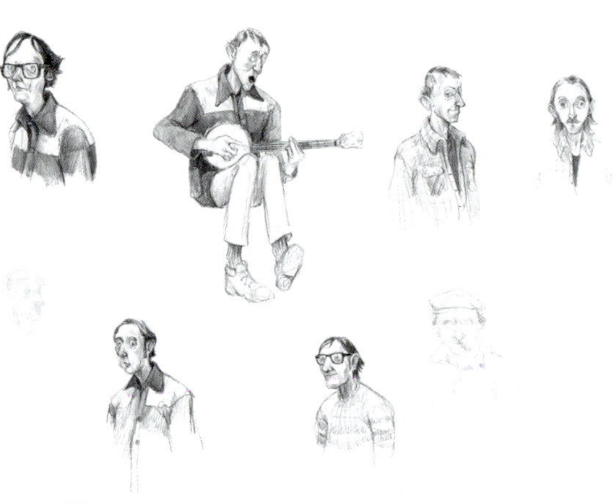

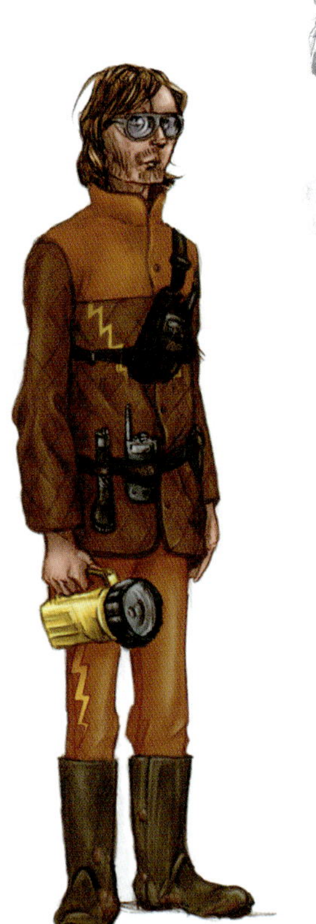

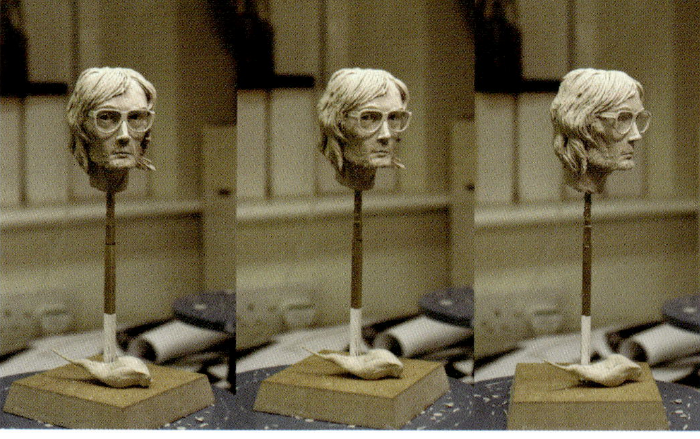

Top right: The Petey puppet head

Right: The final Petey puppet being photographed for approval

Below: Early designs for Petey's costume and glasses by Félicie

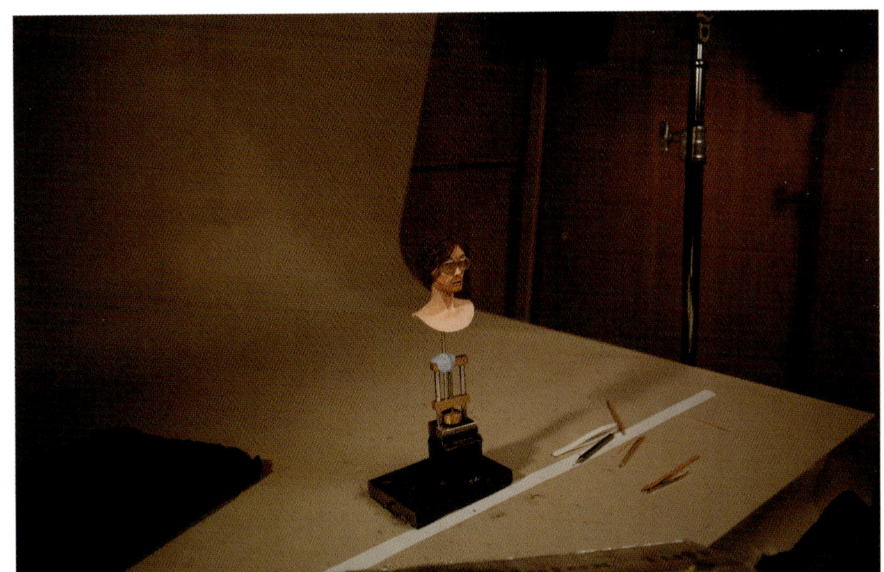

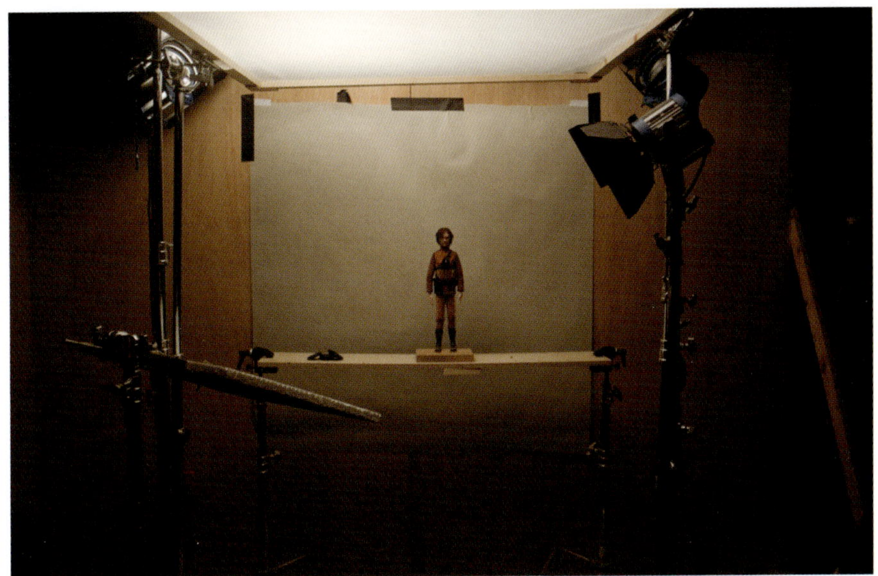

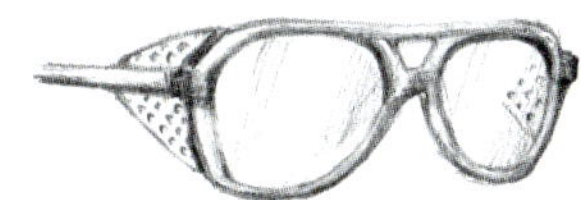

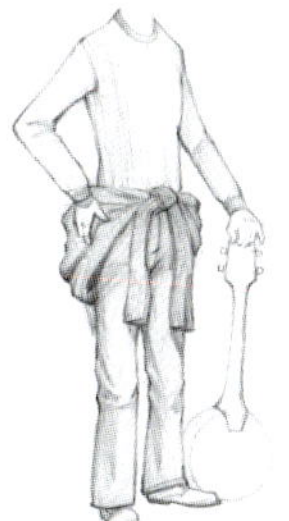

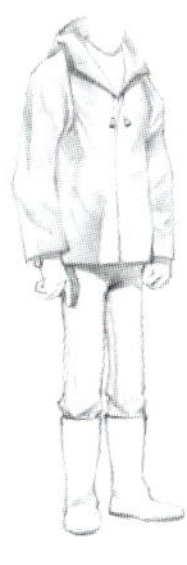

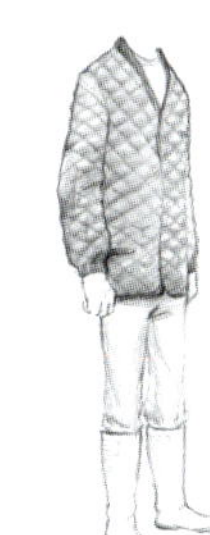

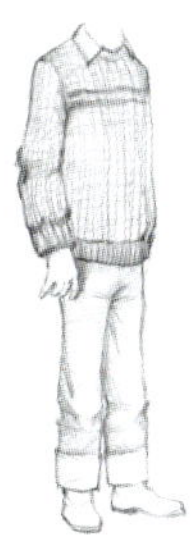

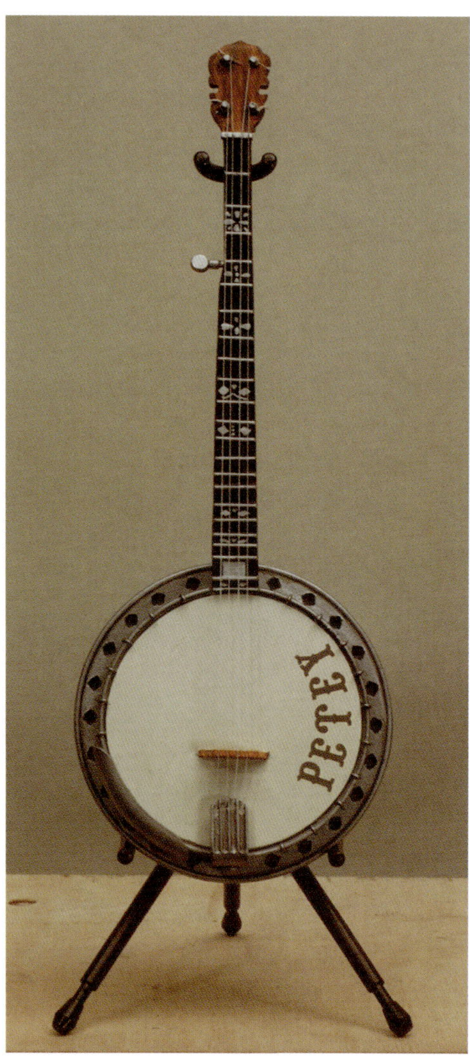

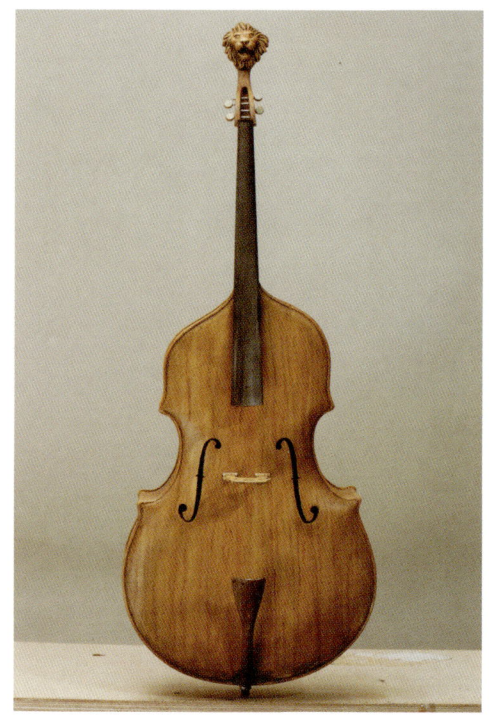

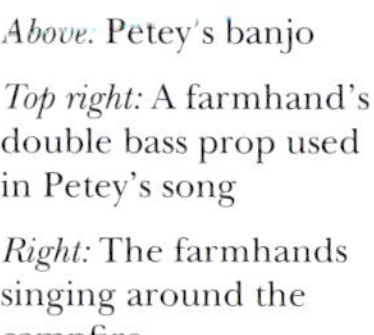

Above: Petey's banjo

Top right: A farmhand's double bass prop used in Petey's song

Right: The farmhands singing around the campfire

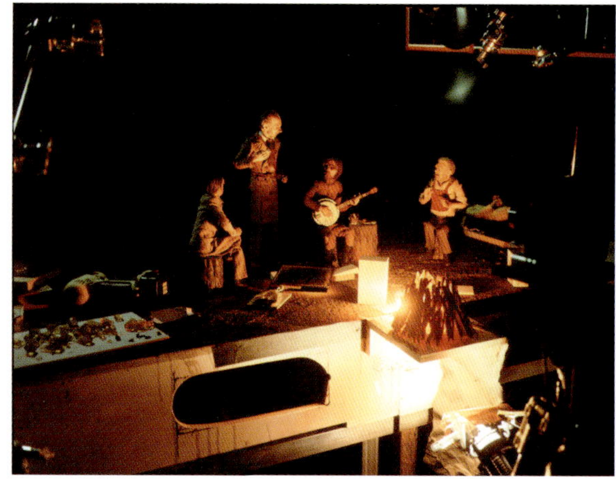

Right: Petey's bicycle

Below: Generic farmhand puppet parts

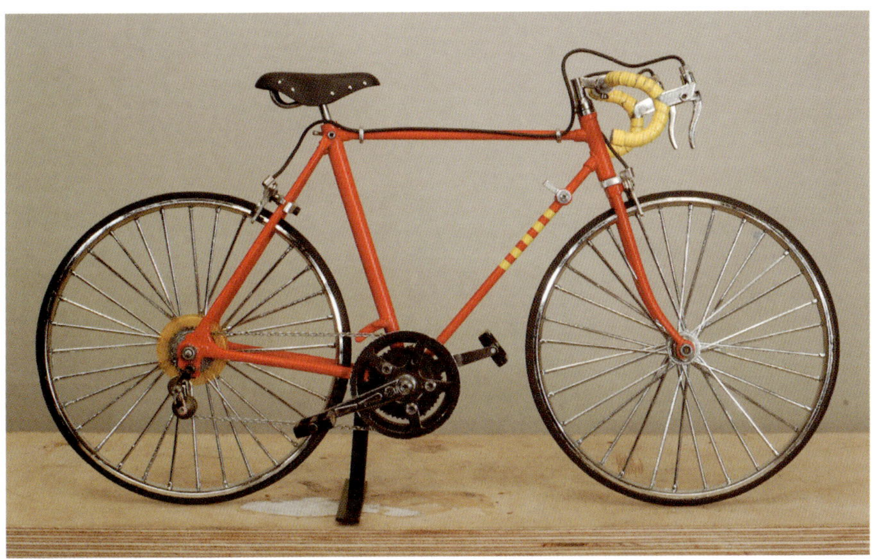

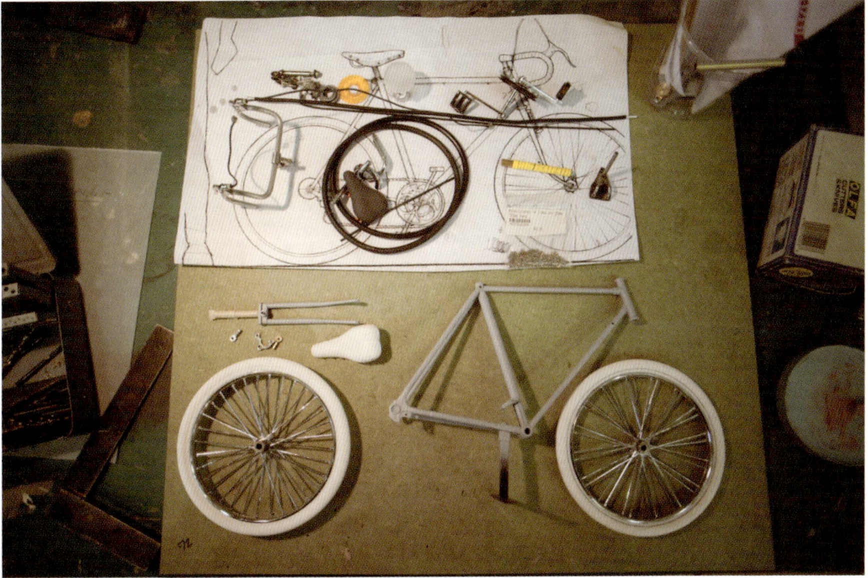

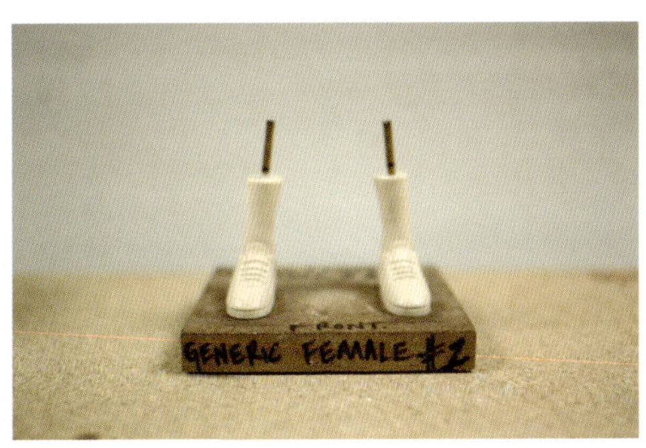

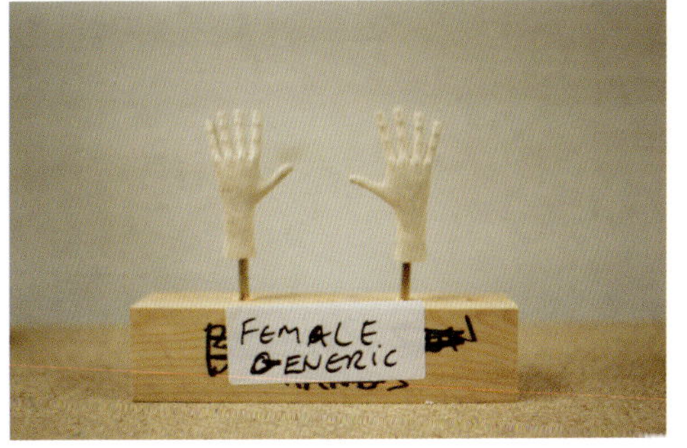

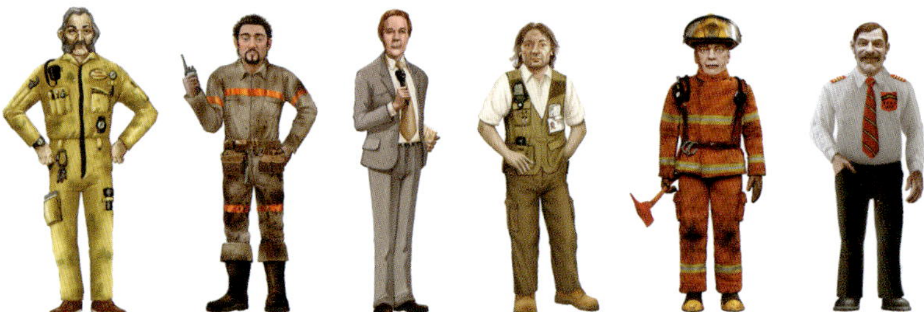

Left: A character lineup for various townspeople

Below: Storage boxes for the farmhand puppets

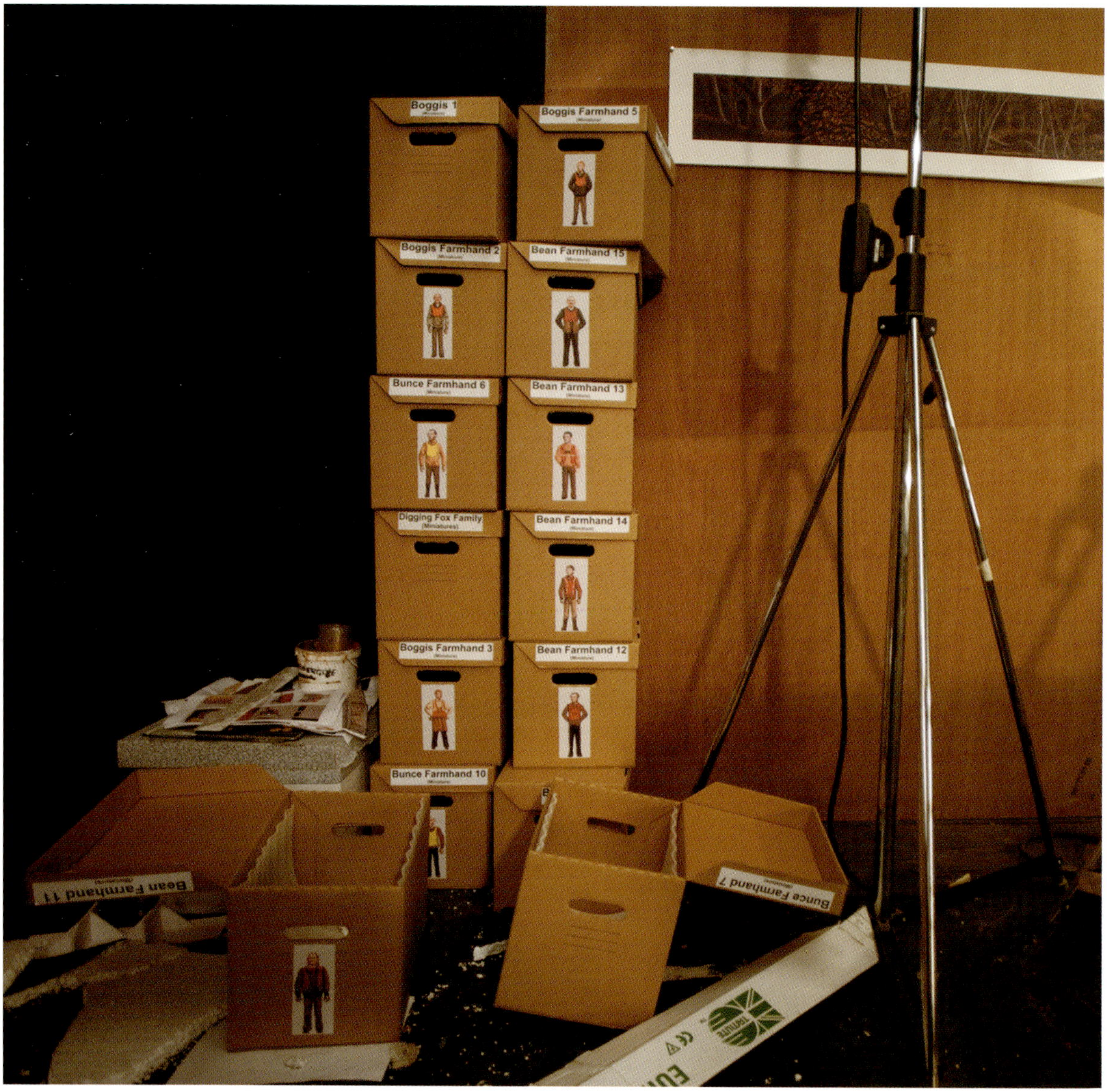

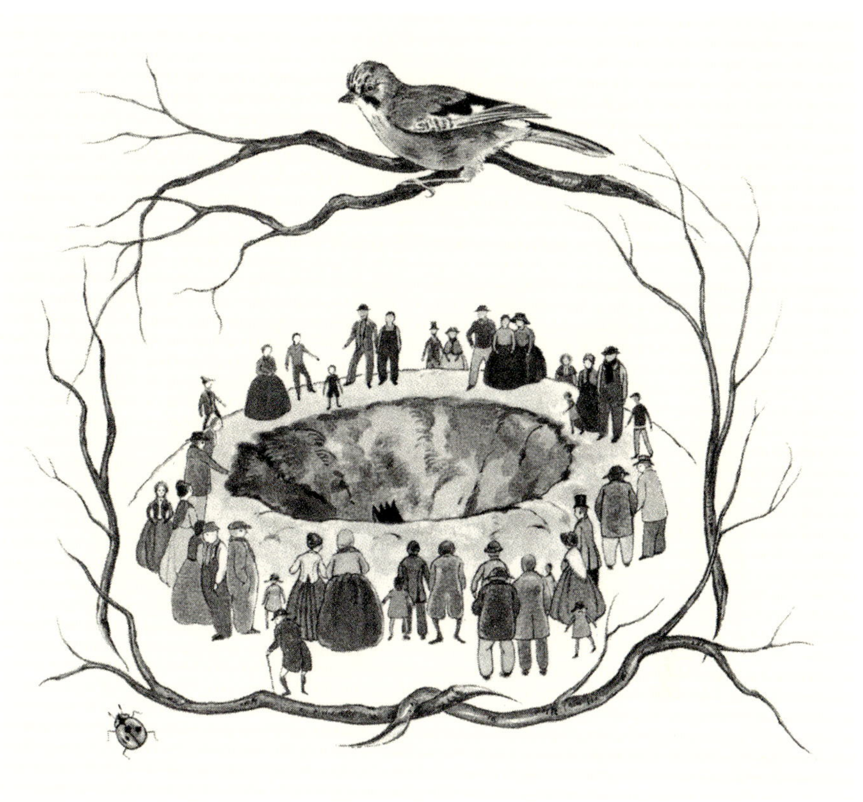

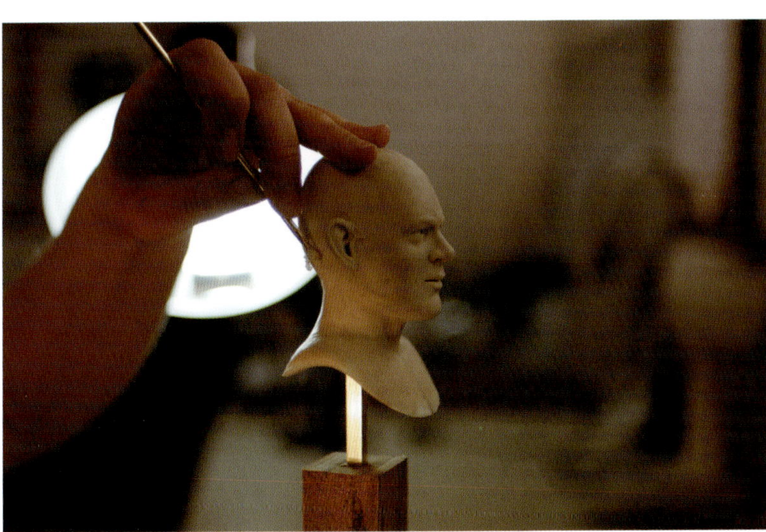

Above: Donald Chaffin's illustration of the townspeople around the foxhole

Left: A farmhand puppet being sculpted in the puppet hospital

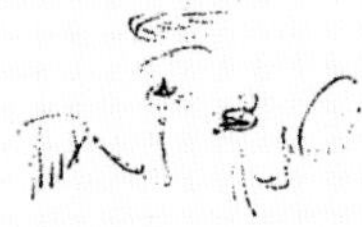

ASH
Boggis Farms is down that way, and
there's the exit to Bean's Apple Orchard,
which means here...

COME TOWARDS US

Ash stops next to a cast-iron chimney-valve sticking out of the side of the tunnel. He points up at the ceiling and whispers:

COME TO A 3-WAY FORK IN TUNNELS,

ASH
Here's where she bakes the cookies.

INT. FLINT-MINE. DAY

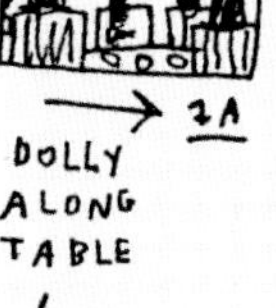

1A

DOLLY ALONG TABLE

END ON BADGER:

Candles glow all around. Everyone is seated at the long dining room table, and a magnificent feast with every variety of fruit, meat, vegetable, and roasted bird has been laid out in front of them. They tear into their meals, eating and drinking ferociously. Crumbs, juices, blood, and bones fly into the air. Jaws snap and chew. There is no conversation.

Badger suddenly stands and rings a knife against his cider glass. Everyone looks up, taking a breather from the frenzy of eating. Badger clears his throat.

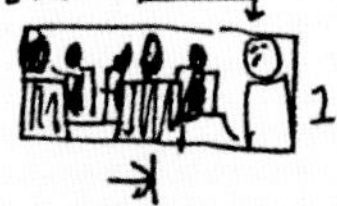

1B.

BADGER
Well, it took a near-catastrophe for all
of you to finally take me up on my offer
to have you over to the flint-mine for
dinner, but I guess we have --

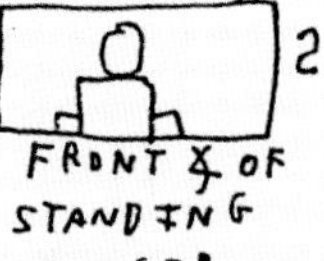

2.

FRONT ¾ OF STANDING BADGER.

FOX
(interrupting)
I'm sorry. Maybe my invitation got lost
in the mail. Does anybody know what this
badger's talking about?

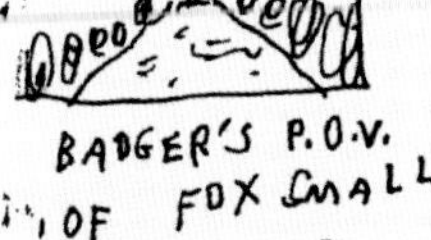

3.

BADGER'S P.O.V. OF FOX SMALL @ FAR END.

Everyone laughs. Fox sits at the opposite end of the table with a crooked smile on his face.

cut back to 2. badger looks thrown

FOX
But Clive's right --
(standing up)
-- in all seriousness --
(aside, to Badger)
-- excuse me, B.

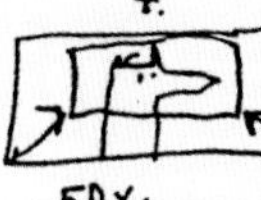

4.

FOX. NO PUSH IN YET JUST MATCH 2.

Fox raises his cider glass. Badger reluctantly sits back down.

2. AGAIN,

FOX
I guess we do have those three ugly,
cusshole farmers to thank for one thing:
(more)

VIII

BADGER'S FLINT MINE

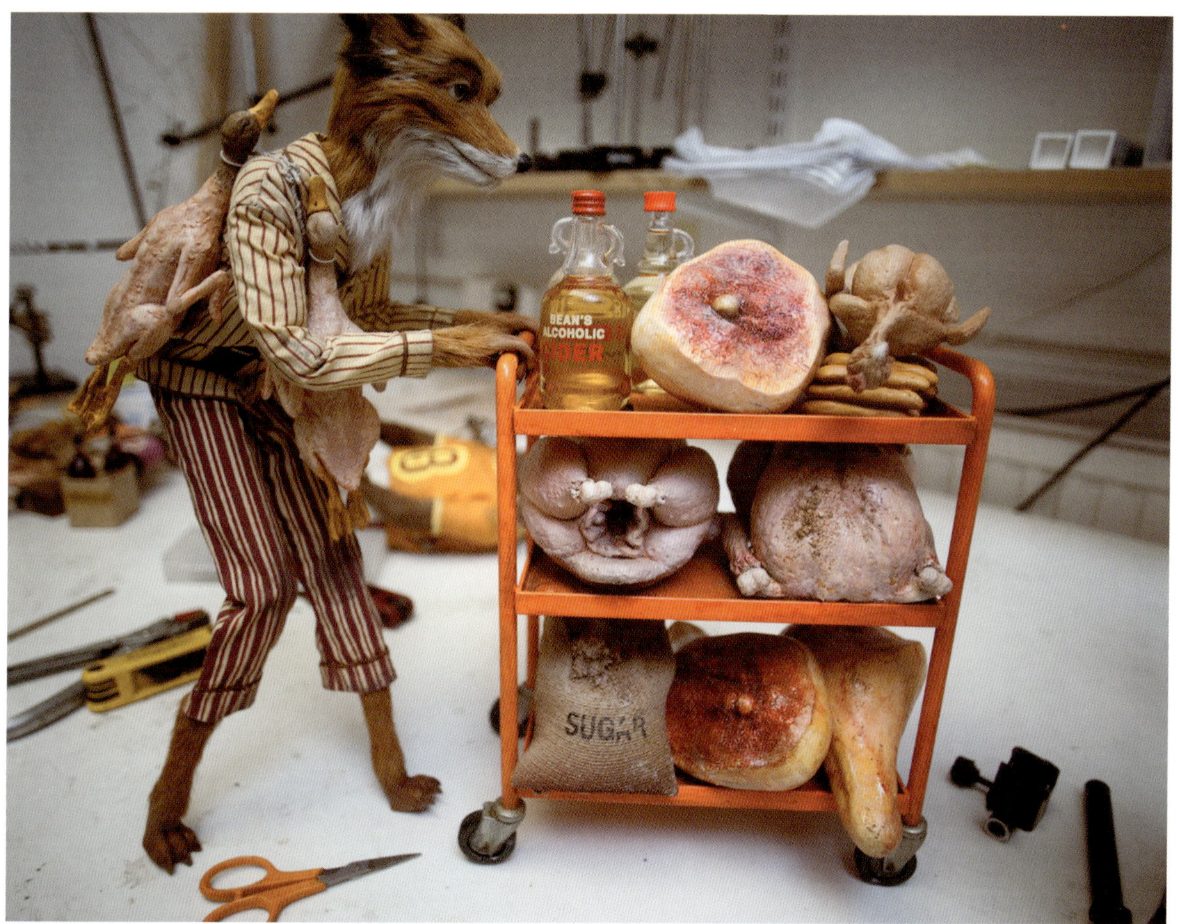

Above: Mr. Fox posed with spoils for the flint-mine feast

Following pages: The flint-mine feast

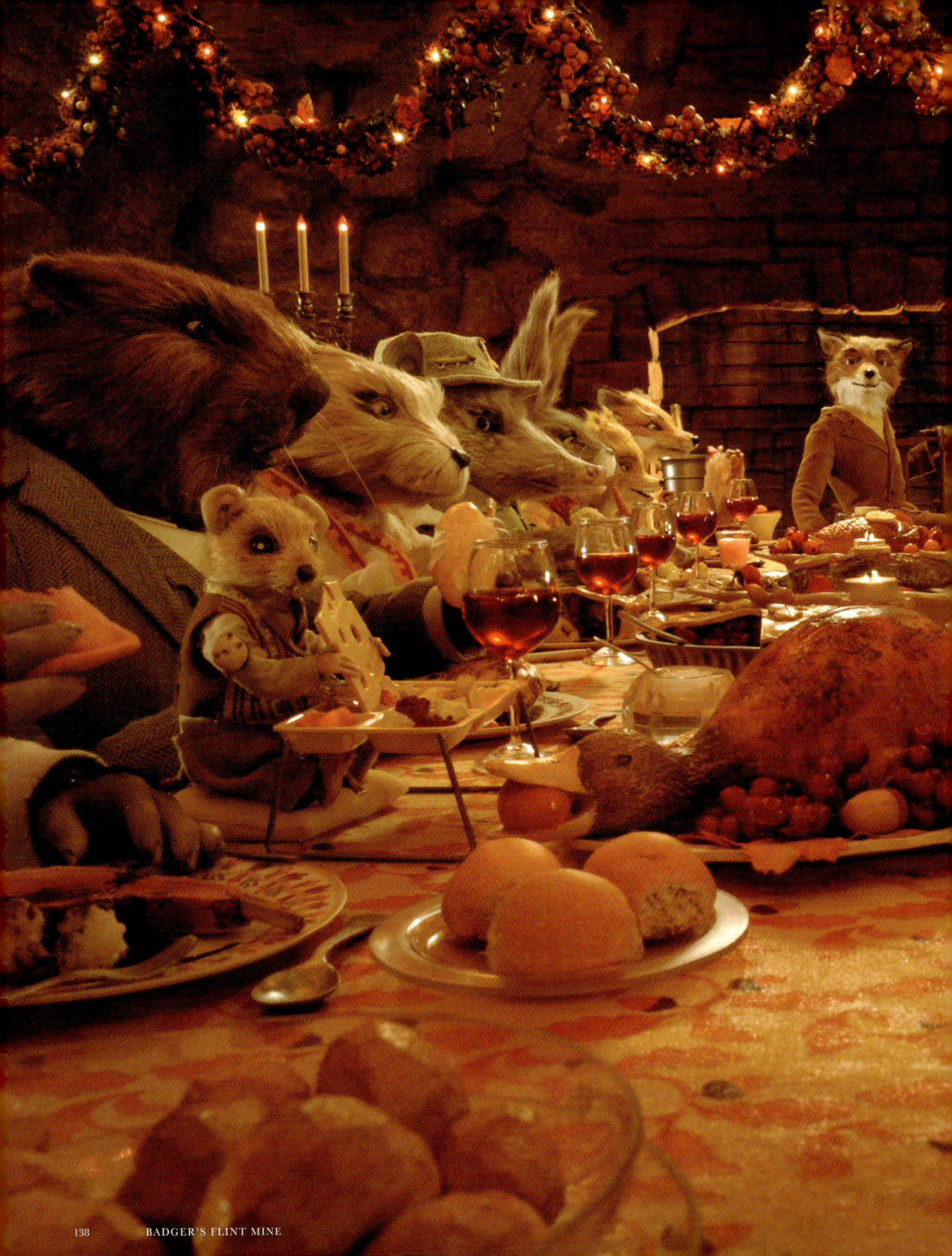

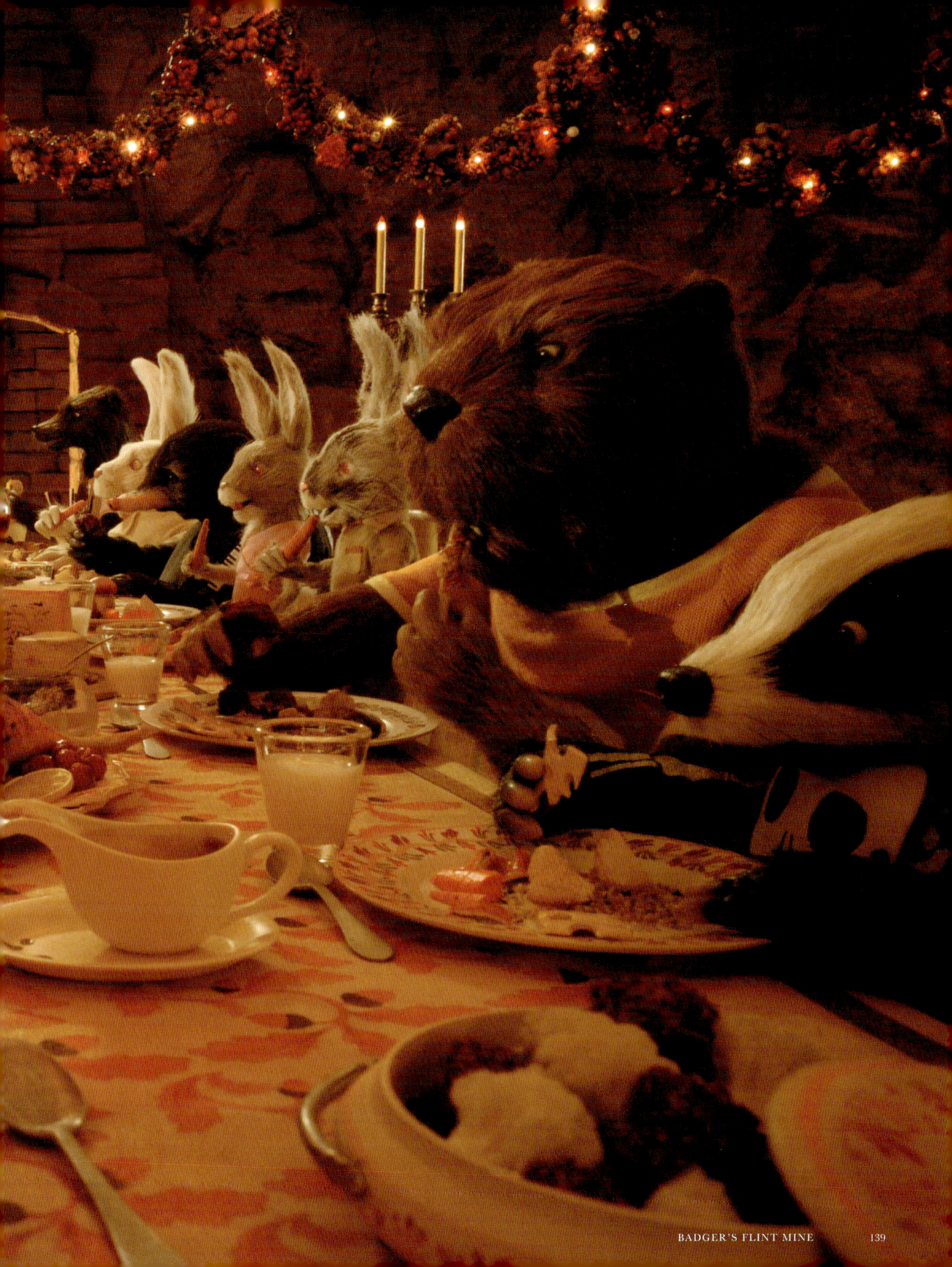

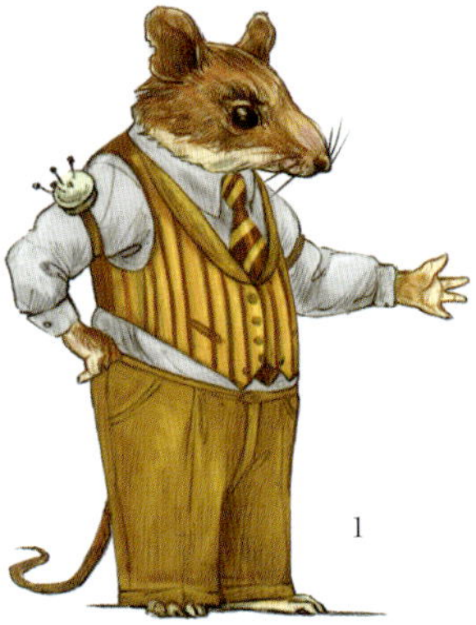

2

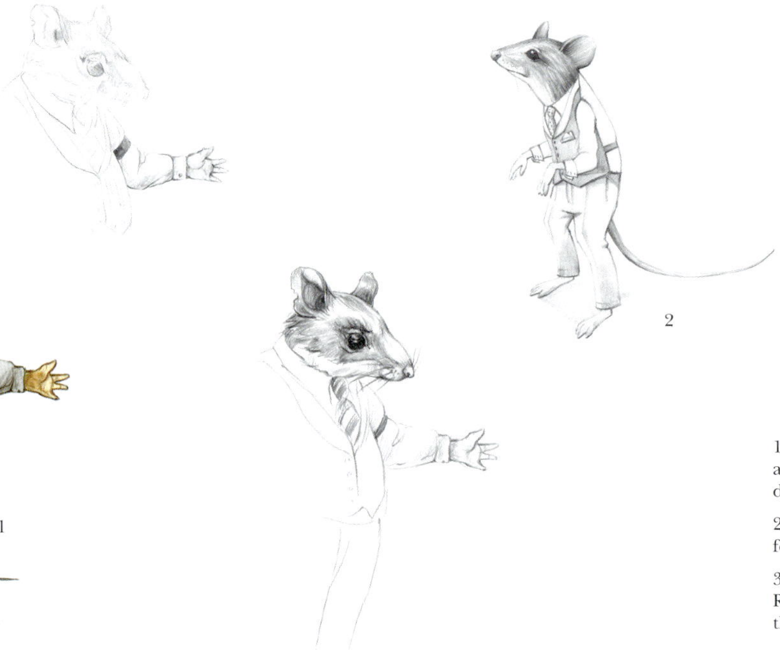

1

RICKITY

1. The final approved color design for Rickity

2. Evolving designs for Rickity by Félicie

3. The full-scale Rickity puppet in the puppet hospital

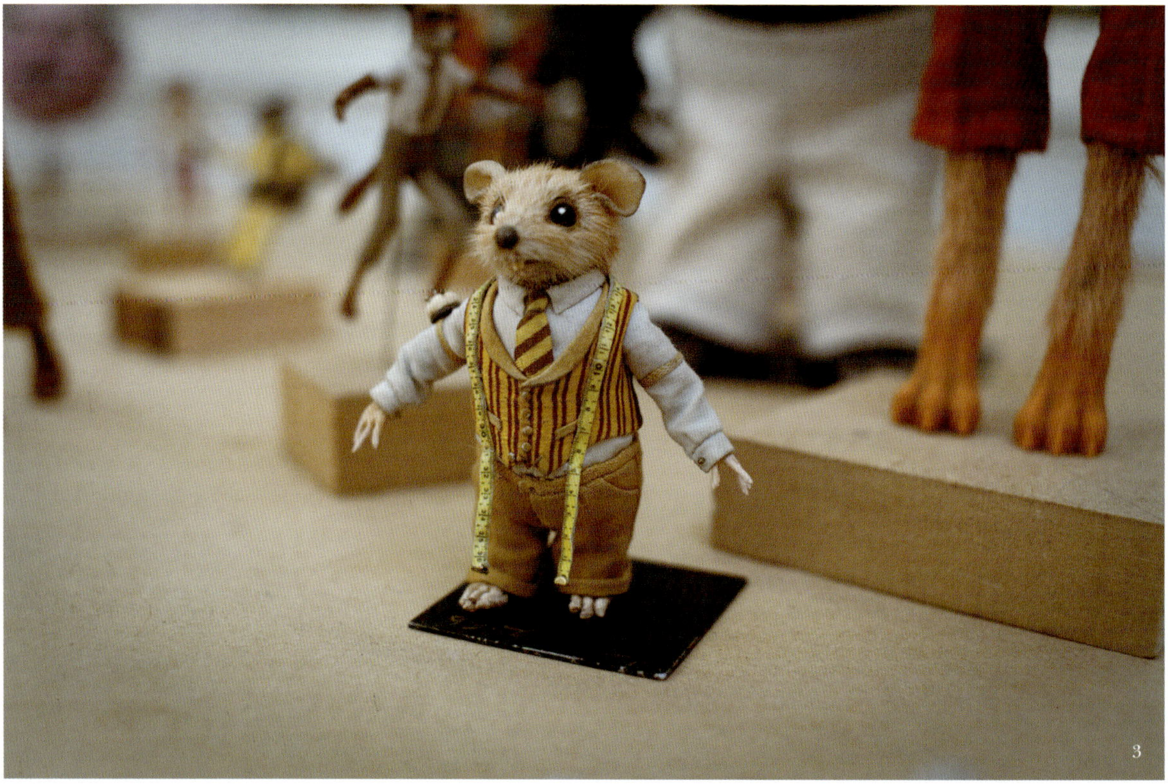

3

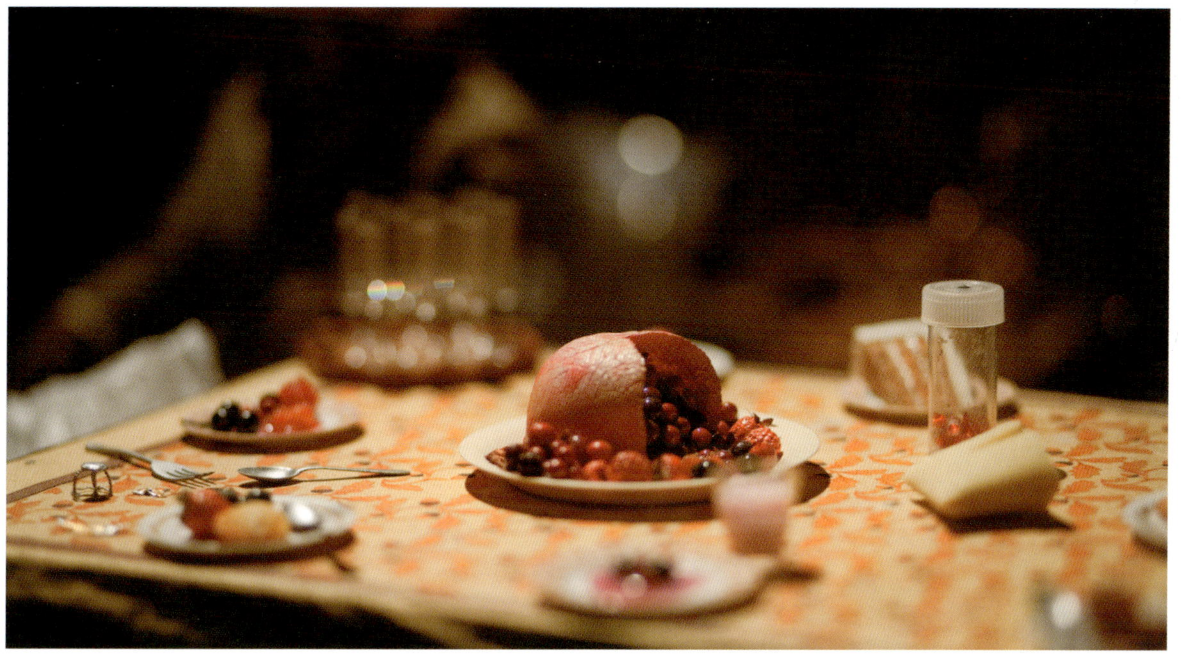

From: Wes Anderson
Subject: **Re: flint-mine dinner menu...ATTACHMENT**
Date: 10 September 2008 16:39:55 BST
To: Chris De Vita

Wonderful. Spectacular. Salad of actual tree leaves might be nice—autumn oak leaf salad with acorns
Also maybe a jar of wheat stalks just to chew on
For dessert a bowl of little red berries poisonous to human but a delicacy for field animals—maybe holly?

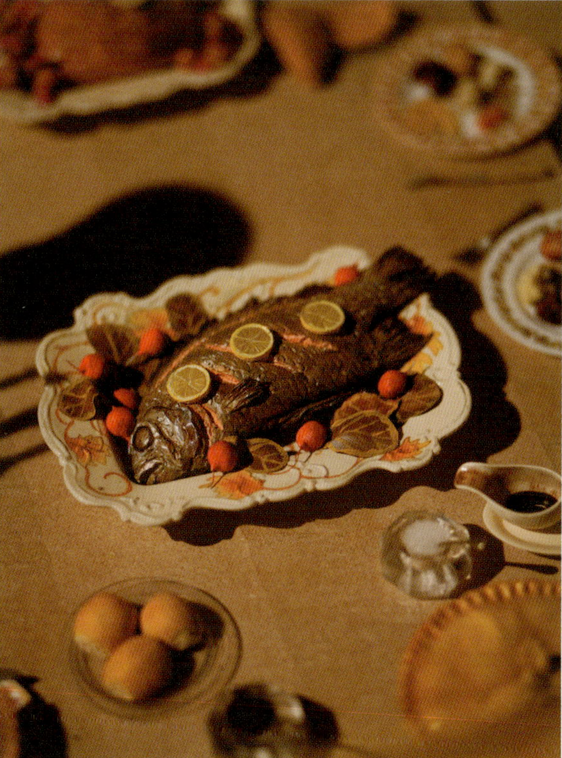

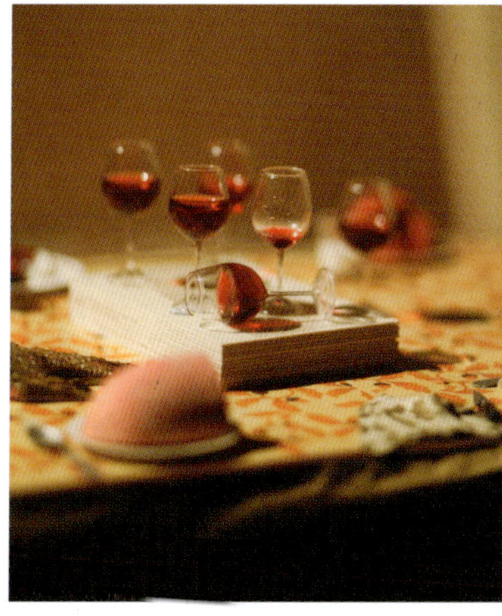

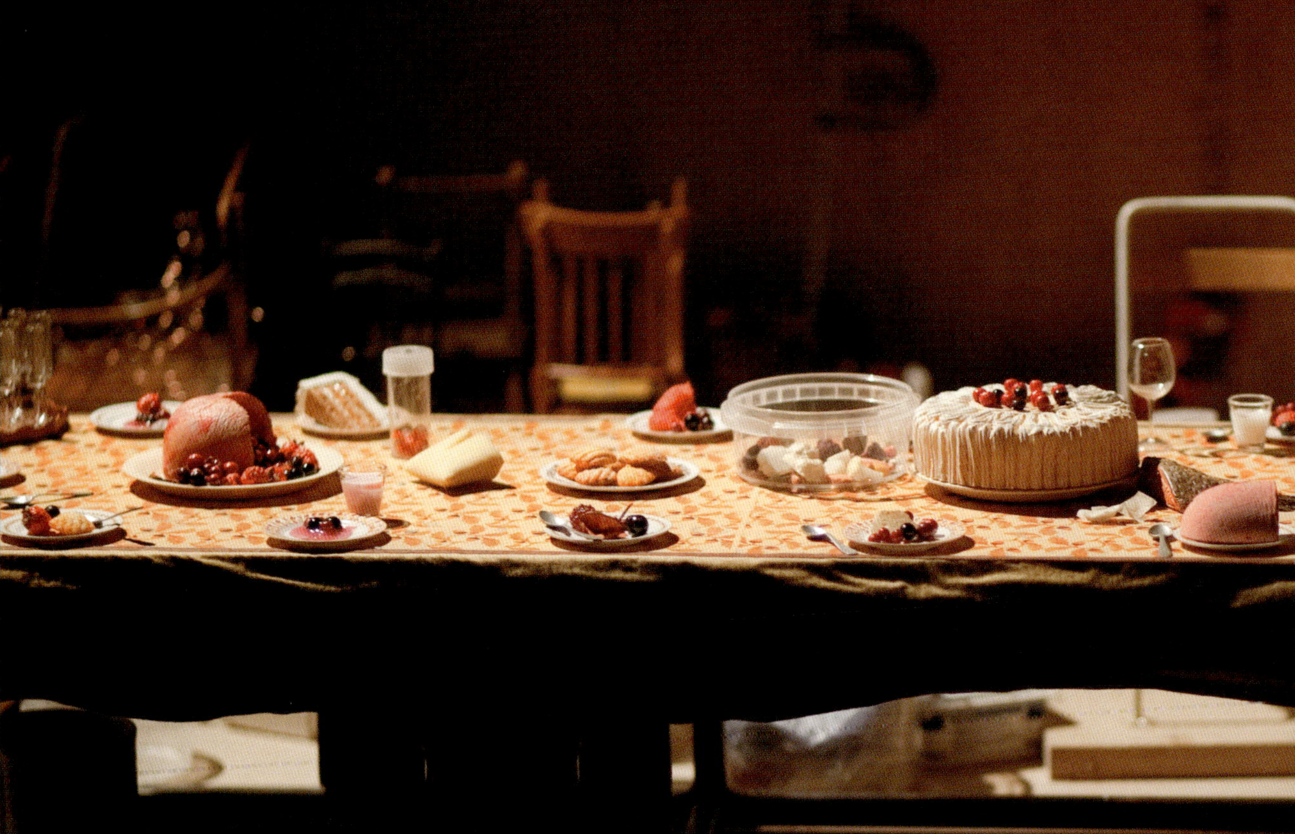

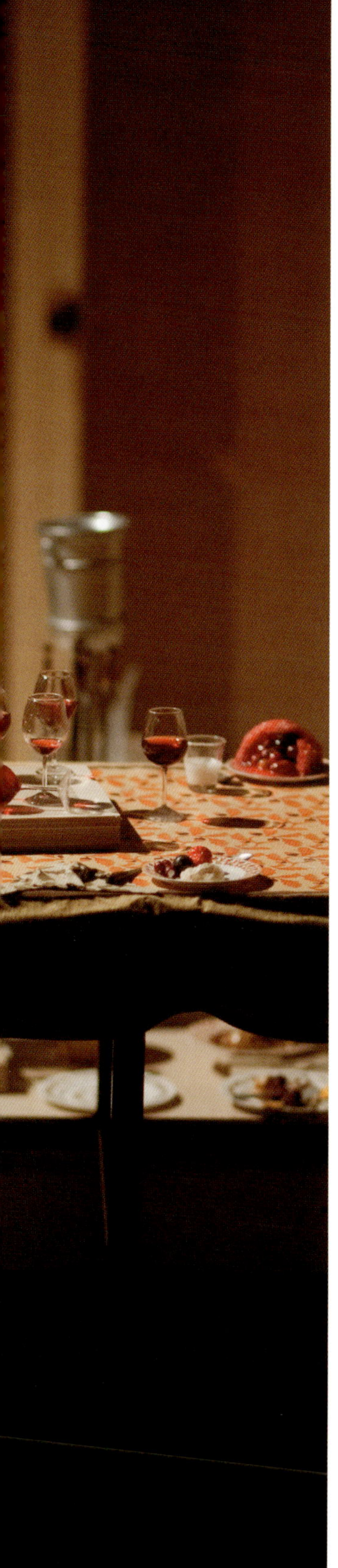

AN INTERVIEW WITH

JASON SCHWARTZMAN

6/28/09

MS: *Now how did this come about for you? How did you get involved in this, or when did Wes first say something to you about it?*

JS: This is a good place to start. So the first time I ever, ever, ever heard about *Fantastic Mr. Fox*, I was shooting, I was working on *Marie Antoinette* in Paris. Wes was on a press tour for *The Life Aquatic* and it was a European press tour that ended in Paris.

I remember it well, because he stayed in Paris afterward.

Well what happened was we were having dinner and I said, "Look, you know, whenever your studio stay expires, whenever this is all technically done for you, you can come stay with me as long as you'd like because I have an extra room in the apartment that I'm living in." And he did in fact stay, he stayed for months and he became my roommate. It was a great time. We would go see movies together, we would do our shopping together, our grocery shopping together. It was wonderful to have Wes with me like that, we basically lived together. Now he moved in very early on in my work stay in Paris, so we were together for six or seven straight weeks, and then he decided to look for his own place because he he was loving Paris so much, and I'm sure that he'd already had thoughts of living there anyway. So he looked for his own place and found his own place and moved out. And one day I asked him what he was doing, if he wanted to go get food, and he said that he couldn't because Noah Baumbach was flying over from America and they were writing this movie, *Fantastic Mr. Fox*. So that was the first time I'd ever heard of it. Noah came and I think they spent a week going over some stuff, or a couple weeks. Then simultaneously he and I and Roman had begun our preliminary screenwriting for *The Darjeeling Limited*, so that was just the way it was presented to me. I didn't forget about *Fantastic Mr. Fox*, but it wasn't really at the front of my mind. Anyway, then we shot our movie, came back, did press for it, and while we were doing press, before the movie was going to be shown at the Venice Film Festival, Wes asked me if I would want to be one of the voices in the script, and I said sure. He said that his dream was that maybe we would try to get all the actors together and record it live, as opposed to, you know, most animated films. Would you call this an animated movie? Is that the way to refer to it?

That's a really good question. I guess so.

Okay, yeah, because every time people have said, "What is the movie?" I say, "You know, they built these furry things, not really a puppet, but maybe a puppet, and they move it"—like I describe the process and then I go, "I guess it's animated."

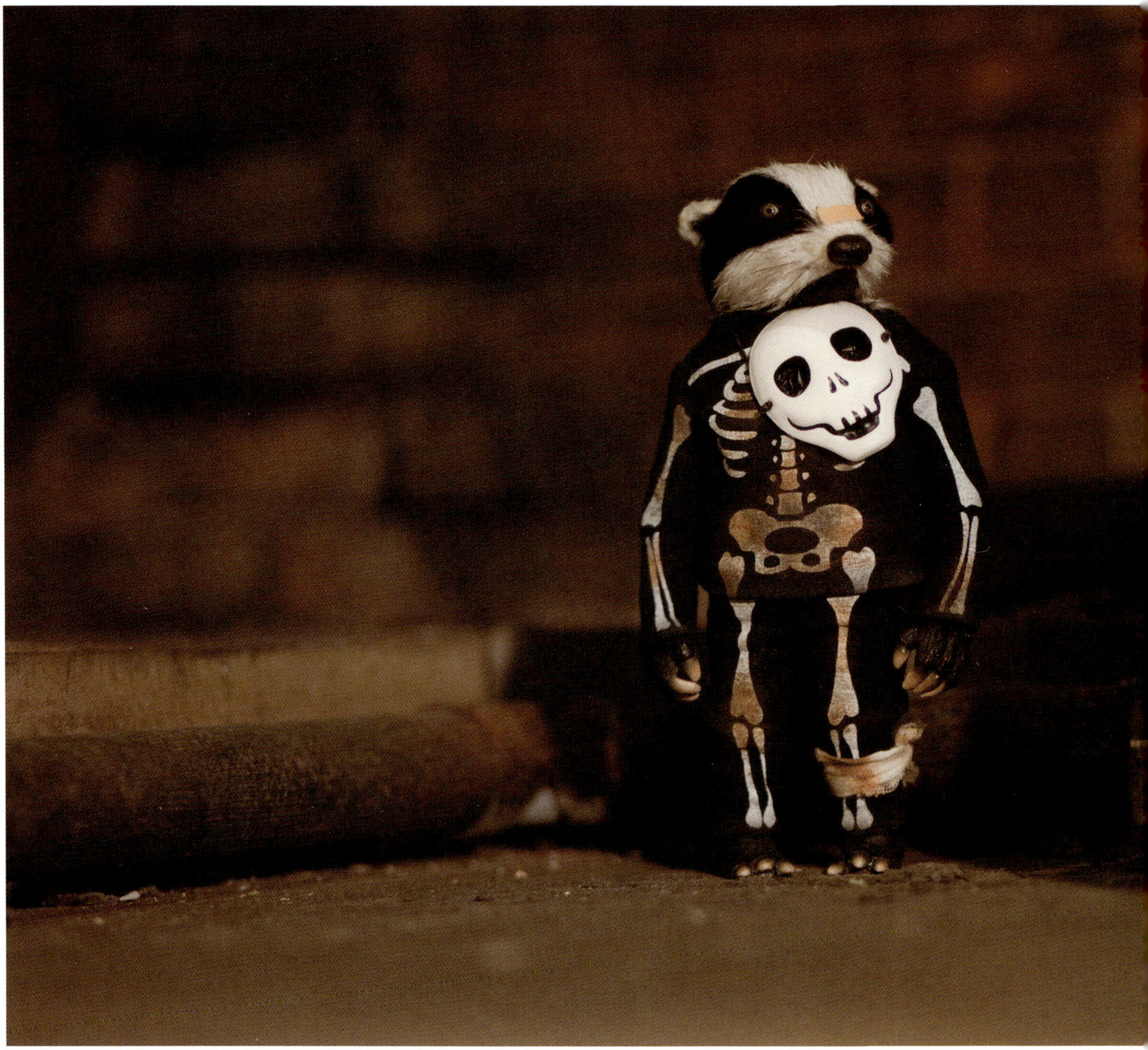

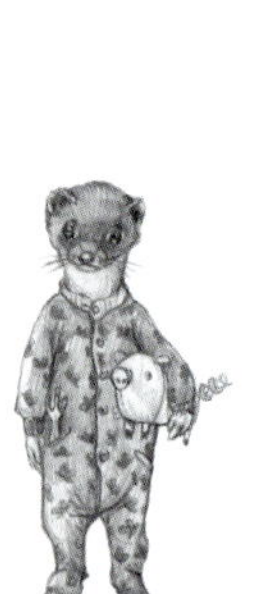
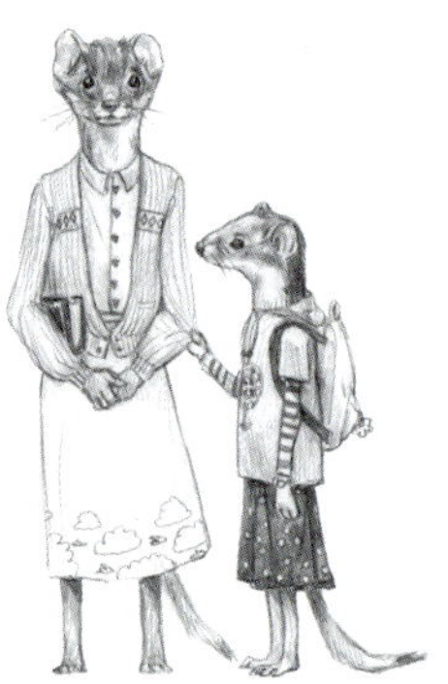
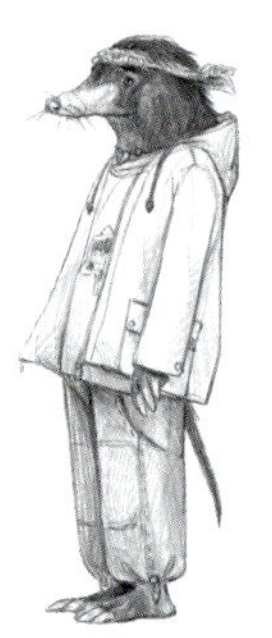
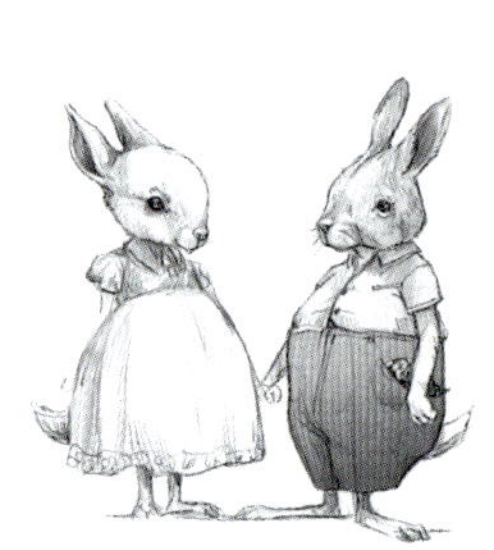
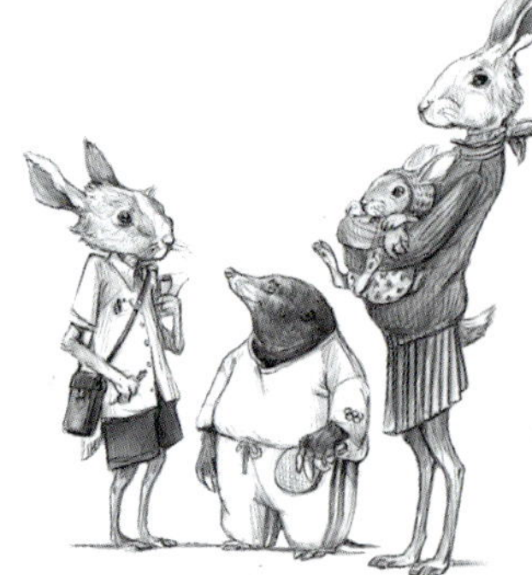

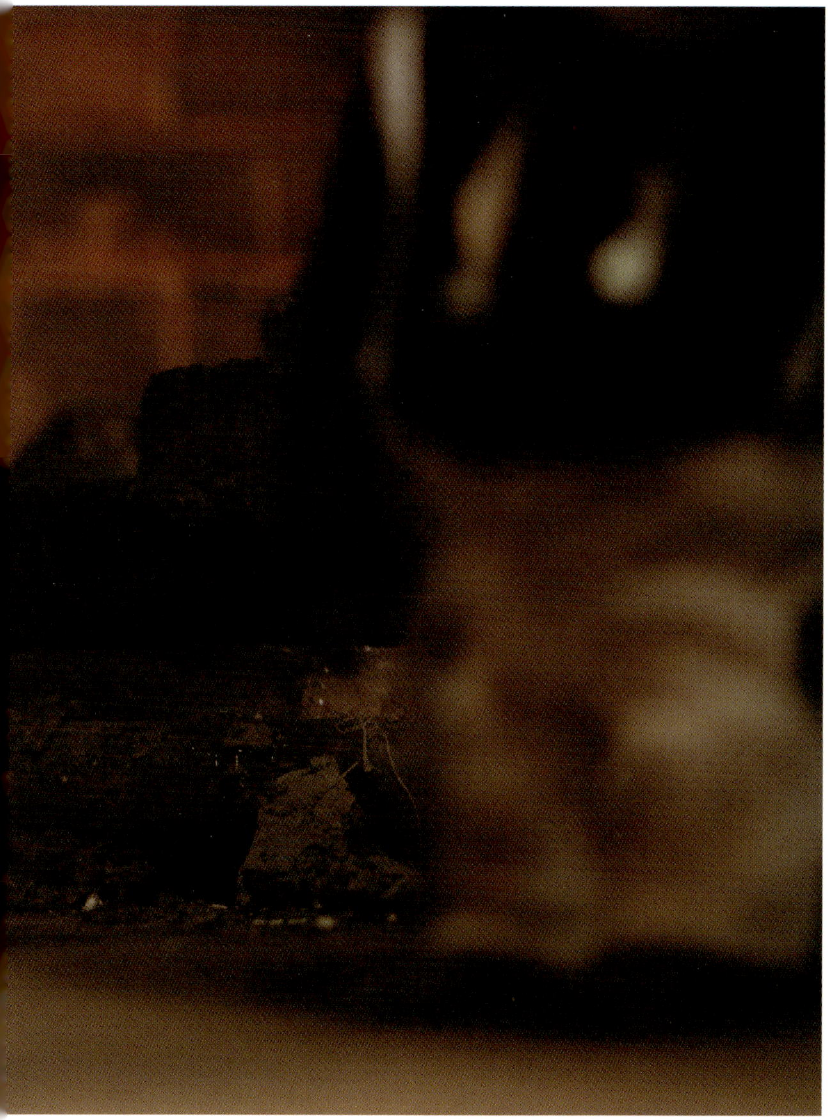

Left: Badger Child on set

Below: Early designs for the animal children by Félicie

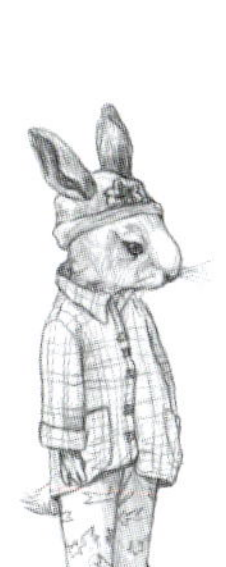
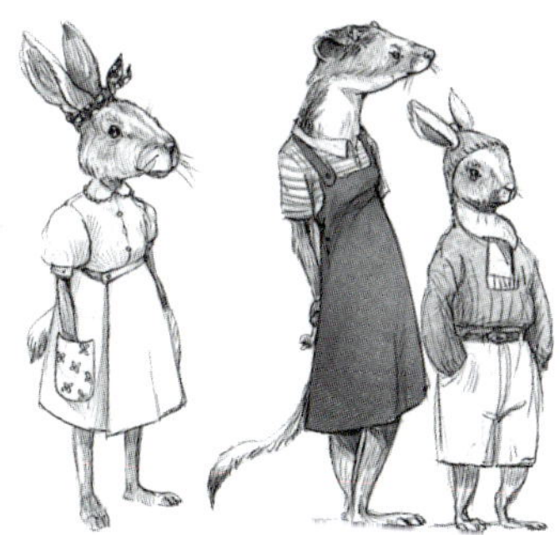
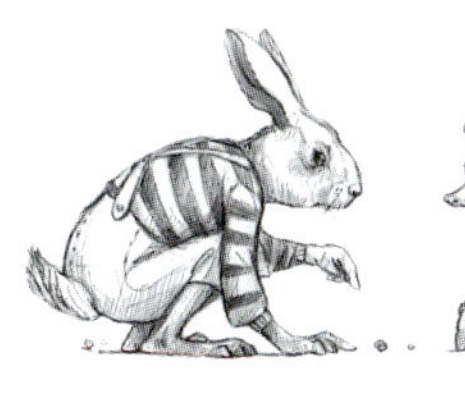
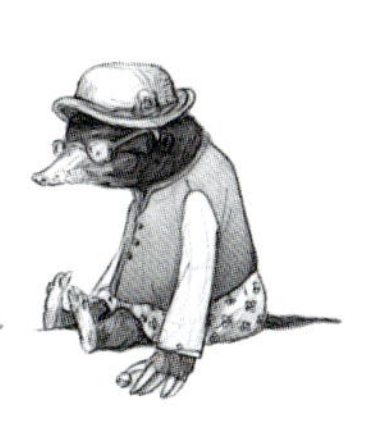
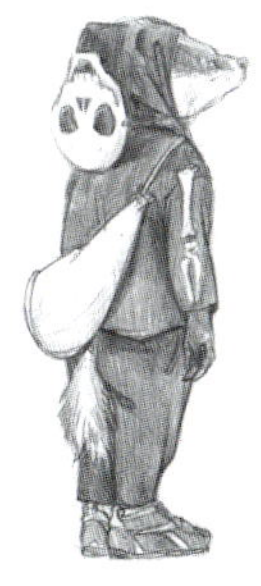

MS: *It's just like nothing else. I guess it is technically animated.*

JS: In most animated movies, a lot of the actors record their voices separately. And from the get-go Wes had this idea that we would try to have as many of the actors together in a group and have one soundman with a boom mike just kind of capturing it all, like you would on a film set, so that actors could overlap and there would just be more interplay and maybe spontaneous things or weird grunts or noises—just things that would almost be impossible to get if people were separated. So we met, a bunch of the actors got together, and for various reasons it was cut short. And the irony is that Wes was always emailing me, "We're going to get everyone together. We've got to try to do this, we've got to try to get your voice for this." And I was doing press for *The Darjeeling Limited* all around America, I was going to different cities talking about the movie. And Wes got Bill Murray, George Clooney, Wally Wolodarsky, and another actor, I forget who, and they found this barn in upstate New York and they all went up and spent a weekend and just went through the entire script a bunch of times.

From: Wes Anderson
Subject: **Re: Water Effects Testing (210_0130B/0140)**
Date: 7 January 2009 16:09:56 GMT
To: Mark Waring

> The first tests were to see how a large volume of water looks when coming down the tunnel towards the camera. (210_0130B)
>
> (210_0130B) Water Test 2 - This has the pipe half full with water but with movement splashing up the sides.
>
> (210_0130B) Water Test 3 - This has a full pipe of water with twice the volume
>
> Do either of these seem right to you? Do you think it should require an even larger volume of water?

AT LEAST AS MUCH AS TEST 3 -- SPLASHING UP SIDES IS GOOD TOO -- AND SOME SHAKING OF THE PIPE HELPS!

ALSO WE NEED LOWER CAMERA ANGLE IN RELATION TO PIPE -- SO YOU CAN SEE THE WATER FROM FURTHER AWAY AND YOU'RE NOT SURE WHAT IT IS YET

> (210_0140) Water Test 5 - This was done with a larger volume of water and a faster shutter speed which gives a different appearance to the look of the water.

I THINK THIS ONE HAS THE RIGHT FEELING -- BUT THE STREAM OF WATER SHOULD BE LARGER/THICKER -- TWICE AS BIG IN RELATION TO TABLE, AND DOES NOT REDUCE AT ALL DURING THE SHOT

> We will test this further with a few levels of water and with some characters in the shot, but do you see the entry of the water into the table shot as a large jet or as a large volume that engulfs them?

I THINK IT CAN COME IN AS A VERY VERY VERY LARGE JET

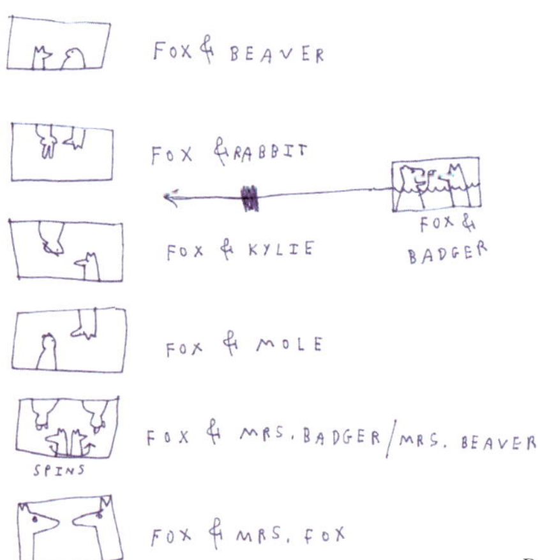

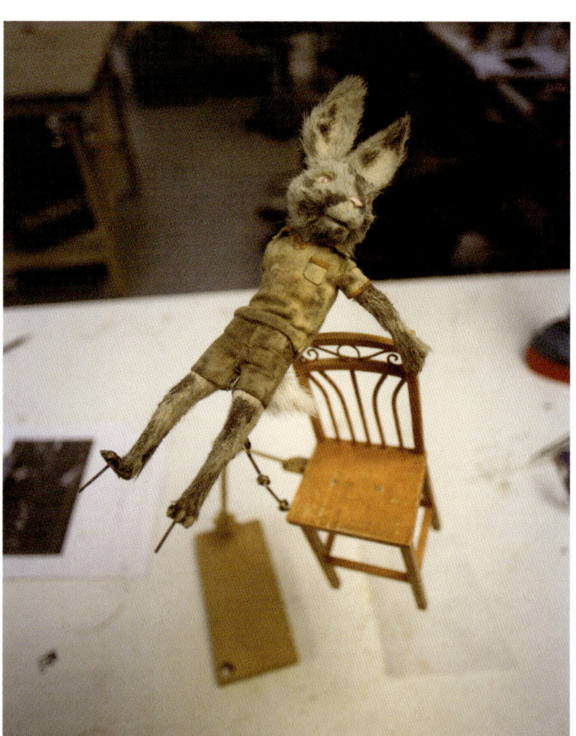

Right: Rabbit Boy posed for the flood shots

Left: Sketches by Wes for the flood shots

Following pages: The flood

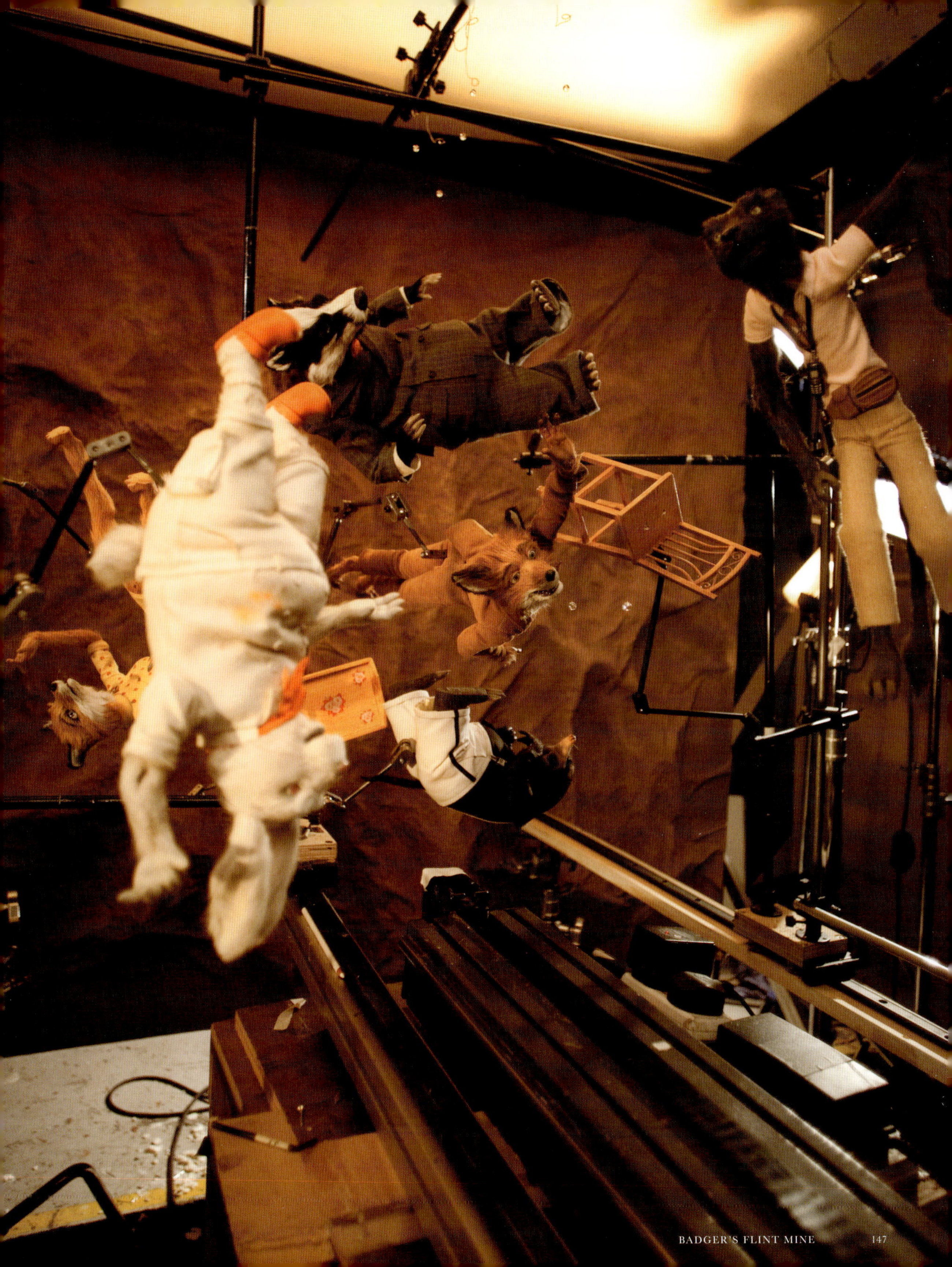

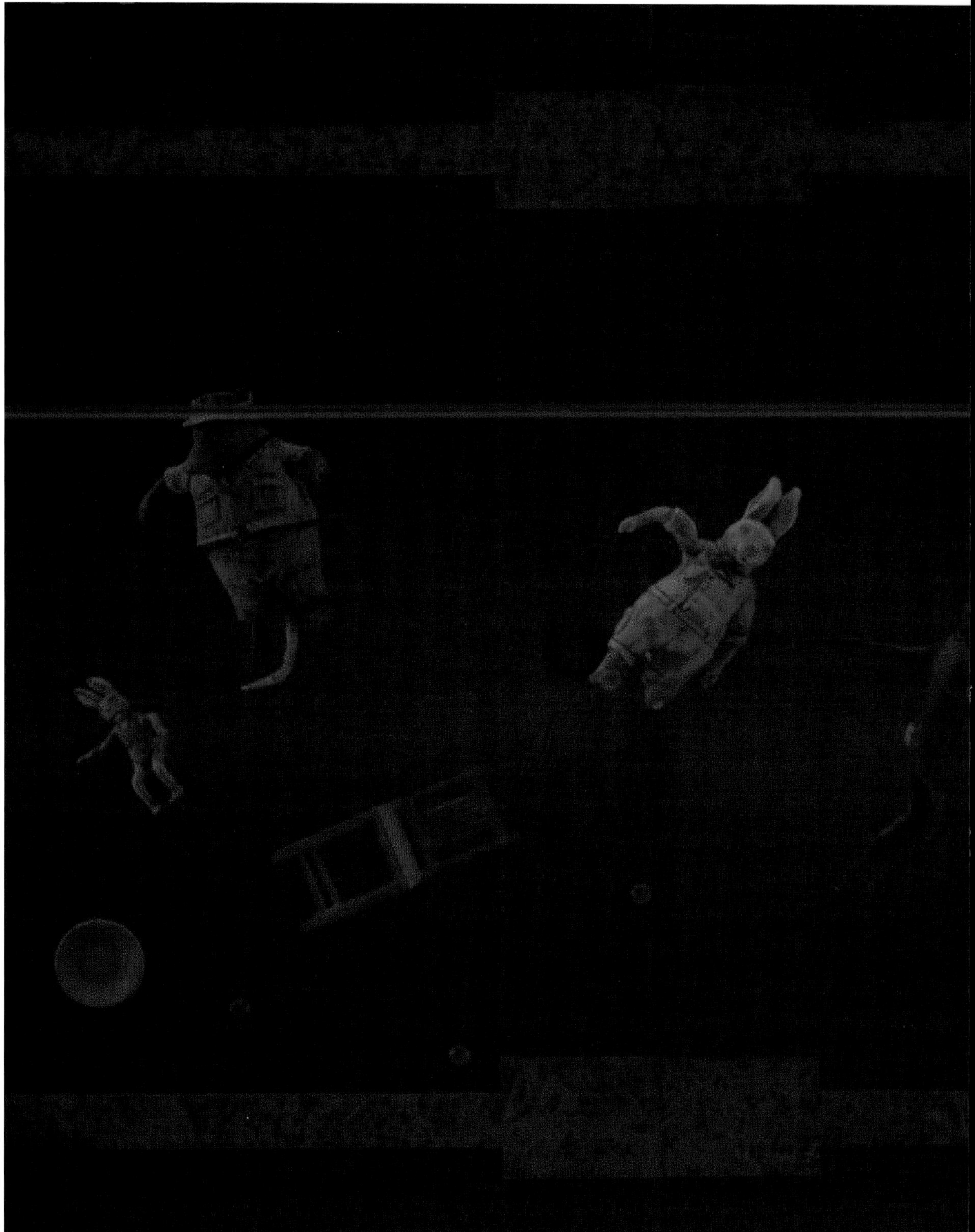

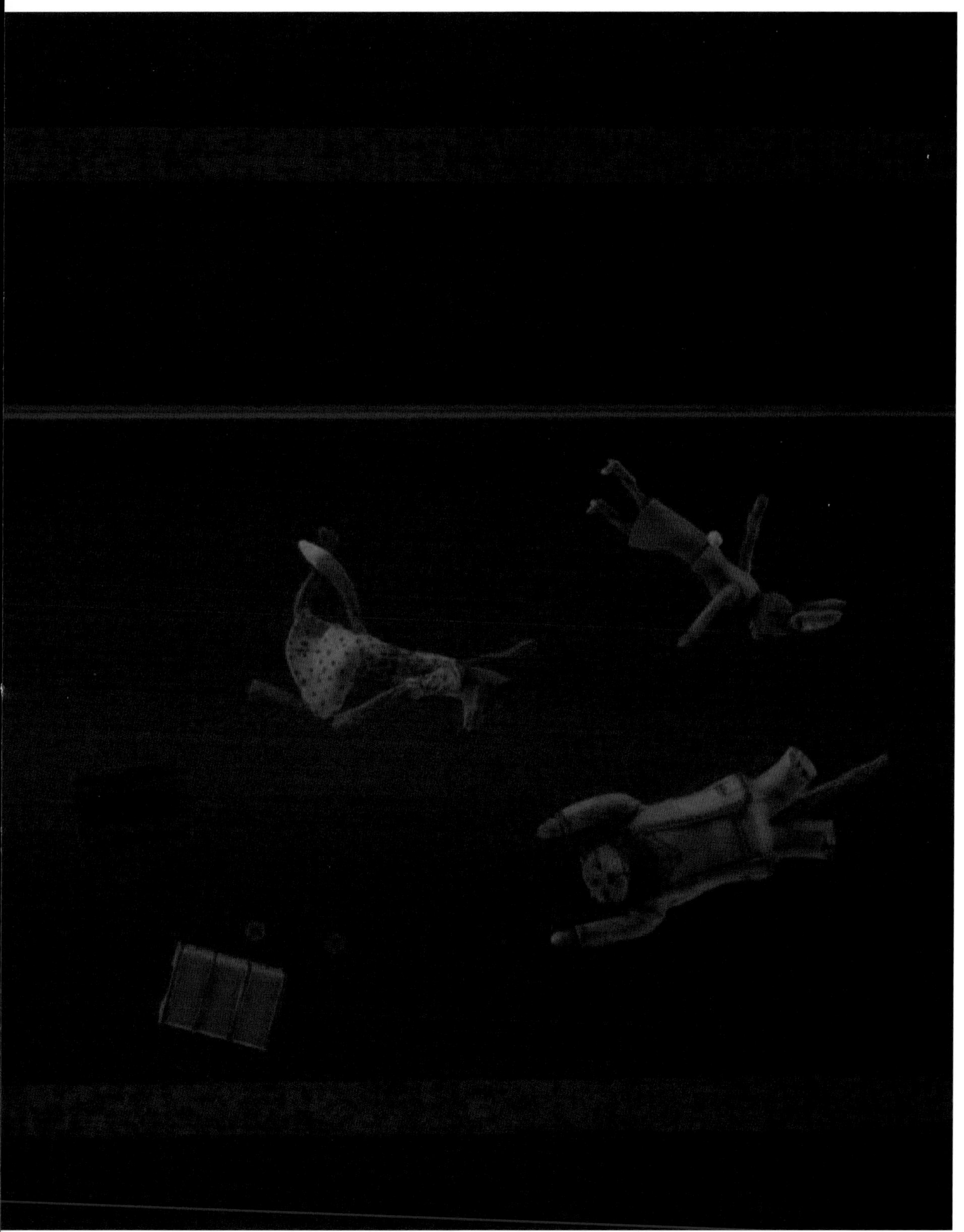

STILL IN SAME SHOT...
Hear KI-YA! & rat comes back into frame curiously.

Rat snaps at Mrs. Fox's shoulder. She ducks away in puzzled terror. Kristofferson hollers:

KRISTOFFERSON
Ki-ya!

CUT TO RAT'S P.O.V.:

Rat stops and turns around. Kristofferson stands across from him in a karate fighting-stance. Ash is behind him. Spit drips from Rat's teeth. Kristofferson's arms shake.

OVER KRIS, LINE, THEN CHARGE.

RAT
What's that? Judo? You want to spar, little fella?

FOLLOW KRIS TO RAT HANDHELD

Kristofferson charges Rat and throws seven kicks and punches in a flurry. Rat dances around him for a minute, then fiercely pins him to the floor by the neck. Kristofferson gasps for air. Mrs. Fox rushes over to them. She grabs Rat's arms and says:

MRS. FOX
Let him breathe, Rat! You're killing him!

Rat squeezes his claws tighter. Kristofferson's eyes close and his body goes limp. Mrs. Fox digs the nails of the fingers of her paws into Rat's arms.

TIGHT OF RAT/ PINNED KRIS

MRS. FOX
Let go!

Rat hisses. He lets go of Kristofferson and turns on Mrs. Fox. Mrs. Fox backs away. Rat smiles.

K STRANGLED

RAT
Keep lookin' good, Mrs. Foxy. I'll be seeing you real, real soon -- at a time T.B.D!

RAT STRANGLING

BOTH SHOTS ARE DIRECT P.O.V.S, DOWN & UP)

Rat squeezes himself into a little tunnel and disappears. Kristofferson opens his eyes. He sits up. Ash says angrily:

ASH
Let me get a couple of licks in for once! Didn't your father ever teach you any manners?
(viciously)
Or was he always too sick?

MRS. FOX
Ash! Stop!

INTERCUT 3 CLOSE-UPS SERGIO LEONE STYLE:

ASH, KRIS, MOM, KRIS, ~~SHOES~~ ASH, SHOES, KRIS.

Kristofferson stands up and kicks off his shoes.

SHOES OFF SHOT.

after rat lets go...

HIGH ANGLE

OVER RAT OF MRS FOX BACKING AWAY

LOW ANGLE

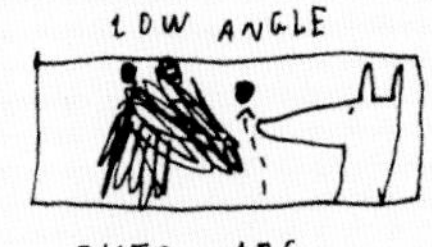

OVER MRS. FOX OF RAT, runs away into little tunnel

then follow mrs. fox quickly to kris as he stands up & ash joins him:

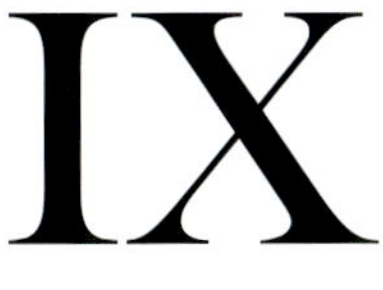

A GO-FOR-BROKE RESCUE MISSION

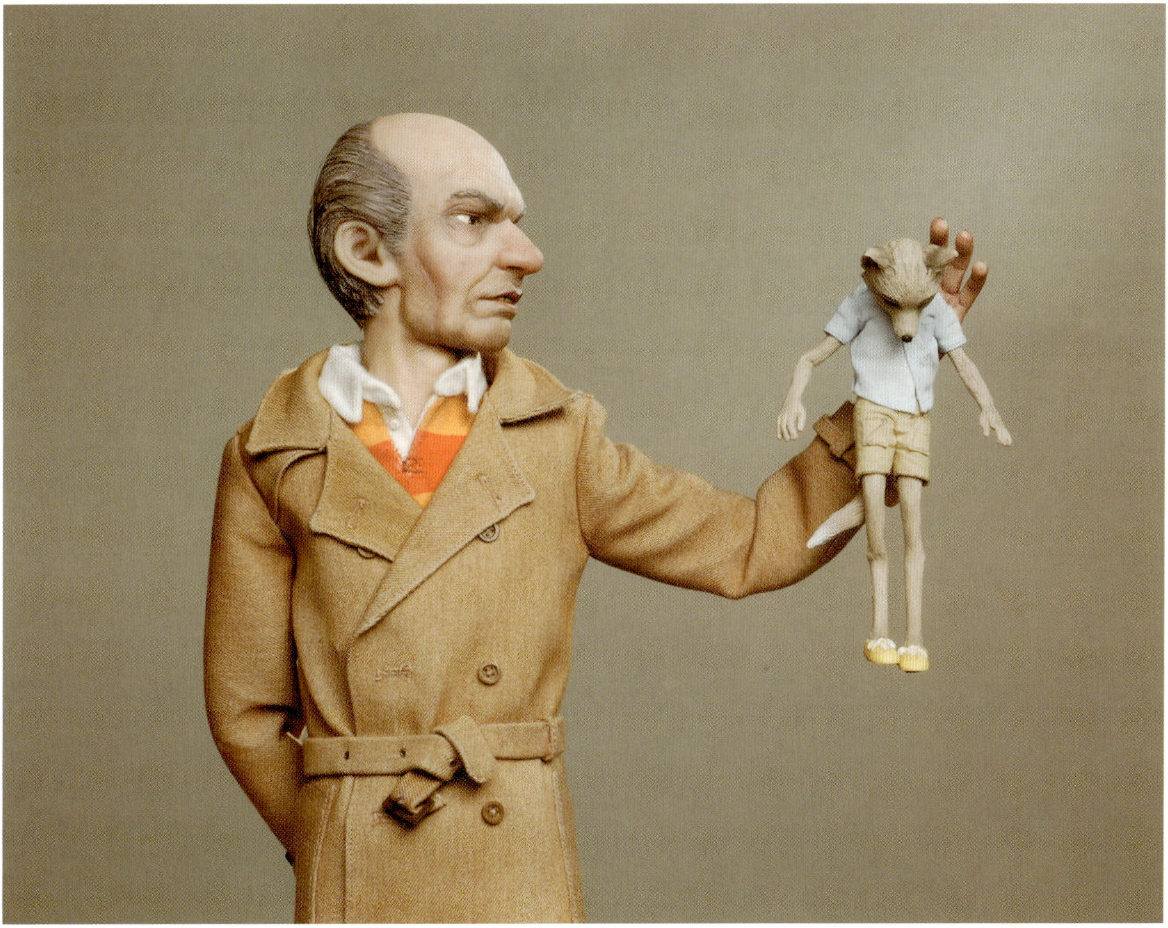

Above: A photograph taken for scale reference of the Bean puppet with a half-scale Kristofferson puppet

MS: *Yeah. I think it was in Connecticut.*
JS: Maybe it was Connecticut. OK good. So they were all digging. And I had heard about it and it sounded like so much fun. Now I went with Wes to the London Film Festival and Wes said, "Let's try to get your stuff I guess while you're here. Unfortunately it'll have to be separate, but let's try to get it while you're here." And so I said okay. At that time the character of Ash, there wasn't a ton of stuff for him, I think. Wes wanted to record it the day after we had had the premiere, and so we kind of got a late start in terms of just communicating from our hotel rooms. He was like, "Let's do it in a half hour, let's do it in an hour, let's do it in two hours," and the day just kind of kept going and I wasn't recording anything. Then at about five, Wes said, "Do you want to drive out to the studio and look at all the puppets?" I was very excited to do that, and we got in a car together and drove forty-five minutes out to this studio and looked at all the puppets, all the sets, I met all the animators and artists, and it was incredible. The funny thing is that we had this dinner at 9 o'clock, and by now it was 7:45. Wes said, "Let's try to go to the recording studio," because they had paid for it of course, the recording studio was booked, "Let's try to go to the recording studio and do some Ash lines." I said, "Well all right, but it's almost 9 o'clock, we might be late for this dinner," and really I was just nervous to record the stuff because I really didn't understand the character. There was very little about him in the script. And Wes kept saying, "No, no, we'll talk about it, we'll talk about it for an hour or two and then we'll record. It's going to be fine." So we drove to the sound studio and I do remember trying to get out of it. "Let's do it another time, let's do it, you know, when you're not so stressed," and really I was just trying to buy time.

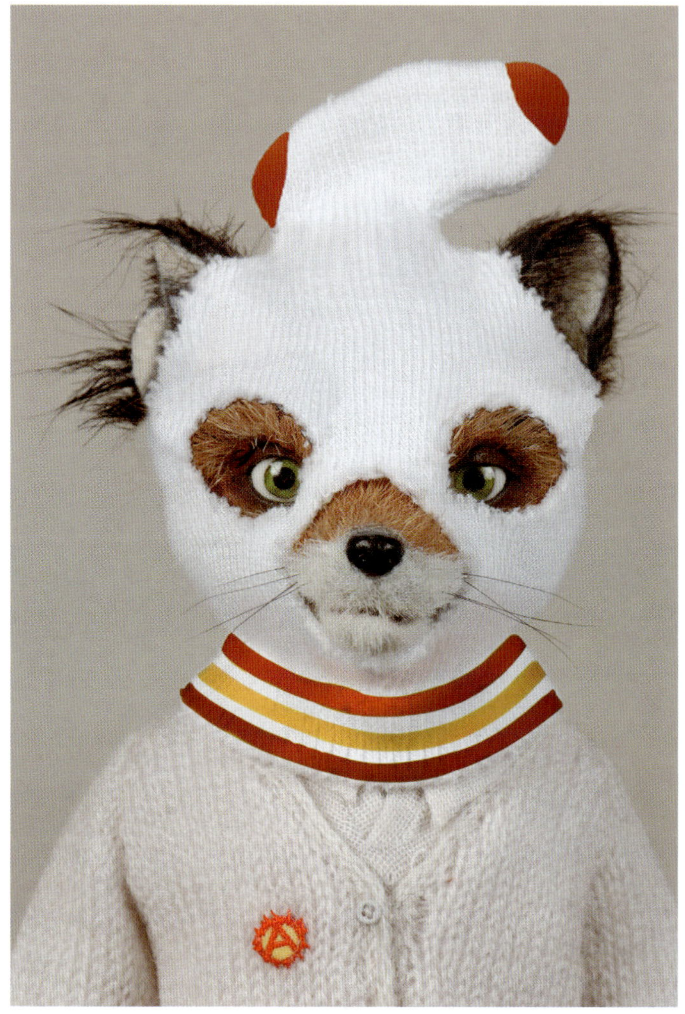

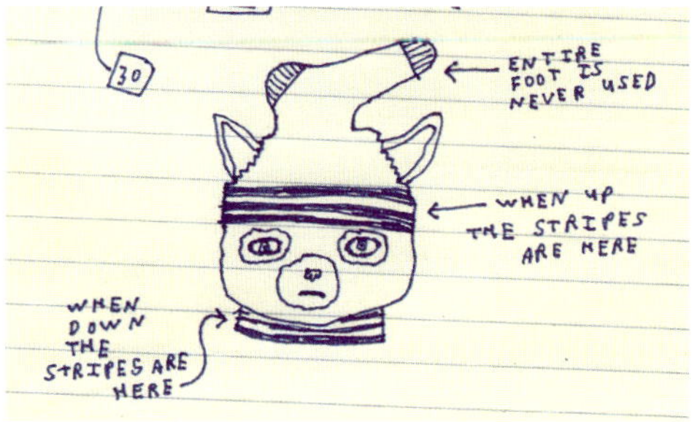

Above: Ash's tube-sock raiding hat

Left: A sketch by Wes for Ash's tube-sock raiding hat

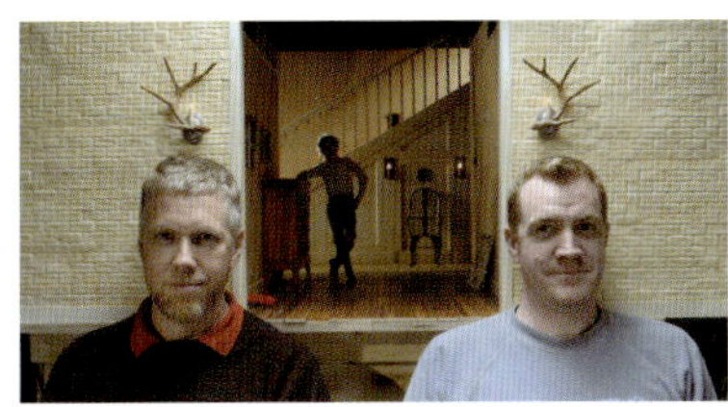

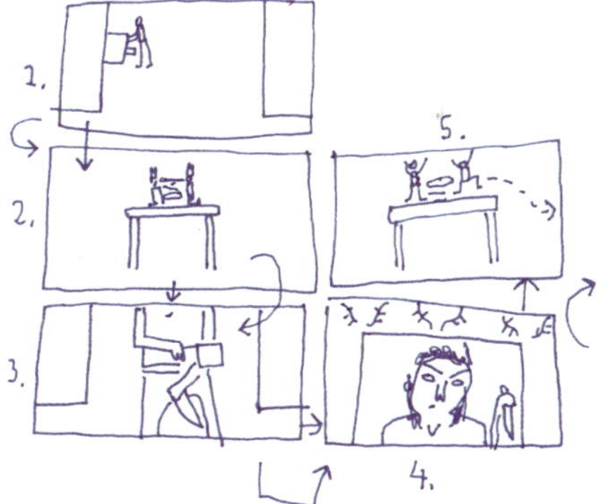

Right: The Kristofferson puppet with raiding hat in the puppet hospital

Top left: Production designer Nelson Lowry and lighting cameraman Toby Howell, who designed and lit this set

Left: Thumbnail sketches by Wes for Ash and Kristofferson in Bean's kitchen

Below: Mrs. Bean's famous nutmeg-ginger apple snaps

Bottom: A still from the movie of Ash and Kristofferson in Bean's kitchen

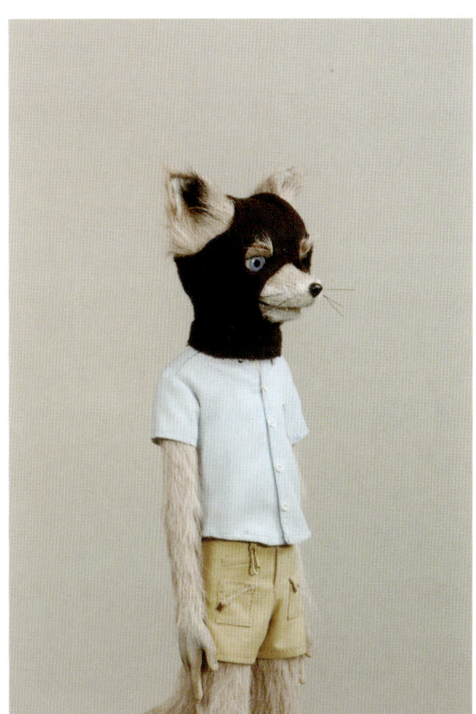

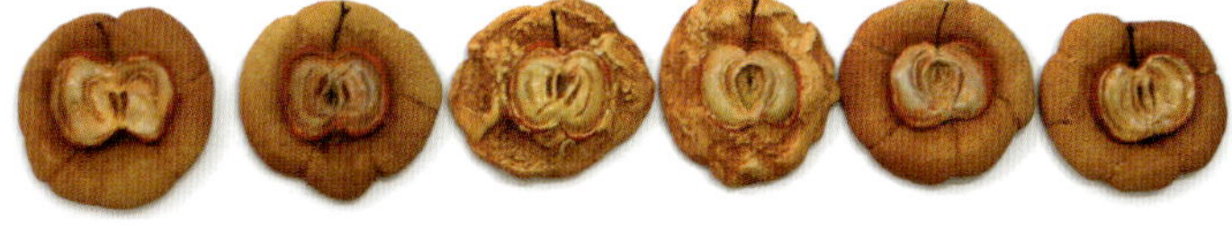

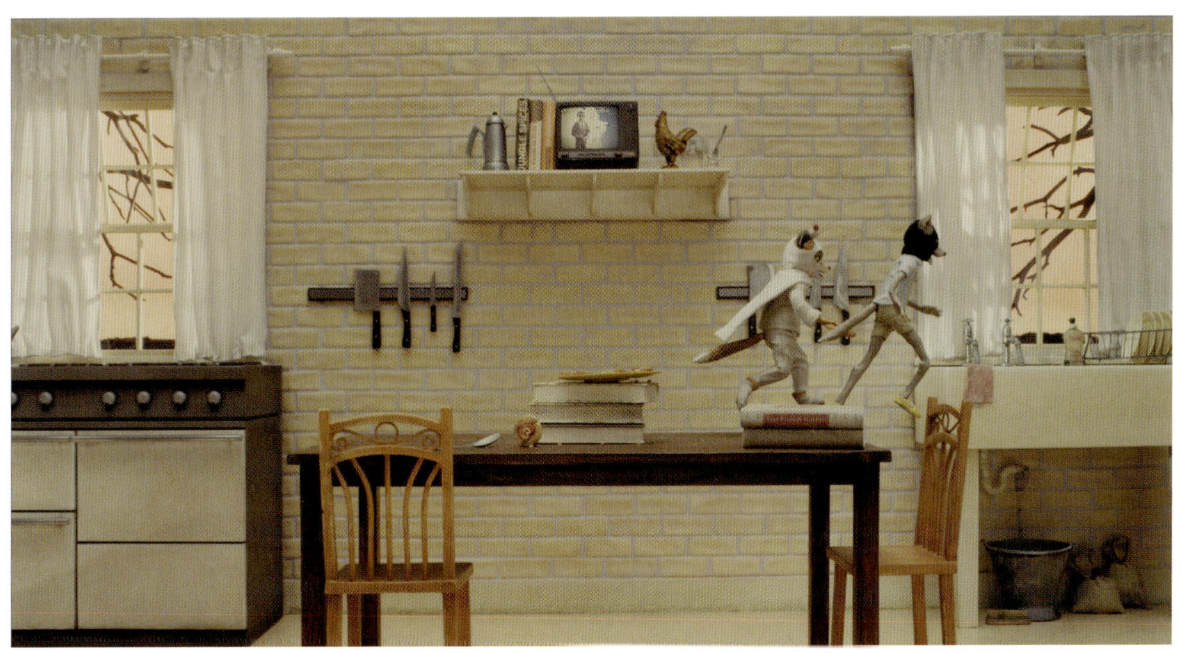

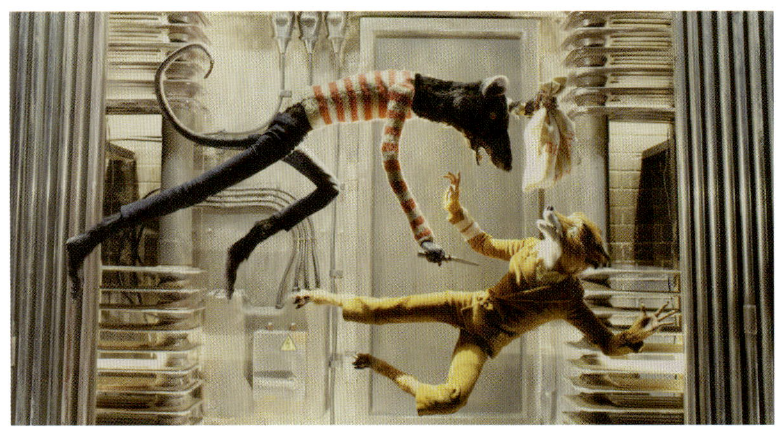

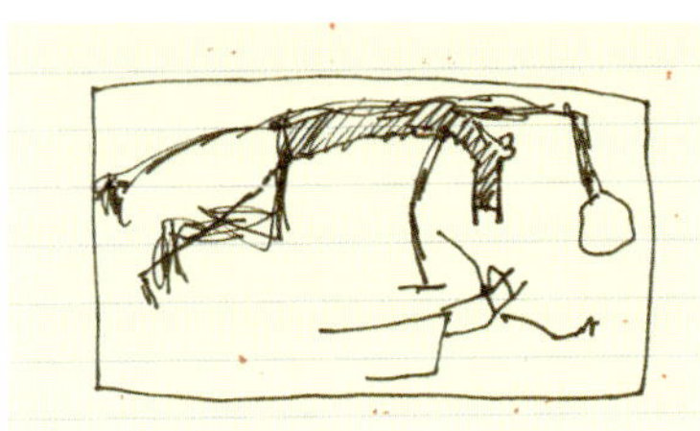

Above: A still from the movie of Rat and Mr. Fox fighting

Left: A sketch by Wes for the above shot of Rat and Mr. Fox fighting

Below left: Early notes by Wes on the fight

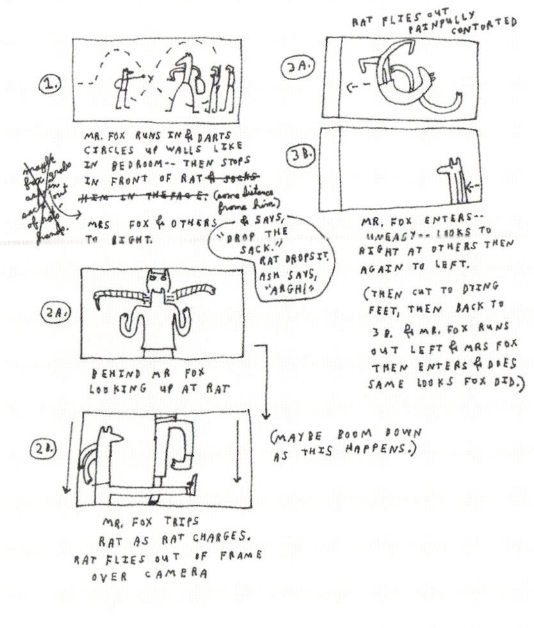

16/03 2009 12:47 FAX 002

1. MR. FOX RUNS IN & DARTS CIRCLES UP WALLS LIKE IN BEDROOM-- THEN STOPS IN FRONT OF RAT ~~& SOCKS HIM IN THE FACE.~~ (some distance from him) & SAYS, "DROP THE SACK." RAT DROPS IT. ASH SAYS, "ARGH!"

MRS FOX & OTHERS TO RIGHT.

2A. BEHIND MR FOX LOOKING UP AT RAT

(MAYBE BOOM DOWN AS THIS HAPPENS.)

2B. MR. FOX TRIPS RAT AS RAT CHARGES. RAT FLIES OUT OF FRAME OVER CAMERA

RAT FLIES OUT PAINFULLY CONTORTED

3A.

3B. MR. FOX ENTERS-- UNEASY-- LOOKS TO RIGHT AT OTHERS THEN AGAIN TO LEFT.

(THEN CUT TO DYING FEET, THEN BACK TO 3B. & MR. FOX RUNS OUT LEFT & MRS FOX THEN ENTERS & DOES SAME LOOKS FOX DID.)

Telephone +44 (0)20 7629 7777 Website radissonedwardian.com/mayfair

THE MAY FAIR

Below: Three stills from the set of the fight

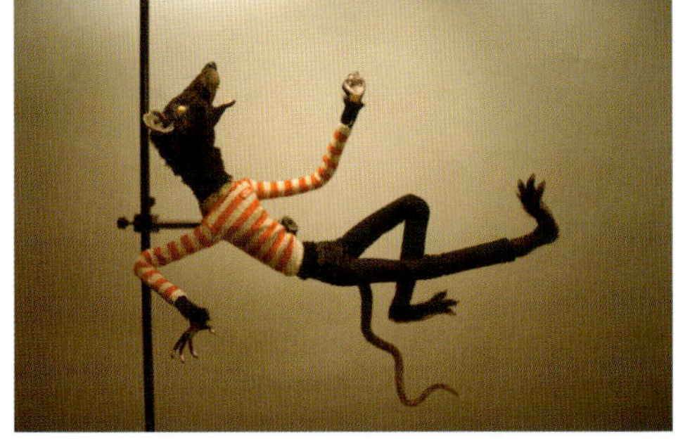

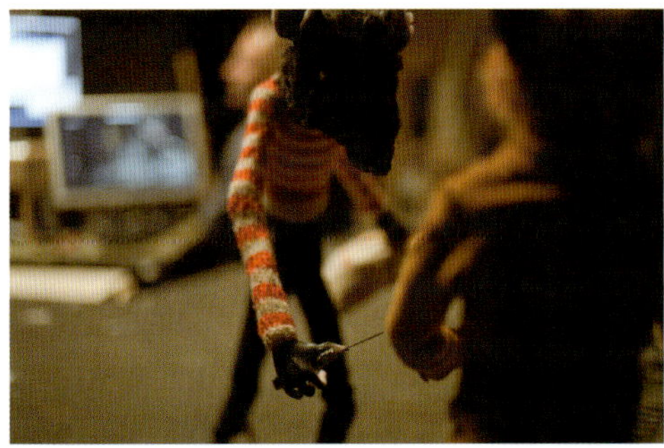

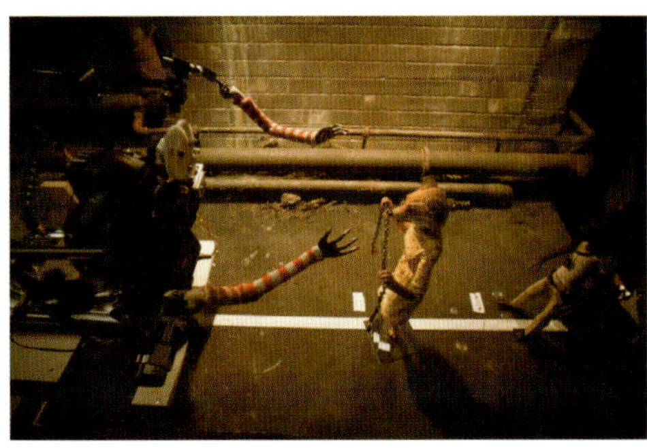

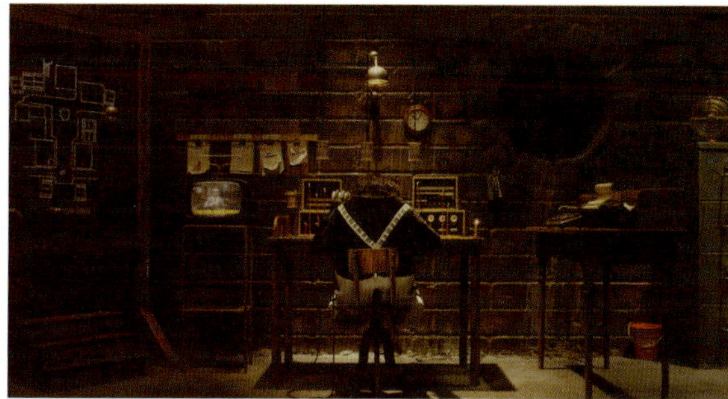

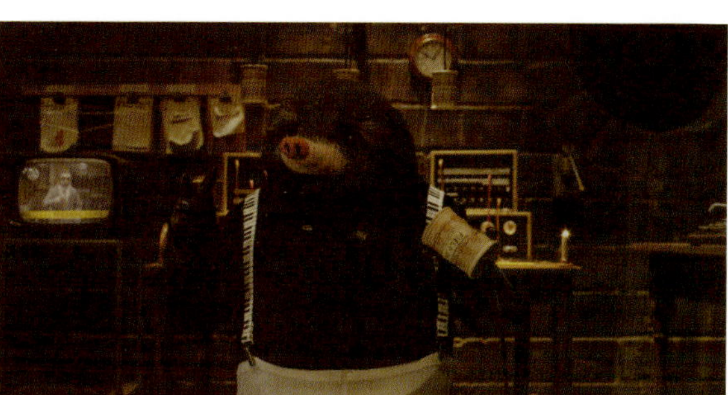

Left: Stills from the movie of Mole in his control room

Right: Props made for Mole's control room

Below: A detail from Mole's control room

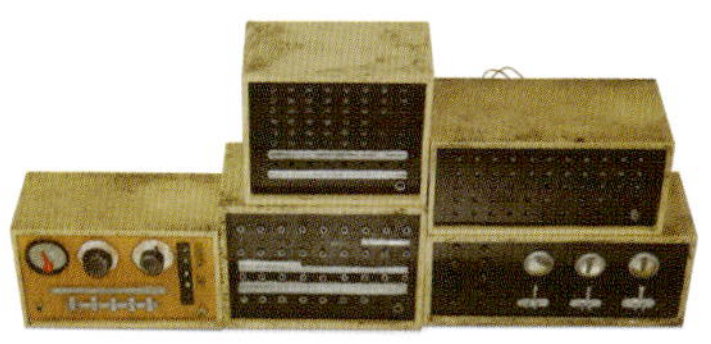

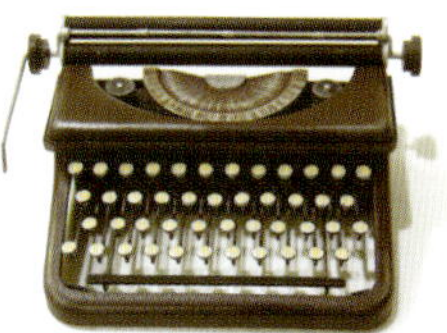

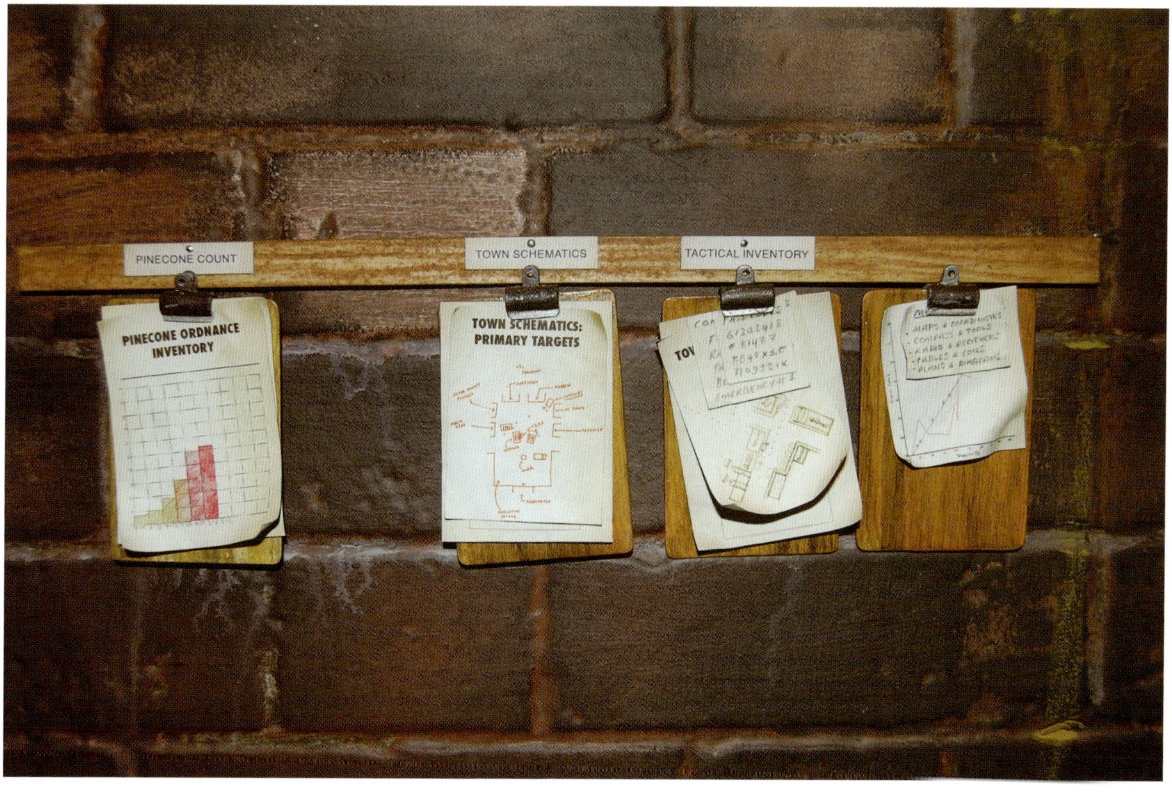

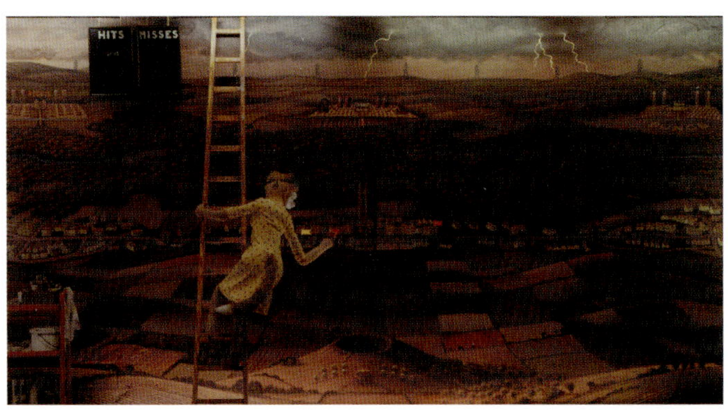
HITS
MISSES

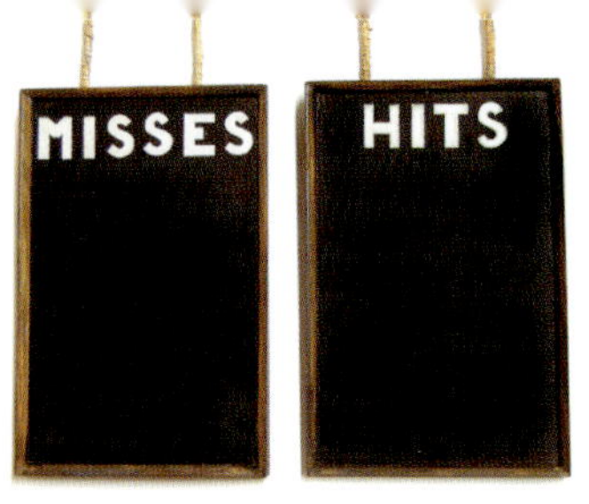
MISSES
HITS

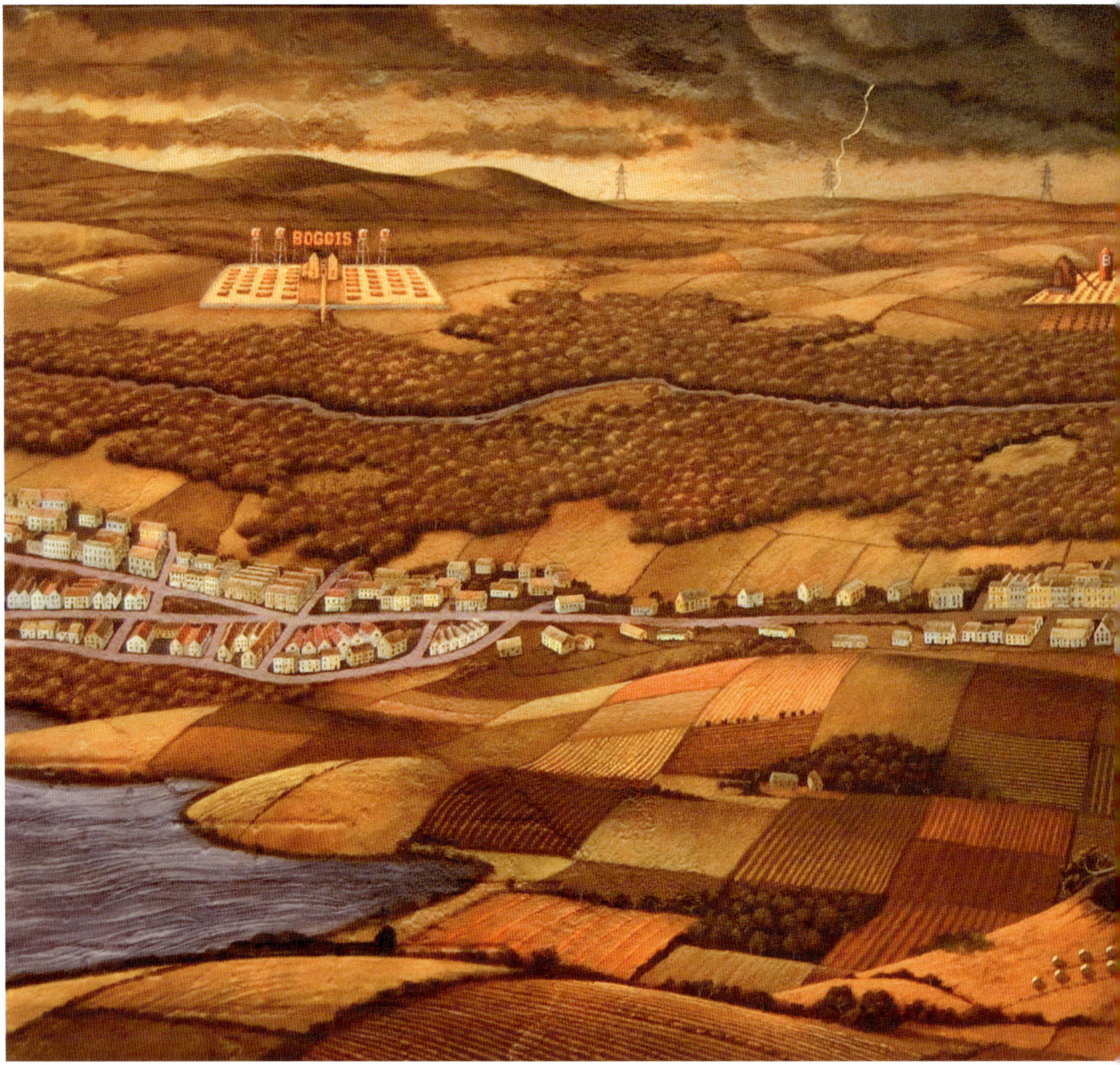

Opposite page: A still from the movie of Mrs. Fox painting the mural and the hits and misses boards from the control center

Right: Mrs. Fox's painting tools and cart

Below: Mrs. Fox's mural, painted by Turlo

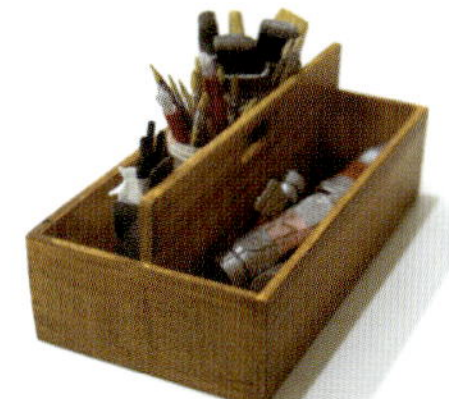

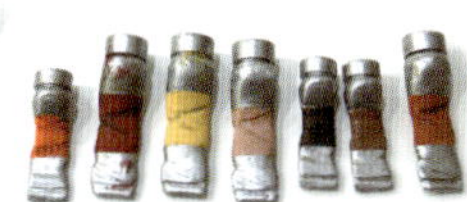

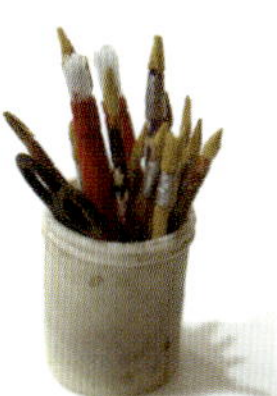

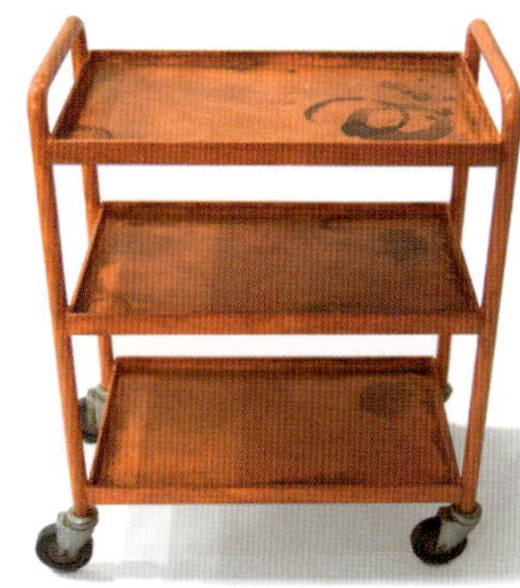

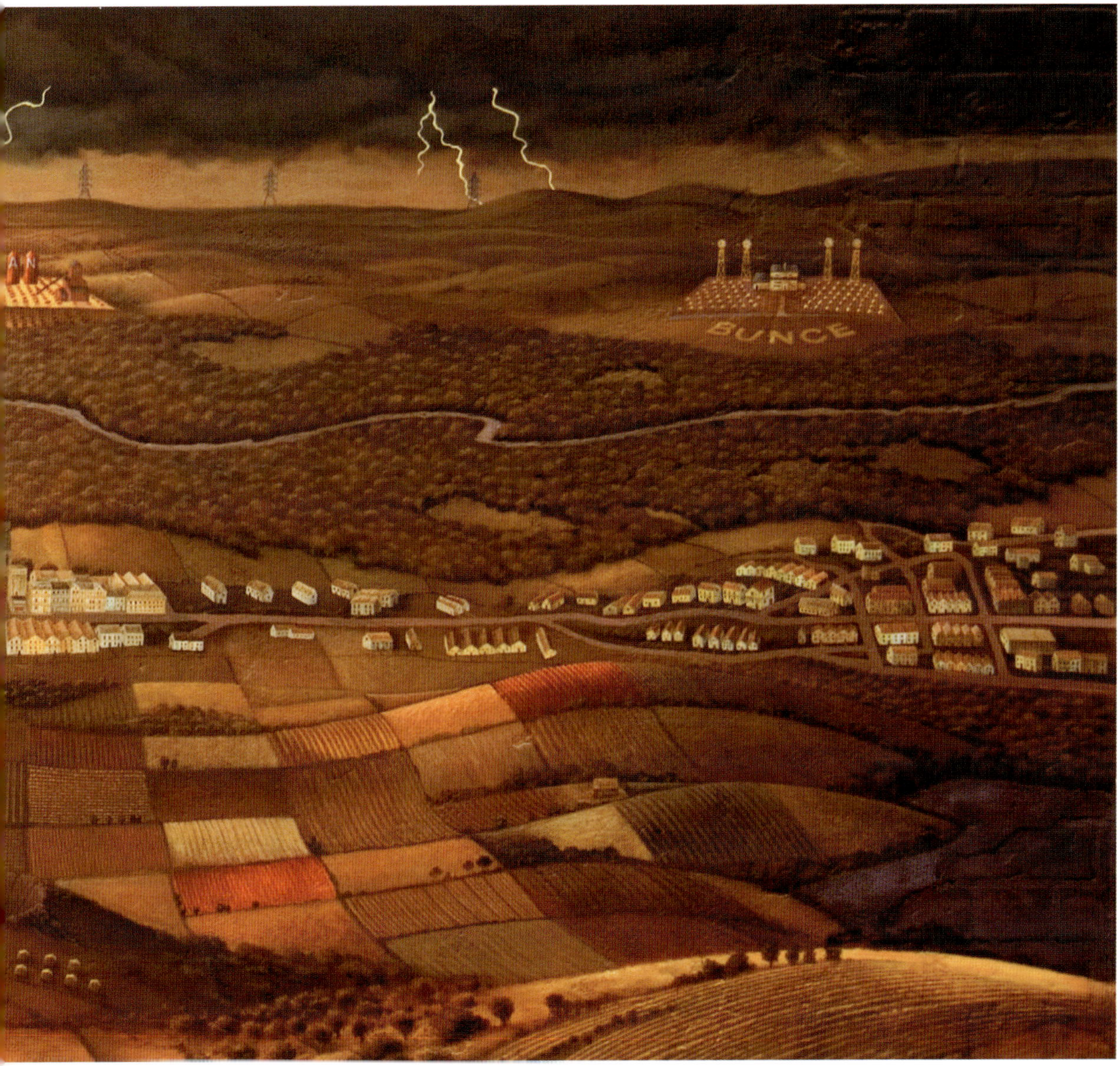

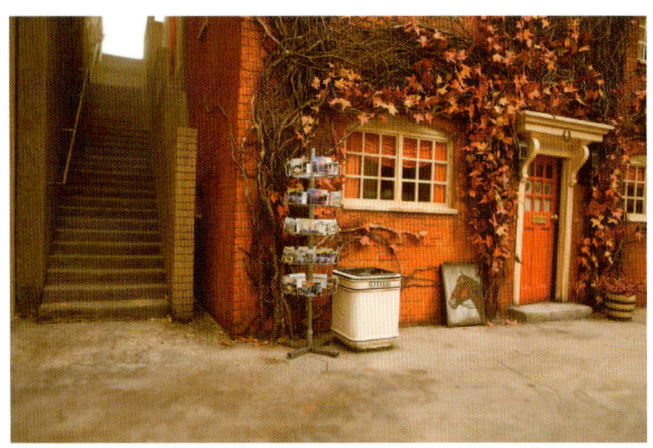

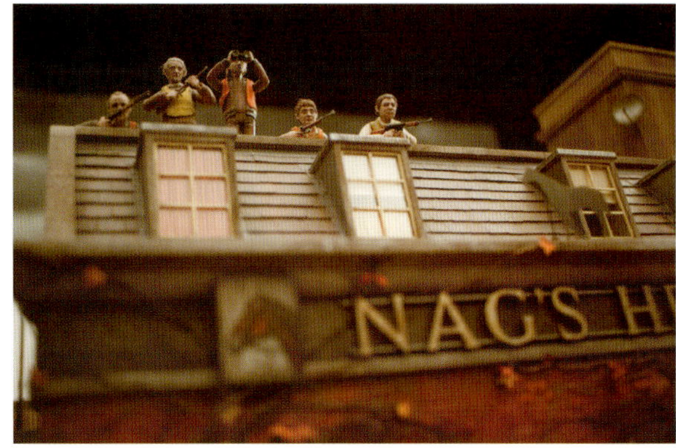
NAG'S

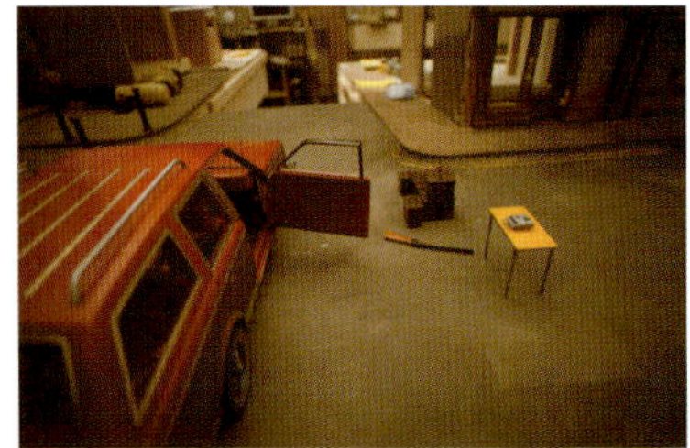

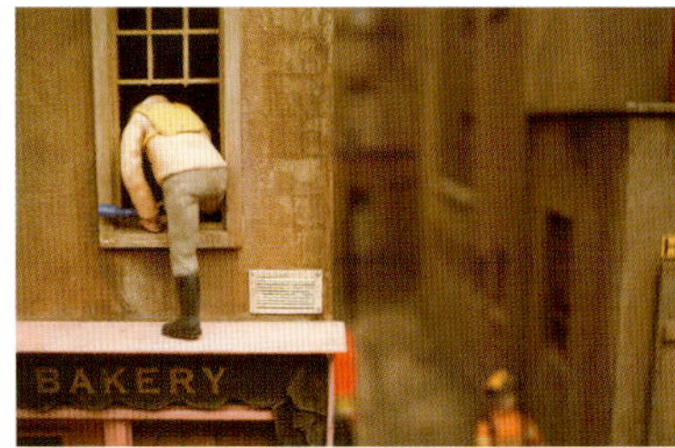
BAKERY

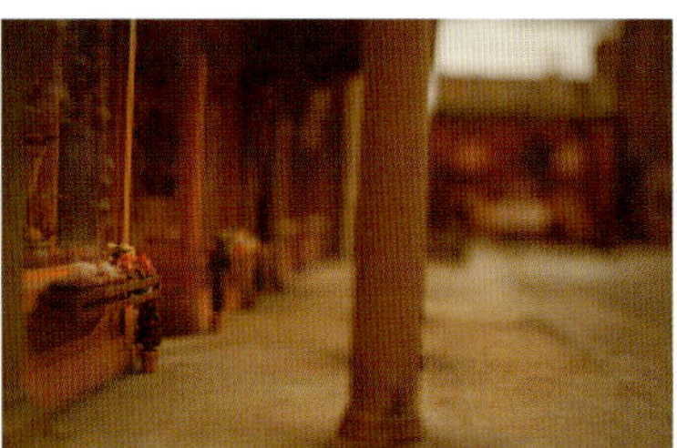

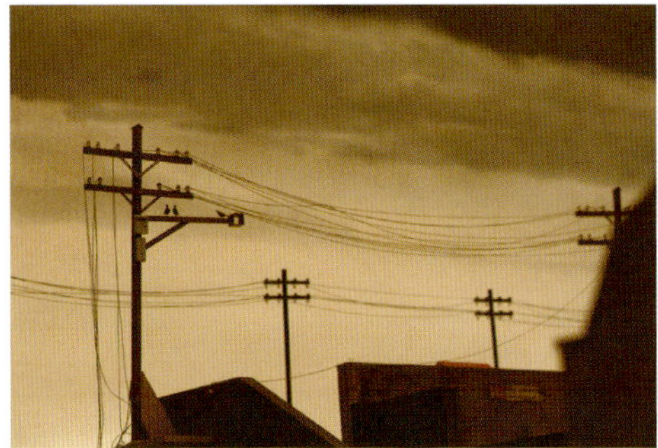

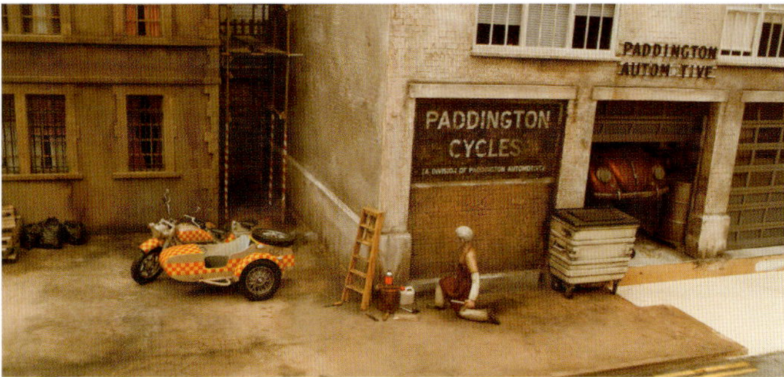
PADDINGTON
AUTOM TIVE
PADDINGTON
CYCLES

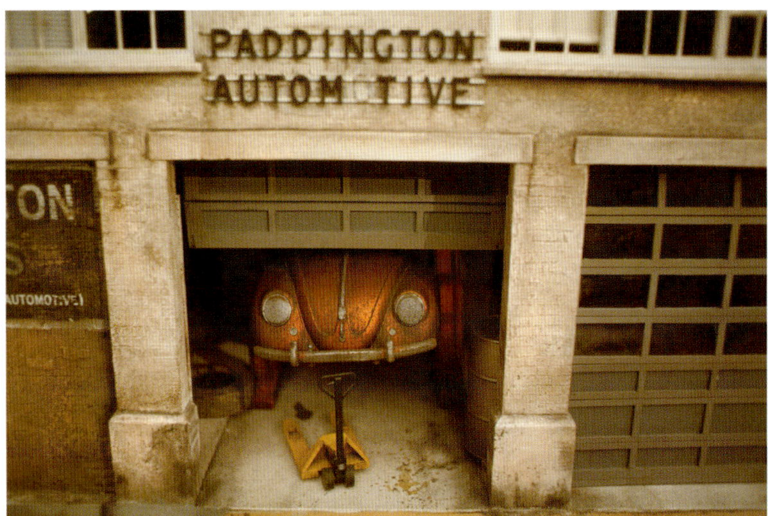
PADDINGTON
AUTOM TIVE

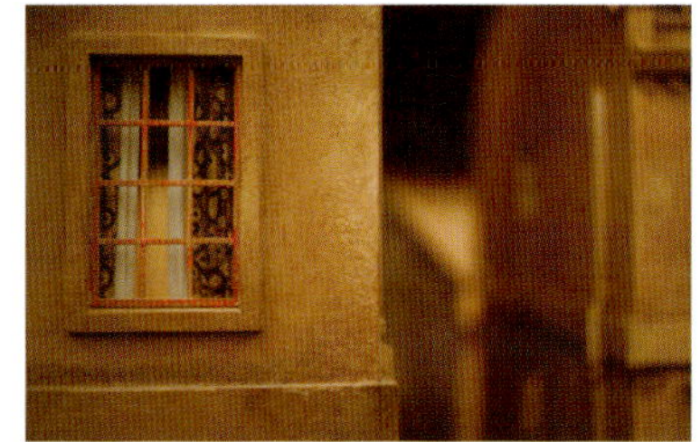

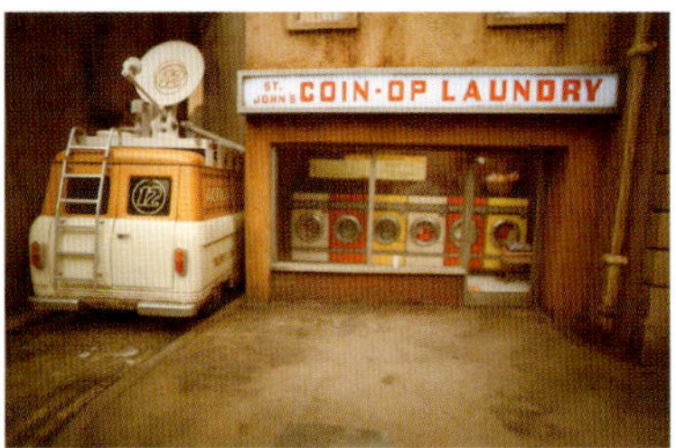
ST. JOHN'S COIN-OP LAUNDRY

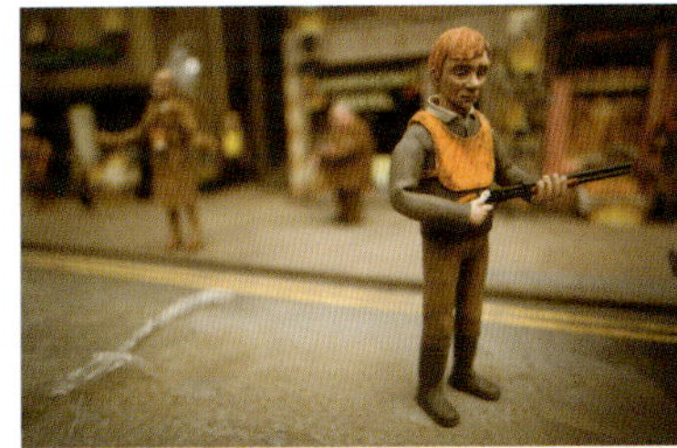

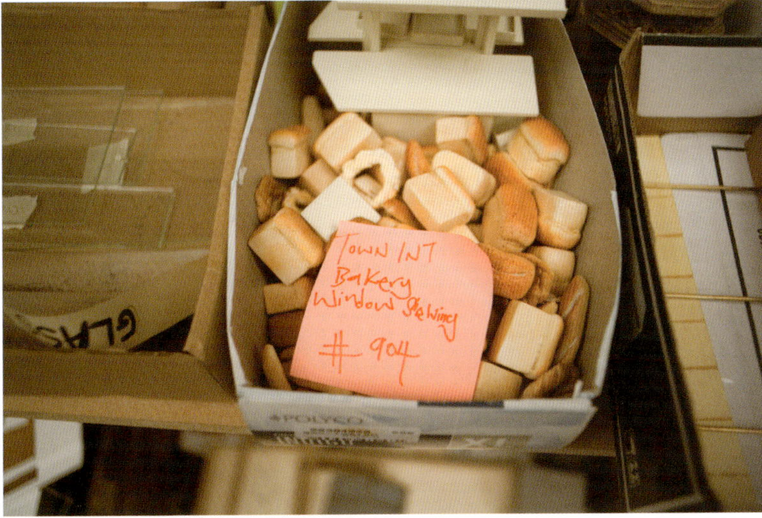

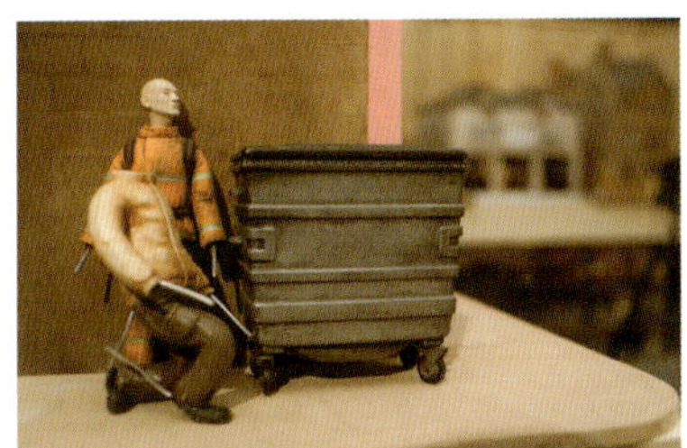

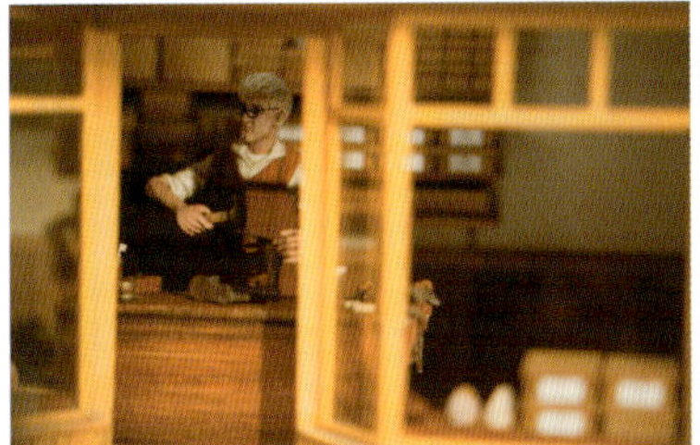

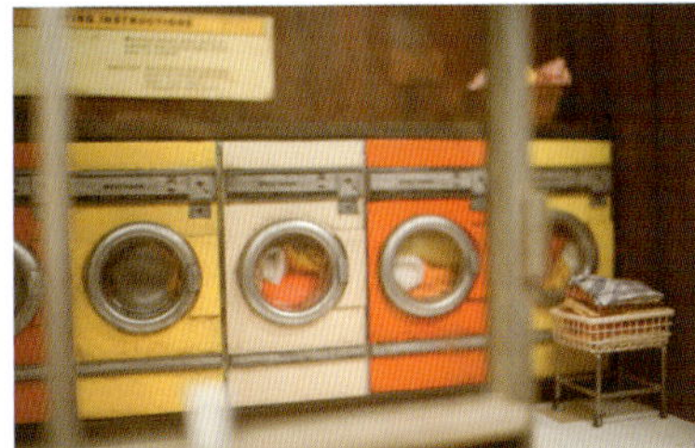

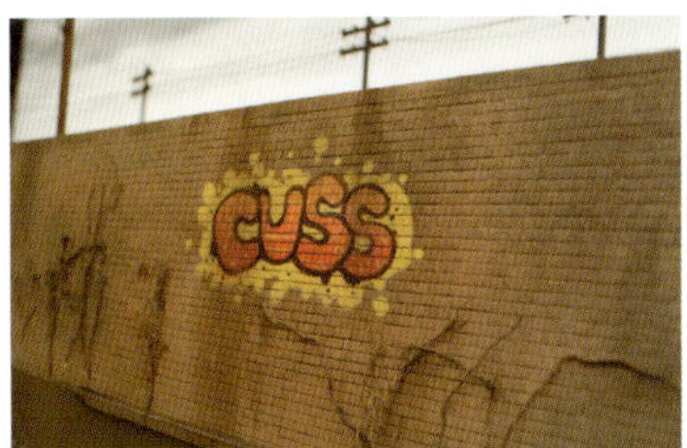

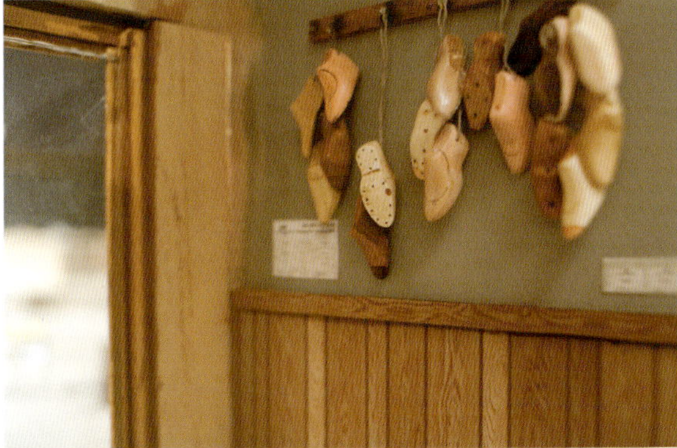

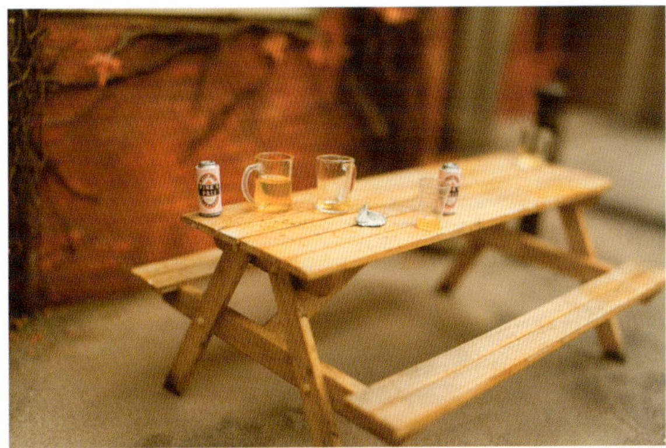

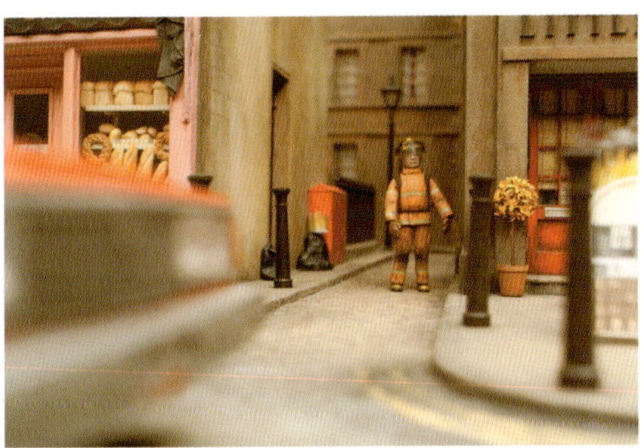

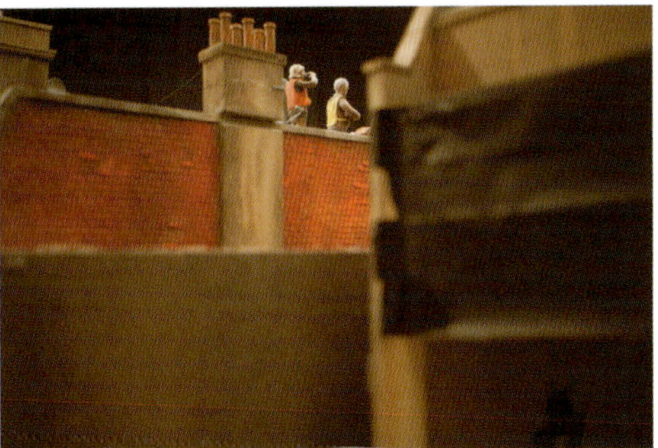

These pages: Photographs of the town square set

Following pages: Wes and Bill Murray on the set of the town square, photographed by Greg

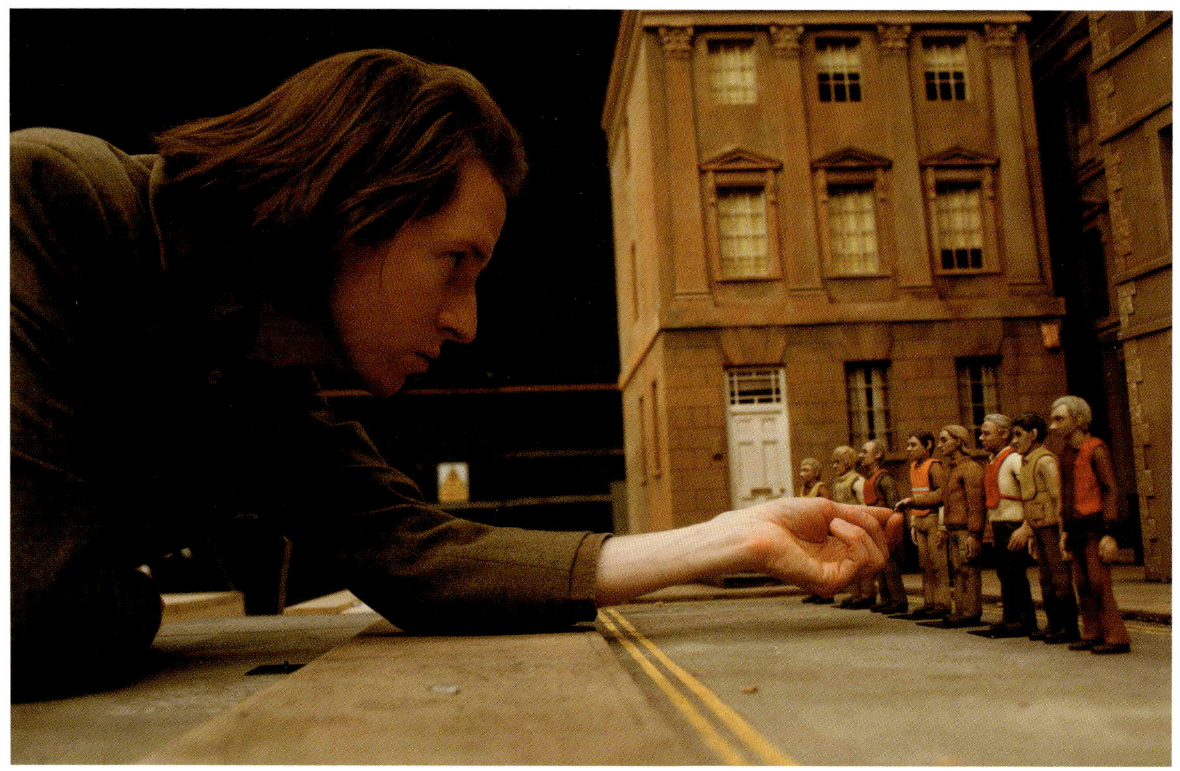

JS: We got to the recording studio and the special microphone that Wes wanted to use, which was his personal microphone I think, was being transported from somewhere, and was stuck in traffic. So we were just sitting at this recording studio and the 9 o'clock hour was approaching and I was getting more and more stressed. Finally the microphone arrived and I had only glanced at the script and I told Wes that. I said, "I've read it but very quickly and I really, you know, I don't know this guy." "We'll talk about it." So Wes and I go into the recording studio, to the actual sound booth, with our scripts in our hands, and Wes orally goes through the entire script. "Okay, now you're in a tree, right, and now the foxes are coming," like he kind of paraphrased the script, but leading me through it. "And the foxes are digging, now they're running through here and ready, go!" And I would read the lines. "Okay, good. Now let's do it again. Now the foxes are coming, now you're running, and go!" He would act, do the scenes with me. We did most of my entire Ash performance in twenty minutes.

Wow.

You know, I've heard about the way silent movie directors worked, where they'd be like, "Now you enter the room, now you enter the room, and you're scared. Then you look up," you know, and they'd act it. They could do that because the director's voice wasn't being recorded. That's what this felt like. Wes was going, "Now you're climbing down the tree, now you're scurrying, now you're scurrying. Let me hear scurrying, now you're eating, let me hear eating."

That's hilarious.

Wes and I, we always talk about that, just how much fun it was to do it. You know, no thought really, not enough time to worry, to overthink it, just complete energy, it was just kinetic. Once we finished a scene Wes would throw the script behind his shoulders, those pages, and in his hand is an ever-diminishing set of neatly organized pieces of paper that are the script. Behind him a floor just filled with complete chaos, these pages out of order. It was just nuts. And that was only the beginning. That was two years ago, that was the press for *Darjeeling Limited*. That was London Film Festival. So then I returned to Los Angeles and Wes kept working on the material and then we met. Wes called me last year, the beginning of June, and said that George Clooney was available to go through the script a couple more times and, could I come and be part of the group of actors for that session. So we all flew and met George Clooney and we just went through all the scenes with a soundman holding a boom mike. It was done completely in the spirit that Wes was trying to go for, which was overlap-

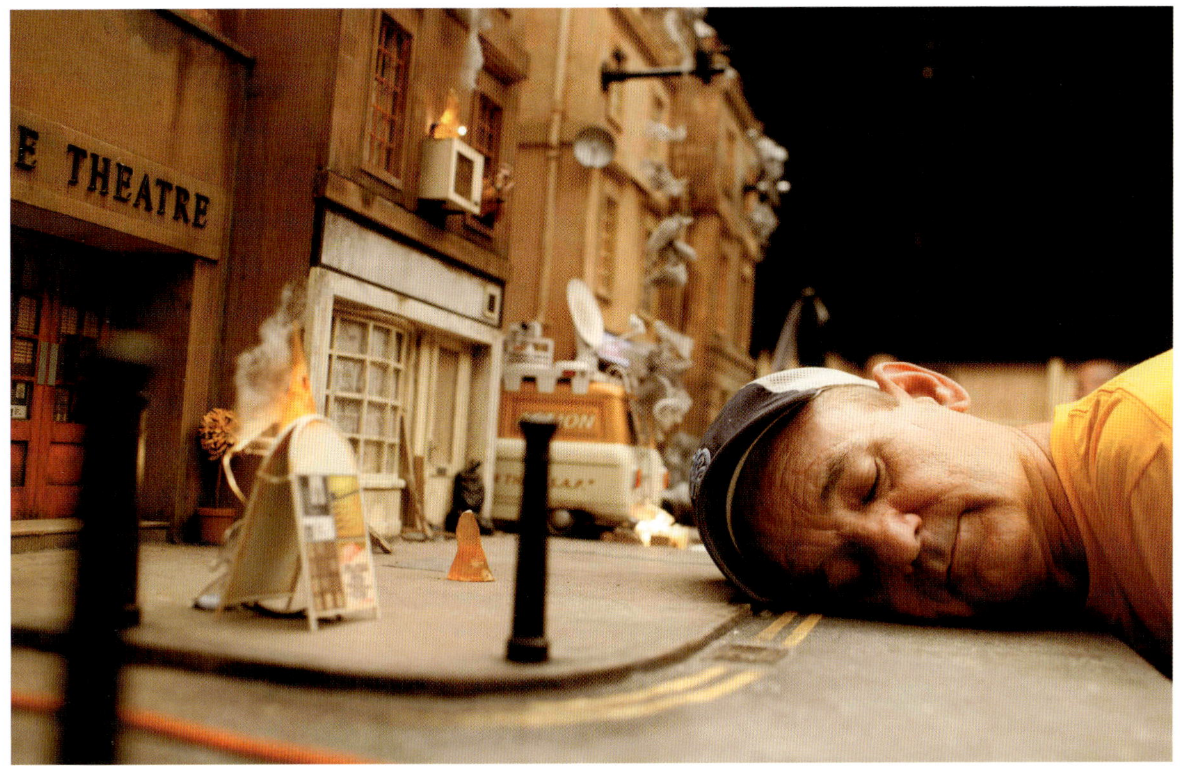

ping, cutting off, just actors really connecting with each other. All the scenes in the movie except for a couple that I do with George, or the Fox character, I did looking at George Clooney, staring at him doing these scenes. The scene where my character is washed, the water washes them all out as he's giving his big speech, that whole thing where it's really panicked—me and Mr. Clooney did that in a bedroom, really panicked, looking at each other, staring at each other, acting. It was really fun and intense, and unlike anything I've ever experienced before. That's always been the best thing about working with Wes, it's always different and it's always its own beautiful experience that's unlike anything else. And yet because it's Wes and now I've known him for so long, it's that perfect combination of familiar and completely brand new and unexpected. But I like that—when you really begin to build up a personal friendship and a working friendship like that, it's so nice, because you build upon your past but you're always going into this unknown area together and there's always a sense of positive uncomfortability. You know what I mean?

Yeah.

If I look back at the ten most amazing moments of my work life, they're all with Wes. Because we have always gone into these brand new, weird, odd situations together. Like we were in India, we were on a train. What were we doing there? We were recording a thing. We did an entire performance in twenty minutes in some weird sound stage. Then we went and ate food and then we were with George Clooney. Just these bizarre experiences. I went home after we did all the stuff with George Clooney, and over the course of the last year I'd get these emails from Wes saying, "Are you available today or tomorrow to go into a sound studio and do some new lines for Ash?" And of course I'll find a way to be available for Wes because I love him and I love this movie. But it's very interesting. You know, when you go to a sound stage or a recording studio to do lines there's a microphone set up, and then a music stand, and on the music stand is a piece of paper with your lines on it. Very rarely with this movie would there be a script in front of me of what I was going to be doing. It would really just be the lines out of context, just hanging there, free-floating lines. I would laugh because I'd get there and I would look at these lines and have no idea what they're about or what they're referring to or where they're coming from or where they're going, anything. So I would just smile and they would patch Wes through into my headphones—they had some kind of a thing where he would be talking from Paris to me on a telephone and I would be hearing it in headphones in the recording studio.

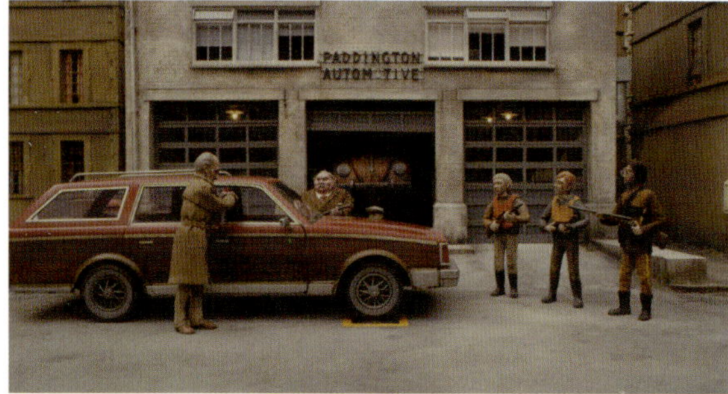

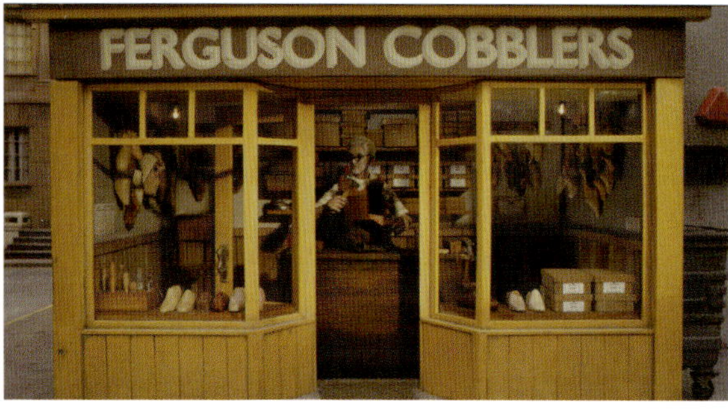

Left: Two stills from the movie

From: Molly Cooper
Subject: **note from Wes on station wagon**
Date: 27 February 2008 16:34:03 GMT
To: Nelson Lowry, Francesca Maxwell, Alice Bird, Luke Sikking

The station wagon at the end is meant to be based on Jarvis Cocker's station wagon—I'll try to get a picture and pass it along as soon as I do.

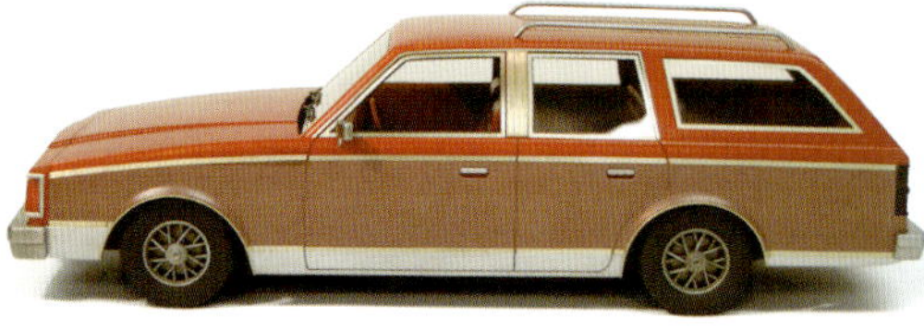

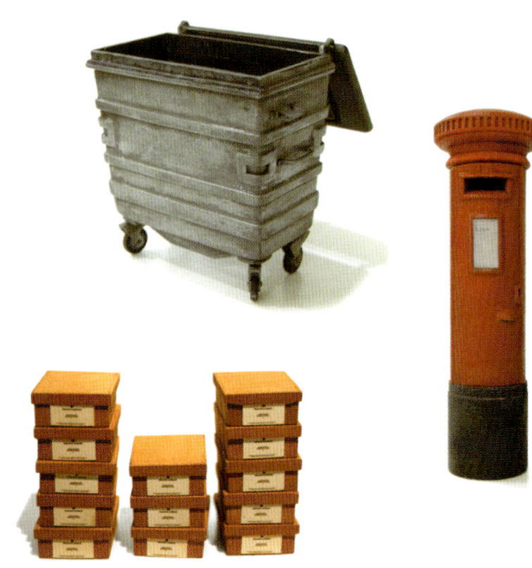

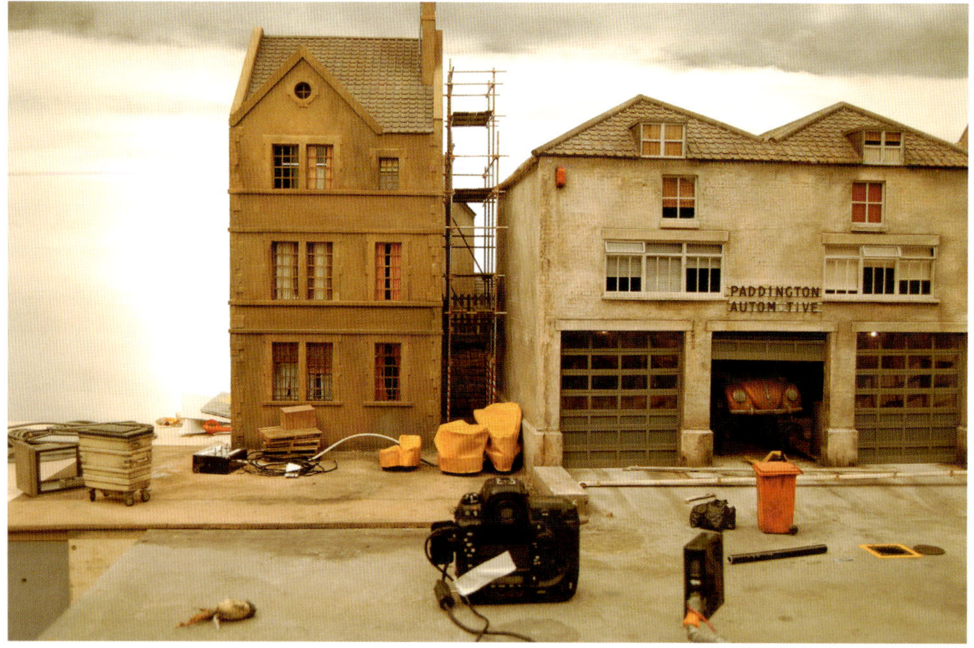

Above: Props from the town square

Left: The town square set

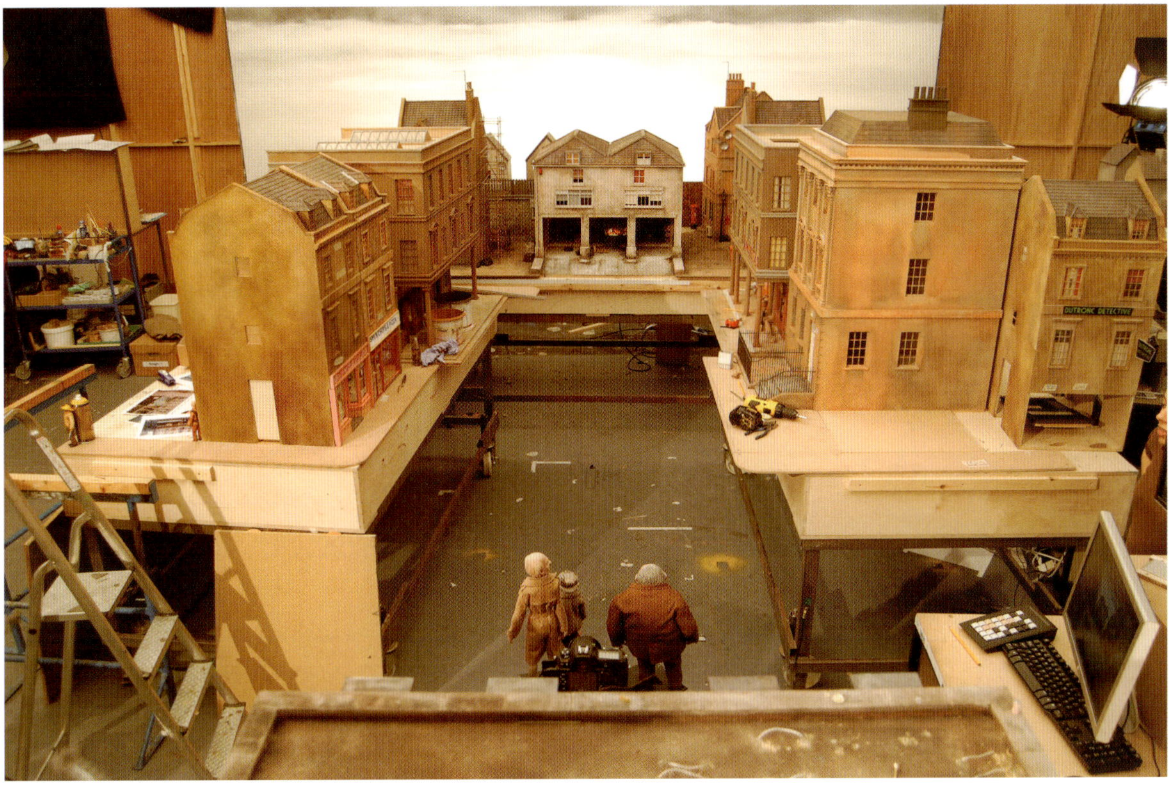

Above: The town square set

Above: The town square set

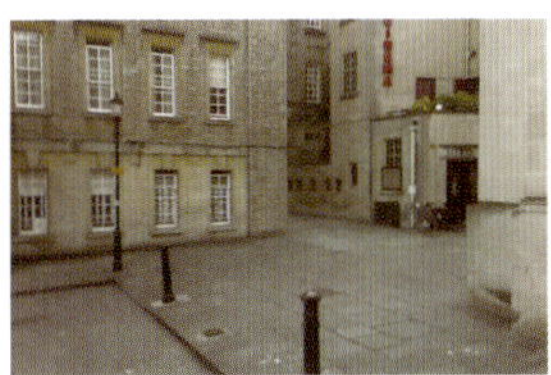

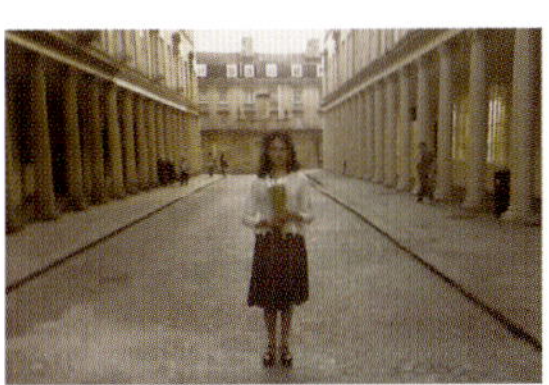

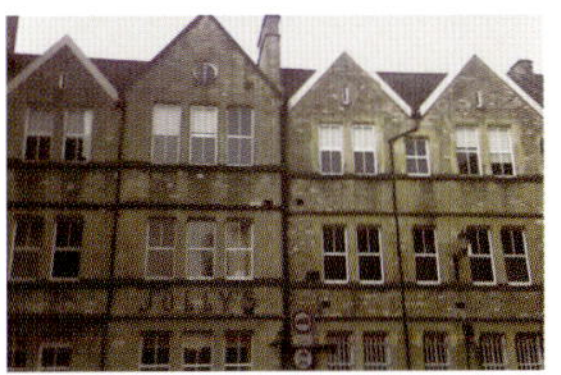

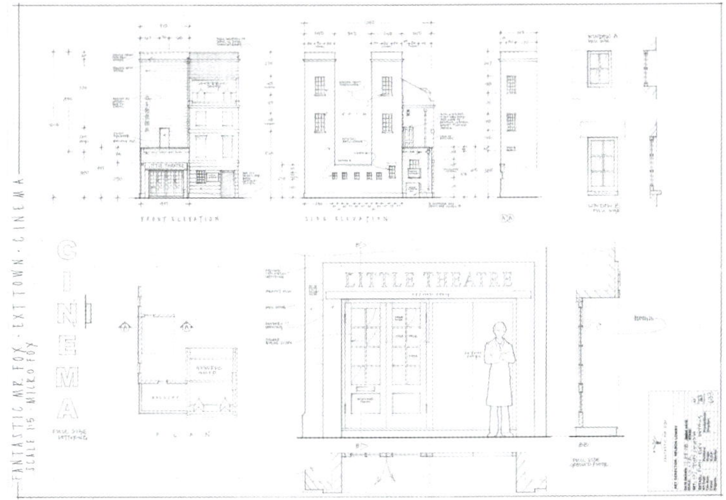

Left: Three photographs taken by Wes on a trip to Bath and used as reference for the town square

Above right: A draft of the town square by Hannah Moseley

MS: *Yeah, Eric mentioned that too.*

JS: He would explain the scenes. "Okay, this is a scene, we have this new scene where you're with Fox, and go!" And that's it. Wes would say, "Could we get some noises of you eating?" I would just be, like, [makes sound]. Meanwhile I'm staring at a guy through glass who has no idea what this movie is and he's going, "What the hell is this guy doing? It's like he's doing nothing." It's a really fun way to make a movie. And as an actor, when you go to see a movie that you've worked on you really don't know what it's going to be because of, you know, because of the nature of a film. You go to work during the day, you do many different takes, many different angles and it's the editor and the director who choose what you're going to see, what's going to be in the final film. When you go to see it to some extent you don't really know what you're going to see, but you have a pretty close idea just because you know the script. With this movie, when I went to go see it, I had no idea what I was going to see. And I'll tell you the really funny thing I observed, because after we were with George I went with Wes back to Paris and, you know, he's in Paris and they're doing the work in London. These scenes take so long to do, just one frame at a time. So before they start working on a scene they email Wes a photo of the set and what it's going to look like and what everyone's wearing and all this stuff, and Wes looks at it, and then he'll give his notes, and then they start working on it. And I was telling Wes—it's like he's directing stop-motion in a stop-motion way. They make a thing, send it to him, he gives his notes, sends it back. He directs via phone call or email notes these scenes. It's very hard work and it takes a long time. So he's actually had to become stop-motion.

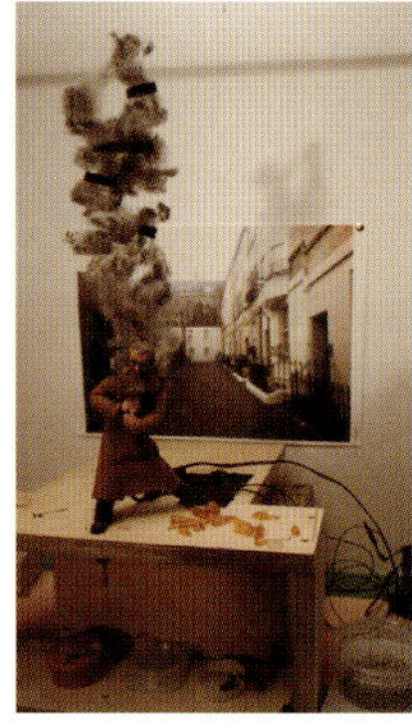

Above: The burning Bean puppet being prepared off set—the flames were made from pieces of soap, and the smoke from steel wool

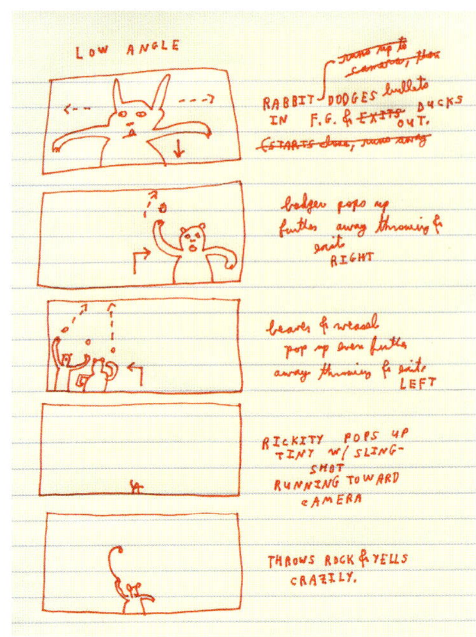

Right: A sketch by Wes of animals coming out of the manhole

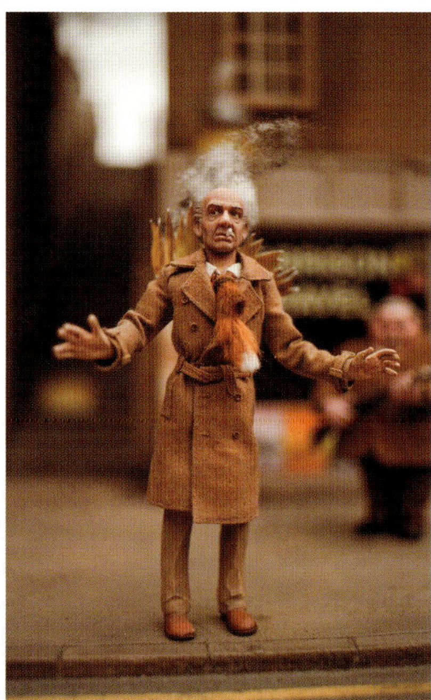

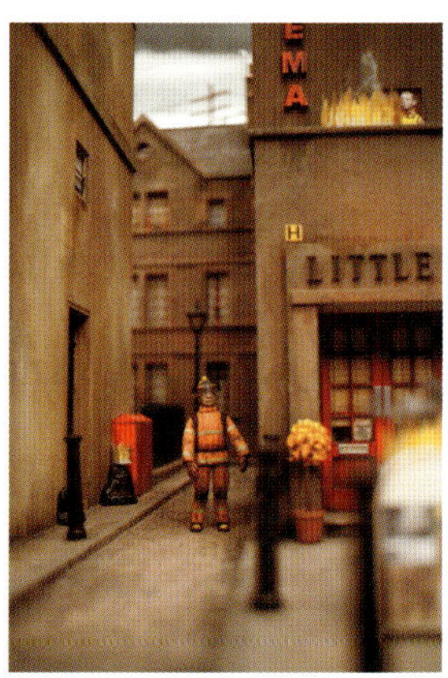

Above: The town square set

Left: Bean on fire

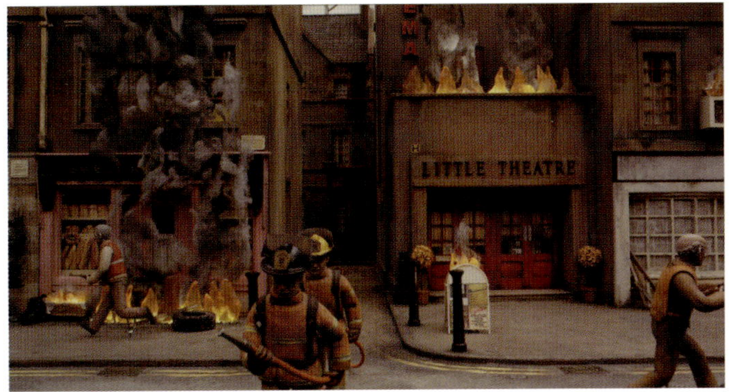

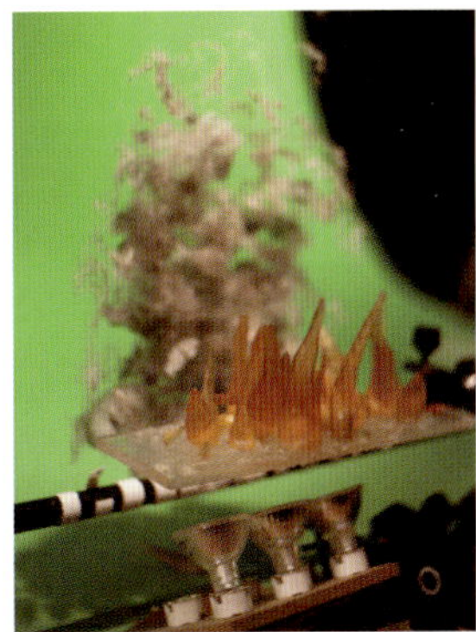

Far left: A still from the movie of the fire in the town square

Near left: Shooting a fire and smoke element

Below: Notes from Wes on the long dolly shot in the town square

From: Wes Anderson
Subject: **Re: Explosion tests to Wes**
Date: 9 October 2008 18:48:19 BST
To: Mark Waring

Mark this is the sort of message only a select few people are ever lucky enough to receive:
"We are sending over a series of different explosions."
Thank you very much for this

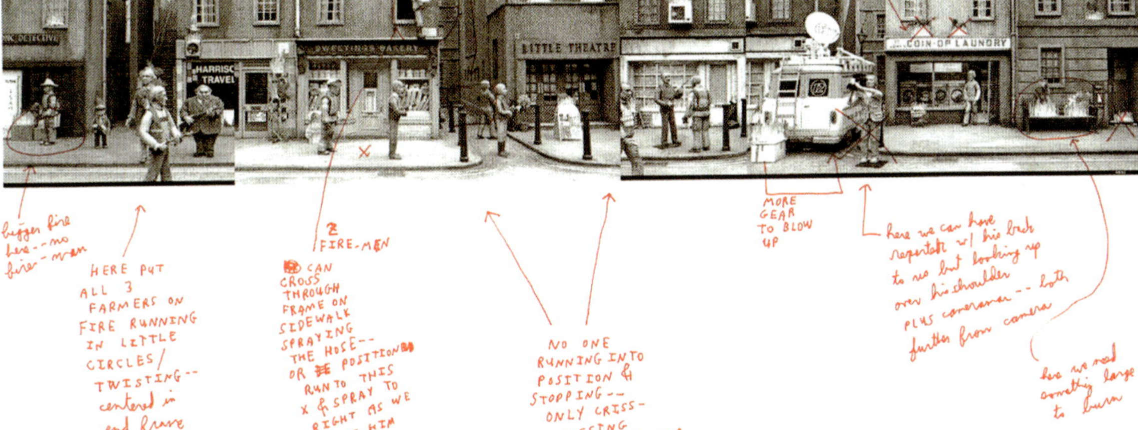

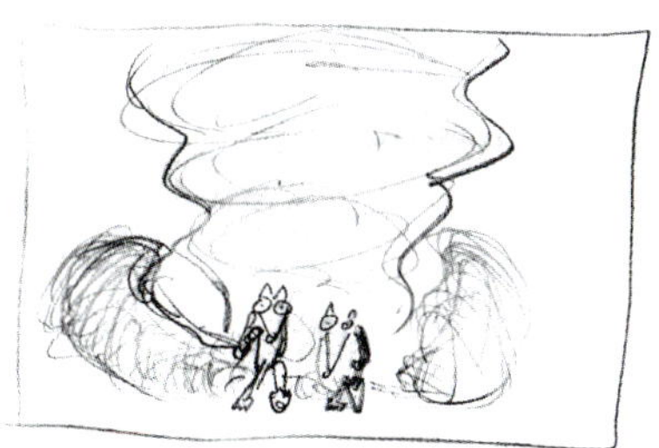

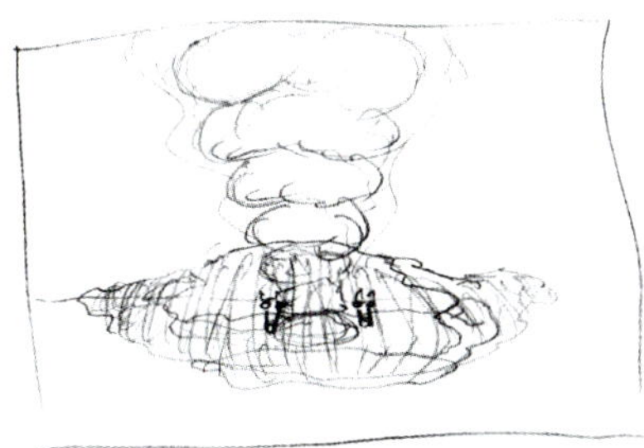

Left: Two sketches by the animator Leo Nicholson of Mr. Fox and Kylie running out of the manhole

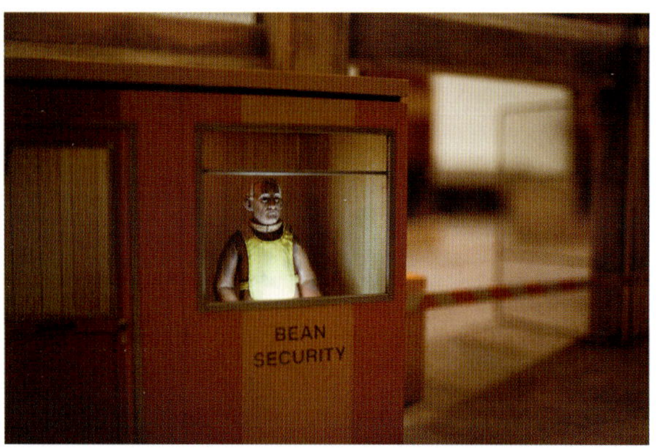

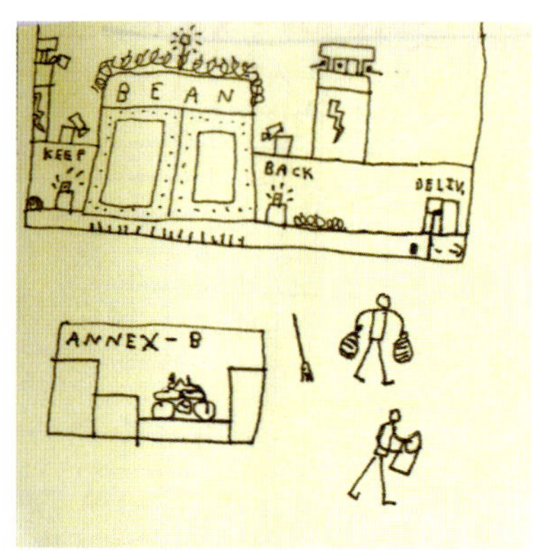

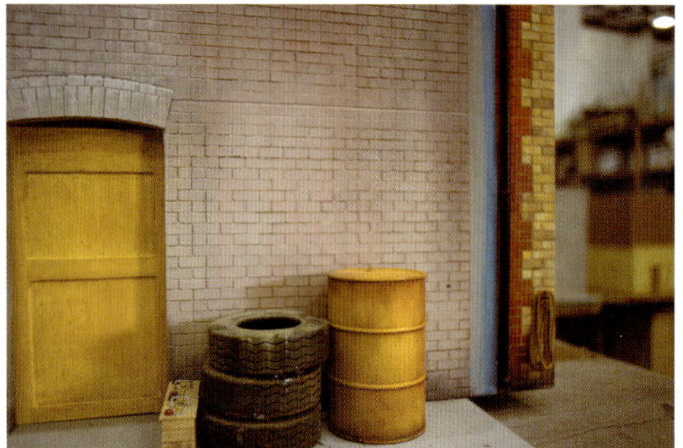

Left: Lighting tests for Bean's security booth

Above: A sketch by Wes of the entrance to Bean Annex

Below: A pill bottle prop for Spitz's rabies medicine

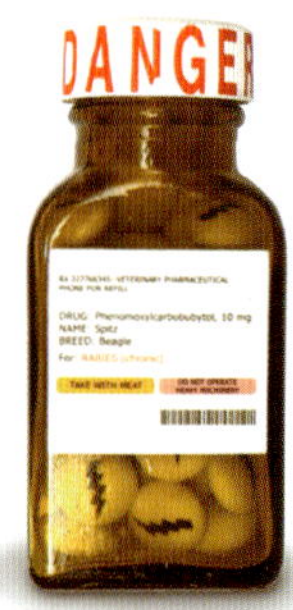

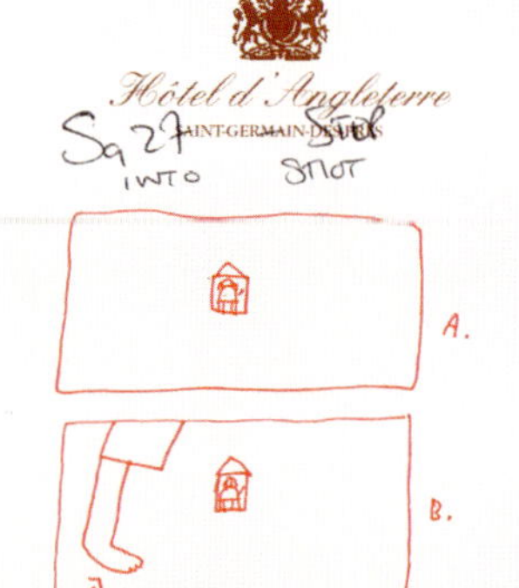

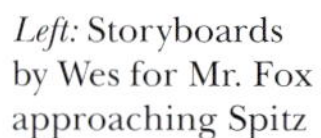

Left: Storyboards by Wes for Mr. Fox approaching Spitz

Below: A set photo of Mr. Fox being chased by Spitz

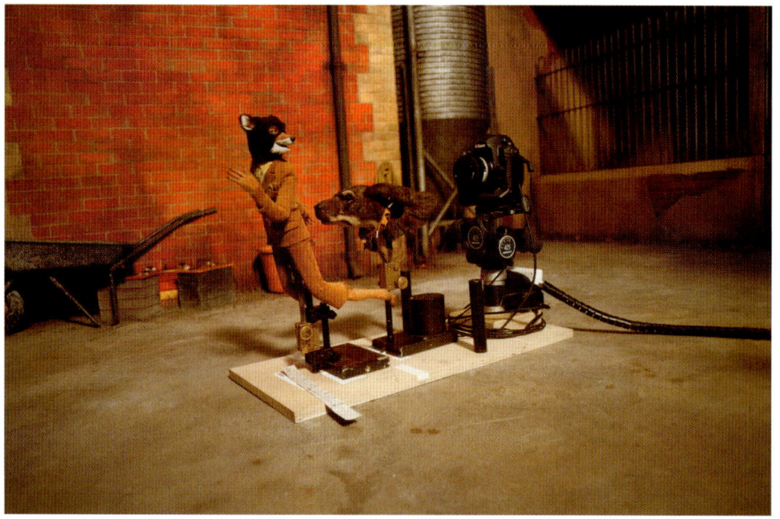

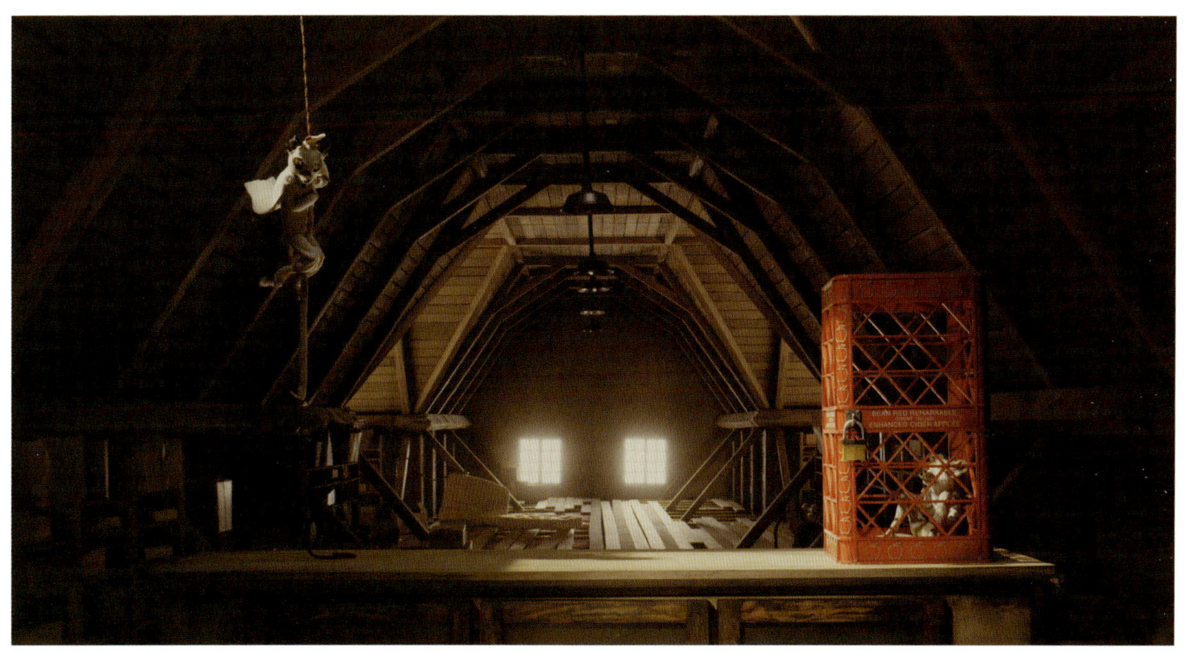

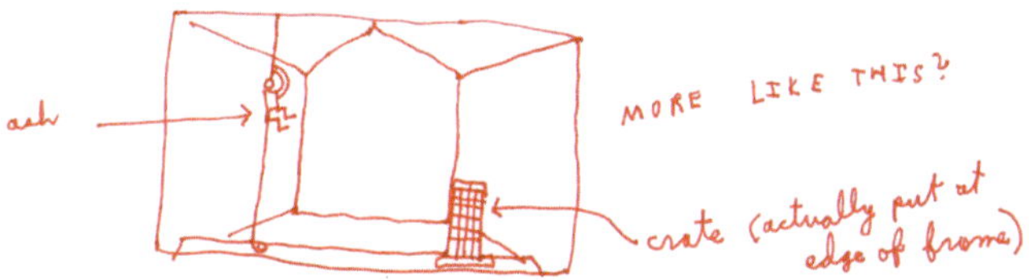

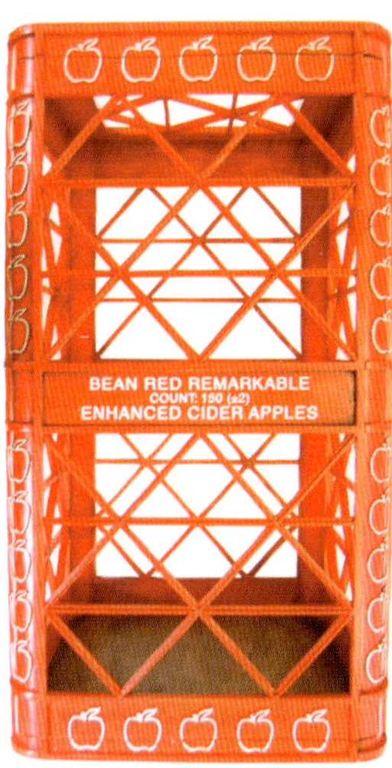

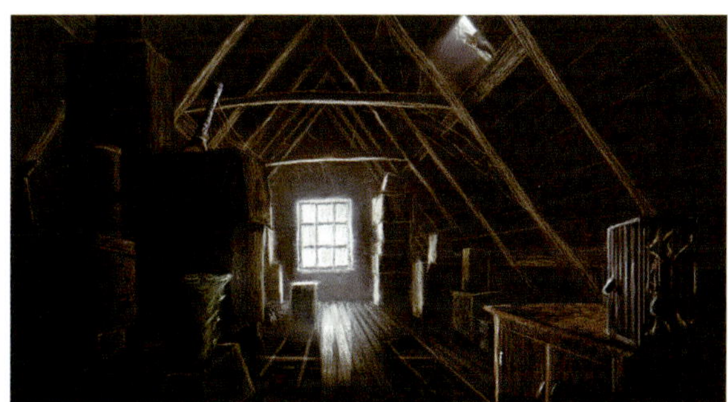

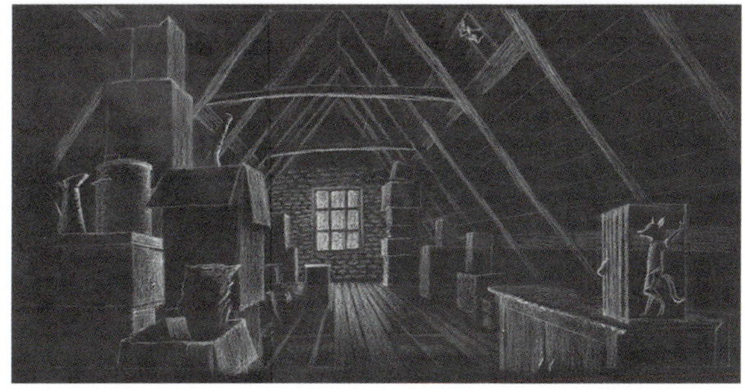

Top: A still from the movie of Ash climbing down the shoelaces

Above left: A sketch by Wes for the above shot

Above right: The apple crate prop

Left: Two concept designs for the attic by Turlo

Right: A test for shooting the boxes

Below left: A sketch and notes by Wes for the Bean Annex shoot-out

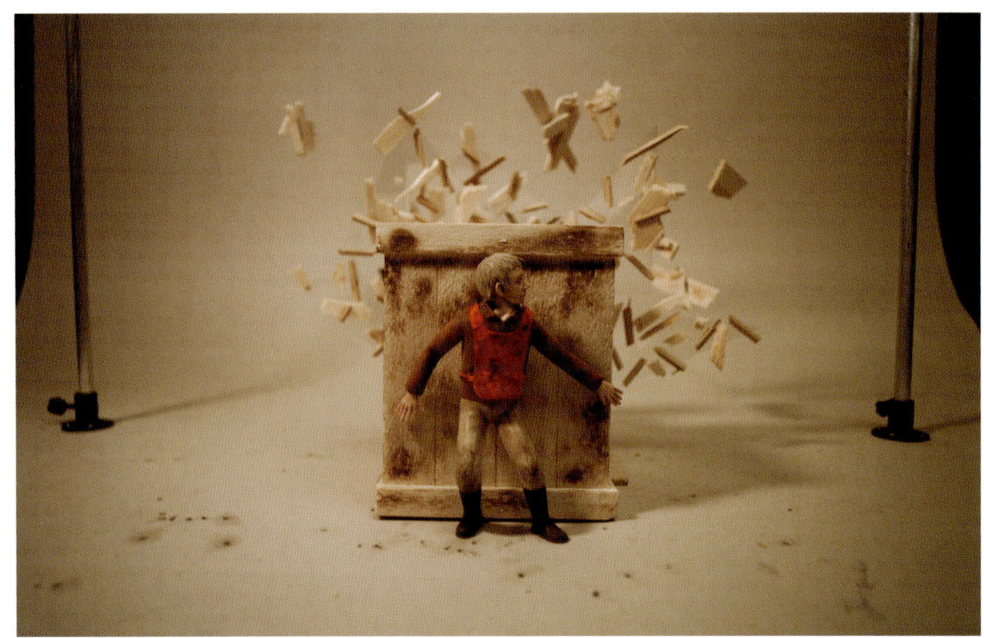

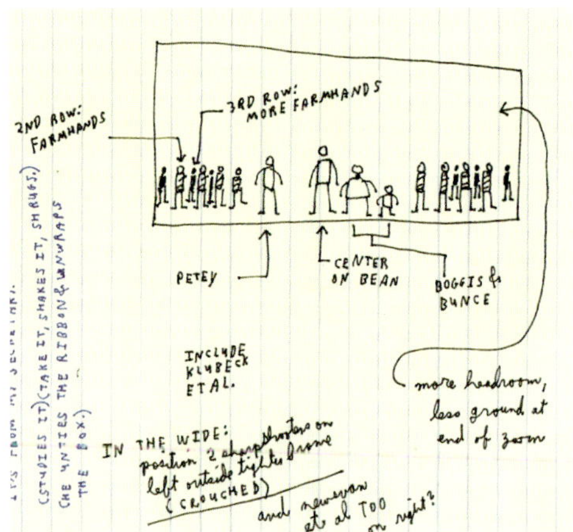

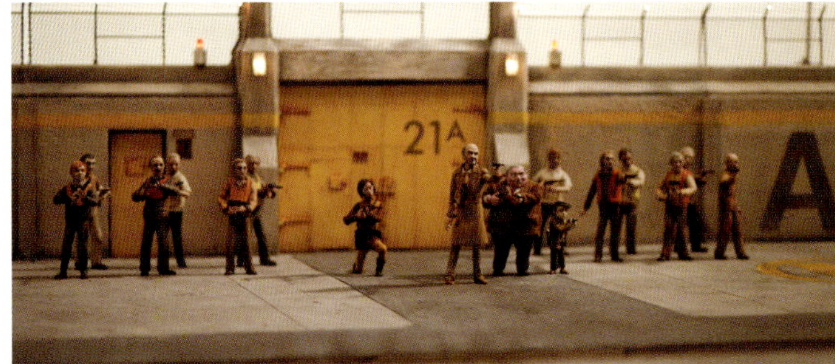

Above and below: Set photographs of the Bean Annex shoot-out

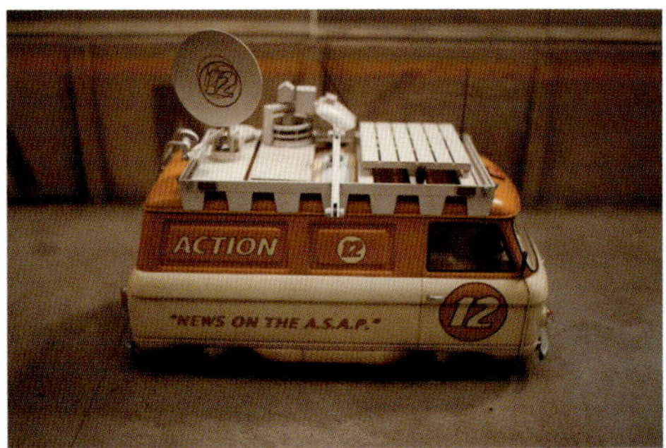

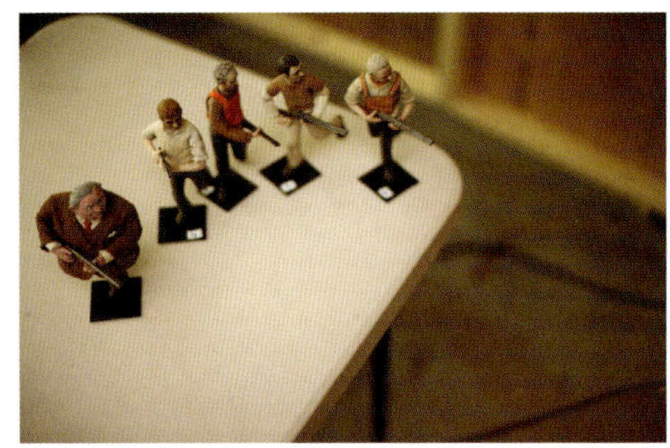

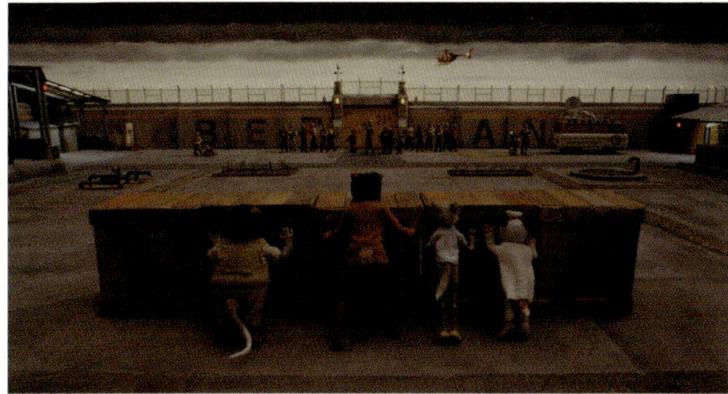

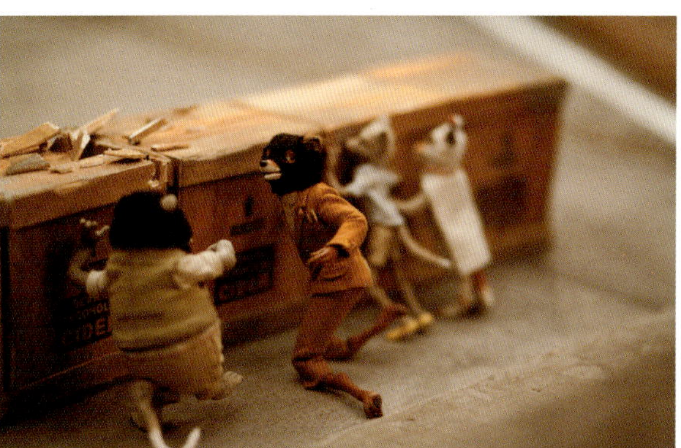

Left: A still from the movie of the Bean Annex shoot-out and a photograph taken on set

Right: Notes and sketches for the shoot-out by Wes

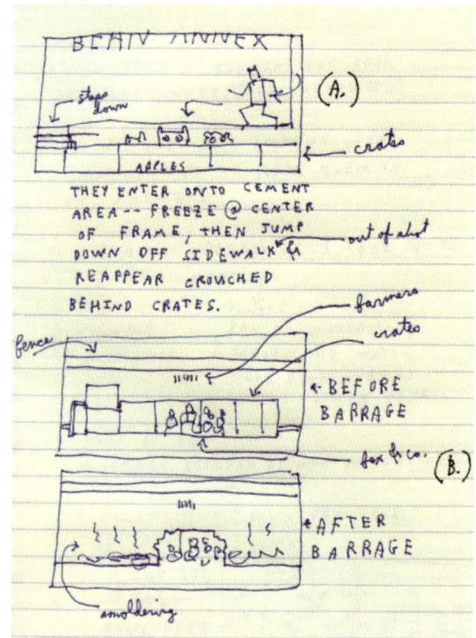

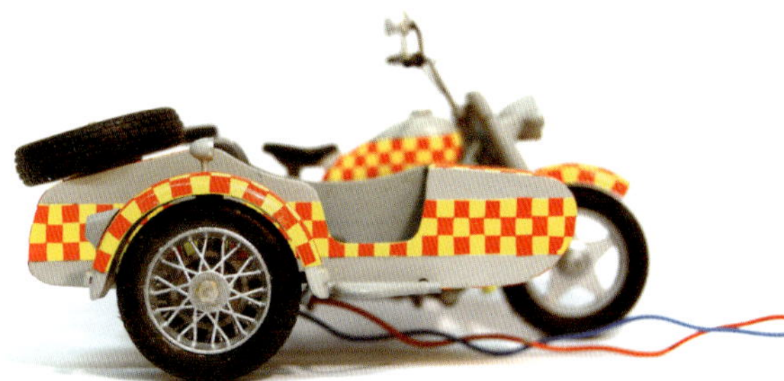

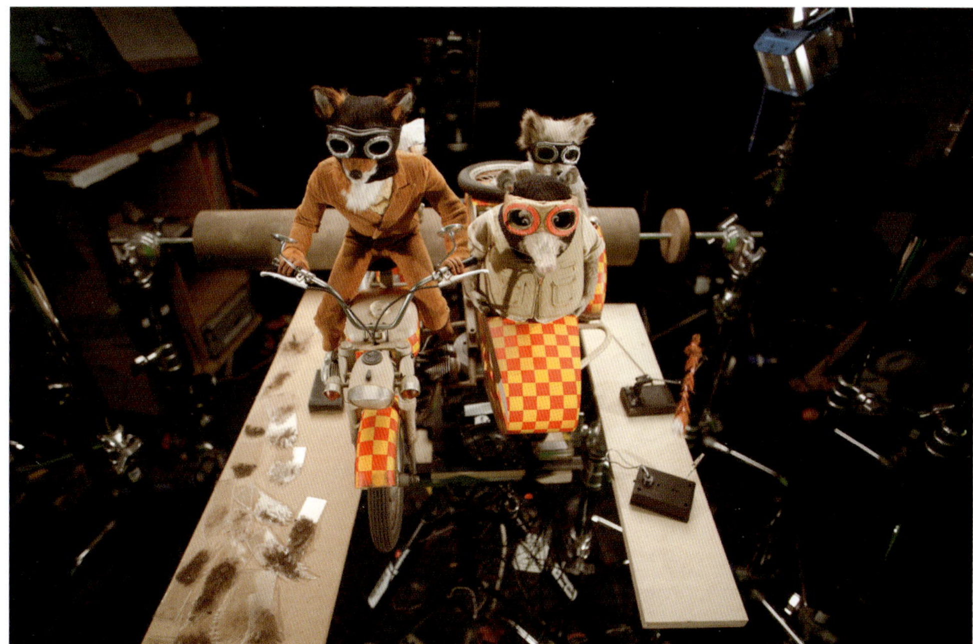

Above: The half-scale motorcycle and sidecar

Left: The motorcycle rigged for a driving shot

EXT. ROAD. DAY

Fox, Kylie, Ash, and Kristofferson ride down a country road. Kylie sees something across the meadow. He says warily:

KYLIE
Don't turn around!

FOX
What?

Fox turns around. A huge, wild, grey wolf with ice-blue eyes stands on a rock fifty feet away from them. Fox slams on the brakes. The motorcycle slides to a halt.

FOX
Where'd he come from?
(loudly)
Where'd you come from? What are you doing here?

Pause. Fox points toward the wolf:

FOX
Canis lupus!

Fox points to himself:

FOX
Vulpes Vulpes!

The wolf does not answer. Fox, Kylie, Ash, and Kristofferson watch idling from the motorcycle.

FOX
I don't think he speaks English or Latin.
(loudly)
Pensez-vous que l'hiver sera rude?
(aside)
I'm asking if he thinks we're in for a hard winter.

The wolf shakes his head. Fox nods.

FOX
He doesn't seem to know.

Silence. Fox shouts to the wolf with a strange hitch in his voice:

FOX
I have a phobia of wolves!

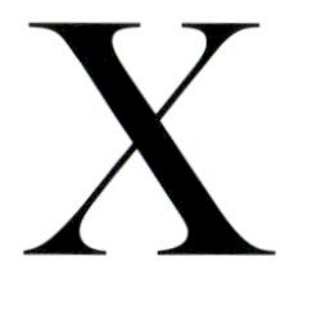

CANIS LUPUS, VOLPES VOLPES

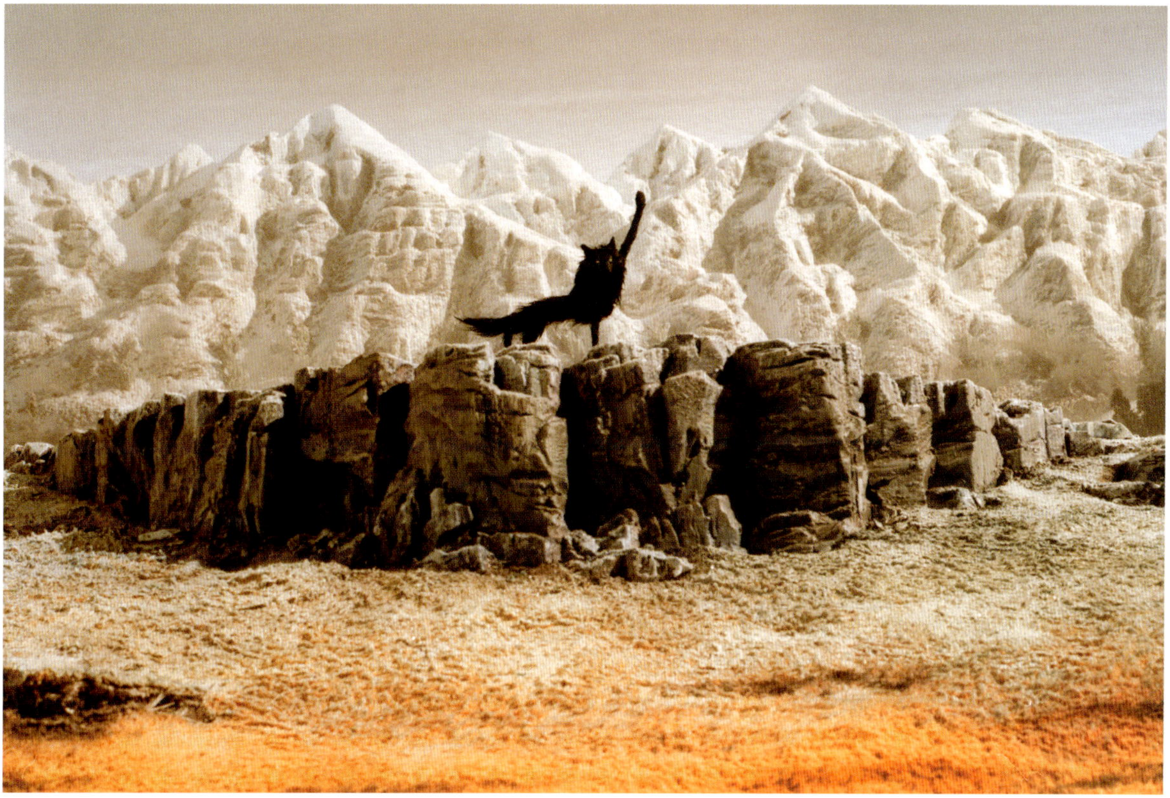

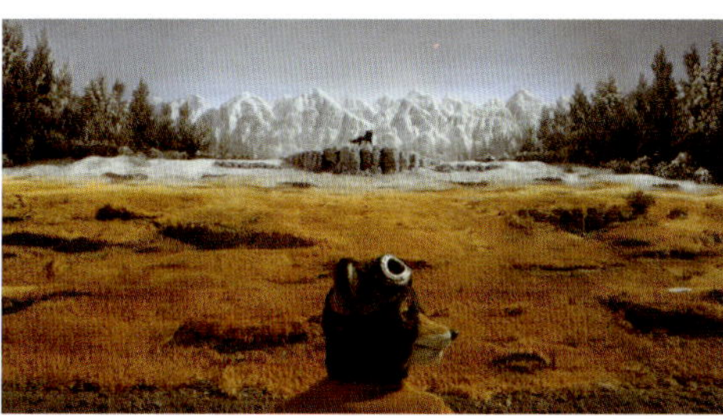

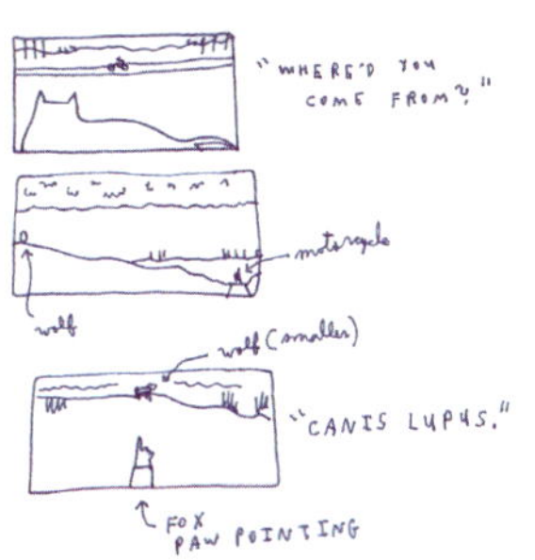

Above: A still of the wolf from the movie

Far left: A still of Mr. Fox from the movie

Left: Storyboards by Wes for Mr. Fox talking to the wolf

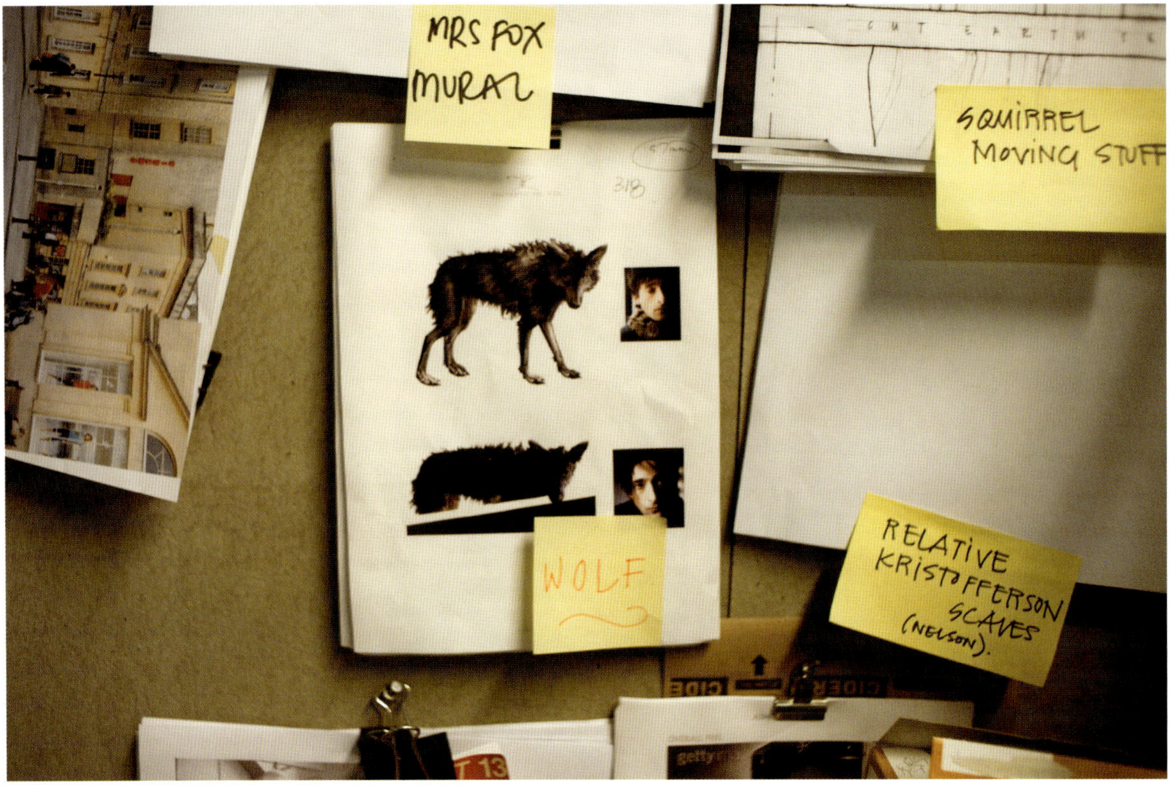

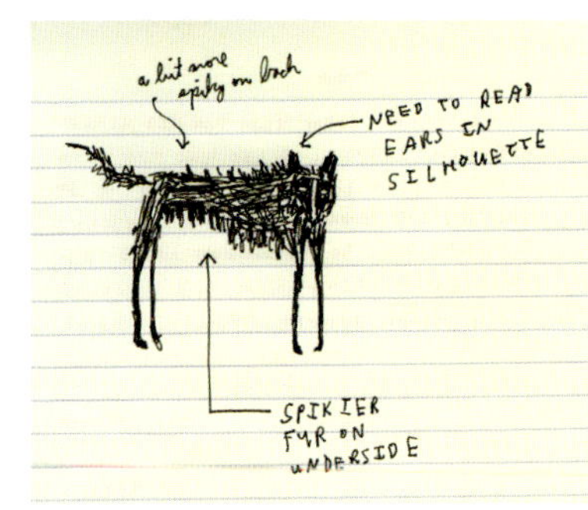

Above: A wall in the art department

Left: A sketch and notes by Wes for the wolf

Below left: Early concept art for the wolf and the mountain ridge by Turlo

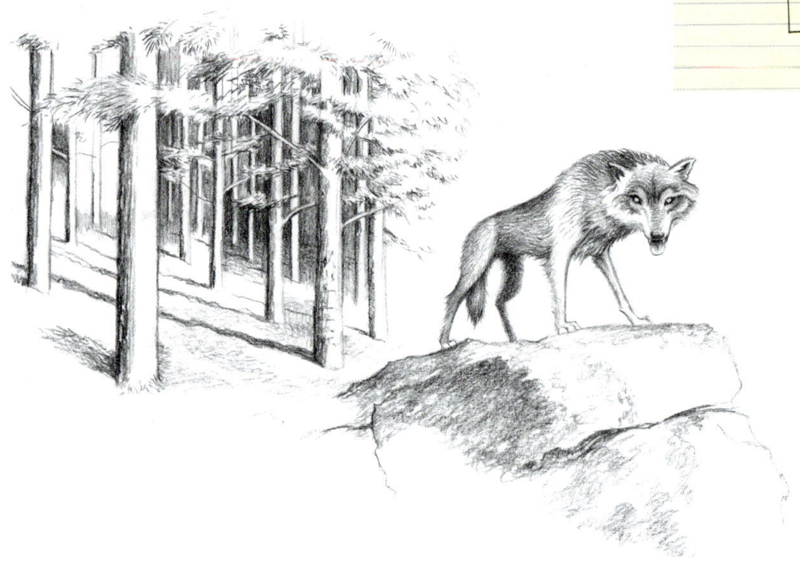

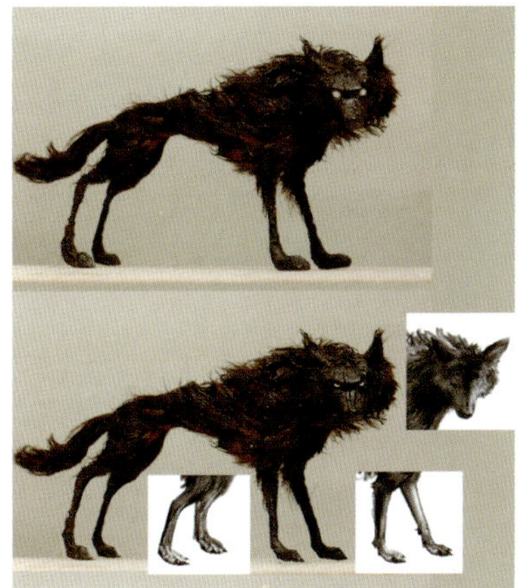

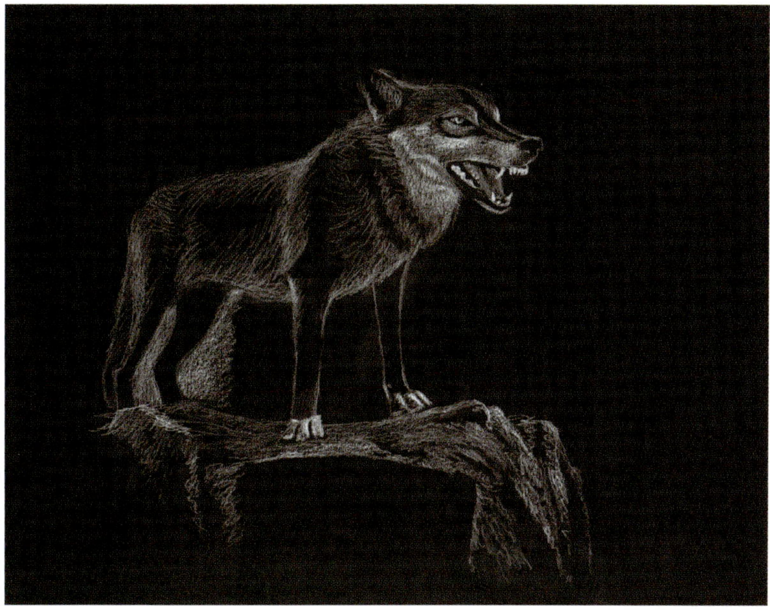

Above and right: Early concept art by Turlo and amendments to the wolf puppet

Below: The sculpture for the wolf puppet

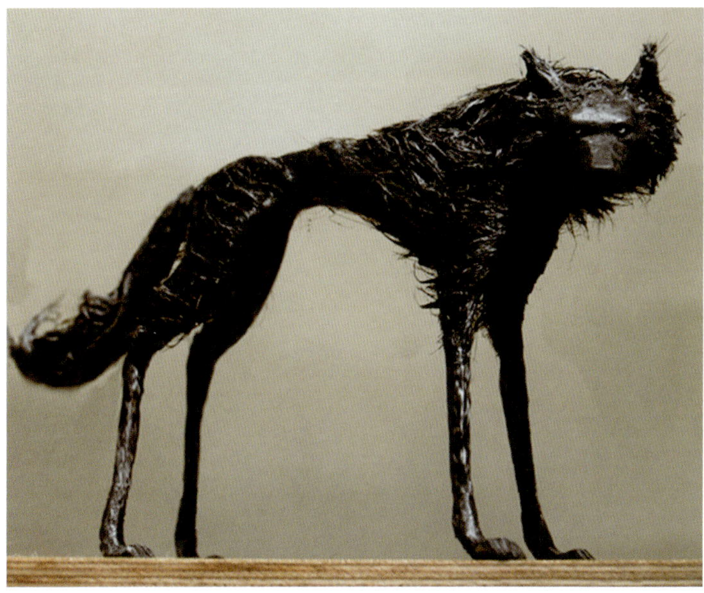

MS: *That's an interesting way of looking at it. I hadn't thought of that. It is amazing, the amount of work, even for Wes, who I think is more into detail than any director alive. Is this a movie for kids or adults?*

JS: Well, I think it has a wondrous look about it and it looks just so beautiful, I feel like adults and kids—I mean, I feel like a little kid, when it comes on, is just going to be floored by the look of it. The movie has a glow about it, it's so beautiful on the eye, and there's nothing like it that I've ever seen before. Kids are so smart and so sensitive and so deeply feeling, I feel like they are really going to respond to it. It doesn't talk down to kids as a film or even just aesthetically, I feel like it comes at the audience with a certain level of respect.

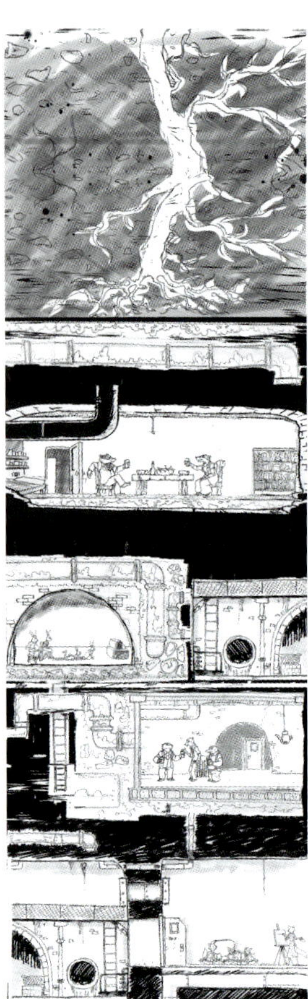

From: Wes Anderson
Subject:
Date: 18 December 2008 18:16:07 GMT
To: Andrew Weisblum

I think we should portray them living not miserably underground, but frugally

Living in some animal version of the projects, bare light bulbs—but trying to stay quite upbeat—"let's sautée these banana peels sweetie"—maybe one of the children says "I'm hungry" and the mother says "well, have a glass of rain-water"—and we already have a bit where one of them is ill

And at the cocktail party could they make apologies for the nature of the hors d'oevres? etc

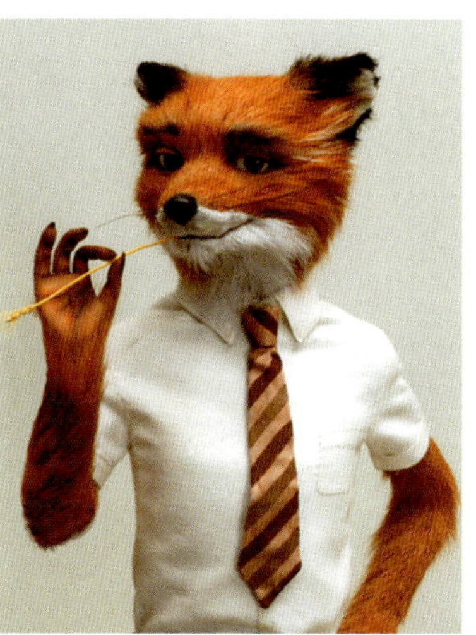

Left: Storyboard images by Christian for the long vertical shot in the drainpipe

Right: A Mr. Fox puppet posed with a stalk of wheat for his newspaper portrait

Opposite page: Early concept art for the drainpipe homes by Turlo

Right: Mr. Fox's new column in the newspaper

The Gazette * 31

BANANA PEEL SPLIT

1 Amazonian jumbo banana
1 pawful summer-sweet chocolate
1 square bark-bitter chocolate
1 pinch butter
2 eggs
3 cups sifted powdered sugar
1 pinch marsh salt
2 pawfuls roasted nuts
2 pawfuls wild marshmallows

Heat Amazonian banana until firm. Peel away top skin and scoop out pawful of banana flesh. Let cool. Melt chocolate pieces, chocolate and butter in large saucepan over low heat, stirring until smooth. Remove from heat. Beat eggs until foamy. Mix in sugar, salt and vanilla. Blend in chocolate mixture. Stir in peanuts and marshmallows. Drop by teaspoonfuls onto waxed paper. Chill two hours until firm. Store in refrigerator. Remove just before serving. Feeds about ½ dozen cubs.

FOX on the Prowl with Fantastic Mr. Fox

We all once lived beneath a meadow where the heather ran wild, and the clover grew thick in the spring-time. Well, life has a way of shuffling the deck from time to time. Is that an industrial-grade waste-water treatment and purification facility bubbling and humming over our heads? Sounds like it to me. Tangentially, what specifically is meant by waste-water? This I have yet to divine. Perhaps the run-off from the Oxford Smokies streams in too cold for those of the human persuasion.

Speaking of cold water, did this reporter ever tell you the story about the Swedish muskrat who got sucked down a whirlpool? The punch-line, which involves ice-cubes, potato-vodka, and 300 yards of unwaxed packing-twine, is both profane and untranslatable – but stop me if you see me strolling down the drain-pipe, and I 'll gladly act out the whole pantomime for you in dialect.

My uncle was a plumber, but he cashed in early. Frankly, he was eaten by a Doberman, or anyway it killed him and ran off with the body in its teeth – but perhaps this is getting a bit gruesome for these pages. Also, my sister-in-law might find the mention of it in bad taste, but fat chance as she reads the Daily Picayune.

I overheard my wife say sadly on the telephone: it 's been a terrible year. Sometimes it 's better not to know, especially if she wasn 't going to tell you. They say things happen for a reason, but they don 't. They happen for a lark and from the well-spring of limitless, infinite chaos. Sometimes this can be hysterically funny, and sometimes it 's a kick in the teeth. My apologies may ring hollow, but they ring frequently. What to do, what to do?

I 'm not the fox I used to be. Not by choice. But these days,

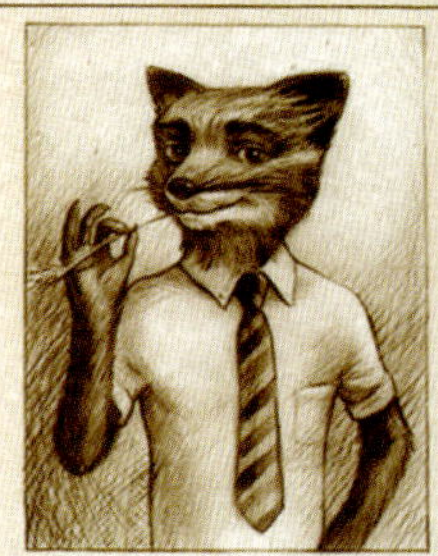

when I look at myself in the mirror, I try to keep a straight face. At some point, maybe I won 't feel the need to turn away.

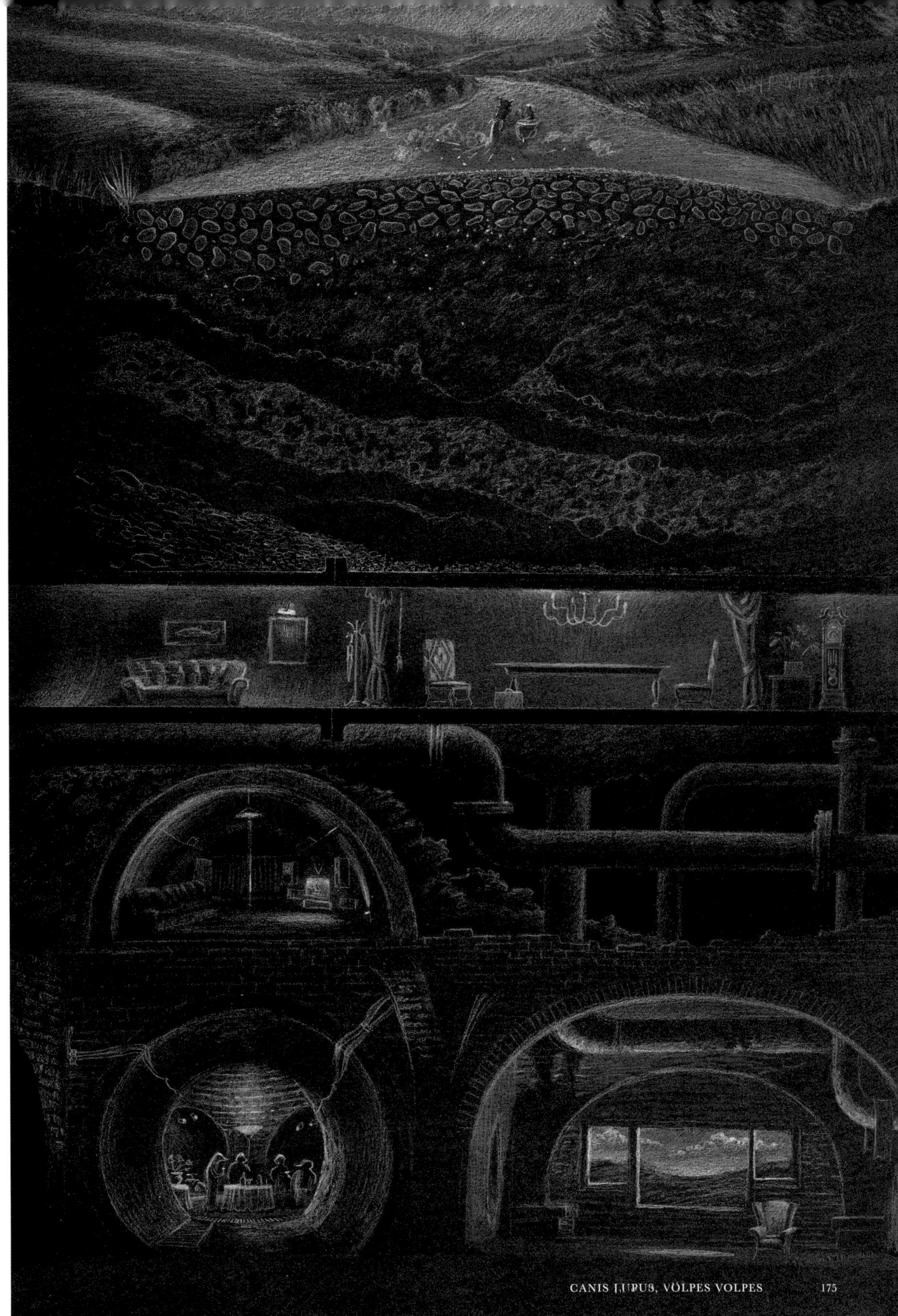

Right: A sketch by Wes of Kristofferson, Ash, and Agnes doing yoga

Below: A still from the movie of Mr. Fox and Kylie coming into the drainpipe home

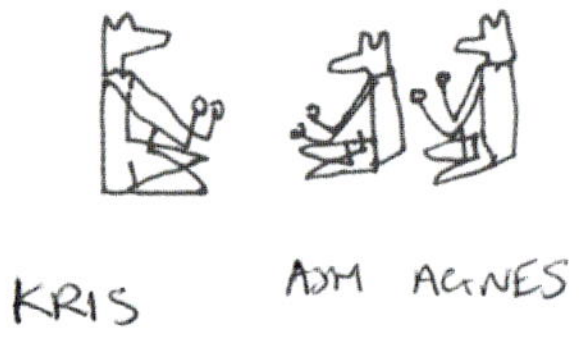

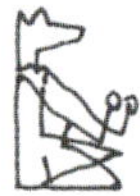

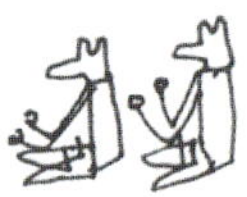

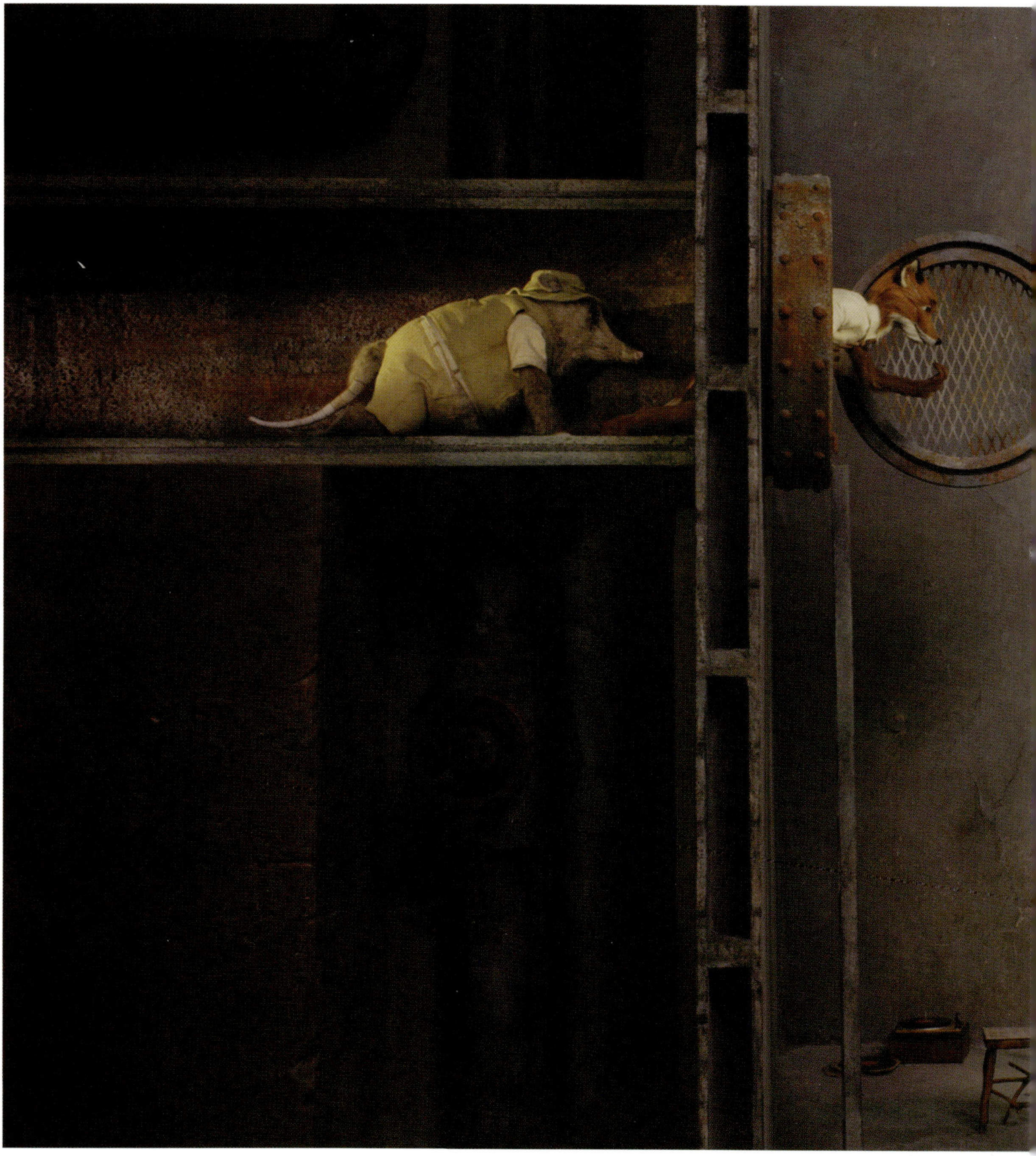

From: Wes Anderson
Subject: **Re: Kristofferson pretzel legs**
Date: 8 August 2008 14:28:30 BST
To: Alice Bird

Let's compare Kristofferson's legs with an actual pretzel reference

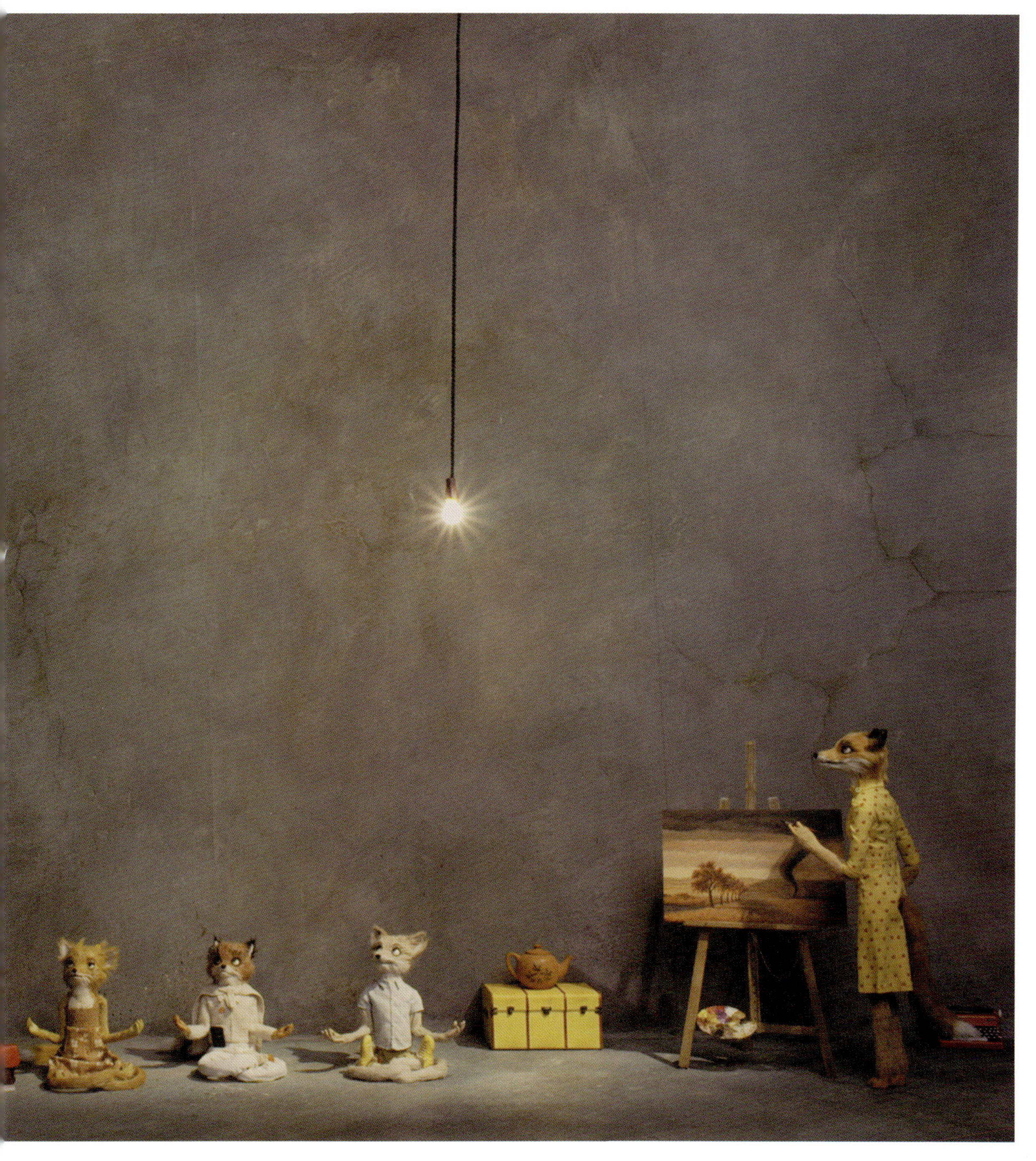

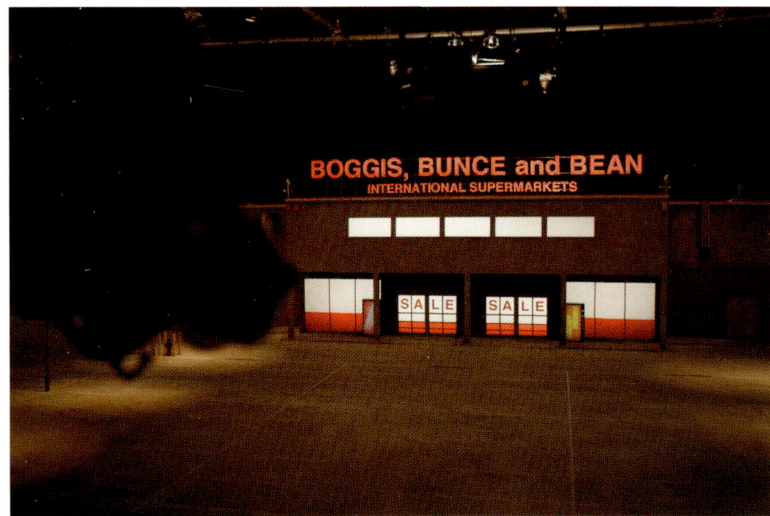

Left: A photograph of the supermarket exterior set

Below: Mr. and Mrs. Fox rigged to walk through the supermarket

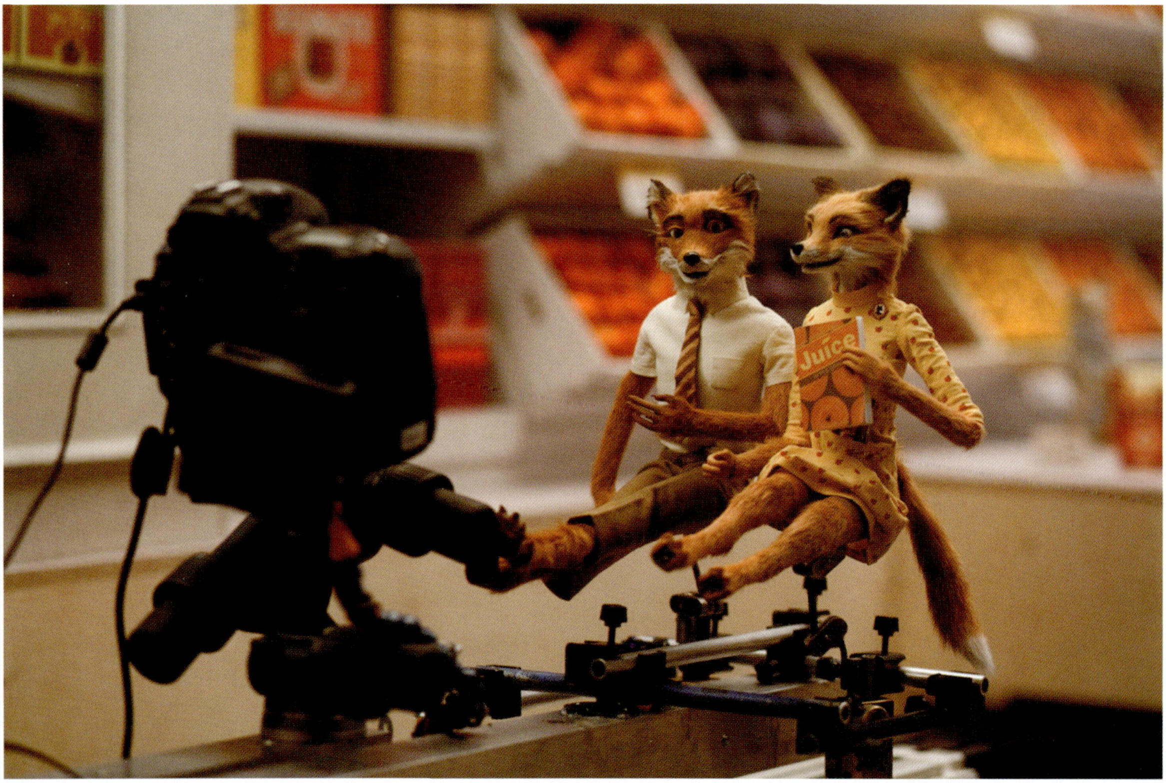

Right: A set photograph of the foxes and Kylie entering the supermarket

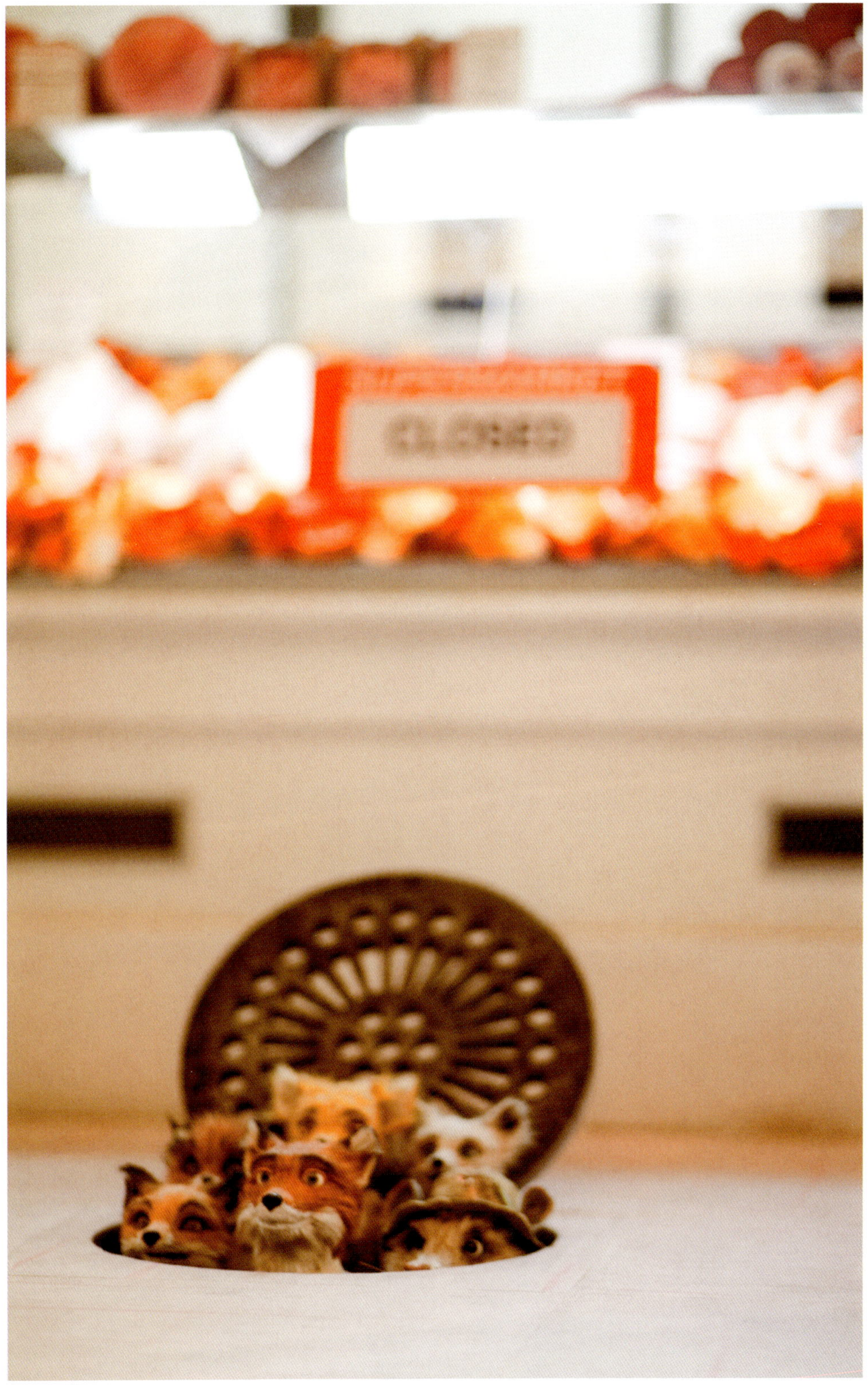

MS: *I agree completely. There was one scene there that I couldn't believe, where Mr. and Mrs. Fox were talking in front of a waterfall. It was near the end. I asked Wes about that—it's just a bunch of Saran wrap. He said they just make this Saran wrap and they crinkle it up and they film it in such a way.*
JS: That's the thing. Look, I'm not by any means an expert in the genre of animated movies. It's so vast, all the great animated work and in this style. I don't know enough about it to say oh, it's never been done or whatever. But I will say that there are things like that—like the scene in the very beginning of the movie, where Mr. Fox is sitting at the table reading a newspaper and Mrs. Fox is walking back and forth and my character is entering. That's like a movie shot to me, with characters coming and going, a newspaper, a piece of a newspaper being flipped and read and crinkled. That seems very complicated. And what I love about the movie is that—I know this is like a dumb thing to say—but it's like Wes's animated movie, meaning there's overlapping, there's characters crossing. It just feels more like a movie, except there are these puppets in front of the camera. I feel like he didn't change the way he made a movie to make an animated movie, he just made his version of an animated movie.

I think you're absolutely right, it's very much like a Wes movie but also, somehow, it's simple in an amazingly beautiful way—even though obviously it's incredibly complex to make. It just moves along like water.
When the lights dimmed in the theater and it started, I started smiling, and nothing had even happened. And I don't know what that is. It made me feel like a kid and an adult. I'm very proud of it. It's not crude, it's smart, but the humor is never—it's just, it's everything. I just think it's so beautiful.

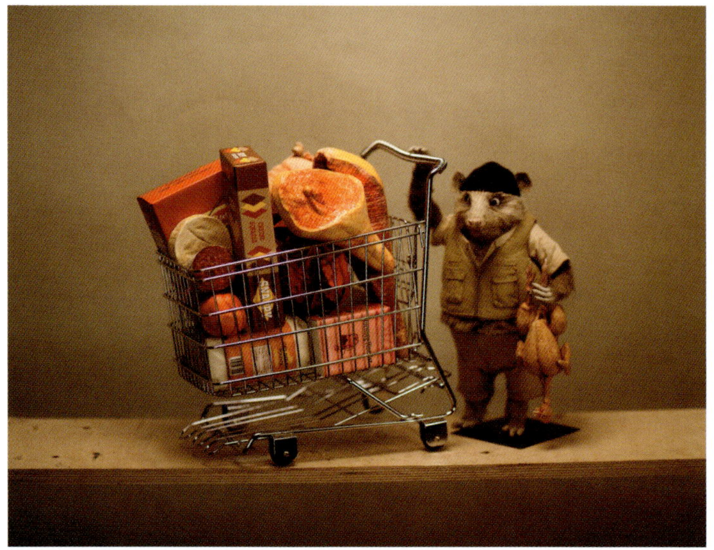

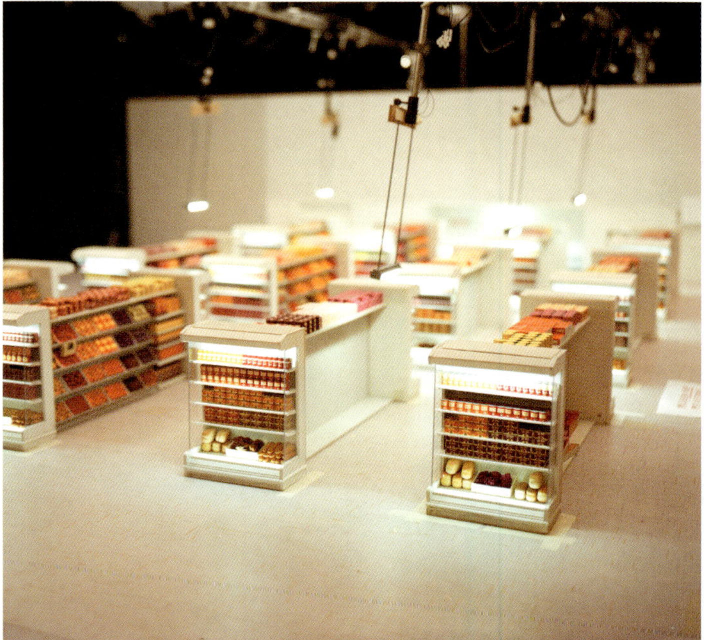

Top: Kylie with his grocery cart

Above: The micro-scale supermarket set used for the wide shots

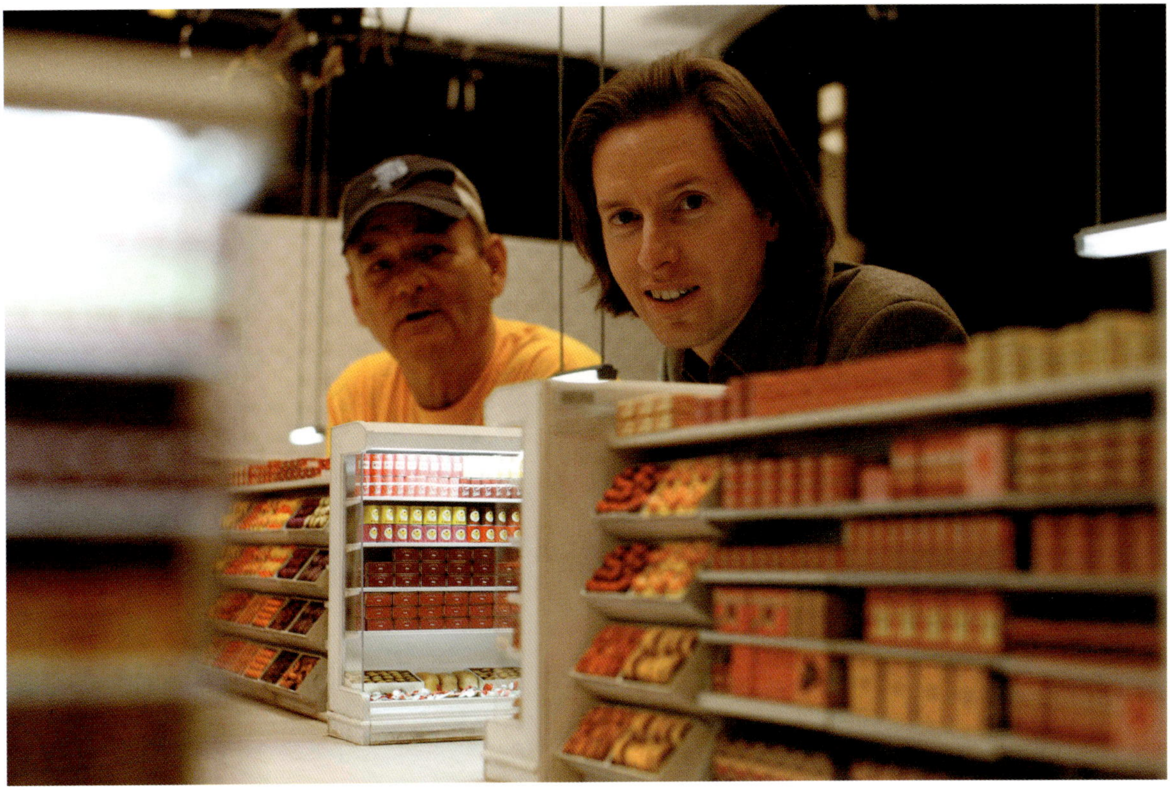

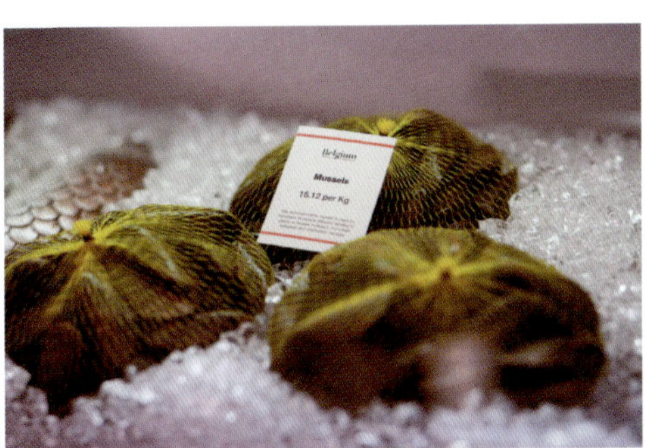

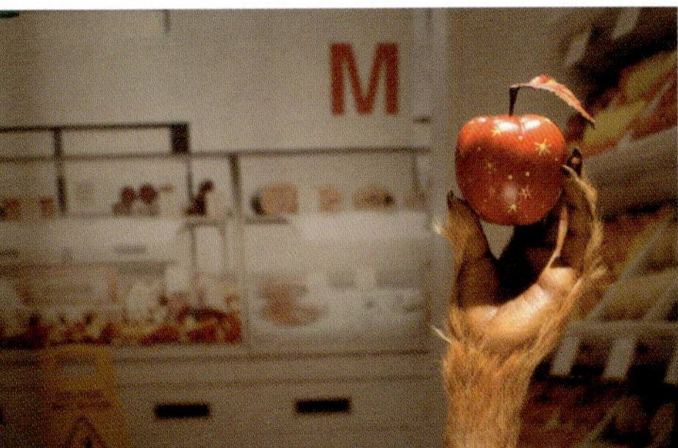

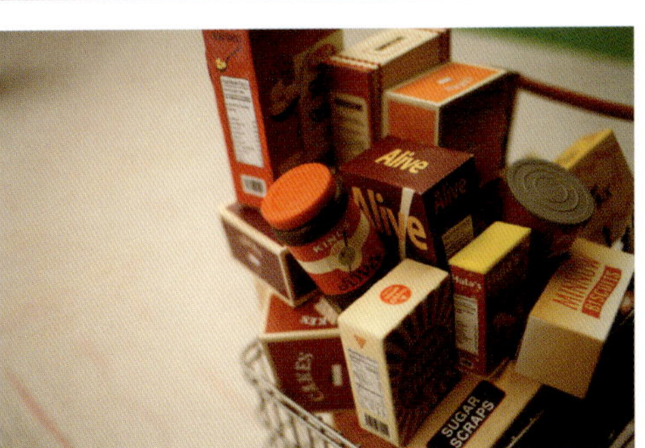

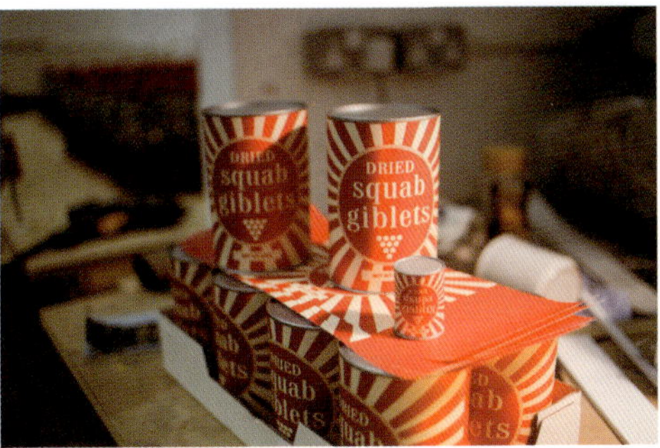

Above: Wes and Bill Murray looking at the supermarket set, photographed by Greg

Left: Supermarket food

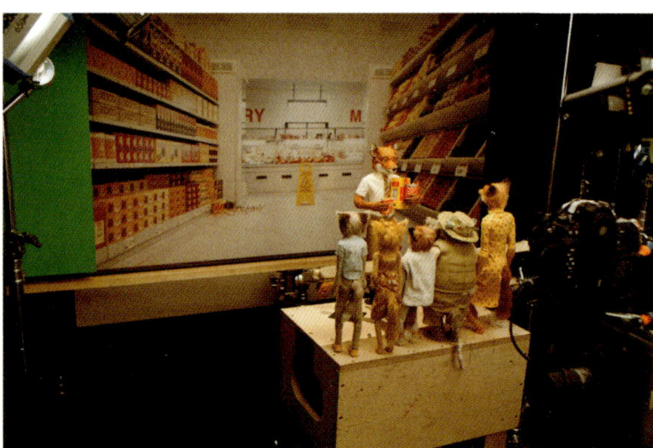

Left: Blocking for Mr. Fox's toast

Below: Early storyboards by Wes for Fox's toast

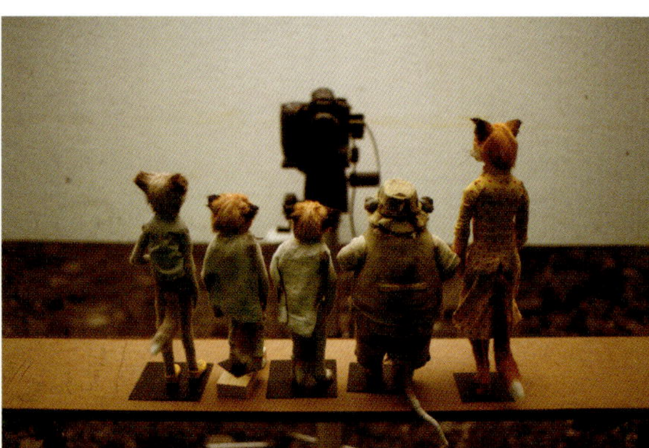

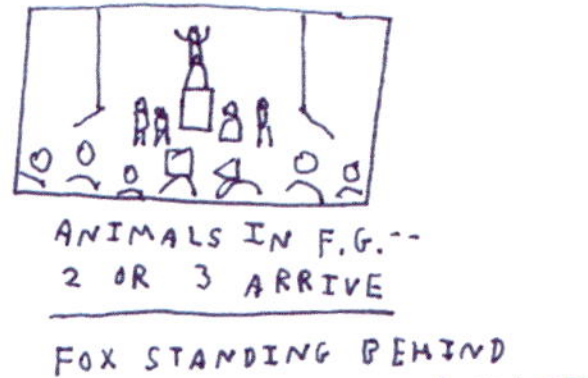

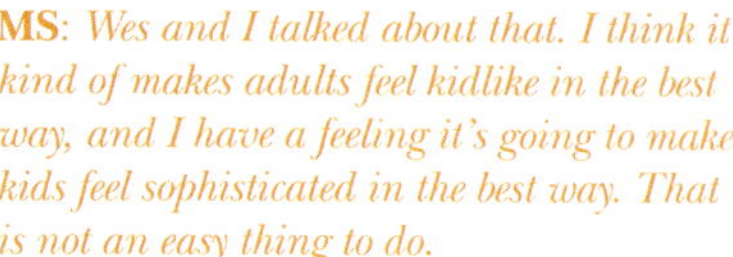

MS: *Wes and I talked about that. I think it kind of makes adults feel kidlike in the best way, and I have a feeling it's going to make kids feel sophisticated in the best way. That is not an easy thing to do.*

JS: What I also noticed about it, which was great, is that Wes really was able to go to a new place in terms of just physical comedy. Because a lot of times in the movies, not only do I find the writing in Wes's films funny but also what the characters do physically, sudden movements, gestures, extreme movements. Those are funny too. Like the way a character will react to something someone said—they'll just walk out of a room. Just that kind of humor he's able to do on a whole other level in this, because there's just stuff actors physically can't do that he's able to get with the puppets. Like there's a moment where two characters are standing, looking at how they're going to break in, and there's an electric fence. And he's like, well, maybe we're going to have to duh, duh, and then Wally's like, "Why don't we just go over there?" And the camera goes way over there and they walk over. He's like, "Let's go there." And they're like, "All right, go." And they walk out of frame and less than a second later they're, like, two hundred yards away. That's funny, that's just funny, and you couldn't do that with actors unless you had people dressed up as them or something. That was a moment where I thought, wow, he can do stuff now because of the nature of this style of film, he can do this now and it's at a whole other level. ⚜

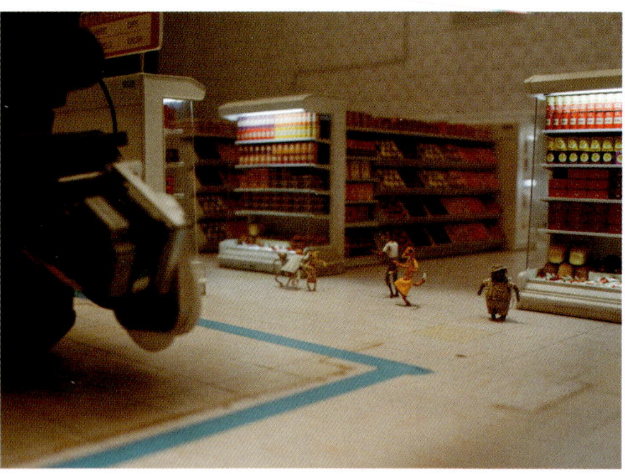

Left: The micro-scale puppets dancing

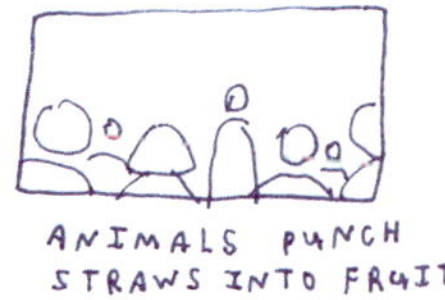

"LET'S RAISE..."

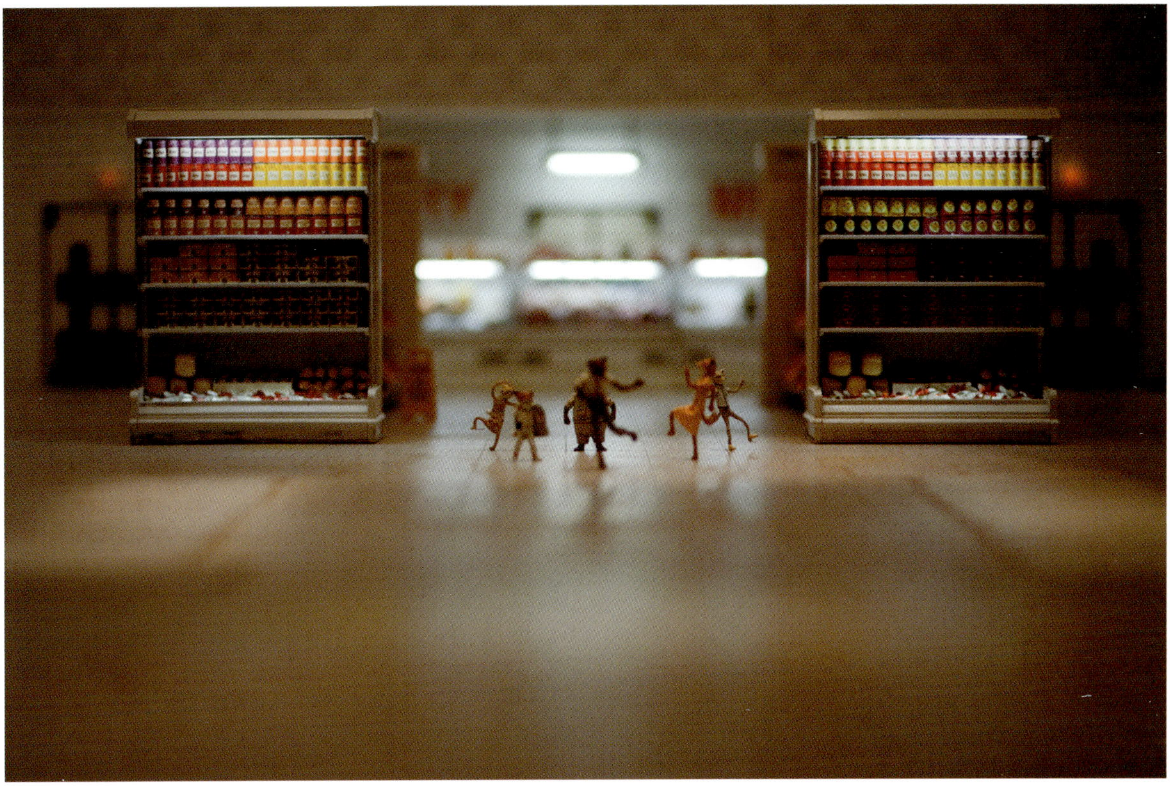

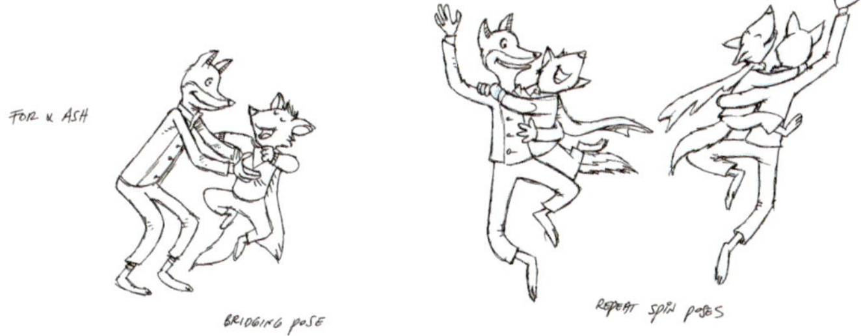

Top: The micro-scale puppets dancing

Above: Storyboard sketches by Christian

Right: A still from the movie of the animals dancing in the supermarket

Following page: A wall in the puppet hospital, photographed by Greg

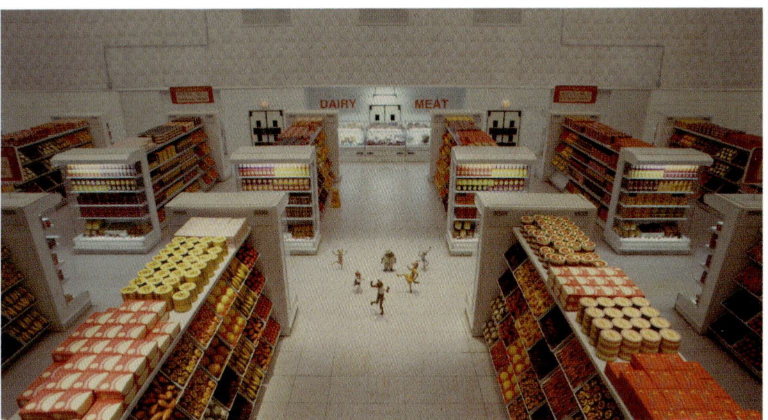

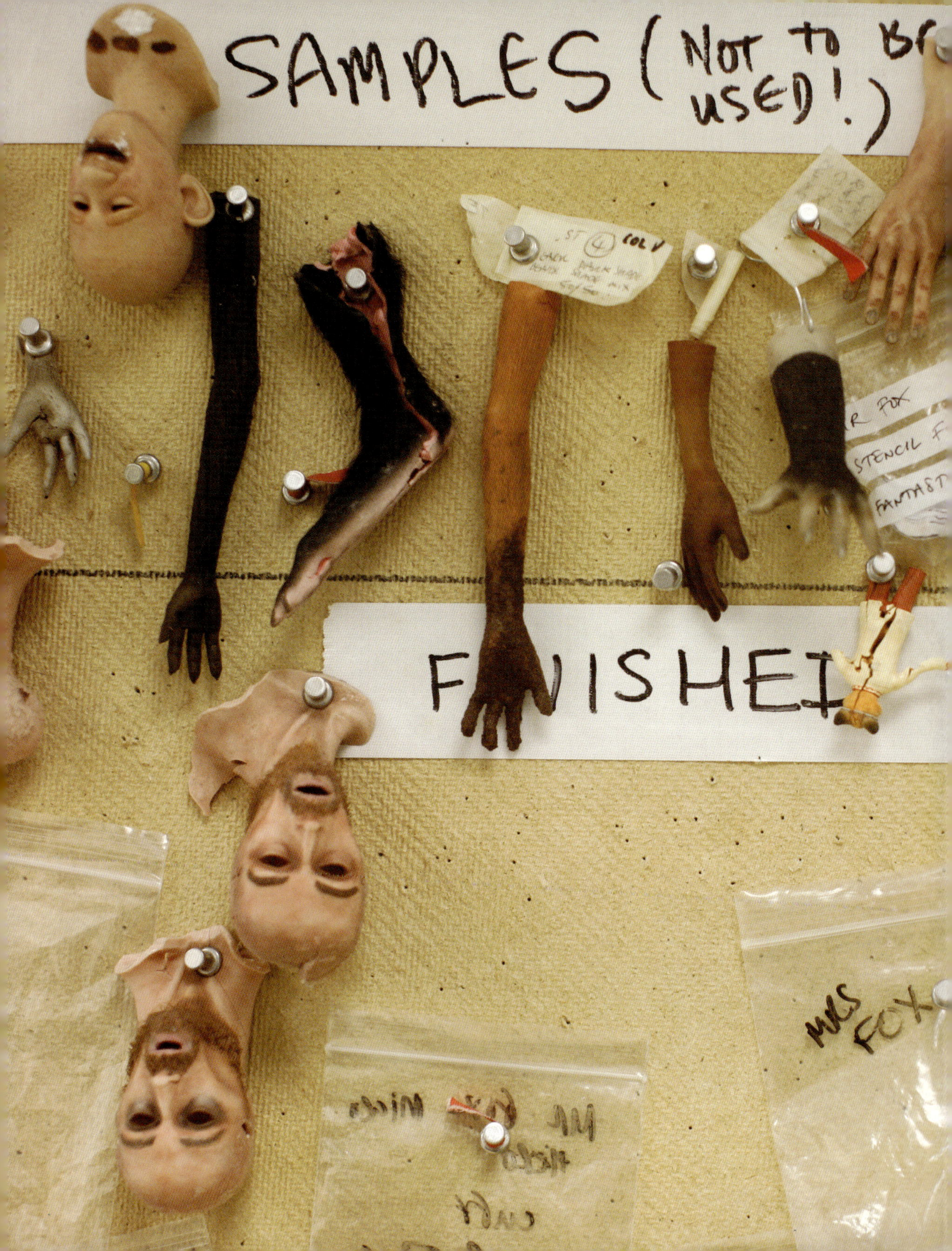

SAMPLES (Not to
USED!)
R FOX
STENCIL
MRS FOX

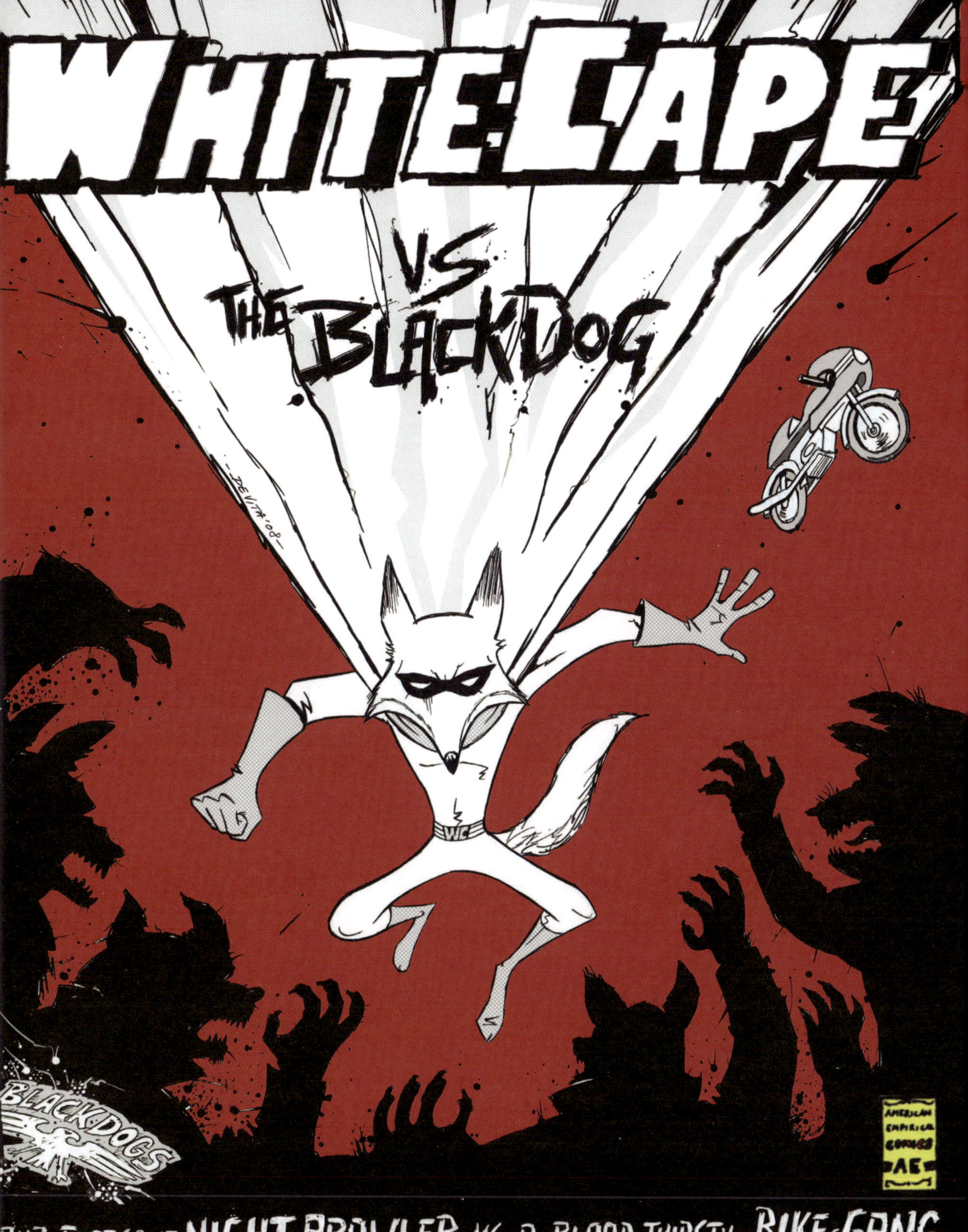
WHITE CAPE
VS
THE BLACK DOG
DEVITA '08
BLACKDOGS
AMERICAN EMPIRICAL COMICS
AE
OUR FEARSOME NIGHT-PROWLER VS. A BLOOD-THIRSTY BIKE-GANG

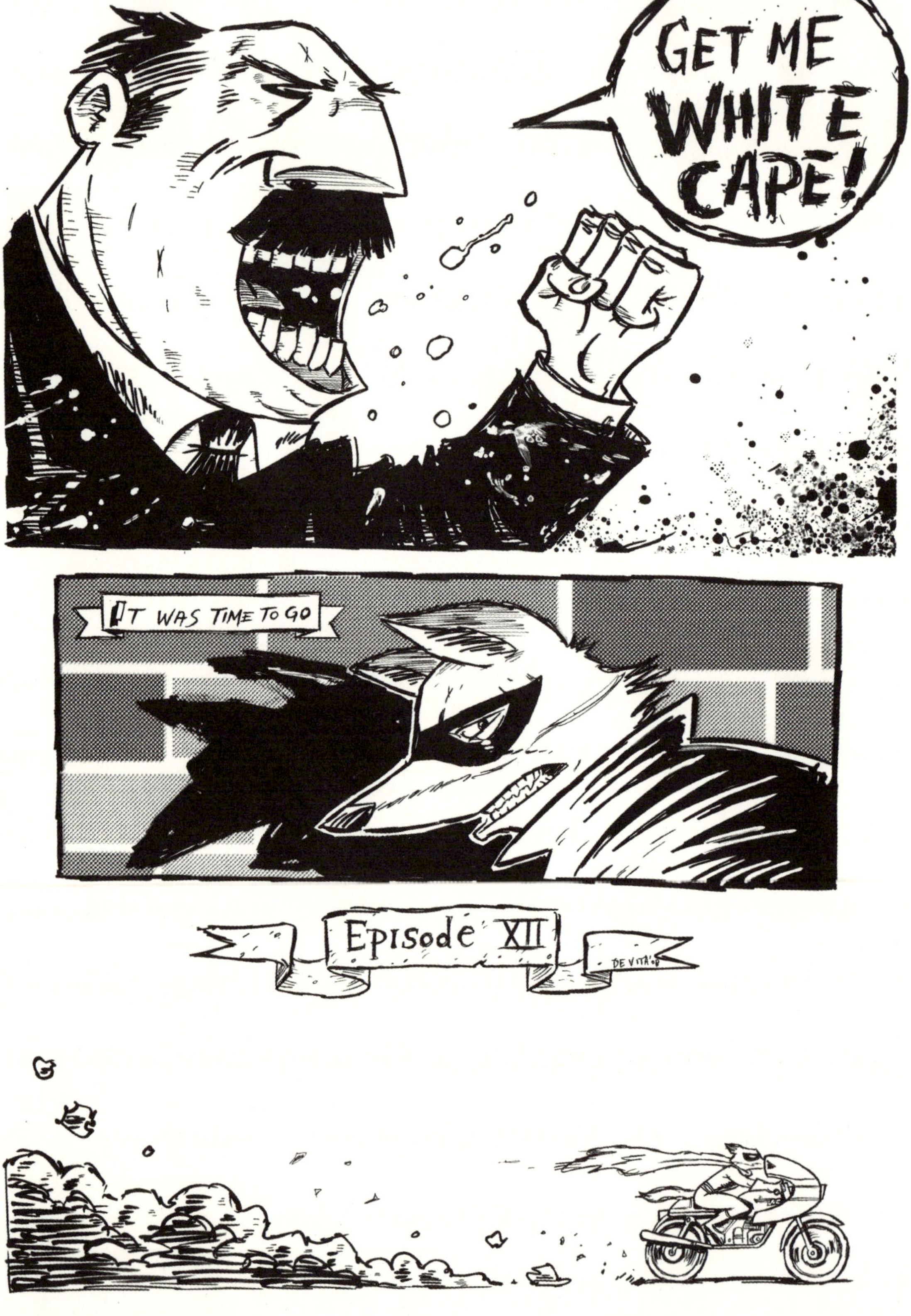

GET ME WHITE CAPE!

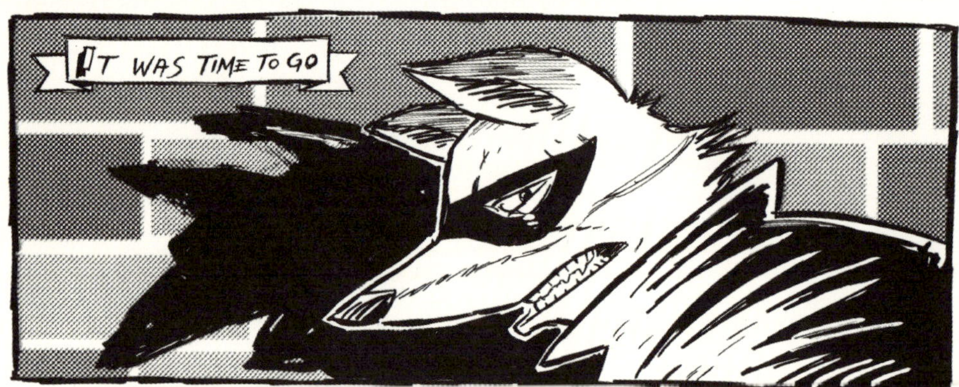

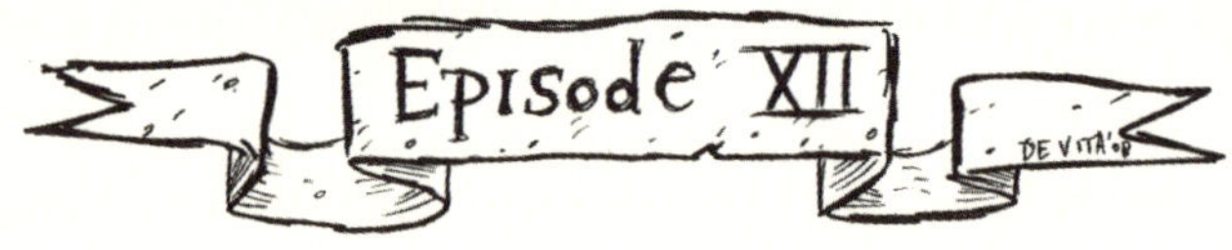

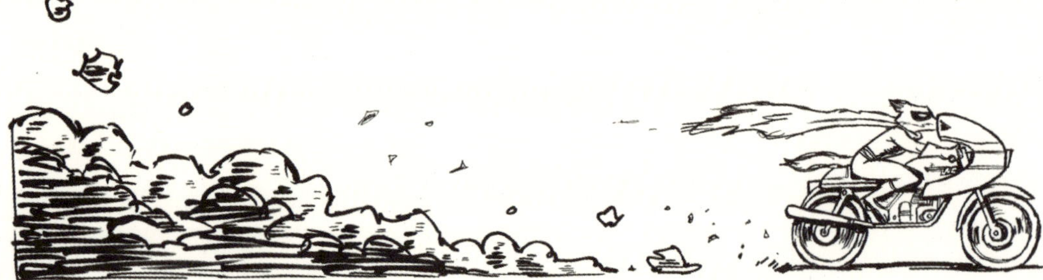

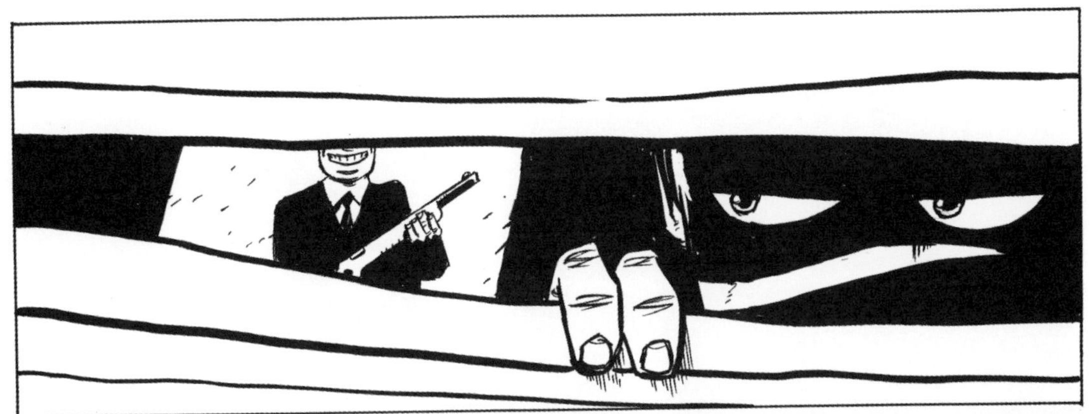

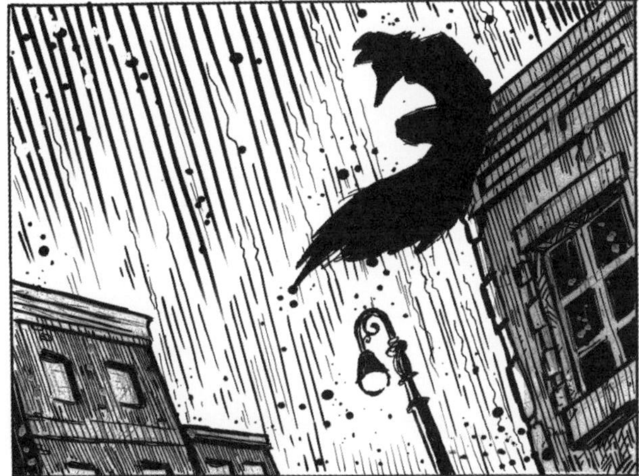

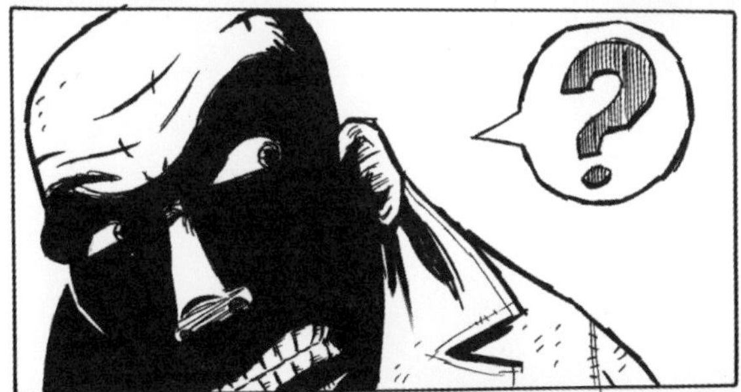

?

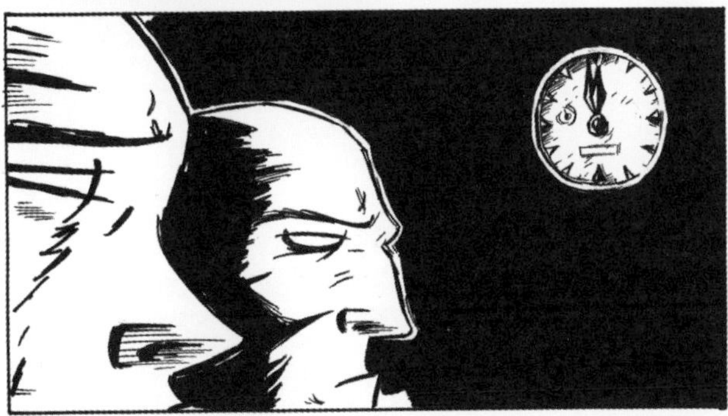

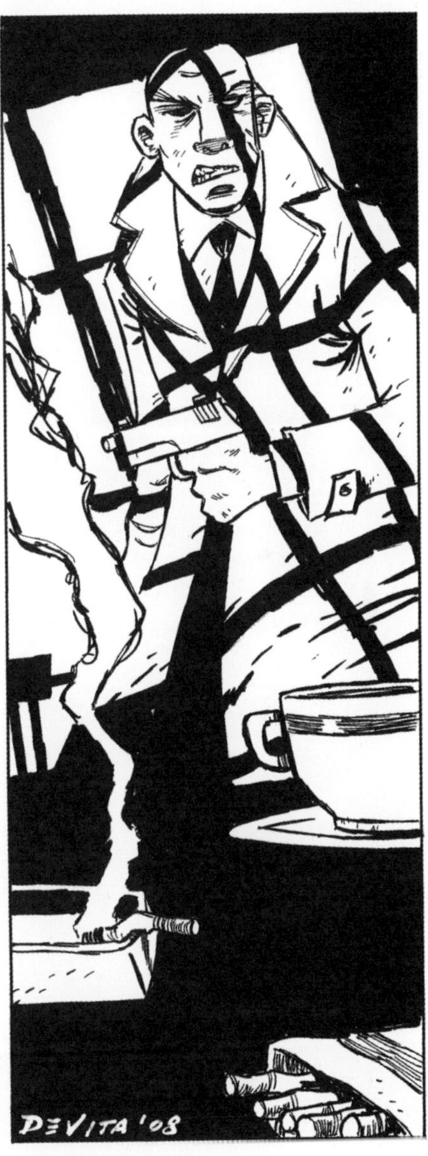

DEVITA '08

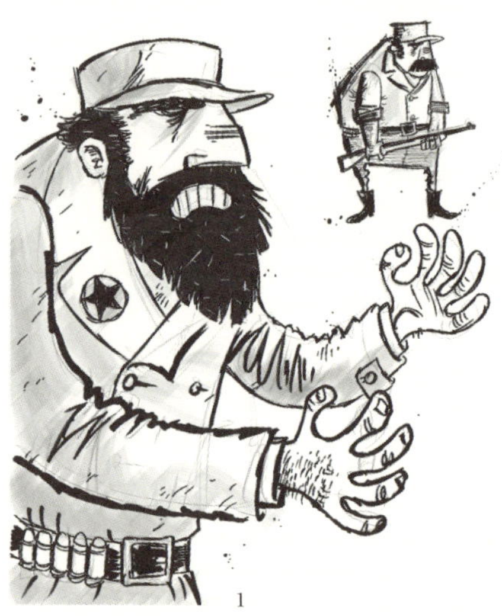

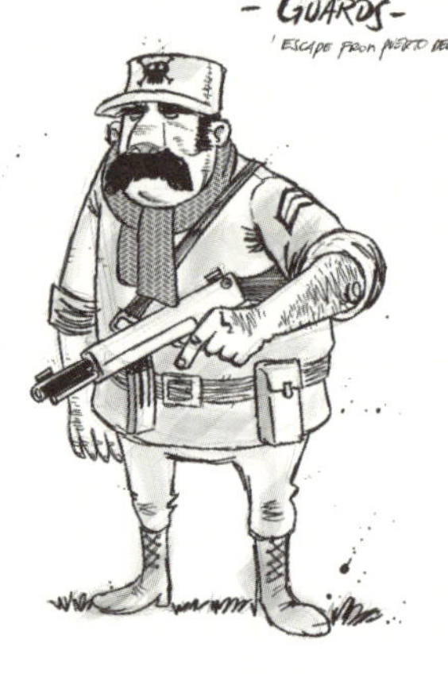

1

All White Cape comic book art by Christian De Vita

1. and 2. Designs for the comic book interior

3. Early *White Cape* sketches

4 and 5. *White Cape* posters from Ash's bedroom

6. and 7. Early *White Cape* sketches

8. Six *White Cape* covers made for the film

9. and 10. Designs for the comic book interior

3

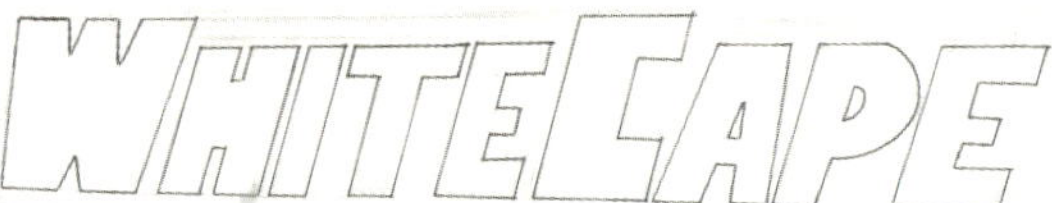

2

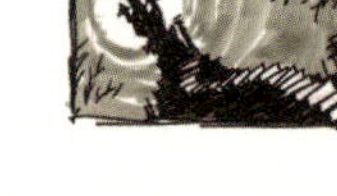

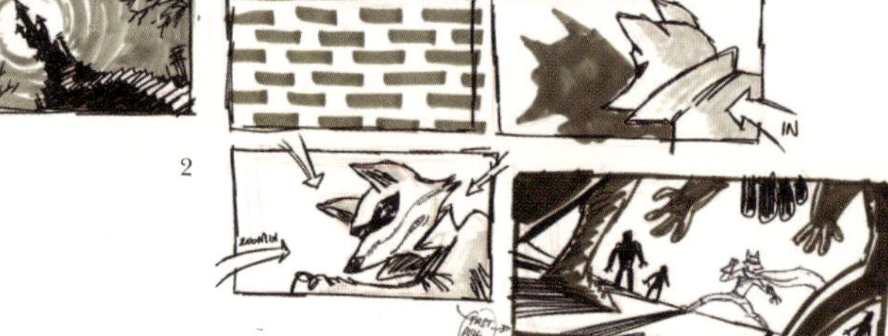

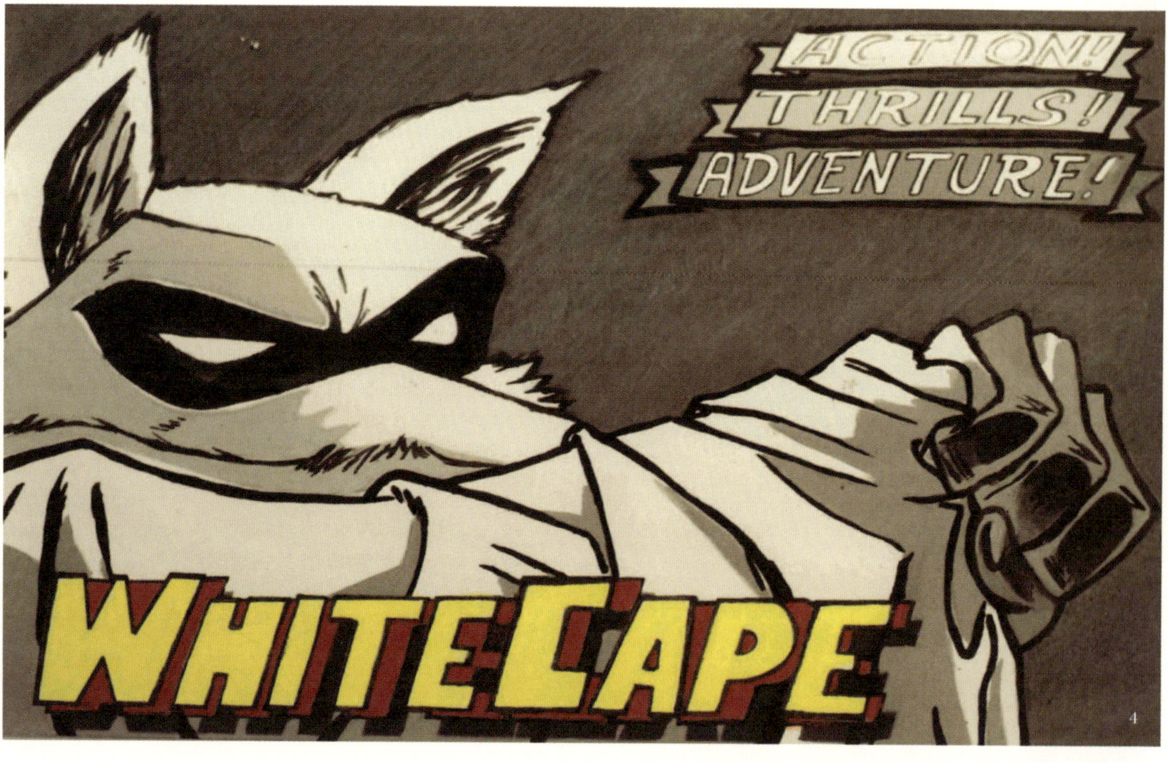

4

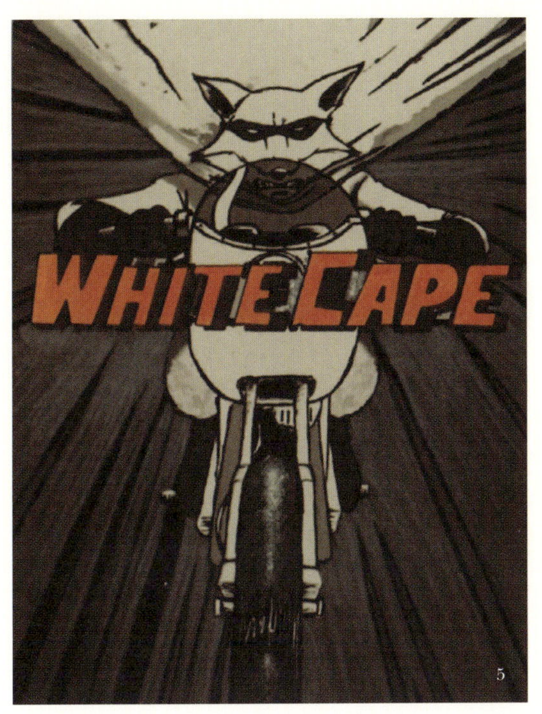

5

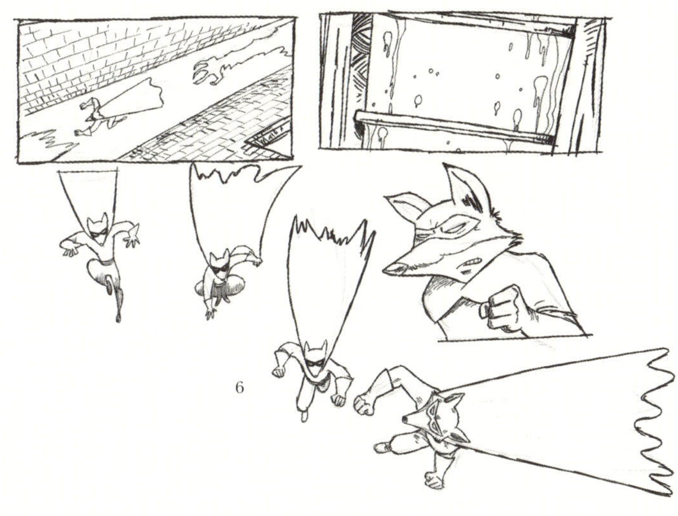

6

7

ACTION!

ADVENTURE!

THRILLS!

8

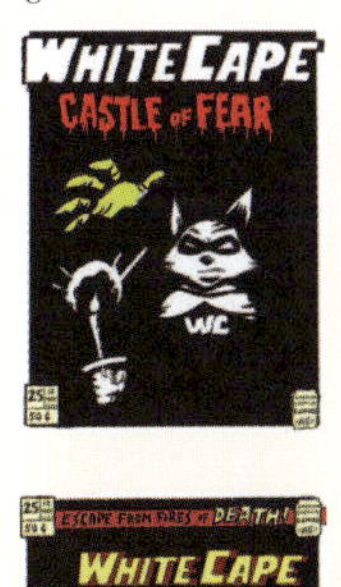

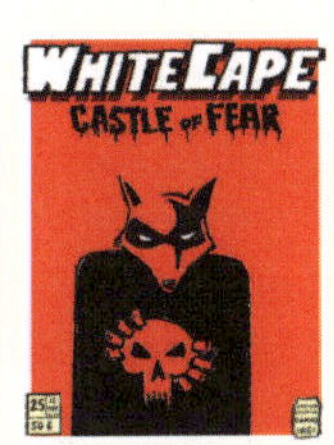

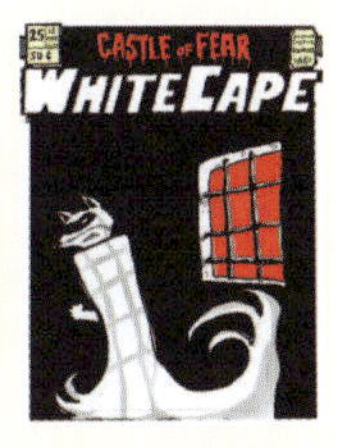

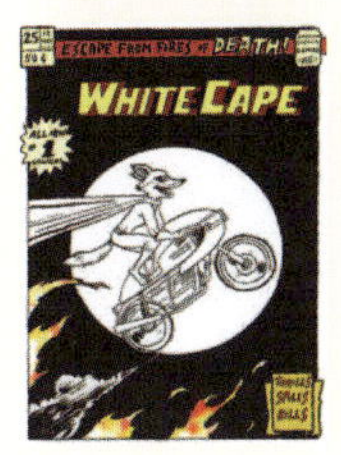

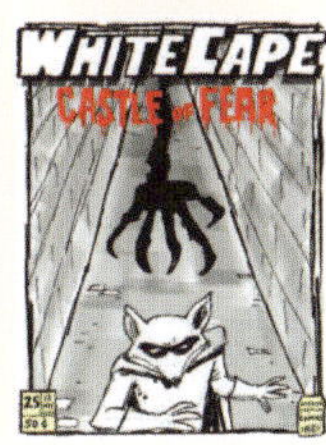

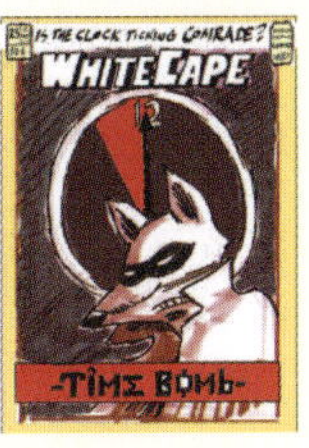

9

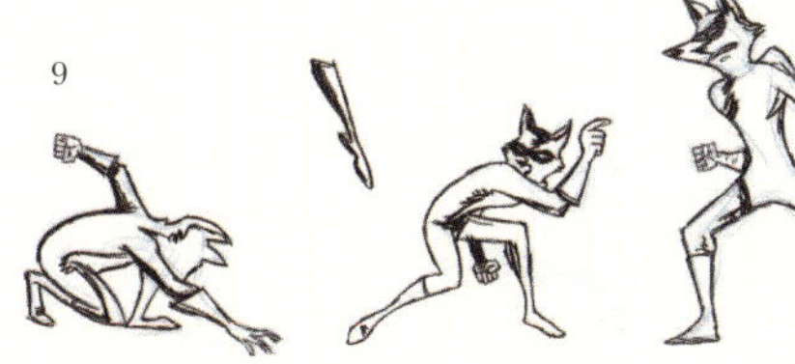

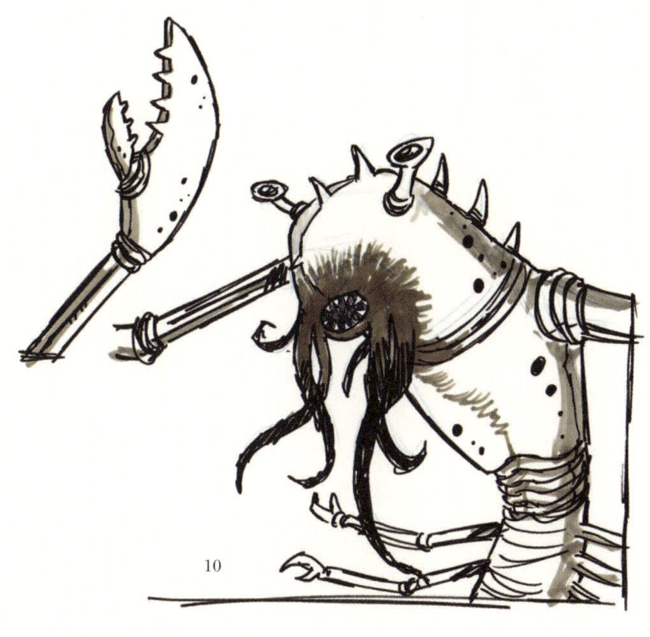

10

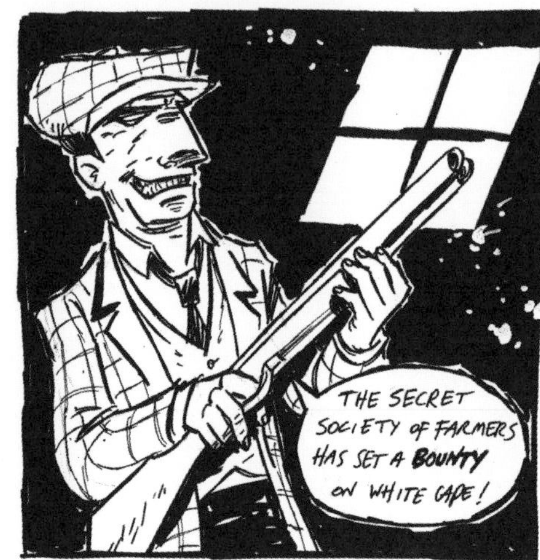
THE SECRET SOCIETY OF FARMERS HAS SET A BOUNTY ON WHITE CAPE!

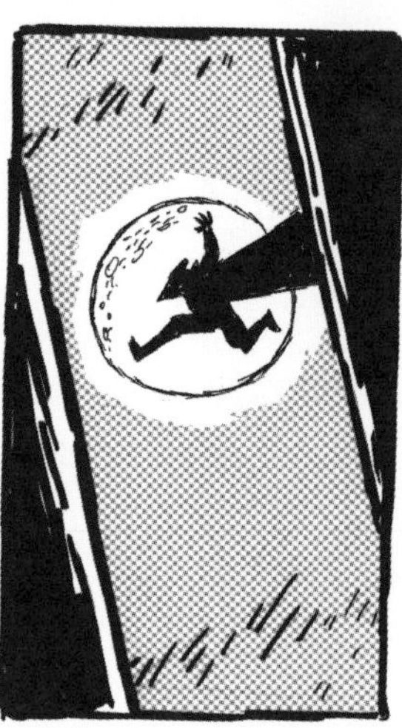

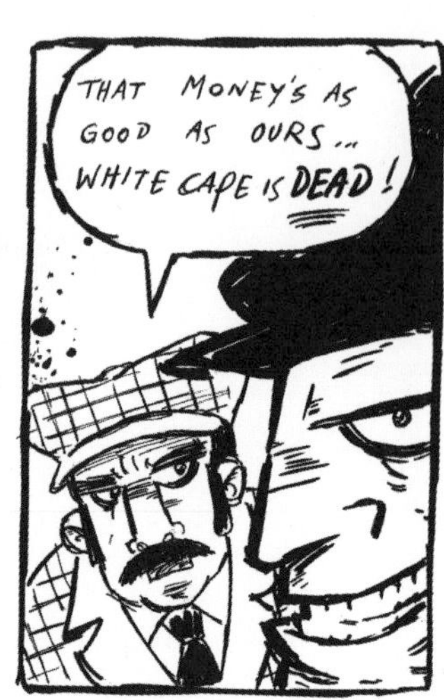
THAT MONEY'S AS GOOD AS OURS... WHITE CAPE IS DEAD!

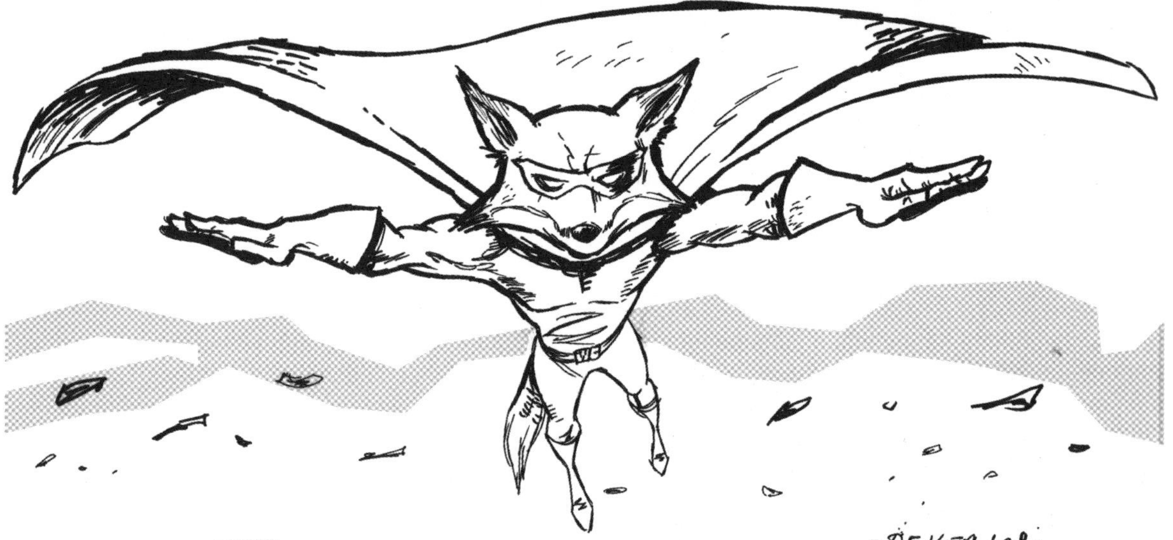
-DE VITA '08-

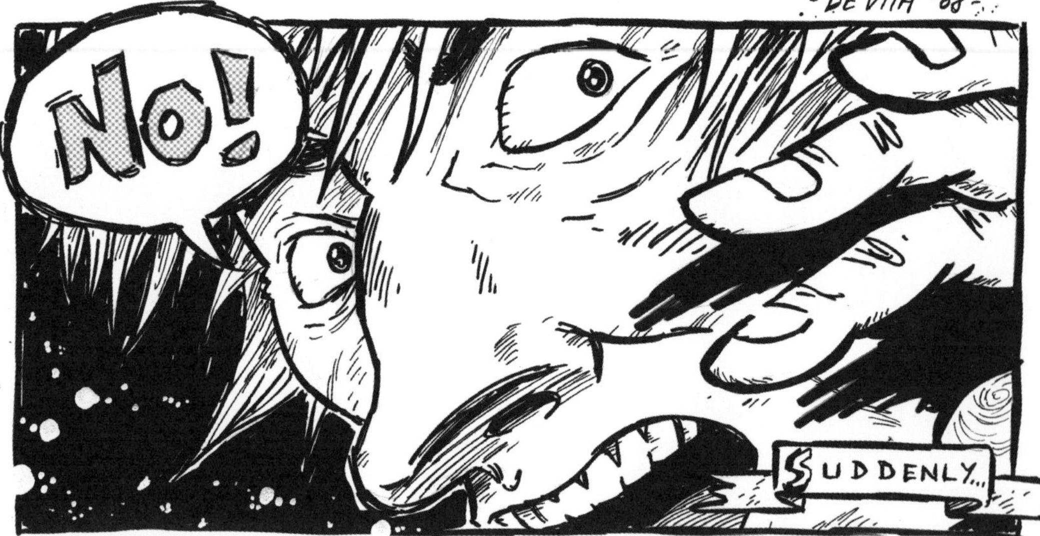
NO!
SUDDENLY...

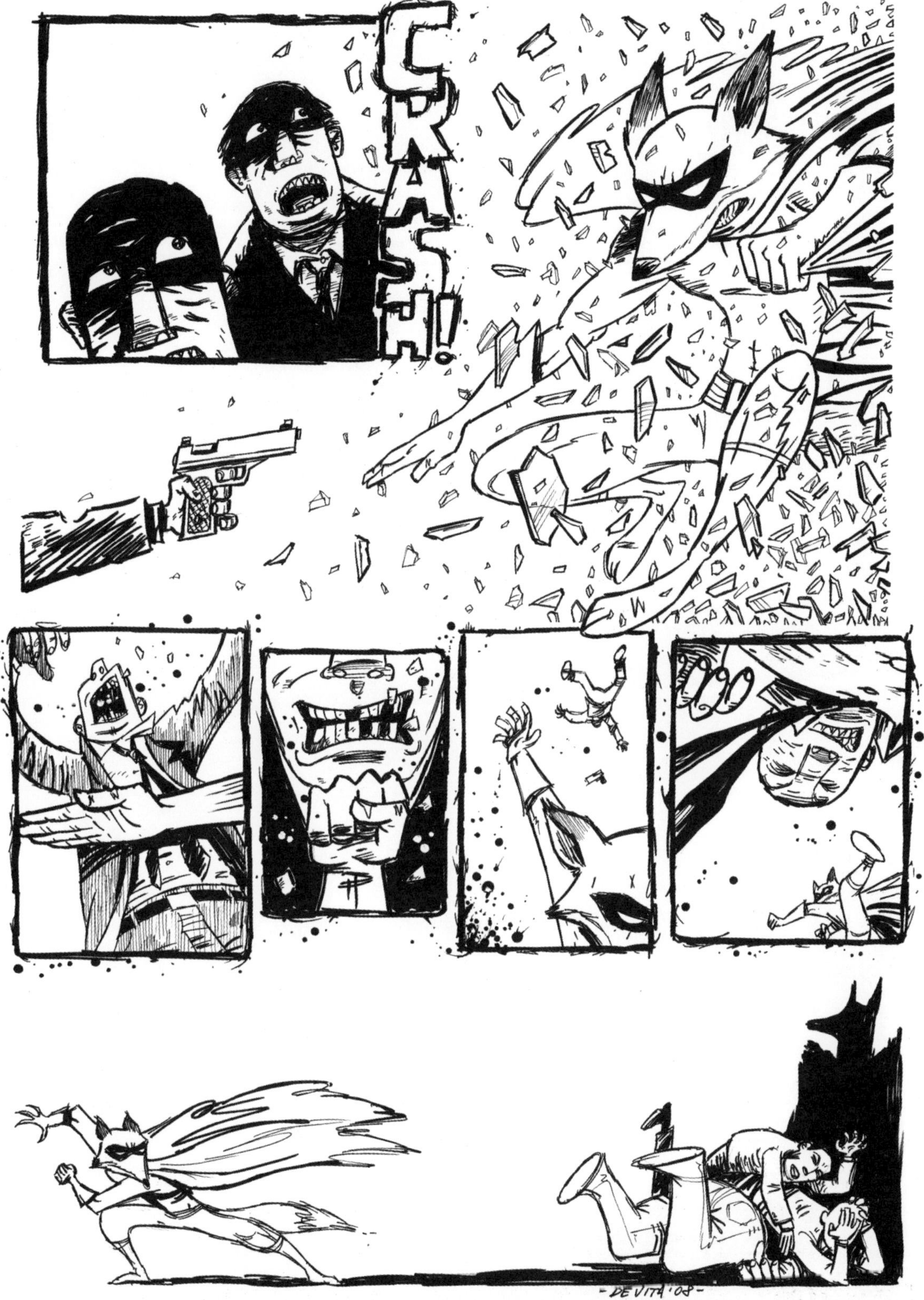
CRASH!
-DEVITA '08-

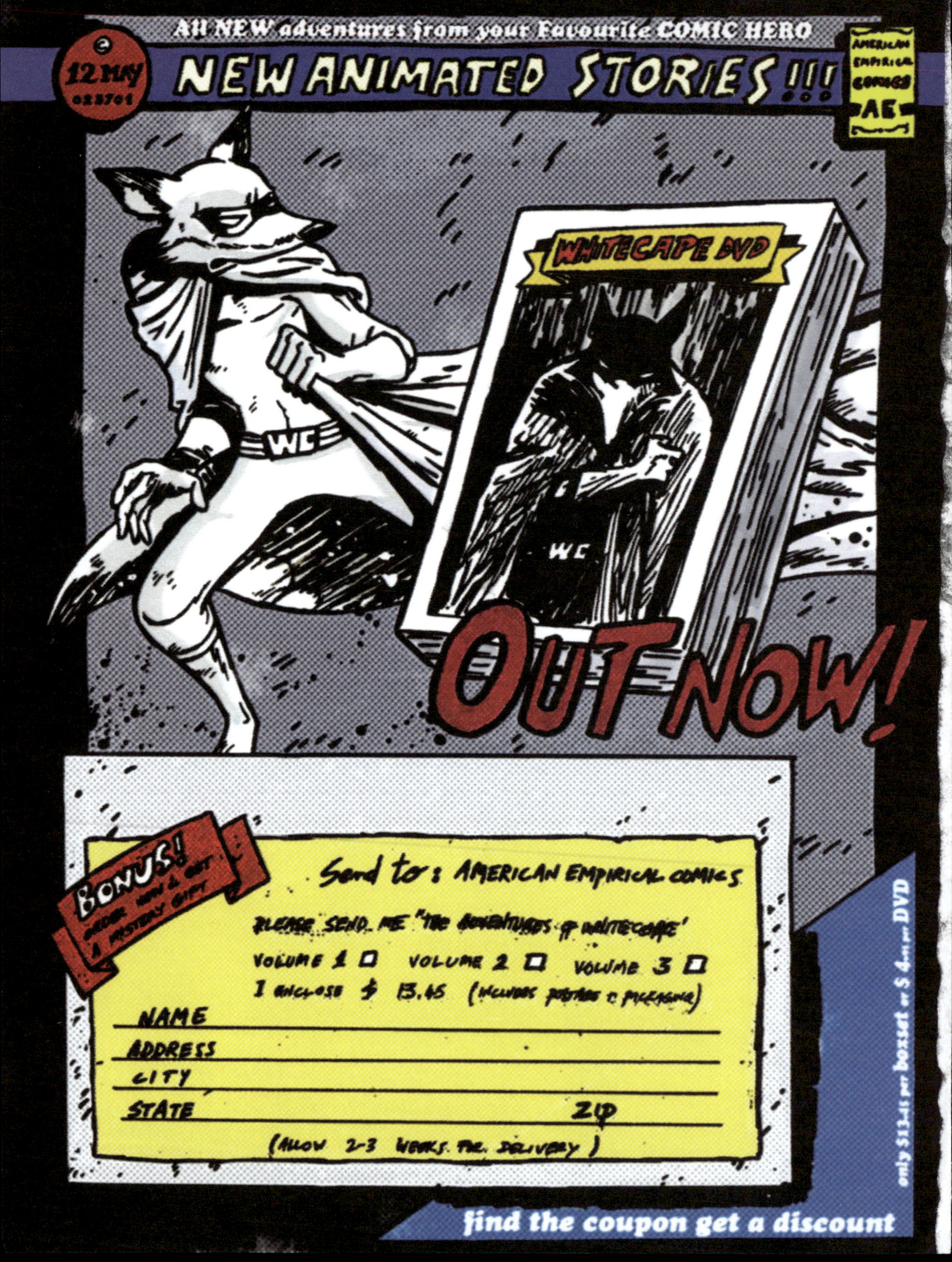

All NEW adventures from your Favourite COMIC HERO

12 MAY
023701

NEW ANIMATED STORIES!!!

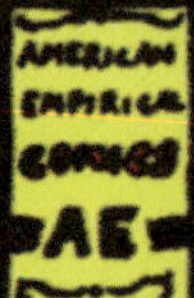

WHITECAPE DVD

WC

OUT NOW!

BONUS!
ORDER NOW & GET A MYSTERY GIFT

Send to: AMERICAN EMPIRICAL COMICS

PLEASE SEND ME "THE ADVENTURES OF WHITECAPE"

VOLUME 1 ☐ VOLUME 2 ☐ VOLUME 3 ☐

I ENCLOSE $ 13.45 (INCLUDES POSTAGE & PACKAGING)

NAME

ADDRESS

CITY

STATE ZIP

(ALLOW 2-3 WEEKS FOR DELIVERY)

only $13.45 per boxset or $ 4.45 per DVD

find the coupon get a discount

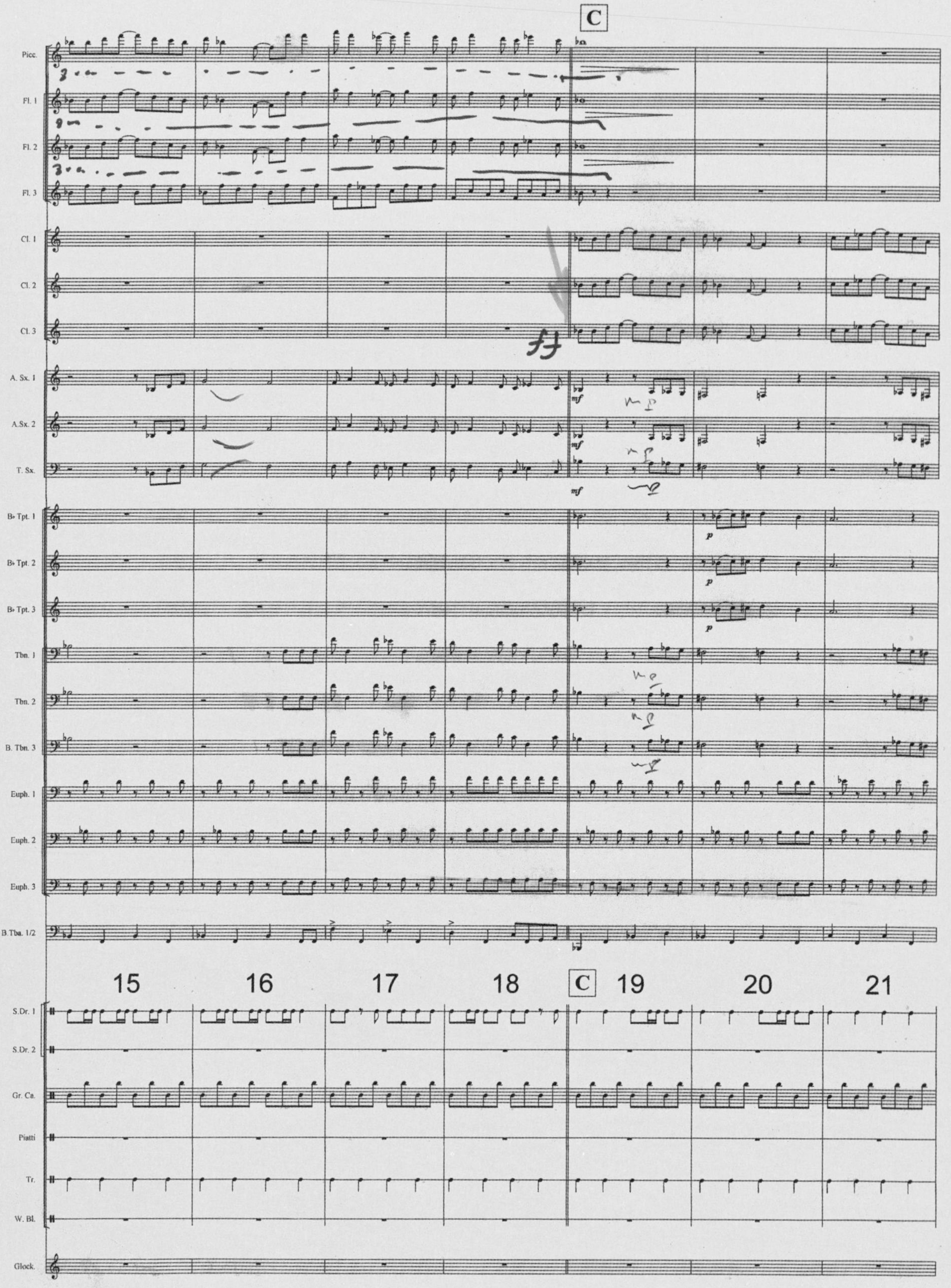
C
Picc.
Fl. 1
Fl. 2
Fl. 3
Cl. 1
Cl. 2
Cl. 3
A. Sx. 1
A.Sx. 2
T. Sx.
B♭ Tpt. 1
B♭ Tpt. 2
B♭ Tpt. 3
Tbn. 1
Tbn. 2
B. Tbn. 3
Euph. 1
Euph. 2
Euph. 3
B.Tba. 1/2
15
16
17
18
C
19
20
21
S.Dr. 1
S.Dr. 2
Gr. Ca.
Piatti
Tr.
W. Bl.
Glock.